# South Africa's Radical Tradition: A documentary history

## Volume 2: 1943 – 1964

# South Africa's Radical Tradition: A documentary history

Volume 2: 1943 – 1964

edited by
ALLISON DREW

Buchu Books: Cape Town
Mayibuye Books: Cape Town
UCT Press: Cape Town

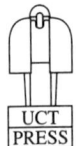

First published 1997
UCT Press, University of Cape Town, Private Bag, 7700 Rondebosch, South Africa,
Buchu Books, P.O. Box 2580, 8000 Cape Town, South Africa and
Mayibuye Books, History and Literature Series no. 71, Mayibuye Centre, University
of the Western Cape, Private Bag X17, 7535 Bellville, South Africa
All rights reserved. No part of this publication may be reproduced, stored in a
retrieval system or transmitted, in any form by any means, electronic, mechanical,
photocopying, recording or otherwise, without the prior permission of the publishers.

The Mayibuye Centre for History and Culture in South Africa is based at the University of the Western Cape. Focusing on all aspects of apartheid, resistance, social life and culture in South Africa, its aim is to help recover the rich heritage of all South Africans and to encourage cultural creativity and expression. The Mayibuye History and Literature Series is part of this project. The series editors are Barry Feinberg and André Odendaal.

© 1997 Allison Drew

ISBN 0-7992-1614-3

Layout and desktop publishing: birga thomas
Cover design:
   Cover concept: Kaleidesign
   Final cover: Jos Thorne
   Cover photograph: Courtesy Mayibuye Centre Archives: *1960 Pondoland uprising*

Printed and bound by Creda Press, Epping II, Cape Town

# Contents

List of abbreviations . . . . . . . . . . . . . . . . . . . . . . . . . . . . . . . 6

Preface . . . . . . . . . . . . . . . . . . . . . . . . . . . . . . . . . . . . . . . . 9

Acknowledgements . . . . . . . . . . . . . . . . . . . . . . . . . . . . . . . 12

Introduction . . . . . . . . . . . . . . . . . . . . . . . . . . . . . . . . . . . 13

**PART ONE**
Building the national movement
   *Political alliances and unity* . . . . . . . . . . . . . . . . . . . . . . . . . 37
   *Uses of the boycott* . . . . . . . . . . . . . . . . . . . . . . . . . . . . . 167
   *National liberation and trade union organisation* . . . . . . . . . . . 205

**PART TWO**
The national question . . . . . . . . . . . . . . . . . . . . . . . . . . . . 235

**PART THREE**
The agrarian question . . . . . . . . . . . . . . . . . . . . . . . . . . . . 295

**PART FOUR**
The turn to armed struggle . . . . . . . . . . . . . . . . . . . . . . . . 343

List of documents . . . . . . . . . . . . . . . . . . . . . . . . . . . . . . 393

Sources . . . . . . . . . . . . . . . . . . . . . . . . . . . . . . . . . . . . . 395

Select bibliography . . . . . . . . . . . . . . . . . . . . . . . . . . . . . 395

Index . . . . . . . . . . . . . . . . . . . . . . . . . . . . . . . . . . . . . . 399

# List of abbreviations

| | |
|---|---|
| AAC | All African Convention |
| ACDWU | African Commercial and Distributive Workers' Union |
| ADP | African Democratic Party |
| ALC | African Liberation Committee |
| AMWU | African Mine Workers' Union |
| ANC | African National Congress |
| Anti-CAD | Anti-Coloured Affairs Department |
| APDUSA | African People's Democratic Union of Southern Africa |
| APO | African People's Organization |
| ARM | African Resistance Movement |
| CAC | Coloured Affairs Council |
| CAD | Coloured Affairs Department |
| CATA | Cape African Teachers' Association |
| CCATU | Co-ordinating Committee of African Trade Unions |
| CFLU | Cape Federation of Labour Unions |
| CLSA | Communist League of South Africa |
| CNETU | Council of Non-European Trade Unions |
| COD | Congress of Democrats |
| Codesa | Convention for a Democratic South Africa |
| Comintern | Communist International |
| CPC | Coloured People's Congress |
| CPNU | Coloured People's National Union |
| CPSA | Communist Party of South Africa |
| CPSU | Communist Party of the Soviet Union |
| ECCI | Executive Committee of the Communist International |
| Fedsaw | Federation of South African Women |
| FCWU | Food and Canning Workers' Union |
| FIOSA | Fourth International Organisation of South Africa |
| FRAC | Franchise Action Committee/Council |
| GNU | Government of National Unity |
| GWU | Garment Workers' Union |
| ICU | Industrial and Commercial Workers' Union |
| ILP | Independent Labour Party |
| ISL | International Socialist League |
| JCATU | Joint Committee of African Trade Unions |

| | |
|---|---|
| MK | Umkhonto weSizwe |
| NCL | National Committee for Liberation |
| NEF | New Era Fellowship |
| NEUF | Non-European United Front |
| NEUM | Non-European Unity Movement |
| NIC | Natal Indian Congress |
| NLF | National Liberation Front |
| NLL | National Liberation League |
| NP | National Party |
| NRC | Native Representative Council |
| Nusas | National Union of South African Students |
| OAU | Organization of African Unity |
| PAC | Pan-Africanist Congress |
| PAFMECSA | Pan-African Freedom Movement of East, Central and Southern Africa |
| PF | Progressive Forum |
| PTU | Progressive Trade Union Group |
| SACP | South African Communist Party |
| SACPO | South African Coloured People's Organisation |
| SACTU | South African Congress of Trade Unions |
| SAFNETU | South African Federation of Non-European Trade Unions |
| SAIC | South African Indian Congress |
| SAIF | South African Industrial Federation |
| SAIRR | South African Institute of Race Relations |
| SALP | South African Labour Party |
| SAMWU | South African Mine Workers' Union |
| SASP | South African Socialist Party |
| SATLC | South African Trades and Labour Council |
| SATUC | South African Trades Union Congress |
| SATUCC | South African Trades Union Co-ordinating Council |
| SOYA | Society of Young Africa |
| Swapo | South West African People's Organisation |
| TARC | Train Apartheid Resistance Campaign |
| TLSA | Teachers' League of South Africa |
| TOB | Transkei Organised Bodies |
| UCT | University of Cape Town |
| Unisa | University of South Africa |
| Umsa | Unity Movement of South Africa |
| UP | United Party |
| WIL | Workers' International League |
| WPSA | Workers' Party of South Africa |
| YCCC | Yu Chi Chan Club |

# Preface

In Volume Two of this documentary history, I have followed the same historiographical and methodological guidelines outlined in Volume One. As noted in the Preface to Volume One, the past is very much part of contemporary South Africa, not only in terms of the legacies which have shaped the present but in terms of the acute controversies which have arisen over conflicting interpretations of the past. In South Africa, the "fetishism of documents" against which the historian E. H. Carr (1987:16) cautioned has taken two forms. First, it has appeared in the struggle to establish ideological hegemony through not merely the adoption, but in some cases the imposition of particular documents on community and trade union organisations, the controversy over the Congress movement's Freedom Charter being the most notable example. Second, it appears in the struggle to establish ideological purity and control by refusing to work with groups which have not adopted particular documents, such as the Non-European Unity Movement's (NEUM) Ten Point Programme.

In addition to these ideological struggles, this fetishism of documents has a historical basis in the lack of a continuous written tradition within the liberation movement and on the Left. Many political activists and radical intellectuals were denied access to formal education and subjected to continual state harassment. Many political documents have been lost or destroyed because of fear of political repression. For political organisations outside the dominant Congress tradition, in particular, the loss of the raw materials from which they could construct a historical record of their own past has exacerbated political defeats and political marginalisation and led to a mystification of missing documents.

Because the remaining accessible documentation of South Africa's liberation movement represents only a portion of the original, no documentary history of the South African liberation movement can claim to be exhaustive or comprehensive. Thus, like Volume One, this volume is intended to complement other documentary histories or bibliographic references of the liberation movement (see, *inter alia*, Carter and Karis 1972-7; African National Congress 1977; Bunting 1981; Bhana and Pachai 1984; Dadoo 1990; Bohmer 1986-7 and Kline 1987 on scope and methodologies of documentary histories).

The selection and organisation of material reflects the multiple aims of this project. Firstly, I hope to demonstrate the existence and indicate the development of a heterogeneous and eclectic radical-left tradition which reflects the articulation of both the socialist and nationalist movements in their international and domestic aspects. The documents are drawn principally from political organisations within this radical tradition. Linked to this, I have attempted to illustrate some of the principal choices, dilemmas and controversies which have confronted South Africa's radical tradition over the twentieth century. As part of this task, I have sought to include documents which indicate the range of positions found within the radical tradition. Many of the issues and problems debated in these documents continue to confront South Africa in its post-apartheid phase.

Most documentary histories of South Africa's liberation movement, like most histories, have reflected the historical predominance of the African National Congress (ANC) and its affiliated organisations or allies. This focus on the majority political tendency has had the effect of underestimating the degree of debate and controversy within the liberation movement. In South Africa, minority political tendencies and organisations have had a political significance which transcends their numbers; majority political tendencies cannot be understood in isolation from the other tendencies which form part of South Africa's political landscape.

The material in Volume Two follows a broadly chronological arrangement, and the documents are organised into thematic or topical subdivisions which illustrate the origins and development of various political concerns and debates. Volume One traced the origins and development of socialism in South Africa until 1950, shortly before the passage of the Suppression of Communism Act which made overt socialist organisation illegal. It covered the dilemmas which socialists faced in confronting a racially-divided working class, their gradual recognition of the national question and their efforts to build political alliances. It also considered the impact of international socialist politics and of World War Two on the South African socialist movement.

Volume Two covers the relationship between socialist currents and the national liberation movement from the 1940s to the early 1960s, addressing some of the main dilemmas facing the national liberation movement – from the perspective of the diverse socialist groups which for much of this period operated in a clandestine and muted manner. It begins in 1943, a focal year for the national liberation movement, which saw an intensification of debates about political strategy and tactics as the Anti-CAD movement, the NEUM, the African Democratic Party and the ANC Youth League were all launched. The documents in Volume Two present the varied approaches to building political alliances, to the national question, to the agrarian question and to armed struggle which were debated within the national liberation movement, particularly by socialists, during these decades.

## Textual treatment

As in Volume One, I have opted for a conservative editing approach and have tried to reproduce the original documents as accurately as possible, including stylistic variations and peculiarities, and grammatical, spelling and typographical errors (Kline 1987:90). Most written political discourse in South Africa's liberation movement has been urban-based and written in English. The varied styles reflect both the different organisational homes and social class backgrounds of the writers, some of whom were highly literate individuals who spoke English as a mother tongue, while others had limited formal education and spoke English as a second or third language. All of these details may be of historical interest, providing insights into both the social backgrounds and modes of communication of the authors of these documents. Generally, the documents in Volume Two have fewer editorial errors and show a more consistent editorial quality than those in Volume One. This reflects their more recent writing and production and the improved access to technology in the post-World War Two years. Many of the documents reproduced here were written for publication and distribution and thus were subjected to editorial scrutiny before they originally appeared.

In cases where the original documents or photocopies of the original indicate editorial changes, I have reproduced what appears to be the most final corrected version, indicating any substantive changes that are not of a grammatical nature in the notes at the end of each section. In their original form, most of the documents reproduced in Volume Two were either typed or typeset, and the correspondence was either handwritten or typed. Letterheads are reproduced in italics and centered at the top of the document.

In terms of physical format, I have standardised the following: document titles; the placement of subheadings within documents; the placement of datelines, salutations and closings in correspondence; paragraph indentations; block quotes; and numbered and lettered lists. I have also supplied missing punctuation that is part of a set, such as parentheses or quotation marks, as well as missing terminal punctuation in cases where the author started a new sentence with a capital letter but omitted the preceding closing punctuation. In the rare occasion where words or punctuation have been duplicated in the source text, the duplicated item has been deleted. Hard hyphens have been carried over from the source texts; hyphens at the end of a line indicate a temporary break due to space, unless otherwise noted.

Aside from these silent emendations, all other editorial interpolations in the text are indicated in brackets and italicised in order to distinguish such interpolations from the occasional use of brackets by authors of the source material. All other editorial notes are to be found at the end of each section. Unrecoverable gaps in original texts, generally due to the poor physical condition of the source material or to illegible handwriting, are indicated by the use of dashes in italicised brackets; where possible, the number of dashes approximates the number of missing words. Missing lines or sections in the original are noted as such in brackets and italicised. Underlining and other emphasis in the source text are indicated through conventional typesetting symbols, e.g. underlined material in the source text has been italicised, and double underlines are indicated by the use of small capitals. The use of bold and of capitalisation in the source text has been reproduced as is. Where I have reproduced an extract of a document, the location of extracted material is indicated by ellipses in brackets.

# Acknowledgements

My thanks to the people who have assisted me with Volume Two of this documentary history: Neville Alexander; Karen Press at Buchu Books; Barry Feinberg at Mayibuye Books and, especially, Rose Meny-Gibert at UCT Press; Lesley Hart; Leonie Twentyman-Jones; Rosemary Neale; birga thomas; Mary Troost and Alex Callinicos. My greatest debt is to David Howell; without his persistent encouragement and assistance this project might not have been completed. Any errors are, of course, my own responsibility.

This project was facilitated by a grant from the Barry Amiel and Norman Melburn Trust in England and by a grant from the Department of Politics at the University of York. I also wish to thank the Borthwick Institute of Historical Research at the University of York for an Honorary Visiting Fellowship during 1995 which provided me with office space and access to their Southern African Archives. The Borthwick Institute provided a very congenial climate for completing this work.

The material in Volume Two of this documentary history has been collected from libraries and archives and from private parties in South Africa, Britain and the United States, to all of whom I am most appreciative. I would like to particularly acknowledge the assistance of the following institutions: in South Africa, the Historical Papers Library at the University of the Witwatersrand, the Manuscripts and Archives Department of the University of Cape Town Libraries, the Mayibuye Historical Papers at the University of the Western Cape and the South African Reference Library in Cape Town; in Britain, the Communist Party of Great Britain Library and Archive; the Borthwick Institute of Historical Research at the University of York; the British Library in London; the Brynmor Jones Library at the University of Hull; the Institute of Commonwealth Studies at the University of London; the Modern Records Centre at the University of Warwick Library; the National Museum of Labour History in Manchester; the Public Records Office in London and the Working Class Movement Library in Salford; and in the United States, the Hoover Institution Archives at Stanford University; the Houghton Library at Harvard University; the Prometheus Research Library in New York City; the Special Collections at the University Research Library, University of California, Los Angeles; and the Manuscripts and Archives office at Yale University Library.

# Introduction

In the 1940s and 1950s, the South African socialist movement faced the strategic dilemmas generated by the tensions between its own avowedly revolutionary goals and the urgency of popular struggles for reforms. Many of these problems were familiar to socialists around the world and concerned the relationship between the struggle for socialism and the appeals of national liberation. But South African socialists also faced the distinctive problems posed by a rigidly divided working class, and they encountered these problems in an increasingly authoritarian political environment. For many Leftists in other societies, the 1940s contained some promise of progress resulting from the successful "war against fascism". In South Africa this promise was always limited and was soon suppressed as the white electorate voted the National Party to power in 1948 on a programme of apartheid. Elsewhere, the harsh dichotomies of the Cold War posed challenges for socialists. Some responded by developing new theories and by finding new causes, often linked to liberation movements in the colonies and former colonies. The South African Left in the 1950s was largely insulated from these developments, and the complexities of South African socialist politics have to be understood within its distinctive and harsh environment.

At the close of World War Two, the Communist Party of South Africa (CPSA) predictably overshadowed the smaller and internally fragmented Trotskyist tendency in terms of practical work, and the CPSA had a foothold in the trade-union movement despite its frequent policy oscillations and ambivalent support for black labour. The Trotskyist tendency engaged mainly in educational and propaganda activity. Neither socialist tendency was prepared psychologically or organisationally to confront the post-war smashing of the black labour movement and the brutal imposition of apartheid, and both tendencies submerged themselves into the national liberation movement; only in the late 1970s, following the revival of the black labour movement, did socialism again begin to manifest itself as an independent political tendency in South Africa. Despite the eclipse of socialism as an overt political tendency in this period, its influence endured in muted form through the work of socialists in class and community organisations. However, the sectarianism which divided Communists and Trotskyists permeated the liberation movement with lasting effects.

Although the Communist International disbanded in 1943, the CPSA continued to look to the international Communist movement, and particularly to the Soviet Union, for guidance. While disavowing the possibility that African nationalism was inherently revolutionary, the CPSA defined itself as the historic representative of the working class and saw itself working in close co-operation with a national liberation movement revitalised under working-class leadership. Thus, it consciously sought to align itself with the ANC, which it had helped to revive in the late 1930s as a challenger to the All African Convention (AAC). In 1950, on the eve of the Suppression of Communism Act, the Party disbanded itself, and when the underground South African Communist Party (SACP) appeared in 1953, the relationship between the Party, the ANC and other Congress organisations became even stronger.

During those three years, South African Communism went through a strategic reorientation. Some Communists who had staunchly advocated the primacy of the class over the national struggle did not join the new underground organisation, which aligned itself squarely with the Congress movement (Everatt 1991). In assessing that period, two prominent Communists, Jack Simons and Ray Alexander Simons, argued that "... the communists could claim the achievement of an objective that had been central to their purpose since 1928. The class struggle had merged with the struggle for national liberation." (1983: 609) But more recently the Party has conceded that the decision deprived it of an independent identity: between 1953 and 1960, it issued no public statements in its own name (SACP 1990: 43; Cronin 1990: 100). The SACP operated on the basis of a democratic centralism whose democratic aspects would, in its view, necessarily require some curtailment during the period of underground activity (Bunting 1981: 210-11; 310-11, 331). The Party's stance and behaviour generated conflict within the Congress movement over allegations of white and Communist domination.

The Trotskyist tendency emerged from the war both regionally and organisationally fragmented. Two independent Trotskyist groups, the Johannesburg-based Workers' International League (WIL) and the Cape Town-based Fourth International Organisation of South Africa (FIOSA), had unsuccessfully attempted to merge in the early 1940s; in 1946 the WIL folded. The other Trotskyist base was the Workers' Party of South Africa (WPSA) which, having ceased public activity in 1939, continued to meet secretly through the 1940s and 1950s and saw itself as the underground, inner core of the NEUM. In the late 1940s, the Fourth International overseas advised the FIOSA and the WPSA to merge, as it had done in the 1930s. Some members of the FIOSA subsequently joined the WPSA and worked in the NEUM. The FIOSA disbanded, with the remaining individuals forming the Forum Club, an independent Left discussion club which met briefly in the early 1950s.

In the 1940s and 1950s South African Trotskyists believed that their main task was to preserve the idea of socialism while they built a democratic mass movement of the oppressed population. This they saw as a necessary first step to building a working-class movement able to draw white workers away from their alliance with white capital. Both Trotskyist groups looked to radical black intellectuals as a political vanguard. They believed that South Africa's class structure – its small black urban proletariat and vast, uneducated, illiterate and politically backwards rural population – necessitated the use of the thin stratum of black intellectuals to disseminate political ideas. This notion bore fruit in the "teachers as a vanguard" thesis expounded by B. M. Kies, a leading intellectual in the New Era Fellowship and the Teachers' League of South Africa (TLSA), at the first National Anti-CAD Conference in May 1943 (Document 4).

When the "teachers as a vanguard" thesis was initially formulated, black teachers were still very much an organic part of the working class – often first generation intellectuals from working-class families who lived in working-class communities and townships. Many teachers played a vital role in conveying political ideas around the *dorps* and towns of South Africa, often suffering intimidation and harassment. Nonetheless, by the late 1940s and '50s this occupational group had crystallised out of the working class into a section of the *petite bourgeoisie*. As teachers became identified with middle-class respectability, particularly amongst the urban coloured population of the Western Cape, the NEUM's teacher constituency meant that it became increasingly aloof from mass action. Mary Simons (1976) and Maurice Hommel (1981) have pointed out that teachers' occupational status as state employees acted as a brake on any radical tendencies. Similar observations were voiced in the Forum Club in the early 1950s (Document 21). The "teachers as a vanguard" thesis not only failed to recognise that the differential social positions of coloured, African and Indian teachers entailed conflicting interests; it meant in affect that ascription to vanguard status was based on occupational status rather than political practice.

The national liberation movement comprised multiple class and political interests, which in turn produced a range of strategic outlooks and tactical preferences. The ensuing tensions were undoubtedly exacerbated by the rigid divisions on the Left and, in the oppressive political climate of the late 1950s, culminated in the rupture of both the ANC and the NEUM. But these tensions also spawned vibrant debates about political alliances, about strategy and tactics, and about the national and the agrarian questions in which socialists played pivotal roles.[1] These debates form part of a radical literature, most of which is virtually unknown today.[2] The documents in this volume illustrate both the richness and complexity of political debates in South Africa and the impressive research and theorising undertaken by people who bore the brunt of political harassment and intimidation and who were often denied educational opportunities and access to universities both as students and teachers during the apartheid era. Some of the literature anticipates the 1970s university-based radical revisionist school, much of which was theoretically influenced by the structural Marxism of Althusser and Poulantzas. In some cases this later literature merely reinvented the wheel.

Two factors explain why most of the earlier literature emanating from the liberation movement remains unknown. First, much of it was lost during the 1960s backlash of repression, as South African political activists buried or burned the documents which constituted much of the primary written record of their own struggle. Second, the political perspectives of radical academics and radical whites must be emphasised. In the 1970s and early 1980s these were heavily coloured by syndicalist sentiments. Subsequently, they became increasingly focused on the ANC and the Congress movement. While the legacy and contemporary importance of the Congress movement cannot be underestimated, its own trajectory and internal schisms cannot be understood in isolation from the NEUM, from the Africanist tendency which formed the Pan-Africanist Congress (PAC) and from socialist currents, all of which formed part of the broader political landscape.

## Building the national movement

### Political alliances and unity

1943 was a pivotal year for national liberation politics. Stimulated by the social militancy of the war years – manifested in strikes, bus boycotts and squatter movements – a new and radicalised generation of political activists sought to reinvigorate existing organisations, such as the ANC, the AAC, the TLSA and the South African Indian Congress (SAIC), or to form new ones. That year saw the establishment of the Anti-CAD movement against the Coloured Advisory Council, the NEUM, the African Democratic Party[3] and the Independent Labour Party,[4] and the groundwork for the ANC Youth League, which was officially formed the following year. Essentially, this generational shift was a response to the government's renewed efforts to remove black people from a common voters' roll based on a qualified franchise and to segregate them into powerless advisory bodies, such as the Native Representative Council (NRC), which had been formed in 1936, the Coloured Advisory Council and South African Indian Council. This systematic disenfranchisement posed questions about methods of struggle, given the inadequacy of earlier appeals and petitions to the white government, and particularly whether participation in these new racial institutions would further or hinder the struggle for democratic rights (Documents 1-5).

The NEUM argued that non-collaboration with racial structures was a fundamental principle of political practice. The NEUM was a federation of affiliated organisations subscribing to a Ten Point Programme of minimum democratic rights which was to be achieved through non-collaboration (Documents 6-8). Its federal structure was conceived as a means of linking the numerous, sectional organisations which had developed in the rigidly divided and stratified society, and the leadership hoped that through political education the need to retain sectional organisations would gradually decline (Tabata 1950). Its two main pillars were the AAC, representing African organisations, and the Anti-CAD, representing coloured organisations; however, an initial hope that the SAIC would affiliate was soon dashed. In the early 1940s a new generation of radicals led by Communists Yusuf Dadoo and H. A. Naidoo wrested leadership of the SAIC from the merchant traders who had previously dominated it. But Dadoo and Naidoo moved the SAIC towards an alliance with the Congress movement rather than the NEUM, and by 1947 this alliance was formalised with the "Doctors' Pact" between the ANC's Dr A. B. Xuma and the SAIC's Dr Yusuf Dadoo and Dr G. M. Naicker, also a Communist (Document 10; Karis and Carter 1973: 272).

The NEUM's political programme was strongly influenced by the tiny WPSA, whose impact on NEUM strategy is seen both in the Ten Point Programme and in the use of non-collaboration. The Ten Point Programme linked the franchise with all other democratic rights. This reflected the WPSA's interpretation of a letter which Russian revolutionary Leon Trotsky wrote to his South African comrades in April 1935 – that all social and economic disabilities flowed from the lack of political rights (Volume One, Document 51). Non-collaboration meant, in practice, the refusal by the oppressed black population to work the instruments of their own oppression, that is, segregated and inferior political institutions. In the WPSA's view, those *quislings* who worked within these institutions represented essentially *petit bourgeois* rather than explicitly

The Cape Anti-CAD was a mass movement in its heyday during the 1940s.

A meeting organised by the Non-European Unity Movement on Cape Town's Parade for the boycott of the Van Riebeeck Tercentenary Celebrations, 1952. At the microphone is S A Jayiya; seated left to right are Phyllis Ntantala Jordan, W P Van Schoor, Dr Goolam Gool, Dan Neethling and Jane Gool.

Delegates from Natal en route to the Congress of the People, Kliptown, for the adoption of the Freedom Charter, 1955.

9 August 1956 - Women from FEDSAW, ANC Women's League, Non-European Women's League, SACPO and COD en route to Mr P J Parsons, Native Commissioner of Cape Town, to protest the extension of passes to African women. They were led by Mrs E Nqose of the ANC Women's League, Retreat, Cape Town (the tall women in the centre). Simultaneous demonstrations took place around the country.

Supporters of the accused, outside the Treason Trial which began in Johannesburg in 1956.

The end of another day in court - supporters outside the Treason Trial.

Mass protest was not only confined to the cities. Here at Bizana, 1960, a group of Pondos protest against the local Bantu Authorities.

The mass funeral after the killing of 69 people by the police at a PAC demonstration at Sharpeville, 21 March 1960.

working-class interests. Hence, the WPSA saw non-collaboration as a means to prevent a multi-class movement from being coopted by *petit bourgeois* and aspirant bourgeois interests in a period when overt socialist propaganda carried high risks.

Convinced that the ANC's traditional petitionary tactics were not successful, the ANC Youth League also adopted a policy of non-collaboration with racial structures. Although this common non-collaborationist stance would seemingly have provided the basis for broader African and black unity, in practice the liberation movement became increasingly polarised between organisations which saw non-collaboration and the boycott in tactical terms, notably moderates in the ANC and other Congress organisations, and those who saw non-collaboration as a principle, like those in the NEUM and some of the Africanists in the ANC Youth League. Thus, by the late 1940s unity talks between the ANC and the AAC had broken down over these conflicting interpretations of non-collaboration (Documents 15, 16).

Apartheid posed in acute form the question of how separate political organisations could fight their common disability: the lack of democratic rights. Following the removal of Africans from the common voters' roll in 1936, the erosion of the few remaining rights of coloureds and Indians made the basis of black unity ever more a reality. Yet the hallmark of the apartheid era has been the continuous breakdown, along organisational, class and colour lines, of efforts to build united anti-apartheid fronts which transcended different political traditions. This problem was seen during apartheid's first years, not only in the breakdown of unity talks between the ANC and AAC, but in the failure of established organisations to come together even on a tactical basis to fight the National Party's racial laws.

The abortive history of the Train Apartheid Resistance Campaign (TARC) is illustrative (Documents 13, 14, 19). The TARC was formed in late 1948 to fight the extension of segregation to trains in the Cape Peninsula. It fizzled out within six months; several months later, following their acquittal in May 1949 of the charge of incitement, the TARC leadership announced its decision to affiliate to the NEUM. On the one hand, the TARC was a forerunner of the Congress movement's tactical campaigns of the 1950s, which, in their use of passive resistance, showed elements of Gandhi's *satyagraha* movement. On the other, it foreshadowed the NEUM's growing reticence, especially in the Western Cape, to engage in tactical campaigns.

The TARC campaign began with massive demonstrations against train apartheid. The African People's Organization (APO), the NEUM and the CPSA all declared their opposition to train apartheid. Initially, the NEUM sought to link the struggle against train apartheid with the broader democratic movement under its Ten Point Programme. But unable to rally sufficient support under its own banner, it entered into a united front with other democratic organisations, including the CPSA and the FIOSA, in which its own representatives formed the majority of the leadership (Document 19).

From the beginning, differences of strategy and tactics began to emerge within the leadership. Given the popular enthusiasm for the campaign, the CPSA argued that small groups of individuals should immediately begin boarding train carriages reserved for whites. The NEUM thought this approach premature and adventurous and called for intensive organisation as a prerequisite for mass action (Document 13). The leaders finally agreed to begin mass boarding of trains by volunteers when a sufficient number had been enrolled, but this compromise broke down in quarrels over what constituted an adequate number. With the NEUM representatives still insisting that mass action was premature, the Communists dropped out of TARC and people began to lose interest.

If the TARC debacle highlighted the problems of the relationship of socialist strategy and tactical participation in working-class struggles, on the one hand, and building united fronts, on the other, the experience of the Franchise Action Committee (FRAC) underscored them and demonstrated the increasing sectarianism characterising the democratic movement (Document 20). Like TARC, FRAC was organised as a single-issue campaign to protest the Separate Representation of Voters Bill of 1950 which, as with Africans in 1936, placed coloureds on a separate voters' roll (Lodge 1983: 40-1; Musson 1989: 108).

FRAC was officially formed in Cape Town in February 1951 by representatives of the APO, SAIC, ANC, and of community groups and trade unions. At its first meeting, indicating a groundswell amongst the coloured population, FRAC called for a programme of militant protest including local political strikes and general strikes. However, the refusal of different political organisations to work on a common platform, a tendency which had manifested itself both in the breakdown of the AAC/ANC unity talks and of the TARC, intensified with FRAC. While the Communist Fred Carneson, a member of the FRAC executive, called for immediate action, the NEUM chose not to protest before the law came into effect, but only to boycott it after the fact.

FRAC's *ad hoc* unity broke down under the pressure to map out a programme of action which in turn raised questions about the basis of political unity. Its very purpose was contentious. Trotskyists in the Forum Club saw the coloured vote – itself a qualified franchise within the coloured population – as "anachronistic and hollow", arguing that its retention could hardly be a victory for democracy. They also criticised FRAC for including George Golding, a member of the widely despised Coloured Affairs Council, when FRAC's purpose was to fight an apartheid law. Carneson, arguing for the broadest possible alliance, countered that retaining the coloured vote could prevent the appointment of special coloured representatives.

Despite its early popularity amongst coloureds, the FRAC campaign faded after a number of months, without achieving its aim. But the Congress movement built upon FRAC's organisational structure: The Defiance Campaign and the Congress Alliance arose out of joint meetings with the ANC, the SAIC and FRAC, much of whose membership soon formed the South African Coloured People's Organisation, later the Coloured People's Congress (Lodge 1983: 69-70).

Essentially, the two traditions represented by the Congress movement and the Unity Movement worked with different and ultimately irreconcilable conceptions of unity. This political difference was reinforced by personality and organisational rivalries. The overriding concern of most Congress leaders was to build the widest possible anti-apartheid alliance, one capable of appealing to all opponents of the National Party and its apartheid policies, including democratic whites and people of all social classes (Documents 22-24, 28). Congress leaders hoped that by uniting people in action, some of these might eventually come to accept the Freedom Charter. Yet the entreaty to the broadest common denominator had its limitations: The continued pleas to whites risked diluting the call for black democratic rights. The slogan "The Nats must go!", designed to grab progressive white voters, was accompanied by a debate as to whether the call for full democratic rights for all was not premature in South African conditions. The frustration felt by John Gomas, who had joined the CPSA as a young man but had been alienated from what he saw as its pandering to whites, is just one example of how the attempt to build the broadest possible anti-apartheid movement could backfire by alienating black radicals (Documents 25-27).

By contrast, the NEUM continued to insist on adherence to its Ten Point Programme as a minimum condition for joint action, labelling all tactical battles as "stunts". This led it into a *cul-de-sac*, as Alexander (1986) has observed. Its leadership became unable to distinguish between the struggles for reforms – which the working class and oppressed engaged in to improve their daily lot and which could form part of a process of political education – and reformist struggles – those which curtailed and deflected the momentum generated by the popular movement, thereby prioritising *petit bourgeois* and aspirant bourgeois interests. This approach did not go unquestioned or unchallenged by those who worked in NEUM affiliates. In 1952, for instance, Seymour Papert, a scientist who was then at the University of the Witwatersrand and who worked in the Progressive Forum in Johannesburg, wrote to I. B. Tabata:

> There is a different of opinion amongst us on the question of U.F. [*united fronts*]. What I say here refers specifically to the Rand situation. We shall have to define our attitude towards the "Day of Mourning" on the 26th. Supposing that the A.N.C.-I.C.-C.P are able to get a mass response (as they did over May Day) we'll risk breaking what contact & confidence we have established if we adopt a completely isolationist position. You must remember that the AAC and UM are scarcely known here and then just as names. Militant struggle is still identified with the C.P. and although there is not much confidence in ANC, the people will follow them before anyone else. We are constantly being asked this typical question: "I agree with you about the faults of Congress & the C.P., but they are doing something, what are you doing?" ... On the other hand any sort of United Front is, as you point out, impossible on a principled basis. ... An alternative for us is to repeat what we were *forced* to do in connection with May Day. That is, not to enter into any organisational unity but to participate actively in the work of leaflet distribution, meetings etc while clearly differentiating ourselves from the principle behind it. The question is: does anyone take notice of the differentiation?[5]

As the 1950s progressed, NEUM youth in the Johannesburg SOYA became scathing about what they saw as the reformist and cult-like practices of the official leadership, whom they accused of selling out the movement (Document 31). As in the ANC, the NEUM leadership refused to listen and scorned these critics as "wreckers" (Documents 24, 30); the late 1950s and 1960s saw a series of expulsions by the NEUM leadership of its generally youthful critics.

## Uses of the boycott

The question of whether participation in racial structures was a viable means of furthering the democratic struggle was posed in a variety of contexts in the post-war years. While eschewing participation in racial institutions, the FIOSA nonetheless saw electoral participation in tactical terms and advocated "critical support for working-class candidates" as a means of political education (Document 32). The NEUM, by contrast, vehemently opposed all participation and argued that their boycott campaigns were a form of political education (Document 38). The Anti-CAD, for instance, began in 1943 as a mass movement against the government's plan to establish a Coloured Advisory Council and a coloured section of the Department of the Interior. It succeeded in forestalling the implementation of the Coloured Affairs Department until after 1948 and kept a boycott tradition alive in the Western Cape (Documents 2, 3, 21, 40, 42). John Gomas, for one, damned the system of separate racial structures known as "Dummy Representation" (Document 41).

Despite the virtually unanimous opposition of African leaders and of democratic organisations to the government's establishment of the NRC in 1936, over the next few years a number of key African leaders stood for election to the NRC. The CPSA modified its initial opposition, arguing that the NRC could be used as a propaganda platform. But in August 1946, after an ineffectual decade, the NRC adjourned in opposition to the government's continuing repressive policies and in particular to its brutal smashing of the 1946 African Mineworkers' Strike.

By the late 1940s, there was a general momentum for boycott amongst Africans as well as coloureds (Documents 33-34). However, in December 1947, Dr A. B. Xuma, then ANC President-General, urged Africans to give the government a second chance by returning the NRC members on a boycott ticket; representatives at the ANC's annual conference were in disarray over the boycott (Documents 35-36). In January 1948 the CPSA endorsed the election of boycott candidates (Document 37).

Within the ANC, the Youth League agitated to secure the adoption of its Programme of Action in December 1949. Although the Programme of Action called for direct African political representation and for the boycott of racial institutions, leading members of the ANC once again began to participate in those institutions. Critics of the boycott argued that it was practised in an abstentionist manner, in that people were organised to boycott institutions but not for further activity, or that the boycott was applicable only at particular periods (Document 39; Davids [1950]; Mettler 1957; Alexander 1986: 10-13). Those who advocated participation in local Advisory Boards argued that they offered the Congress movement and the Communist Party a platform for propaganda at a time when other opportunities for political mobilisation were being curtailed. The potential propaganda gains, they argued, outweighed the risk of losing popular support, especially since Africans, in their view, did not have the strong boycott tradition of the coloureds (Lodge 1983: 78). Yet the widespread practice of the boycott in Transkei, and the success of the Society of Young Africa (SOYA), an AAC affiliate, in organising advisory boards boycotts in Soweto and Sharpeville, suggests that the boycott remained an accepted grassroots tactic in African areas (Phahle 1987). SOYA pointed to the boycott of beer-halls directed by African women in Durban as an example of how a specific use of the boycott could develop into a more generalised opposition (Document 44).

This tactical approach to the boycott and the trend towards participation in racial structures exacerbated tensions between ANC moderates, who favoured a multiracial alliance, and Africanists in the Youth League, who maintained that whites were encouraging participation in racial structures and trying to reorientate the ANC towards white politics. The failure of the ANC's 1958 election stay-at-home, with its white-orientated slogan, "The Nats must Go!", indicated that ANC leaders were out of touch with grassroots feelings, Africanists argued. They were not alone in their opposition to these practices. The tiny Socialist League of Africa tried to provide a left critique within the Congress movement against what it saw as the moderating influence of Communists. It argued that COD members, by resisting the demand for immediate, universal franchise and by using their organs to raise the possibility of electoral participation, had a disproportionate influence on the electoral policy of Congress Alliance affiliates (Document 43; Karis and Carter 1977a: 76-7).

## National liberation and trade-union organisation

World War Two marked a peak for the black labour movement. The Council of Non-European Trade Unions (CNETU), a federation of black trade unions, was formed in 1941. As a stark indicator of the dramatic turnaround in the post-war years, in 1945 CNETU claimed 158 000 members from 119 trade unions – a figure not reached again until the 1980s. The brutal crushing of the 1946 African Mineworkers' Strike and the ensuing repression faced by its leaders left the black trade-union movement severely weakened on the eve of apartheid, and CNETU went into decline and collapsed, a victim of external repression from the state and internal left-wing rivalries (Callinicos 1993: 75, 86, 105-7). Apartheid laws restricted African trade-union organisation and entrenched divisions between black and white workers. The 1950 Suppression of Communism Act was used as a pretext to ban trade unionists. The 1953 Native Labour Act outlawed strikes by African workers. The 1956 Amendment to the Industrial Conciliation Act prohibited strikes in industries designated as essential, reaffirmed job reservation for whites, strengthened racial segregation under white leadership within trade unions and prohibited any future registration of "mixed" unions (Fine and Davis 1991: 156-7; Berger 1992: 182-3).

Both the leadership of the Congress movement and the NEUM shared the similar conviction that trade unions should be integrated into the national liberation movement through affiliation to particular organisations. The Trotskyist Eric Ernstzen, for instance, bemoaned the fact that only one trade union was represented at the Second National Anti CAD conference in 1944, and he called on the trade-union movement to call a conference to consider the impact of the CAD on organised coloured workers and on the entire trade-union movement (Document 9). NEUM affiliates like the Anti-CAD regularly called for the integration of trade unions into the national movement through their adherence to the Ten Point Programme (Document 48). The Congress movement and the NEUM diverged, however, on the question of practice. While Communists and activists within the Congress movement maintained their tradition of trade-union work, NEUM resolutions on labour were accompanied by a distinct lack of practical support. NEUM leaders rationalised their lack of trade-union work on the grounds that the trade unions were Communist-dominated (Document 9), and in 1948 they passively allowed trade unions to pull out of the TARC following the Communist Party's departure. Although NEUM youth became increasingly disenchanted with the leadership's reticence towards and even disdain for mass struggles in the 1950s, the more activist NEUM youth generally worked in community rather than trade-union organisations.

In the early 1950s, left-wing debates about trade-union organisation concerned the question of whether to build trade-union unity across the colour bar or to build the black trade-union movement. Not surprisingly, veteran trade unionist Ray Alexander, who organised for the Food and Canning Workers' Union (FCWU), argued, in December 1952, for working-class unity across the colour line through the affiliation of the

CNETU to the South African Trades and Labour Council (SATLC). At that time the SATLC was, in her view, the most representative of South African trade-union federations, where progressive white unions had recently successfully fought the imposition of a colour bar policy; subsequently, though, the FCWU criticised the SATLC for caving in to racialism. Trotskyists in the Forum Club countered that any unity between black and white workers would necessarily be on conditions detrimental to blacks; hence the focus should be on strengthening black trade unions (Document 45; see also Berger 1992: 205). A few months later, another Communist and trade-union leader, Daniel Tloome, attributed the weakness of organised labour to its exclusive concern with economic issues and its reliance on formal appeals to government machinery such as Wage Boards. His argument that black workers build up their trade unions and join the national liberation movement to fight the political disabilities which hampered them foreshadowed the establishment of the South African Congress of Trade Unions (SACTU) in 1955 (Document 46).

SACTU was formed from remnants of the SATLC and CNETU following the exclusion of African trade unions from the white-dominated Trade Union Council and further restrictive Industrial Conciliation legislation (Bunting 1981: 309-10). Ray Alexander and other Communist trade unionists helped to build SACTU, which became the fifth affiliate in the Congress Alliance. Fine and Davis (1991: 165) describe SACTU's style as one of "political unionism" in which "... working-class organisation was limited to the trade-union sphere, while the political struggle was conducted in national rather than class terms". Certainly, the Congress Alliance downplayed characteristically working-class forms of protest like workplace strikes, while stressing community-based forms of protest such as the stay-at-home.

Following the police massacre of unarmed protesters at a PAC demonstration in Sharpeville on 21 March 1960 and the government's subsequent imposition of a State of Emergency, the liberation movement was forced to reappraise its strategy and tactics, and particularly its use of non-violent civil disobedience. The stay-at-home tactic had been used with varying degrees of success: a stay-at-home the week after the Sharpeville massacre had been a success, but the ANC's call for another stay-at-home the week of 18 to 25 April failed to materialise. The Emergency Committee of the ANC offered an explanation for the poor showing (Document 49). It did not criticise the stay-at-home as a general tactic, but instead pointed, on the one hand, to the climate of extreme intimidation produced by police and army control of the townships and the mass arrests of Congress leaders and, on the other, to confusion and disarray amongst the remaining leadership.

The Socialist League of Africa, by contrast, stressed the limitations of the stay-at-home tactic for the development of working-class consciousness and organisation (Document 50). The tactic was a plausible response to conditions where strikes by African workers were illegal and trade unions were weak, it wrote. It was not, however, a viable means to build working-class strength over the long term: It reinforced divisions amongst workers and was necessarily of limited duration because townships were designed to be easily sealed off.

If the Congress movement's sectional mobilisation and the prominent role of whites, especially Communists, exacerbated tensions between Africanists and ANC moderates, its passive resistance tactics, which subordinated working-class interests to a broad class alliance, proved ineffective in stopping state repression. Throughout the 1950s, the state put more and more obstacles in the way of open political work. Many activists were banned during this period, and the five-year Treason Trial, which lasted from 1956 to 1961, kept the top layer of Congress leaders from their political work. Stripped of experienced cadre, democratic practices began to break down. In the late 1950s, ANC elections were pre-arranged, rank and file criticism stifled and dissenters expelled (Gerhart 1978: 173-9), practices which the NEUM was similarly accused of by numerous critics. Disputes within the ANC were especially intense in the Transvaal, an Africanist stronghold, where 1957 saw a severely contested attempt by the Provincial Executive to get itself reelected *en bloc*. These practices were deplored even by loyal Congress members (Karis and Carter 1977a: 242-5, 273, 308-9; Lodge 1983: 82). For Africanists, they confirmed their critiques of multiracialism.

Within the NEUM tensions were mounting between a leadership whose political caution was seen as abstentionist and a militant youth who argued for greater participation in localised grassroots struggles and for more emphasis on class rather than purely national struggle.

## The national question

In South Africa of the 1940s and 1950s, the overwhelming majority of the nationally oppressed were proletarians and land-hungry peasants; most socialists, therefore, believed that the national question was inextricably linked to the working-class struggle. Beyond that basic agreement, however, socialists used different paradigms to evaluate South Africa's political dualism, characterised as a democracy for whites and a slave colony for blacks, or as the Forum Club (1952:4) described it, "... democratic independence in *form* but not in *content*". Communists saw social change occurring in stages, an approach elaborated in the theory of "colonialism of a special type". Trotskyists analysed the divided polity in terms of South Africa's combined and uneven development.

These theoretical points of departure had important implications for conceptualising the national question and for strategies of national liberation. "Colonialism of a special type" lends itself to a two-stage process of social change in which a multi-class alliance for national liberation is seen as a necessary pre-condition to the struggle for socialism. The notion of combined and uneven development rejects the colonial analogy, arguing instead that British imperialism refashioned pre-capitalist remnants to its ends. Because most South African Trotskyists agreed that the colour bar was "... the iron hoop which binds together the whole structure of imperialist-capitalist exploitation and oppression" (Volume One, Document 121), they have generally seen the struggle against the colour bar and for democracy as a direct assault on capitalism.

The implications of these theories, and their articulation with conflicting approaches to non-collaboration, can be traced in the various approaches to the national question within the liberation movement. The NEUM saw building a non-racial nation as the road to national liberation and democracy; the moderate wing of the Congress movement, along with Communists, used a multiracial or multinational paradigm; Africanists saw building an African nation as a precondition for broader black unity and for the overthrow of white supremacy.

The NEUM, with its slogan, "We build a nation", was the first organisation to directly challenge the state ideology that South Africa was a multi-racial or multi-national society (No Sizwe 1979: 54-60). In *The Background of Segregation*, written in 1943, B. M. Kies articulated what would be the dominant approach to the national question within the NEUM, stressing the significance of racial ideology and political education. If the cause of the majority's subordination lay in their acceptance of the ideology of segregation, argued Kies, the solution lay in the rejection of segregation through Non-European unity. Only after their common oppressor was overthrown, Kies contended, could the national question be resolved, "ON OUR TERMS, NOT THE TERMS OF THE EXPLOITER" (Document 4). In 1950 the teacher and educationist W. P. van Schoor, a former member of the FIOSA who joined the NEUM, challenged conventional South African historiography with the argument that twentieth-century *Herrenvolkism* had its economic and political roots in the British Cape Colony and Natal plantation systems, and its emotional basis – colour prejudice – in Boer society (Document 51).[6] The following year, the NEUM leadership produced "A Declaration to the People of South Africa from the Non-European Unity Movement". Rejecting Stalin's definition of nationality based on common culture, language and traditions, the NEUM defined the South African nation as comprising "... the people who were born in South Africa and who have no other country but South Africa as their mother-land" (Karis and Carter 1973: 495). The struggle to build a nation must begin with principled rather than *ad hoc* Non-European unity against the *Herrenvolk* notion of a master race, argued the NEUM. This required repudiating the *quislings* who collaborated with the state's divide-and-rule policies by working within racial structures like the NRC. The NEUM's federal structure was an attempt to deal with the national question on an organisational level by uniting African, coloured and Indian organisations in one large federation, but it never drew in an Indian pillar. Although the leadership had hoped that the federal structure would wither away as sectional divisions broke down, in practice it proved to be top-heavy and long-lasting (Tabata 1950; No Sizwe 1979: 112).

Differences between the NEUM and its external Trotskyist critics emerged over the theory and practice of nation-building. Kenneth Jordaan, for instance, a member of the FIOSA and the Forum Club, criticised Van Schoor for his assumption that colour, rather than a common lack of democratic rights, was the basis for Non-European unity (Document 52). Van Schoor's argument, Jordaan maintained, buttressed the NEUM's use of the term *Herrenvolk*, which in practice obscured class divisions and implied that blacks and whites constituted two inherently antagonistic blocs. Van Schoor suggested that South Africa had passed through a feudal stage and still retained feudal remnants, a position which was reflected in the NEUM's stress on agrarian revolution, Jordaan wrote. But the twentieth-century racial system, Jordaan countered, was the result of rapid imperialist intervention in a white settler society. Accordingly, the political demands of the national liberation movement, he concluded, must coincide with the economic tendency towards increasing black proletarianisation.

This debate intersected with and influenced debates on the national question within the Congress movement. The ANC's "old guard" leadership still saw South Africa as a multiracial and multinational society in which racial equality would be won through incorporation in the existing political and socio-economic system, achieved through tactical alliances along sectional lines. For the ANC old guard, Gail Gerhart has explained, building the nation meant uniting Africans across tribal groupings. But in the 1940s the ANC Youth League broke from the prevailing idea of an African nation within a multinational South African society, counterposing the idea of a single South African nation created on terms established by the indigenous African majority (Gerhart 1978: 67; Karis and Carter 1973: 323-4, 335).

The ANC Youth League's nation-building project had striking parallels with that of the NEUM. Both the NEUM and the Youth League believed that building a non-racial nation was premised on non-collaboration with racial institutions, and the ANC's acceptance of the Programme of Action in 1948 symbolised a temporary convergence of the old guard's tactical use of the boycott and the Youth League's espousal of non-collaboration. Yet the NEUM hoped to achieve Non-European unity through a federal structure uniting sectional groups under a common programme and saw Non-European unity as a precondition for drawing white workers from their historical alliance with the bourgeoisie into the ranks of the democratic movement. The Youth League, without rejecting Non-European co-operation in principle, saw "... the creation of a single powerful African National Front ..." as a precondition for future alliance with other social and political groups (Karis and Carter 1973: 322, 317-8). The Youth League's conception of the South African nation contained an ambivalence which foreshadowed the developing tensions in the ANC: In some of its writings, nationhood is determined by right of birth and shared geographical and social experiences; in others, it is based on colour.

Within the ANC, tensions over the national question mounted through the 1950s, reinforcing the related tensions over strategies and tactics and finally culminating in the breakaway of the Africanists and the formation of the PAC. In 1952 Oliver Tambo and Walter Sisulu of the ANC and Yusuf Cachalia of the SAIC called on whites who had supported the Defiance Campaign to form an "alliance of Europeans" to work with the Congress movement (Lazerson 1994: 68-75). This became the all-white Congress of Democrats (COD). Communists were prominent in the COD leadership, and Africanists believed that the COD exercised a disproportionate and moderating influence over the Congress movement. The adoption of the Freedom Charter by the Congress of the People in June 1955, and by the ANC in 1956, became a basis of further dispute within the Congress movement (Document 23). The Natal ANC's Provincial Council argued that the Freedom Charter's national clause emphasised racial distinctions rather than nation-building (Karis and Carter 1977a: 65-6; Lodge 1983: 74). Similarly, at the launch of the PAC in 1959 Mangaliso Sobukwe argued that multiracialism negated democracy by promoting group rather than individual rights, giving disproportionate representation to whites while denying the indigenous majority their rightful possession of the land (Document 58; Gerhart 1978: 190; Lodge 1983: 211-2). Within a few years, however, Sobukwe's aspiration for a non-racial South Africa was eclipsed with the formation of the overtly racialist *Poqo*, the PAC's armed wing (No Sizwe 1979: 116-7).

Although most socialists concurred that socio-economic development was laying the material basis for national unity, Communist support for the Freedom Charter and the Congress Alliance suggests that in practice a multiracial or multinational approach to the national question prevailed in the Party.[7] Here, the theoretical influence of Soviet scholars can be seen. In the late 1940s Soviet scholars had been sceptical about the progressive potential of national bourgeoisies of oppressed or colonised countries. By the early 1950s, though, they were promoting the concept of People's Democracies as anti-imperialist and potentially pro-Soviet transitional forms to socialism. Hence, the Soviet Union's support for national democratic movements premised on a broad alliance of the bourgeoisie, *petite bourgeoisie* and working class (Hudson 1986: 11-5). I. I. Potekhin's work was particularly influential amongst South African Communists. Potekhin argued that the African bourgeoisie in South Africa lacked the national consciousness necessary for self-government and that this laid the basis for the growth of working-class and Communist influence in the liberation movement. However, he added, Anglo-Afrikaner imperialism impeded the development of a single African nation by artificially preserving feudal remnants in the form of tribes or "territorial-administrative units". Potekhin's contention that the South African national struggle was developing into a conflict between an Anglo-Afrikaner imperialist nation and an African nation supported by other national groups echoes the colonial conception of the Native Republic thesis and is seen later in the "colonialism of a special type" thesis (Potekhin [c. 1953]: 1-3, 12-16; No Sizwe 1979: 97-8).

The years between the disbanding of the CPSA in 1950 and the appearance of the SACP in 1953 marked a period of relative intellectual fluidity amongst South African Communists, who debated the national question in forums such as the Johannesburg Discussion Club. As Lazerson (1994: 124-9) has noted, much of the debate at the Johannesburg Discussion Club concerned the class structure of the national liberation movement and the degree to which this class structure, particularly the absence of an African bourgeoisie, influenced its political trajectory. Two main positions can be discerned in the club's proceedings, *Viewpoints and Perspectives*: one maintained that the national struggle obscured the primacy of the class struggle; the other, which became SACP orthodoxy, argued that the road to socialism lay through the national struggle, i.e., that South Africa's distinctive conditions constituted "colonialism of a special type" and that, after national liberation, the predominantly proletarian composition of the national movement would push the movement towards socialism. Michael Harmel, an influential Party ideologue, elaborated an early analysis of "colonialism of a special type" (Document 53).

The urgency of the national question in the early 1950s meant that, unusually, Communists and Trotskyists met at a symposium in Cape Town organised jointly by the South Africa Club and the Forum Club. Jack Simons and Lionel Forman of the SACP, Kenneth Jordaan of the Forum Club and Thomas Ngwenya of the ANC presented papers (Documents 54-6; Forman and Odendaal 1992: 179-89; Lazerson 1994: 130-2). The arguments of Jack Simons and Lionel Forman both showed the influence of Stalin's views on nationality. Simons argued that South Africa's national question could not be solved by the traditional demands of oppressed nations for autonomy, self-determination or secession, but by legal and social equality (Document 55). Because the colour bar stifled the development of a black bourgeoisie and prevented any significant class differentiation amongst the oppressed, the working class would play the dominant political role within the liberation movement, which would, accordingly, reflect the common interests of all workers rather than specific group interests, reinforcing South Africa's tendency to develop into one nation rather than a multinational society. Forman, by contrast, stressed the idea of a multinational society. In an article written in 1954 but only published in 1959, Forman evaluated the political content of nationalism in terms of the class interests it served, distinguishing between people's nationalism and oppressive "rich man's" nationalism. Forman argued that in South Africa the rapid growth of the black proletariat raised the possibility of a "people's movement" along Chinese lines. South Africa, he believed, comprised both nations and aspirant nations, and working-class policy should guarantee those nations their right to territorial and administrative autonomy. Because national autonomy would be combined with individual freedom of movement, this would not be another form of apartheid (Document 57; Forman and Odendaal 1992: 190-215).

Kenneth Jordaan argued that South Africa's national question was not one of conflicting nations within the same borders, but of peoples of the same nation oppressing other peoples (Document 54). Hence, the national question could not be solved through formal independence but through the struggle for democracy, and in this respect the national and democratic struggles converged. Even though South Africans perceived themselves as comprising four national groups, these were not aspirant nations, as they showed no movement for autonomy, but considered themselves to be part of the South African nation. In contrast to India, where national groups had a long history as distinct cultural groupings, South Africa's combined development – the rapid development of industry and proletariat – precluded a distinct cultural and historical tradition by any national group.

Unlike France, India or China, where the bourgeoisie had led democratic struggles, in South Africa, Jordaan continued, the colour bar had stifled the development of a black bourgeoisie and blacks were overwhelmingly workers or impoverished rural cultivators. Reflecting this uneven class development, he argued that leadership of the democratic struggle must fall to the proletariat whose aspirations could only come into conflict with capitalism. Consequently, he concluded, South Africa's national democratic struggle could only be solved through an uninterrupted permanent revolution.

This joint symposium marked the only formal co-operation by Communists and Trotskyists on the national question. The establishment of the SACP in 1953 marked a political reorientation for the South African Communist movement. Many of those Communists who had argued for the primacy of the class struggle and for the organisation of workers along class lines did not join the new Party, and discussion of the national question was marginalised. Forman's interpretation of a multinational society was considered divisive, the prevailing position being that to speak of national autonomy for South Africa's national groups while the government was developing its bantustan policy, risked encouraging separatist tendencies (interviews with Turok and Forman). The Freedom Charter's national clause, with its emphasis on group rights, omitted any question of national development or integration and thus was open-ended enough to lend itself to a variety of interpretations. Or, as Nelson Mandela (1956: 7-8) put it, the Charter's force lay in its democratic appeal to all classes and strata of the oppressed, a view which dovetailed with the SACP's two-stage approach.

## The agrarian question[8]

White control of land has been a hallmark of South African development this century. The 1913 Natives' Land Act established the principle of territorial segregation in the new Union of South Africa; the 1936 Natives' Trust and Land Bill stipulated that the African majority be restricted to 13 per cent of the total land in South Africa and prevented Africans from acquiring land outside reserved areas, later called bantustans. Development in the reserves was linked to that in urban areas and on white farms through the migrant-labour network; the movement of Africans to and from the reserves was controlled through the pass system. In 1942 the government temporarily relaxed the controls on African movement to towns as part of its efforts to promote war-fuelled industrialisation. For white farmers, who relied on cheap, servile labour, this sparked fears of a labour shortage. Hence the proposals by the Transvaal Agricultural Union for tightening controls over African farm labour and over the labour of African youth, to which both Ruth First of the Young Communist League and I. B. Tabata of the WPSA referred (Documents 59, 60, 62). In the 1940s and 1950s, however, most socialists who addressed the agrarian question were concerned with organising in the reserves rather than on white farms. The virtual impossibility of organising black farmworkers or labour tenants on white farms left the reserves as the only option for rural organising (Hofmeyr 1985: 281-311; interview with Alexander).

Even though the principal efforts to address South Africa's agrarian question and to organise in the reserves have come from socialists concerned with the revolutionary potential of the rural population, the socialist movement's theoretical and practical attention to the agrarian question has been sporadic. The South African Left has been divided between a majority giving primacy to the urban working-class movement and a minority which saw the agrarian question as the backbone of any social revolution. This dichotomy resulted in an oscillating practice between town and countryside.

The first systematic attempts to address the agrarian question came with the CPSA's adoption of the Native Republic thesis in 1928, which saw land-hunger as the driving motivation for South Africa's rural majority. But in the late 1930s, with the adoption of the Comintern's People's Front strategy, the CPSA put the Native Republic thesis on the back-burner and turned its attention again to trade-union work and electoral politics. By contrast, the WPSA saw the agrarian question as the "alpha and omega" of the South African revolution. As a result, socialist attention to the agrarian question in the 1940s and '50s was mainly the work of Trotskyists and of individual Communists like Alpheus Maliba in Zoutpansberg, Northern Transvaal, Flag Boshielo in Sekhukhuneland, Eastern Transvaal, and Govan Mbeki in Transkei. Using the notion of "teachers as a vanguard", Trotskyists and others in the AAC worked with teachers in Transkei to disseminate political ideas. Those Communists who engaged in rural organising tended to be migrant workers who later gained trade-union experience through employment in urban industry; as Delius notes, they were far more sensitive to the possibilities of rural organisation than the largely urban-based Party leaders (Delius 1993: 306-10; Hirson 1977: 4-7; Basner 1993: 105-8; Bunting 1981: 138).

With the significant exceptions of the writings of Alpheus Maliba (Bunting 1981: 138-47) and Govan Mbeki (1964), there is little indication of Communist attempts to theorise the agrarian question (Delius 1993: 303). In the proceedings of the Johannesburg Discussion Club published in *Viewpoints and Perspectives* only one paper addressed the agrarian question; this showed some intriguing overlaps with Trotskyist perspectives on the subject (Document 65). Trotskyists, by contrast, were consumed with the agrarian question and the strategic problem of linking urban and rural movements. At the same time, South Africa's organised urban proletariat was overwhelmingly white and racist, pursuing labour protectionist policies. Hence, most Trotskyists saw migrant labour, because of its unique social position and exposure to urban ideas, as the most advanced section of the rural population and a vector for transmitting political ideas from town to countryside.

The FIOSA stressed the centrality of objective economic conditions in ascertaining the class nature of the reserve population. M. N. Averbach argued that aside from a minute layer of farmers scattered about some reserves, rural landless Africans were peasants in aspiration only and those on white farms were agricultural proletarians. He coined the term "tribal proletariat" to characterise South Africa's migrant labour and rural proletariat, indicating their Janus-faced character: proletarian in outlook; peasant in aspirations (Document 61).

The WPSA, by contrast, believed that most Africans were driven by land hunger and that political mobilisation in the countryside should begin with a recognition of Africans' peasant aspirations. In the late 1930s the urban-based WPSA made some stabs at organising migrant labour at its point of production on the mines but the rigidly guarded compounds which housed migrant workers made trade-union organisation on the mines extremely difficult. As a result, the WPSA began to consider the organisation of migrant labour in the countryside, in the belief that as long as the reserves remained unorganised, migrant labour could easily be used by capitalists to break the strikes of black workers in towns (interview with Tabata and Gool). However, activists in the WPSA and the AAC organised reserve-based Africans as peasants rather than as rural proletarians, evoking considerable criticism by FIOSA Trotskyists (Document 67; Ernstzen 1950).

The 1940s and 1950s saw a series of rural protests and uprisings across South Africa's reserves, including Zoutpansberg in the Northern Transvaal in the 1940s; Witzieshoek in 1950; Zeerust in the Western Transvaal and Sekhukhuneland in the Eastern Transvaal in the mid-1950s; and Pondoland in Transkei at the end of the decade (Hirson 1977; Lodge 1983: 261-94; Basner 1993: 99-108; Hooper 1989; Mbeki 1964). This rural discontent reflected the long-term economic deterioration produced by state policies which locked Africans in the reserves while stifling the development of an African peasantry. More specifically, the protests were catalysed by the increased state intervention of the post-World War Two period which imposed conservationist policies without local consultation, political restructuring and controls on movement.

These protests reflected the mass rejection of the government's 1945 Rehabilitation Scheme and the Bantu Authorities Act. The Rehabilitation Scheme ostensibly aimed to rehabilitate the depleted reserves by resettling people into newly constructed villages where afforestation and soil conservation programmes would be implemented. In effect, the scheme aimed to create reserve-based proletarian settlements for the families of migrant labourers and to impede the development of an urban African working class. The Bantu Authorities Act laid the foundations for the future bantustan system. While curtailing popular electoral participation and prohibiting unauthorised public meetings of more than ten, it expanded and consolidated the powers of chiefs, whose legitimacy declined as they became direct symbols of the oppressive state (Mbeki 1964: 34-42; Beinart and Bundy 1980: 305-6).

Initially, people responded by protesting against the specific measures designed to strip them of land and cattle and turn them into perpetual migrant labour. The AAC concentrated on the struggle against rehabilitation. I. B. Tabata, for instance, who was born near the farming community of Queenstown and organised for the AAC in Transkei, argued that the reserve policy was premised on the restriction of land as the basis of ensuring a cheap migrant workforce. Thus, the means to rehabilitate the reserves was not to reduce cattle stocks, as this would only intensify hunger and malnutrition, but to increase the land – a view propounded by the Johannesburg Progressive Forum, which poured scorn on Eddie Roux's ideas of developing Transkei (Documents 62-5).

Later, these protests merged into struggles against Tribal Authorities who, in addition to enforcing rehabilitation, controlled labour influx and efflux. Virtually all protests in the reserves during these years indicated the social class antagonisms emanating from the relationship between collaboration and capital accumulation. In the Pondoland revolt of 1960-1, for instance, people attacked chiefs both because they collaborated with the regime in enforcing these unpopular measures and because their collaboration was a means to accumulate wealth (Chaskalson 1987: 51-52; Beinart and Bundy 1980: 309-10).

Against this backdrop, socialists became increasingly concerned with the practical problems of organising in the reserves. Through this work they developed and modified their ideas about the role of migrant labour in the countryside. Despite differences in social background and organisational allegiance, rural activists displayed striking similarities both in their attention to the reserves and their analyses of rural mobilisation and protest.

It is in the analyses of Tabata and of Govan Mbeki, another Transkeian-born activist who was secretary of the Transkei Voters' Association in the early 1940s and General Secretary of the Transkei Organized Bodies from 1943-8, that the South African Left came closest to developing an indigenous theory of rural mobilisation that reflected local empirical conditions. Given the intense sectarianism dividing Trotskyists and Communists, mirrored in the relationship of the NEUM and the Congress movement, the similarity of Tabata's and Mbeki's analyses of rural protests is striking. Both conceived the relationship of urban and rural protests as one of intense, short-lived urban protests which periodically intersected with slower, longer-lived rural protests, with migrant labour as the critical link. Both also stressed the virtually unanimous solidarity of the reserve population, rather than differentiating its actual or potential differences or assessing which strata might potentially support a socialist movement. Both believed that it was in the reserves rather than in towns that social protests transformed into sustained mass-based uprisings potentially capable of challenging state power (Mbeki 1964: 128; interview with Tabata and Gool).

Despite the broad conceptual agreement of Tabata's and Mbeki's ideas, within the NEUM theoretical divisions over the strategies and tactics of rural mobilisation became starker and more vituperous in the 1950s, a decade of virtually continuous upheaval in South Africa's reserves. The AAC's rural mobilisation on a classically democratic rather than socialist programme provoked a controversy within the NEUM which catalysed its split in December 1958. To a large degree, but with significant exceptions, the NEUM split between its two main organisations, the AAC, strongest in Johannesburg and the Eastern Cape, and the predominantly Western Cape-based Anti-CAD. Both sides concurred in the essential unity of the land and national questions; hence, their joint use of the Workers' Party slogan "Land and Liberty" to link the two struggles. The dispute boiled down to an interpretation of Point 7 of the NEUM's Ten Point

Programme (Document 8), reflecting polarised conceptions of the rural population. Essentially, the two factions differed in their assessment of the extent to which the mentality of rural cultivators had been affected by the market, a polemic amongst South African Trotskyists since the 1930s.

The majority in the AAC saw rural Africans as peasants or aspirant peasants and interpreted the abolition of restrictions on acquiring land to mean the right to buy and sell land. Tabata argued that people in the reserves could not be mobilised on a slogan of nationalisation as from their perspective the state's trusteeship of the land was tantamount to nationalisation. But because the legal right to buy land without the means to do so could never satisfy popular land hunger, Tabata contended, that realisation would push people beyond capitalism. In this sense, he saw the achievement of the right to buy and sell as the pivot of a permanent revolution. The new division of land enacted by a democratic parliament would be determined by the existing balance of class forces at that time and could not be stipulated beforehand (interviews with Tabata and Gool and with Alexander).

The other dominant position, articulated by Hosea Jaffe and the majority of the Anti-CAD, also assumed a high degree of African peasant consciousness (Document 66). Because the Ten Point Programme was a minimum programme, Jaffe argued, Point 7 implied firstly a democratic redivision of the land rather than a maximum socialist demand of collectivisation. Redivision meant the expropriation of large landowners, abolition of white control of land and of exploitative practices like speculation and landlordism, and the allotment of land to smallholders on an equal household basis. The question of nationalisation or private ownership could only be settled after expropriation and the elimination of all racial laws. Undoubtedly influenced by Averbach's "tribal proletariat" concept, Jaffe believed that migrant workers or "peasant-workers" would return to the land, opt for individual titles to non-marketable land and apply the technical and co-operative practices learned in their urban worksites to agricultural production.

From outside the NEUM, Kenneth Jordaan argued that unlike classical peasant-based democratic revolutions, the land question was not the sub-soil of the South African revolution, because most South Africans had been uprooted and those still on the land were a proletarianised reserve labour force and did not look to land for their subsistence. Whereas the bourgeoisies of classical democratic revolutions had been able to satisfy popular democratic demands, albeit in a delayed, top-down manner, South Africa's white bourgeoisie, Jordaan maintained, could not satisfy the democratic demands of the black majority. Indeed, because capitalist development has been premised on the lack of democratic rights, he believed that democracy would undermine capitalism in South Africa.

Point 7, Jordaan argued, contained elements which, from the point of view of capitalist development, were both progressive and backward. It did not address social relations on the land after the initial reallocation of land; thus it side-stepped the class nature of the future state. Underlying the AAC's demand for the right to buy and sell land, Jordaan continued, was the aim of creating a yeomanry. But industrial South Africa lacked the large peasantry upon which to develop a yeomanry: The bourgeoisie relied on the super-exploitation of proletarianised reserve-dwellers and would never allow sufficient numbers to withdraw from the labour market to develop as independent farmers. To call for the development of a small stratum of black capitalist farmers or peasants in South Africa's conditions, as the AAC did, was not historically progressive from the point of view of the working class, even if it accorded with the laws of capitalist development. But the Anti-CAD's call to break up and redistribute large, productive capitalist landholdings using a quantitative yardstick was economically unviable and utopian, assuming that Africans had a prior land claim and would abandon industrial employment for small-scale agrarian cultivation. Jordaan suggested that nationalisation would allow the continuation of large, mechanised farms conducive to agricultural productivity, enabling a gradual transition to collectivisation (Document 67).

The intensity of the theoretical disputes masked the political crisis facing socialists which related to the theory-practice problem. Fuelling the disputes were two practical problems. The first concerned whether to organise in the reserves on the basis of a democratic or socialist programme, a problem which became more acute after the passage of the Suppression of Communism Act in 1950, which pushed the entire socialist movement underground. The second concerned whether to actively support armed struggle in the Pondoland uprising against state repression. Neither the NEUM nor the ANC supplied arms requested by Pondoland militants during their uprising.[9] Hence, despite fierce theoretical disputes amongst socialists, the Left did not give practical support to rural people fighting the state. Although armed resistance in South Africa began in the countryside, only in the aftermath of the Sharpeville massacre and the ensuing nation-wide uprising, when the state banned political opposition, did urban-based socialist organisations seriously consider the question of armed struggle.

## Underground and armed resistance

Armed struggle against apartheid began in the rural areas; in Pondoland it accelerated after March 1960, with the formation of hill or mountain committees which voiced local demands such as non-collaboration with the Bantu Authorities and non-payment of taxes and took over functions of local governance (Documents 68, 73, 74). March 1960 also marked a transition for the urban-based liberation movement: The non-violent phase of the struggle came to a close, catalysed by a police massacre of unarmed people at an anti-pass protest in Sharpeville organised by the PAC. Shortly thereafter, following mass upheavals around the country, the government imposed a State of Emergency and banned the ANC and PAC. This catalysed a perceptual shift within the liberation movement, as urban activists recognised the ineffectiveness of non-violent protest as a means to achieve social reform and began considering armed struggle as a means to contest the repressive state. Small study circles and socialist groups mushroomed around the country. However, political organisation became increasingly clandestine, and the State of Emergency and the banning of organisations and activists muted political debate and pushed political work underground (Document 69).

Despite the transition from non-violent protest, there were continuities both in terms of political rivalry and in the approaches adopted by diverse political traditions to armed struggle. An "All-In Conference" meant to include representatives from all democratic organisations was held in March 1961, even though the PAC and Liberal Party had withdrawn from the Continuation Committee planning the conference alleging ANC domination. The Congress movement saw armed struggle as a tactical means to pressure the South African state for democratic reforms and to inspire the oppressed majority, while the NEUM initially claimed that armed struggle was adventurist. Other small groups of radicals envisioned a people's war which would lay the basis for socialist transformation. Some socialists believed that a South African revolution would not be a two-stage process, but that the national movement would transform itself into a socialist revolution. For them the question was, given South Africa's racially-divided working class and small black urban proletariat, how to spark off that revolution and conquer power (Johns 1973: 272-3; Turok 1974: 359; interviews with Alexander and Mohamed).

*Umkhonto weSizwe* (Spear of the Nation) (MK) was formed in November 1961 by members of the ANC and SACP. Despite broad consensus within the SACP on this move, not all members were convinced: Rowley Arenstein, for one, ardently criticised the turn to armed struggle as anarchism. MK launched its sabotage campaign on 16 December 1961, an official holiday commemorating the Afrikaner massacre of the Zulus at Blood River, Weenen in 1838 and popularly known as Dingaan's Day. During 1962 Nelson Mandela secretly went abroad to raise funds for training and supplies (Bunting 1981: 274-6; Kasrils 1993: 41-5).

The SACP's 1962 programme elaborated the "colonialism of a special type" thesis which laid the theoretical basis for its insistence that national democracy would be a precursor to socialism and for its continued alliance with the ANC during this underground period (Bunting 1981: 284-320). At its Sixth Conference in 1962 the SACP reiterated its belief that repressive conditions in South Africa necessitated a turn to underground and armed struggle (Document 72; Bunting 1981: 314-5). It conceded that political repression impeded effective organisational work, but as it had in 1949, it anticipated that increasing repression would radicalise the masses and provide favourable conditions for the Party's growth. It viewed small-scale sabotage as a first step to be followed by a mass struggle combining both violent and non-violent methods.

MK engaged in the sabotage of key government installations in vital industries or communications or infrastructure as a means to demonstrate the consequences of apartheid to whites and to inspire popular support amongst blacks. Its hope that sabotage would have a "demonstration effect" as a form of propaganda showed a continuity with the appeals to whites which had marked the Congress Alliance's civil disobedience campaigns of the 1950s. Yet MK also saw sabotage as a facet of guerrilla war in that it was meant to create the necessary conditions for the formation of guerrilla units amongst the people. The first phase of armed struggle was one in which a well-trained underground group would engage in spectacular acts of sabotage to generate mass support. This "armed propaganda" would be followed by a broadening into mass resistance through a people's war, in which the small MK cadre would attract and train new recruits inside the country, engaging in hit-and-run guerrilla tactics and merging back into the people. It was assumed that this guerrilla struggle would begin in the countryside and would gradually gain the active support of urban black workers, who remained a minority in white-dominated towns (Document 76; Bunting 1981: 274-6; 380-93; Barrell 1990; Kasrils 1993: 35-63; Ellis and Sechaba 1992). However, on 11 July 1963 much of MK's top leadership was arrested in a security police raid on a farm in Rivonia, near Johannesburg, where they were formulating strategy and tactics. A series of other arrests followed the Rivonia raid, leading to the imprisonment or escape into exile of much of MK's leadership.

The turn to armed struggle made the Congress Alliance and the SACP more dependent on external sources for funding. With the banning of the ANC, the nature of the Congress Alliance became increasingly contentious, as public campaigns undertaken by the remaining legal organisations of the Alliance might promote the perception of non-African domination within the Congress movement (Document 72; Bunting 1981: 274-6). This was a point raised by the PAC in its appeals to external sources for funding. The issue indicated that the national question was far from resolved, either in theory or practice.

The PAC's armed wing was known as *Poqo* ("We stand alone"). Reports of *Poqo*'s activities begin to circulate in early 1962. In explaining the relative scholarly neglect of *Poqo*, Tom Lodge (1978: 94-5) has noted that in contrast to MK and other groups concerned with armed struggle in which literate intellectuals played a leading role, *Poqo* itself did not produce written records and few of its members have written about it. The PAC, however, had an intellectual cadre; although leaders like Sobukwe espoused a socialist viewpoint, the organisation was strongly anti-Communist, a legacy of the distrust of whites and Indians in the Congress Alliance. This anti-Communist stance attracted radical liberals like Patrick Duncan, who joined the PAC and represented it in exile.

In contrast to MK's tight organisational structure, *Poqo* was a loosely organised network with a populist orientation whose activists used home-made weapons and relied on intimidation when recruiting membership. It attacked black collaborators and engaged in random attacks on whites. Its random use of terror and lack of strategy attracted criticism from both MK (Document 76) and the National Liberation Front (NLF), a network formed by the Yu Chi Chan Club, a group of youth who had been expelled from or left the NEUM. Describing *Poqo*'s use of terrorism, the NLF (1963b) wrote:

> This practice, i.e., forcing people into the organisation, is very unhealthy, since they never really understand, or feel the necessity of understanding, the aims and policy of the organisation. The organisation can never depend on their loyalty and sincerity, as can be seen from the many Poqo members who are prepared to give evidence against Poqo in the trials proceeding throughout the country.

*Poqo* attracted support in the Western Cape and Transkei, particularly from migrant workers. It produced no clear-cut view of social transformation but appealed to traditions of primary resistance which sought the return of land to Africans as the indigenous occupants. Some members envisioned a spontaneous insurrection ignited by the leadership; others, a protracted guerrilla struggle. By 1963 it was experiencing serious organisational problems (Lodge 1977: 102-7).

In March 1963 Potlako Leballo, PAC's deputy leader in Maseru, Basutoland, held a press conference declaring that 150 000 PAC supporters were preparing for a general uprising the following month. His communications with South African PAC members were intercepted by the South African police, leading to massive crackdowns and the arrests of thousands of PAC members. Nonetheless, PAC leaders continued to make plans for using Basutoland as a base from which to launch guerrillas into South Africa, seeking funds from anti-Communist sources (Document 78). Despite this optimism, the organisation was plagued by internal rivalries and corruption from which it never recuperated.

Through 1962 all efforts to discuss armed struggle within the NEUM were suppressed. Those who refused to drop the matter were expelled or left. In late 1961, the NEUM leadership reiterated its conviction that the 1960 Pondoland uprising had been premature and that it had wisely refused to assist the peasants who had appealed to them for arms. The same year the African Peoples' Democratic Union of Southern Africa (APDUSA) was formed by the Tabata faction of the NEUM. Its core was composed of the AAC elements from the old WPSA. Its formation can be seen as an attempt by Tabata to broaden his organisational base following the NEUM's split and in response to the PAC's success at popular mobilisation. APDUSA's unitary structure and its non-racial definition of the African nation reflected both a recognition of the criticisms of NEUM's federal structure and its effort to be a viable alternative to the PAC, with its unitary organisation. However, within a few years it was clear that APDUSA had difficulties mobilising working-class people and retaining its younger members.

APDUSA belatedly accepted the idea of armed struggle in early 1963. Yet this decision was an ambivalent one, with many members still believing in the viability of non-violent transition. By April 1963, the initial interest which APDUSA's "New Line" on armed struggle had sparked had evaporated as, in the eyes of critics, the leadership stalled on making military preparations (NLF 1963a). In 1970, however, APDUSA leadership exiled in Zambia infiltrated guerrillas back into the NEUM's traditional rural base in Pondoland. These were soon captured (Unity Movement of South Africa 1972).

Two smaller and independent groups emerged alongside the efforts at armed struggle undertaken by the older political traditions. The NLF emerged shortly after MK, formed by members of the Yu Chi Chan Club, a discussion club composed of youth who broke from the NEUM due to its practical inactivity and its unwillingness to discuss socialism and armed struggle: Amongst its members were Neville Alexander, Kenneth Abrahams and Dulcie September. Seeking to avoid the sectarianism which resulted from requiring strict adherence either to the Freedom Charter or the Ten Point Programme, the NLF retained the concept of a minimum programme as a basis for unity and hoped to attract members from diverse groups. Its conceptions of armed struggle influenced by the experience of China, Vietnam and Algeria, it began to develop a network of cells in order to link up and co-ordinate the numerous and continuous local revolts which, it assumed, would begin in the countryside and spread to the towns (Document 77). However, its leadership was arrested in July 1963, the day after the Rivonia raid, and although it claimed several hundred members, the hierarchical nature of its cell structure meant that those who were not caught were unable to put the organisation back in operation.

The National Committee for Liberation (NCL) was formed in 1961 around the figure of Monty Berman, who had been recently expelled from the SACP. It announced its sabotage campaign on 20 December 1961, adopting an approach similar to that of MK, in the hopes of a rapprochement and a working relationship. In May 1962 the NCL merged with two other tiny groups, the Socialist League of Africa and the African Freedom Movement, and various radical dissidents from the Liberal Party. The reconstituted NCL advocated a political pluralism amongst organisations engaged in armed struggle. Although non-racial in principle, its membership was disproportionately white and its leadership virtually all-white, Eddie Daniels being the significant exception. The Rivonia raid provoked a debate within the NCL about the continued feasibility of armed struggle. In 1964, a faction successfully argued for the continuation of its sabotage campaign under the name of the African Resistance Movement (ARM).

Shortly thereafter its leadership was arrested and the organisation broken (Documents 71, 79; Lewin 1976; Du Toit 1991 and 1994; Lazerson 1994: 235-39; Hirson 1995: 302, 310-24; Vigne 1971; interview with Daniels).

The bifurcation which developed in South Africa's socialist movement in the 1930s coincided with the emergence of opposing positions on how to fight South Africa's racial system. This divide was continually reproduced within the Congress movement and the Unity Movement throughout the post-war era and left its mark on the complex responses to the post-Sharpeville situation. Nonetheless, reflecting the structural conditions in which these diverse traditions developed, common motifs are apparent. Both traditions sought answers to South Africa's most pressing social problems, the national and the agrarian questions and the problem of how to fight apartheid, and the debates produced a wide spectrum of responses. Both were eventually ruptured by the combined pressures of internal contestations and of state repression.

**NOTES**
1 The marked absence of a discourse on women indicates the lack of a movement for women's rights and liberation at that time. The liberation movement was historically male-dominated, appealing to women to form auxiliaries, leagues or brigades to support political programmes developed by men. Since the 1980s, however, women have been explicitly challenging unequal gender relations. See Hassim (1991) and Walker (1991).
2 Saunders (1988) and Nasson (1990) discuss some of these works.
3 The ADP was launched on 26 September 1943 by, amongst others, Paul Mosaka, Self Mampuru and Dan Koza. It had a social-democratic programme and hoped to provide a counterpart to the ANC. Former Communist Hyman Basner addressed its inaugural meeting, criticising the ANC-CPSA alliance. It was influential in Alexandra and Orlando and lasted about five years. For its manifesto see Karis and Carter (1973: 391-5).
4 The ILP, described by Witz (1987: 267) as the "... child of the Garment Workers' Union", was formed by trade unionist and former Communist Solly Sachs in order to draw GWU members away from electoral support for the waning SALP and the UP and move them towards the left. Sachs believed that it was necessary and possible to transform the racial attitudes of white workers by stressing economic issues. However, GWU members' support for their trade union did not translate into electoral support for candidates endorsed by the union's leadership. Following the ILP's ignominious defeat in the 1943 general elections, the ILP merged with the Progressive Labour Group to form the SASP, another short-lived venture.
5 Letter from Seymour Papert to I. B. Tabata [c. May/June 1952], Unity Movement of South Africa Papers, 1952, BC 925, Department of Manuscripts and Archives, University of Cape Town Libraries. The ANC's Day of Mourning took place on 26 May 1952.
6 Two significant radical histories written by NEUM members soon followed Van Schoor's pamphlet; see Majeka (1952) and Mnguni (1952). Majeka was the pseudonym of Dora Taylor, a writer who worked with the NEUM in Cape Town. Many of her essays are found in *Trek*.
7 The South African Communist Party officially endorsed the Freedom Charter in its 1962 Programme (Lerumo 1971: 100).
8 This section draws on Drew (1996).
9 For the NEUM's response to the request for arms see Document 70 and Drew (1991: 474-505) and interview with Mqotsi; for the ANC, verbal communication from Howard Barrell, St Antony's College, Oxford, 4 April 1992.

# Part One

## Building the national movement

*Political alliances and unity*

**EDITOR'S NOTE**

*Any pursuit of effective radicalism necessarily raises the question of constructing alliances. One tradition on the Left emphasises the need to develop the broadest possible coalition across class and sectional lines, uniting on points of agreement and on specific issues, while marginalising the potentially divisive questions of principle. Its proponents would see this as a choice of effective pragmatism over purist principle. In the South Africa of the 1940s this perspective was seen in the politics of the Congress movement and its associated organisations, including the CPSA and its successor, the SACP. In contrast, other radicals have argued that such alliances run a continual risk of degenerating into opportunism where the underlying purpose is lost in the pursuit of immediate benefits or in the preservation of organisational positions. They suggest that any effective alliance requires agreement on some basic issues of principle. This position was represented by the NEUM and its affiliates and was expressed in the policy of non-collaboration. The documents in this section consider these basic strategic problems and their application to particular campaigns undertaken in a context of increasing state repression. They address, as well, the involvement of particular groups such as women and the relationship between workers and intellectuals. The climate of escalating repression inevitably generated an intolerance of criticism within both movements, and by the late 1950s both traditions showed significant divisions which were characterised by bitter denunciations and which culminated in organisational splits.*

## Document 1
## Harry Snitcher[1], *Unite Against Segregation!*
## Communists Condemn the C.A.C. [1943]

In spite of protest by many leading representatives of the Coloured and Malay people, the Minister of the Interior, Mr. Lawrence, has declared that the Government will carry out its proposal of appointing a Coloured People's Council, to be "the only body recognized by the Government to express the views of the Coloured community."

Mr. Lawrence says this step has been taken only after consultation with "leading members of the Coloured community".

*Who are these leaders, and why the secrecy about this "consultation"?*

*If the so called leaders do really represent Coloured opinion, they should at least have found what the view of the great mass of non Europeans is on the matter.*

*Why did they not call a representative conference to work out proposals to place before the Government?*

In spite of the statement by the President of the A.P.O. that his Executive supports the Lawrence Commission, the great majority of members of the A.P.O. are opposed to it. This is shown by resolutions passed recently by numbers of branches.

*This is a matter of great importance to the masses of the Coloured people. No Executive Committee has the right to decide the fate of the people without consulting them. The voice of the people must be heard.*

The Communist Party considers this issue must be approached in the light of statements that have been made in recent years by the heads of Government. Our Party's standard by which we judge this action is in the first place an uncompromising opposition to all forms of segregation. We are of the opinion that the setting up of such a Council is essentially a big step towards the segregation of the Coloured community which has been foreshadowed in the statements of Government spokesmen.

## SEGREGATION

Why do we think this? Why do we say this Council is a segregation measure?

In the first place, Mr. Lawrence has stated that the Government is carrying out the policy laid down by General Hertzog in 1938 regarding the Coloured community.

*This policy was one of residential and social segregation and political discrimination.*

General Smuts, in the House of Assembly, has repeated that it is the Government's policy to segregate the Coloured into separate residential areas.

When statements such as these are linked up with the colour bar clauses in the Factories Act that was passed two years ago, with the undemocratic and unjust discrimination against African and Coloured soldiers in the army, and with the maintenance of Colour discrimination in education and social legislation generally, the Communist Party can come to only one conclusion, which is that the Government is carrying out, and determined to carry out, a policy of segregation.

It is necessary the people of South Africa should be made to understand the dangers that lie in this scheme of a separate Council.

It introduces the principle of communal representation, i.e., that the political system of this country should be organized along purely racial lines. This is absolutely a violation of every principle of democracy, and is in essence a Fascist conception.

THE ACCEPTANCE OF THIS PROPOSAL, IN OUR OPINION, WILL OPEN THE WAY TO A DIRECT ATTACK ON THE EXISTING POLITICAL RIGHTS OF THE COLOUREDS; THEY WILL BE THREATENED WITH THE LOSS OF THEIR FRANCHISE, JUST AS THE AFRICANS LOST THEIR VOTE AFTER THE NATIVE AFFAIRS COMMISSION HAD BEEN SET UP.

It is all the more regrettable that the Government should come forward to-day with a proposal of this kind, which expresses the Fascist ideas against which the country is mobilized. This will have the effect of undermining the morale of the non-Europeans and their enthusiasm for the war. They have proved their willingness to sacrifice their lives in this struggle for human liberty against Fascism and its bestial forms of racial oppression and intolerance.

IS THE ONLY REWARD FOR THEIR COURAGE AND SELF-SACRIFICE TO BE THE APPOINTMENT OF A COLOURED ADVISORY COUNCIL?

## SEPARATE REPRESENTATION

The coloured people do not want separate representation nor will it be in their interests.

What they want are political rights, decent wages, the right to work, better housing, compulsory education, equal pay and allowances for their soldiers and dependants.

These are things they have asked for, which authorities of different kinds have stated over and over again the Coloured peope require. The Government can give them these things.

*It is our job to see it does so, instead of continuing the policy of appeasing the Malans, Pirows, Louws, and Van Rensburgs.*[2]

The Communist Party has on all occasions declared its uncompromising opposition to all segregationist measures, and will throw all its energies into a struggle against this one and for the achievement of the positive demands of the non-European peoples. Racial harmony in South Africa can exist only if the non-Europeans are given those rights which are denied them to-day.

The Communist Party will co-operate with all bodies and persons who are fighting for these things, and it calls upon all non-Europeans in the Cape, as well as progressive-minded people of all other races, to join in a united and determined struggle against the Lawrence Segregation Scheme.

> *We welcome those steps which have already been taken by non-European organizations to carry out a united struggle against this scheme.*

### Democratic Rights for All!

At a conference of the Cape District Branch of the Communist Party, held at Cape Town on MARCH 14, the following resolutions were adopted:

**RESOLUTIONS**
"This Conference views with alarm the recent statements by General J.C. Smuts and Mr. H.G. Lawrence, declaring the Government's support of a policy of social, political and residential segregation. It calls for the immediate withdrawal of these statements as contrary to the Atlantic Charter and the democratic principles for which the non-European soldiers have been asked to sacrifice themselves in the war.

"This Conference unreservedly condemns the establishment of the Cape Coloured Permanent Commission as a measure designed to facilitate further segregation of the Coloured and Malay peoples. It draws attention to the fact that the members of the Commission are arbitrarily appointed by the Government and not democratically elected by the Coloured and Malay communities, and that the Commission has no administrative or executive powers whatever, but is purely advisory. It calls upon the Coloured and Malay peoples and all progressive sections of the population to wage a united struggle against the Commission, and urges every non-European to boycott the Commission by refusing to accept appointment as a member."

The Communist Party reiterates its demand for democratic rights for the non-Europeans. Victory over Fascism can be secured only if all sections of the people are allowed to play their full part in the great struggle for human freedom. The Government must act NOW.

Issued by the Communist Party of South Africa, Cape District Committee, P.O. Box 1176, Cape Town

## Document 2
## Against the C.A.D. *for* Full Democratic Rights [1943]

**THE PURPOSE OF THIS PAMPHLET**
In this pamphlet the "Anti-C.A.D. Committee" is going to tell you the TRUTH about the Government's latest moves against the Coloured People, a section of the non-European oppressed of South Africa.

We tell you this so that you may be WARNED of the new danger threatening the non-European people, and so that you will PROTEST AND FIGHT against it in your trade unions, in your Civic Associations, your Vigilance Societies, Churches, and in any political, social, benefit or sporting organisations to which you belong.

We know for a fact that you, like all honest non-Europeans, are striving for the full rights of a citizen in the land of your birth; and we know that you will reject the C.A.D. as soon as you know what it means; but that is not enough, FOR WE MUST ALL REJECT IT AND PROTEST AGAINST IT PUBLICLY IN OUR THOUSANDS AND TENS OF THOUSANDS, BECAUSE IT IS DEFINITELY A BRAKE ON OUR ADVANCEMENT TOWARDS FULL CITIZENSHIP.

**WHAT IS THE C.A.D.?**
According to a statement made by the Minister of the Interior on January 28th, the Government intends to create a special section within the Department of the Interior "to deal exclusively with matters affecting the Coloured people", because "There was a special Government Department to deal with matters affecting the Natives and a Commission for Asiatic Affairs. There was, however, no such provision for the Coloured people." – ("Cape Times", 29/1/43.)

But this is not all, for: "In addition a standing Commission – to be known as the Cape Coloured Permanent Commission – would be appointed to form a link between the Government and the Coloured community. Members of the Commission would consist of representatives of the Coloured people throughout the Union. The Commission would co-operate with the special Coloured section of this Department. It would meet at various centres as the need arose, and put forward suggestions and recommendations on matters affecting the Coloured population." – "Cape Times", 28/1/43.)

**HOW ARE THE C.A.D. AND THE C.C.P.C. SUPPOSED TO BENEFIT US?**
In this same statement the Minister said:
(i) "It was an experiment which he hoped would prove successful in bridging a gap which had existed and been widening over a period of time", and
(ii) "He looked forward to this experiment as opening a new page in the history of the Coloured people, and trusted that it would help them to reconcile the interests of the Europeans and Coloured people in a very much better manner than in the past."
According to a sub-leader in the "Cape Argus", 30/1/43, "A Permanent Commission will receive and co-ordinate all the requests, complaints and suggestions affecting the welfare of the Cape Coloured, and a Government official, well versed in the mysteries of departmental activity, will see that all these are carried to the correct quarter."

**DID WE EVER ASK FOR THIS**
We have never at any time asked for a special Coloured Affairs Department, nor yet a Permanent Commission. Similarly, the Africans have never asked for a Native Affairs Department, nor a Native Affairs Commission, nor a Native Representative Council, nor a separate Native Voters' Roll – but have had all these thrust upon them.

We have always insisted on our right to be full citizens of South Africa, and have always fought against any political move or legislation which wanted to treat us as "special" creatures who need "special" political, economic, educational and social institutions. For example:
(i) In 1909 the non-Europeans of the Union protested strongly against the Colour Bars

in the Act of Union whereby only Europeans could be elected to Parliament, and whereby non-Europeans, except in the Cape and to a limited extent in Natal, were debarred from all political rights; and deputations even went to England to protest there.

(ii) In 1922 a petition signed by fifty thousand Coloured people of the Union was handed to General Smuts, the Prime Minister, for submission to the Union Parliament; the petition asked for the removal of the "special" political treatment given the "non-European sections of the population" by the South Africa Act, 1909.

(iii) The Coloured people rejected and utterly defeated the Coloured Persons' Rights Bill of 1926, whereby a special "Board" was to be set up (an earlier form of the C.A.D.), one of whose functions was to draw up a separate voters' roll, and whereby Coloured persons outside of the Cape Province were to have one European representative in Parliament.

(iv) In 1936, all non-Europeans rejected the three Native Bills which were to segregate the African still further, to push him out of the towns, to put him on a separate voters' roll and to give him a dummy Native Representative Council and a few European representatives in Parliament. The African people, united as never before in history, rejected this "special" treatment, and they would have won the day if their leaders had not been so weak-kneed and compromising.

(v) In 1939, the widespread and insistent protests and the mighty Parade demonstration against the Segregation Ordinance again showed that WE ARE ALWAYS AGAINST ANY FORM OF "SPECIAL" OR SEGREGATED TREATMENT.

**WHY WE OPPOSE THE C.A.D. AND THE COMMISSION**

We oppose and unconditionally reject the C.A.D. and the Commission because:

(i) We are men and women with the same needs and desires as any other men or women of this country; but these proposals are based upon the despotic idea that we are not fit to be governed by the ordinary law or to take part in the ordinary legislative and administrative institutions of the country, SO WE ARE INTENDED TO OCCUPY PERMANENTLY A PLACE OF INFERIORITY, OUTSIDE OF THE ORDINARY CIVIC SYSTEM OF THE COUNTRY. THEY say that we are inferior and that we have a lower standard of living. But WE know that it is they who keep our wages down, who herd us into slums and reserves, it is they who give us inferior educational opportunities, who keep us out of the professions, the libraries, the art galleries and theatres. Our needs and our aspirations are the same as theirs, but they have denied us the opportunity of satisfying these, and now they wish to continue this permanently.

(ii) The Native Affairs Department carries out the Government policy of keeping the African in a permanent position of servility, and the Native Affairs Commission does the scouting to find out whether to go "Full speed ahead" or "Half speed ahead". THE COLOURED AFFAIRS DEPARTMENT AND THE CAPE COLOURED PERMANENT COMMISSION WILL DO THE SAME FOR THE COLOURED PEOPLE. THIS IS WHAT IS MEANT BY FORMING "A LINK BETWEEN THE GOVERNMENT AND THE COLOURED COMMUNITY".

(iii) The fact that willing tools are to be found amongst the Coloured people to serve on the Commission does not alter its sinister nature and purpose in any way. Every nation has its Judases, and certainly a few Coloured "leaders" will be found to betray their people. But we will know them for what they are, and we already know the only proper name for them – Judases. Their betrayal only makes us fight the harder.

(iv) WE CAN NEVER HAVE ANY TRUST IN AN OFFICIALLY APPOINTED COMMISSION WHICH WILL MEET AT VARIOUS CENTRES "AS THE NEED ARISES" AND "PUT FORWARD SUGGESTIONS AND RECOMMENDATIONS ON MATTERS AFFECTING THE COLOURED POPULATION". WE DO NOT TRUST IT, WE DO NOT NEED IT, AND WE DO NOT WANT IT.

(v) This Permanent "experiment" can never "bridge the gap" which has existed and has "been widening over a period of time" because the gap was created against our wishes and despite our protests at the Act of Union, when all non-Europeans were deprived of direct representation and when all non-Europeans outside of the Cape and (with limitations) Natal could not even vote. THE GAP HAS BEEN WIDENED ECONOMICALLY by the Colour Bar Act, the Apprenticeship Act, the Civilised Labour Policy, the Industrial Conciliation Act, and the latest amendment to the Factories Act; THE GAP HAS BEEN WIDENED POLITICALLY by the Women's Enfranchisement Act of 1930 (which gave only European women the right to elect and to be elected to the Houses of Parliament), by the Franchise Laws Amendment Act of 1931 (which gave every White male person over 21 years of age the franchise), by the Native Bills of 1936 (which cast out the African by taking away the Cape Native Franchise, by placing him on a separate voters' roll, by giving him three M.P.s and four senators who, on account of their insignificant voting power – three in a House of 153 – could never achieve anything worth while, and by giving him a Native Representative Council, undemocratically elected, Government controlled and able only to advise – its advice has always been very feeble, but, still, it has never been taken).

(vi) We say that the gap can only be bridged by starting with the South Africa Act and all the gap-widening laws like those mentioned above, amending some, e.g., South Africa Act, Apprenticeship Act, Women's Enfranchisement Act, Franchise Laws Amendment Act, Industrial Conciliation Act, Factories Act, and abolishing others, e.g., Colour Bar Act, Civilised Labour Policy, and the three Native Acts of 1936, i.e., the Representation of Natives Act, Urban Areas Act and the Native Land and Trust Act. THE GAP CAN NEVER BE BRIDGED OR IN ANY WAY NARROWED BY A WRETCHED C.A.D. AND PERMANENT COMMISSION. IT CAN ONLY BE WIDENED. WE WANT THE REPEAL OF ALL THESE REPRESSIVE MEASURES, NOT THE CREATION OF FRESH ONES LIKE THE C.A.D. AND THE C.C.P.C.

(vii) This "experiment" can never "reconcile the interests of the Europeans and Coloured people in a very much better manner than in the past", because it is a continuation of the policy of the past. THE "INTERESTS" OF THE EUROPEAN AND NON-EUROPEAN CAN ONLY BE RECONCILED WHEN THEY ARE ONE AND THE SAME, I.E. WHEN THE EUROPEANS DISCARD THEIR ATTITUDE OF "TRUSTEESHIP" WITH ITS MASTER AND SERVANT OUTLOOK, AND RECOGNISE THE NON-EUROPEAN AS A FULL AND FREE CITIZEN OF SOUTH AFRICA.

(viii) The suggestion that the retardation of the Coloured people is due to ignorance of the "mysteries of departmental activity" is too absurd to justify a serious reply, because we have always known, and we still know, who does the damage to us.

**WHAT WE REALLY WANT**

We have shown very clearly what we do NOT want, so, let us now say what we non-Europeans are really striving for. WE ARE STRIVING FOR FULL DEMOCRATIC RIGHTS. When we say this we mean that we struggle for:

(i) FULL AND EQUAL POLITICAL AND CIVIC RIGHTS FOR ALL THE PEOPLE OF THE UNION. This includes:
(a) The granting of the vote to all adults, irrespective of race, religion or sex.
(b) The right of all voters to be elected to National Assembly.
(c) The right of all persons to travel freely and without restriction through any part of the country – this implies the abolition of the pass system.
(d) The right of all persons to reside wherever they wish and to purchase land or other property in urban or rural areas – this implies the abolition of the segregation of the Native (which already exists) and of the Coloured and Indian (which is almost complete).
(e) The release of more land for African, Coloured and Indian peasants.
(ii) Full and equal rights for all workers to form trade unions for the purpose of protecting and furthering their interests – this implies the abolition of all discrimination in industrial legislation based on colour.
(iii) Full and equal rights in, and access to, all skilled occupations and professions.
(iv) Equal taxation of all persons according to their income – this means the abolition of the Poll Tax and other discriminatory taxes.
(v) Equal, free and compulsory education for all children up to the age of sixteen, and the abolition of the present discrimination in the subsidies.
(vi) Equal rights in, and access to, trade.
(vii) The equal right of all persons to hold office in any governmental, administrative, juridical and educative institution of the country.

**WHY EVERYONE MUST OPPOSE THE C.A.D. AND THE C.C.P.C.**

Do not fool yourself that the C.A.D. is "not your concern". It is very much your business, whether you are Coloured, African, Indian or White. These proposals are part of a process which aims at keeping the non-European politically voiceless (except for ventriloquist dolls like the N.R.C., the C.C.P.C. and the Indian Commission), and economically segregated and controlled, and then at reducing the relatively high standard of the White worker.

This process affects all of us. It was "completed" for the African by the 1936 Acts; it is being completed for the Indians by the Indian Commission of Natal (which will soon be extended), and for the Coloureds by the C.A.D. and the C.C.P.C. Then it will be the White workers' turn.

So we must all realise that while these proposals are aimed at one section of the non-European oppressed, they are the direct and vital concern of ALL NON-EUROPEANS, for an injury to one limb of a body is an injury to the whole body. We must not allow ourselves to fall into the trap of being artificially divided into three groups, oppressed African, oppressed Coloured, oppressed Indian – segregated even in suffering.

## WHAT WE ARE DOING TO OPPOSE THESE MEASURES

These measures have been sprung upon us in a bad time, for they find us in a very poor state of organisation. We are still prepared, every man and woman amongst us, to resist all existent and proposed attacks upon our rights, but let us be quite frank and realise that from the point of view of organisations, we are at a very low ebb. Unfortunately, there exists no militant national organisation of the non-European people taking up and fighting bravely any and every issue concerning the rights of all non-Europeans, African, Coloured, or Indian. If such a national organisation did exist, there could be no need for an "Anti-C.A.D. Committee" – in fact, the C.A.D. proposals would never have been made. More unfortunate still, such a militant national organisation cannot be created overnight, and certainly cannot be created just to fight the C.A.D. and side-step the fundamental issues that we outlined in the section headed "What We Really Want".

But, just because we have no fighting national organisation, and just because fighting national organisations do not sprout like mushrooms, we cannot lie down and let the steamroller of oppression flatten us out. We must realise that we are faced by an emergency at a bad time, and we must jump to it and see what can be done to save the situation.

So we have formed the "Anti-C.A.D. Committee". This Committee consists of all organisations which are opposed to the C.A.D. and the Permanent Commission. On this Committee we have political parties, branches of political parties, civic associations, trade unionists, churches, welfare societies, teachers' organisations, student and past-student societies and sporting bodies. There are Coloureds, Africans, Indians and Whites, men and women, old and young, on the Committee – in fact, all people who are opposed to the C.A.D. and the C.C.P.C.

The Committee has sent a telegram to the Minister of Interior, unconditionally rejecting these proposals, and has called upon all other organisations to do likewise. FURTHERMORE, THE COMMITTEE IS:
(i) Holding meetings of protest as often as possible, and wherever it can.
(ii) Calling upon you to get your trade union, civic or vigilance association, church or club to reject these proposals publicly, to hold public meetings of protest, to pass resolutions AGAINST these proposals and FOR full democratic rights, and to make these resolutions known to all the people, to the Press, M.P.C.s, M.P.s, and to the Government itself. For it is only the mass protests of the people that can protect us.
(iii) Calling upon ALL trade unions which have not yet joined and all political, social and religious organisations opposed to these measures, to join the Anti-C.A.D. Committee.

## WE CAN STOP THE C.A.D.

WE CAN DEFINITELY STOP THE C.A.D. AND THE C.C.P.C. IF THE PEOPLE PROTEST LOUDLY AND UNCOMPROMISINGLY AND PUBLICLY, IN THEIR TENS OF THOUSANDS. SO YOU MUST DO YOUR SHARE THROUGH WHATEVER FORM OF ORGANISATION YOU CAN.

## HOW WE CAN BE SAFE FROM ALL SUCH MEASURES

IF OUR PROTESTS ARE STRONG ENOUGH, the C.A.D. will be withdrawn and shelved, even if the "terms of reference" or the names of the Commissioners will have been announced.

BUT IT WILL ONLY BE WITHDRAWN AND SHELVED FOR THE TIME BEING, AND IT WILL BE BROUGHT OUT AGAIN WHEN IT IS FELT THAT THERE IS A CHANCE OF GETTING IT PAST THE PEOPLE. So, WHAT ARE WE TO DO? We are to fight tooth and nail NOW, but we must realise clearly that we will never be safe from such legislation and we will never obtain full democratic rights until we have built up a militant national organisation which will take up the struggle of all the non-Europeans, African, Coloured and Indian.

**YOUR TASK**
Your task is clear. You must:
(i) Understand clearly the implications of the C.A.D. and the C.C.P.C.
(ii) Explain this to the people.
(iii) Protest individually and organisationally in every way that you can.
(iv) Get your organisations to join forces with the Anti-C.A.D. Committee.
(v) Show the people why it is our most urgent and responsible task to build a national organisation, and YOU MUST WORK TOWARDS THIS END.

.......

Since writing this pamphlet, the "Cape Argus" of the 10th March has announced the establishment of the C.C.P.C.:

**"Having heard the opinions expressed by leading members of both communities ... the Government therefore decided to establish a C.C.P.C.**

Thus, against the wishes of the people, but in consultation with certain leading members" (unnamed, read "Judases"), the C.A.D. and C.C.P.C. are foisted upon us.

Mr. Lawrence is anxious to remove the stigma attached to the C.A.D. by telling us that the Department of Interior will be extended and strengthened, and will act as the "channel of communication"; in other words, that part of the Department of Interior will function as a Department of Coloured Affairs in actual fact, but not that obnoxious name C.A.D.

**WHATEVER WE HAVE SAID IN THIS PAMPHLET, THEREFORE, REMAINS VALID: A MERE WORD JUGGLERY DOES NOT ALTER THE FACT.**

Issued by the ANTI-C.A.D. Committee; Secretary, Miss H. Ahmed[3], Constantia Road, Wynberg.

## Document 3
## National Anti-CAD Conference Agenda,
## Oddfellows Hall, Hope Street, Cape Town, Saturday, 29 May [1943]

*AFTERNOON SESSION:* 2 p.m. to 6 p.m.
2 p.m. to 3 p.m.        Registration of Delegates.
3 p.m.    Opening Remarks by the Chairman, Dr.G.H.Gool.[4]
3.30 p.m. *Address:* Mr.E.C.Roberts: "WHAT THE ANTI-C.A.D. MOVEMENT HAS ACHIEVED TO DATE"
Questions and Discussion.

*Resolutions:* That this National Anti-C.A.D.Conference, representing vigilance, social, political, sporting, trade union, educational and religious organisations:
(a) Emphatically and unconditionally rejects the Government Segregation Schemes, known as the C.A.C. and the C.A.D.
(b) Resolves to continue the struggle unabatedly throughout South Africa until these Segregation Measures are defeated.
(c) Demands the extension of Full Democratic Rights to all sections of the Non-Europeans.
(Mover: Cape Town. Seconder: East London)
That this Conference recognises the C.A.C. as an integral and inseparable part of the whole system of Colour Bar oppression directed against the entire Non-European population of South Africa.
(Mover: Fourth International, C.Town)

*EVENING SESSION:* 8 p.m. to 10.30 p.m.
8 p.m.　　Address: Mr. B. M. Kies: "THE BACKGROUND OF SEGREGATION".
Questions and Discussion.

SUNDAY, 30th MAY.
BANQUETING HALL, CITY HALL, CAPE TOWN.

*MORNING SESSION:*　10 a.m. to 1 p.m.
10 a.m.　*Address:* Mr. A. B. J. Desmore: "METHODS OF DEFEATING THE C.A.C. AND THE C.A.D."
Questions and Discussion.
*Resolutions:* That this Conference calls upon the people to extend and intensify the boycott of the C.A.C. and its men, socially, educationally, economically and politically, on a national-wide basis.
(Mover: Cape Indian Congress; Seconder: Stellenbosch.)
That this Conference undertakes to draw up a Union-wide petition for the withdrawal of the C.A.C. and the C.A.D., for submission to the Union Government.
(Mover: Kimberley)
*DISCUSSION:* THE GENERAL ELECTION, introduced by a member of the Working Committee
1 p.m. to 2 p.m. Adjournment:　Light Lunch to be provided.
*AFTERNOON SESSION:*　2 p.m. to 6 p.m.
2 p.m.　*DISCUSSION:* ORGANISATION.
*Resolutions:* That this Conference appoint a National Anti-C.A.D. and Anti-C.A.C. Committee.
(Mover: General Committee, Anti-C.A.D. Comm.)
That the Anti-C.A.D. Committee shall be the officially recognised mouthpiece in the struggle for the defeat of the C.A.C. and the C.A.D.
(Mover: Kimberley)
That this Conference urges the establishment of local Anti-C.A.D. Committees throughout the Union on the same lines as the Central Anti-C.A.D. Committee.
(Mover: Claremont)
4 p.m.　Adjournment: Tea
4.30 p.m.　FINANCE: Treasurer's Report.

GENERAL BUSINESS.
6 p.m.   Close of Conference.
MONDAY, 31st MAY.
ANTI-C.A.D. DANCE.
DRILL HALL, at 8 p.m.
ADMISSION:
SINGLE: 3/-; DOUBLE: 6/-.

## Document 4
## B. M. Kies[5], "The Background of Segregation", Address delivered to the National Anti-CAD Conference, 29 May 1943

*[....]* The determined stand at present being made by the Coloured People is but one very, very humble example of that new and militant spirit which is being shown by those who have suffered under the Herrenvolk.[6] It is a part, however small at present, of the new spirit of manhood and brotherhood which has already shown itself in China and India, and which must inevitably sweep the Colonial countries and the whole of the world. *[....]*

While it is true to say that the Coloured People have learned more in the past three years about their rulers than they have learned during the past thirty years, it is a grim necessity that we should recognise the fact that we are only at the very beginning of things and that there is much, very much, to learn and to do before we can consider ourselves anywhere near the road to emancipation. *[....]*

The bitter truth is that white South Africa still dominates because it has been able to enslave the mind, the ideas of the non-European. It is a known historical fact that in any society, the prevailing ideas, manners and customs of even the oppressed section, are the ideas manners and customs of the ruling class. South Africa is no exception. Segregation is the prevailing idea of the South African ruling class and it has created segregationists in our own ranks. So, we can distinguish the three main causes of our defeats.

(1)   The segregationist outlook of the non-Europeans.
(2)   The segregationist political organisations and efforts of the non-Europeans.
(3)   The segregationist and reformist leadership.

The fact that 291 years after the advent of the European in this country, one still has to speak of African oppressed. Coloured oppressed and Indian oppressed is sufficient evidence of the sad fact that the slaves have taken over the segregationist ideology of their master. The white minority looks upon the African as a "raw kaffir," and such he has been to the majority of Coloureds and Indians. The white minority looks upon the Coloured man as a "bastard Hottentot" and such he has been to most of the Africans and Indians. The white minority looks upon the Indian as a "bloody coolie," and such he has been to most Africans and Coloureds. The African is told that he is superior because he is "pure blooded" – and he has believed this. The Coloured man is told that he is superior because the "blood of the white man" flows in his veins – and he has believed this. The Indian has been told that he is superior because he belongs to a great nation with a mighty culture and he has believed this. The Herrenvolk of South Africa have nothing to learn from Dr. Goebbels, for their vicious racial myths have bitten deep into the life and ways of non-Europeans. *[....]*

Let us turn now to the segregationist political organisations and efforts of the non-Europeans. There are three organisations which immediately spring to mind: the African National Congress, the A.P.O., and the S.A. Indian Congress. We are not concerned with the pious protestations of these bodies, but with their practice; we will not worry about what they said, but only about what they did. What they still say they are going to do is not our concern at the moment, but only what they have done.

And the bald fact is that each one of these organisations, as their very names imply, has had a sectarian approach towards the political emancipation of the non-European. The African National Congress ploughed its lonely furrow, trying to turn up a few reforms; the A.P.O. was never actively concerned with anyone except Coloured voters, handing them over to this or that Party in the hope of getting some concessions by way of gratitude.

They always were rewarded with further repressive measures, but still they continued with their separatism. We have just had the C.A.C forced upon us, but at this very moment they have an organiser doing a pre-Election trip around the country. He is concerned only with votes for the master, and so it does not matter to him whether a Branch is pro- or anti-C.A.C. The S.A. Indian Congress was always more concerned with trade licenses for their merchant members, with welcoming Agents-General or sending cablegrams to Mother India, than with a broad mass struggle at home. They looked everywhere for aid except to their own workers and peasants, or to the Coloureds and Africans.

From time to time the A.P.O. and the S.A. Indian Congress have uttered the dire threats of unity with the African. From time to time they did enter into what they called a United Front. But it was never more than an empty gesture, a token, a threat to the rulers that terrible things might happen. It was used by Coloured and Indian leaders to increase their bargaining powers for petty concessions, and naturally, the African became suspicious of the little game of using him as the monkey's paw to take the chestnuts out of the fire. And it was a little game played by the top leadership; it was a little tin trumpet that they used to try and peeve the whites. It never touched the masses and it was not meant to do so.

If either the A.P.O. or the S.A. Indian Congress had anything but a sectarian conception of the political struggle, they would have roused the people in 1935-36 at the time of the three Native Bills, a smashing attack on the non-Europeans' main line of defence: they would have gone into the All-African Convention and built it up into a real united front with a mass base, and they would have opposed and defeated the disgraceful "compromise" by Jabavu and company. It was because they allowed the defeat of the African in 1935-36 that to-day we have the C.A.C. and the Indian Pegging Bill.

However, we are not here to discuss what might have been, and we must go on to the third important reason why we have failed – the fact that our leadership has been both segregationist and reformist. We have only to recite the names of a few of them and you will immediately recognise them as such – the Jabavus, Abdurahmans, Gows, Ka Semes, Kajees, Dubes and Nanas who have landed us in the wretched plight we find ourselves in today.[7] They were all sectarians, as we have already shown. But more than this, they were petty reformists. They took over the ruling-class ideas of what was and was not political cricket. To them politics was a gentleman's game with gentlemen's agreements written in flowery language and decorated with red seals and green ribbon. It was never a grim life-and-death struggle between oppressor and oppressed. In fact, there was no struggle at all, only resolutions and petitions and deputations. It is said that the servants of the aristocracy are more snobbish and highbrow than the aristocrats themselves. That may or may not be true, but it is certainly true that the so-called leaders of the African, Coloured and Indian oppressed have been greater upholders of constitutionalism than the Government itself. They were better policemen to the people than the police and lawcourts themselves.

The main bee in their bonnet was that the Colour Bar was all a misunderstanding. One half of the Government did not know it was there and had to be informed about it; the other half knew of its existence and so had to have their hearts changed. And so they went on, generation after generation, informing their masters that they were being lashed, and respectfully begging for a change of heart.

A change of heart, indeed! They were asking the Unionist Party, the South African Party, the Nationalist Party, the Labour Party, and the Coalition Party for a change of heart! Fancy making such a request to the Unionist or South African Party, which represented British Capitalism in the form of the Chamber of Mines and the Chamber of Commerce, and who had built and maintained an Empire on the sweat and toil of the non-European! Fancy talking such arrant nonsense to the Nationalist Party which represented the farming interests, which wanted only one thing, cheaper and cheaper black labour until they had returned to slavery where they did not have to pay any wages at all! Fancy talking at all to the most disgraceful Labour Party in the world! For, while we all know that the international Labour movement has been at a very low ebb for the last decade, nowhere has it sunk to such depths of shame as in South Africa, where it has its own segregation scheme and where, together with its Minister of Labour and the Trades and Labour Council, it has deliberately held up the recognition of African Trade Unions.[8] And what honest man can expect anything but more oppression from the Coalition or Fusion or United Party – call them what you will? For they came together in their unholy alliance for one purpose, and one only, to make mutually agreeable arrangements for the unhindered exploitation of non-European labour. This is their record – the Native Acts, the Wireman's Act, the amendment of the Factories Act, the C.A.C., the Housing Bill, and the Indian Pegging Bill. In fact, every Act since Fusion has a Colour Bar. And fancy appealing to them to change their heart when they themselves say that their aim is to make South Africa a white man's country. United Party, Nationalist, Dominion or Labour Party – they are all equally fascist towards the non-European: there may not be a Non-European United Front but there certainly is a United Front of European political parties. A plague on all of them! *[....]*

During all this dark and dreary history there was only one bright spot. There was only one organisation and one movement that made a clean break in deeds as well as words, with the sectarian and petty reformist leadership of the past. It was the first real mass movement which in fact and not in mere talk, took in all the non-Europeans. I refer to the I.C.U. (the Industrial and Commercial Workers' Union).[9] It started humbly as a little trade union but soon grew to a mighty organisation which swept the country and made the rulers tremble. Significant about the I.C.U. was the fact that, while the old Coloured leaders were still having academic discussions as to whether Coloureds should unite with Africans, the Coloured workers had long ago taken matters into their own hands and were fighting side by side with the African workers. They did not lose their identity and they did not lose their personality. But they DID lose some of their economic chains! Another significant thing was that while the reformist African leaders were also having abstruse discussions on the advisability of this, that and the other, thousands upon thousands of African workers were already putting up a militant fight in the I.C.U. Unfortunately, the Government succeeded in corrupting the top leadership, and this together with the "reorganisation" by Mr. W. G. Ballinger on reactionary and docile British Trade Union lines, resulted in its collapse.[10] But the brief episode of the I.C.U. has taught us four things: First, that the masses want the unity of all oppressed in their struggle for emancipation. Second, that sectarian and reformist leadership is always more worried about its own hide than about the liberation of the oppressed. Third, that what the rulers of this country fear most is the unity of all the oppressed non-Europeans for the furtherance of their struggle. Fourth, that when such unity is established upon a militant mass basis, the Herrenvolk tremble in their boots and use hook and crook to stop it. *[....]*

The question now is: WHAT ARE WE GOING TO DO ABOUT IT?

There are only two things that can be done about it. There are only two paths to take. We are free to take either, because we are all at the cross-roads. African, Coloured and Indian, we are all at the cross-roads. It is a crisis in world history, and it is a crisis in our history. We must choose .......

The choice is this. We can continue in the old way, each travelling along his own lonely ditch which leads into his own segregated camp. This means that we accept the idea of trusteeship and segregation. We accept A. C. Petersen's idea that some races are superior to us. We each keep to ourselves and see what we can get for "our own people." We take his motto. "Charity begins at home," and therefore segregation should begin at home. We go on like this until we have Africans, Coloureds and Indians all completely enslaved by the same master, but content to remain segregated and content to remain slaves. That is one alternative.

The other one is this. We must take the road to unity. We must unite the struggles of oppressed Africans, oppressed Coloured, oppressed Indian, into the unified struggle of the oppressed non-European. We must build up a real and militant United Front of the PEOPLE.

Let us be quite clear as to what we mean. Let us realise that throughout our whole history there has never, at any time, been a real united front. The nearest approach was the I.C.U. There have been several attempts at a United Front, sometimes sincere and sometimes not sincere. But there has never been a REAL United Front. There have been threats of a United Front. The Coloureds have threatened and the Indians have threatened. There have been united fronts of a few of the leaders at the top and a few of the organisations at the top, but this does not make a REAL united front. A REAL United Front is not something which can be made by the collaboration of a few isolated leaders, nor yet by a few organisations of indeterminate membership. A REAL United Front cannot be made by declaration or by passing any amount of resolutions. It cannot be created overnight by loud shouts for a national organisation or any other sort of organisation. A REAL United Front cannot suddenly be called into being by Coloureds or Indians whenever they are faced by a new piece of repressive legislation. A REAL United Front cannot be created out of spite or panic or despair.

The fact of the matter is that a REAL United Front cannot suddenly be called up or created, but it has to be BUILT. And it can only be BUILT UP from below. It can only be BUILT UP by the slow and steady unification of the African, Coloured and Indian workers in and through the struggle for their full democratic rights. This is the first condition for a REAL United Front: it must have a mass base, and its aim must be to fight for national emancipation and equal rights for All peoples in South Africa. It is a fact that in South Africa the national and agrarian questions are inseparable from each other. The question of land and of political rights go hand in hand and cannot be separated. This, then, is the common basis upon which a REAL United Front can be formed, otherwise there is no use trying to form it at all. Its programme must have this common minimum basis: for this alone embraces both the needs of the day and the needs of the future, and can arouse the masses to action. Second, it cannot have leaders who speak with two voices, one to the Government, the Liberals and the Conservatives, and another to the people. Its leaders must have one loyalty and one loyalty only – to the oppressed people, not the rulers. Third, it must rid itself of the reformist methods which have only bred failure after failure. It must use every means at the disposal of the oppressed people to rid themselves of their exploiters.

These are the essentials for a REAL United Front, built upon a solid foundation. It will take a long time, but it is THE ONLY ROAD that we can travel if we non-Europeans really wish to liberate ourselves and if we really wish to enjoy full democratic rights. It is the ONLY ROAD for honourable men and women. It is the ONLY ROAD for honest fighters against tyranny.

At this stage it might be well to strike two notes of warning. Firstly, when we speak of a united front of ALL non-Europeans we do not mean lumping ALL non-Europeans holus-bolus together and fusing them all together in the belief that, since ALL are non-European oppressed, the African is a Coloured man, an Indian is an African, and a Coloured man is either Indian or African, whichever you please. Only those who are ignorant of both politics and history can believe in this nonsensical type of unity. When we speak of the unity or the united front of all non-Europeans, we simply mean this: they are all ground down by the same oppression: they have all the same political aspirations, but yet they remain divided in their oppression. They should discard the divisions and prejudices and illusions which have been created and fostered by their rulers. They should remember only that they have a common foe and they should unite to liberate themselves. When they have thrown off the chains, then they can settle whatever national or racial difference they have, or think they have. After we have rid ourselves of our common oppressor, the national question will remain. BUT THE NATIONAL QUESTION MUST BE SETTLED ON OUR TERMS, NOT THE TERMS OF THE EXPLOITER. As long as we allow these national or racial differences to keep us apart NOW, then we will never liberate ourselves. A simple analogy ought to suffice. Take the case of the Moslems and Hindus in India. Everyone knows that the faction fights between Moslems and Hindus have been actively fostered by Great Britain, for she knows that as long as she can segregate the Moslem minority from the Hindu majority, so long will she rule. If the Moslems and Hindus were to bury all their real and imagined differences and unite, then it would be the end of the British Raj in India. Then they could solve the Hindu-Moslem question on their own terms and in their own time. Exactly the same applies to Africans, Coloureds and Indians in South Africa.

The second note of warning is this: when we speak of a united front of ALL non-Europeans, it is not for the purpose of putting white against black and stirring up race hatred. It is for the purpose of uniting ALL non-European oppressed, so that they may bring the white working-class to its senses, and demonstrate that its real place is with us and against the Imperialist exploiter. It may seem fantastic to some of us at the moment. It may seem to us that all the whites are living on milk and honey. That is not so. They are better off than we are, but they are exploited all the same. They may all appear to be little bosses TO-DAY, but that is because they are bribed at our expense. TO-MORROW, by means of a united front of all oppressed non-Europeans, they will learn where they really belong, because the majority of them are also workers. This may seem fantastic to some of us. It is probably even more fantastic to the white workers. That need not deter us. Let us get on with our main task, the building up of the REAL United front, and we will settle the other problems as they arise. We are not trying to paint a dream world, a Utopia. We are only honest and fearless men, seeking the right road to freedom and equality, and finding that the road of the REAL United Front is the right road and, therefore, the only road that we can travel.

There is one last matter that we must deal with, and that is the question of leadership.

It is a known historical fact that the emancipatory theory and the practical leadership always come from the intelligentsia. The workers and peasants have always been so exhausted and bowed down by their arduous toil, that they have never had time to study and look deeply into the why and wherefore of their miserable condition. More than that, even if they had the time, most of them had not the education. So it was always the intelligentsia, who came of a more leisured and educated class, who took the ideas to the working class and who provided that fusion of theory and practice which is known as leadership.

We have no leisured class, except amongst the sons and daughters of a few merchants. But we certainly have an intelligentsia. And we are luckier than that, because our intelligentsia has sprung straight form the loins of the working class. They do not have to go to the people. They belong to the people and the people are all around them.

I refer, of course, mainly to the teachers. For almost the only persons amongst the non-Europeans who have had more than just a mere smattering of education, are the teachers. And they are certainly almost the only ones who have a certain amount of leisure. The leadership will come mainly from them. You can overlook the seven teacher traitors on the C.A.C. But you can never overlook the fact that in every part of the country, in the large towns and in the small dorps, the teachers have played a very great part in telling the Coloured People the truth about the C.A.C. swindle. There have been waverers and cowards. Some of them, and some Branches of the T.L.S.A. are still sitting on the fence, too scared to come off. At least one of them, Wynberg Branch, is running with the traitors. But many, many more of them are standing firmly by the people, enlightening them and helping to organise them.

This augurs very well for the future. It means that the intellectuals are realising the role that they have to play, and they are beginning to fulfill that role. It is a very healthy sign also to see how keen an interest the students are taking in the Anti-C.A.D. movement and that several University and other student groups have actually affiliated to the Anti-C.A.D. Committee. All these are promising signs that the leadership will come from those whose historical duty it is to provide such leadership.

And so I wish to turn for one moment to the young men and women teachers, and I wish to say to them: "We have a very responsible task within and without the classroom. We are not pioneers in this field for many men and women teachers in other parts of the world have gone before us. We walk in their tradition and **our** generation of teachers is the pioneer in this country. We should keep constantly before us the example of those mighty teachers in France, who for decades and decades fought against darkness and despotism until the dawn of French Revolution; we should always remember and follow the generations of teachers who for a full hundred years prepared the way for the Russian Revolution. You will not find their names in the official manuals of education, because officialdom is always opposed to the forces of real progress. But without the teachers there would never have been a French or a Russian Revolution. For it is the duty of the true teacher to pull off the mask and scrape off the scales of ignorance that blind the youth. It is the duty of the true teacher to give his pupils knowledge so that they may KNOW the world and so that they may CHANGE the world. For it is not enough for them to know: they must also change things for the benefit of humanity. And more than this, the true teachers's duty does not end with his pupils. He has a vital and active part to play in the liberation of the people. He has to help to educate the people in the struggle. He has to help to lead them along the right road. We are all in chains, teacher and worker: we can never throw them off individually. But if we both play our part to the full, we will break those bonds.

So we teachers, men and women, must make up our minds whether we are going to be true teachers, or whether we are going to be traitors and cowards, whether we are going to be WITH our people or AGAINST our people. For those who are both honourable and courageous there can be only one answer: WE STAND WITH OUR PEOPLE. First, we must see to it, then, that we fit ourselves for our task. The ignorant can never lead. We must see to it that we study the problems of the people and that we understand them clearly. Liberation is never achieved by raving or passing violent resolutions. It is only achieved by those who KNOW HOW. Second, we ourselves must practice what we teach our students and our people, namely, that it is not enough to know how the world must be changed, but that WE must also change it. In other words, it is only unity of theory and practice which can produce sound leadership. Theory without practice is useless: practice without theory is suicide. Third, we must have courage. It is a sad fact that, while the intelligentsia of the world has produced some of its greatest heroes, sung and unsung, it has also produced some of the greatest intellectual cowards. Let this not daunt us, but rather let it inspire us to see to it that we are not the ones to falter and to betray. For he who wavers and falters in his allegiance to the people is no longer with the people, but with the enemies of the people.

We must make a break with the past. We must blot out the shame cast upon our profession by those teachers who have helped to mislead and betray the people, who have helped to put on the chains and to keep them on. WE MUST TURN OUR FACES TO OUR PEOPLE AND WE MUST BE AMONG THEM AND WITH THEM AND OF THEM, TEACHING AND LEADING THEM.

One last word: The leadership must choose and the people must choose the road that we are to travel. We have trodden the mud and the slush of the road to segregation. Are we going to choose to continue along that road? Or are we going to take the only road to liberty and equal rights for all – the road which leads to the unity of all the oppressed people against those who oppress us. We stand on trial.

We must choose – either LIBERTY OR SLAVERY. WE CAN ONLY CHOOSE

ONE. WE MUST CHOOSE LIBERTY.
Issued by Anti-C.A.D. Committee, Secretary, H. Ahmed, Constantia Road, Wynberg.


## Document 5
## Johannesburg Anti-CAD Committee,
*Bulletin Number One* [1943]

FOR THE LAST HALF YEAR a strong movement has sprung up in the Cape Province to fight the Coloured Advisory Council. This council was set up by Lawrence, acting on the behalf of the government. At first it was a mere promise by Lawrence, in 1943. Then, before the Coloured people could turn round, the Council was no longer an ugly promise but a fact and an institution. The Non-European people in the Cape took up the challenge of the government and have been waging a hard struggle against the C.A.C. for months on end. The Anti-C.A.C. movement has now spread to other provinces, outside the Cape, and in these provinces, too, the oppressed are lifting up their heads and rising from their knees to face and to fight the oppressor, the ruler, the government. The Anti-C.A.D. Committee in the Transvaal is now openly beginning the struggle in the northern province. Already it has received the support of many trade unions, of anti-segregation organisations, of political parties, of sporting bodies, social clubs, etc. It has won the support of organisations containing African, Indian, Coloured and sympathetic White workers and oppressed.

The fact that in all the provinces where the Anti-C.A.C. movement has joined battle with the authorities not only Coloured, but also Indian and African organisations have entered the Anti-C.A.D. Committees, shows clearly to the whole nation that the Non-Europeans are beginning to realize that "an injury to one part of the body is an injury to the whole body". The oppressed are starting to see that the government is trying to carry on its old policy of dividing them in order to rule them; and that when it tackles the Non-Europeans one by one, first the African, then the Indian and finally the Coloured and Malay, it is harming not only the section which it is attacking at the time, but all the sections of the Non-Europeans and workers. The history of the way in which the government has dealt with the Non-European people during the last 7 years, for instance, shows this clearly.

Some people in ivory towers, which can be found even in the dirtiest slums, delude themselves and others by imagining that the C.A.C. will help them, even while they admit that it tries to divide them from the African and Indian by treating them separately. If, however, we look back a little bit, we behold a string of growing colour bar laws against every single section of the Non-Europeans, including the Coloured. In 1936 the government hit out brutally at the 8 million Africans, by passing the 1936 Native Bills, which tore at the rights of the African on the land, and in the towns and gave him a segregationist voters' roll. Then the government turned on the Indian people, passing the most vicious anti-Asiatic laws, especially dealing with trade, property and land. The recent Pegging Act is still fresh in our memories.[11] Having dealt hammer blows of segregation at the 8 million Africans, at the Asiatics in their 1/4 million, the government brought down the hatchet of the colour bar over the heads of the Coloured peoples.

The first big attempt to segregate the Coloured people nakedly took place in 1938-'9, when the Hertzog government tried to bring in the segregation laws against the Coloured people. Thanks to the organisation of the Coloured toilers, to mass meetings, and to the giant demonstration and unforgettable march on the House of Parliament in Cape Town on March 27, 1939, the government was forced to withdraw its segregation laws of 1939. But the government had only put these laws in cold storage, and had not buried them forever. Sooner or later, it was sure to bring the laws out again. But it could not do so openly, otherwise the Coloured people, whose eyes had been open by their mass action in 1939, would give the government a repeat performance of March 1939.

And so the rulers of the land had to work out a new way of imposing segregation on the necks of the Coloured people. IT HAD TO BRING IN THE 1939 HERTZOG BILLS THROUGH A BACK DOOR. The door had to be well-oiled, had to open quietly and unobserved. THIS DOOR IS THE COLOURED ADVISORY COUNCIL. It has hinges which are well oiled, taking the shape of the Coloured members of the C.A.C. traitors to the people whom they claim to represent. Through this back-door will come the old 1939 Segregation Bills, if the Non-Europeans as a body do not unite to fight segregation. And if these bills take effect, and reduce the Coloured and Malay standard of life and rights to those of the Africans, it will weaken the entire front of Non-European struggle for full democratic rights. It is in order to hold and to strengthen this front that the C.A.C. has to be fought and exposed. It is in the interests of every Non-European and worker to take up and carry this fight and exposure.

It is false to say that the C.A.D. will improve the conditions of the Coloured people, for the history of the last 33 years since Union shows that the conditions of the oppressed and the exploited have not improved but grown worse and worse. Under the present social system there cannot be lasting reforms.

It is equally false to say that the C.A.C. will bring free compulsory education to the Coloured children. This empty promise is a red herring to draw the workers away from the fight for higher wages. The government has never, in all its history, carried out such a promise to the oppressed, and there is less reason than ever before why it should do so now.

It is a crude deception of the people when the C.A.C. blabbers about helping the starving people of Namaqualand. Far from helping the starving and dying people, it has set-up a useless Advisory Council which feeds the starving people with hollow promises.

Not only is the C.A.C. doing absolutely nothing to help the Coloured people, but it is coming out more and more openly as an agency of stirring up race-hatred between the Coloured and the African. For the C.A.C. is egging the Coloured people in the Cape on to oppose the Africans now entering the Cape for work. The C.A.C. is doing what the British imperialists have long done in India, in stirring up feuds between the Hindus and Moslems. One of the main purposes of the C.A.C. is to draw the attention of the Coloured toilers away from their real bosses and rulers, and to focus this attention on the savagely oppressed Africans.

The C.A.C. will not improve conditions; will not bring in compulsory education; will not help the starving people. Instead it tries to stir up race hatred; it will bring in industrial, residential, educational and political segregation even more than already exists. It will bring in a separate voters' roll for the Cape Coloured males and do nothing helpful about the Transvaal Coloured franchise. All that Hertzog dreamed of, and that Smuts is trying to practice, will come pouring in through the silent door of the C.A.C. This is the meaning of any part, any organ, of the government which rules for the exploiters and not for the workers; which is voted in by a tiny 20% minority, and which is filled with "Europeans only".

We are carrying on with the fight. We are bringing to the Transvaal something of the fine spirit which has sprung up from the militancy of the toilers of the Cape during the last months. We appeal with all the urgency of which we are able, to all organisations and individuals that are against segregation, to come into the Anti-C.A.D. and help in its fight which is:

THE STRUGGLE FOR FULL DEMOCRATIC RIGHTS.

Issued by the Johannesburg Anti-C.A.D. Committee, c/o The Sec., 13 Progress Buildings, JHB.

## Document 6
## Report of Delegation to All-African Convention and Unity Conference 16-17 December 1943. Presented to 2nd National Anti-CAD Conference, 4-5 January 1944

Members of the Conference,

Your delegation has much pleasure in presenting this Report of their visit to the All African Convention and their participation in the preliminary Unity Conference held in Bloemfontein on December 17th, 1943.

We consider that the Anti-C.A.D. has taken a wise and momentous step in sending a delegation to these Conferences, and that thereby we have moved nearer towards the Unity of all Non-Europeans.

The meeting of the A.A.C. was the most important one since 1935, which was the peak point in the resistance of the Africans to the three Native Acts (the Representation of Natives Act; the Land and Trust Act and the Amendment to the Urban Areas Act). It might be explained at this stage that the A.A.C. is a federal organisation which came into being in 1935 by rallying around it all the different African organisations and churches opposed to the three Acts. In 1936, it was decided to make it a permanent body to act as the mouthpiece of the African people. It met triennially so that the various affiliated organisations could lay down the general lines of policy for the ensuing period. Although the A.A.C. has always defined the term African as meaning all Non-Whites, and has affiliated members of the Coloured and Indian minority groups, no special effort was ever made to embrace all sections of the Non-Europeans.

The meeting of this occasion was made important because it marked the striking out on a new road after eight years bitter experience of the three Acts. This new outlook of the A.A.C. might be summarised as follows: (i) The A.A.C. reaffirmed it rejection of the three Acts and of the principle of trusteeship and declared that it has never been a party to the acceptance or working of these Acts; (ii) It determined to renew its resistance to these Acts and the principle of Trusteeship and to fight for full democratic rights; (iii) It welcomed the expressions of Unity which had come from the Coloureds and the Indians during the year, and endorsed the Executive's decision to invite these two groups to a preliminary Unity Conference; (iv) It decided to meet annually instead of triennially, and to form branches particularly in rural areas where people are unorganised or do not desire to join any existing organisation.

After 10 months of vigorous campaigning against the C.A.C. and for full democratic rights, and after the active political education which we have received during this period, we may be prone to underestimate the really great step forward which has been made by the A.A.C. We should avoid falling into this error, and we would do well to remember our own general political level before the Anti-C.A.D. Movement commenced, and realize that the Africans are rallying to their present position after a regression of eight years.

The significant features to notice are the rejection of advisory or representative councils and allied forms of segregation, and the emphasis on the struggle for full democratic rights. This, together with the active realisation of the need for the Unity of all Non-Europeans points to a basic similarity between the aims of the Anti-C.A.D. Movement and the policy now adopted by the A.A.C. It is of very great importance for us to recognise this basic identity of needs and aims between the emancipatory movement of the Africans and that of the Coloureds. It is of still greater importance for us to give further effect to this in practice.

Before reporting upon the Unity Conference, we must give prominence to the decision of the A.A.C. to reaffirm its previous opposition to the inclusion of the Protectorates in the Union. The reasons are that as long as the Africans in the Union are denied their full citizenship rights and the policy of the Government remains Segregationist, the incorporation of the Protectorates into the Union will bring a still greater enslavement of the Non-Europeans both in the Protectorates and in the Union, and must, therefore, be sternly opposed by our people in the Union and firmly rejected by the people in the Protectorates. Only in a country based on full democracy for all the people, do we wish to be united with the people of the Protectorates and, until then, we wish to be united with them only in our mutual struggle for full democratic rights.

This matter is just as important for Coloureds and Indians as for Africans, and we must give it due attention for it is going to loom very large during the coming months. If the Union Government succeeds in getting the Protectorates as part of its spoils of war, then the Africans in the reserves, the so-called "black-spots" in white South Africa, will be shifted to the Protectorates which will then become the Reserves – the reservoirs of black labour and the dumping ground for "redundant" labour. Moreover, the shifting of Africans from the present Reserves will then give the Union Government sufficient land for the removal of the remaining black-spots, the Coloureds and Indians, into segregated areas. It is necessary, therefore, that all Non-Europeans should stand firm in opposing the inclusion of the Protectorates into the Union until such time as everyone enjoys full democratic rights.

The Unity Conference took place on the evening of the 17th, immediately after the Convention had ended. We had anticipated that it would only meet on the 18th, but this was deemed inadvisable as many of the African delegates had to leave by that time. However, the sessions of the A.A.C. had in very large measure prepared the ground, so that we were able to assume the necessity for Unity and thus proceed to the practical task of finding a working basis.

The Convention had chosen a delegation which included their President, Vice-President, Secretary and Treasurer. Our delegation consisted of the official delegation of 7 from the Provisional National Committee and representatives from the Kimberley, De Aar, Port Elizabeth and Johannesburg local Committees. Councillor A. Ismail was prevented by ill-health from atteding on behalf of the Cape Indian Congress. Messrs. Kajee and Pather had signified their intention of attending from the Natal Indian Congress, but sent word to say that they were unable to attend as they were busy as the time with certain matters affecting the extension of the Pegging Act. This was a disappointment to the delegations, but it was felt that there is no present justification for thinking that the Indian Congress is intentionally keeping itself aloof from the other two sections of the Non-Europeans, or that the Indians of Natal have been taken in by Senator Clarkson's bait of a sham Municipal vote on a communal basis. Therefore, arrangements were made whereby the chairman of the Conference, Professor D. D. T. Jabavu, and the secretaries were to give the Indian Congress a full report of the proceedings, keep them acquainted with subsequent decisions and make certain suggestions as to their full participation in our further work.

A 10-Point Programme for full democratic rights was provisionally adopted as a basis for Unity. It was considered that this provides a minimum programme to which all three sections of the Non-Europeans can subscribe and which should be the programme around which propaganda for Unity should now be made. It was considered that all three sections should, wherever possible, hold joint-meetings, throughout the Union in order to make the people acquainted with the programme upon which Unity of struggle may be achieved and in order to fight together upon matters fundamentally affecting the needs and aspirations of all three sections. It was decided that another Unity Conference shall be held within six months and it was urged that all three sections should start a Unity campaign to prepare the ground for this Conference by explaining to the people what is meant by unity, how it may be achieved and demonstrating this unity by practical defence of the rights of Africans, Coloureds and Indians, commencing with the coming Parliamentary session when further attacks will certainly be made upon all three sections. It was considered that such active campaigning for unity, by demonstrating how unity of action may be achieved upon the basis of the 10-Point Programme, would be the best possible preparation for the next Unity Conference when the furtherance of the Unity Movement may be decided upon in light of our further experiences.

A provisional Unity Executive Committee was appointed in order to coordinate the work as far as possible. This consists of a Chairman, Professor Jabavu and 2 Vice Chairmen; Dr. G. H. Gool of the Anti-C.A.D. is one, and it was decided to invite Mr. A. I. Kajee to be the other; a joint-secretariat was appointed consisting of Mr. S. Jayiya, Mr. E. Ramsdale, and one to be invited from the S. A. Indian Congress. It was decided to invite Councillor A. Ismail to be treasurer. The rest of the Committee is to consist of 8 members of the A.A.C. and 4 each from the Anti-C.A.D. and the S.A. Indian Congress. The 4 provisionally appointed from the Anti-CAD are Mrs. Z. Gool, Mr. E. C. Roberts, Mr. E. Marthinus, Mr. B. M. Kies. Those from the A.A.C. are Messrs. T. Sinyogo, Sesedi, Koza, Tabata,[12] Sondlo, Dr. Moroka, Tsotsea, Morani, and the Indian Congress is asked to appoint 4. This provisional Executive should meet by Easter in order to decide upon the venue and other matter affecting the 2nd Unity Conference. A copy of the 10-point programme is attached and we feel sure it will play an important part in our movement for liberation.

## Document 7
## Draft declaration on unity provisionally adopted at Unity Conference, Bloemfontein, 17 December 1943

These organisations of the Non-European, which in themselves are not political parties but federal bodies embracing various political, economic and social organisations and parties of all shades of opinion from every walk of life, have met together in Conference upon 17th December at Bloemfontein.[13]

After frank and friendly deliberations on questions affecting all Non-Europeans in South Africa, the conference has come to the following conclusions:–

1. That the rulers of South Africa, who wield the economic and political power in this country, are deliberately keeping the non-European people in political and economic oppression for the sake of their own selfish interests.
2. That the entire constitutional and economic structure, the legislative, educational, fiscal, judicial and administrative policy, is designed to serve the interests of the European ruling-class (the minority) and not the interests of the people of the country as a whole.
3. That despite protestations to the contrary, it is the firm determination of this ruling-class to prevent the economic advance and upliftment of the Non-Europeans.
4. That during the 33 years since the formation of the Union, the promises of the rulers (who have assumed the self-appointed role of "trustees") that they would use the economic resources of the Union for the benefit of the underprivileged (those in "trust") have been flagrantly broken. Instead of a process of civilisation, of reforms leading to a greater share in self-government and government, to a greater share in the national income, to a greater share in the material and cultural wealth of South Africa, to a more equitable distribution of the land – these 33 years have been marked by a process of cumulative oppression, of more brutal dispossession of the Non-European, of more crippling restrictions in every sphere.
5. That not only the future wealth of the Non-Europeans in South Africa, but their very existence as a people demands the immediate abolition of "trusteeship", of all constitutional privileges based on skin-colour, privileges which are incompatible with the principles of democracy and justice.
6. That the continuation of the present system in South Africa, so similar to the Nazi system of Herrenvolk, although it may lead to temporary prosperity to the ruling class and race, must inevitably be at the expense of the Non-Europeans and lead to their ruination.
7. That the economic prosperity and all-round advancement of South Africa, as of other countries, can only be achieved by the collaboration of free people: such collaboration can only be possible and fruitful as between people who enjoy the status of citizenship, which is based on equality of civil and political rights.
8. The recognition that Segregation is an artificial device of the rulers, and an instrument for the domination of the Non-European, is at the same time a recognition that the division, strife and suspicion amongst the Non-European groups themselves is also artificially fostered by the ruling-class. From this it follows:–

(a) That no effective fight against Segregation is possible by people who tacitly accept segregation amongst themselves.

(b) That the acceptance of Segregation, in whatsoever form, serves only the interests of the oppressors.
(c) That our fight against Segregation must be directed against the segregationists within as well as without.
(d) That the Unity of all the Non-Europeans is a necessary pre-condition for this total fight against Segregation.
9. As representatives of the Non-European oppressed people, we have come together in the full recognition of the above, in order to lay the foundation for real unity amongst the Non-Europeans. As the purpose of this Unity is to fight against Segregation, discrimination and oppression of every kind and to fight for equality and freedom for all, such a Unity movement cannot and must not for one moment be considered as directed against the Europeans (an anti-European front). It is an *anti-Segregation front* and, therefore, all those European Organisations and Societies which are genuinely willing to fight Segregation (as distinct from those who profess to be against Segregation but in reality are only instruments of the Ruling Class) are welcome to this anti-Segregation Unity movement.
10. In view of the heavy legacy of the past still in the ranks of the Non-Europeans, the task of this movement will be the breaking down of the artificial walls erected by the rulers, walls of distrust and suspicion between the Non-Europeans. This breaking down must start from the top and come down right to the bottom. This is the organisational task of Unity. Provincial Committees must follow, then Regional Committees and finally local Committees, where this Unity will become a living reality.
11. Indeed, all Non-Europeans suffer under the same fundamental disabilities – the lack of political rights. This lack of political rights is the main cause of the poverty of the Non-Europeans, the main impediment to their progress and future. It is through lack of political rights that laws were passed, Land Acts were passed, depriving the Non-European of his land, prohibiting him from buying land and forcing him to stay on the land as a semi-labourer and semi-serf. It is through lack of political rights that laws were passed making it virtually impossible for a Non-European to become a skilled worker (the white labour policy Apprenticeship Acts, etc.) and keeping unskilled and semi-skilled labour on the very lowest plane and even below the minimum subsistence level. It is through lack of political rights –
(a) that his education is deliberately starved;
(b) that he is starved of medical facilities, hospitals, maternity homes and clinics;
(c) that he is forced to live in locations, bazaars, hovels and sheds;
(d) that he is forced to carry passes and cannot move freely;
(e) that the system of taxation is unjustly applied against him;
(f) that he is not allowed to form Trade Unions.
12. In view of the fact that all the above disabilities, economic, educational, social and cultural all flow from the lack of political rights, the struggle for full democratic rights must become the pivotal point of our struggle for freedom. But while recognising that our struggle is chiefly a political struggle, we must not neglect any other form of struggle so long as it serves the cause of liberation. Thus it is the duty of every organisation attached to this Unity movement to unfold to the people the meaning of the following programme, a programme not for bargaining but representing the minimum demand and fundamental needs of all sections of the people.

## Document 8
## *The Ten-Point Programme* [1943]

The aim of the Non-European Unity Movement is the liquidation of the National Oppression of the Non-European in South Africa, that is, the removal of all the disabilities and restrictions based on grounds of race and colour, and the acquisition by the Non-European of all those rights which are at present enjoyed by the European population.

Unlike other forms of past society based on slavery and serfdom, Democracy is the rule *of* the people, *by* the people, *for* the people. But as long as a section of the people are enslaved, there can be no democracy, and without democracy there can be no justice. We Non-Europeans are demanding only those rights for which the Europeans were fighting more than 100 years ago.

These Democratic demands are contained in the following 10 Points –
1. The franchise, i.e. the right of every man and woman over the age of 21 to elect and be elected to Parliament, Provincial Council and all other Divisional and Municipal Councils.
2. Compulsory, free and uniform education for all children up to the age of 16 with free meals, free books and school equipment for the needy.
3. Inviolability of person, of one's house and privacy.
4. Freedom of speech, press, meetings and association.
5. Freedom of movement and occupation.
6. Full equality of rights for all citizens without distinction of race, colour and sex.
7. Revision of the land question in accordance with the above.
8. Revision of the civil and criminal code in accordance with the above.
9. Revision of the system of taxation in accordance with the above.
10. Revision of the labour legislation and its application to the mines and agriculture.

*EXPLANATORY REMARKS ON THE PROGRAMME*
1. This means the end of all political tutelage, of all communal or indirect representation, and the granting to all Non-Europeans of the same, universal, equal, direct and secret ballot as at present enjoyed by Europeans exclusively.
2. This means the extension of all the educational rights at present enjoyed by European children, to all Non-European children, with the same access to higher education on equal terms.
3. This is the elementary Habeas corpus right. The present state of helplessness of the Non-European before the police is an outrage of the principles of democracy. No man should be molested by the police, nor should his house be entered without a writ from the magistrate. The same right to inviolability and privacy at present enjoyed by the European should apply to all Non-Europeans. All rule by regulations should be abolished.
4. This point hardly needs explanation. It is the abolition of the *Riotous Assemblies Act*, directed specifically against the Non-European. It embodies the right to combine, to form and enter Trade Unions on the same basis as the Europeans.
5. This means the *abolition* of all *Pass Laws* and restriction of movement and travel within the Union, the right to live, to look for work, wherever one pleases. It means the same right to take up a profession or trade as enjoyed by Europeans.
6. This means the abolition of all discriminatory Colour Bar Laws.

7. The relations of serfdom at present existing on the land must go, together with the *Land Acts*, together with the restrictions upon acquiring land. A new division of the land in conformity with the existing rural population, living on the land and working the land, is the first task of a democratic State and Parliament.
8. This means the abolition of feudal relations in the whole system of justice – police, magistrates, law-courts and prisons – whereby the punishment for the same crime is not the same, but is based upon the skin-colour of the offender. There must be complete equality of all citizens before the law, and the abolition of all punishment incompatible with human dignity.
9. This means the *abolition of the Poll-Tax*, or any other tax applicable specifically to the Non-European, or discriminating between Europeans and Non-Europeans. There should be one, single, progressive tax, and all indirect taxation that falls so heavily upon the poorer classes should be abolished.
10. This means specifically the revision of the Industrial Conciliation and Wage Acts, the elimination of all restrictions and distinctions between a European worker and a Non-European worker, equal pay for equal work, equal access to Apprenticeship and skilled labour. This means the liquidation of indentured labour and forcible recruitment, the full application of Factory Legislation to the mines and on the land. It means the *abolition* of the *Masters and Servants Act* and the establishment of complete equality between the seller and buyer of labour. It also means the abolition of payment in kind, and the fixing of a minimum wage for all labourers without a distinction of race or colour.

Document 9
Report of the proceedings of the
Second National Anti-CAD Conference held at
Banqueting Hall, City Hall, Cape Town, 4-5 January 1944

*TUESDAY 4th JANUARY, 1944*
*Morning Session. 10 a.m.*
I. Registration of Delegates.
II. Chairman's Opening Remarks: The Chairman (Dr. G. H. Gool) opened the Conference. He said that the First National Anti-C.A.D. Conference had set us many tasks, and these had been set about with energy and enthusiasm. Much had been done, and we could look back upon the past year with a great deal of satisfaction. One of the most urgent tasks was the extension of the movement throughout the Union – to deepen and consolidate the movement among the people. The Anti-C.A.D. was rapidly becoming completely representative of the people. This fact gave added emphasis to the wise step of deferring the elections of the National Anti-C.A.D. Committee until the second Conference.

At no time did we lose sight of the fact that the C.A.C. could not be treated in isolation and divorced from the rest of the repressive legislation affecting the Non-European people as a whole. It was necessary always to link up this latest move of the Government against the Coloured people with the whole past policy, and show how it had a direct and vital bearing on the ultimate aim of the Government – that of complete segregation of the Coloured people, politically, socially and economically.

He drew attention to another aspect that has not been stressed sufficiently, namely, that although the C.A.C. and C.A.D. may be regarded by many as not constituting the most important of the various segregation measures, in actual fact it takes precedence over all others. The C. A.C. is the measure that crowns all other efforts of the Government – it is the channel through which the Government would like to tow all the repressive laws against the Coloured people. The C.A.C. is the rubber stamp of the Government; the C.A.C automatically endorses all Government segregation schemes whether political, economic or social. That is why there must be no relaxation in the building of the Anti-C.A.D. Movement.

III. Notices of Motion: No notice of motion were received.
IV. The Secretary's Report was then read. (Addendum I).
V. Mr. E. Ramsdale reported on behalf of the Credentials Committee that there were 94 delegates present, representing 59 organisations.
VI. The Chairman read the report of the delegation to the All-African Convention and Unity Conference, Bloemfontein, 1943 (Addendum II). The report was then discussed. Mr. S. Rahim asked for the actual reason why the Indians had not attended. The Chairman said that he understood that Councillor A. Ismail had been ill and he assumed that the Natal Indian Congress was busy with matters in connection with the Pegging Act. Mr. Rahim replied that the All-African Convention had issued the invitation to the South African Indian Congress and not to the Natal Indian Congress or Councillor Ismail. As no official reply had been received, he could not understand why the Unity Movement should be delayed by them. We should get down to the Indian masses for the purpose of unity and not worry about the so-called leaders. The Anti-C.A.D., he pointed out, had started on that basis.

Councillor Mrs. Z. Gool[14] replied that the leaders of the South African Indian Congress had spoken very warmly of the Anti-C.A.D. and, whilst direct advances had been made to the S.A.I.C. leaders, the federated organisations were not being forgotten.

The adoption of the report was proposed by Mr. Basson (Kimberley) and seconded by Mr. Hansby (Bellville Ratepayers Association). The Report was unanimously accepted.

*Mr. A. J. B. Desmore* introduced Article VIIa on the Agenda, headed "Unity of All Non-Europeans", and on behalf of the National Committee, formally moved resolution VIIa (i): "That this Conference thanks the Delegation to the A.A.C. and the Unity Conference for work accomplished at Bloemfontein, adopts the Report and accepts recommendations of the Unity Conference with regard to the Unity Campaign upon the basis of the 10-Point Programme

Seconder: *Mr. Hansby* (Bellville Ratepayers Association). The *Rev. Abrahamse* (Diep River Welfare Association) said that the Coloured people had taken a great step forward in attending the Unity Conference and consolidating with the Africans. The Coloured people and Africans could really say now that they were beginning to understand one another. *Mr. F. Grammer* (Livingstone Past Students Union) said that the Anti-C.A.C. was definitely showing which way they were moving and although their policy may have appeared nebulous in the past, we could now see how the Anti-C.A.C. was blossoming out. He stressed the urgent necessity for unity of the oppressed and exploited. *Mr. A. Fataar* said that much of the praise for the Unity Conference must go to the Africans. This was supported by *Mr. H. Jaffe* (4th International Club, Johannesburg) who declared that the African had always been the one section of all the South African peoples to come out for unity. The Africans constituted 6 1/2 million allies ready to spring into the struggle of all the oppressed. He quoted several instances of African support for Coloured and White workers. *Mrs. Z. Gool* said that Mr. Jaffe was not quite right in his contentions and was guilty of a certain measure of wishful thinking. Thousands of Africans were slavishly following their chiefs. There was much understandable suspicion amongst them. We were glad, however, to have the support of Professor D. Jabavu, who had come out openly for unity. *Mr. E. Marthinus* (Kimberley Anti-C.A.D.) said that the African people were to be thanked for their part in the Unity conference, and moved an unopposed motion that we thank the A.A.C. for their invitation and the work accomplished at Bloemfontein. *Mr I. Amra* (Communist Party) spoke at length on the Unity of the masses through their trade-union and other organisations. He declared that no Unity would ever come from the top. The rank and file should be harnessed. *Mr. B. M. Kies* said that a more sober view of the subject should be taken. There was no need to join in the dizzy elation of Mr. Jaffe or the gloom of Mr. Amra. We should not sit down to bewail the fact that there were differences and cross-currents among the people. Life was life and we had to get on top of it. He maintained that the Unity Campaign, upon the basis of the 10-Point Programme, had been set afoot and it was now for us to carry out the principles we had adopted and ensure greater unity before the next Unity Conference. The First Unity Conference, he concluded, had given us something to work on, to build upon, and we should make up our minds to set to work seriously.

*Rev. E. Jason* (Goodwood Ratepayers Association) supported Mr. Kies. He said it was essential to maintain contact with the people and at all times convince them that we are 100% sincere. He reminded the delegates of the Government's determination to carry out its segregation scheme.

The resolution was carried unanimously.

Upon a resolution by *Mr. Marthinus* (Kimberley) seconded by *Mr. Basson* (N. Cape Anti-C.A.D.) It was agreed that resolutions (a) ii (National Liberation League, Windermere and Kensington Branch) and (a) iii and (a) iv (Northern Cape Anti-C.A.D.) should be considered as covered by (a) i, already accepted by Conference.

*Mrs. Z. Gool* on behalf of the National Committee, introduced motion (b) i, dealing with the inauguration of the Unity Campaign "That the Anti-C.A.D. Movement shall inaugurate its Unity Campaign on the day of the opening of Parliament, by holding Joint Mass Meetings with African and Indian organisations throughout the Union, and that this Campaign shall be continued up to the time of the Second Unity Conference". The mover felt that it was right and proper that the Unity Campaign should be inaugurated in Cape Town. This should begin with a mass meeting coinciding with the next Parliamentary session as the Emergency Regulations made it difficult to hold demonstrations. Other groups should be urged to do likewise. Mr. E. C. Roberts seconded the motion. Mr. E. Ernstzen (Fourth International Club) differed with Mrs. Gool that the Emergency Regulations should act as a brake on the use of demonstrations as a weapon of protest.

*Mr. B. M. Kies* urged that the inauguration should be worthy of the campaign which was to follow, and he urged the delegations to realise that they were embarking upon a serious struggle; they should not merely bask in the reflected glory of any huge demonstration in Cape Town, but should organise similar demonstrations together with the Africans and Indians. This, he maintained, was the implication of the resolution. *Mr. Z. Gamiet* (Anti-C.A.D. Johannesburg) felt that time should be spent in organising demonstrations and mass meetings again and again, and not necessarily at the opening of Parliament as if that were a great occasion. More repressive legislation could be anticipated and the question of demonstrations should not be shelved. *Mr. A. Abdurahman* (A.P.O.)[15] felt that Mr. Z. Gamiet was wrong in feeling that the question of demonstrations was being shelved. *Mr. S. Rahim* stressed the fact that we intended gaining unity not merely demonstrating to Parliament. *Mr. Amra* felt that the localised nature of Anti-C.A.D. strength would result in a demonstration in Cape Town and its environs and would not affect the rest of the country. *Mr. Fataar* reminded the delegates that the proposed demonstration would be the fore-runner of many like demonstrations by all Non-European groups throughout the country. It was then pointed out by the Chairman that the programme necessitated many such demonstrations. The resolution was then put and carried unanimously.

*PROGRAMMATIC BASIS OF ANTI-C.A.D.*
On behalf of the National Committee, Mr. B. M. Kies inaugurated the discussion on the Programmatic Basis of the Anti-C.A.D. Movement, and moved the resolution (c) i "That the Anti-C.A.D. Movement shall adopt the 10-Point Programme as the basis of its fight against the C.A.C. and C.A.D. and for full democratic rights for all".

*[....]* Mr. Basson seconded the resolution. Messrs. W. Parry, Rev. E. Jason and Mr. E. Marthinus spoke in support of the resolution. It was then put to the vote and carried unanimously.

The resolution c (ii) "That this Conference upholds the policy of the Anti-C.A.D. Committee in it endeavours to obtain equal rights for our people". (Diep River and District Coloured Welfare Association) was formally accepted as being covered by the preceding one, c (i).

Mr. Rex Close (Cape District Committee, Communist Party) moved c (iii): "This Conference resolves: (i) That the name of the organisation be changed to "League of Struggle for Coloured Peoples' Rights"; (ii) Membership of the League shall be open to all organisations that accept the Programme of aims, which shall be as follows:

(a) To co-ordinate all activities of Coloured social, political and industrial organisations; (b) To formulate a common policy of struggle; (c) To promote unity of action amongst the Coloured people and all other Non-European oppressed; (d) To conduct the fight for (1) The extension of democratic rights; (2) The removal of Colour Bars; (3) To combat all forms of segregation; (4) To fight against the C.A.C. and other similar bodies which divide the people and prevent the attainment of full democratic rights; (5) The improvement of the conditions of the Coloured people". (Cape District Committee, Communist Party.)

The mover pointed out that this omnibus resolution had been drafted before they were in possession of the other Conference resolutions and this would account for some measure of repetition. He congratulated the Anti-C.A.D. on the success of the struggle and the broadening out of its basis. He felt that the organisations of each group, while aiming at unity, should attempt to co-ordinate the social, political and industrial organisations of their own group.

*Mr. I. Tabata* (All African Convention, Western Province) declared that the political side of the omnibus-resolution had already been more than covered by the 10-Point Programme, and, if Mr. Close would agree, the rest of his resolution could be referred to the discussion on "Organisation". Mr. Amra objected to this proposed change to the Agenda, but Mr. Close agreed to defer the question until later in the Agenda.

*Mr. E. Ernstzen* introduced resolution c (v): "That this Conference considers our fight for full democratic rights inseparable from the fight against imperialist domination, and, in opposition to the imperialist aims of Smuts' Pan-Africanism, supports the fight for self-determination for all oppressed colonial peoples" (4th International Club, Cape Town). He felt that the full implication of accepting the 10-Point Programme was not understood by all. The nature of our struggle and the economic struggle of our country meant that our fight was a fight against Imperialism, since South Africa was, in spite of its dominion status, a semi-colonial country like India. A nationally independent South Africa alone would be a South Africa without colour bars.

*Mr. H. Jaffe* in seconding the motion, maintained that in accordance with Article IV of the Draft Declaration on Unity issued at Bloemfontein, the fact of imperialist domination must be recognised. Our political oppression was but an expression of the economic exploitation of the African. Smuts with his Pan-African policy is the mouth-piece of British Imperialist policy to exclude American competition and for the more thorough exploitation of Africa. *Mr. H. van Gelderen* (Council for the Advancement of Non-European Education) felt that we should be ready to support the struggle of colonial peoples throughout the world. Mr. Jacobs (League of Friends of the Blind) felt that we should not make the mistake of flying before we could walk. We should confine our programme to what the masses can understand and avoid the error of putting forth high-sounding phrases which no one could make out. *Mr. W. van Schoor* in replying to Mr. Jacobs pointed out that the acceptance of the resolution moved by Mr. Ernstzen was basic for a real understanding of the 10-Point Programme. Conference had accepted the Programme and so it should logically accept Mr. Ernstzen's resolution. To reject the motion meant rejecting the Programme.

*Mr. A. Fataar*, pointed out that neither the mover nor the seconder nor yet their supporters had made the issue very clear. They should guard against the danger of mistaking aggressive wording, for real progressiveness. The fight against the C.A.C. was definitely a stage in the fight against imperialism. One step of the real struggle was worth a dozen programmes and a score of high-sounding resolutions. In theory no one could disagree with the principle embodied in the resolution. In practice it was unnecessary as it was already implicit. *Mr. S. Rahim* congratulated the mover and seconder of the motion and felt that it was in keeping with the 10-Point Programme. *Mr. F. Grammer* associated himself with the remarks of Mr. Fataar and declared that the movers were crossing bridges before they had properly set out on the journey. *Mr. Z. Gamiet* declared that the motion implemented the 10-Point Programme with realism. *Mr. van Noie* (Stellenbosch Anti-C.A.D.) supported Messrs. Grammer and Fataar and asked Conference to bear in mind the backwardness of the Platteland and the effect that the brandishing of Anti-Imperialist slogans had upon the mind of the average farm labourer. *Mr. E. Marthinus* (Kimberley) asked for the acceptance of the motion. Rev.

E. Jason asked Conference, to keep close to the masses; leadership implied leading but not racing ahead of the people or confusing them. *Mrs. Z. Gool* felt that while most people would be in sympathy with the resolution, which was brought forward in all good faith, they should be guided by the country speakers and their emphasis upon the political backwardness and slow orientation of many country people. The Anti-C.A.D. was not a revolutionary party but yet the Conference could safely accept the motion since it was not really in conflict with the 10-Point Programme and in practice would not affect the steps Conference had already decided to take. *Mr. B. M. Kies* said that Conference need not be frightened by the aggressive wording of the resolution or the tone of its supporters. Mr. van Schoor's posing of the question to the effect that because we had passed the 10-Point Programme we must of necessity pass the resolution, implied a threat and should be ignored as irrelevant. He did not question the good intentions of the movers but he certainly was not impressed by their political understanding. They should try to find out the real stage that the movement had reached, instead of substituting wishful thinking whenever confronted by a new turn in the movement. The 10-Point Programme was a very sober step forward and they should not allow themselves to be intoxicated by it. People should always find out whether they were attending a birth or wedding.

The vote was taken. The motion was accepted with one dissentient, Mr. Jacobs. [....]

## BOYCOTT

*Mr. E. Viljoen*, on behalf of the National Committee, led the discussion on the Boycott by moving the following resolutions:

(i) "That while the Conference is of opinion that the Boycott of the C.A.C. as an organisation is working satisfactorily, it urges all local committees and other organisations to intensify their vigilance in this respect, as the C.A.C. adopts many cunning and fascist methods of deceiving the people into working through the C.A.C.

(ii) That this Conference instructs all organisations to make a special drive to perfect the boycott of the C.A.C.-men and their accomplices, and urges all organisations to impress upon their members that the personal boycott is not a matter of individual preference, but of whether they are prepared to fraternise with the enemies or not".

The mover stressed the importance of isolating the C.A.C. so as to make it useless to its creators, the Government. The Boycott is an integral part of the Anti-C.A.D. movement, it is a weapon of struggle and no man had the right to elevate his personal or sentimental feelings above the interests of the people. The Boycott had to be intensified in all its aspects. *Mr. F. Grammer* in seconding the resolution urged for a tightening up of the Boycott. Some people had declared that the Boycott was unchristian, but he had yet to learn that being a Quisling and betraying one's people was a form of Christian behaviour. *Mr. Amra* felt that the motion was too optimistically worded. There was a tendency to relax our efforts after the first wave of enthusiasm – the Dollie-Willemburg election showed this. The Anti-C.A.D. should go to the masses, the peasants and workers. The boycott must be applied but it required a strong organisation that would discipline the people. He felt that the fact that the Anti-C.A.D. was formed on a federal basis largely prevented it from enforcing such discipline. *Mrs. Z. Gool* outlined, in reply to Mr. Amra, the work of the members of the National Committee who had travelled all over the country and had combed the South Western Cape in order to organise and enlighten the people – workers and peasants. They did not talk vaguely about the masses, but went to them and spoke to them and brought them into the movement. *Mr. Wilson* (Lansdowne Ratepayers Association) also spoke of the work which had been accomplished especially amongst the illiterates and semi-literates. Before criticising so airily, people should compare the present, advanced political level with that which existed prior to the Anti-C.A.D. movement. *Miss Ruth Pienaar* urged a boycott of the accomplices of the C.A.C.-men – those who consciously did the work of the C.A.C. where the C.A.C.-men could not gain entry. *Mr. E. Ramsdale* told how C.A.C.-man No. 1 had gone on a vain mission to find a new C.A.C.-man in Bloemfontein and had been afraid to address a public meeting. *Mr. E.C. Roberts* suggested that those who were not fully aware of the success of the boycott should inquire from the nearest pro-C.A.C. Even if all the people had not realised it, the Government already knew that its dummy was useless. *Miss J. Gool*[16] (T.L.S.A., Cape Town Branch) corrected Mr. Amra's statement that the Anti-C.A.D., because it was a federal organisation, was therefore too loose to exercise the boycott. Not a single organisation that had affiliated to the Anti-C.A.D. had approached the C.A.C. on any issue, in spite of the overtures made to many organisations. The level of the struggle had been raised and we could look forward expectantly to 100% boycott in future if we but applied ourselves diligently to the task. *Mr. I. Tabata* showed how the success of the boycott was relative to the political education of the people. The two things were inter-dependent and the success of the boycott was largely dependant upon the success of the local Committees. *Mrs. R. E. Viljoen* said that she had found from personal experience that the boycott came very easily if people sincerely faced up to the question of whether the welfare of the people was more important than their personal friendships. *Mr. Fataar* moved that the words "and all Anti-C.A.D. Committees" should be inserted in Resolution (ii) after the words "instructs all organisations". *Mr. A. Abdurahman* seconded.

The amended motion was then put and unanimously accepted.

Close of Session, Tuesday, 4th January, 1944.

*WEDNESDAY, 5th JANUARY, 1944*
*Morning Session.*                 *TRADE UNIONS*

*Mr. E. Ernstzen* led the discussion on Trade Unions, on behalf of the National Committee. He held that it was an unhealthy state of affairs that only one trade-union was represented at the Conference. It was imperative that local committees should be instructed to get trade unions to join the Anti-C.A.D. movement. In the Non-European trade unions there was an economic as well as a colour-bar fight. The political organisations should, therefore, lend aid to trade unions and actively participate in their everyday struggle. The unorganised workers should be organised, and in this the Anti-C.A.D. should help the trade unions. It was not necessary for the Anti-C.A.D. to interest itself in the domestic affairs of the trade unions.

The C.A.C. would attempt to be the spokesman of the Coloured workers and advise the Government on "Coloured trade union" problems. If the trade unions allowed that to happen they would lose their right to bargain and even the whole position with regard to the White workers would be jeopardised. The C.A.C. was also trying to drive a wedge between African and Coloured workers. The C.A.C. was a direct threat to workers' unity. He then moved (i) "That this Conference instructs all local committees and individual organisations to make every endeavour to enrol the organised workers, the trade unions, into the Anti-C.A.D. movement, and calls upon all trade unionists to assist in this task. (ii) That this Conference urges the organised trade union movement as represented by the Cape Federation of Labour Unions, the S.A. Trades and Labour Council, the Western Province Council of Trade Unions, and the Non-European Councils of Trade Unions (Port Elizabeth, Johannesburg, Pretoria) to call a special conference to consider the disastrous effect of a C. A.C. and C.A.D. upon the status of Coloured workers in trade unions and thus upon the trade union movement as a whole".

In seconding the motion, Mr. Jaffe made mention of the wedge that the C.A.C. was driving between Coloured and African workers. At the two conferences of "The Rights and Justice" many trade unions attended and were duped by the Liberals and the heads of the Churches who engineered the Conferences. Many problems affecting the Non-Europeans were discussed, and many resolutions were accepted by the trade unions. The fact that the Conference passed a resolution calling for a minimum wage of £2. per week for African workers, showed the segregationist line of the Conference. This was not a just demand, and only aimed at driving a wedge between Coloured, White and African workers. He contended that the demand should be "Equal pay for equal work". *Mr. M. Arendse* (General Workers Union) agreed with the views of Mr. Ernstzen and urged that the Anti-C.A.D. should worry itself less about political problems and pay more attention to "bread and butter" problems. At this stage the Chairman reminded the delegates that, from its side, the Anti-C.A.D. had made every effort to get the trade unions to link up with the AntI-C.A.D. but had not received very much help from those who had control over the trade unions. Mr. E. Viljoen said that there were people standing between the organised worker and the Anti-C.A.D.

*Mr. R. Close* held that the Anti-C.A.D. offered no practical and concrete leadership in the day to day problems of the workers. There was nothing practical and material that the workers could follow. This was the reason for their apathy. He disagreed with Mr. Jaffe that in demanding £2. as a minimum wage for African workers, he was supporting a segregationist move. It was wrong to attack Liberal Churchmen of the type of Bishop Lavis, who were really interested in the lot of the poor. The *Rev. D. Wessels* said that he was amazed to hear Mr. Close commend Bishop Lavis to the Coloured People, as he and many other so-called liberals, churchmen and otherwise, had either given tacit support in the open or active support behind the scenes to the Government's C.A.C. and other segregationist moves.

*Mr. I. Tabata* said that Mr. Close belonged to an organisation which had a controlling interest in many trade unions and he might be able to offer an explanation of the fact that the workers were strongly Anti-C.A.D. and found that the Anti-C.A.D. provided practical and concrete leadership. But suddenly when they were banded together in trade unions they were alleged to find the Anti-C.A.D. movement lacking in "practical and concrete" leadership. There was something there which required careful consideration. Mrs. Z. Gool, Mr. Fataar, Mr. Basson, Mr. van Gelderen and Mr. Grammer all spoke against Mr. Close's defence of the liberals and the "Rights and Justice" Conference. *Mr. J. Phillips* (Johannesburg) supported the resolutions, but disagreed that in accepting £2. they were forwarding a segregationist demand. After *Mr. van Noie* (Stellenbosch) had reminded Conference of the fact that the chief fight at present was still the fight against the C.A.C., the resolutions were unanimously carried.

*ORGANISATION*

*Mr. E.C. Roberts*, on behalf of the National Committee, led the discussion on organisation, and formally proposed "That this Conference urges the formation of more Local Anti-C.A.D. Committees and impresses upon all existing Local Committees the necessity for detailed house-to-house combing of their areas in order to make the masses fully conscious of the struggle".

The mover traced the history of the Anti-C.A.D. movement since 13th February, 1943, and stressed the necessity of establishing Anti-C.A.D. Committees in areas or districts that are more densely populated, *Mr. E. Marthinus* seconded the motion and requested the issue of a children's bulletin for the education of younger students especially in matters affecting the true history of the country. *Rev. Abrahamse* asked the Chairman whether the motion meant the organisation of Coloured people exclusively. He was assured that the ranks are open to all. The motion was carried.

*Mr. R. Close* then moved Resolution c (iii) (see text above). It was seconded by *Mr. E. Railoun* (Someset Strand). *Rev. D. Wessles* strongly opposed any attempt to tamper with the name. He said that the term "Anti-C.A.D." now meant so much to the people that it stood for an idea, a new conception of struggle and a new aim in life. *Mr. Ernstzen* pointed out that the Communist Party was pleading for a segregationist organisation for Coloureds only. *Mrs. Z. Gool* maintained that the Communist Party was rather behind the times because while we were emphasising "Non-European" their resolution returned the emphasis to "Coloured". *Mr. Fataar* declared that this was the raising of the old skeleton – the formation of a single organisation to liquidate all others, *Mr. Amra* contended that the resolution was an attempt to give the Anti-C.A.D. a national organisational basis. Hitherto the Anti-C.A.D. could not claim to be a national organisation. The motion was lost by 5 votes to 42.

*Afternoon Session.*
*Mr. van Schoor* introduced motion VIII (ii) a and b: (a) "That this Conference give formal recognition to the new status of the Anti-C.A.D. Movement as a general anti-segregationist movement, by empowering each local Anti-C.A.D. Committee henceforth to function as an anti-segregationist committee in its area, with provisions for individual membership thus creating the basis for a National Organisation fighting for full democratic rights for all Non-Europeans. (b) That this Conference empowers its delegates to the forthcoming Unity Conference to change the local Anti-C.A.D. Committees into local committees of the proposed Federal Unity Organisation should this latter be decided upon at the Unity Conference". (Fourth International Club, Cape Town). (The mover claimed that the Anti-C.A.D. had now broadened its activities and policy – witness the 10-Point Programme. The aim of the first part of his resolution was to give formal recognition to the fact that the Anti-C.A.D. was assuming a new role. This new role was also being played by the various committees. The purpose of (b) was merely to change the Anti-C.A.D. committees in name when once they had become anti-segregationist committees with provision for individual membership, and these would now link up with other organisations in the area concerned, and these larger committees would become affiliated to the still larger Federal Unity organisation.)

He was seconded by *Mr. J. Marais* who stressed the point that it was essential to the progress of the oppressed that a National Organisation should be formed.

*Mr. E. C. Roberts* held that the motion meant a formal strangulation not strengthening. The remarks of the mover were familiar as they harked back to the early days of the Anti-C.A.D. movement when the Fourth International Club felt that one couldn't be Anti-C.A.D. without a National Organisation, which later boiled down to a National Organisation in the Cape, which letter reduced itself to mere idle talk and no work. Their proposals were as invalid now as they were 12 months ago. *Mr. A. J. B. Desmore* felt that the Anti-C.A.D. had not suddenly altered its status in the sense that it had made any sharp turn. What we had done in the past, namely, to oppose the C.A.C. and to fight for democratic fights, was now being more fully formulated and more clearly defined.

*Mr. Z. Gamiet* differed from Mr. Desmore. He maintained that Anti-C.A.D. representation at the All African Convention was definitely a precedent, and failure to form an organisation was a negation of that policy and spirit.

*Mr. E. Ramsdale* said that the first part of the resolution was contradicted by the second. Part (a) proposed to change the local committees into anti-segregationist committees to form the basis of a National Organisation for all. Part (b) wanted to change those same local committees into something else – into local committees of a *federal* organisation. How could one and the same committee serve in (a) as a mouthpiece of all Non-Europeans and in (b) as a part of a Federal organisation which claimed to be the mouthpiece. *Mrs. Z. Gool* and *Mr. Fataar* spoke in support of Mr. Ramsdale. Mrs. Gool suggested that the whole matter of organisation form be left over until after the Unity Conference. *Mr. Parry* maintained that the Anti-C.A.C. had been changed entirely and that to deny this was false. The motion was put to the vote and defeated. [....]

## ELECTION OF OFFICIALS TO NATIONAL COMMITTEE

*Rev. D. M. Wessels* and *Mr. Basson* were nominated and elected scrutineers.

On a resolution by *Mrs. Z. Gool* seconded by *Rev. Abrahamse*, *Dr. G. H. Gool* was nominated Chairman. There were no other nominees. On further resolutions the following were elected unopposed: *Miss H. Ahmed*, Secretary; *Mr. S. Edross*, Assistant Secretary; *Messrs S. Rahim and E. Viljoen*, Trustees; *Mr A. Fataar*, Treasurer; *Mr. B. M. Kies*, Director of Publicity.

The nominees for the position of Vice-President were *Mr. E. W. Ernstzen* and *Mr. E. C. Roberts*. A ballot was taken (ballot papers were issued) and *Mr. E. C. Roberts* was duly elected. [....]

## GENERAL

[....] *Mr. R. Close* then moved: "That this Conference pledges its fullest support to the National Anti-Pass Campaign of the African National Congress". *Mr. Holmes* seconded. *Mr. L. Phillips* supported the resolution. *Mr. I Tabata* said that the resolution was in order except for the fact that its tail attempted to claim that the struggle against the Pass Laws was the monopoly of a particular, sectarian organisation. He moved the amendment: "That this Conference pledges its fullest support to the National Anti-Pass Campaign or any campaign against the restrictive measures concerning the Africans". *Rev. Abrahamse* seconded. *Mr. A. J. B. Desmore* moved the further amendment: "That this Conference re-iterates that the Anti-C.A.D. movement is in principle against the Pass-Laws and in practice will support any effort to have them abolished". *Mr. Tabata* withdrew his amendment in favour of Mr. Desmore's. This latter, seconded by *Mr. Kies*, was accepted by an overwhelming majority.

It was moved by *Rev. D. Wessels* and seconded by *Mr. Tabata* that the National Committee should meet at 10 o' clock, Thursday, 6th, to elect the Working Committee. Agreed. [....]

## Document 10
## Y. M. Dadoo[17], "The Non-European Unity",
## Freedom, 4, 1, February 1945

THE Unity Conference which met at Cape Town on the 4th and 5th January aroused a great deal of interest among politically conscious circles, particularly among the non-Europeans. They were expectantly waiting for results to flow from the Conference, which would help in forging the unity of the different non-European sections in their struggle against oppression and for full democratic rights.

Are these hopes going to be realised? The Conference gave some indication of the aims and object which the sponsors of the Conference had in mind during discussion of the two main resolutions on i) the basis of unity and (ii) the building of unity.

### BACKGROUND OF THE UNITY MOVEMENT
In order to obtain a clear picture of this Conference, it is necessary to give a brief outline of the events which led up to it.

The Executive Committee of the All-African Convention at a special meeting held on 26th August, 1943. decided to invite "representative bodies of the other non-European Groups", the Anti-C.A.D. and the South African Indian Congress, to send guest delegates to the All-African Convention with a view to meeting them in a Unity Conference after the Convention session in order to discuss practical steps for united efforts in the struggle for liberation.

Representatives of the Anti-C.A.D. and the All-African Convention met at Bloemfontein in December 1943 under the chairmanship of Professor Jabavu.

The South African Indian Congress excused itself on the grounds that their delegates were unavoidably engaged in matters arising out of the Pegging Act and therefore could not attend.

The Conference decided on a Minimum Ten Point Programme on which to build Unity and a Provisional Committee was elected to work towards the calling of an "All-In Unity Conference".

A second Unity Conference was held at Johannesburg between the representatives of the All African Convention, the Anti-C A.D. and the South African Indian Congress.

At this Conference, a virtual ultimatum was presented to the South African Indian Congress representatives; they were told to come into the Unity Movement on nothing less than the 10-Point Programme. The Indian Congress' suggestion of a "broad co-ordinating committee to co-operate on issues as they arise" was turned down and no settlement was arrived at.

The Conference, however, decided to call an All-In Unity Conference in Cape Town in the first week of January, 1945.

### ALL-IN UNITY CONFERENCE
**Composition:** 212 delegates, representing 102 organisations, attended. Amongst the 102 organisations were the Executive plus 25 branches of the Teachers' League, Executive of A.P.O and 7 branches, 11 trade unions and 30 political organisations. No detailed report was submitted by the Credentials Committee, and therefore it is difficult to analyze the real African representation at the Conference. It would be interesting to know the names of the thirty political organisations which, it was claimed, were represented.

**Ten-Point Programme:** Mr. B. Kies moving the resolution on the Ten-Point Programme as the minimum basis of unity stated there could be no unity except on a programme and that the 10-Point Programme constituted the absolute **minimum** for unity. The Ten-Point Programme starts off by laying down the aim of the non-European Unity Movement as "the liquidation of the national oppression of the non-European in South Africa" – and includes demands such as full franchise, compulsory, free and uniform education for all children up to the age of 16, inviolability of person, freedom of speech and assembly, freedom of movement and occupation, revision of the land question, revision of civil and criminal code, revision of the system of taxation and of labour legislation so as to apply equally to all without distinction of race, colour or sex.

In other words, the Ten-Point Programme set out the demand for full democratic rights of non-Europeans on a par with Europeans. It demands radical changes in the system of taxation, so as to eliminate all forms of indirect taxation, redivision of the land and amendments to labour legislation so as to abolish all form of colour discrimination and the full application of factory legislation to the mines and the farms.

It is an excellent and essential programme if South Africa is to go forward with the rest of the world and if South Africa is to avoid unemployment, depression, reaction and bloody racial strife in the immediate post-war period. It is a programme which every politically-conscious non-European supports from the bottom of his heart and tries to translate into practice through his activities in political, trade union, peasant and other bodies. But surely it can scarcely be considered a **minimum** programme.

The pertinent question that arises is:–

"Is the programme of such a nature as to be capable of bringing together the non-European national movements into united action?" The test of the pudding is in the eating. We have already seen that the South African Indian Congress could not agree to the programme. Now, we do not hold any brief for the compromising, reactionary leadership of the Indian Congress but it should have been possible to draw them into united action on common issues. Wouldn't it be far better to secure their active co-operation on urgent questions like the Anti-Pass Campaign and the C.A.C. than to wait until such time as they have been reconciled to the 10-Point Programme? After all, those who have any experience of mass movements know that unity is built in the process of united action and not on any paper programme no matter how excellent it may be.

## BUILDING OF UNITY

The resolution on this subject as well as the outline of the scheme put forward by Mr. Tabata on behalf of the Provisional Committee and accepted by Conference laid down the policy on how to build unity. The whole structure of unity is apparently to rest on three federated organisations of the non-European people, namely, the Anti-C.A.D., for the Coloureds, the All-African Convention for the Africans and the South African Indian Congress for the Indians.

This formula pre-supposes:
(a) that the three federated organisations are sufficiently representative of the three groups, and therefore,
(b) the unity of their three organisations will bring about the unity of Africans, Coloureds and Indians.

Let us briefly examine the status and position of the three organisations – ...

**The Anti-C.A.D.** – This organisation came into being in order to defeat the C.A.C. It can in no sense of the word be called a permanent federal body of the Coloured people.

The A.P.O. has been relegated to a sub-ordinate position. The A.P.O. is the oldest functioning body which can claim to be a national organisation of the Coloured peoples. Although some executive officers accepted the scheme, there was disappointment among the delegates representing A.P.O. branches at the Conference.

**All-African Convention.** – It is misleading to claim that the All-African Convention is the representative body of the African people. It has very little support among the African people. The last two Conferences in 1943 and 1944 were sufficient to expose its non-representative character. It was formed in 1936 to fight the Hertzog Native Bills but failed and since then has remained an empty shell.

Moreover, the African National Congress has to all intents and purposes been ignored. The Congress may not as yet be a very powerful organisation with well-oiled machinery nor may the leadership be what we would like it to be, but it most certainly has roots among the African people as their premier national body. To reckon without the Congress in any unity move is to reckon without the representative support of the African people.

**South African Indian Congress.** – This is not a federal organisation in the same sense that the Anti-C.A.D. or the A.A.C. is supposed to be. The Provincial bodies of the Indian Congress are based on individual membership and the S.A. Indian Congress is a co-ordinating body.

The African National Congress functions in the same manner. Therefore, if the S.A.I.C. can be considered a federal body for the purpose of unity the African National Congress can be placed in the same category.

## LACK OF REALISM

Most important of all, the Conference betrayed a complete lack of realism – a failure to come to grips with live issues which in the main direct the course of unity.

For example, not a word was said about the Anti-Pass Campaign.

The Pass Laws System constitute the most burning grievance of the African people – it goes to the root of the restriction of movement, of forced migratory labour, non-recognition of African trade unions, low wages, etc.

The African people have united as never before in one big campaign to fight against this pernicious system. The Anti-Pass Campaign has been a **living example** of how unity can be built in action on some definite, concrete issue. And yet it was wholly ignored. It would have been possible to further the cause of unity if steps had been taken to unite all sections on the practical issues of the Anti-Pass Campaign, the Pegging Act and the C.A.C.

## CONCLUSIONS

The activities of the Unity movement prior to, and during the Conference reveal two basic implications to a critical observer. It is an attempt:

(i) to build a permanent basis for the Anti-C.A.D. Movement by broadening out its appeal;

(ii) to isolate the African National Congress and to revive the defunct All-African Convention.

**THE REAL SOLUTION**
Practical ways of attaining unity in the common struggle for liberation lie in:–
1. The building and strengthening of existing national liberatory organisations, by making them live and active bodies; and
2. The calling together of the executives of these organisations which must include the African National Congress, the A.P.O., the South African Indian Congress and the anti C.A.C Movement.

Document 11
Peter Meissenheimer, "Smuts' Anti-Indian Bill: Economic Sanctions or Non-European Unity?" *Workers' Voice*[18], April 1946

*[....] SANCTIONS: THE WAY TO FIGHT SMUTS?*
Ever since the time of the Pegging Act of 1943, and more so since the announcement of the new anti-Indian Bills, a controversy has been raging in National-liberatory and socialist circles on the question how best to fight Smuts. The line put forward by both the old and the new leadership of the S.A. Indian Congress, as well as by the S.A. Communist Party is for appeals to be made to the U.N.O. (the new "kitchen of thieves") and to Wavell, Military Dictator of India.[19] They appeal to the latter to apply economic sanctions against S.A. This, they think is the best method of combatting Smuts and his fascist-like Bill.

Now, to the student of history, economic sanctions by one state against another state is nothing new. Invariably, if carried to the logical conclusion, sanctions lead to armed conflict. When the ruling class of one country discards diplomatic means in its struggle against the ruling class of another country, then war is just around the corner.

In the present case we find mention made of economic sanctions against South Africa in October 1944. At the time world-wide indignation was aroused against the Natal Residential Licensing Ordinance which attempted to introduce official segregation against the Natal Indians; and Indians in the "Mother" country were thinking of ways and means of assisting their brethren in this country. There the masses in the All-India Congress especially were determined that at the same time as they were struggling for their own national emancipation and Independence from British Imperialism they would not tolerate the further enslavement of their kin in other parts of the Empire.

When it was stated above that economic-sanctions were the prelude to armed conflict between states, it was assumed that both of them were independent, and that their respective ruling classes were pursuing mutually conflicting policies. The same cannot be said of South Africa and India, because neither of them are independent; but India is a colony, and S.A. virtually a colony, as far as the Non Europeans are concerned (although nominally a dominion). The masters of India are at the same time also the masters of South Africa. It is in this light that economic sanctions between the two countries must be viewed: a retaliatory measure taken by one colony against what is virtually another colony, with the British Imperialist master acting the part of the cynical, although ostensible impartial, bystander.

At the time of the passing of the 1944 Natal Residential Licensing Ordinance, a tremendous wave of indignation arose, especially in view of the fact that both India and S.Africa, as part of the British Empire, were engaged in a war fought "for the preservation of human freedom, and liberty", and the masses of India could not countenance oppressive laws being passed against their brethren by one of "their country"'s "allies". Then it was that the cry arose for retaliatory measures against S.Africa. Simultaneously, of course the fight was waged against Britain to "quit India". And in order to deceive the masses, and to give them a false sense of Indian autonomy in foreign affairs, Britain's Indian-quislings raised the cry of economic sanctions, knowing full well that such a step would not in the least be of any practical utility, and that it would mislead the Indians with the illusion: India can apply sanctions against S.Africa, this shows that we have some measure of independence!

The volume of trade between the two countries, in relation to their total volume of foreign trade, is so small that neither can be seriously affected by sanctions; and less so S.A. whose balance of trade has favourable. And while India is S.Africa's sole source of jute and hessian, a rupture of trade will not deprive S.A. of these goods. There are a thousand and one ways of obtaining them from India.

This slogan of economic sanctions has a twofold deceptive purpose. Firstly, it tends to deceive the Indian masses, in particular, with the illusion of Indian independence, before Independence has been won. With Britain's Indian quislings beating the drum of sanctions, large sections of the masses may be deceived into thinking that even under the British jackboot India is able to protect her interests and nationals in other parts of the Empire and the world. In this way the struggle for complete and full national independence may be weakened.

Secondly, it arouses amongst S.African Indians the treacherous belief that their burdens will be lightened for them, not by their own struggles, but by the Indian bourgeoisie across the ocean. In this way the movements for the unity of the three Non European "sections" – African, Coloured and Indian – is sabotaged, and the Indians isolated from the rest of the oppressed masses. This is the value of economic sanctions: a means of deceiving the masses both here and in India.

*NON EUROPEAN UNITY*
Imperialist domination and exploitation, in South Africa, is based on the naked and brutal enslavement of 10 million Non Europeans with the assistance and support of two million Whites. Correctly did Trotsky sum up the position here when he wrote that S.Africa was a Dominion only for the Whites, but for the Non Europeans it is a slave-colony.[20] This naked enslavement of the Non Europeans is made possible by maintaining the Whites, in their majority, through the super-profits extracted out of the sweat of 10 million black brows.

The first great step to end this enslavement and free the Non Europeans of their chains, is the unification of the three "sections" of the Non Europeans, Africans, Coloured and Indian, united in one national organisation to struggle for full democratic rights and national independence from British Imperialism. An oppressed people cannot free itself while it is divided among itself. "Divide and Rule" had been the universal formula since time immemorial for keeping a subject people in chains. In S.A. this division takes place along racial lines, in India along religious lines: in South Africa, African, Coloured and Indian against each other, and the Whites against all; in India Hindu and Muslim against each other. Whoever in any way, either directly or indirectly, causes division in the ranks of the oppressed people, or maintains the division, he can do so only at the behest and instance of the oppressor.

It is here that the treacherous role of the S.A. Indian Congress and the S.A. Communist Party leaderships comes in. Both leaderships parrot-like repeat the cry of Britain's Indian quislings for economic sanctions against South Africa. The oppressed masses are beginning to realise that the only road to freedom lies along the path of Non European Unity, and that a blow against one section is a blow against all three. These gentlemen-leaders, now come forward with the slogan: "Go to Mother India. She will help you out of your troubles by applying sanctions against the Smuts Government."

This is a betrayal not only of the Indians, but of the whole national liberatory struggle, for by pinning their hopes on "Mother India", herself in chains, the treacherous leadership isolates the Indians from the Africans and Coloured, thereby impeding the process of unification. In any case, the Indian capitalists would only exert themselves on behalf of the S.African Indian capitalists, and not on behalf of the Indian workers. This "eyes across the sea" policy is being justified on the grounds of the cultural identity of the Indians here and in the homeland. Identity of culture, therefore identity of interest.

This theory of the identity of the interests of all members of any one national group is not put forward only by the Stalinists in this country, but the world over today. During the war it found expression in "No strike" and "support the war effort" etc. By these means the workers' movements are being castrated and tied to the capitalist state apparatus. There is only a difference of degree, but not of quality, in the Stalinist's advice to Indians to appeal to "India" (i.e. Wavell) for help, and in the Stalinists being Cabinet Ministers in a French Government which shoots the Arabs in North Africa and the Levant, and engages in full-scale war of intervention against the people of Indo-China.[21] They have abandoned the class struggle in favour of collaboration between workers and capitalists, oppressed and oppressor, with the latter in the saddle. But because we point to the slogan of "cultural-ties" as obscuring the class differentiations among the Indians in this country itself, and between the workers here and the Indian capitalists in India, and therefore a deception of the toilers, it must not be assumed that we ignore the cultural factor.

Quite the contrary. As socialists we point not to the "identity of cultural interests" between opposing classes of one nationality; but we point to the disharmony existing within any one "cultural entity", the conflicting interests between exploited and exploiter within one "cultural entity". We point out that there are in this world only 2 sets, generally, of cultural ties: the one which binds the exploiters of all lands, and the other which binds the exploited the world over.

The programme of the Fourth International Organisation of South Africa stands for the total abolition of the colour bar, for full democracy and national independence. The struggle for the attainment of these can be waged only on the basis of the unity of the toilers of different races and colours, and, in particular, on the basis of the unity of the Non Europeans.

Any struggle waged on any other basis, such as "passive resistance" of the Indians only, dooms itself to utter failure. The attempt to keep the Indians out of the movement to unite African, Coloured and Indians, is a betrayal of the national-liberatory struggle. This is precisely what the Stalinist leaders, of the S.A. Communist Party, are doing when they put forward the "Mother India" and sanctions slogan.

But while the Stalinists have to be exposed for continuing the anti-unity role of their openly reactionary predecessors in the Indian Congress, the present Unity Movement leadership is not without blame or fault. Indeed they should be exposed for their failure to establish a real Unity, a real unity organisation, and, still more, for deceiving the masses (or rather those who lend an ear to the Unity tops) that such a real Unity movement already exists. With their semi-segregationist 3-pillar "federal" structure, they are holding back the growth of the Unity Movement.

The F.I.O.S.A. has for long been demanding that unity be built not on hot air (or international declarations), but by broadening out from a "United Front" type of Unity body into a mass national organisation with individual membership. Without such a national organisation unity cannot be realised. In spite of the hostility of the "Unity Movement tops", the F.I.O.S.A. will continue its fight for a mass national organisation to fight for full democratic rights and national independence, and for the destruction of the colour bar, including the Indian Bills now being passed.

## Document 12
## Non-European Unity Movement.
## Resolutions passed at 6th National Unity Conference, Cape Town, 29, 30 and 31 March 1948

**1. Resolution on Elections**

In view of the fact that the Parliament of South Africa is composed of Europeans only, and that only Europeans (men and women) have a full franchise without qualifications; and in view of the fact that any segregatory vote accorded to the Non-Europeans is a travesty of the franchise and is designed to render their voice in Parliament completely ineffectual; and in view of the fact that Parliament, as it is to-day, constitutes a machine for the domination, oppression and the complete exploitation of the Non-Europeans; this Conference, after full deliberation, has come to the conclusion that the participation of the Non-Europeans in these mock-elections signifies their acceptance of an inferior position and in fact amounts to operating the machinery of oppression against themselves.

**2  The Balance-sheet of the Non-European Unity Movement**

(a) The Conference is satisfied that the Executive has made every possible effort to draw into the Unity Movement all organisations which claim to be struggling for the liberation of the Non-Europeans from the yoke of national oppression and economic exploitation, and considers that the blame for not joining the Unity Movement lies with these organisations and not with the Executive.

(b) The Conference condemns the attempts of these organisations to form a rival Unity Movement on lines not only hostile to the 10-Point Programme, but without any principled basis at all, which attempts can only split the Non-Europeans and thus serve the interests of the rulers.

(c) This Conference deplores the outcry during the past year of some vacillating elements for an all-in Unity Conference, as being void of substance, injurious to the real interests of the Non-Europeans and inspired by the enemies of Unity on a programmatic basis.

### 3. The Coming War and the Non-Europeans

Since all the noble aims for which the 2nd World War was allegedly fought; since all the fine talk of Atlantic and San Francisco Charters, of the "Four Freedoms", "inalienable human rights" and the United Nations, now stand exposed as a cynical sham; since the world is to-day divided into two irreconcilable camps, the camp of the Imperialists who wish to exploit and oppress, and the camp of the peoples fighting for liberation from exploitation and oppression; since the Imperialist camp is now trying to provoke a 3rd World War as soon as possible in order to defeat the aspirations of the oppressed and exploited peoples; since the Imperialists are lining up all reactionary forces throughout the world, embracing Franco's Spain, reviving Nazi Germany, Fascist Italy and Japan against the peoples of China, Indonesia, Indo-China, Korea, Greece and the rest of Europe, the colonial and semi-colonial world, this Conference declares:

(a) that the interests of the Non-Europeans of South Africa are akin to the interests of the people of China, India and the other peoples struggling for their liberation;
(b) that the victory of Imperialism can only mean the continued subjugation of all the Colonial countries and consequently our own enslavement by the Herrenvolk;
(c) that under no circumstances can the Non-Europeans in South Africa line up in the coming war on the side of the enemies of the Non-European peoples of Asia and the Colonies;
(d) that under no circumstances can the Non-Europeans support Smuts-Malan and the Herrenvolk in their aim of perpetuating White domination of South Africa for another 300 years;
(e) that under no circumstances can the Non-Europeans enlist on the side of the Herrenvolk for their own enslavement.

### 4. Resolution on Immigration

In view of the declared aims of the Government's Immigration policy, namely, the strengthening of the White Herrenvolk against the Non-Europeans, this Conference is uncompromisingly opposed to all Immigration under the present circumstances.

### 5. The New Menace to Africa – The Bevin Plan[22]

This Conference of the Unity Movement expresses its uncompromising condemnation of the Bevin Plan and all the Plans of the British, French, Belgian and other Imperialists – the so-called Western Powers – for the more thorough and co-ordinated exploitation of the African Continent. It considers that these plans are not all for the development of Africa in the interest of its inhabitants, but are intended for the purpose of plundering the resources of Africa in the interests of bankrupt Imperialisms, and can only lead to a more ruthless subjugation and exploitation of the peoples of Africa. It stands for the complete independence of all African territories and supports every struggle of their peoples for liberation from the yoke of Imperialism.

### 6. The Ciskei

This Conference of the Non-European Unity Movement –

(a) Has heard with deep concern and disapproval of the actions of the Native Affairs Department in forcing the provisions of the Native Trust and Land Act (1936) upon the unwilling people of the Ciskei, and in compelling them to reduce their stock and concentrate their homesteads.
(b) Has heard with deep regret and condemns the collaboration of certain chiefs, headmen and Bunga Councillors with the Government in foisting the so-called Rehabilitation Scheme on the people against their will.

(c) Has heard how in their despair the people have resorted to violence in defence of their land and stock, and how this has led to the condemnation of 12 men to death. The Non-European Unity Movement regards these men as martyrs of the vicious Government policy of oppression and exploitation.
(d) Has heard with great joy and approval of the formation of people's committees in the various locations to fight the oppressive measures of the Government and its collaborators, and strongly recommends the formation of such committees in all locations, and their affiliation with the N.E.U.M.
(e) Extends the hand of fellowship to the suffering masses of the Ciskei in their struggle against oppression and pledges its assistance in their struggle to the best of its ability.

**7. The Transkei**
This Conference acclaims the actions of the Transkeian Organised Bodies and the Transkei Voters' Association in expelling the Quisling members who offered themselves for election to the dummy Native Representative Council.

**8. Organisation**
That the Unity Movement continue negotiations with the major Non-European organisations with a view to bringing about a Federal Organisation representative of all sections of the Non-Europeans.

**9. Industrial Conciliation ("Native") Bill**[23]
That this Conference calls for the withdrawal of the proposed Industrial Conciliation ("Native") Bill and that this measure be fought on the basis of the 10-Point Programme.

## Document 13
## Sarah Mokone [Victor Wessels] "The T.A.R.C.", *Majority Rule: Some Notes*, Chapter XIX[24]

The best shorthand introduction to what the struggle against train apartheid was all about, what its difficulties were from the very beginning and why it is inevitably ran into the sand, is provided by a document, **"The T.A.R.C. Reports", published by its Secretary, A.E. (Sonny) Abdurahman**, a bare two months after the Train Apartheid Resistance Committee was formed (August 18, 1948).

The TARC was an *ad hoc* Committee. The Anti-CAD and the Local Committee of the NEUM, opposed in principle to *ad hoc* committees and *ad hoc* campaigns which highlighted one or other aspect of oppression and failed to struggle against it as part of the whole system, nevertheless joined the TARC. The first reason was to demonstrate that, although it was politically strong in the Western Cape particularly, it was not sectarian and divisive. There was a widespread and angry reaction to the introduction of train apartheid in the Peninsula, and the move was regarded as an arrogant provocation by an intoxicated Nationalist government. The second reason was that the Anti-CAD and Local Committee hoped to broaden the relatively narrow struggle into a mass struggle of an all-embracing nature.

In the "T.A.R.C. Reports", the Committee states that after existing for two months it wanted to report to the people on how things stood. It reported that it had held crowded meetings throughout the Peninsula, that there had been financial and moral support locally and from other parts of the country. It said that "After a tremendous mass rally on the Grand Parade on September 5th, the Government decided to prosecute 10 members of the TARC on charges of inciting to public violence, inciting to break railway regulations, and fomenting ill-feeling between Europeans and Africans. Nine of these were found 'not guilty' on all counts. One was found guilty on the second charge, and fined £5. We are appealing against this on the grounds that the Railway Regulations under which the latest apartheid measures have been introduced are ultra vires (not valid in law). This will be the nature of a test case on the regulations." This was the case of R. v. Abdurahman.

**"The Purpose"**
Then the Report goes on to say: "But the TARC was not formed merely to make a test case to prove Train Apartheid invalid. It was formed to organise ACTIVE, DISCIPLINED, MASS RESISTANCE by boarding the marked coaches on the trains, and making the regulations unworkable. It was formed to DEFEAT the regulations by every means at our disposal. This was and is the purpose for which TARC exists. This is what we are working to bring about as soon as possible. The TARC is convinced that this CAN be done. Why, then, the delay? Why hasn't it started yet?"

**"Two Reasons"**
It says "There are two reasons why the mass boarding of the marked coaches has not yet begun. It is important that YOU should know these reasons, because YOU alone can help us to remedy the position and mass action cannot but be delayed until YOU get moving.

"The first reason is that, despite the enthusiastic support we have received from tens of thousands of people all over the Peninsula., WE HAVE RECRUITED ONLY 450 VOLUNTEERS. We are, of course, pleased that these 450 have come forward and every credit is due to them. But with such a small number we cannot start MASS resistance to train apartheid, we cannot have MASS boarding of the coaches marked 'Slegs Blankes'. To attempt such a move would be foolhardy, and ineffective and the whole movement may suffer a severe setback. We could, of course, send in tiny batches of 10-20, but these would not achieve anything and would merely be offering a TOKEN resistance. We don't want mere token resistance. We want REAL resistance, MASS resistance so that the regulations will be unworkable. We are up against a Government which is determined to carry out its plans irrespective of our resolutions. Token resistance would not 'soften our hearts' or change their minds. They will move only when organised, disciplined, determined mass resistance makes it impossible for them to carry on with their train apartheid.

So we must have an army of volunteer-resisters. We must have thousands of people determined to ride in the marked coaches regularly, day after day, week after week. Until we have such an army, nothing can be done to bring about EFFECTIVE resistance. Thus the question, 'Why the delay?' resolves into a question which YOU should ask yourself. Have YOU volunteered? Has your fellow-worker volunteered? Your neighbour? Your brother? Your sister? Your father and mother? Your son and daughter? Or are you depending on someone else to volunteer? Are you waiting for someone else to go into action, while you are content to remain aloof or to cheer and pass resolutions at meetings?

The second important reason why mass action has not been launched yet, is that only nine trade unions have come forward to join the TARC. In other words the majority of the organised workers are still standing aloof, outside the TARC. Some unions say it is none of their business. Some say they can't have 'politics' inside their union. Others say that they will fight apartheid when it reaches their union. Others say that they are waiting for the S.A. Trades and Labour Council Local Committee or the W.P. Federation of Labour Unions to give a lead. And only NINE have come into the TARC.

WHAT ARE YOU GOING TO DO ABOUT IT? Into which group does YOUR trade union fall? Have YOU been consulted, or has someone else decided that YOUR trade union should not join the TARC?

Very many of the unions which are not yet in the TARC have a large Non-European membership. Some of them are predominantly Non-European. But yet SOMEONE has decided on behalf of these workers that their union should stay out of the TARC and thereby accept train apartheid.

There are unions which have boasted for year that they allow no racialism and no politics inside them. It is about time that the workers examined this boast a little more closely. In very many cases, in fact in most cases, they will find that it is a lie. Every trade union which claims to be non-racialistic and non-political but refuses to join in the fight against train apartheid, which affects every Non-European worker, is in fact supporting the racialistic doctrine of apartheid. Every such union HAS a political policy – it supports the politics of the Government, the Nationalist Party, or the politics of the United Party."

**"The Irresponsible"**

In conclusion the leaflet says: "You have heard accusations that the TARC is shilly-shallying, avoiding the issue, afraid of action. This accusation comes from two sources: (1) from those who are eager to see the People's cause defeated so that they may justify their own policy of collaboration with, and submission to, apartheid; and (2) from elements who are prepared to plunge the Non-Europeans into any irresponsible and adventuristic action, just to be able to boast that 'we are up and doing', even if this action must inevitably lead to disaster. This is the line of the Communist Party against which the majority of the TARC have had to fight for the past two months. We are not prepared to send into action the few volunteers whose self-sacrifice would not make any impression on the train-apartheid issue, as their small number could only lead to their imprisonment WITHOUT anything being achieved thereby, except the fizzling out of the movement in a miserable defeat.

The issue is much too big, and much too important for all the Non-European oppressed, for any display of individualistic heroics. And as responsible leaders we can think only in terms of MASS resistance, Mass action ..."

Document 14
"Short History of Betrayal",
*Freedom*[25], New Series, 1, 5, 1 November 1948

THE introduction of apartheid regulations on the Cape suburban trains nearly three months ago was the signal for intense political activity amongst the Non-European people of the Peninsula particularly amongst the Coloured people. Not since 1938, when militant demonstrations forced Hertzog to drop his Bill for residential segregation, had the Coloured people been so stirred. The vigorous protests which were voiced by a large number of politically differing organisations, including powerful religious bodies, illustrates the intensity of feeling aroused amongst all sections by the Government's insulting action.

Realising that mere verbal protests would not by themselves prove sufficient, the Communist Party and others advocated the formation of a united front for the purpose of launching a campaign of resistance which would force the Government to withdraw the regulations and thereby make the introduction of further apartheid measures a great deal more difficult. This policy was carried a stage further at a conference convened by the Unity Movement, when the two main political organisations present, the Unity Movement (which includes the A.P.O.) and the Communist Party, agreed to ignore differences on wider issues for the purpose of defeating the regulations. A Train Apartheid Resistance Committee was elected, charged with the task of getting resistance under way. The committee consisted of a majority of Unity Movement adherents, with a small Communist minority. It was understood by all present at the conference that resistance would take the form of organised breaking of the regulations.

There is no doubt that what would have been in effect a movement of civil disobedience would have had important political repercussions both internally and externally. Comment by the Government Press and by Government spokesmen indicated that the Nationalists were very worried by the prospect. The entire democratic movement waited expectantly and hopefully for the committee to give the signal for the start of a significant counter-attack against the Government's reactionary offensive.

Nothing happened. The regulations have become more firmly entrenched, and the Government has renewed its offensive all along the line. Train apartheid has long since ceased to be the dominant political issue, and a glorious opportunity of wresting the initiative for the democratic forces has been lost. It must now be admitted that the Train Apartheid Resistance Committee failed hopelessly to fulfil the mandate given to it by the people.

The collapse of the promising resistance movement cannot in any way be attributed to public apathy. Packed meetings throughout the Peninsula and the inspiring demonstration on the Grand Parade, when hundreds, in spite of the "do-nothing" policy of the speakers, spontaneously broke the regulations, clearly, proved that the people were willing to follow a militant lead.

The failure of the Train Apartheid Resistance Committee to give such a lead amounts to a gross political betrayal of the entire democratic movement, and led directly to the recent resignation of the Communists on that committee. To avoid similar betrayals in the future, and to place the blame where it belongs, it is necessary to analyse the policies advocated by the different political groups inside the committee itself.

**SERIOUS DIFFERENCES**
The first serious difference of opinion revealed itself two days before the mass demonstration on the Grand Parade at a committee meeting called to discuss what positive lead could be given to the people and to the volunteers. The Communists proposed that the volunteers be organised into groups and that the first group or groups, led by members of the committee, should go into action either immediately after the

demonstration or the following Monday, or at least on a definite date which could be announced to the assembled people.

The Unity Movement adherents, led by Dr. Gool, Messrs. Kies and Fataar, rejected the proposal. They argued that the time was not yet ripe, that there were not sufficient volunteers (although over 200 had already been enrolled) and that in any case they were opposed to sending in individual batches of volunteers. Defiance of the regulations was not sufficient. The regulations must be made "unworkable" by organising groups in the different areas and in the factories so that on a given date thousands would begin to break the regulations every day on their way to and from work.

To the suggestion that members of the committee give the lead in breaking the regulations the Unity Movement stalwarts replied that that would only be "helping the Government to cut off the head of the movement". It would be suicide, they said, to move before victory was certain and the people 100 per cent. organised!

The Communists pointed out that no democratic movement had ever waited until victory was certain or the people 100 per cent. organised before taking action on a specific issue. To delay action by single groups now would make it virtually impossible to organise the wider mass breaking of the regulations hoped for by all members of the committee. The people had been told that action would be taken, and they would come to the demonstration expecting to hear something definite in this respect. If action were long delayed there was a grave risk that interest would fall off and that the people and the volunteers would lose confidence in themselves and in the sincerity of the committee.

In spite of all the arguments, however, the majority of the committee refused to fix any definite date for the commencement of resistance, and adopted instead a proposal calling upon the volunteers to enrol more volunteers.

This difference of opinion in regard to tactics manifested itself at all subsequent meetings of the committee. The Unity Movement members continued to reject the Communist demand for action, even after the experience of the committee itself had proved the impracticability of organising the form of struggle proposed as an alternative to sending in batches of volunteers. Their arguments wearing thin in the light of experience, the Unity Movement spokesman began to take refuge in completely unrealistic proposals for a general strike! Without, of course, suggesting a definite date!

When it became quite clear that the majority of the committee was paying only lip-service to resistance while in fact pursuing a policy which led away from action, the Communists decided that the time had come to place the matter before the volunteers themselves. But even the proposal to call a general meeting of volunteers was repeatedly rejected, and up to the time of writing only one general volunteers' meeting has ever been called – the one preceding the demonstration – at which they were told that the time was not yet ripe and to go out and enrol more volunteers.

The action of one Unity Movement member of the committee who tried to pull the people out of the forbidden carriages after they had taken matters into their own hands accurately sums up the practical effect of their policy – stir the people up, then hold them back when the time comes for action. The facts speak for themselves. There has been no organised breaking of the regulations, as a result of which they have become more firmly entrenched, and train apartheid has ceased to be a burning issue amongst the people.

Attendances at public meetings and the enrolment of volunteers have fallen off.

There is nothing left of the movement except a group of political megalomaniacs shouting "Resist! Resist! Resist!"

The false organisational and political concepts of the Unity Movement have betrayed the Coloured people. It is time to look elsewhere for a new leadership capable of giving a positive lead in the further struggles which lie ahead on a number of extremely important issues. How that leadership is likely to arise can well be the subject for a further article in this paper.

## Document 15
Ruth First[26], "Progress in Unity Talks: African Organisations Agree in Principle", *The Guardian*[27], 23 December 1948

BLOEMFONTEIN

**The two premier African organisations in this country, the African National Congress and the All-African Convention, meeting here in joint session last Friday, agreed after three hours' tense debate on the principle of uniting the two bodies.**

Their executive committees were authorised to meet jointly to work out the details of unity, and to report to their next annual conferences.

Presided over by President D. D. T. Jabavu, of the Convention, together with Dr. A. B. Xuma,[28] of the Congress, the joint session agreed to endorse the October 3 statement of the 12 African leaders, which called for unity against the threat of apartheid, and initiated this unity conference.[29]

"A direct attack on democracy has accelerated the desire of all of us to come together," said Dr. Xuma, outlining the history of the unity negotiations which dated back to August, 1943.

On Thursday afternoon when the joint session was due to begin, Prof. Jabavu asked that it be postponed to the Friday. Some of his followers were still meeting at a conference of the African Voters' Association in Queenstown, he said.

Here, The Guardian understands, a vote of no confidence in Prof. Jabavu for being a party to the October unity declaration, was defeated.

### "UNITY RESOLUTION"
When the talks opened, the Convention delegation placed a "unity resolution" before the session. "In view of the political crisis facing the African people and the crying demand for unity from the people," it said, **"the African National Congress should be approached to join the other organisations already in the All-African Convention."**

This unity should be subject to four Convention conditions:
(1) It should be based on the Convention's 10-point programme.
(2) The federal structure of the Convention should be retained.
(3) The unity should be based on the acceptance of the principle of the unity of all the Non-Europeans.
(4) It should be based on a policy of "non-collaboration with the oppressor." (Here the Convention referred to its policy of the boycott of the 1936 Native Representation Act, for instance.)

The Convention's chief spokesman, Mr. I. Tabata, said "we are prepared to ensure the Congress a given percentage of the seats on the Convention executive."

## NO DIFFERENCE

Arguing his organisation's thesis, Mr. Tabata said the Herrenvolk parties were united in their oppression of the Non-Europeans, and there was intrinsically no difference between them. On May 26 "the velvet glove was replaced by the brutal, mailed fist. For us it produces the same kind of blow."

The unity demanded at the present time must be based on certain fundamental principles. "We must say we do not want separate institutions. We want to go to the only councils recognised in the land – Parliament, provincial and municipal councils."

**Prof. Z. K. Mathews rose to put the Congress viewpoint.**[30] **"To the average Congress person this (proposal) seems to mean that one mouthpiece of the African people (the Convention) is wanting to swallow up the other mouthpiece (the Congress),"** he suggested.

As the unity they were both seeking could not be achieved overnight, Congress placed a resolution before the session that a committee of representatives of the two bodies be set up to examine the details of unity. "There are also other organisations which must be drawn into the process of unification," he said.

## ONE ORGANISATION

Mr. Moses Kotane said the two groups had different conceptions of unity.[31] "Some of us feel a federal organisation is not a source of strength. We want to eliminate conflicting direction, interests and ideologies. We want one political organisation that will speak for the individual members of that organisation."

**"A federal body tends to be an organisation of different interested bodies that come together to consult but have always to go back to their executives for directions. We conceived of one political organisation."**

Convention speakers insisted that agreement on policy be reached that afternoon.

## Document 16
## Joint Sitting of the Executive Committees of the All-African Convention and the African National Congress, 17 April 1949

A meeting of the above committees was held in the Boardroom at the Batho Location, Bloemfontein, on Sunday morning, 17th April, 1949, at 10 a.m.

Present were:–

African National Congress.

1. Messrs J. B. Marks; 2. A. P. Mda; 3. R. V. Selope-Thema; 4. L. K. Ntlabati; 5. Moses Kotane; 6. J. Malangabi; 7. G. Mkabeni; 8. L. S. Phillips; 9. O. R. Tambo; 10. Prof. Z. K. Matthews; 11. Dr. A. B. Xuma.

All-African Convention.

1. Messrs R. M. Canca; Mda Mda; A. K. Mazwai; S. A. Jayiya; 5. I. B. Tabata; 6. Leo Sihlali; 7. W. M. Tsotsi; 8. Jas Mdatyulwa; 9. Rev. Z. R. Mahabane; 10. Dr. G. H. Gool; 11. Mrs. Elizabeth Benjamin; 12. Mr. Robert Sello; 13. Mr. C. M. Kobus.

The meeting was under the joint chairmanship of Mr. W. M. Tsotsi, President of the All-African Convention, and Dr. A. B. Xuma, President of the African National Congress.

The meeting was opened with prayer by Rev. Mahabane.

Dr. Xuma in his opening remarks welcomed the delegates and expressed the hope for a successful meeting. In his remarks Mr. Tsotsi said that unity could be approached from two angles. It could be approached from the emotional as well as from the rational angle. The ordinary man's approach was emotional. We were all oppressed, he argued, and therefore we should all unite. But there were real differences which could not be ignored. Unity was a means to an end. It could also be a source of weakness if there was no common aim. We wanted unity in the fight against oppression and therefore we should be prepared to accept as allies all those people who were fighting the common enemy. There were those who did not accept road of struggle because of the travail through which the road led. We had therefore to define unity. Unity for what? Some were stumbling blocks to unity, and others, through a mistaken analysis, took the road to oppression for the road to unity and freedom. We should waste no time on the form of the organisation we intended to build, but first of all we should discuss the principles upon which unity is to be based.

The meeting decided that the principle upon which the proposed unity was to be based be discussed first.

In leading the discussion on Non-collaboration, Mr. I. B. Tabata said that we should agree that we reject inferiority and therefore we reject the institutions created for an "inferior" race and demanded full democratic rights and only those institutions which were recognised in democratic government. By non-collaboration, he said, we meant an unwillingness on our part to work those institutions which were created for our own oppression. A collaborator was one who voluntarily supported and worked political institutions created for the oppression of the Black man. We should support the freely created organisations of the people. That was what we meant by Non-collaboration.

Speaking for the African National Congress, Mr. J. B. Marks said that there were fundamental differences between the All-African Convention and the African National Congress.[32] We knew the strength of our armies and we had to unite eight million people. We should have in mind the immediate and ultimate aim of the struggle. For instance a demand for unity on the basis of socialism would be absurd where the position was not ripe. It would be wrong to stigmatise as collaborators those who did not agree with Non-collaboration at this stage.

Mr. R. V. Selope-Thema, M.R.C., supported Mr. Marks and said that if the Convention delegates advocated a boycott of Government institutions then they should carry out their policy to its logical conclusion. Did the delegates believe that they could tell the people of the Transkei to abolish the Bhunga?[33] (Several Transkei delegates replied "Yes"!) Some of them believed that they could fight these institutions that was why the government was afraid of the Native Representative Council. If we accepted the policy of Convention then we should have nothing to do with Europeans. If a lawyer who defended an African in a European Court was not collaborating but earning a living, then the M.R.C.'s were not collaborating. The people did not appreciate the demand for parliamentary representation, what the people wanted was land. We should think of the eight million Africans who still wanted these things. The Bhunga had done many things. It had granted bursaries and planted trees. If he were to go to his own area,

Pietersburg, and tell the people to have nothing to do with the Bhunga, they would think he was mad. We sat in our various homes and cried "Don't collaborate," while in the meantime the people accept these things. Non-collaboration was alright as a long term policy. These things could not be overthrown overnight. We were all agreed. The difference was merely one of approach.

With regard to unity, Mr. Thema said that if by unity we meant the unity of all the oppressed, then we might as well go home. They regarded the unity of the African people of primary importance. Charity began at home. They the Africans, wanted to unite in their economic and social life, and therefore they had to unite as a race. If we wanted to unite with other people, we could form an alliance with them. We had a purpose to fulfil as a united African race. Our aims might be opposed to those of other people, it did not matter. We should follow the law of self-preservation. We should love each other first before we loved other people.

Mr. R. M. Canca explaining the meaning of collaboration, said that laws were not enough to rule. Institutions had to be created to create a mental attitude of acceptance of the laws. These institutions were the N.R.C., the Bunga and Advisory Boards. A collaborator was one who contested a seat in one of the above institutions. He was engaged in a mental swindle. He knew participation in these institutions could not free the African, yet he pretended that it could. The delegates should not confuse issues. A teacher in a segregated school and an African boarding a reserve coach in a train could not be called collaborators because they had no choice in these things.

Mr. G. Makabeni felt that policy was most important.[34] The word "Non-collaboration" was vague. They represented the masses and were concerned with freedom and not with words. The expression was meaningless, it was not honest and it would not rally the people. The duty of a trade-unionist was to represent the interests of the people wherever those interests were. Trade unionists had to state their case before Gov. Commissions when necessary. They had to present the case of the people honestly. We should unite and not weed out leaders even before we had formed an organisation. If we could not look at realities then there was no point in further discussion.

Mr. Moses Kotane said that they could not reply by "Yes" or "No" to the question of acceptance or non-acceptance of Non-collaboration. They were fighting for freedom. Congress did not want to collaborate. The worker in production was operating the machinery of oppression, but he formed another instrument whereby the same instrument could be overthrown through strikes and revolutions. Congress did not want to collaborate, but the people were not ready. We could not carry out "Non-collaboration." The A.A.C. itself had not been able to carry out "Non-collaboration." In some cases non-collaboration might be possible, determined by the preparedness of the people at the particular time. Congress stood for Non-collaboration – when the people were ready. They went into the N.R.C. to abolish it from within. They could not accept an inflexible term.

Rev. Z. R. Mahabane replied that the analogy of the worker did not apply. Non-acceptance of collaboration because the people were not ready was defeatism. Words were vehicles of ideas which the world eventually followed. Democracy was first a word and then a reality. It was the Apartheid term which had brought Malan into power. We should not drop the term because the people did not follow it. People were already beginning to accept non-collaboration. It was the intention of the Government to establish tribal councils, and we should express ourselves unequivocally against the system. Until the Africans were represented in parliament by their own people they could not abolish their oppression.

Mr. A. P. Mda said that there was much weight in what Convention said on Non-collaboration. There was also much weight in what Congress said. But we shall all be forced in time to accept Non-collaboration.[35] The discussion should boil down to whether Congress was prepared to accept Boycott as a long term policy. In 1946 the African National Congress had resolved to boycott the N.R.C. and Advisory Boards. In 1947 there was a slight change in the attitude of Congress. They advocated the election of "Boycott candidates" They felt that the time was not ripe and that the present instruments should be used to further the boycott weapon. We should decide whether we were going to accept boycott or not, and when we were going to apply it. Some thought we should boycott now, others thought we could use these institutions to teach the people boycott. Mr. Mda felt that not sufficient work had been done to educate the masses. He proposed the acceptance of the boycott weapon on principle.

Mr. O. Tambo said that it had not been suggested that getting into these institutions to wreck them was collaboration.[36] We should accept the principle and then decide when to apply it and where. Unity should not break on acceptance or non acceptance of non-collaboration.

Mr. I. B. Tabata then moved: the following resolution for the All-African Convention:

"In view of the political crisis facing the African people today, In view of the urgent necessity to unite the people to fight oppression and for full democratic rights, this joint session of the All-African Convention and the African National Congress executive committees meeting in Bloemfontein this 17th day of April, 1949, resolves that this unity be based on:
1. A demand for full citizenship rights equal to those of the European.
2. A rejection of inferior status as expressed in the segregated and inferior political institutions created for a so-called child race and for the perpetuation of white domination, viz, the N.R.C., the Bhunga; Location Advisory Boards; and any other institution of a similar nature which may be created to substitute, supplement or strengthen existing institutions.
3. The acceptance of Non-collaboration, i.e. the rejection of the N.R.C.; Bhunga; Location Advisory Boards; The Natives Representation Act, etc."

In moving this resolution Mr. Tabata said that the term "Non-collaboration was open to many interpretations. We, the African people had decided to use it in this particular sense. We were not concerned with the dictionary meaning of the term in our interpretation of it. He did not understand what the Congress speakers meant by long-term policy. The duty of leadership was the interpretation of the aspirations of the people. We should go out to the people therefore and preach Non-collaboration, and not wait for the people to lead us. We want to eliminate internal strife by agreeing now. We could not accept the statement that the people did not want to go to parliament. If the question were properly put to them they would all say they wanted to go, because that was what they were used to. They were used to making laws in their own Inkundlas, and it is surprising to hear anybody say African men did not want to go to a National Inkundla. That was why we wanted to be agreed on the question. Convention has come to Congress because we realise that unless responsible organisations agree on the boycott it will be difficult for the people to follow. They were suspicious of government institutions, but it was the intellectuals who went to the people and asked to be elected. The intellectuals must therefore be agreed on non-collaboration. If the position were to be reversed, and Europeans were to elect three Black men to represent them in parliament, they would not accept the position. We must create such an attitude of mind as will make these institutions stink in the nostrils of the people. The people will follow if the leadership gives expression to the aspirations of the people.

The resolution was seconded by Mr. S. A. Jayiya.

Mr. R. V. Selope-Thema said that so far as the meeting had not discussed policy but a programme. He proposed the appointment of a committee.

Mr. L. K. Ntlabati said that we should be agreed on the principle of non-collaboration, but if we found that it would serve our purpose to contest seats in these government institutions we should not be called collaborators.

Mr. Moses Kotane wanted to know whether, if the policy was accepted it would be carried out immediately.

Dr. G. H. Gool replied that the government would always find quislings to sell the people. We should let them know that all those who went into those institutions would be nailed on to the wall as traitors. He appealed to the delegates to be open with each other.

Mr. R. M. Canca said that we could not support something against which we spoke. There was a school of psychologists who doubted the mentality of the Africans. They don't understand how the African can put up with so much oppression. If we decided to boycott we should boycott.

Mr. Thema said that unity would be destroyed by non-collaboration as a basis. We should merely agree on the principle of unity, i.e. non-co-operation with the authorities and not mention the institutions to be boycotted.

Professor Z. K. Matthews said that para. 1 of the resolution was comprehensive. It dealt with the political, economic & social institutions. Para. 2 & 3 were not consistent with para. 1. They narrowed the question to the political aspect. The joint resolution should incorporate the desire of Congress to broaden the definition. We have to be consistent.

Dr. G. H. Gool explained that we brought in the political aspect because if we succeeded in that field all else would follow. In India Ghandi had advocated the boycotting of government schools. It had failed. The argument was merely a red-herring to confuse the issue more and more.

Mr. C. M. Kobus said that the acceptance of Non-collaboration meant the carrying out of non-collaboration straight away, not at some dim and distant future. We would not speak of fighting segregationist institutions from within, because we could not accept Non-collaboration and still help to work segregationist institutions.

Rev. Z. R. Mahabane moved the acceptance of the original resolution as moved by Mr. Tabata. The resolution was accepted.

Leading the discussion on the structure of the proposed body, Mr. A. P. Mda said that the time had come for the establishment of a basis for total struggle against oppression. We should lay such foundation as would make the force gain momentum as struggle continued. The most effective way of appealing to the Africans would be to appeal to them as oppressed people. We should base our appeal on colour. The basis of the organisation should be nationalistic. We could meet oppression by organising on the basis of African Nationalism. This pre-supposed a unitary organisation. The advantages of this would be first of all that we would be able to mobilise the majority of the people in a language they could understand. Secondly, there would be no contradictions within the body caused by groups which may place certain interpretations on certain principles because of differences in political outlook. There was a danger in admitting different groups in the same organisation, particularly was this the case when major decisions had to be made. The Miners' strike confusion was as a result of this weakness. We should appeal to Africans as such, to unite as Africans. An African united front would not be opposed to an alliance with other oppressed groups organised in their national organisations.

Mr. W. M. Tsotsi wanted to know whether if Mr. A. P. Mda was speaking for Congress, as his speech seemed to be contrary to the Congress resolution.

Messrs A. P. Mda, Dr. Xuma and Moses Kotane stated that Congress had intended the resolution to mean unitary organisations. It meant that other organisations were to be invited to disband themselves and join the unitary organisation.

Dr. G. H. Gool, in reply said that it would be the ideal thing to have a unitary organisation. There had been such in the past, e.g. the I.C.U., but these could not carry the country with them, hence the adoption of the Federal structure in 1935. If in 1935 we had established a unitary organisation we would have been charged with competing with local organisations for membership. There were old organisations long established in their own areas, hence the decision of the Anti-CAD to form a federal organisation, so as to be able to accommodate other organisations. Convention was prepared to guarantee the leadership of the organisation to Congress by granting a certain number of seats in the executive of the new federal body, to Congress.

Mr. I. B. Tabata: Creating a unitary organisation would mean creating one mass political party dictating to the African population. We would be arrogating to ourselves the right to dictate that no African shall have ideas different from our own. We should fight that, for who would determine this outlook? We wanted the greatest amount of unity among the Africans, and we could achieve this only by inviting other organisations to come in and work with us. No political party could dictate to all the people. We should agree on the minimum demands, then the people would not run away from us because they feared competition. When people wanted to fight they formed federal organisations. That was what had been done in the past, e.g. the bus strike. We should have a permanent structure because we were in a state of permanent emergency. A mouthpiece should represent all strata of society. We did not want to see Congress abolished. We wanted to see it strengthened. We should all go out to organise together. Where Congress existed, we should let people join Congress. But these organisations should meet in a federal organisation. This would eliminate mutual competition. If one unitary party were formed, another would crop up. No single party could be a mouthpiece. The mouthpiece of the whites was parliament and we should build a similar organisation.

Mr. L. K. Ntlabati: said that by a unitary organisation Congress did not mean a political party. We were dealing with national organisations to fight for freedom. The All-Indian Congress was mainly a unitary organisation, until India achieved independence. Only where people had attained national autonomy could they form political parties. When the Dutch fought the English, the Dutch had different shades of opinion, but they were united in their aim of fighting the English. It had been claimed that Convention had been formed to accommodate different shades of opinion. A political body formed to fight for political rights would not object to bringing in Teachers Associations in a political body. We should not have a conglomeration of organisations which were not political. He would concede the inclusion of Voters Associations and Vigilance Associations, but teachers should not discuss politics as teachers organisations. They should join political parties.

Mr. O. R. Tambo said that the danger in the suggestion of a federal structure was that it opened up avenues for division. The masses could be united on the fact that they were oppressed because they were black. We should recognise our strength. We should not preach to the masses division which did not exist in their minds. The unitary was the strongest form of organisation, he said.

Mr. W. M. Tsotsi said that the discussion was in the air. The Congress had been a unitary organisation since 1912, and yet it had not built up a worthwhile following. The mere fact that an organisation was unitary and black was no guarantee that we would have a following. The people formed their organisations for local purposes, and Convention had shown that it was possible to politicise these organisations and show them that their disabilities flowed from the general oppression. We should built on what existed and not on a unitary organisation whose future we did not know. Mr. Leo Sihlali pointed out that even where there is one political party one does find splits on personalities. Even women's organisations split on personalities, e.g. the East London Congress split into two and both groups wanted to affiliate to the Provincial Congress. We wanted to appeal to organisations because we could not appeal to the people in vacue. It had been said that organisations had specific interests. Could not these organisations be orientated? Ordinary leaders of organisations were not going to accept competition. We could not force the people to disband their organisations, moreover, people would not be prepared to join new organisations, as these would mean more subscriptions.

Mr. G. Makabeni complained that the delegates were not serious. When the president of the A.A.C. said we were not oppressed because we were black, then we wondered whether we were serious. All forces should be centred in one place, namely, a unitary body. He was not sure what the nature of the proposed federation was going to be, but he wanted the Africans to be taught African nationalism and be taught to fight as Africans.

Mr. A. K. Mazwai said that a unitary organisation was not practical. We could not have all Africans owning allegiance to one organisation.

Mr. Moses Kotane said that the Congress was committed to advocate that the organisation be unitary. The point raised, that Congress, a unitary organisation, did not have a large membership was irrelevant, because the small membership was not due to its unitary structure. There could be no stability in a federal organisation because interest in the federal structure remained only while there was a burning question. Why should even ping-pong players be brought into a political organisation. There would be the difficulty of being unable to decide important issues because the constituent issues had no mandate. In our crisis we wanted a unitary organisation which would be a source of strength. We should have one mouth-piece. The question was not the structures of the two bodies, but which body was to be the mouth-piece. The people should be instructed to one organisation.

Mr. S. A. Jayiya said that it would not be easy to disband local organisations. The people formed their local organisations to fight local questions. This was alright as long as they linked up with other organisations in a federal body to fight the bigger issues.

Mr. R. V. Selope-Thema said that it seemed that the two sections had conflicting mandates and there was no spirit of give and take. Would both the A.A.C. & the A.N.C. retain their respective identities? The League of Nations had gone to pieces and the United Nations was also going to pieces. We could not encourage divisions by allowing separate organisations to exist. According to its new constitution, Congress demanded 50% of the funds of an affiliating organisation.

Dr. G. H. Gool said we should try to create such an organisation as would make it possible for Congress and Convention to work together. All the organisations in the All-African Convention would have to be brought into the new organisation. The question of the name was unimportant.

Mr. L. K. Ntlabati said that it would be a sad spectacle if we were to go back to the people without concrete decisions. People were not interested in structure. They wanted to see unity. The country was expecting some form of unity. America was a federation, so had South Africa some federal features. We should come to some compromise, so as to inspire the ordinary man with confidence, we should form a unitary organisation with federal features. There had been no meantion of destroying existing organisations. Farmers organisations had a purpose, but they should not be brought into politics. Mr. Ntlabati then moved that: "Unity be accepted on the unitary organisation with federal features."

The motion was seconded by Mr. O. R. Tambo. When asked what the federal features would be, the movers said that some organisations would be allowed to affiliate, but the new organisation would decide which organisation to affiliate and which not to affiliate.

The Convention delegates wanted to know the basis on which the deciding would be made, and Mr. R. M. Canca, seconded by Mr. I. B. Tabata, moved as an addendum: "Organisations accepting the policy of the new organisation would be allowed to affiliate."

The Congress delegates refused to accept this addendum, whilst the Convention delegates felt that the Congress resolution left as it was would lead to an arbitrary cutting out of certain organisations from the new body, even if they accepted its policy.

As no agreement could be arrived at, Rev. Mahabane proposed that the joint-committee should meet before the next conference to continue the discussion. This proposal was not accepted by Congress.

Mr. I. B. Tabata proposed that we report to the joint conference. Mr. O. R. Tambo felt that we could not report to the joint conference until an agreement between the two executives had been reached.

The conference was adjourned sine die, at 3.30 a.m. on the 18th day of April, 1949.
(Sgd) C. M. Kobus.
Recording Secretary Joint Meeting

## Document 17
## Letter from I. B. Tabata to
## Robert Mangaliso Sobukwe[37], 13 August 1949

80 Harrington St.
Cape Town.
13th Aug. 1949

Dear Sobukwe,

This is just a note to congratulate you on your fine performance at the Conference of the Cape African National Congress held in P.E. last June. I know this is somewhat belated, but I only saw a report of the proceedings in one of the recent issues of the Inkundla. Since then I have been so busy with work here, – what with raising funds for the Torch case, the Trains Apartheid case, etc and holding public meetings to gather the people together in readiness for resistance.[38] All this kept me from communicating to you sooner my appreciation of the good work which the youth carried through at the Conference.

Since the last time I addressed the students at Fort Hare[39], I have been thinking of getting in touch with you with a view to discussing some of the problems which I realised were troubling the students. But somehow up to now I have failed to get down to the matter. As a first step I am sending you a copy of a letter I wrote to a friend some time ago.[40] In it I make a few observations on the organisational problems for your consideration. I hope that the letter will serve as a basis for discussion by correspondence between us.

I am vitally concerned with the activities of the youth. In the past nobody has taken any interest in their development. Each successive generation has been left to grope and laboriously and painfully find out things for itself. This has entailed a great waste of human spirit. All the young people on leaving college are full of high ideals and enthusiasm, but almost invariably these at first are directed into the wrong channels, mainly through ignorance. In the harsh school of experience they gradually realise that their activities are at best ineffectual. The nett result of all their expenditure of energy, far from advancing the cause of freedom, actually has the effect of assisting the oppressor in so far as it immobilises the forces of the oppressed by creating confusion in their minds. This realisation often produces in the young student a sense of frustration, a feeling of bitter disillusionment. Many of our young men and women never recover from this experience. Some become cynical while others turn their backs on politics and drown themselves in sport and drink, or divert all their energies into selfish ventures, building up profitable businesses for the aggrandisement of their own petty selves and lording it over their less fortunate brothers. These creatures batten on their own people as relentlessly as any white blood-sucker.

Only the most ardent and determined spirits survive this period of disillusionment and pursue the search for the right course of action. It is to avoid this waste of energy and valuable human material that it is the duty of the older ones to give the benefit of their experiences to the young students standing on the threshold of life. Enthusiasm by itself is not enough. They must have a proper political orientation. It is essential to acquire a knowledge of the psst political development of the people and a proper appreciation of each stage reached in this development. The exerience of the past 15 years has brought home to me the absolute necessity for a clear picture of the past development and the danger of ignorance in this matter.

Withe the introduction of the Hertzog "Native" Bills, when the Africans came together and formed the All-African Convention with the express purpose of resisting not only those notorious Bills but oppression as a whole, the Government-controlled Press released a flood of propaganda designed to smash the unity of the people. The so-called Bantu Press took the lead in distorting the historical facts and sowing confusion in the minds of the people. The students who left college during this period, therefore, (i.e. 1937-1945) could not have a clear picture of what had transpired. The result was that, acting under the influence of the European-controlled Press, they gave their allegiance to those forces which helped to destroy the unity of the people and thus threw the movement for liberation back at least a decade.

Thanks to the efficiency of this Government agency, the Press, we were thrown into the swamp; for ten years we have been struggling to pull ourselves out of it. And now the African people are on the upsurge. They are gathering their forces together. They are forging organisational unity. But for that very reason the forces of reaction are scheming to destroy it. Once more history is being distorted. And strangely enough this time the Inkundla seems to be taking the lead in this process. I do not know what exactly is actuating the Inkundla to take this course. But, whatever the motive may be, one thing certain is that the insidious distortion of facts can only lead to disaster – unless we arm ourselves against it. It behoves us to be on the alert and prevent a repetition of those dark days, from which we have just emerged.

I am looking forward to a reply from you in the near future.

Yours sincerely,

I. B. Tabata.

## Document 18
### Letter from C. I. R. Fortein to John Gomas[41], 29 April 1950

C.I.R. Fortein,
Box 110,
Kokstad.
29th April, 1950.

Dear Mr. Gomas,

I certainly owe you an apology for not having written earlier. I have no doubt disappointed a number of Cape Town friends who expected me to write.

The reason for being such a bad correspondent is that I am harnessed as only a slave can be and my manifold duties have even robbed my family of my company at times. This is due to the fact that the weight of the struggle for a square deal and the organising of our people who are widely scattered has fallen on me alone. There is no other man who can assist – all they know of course, is to talk big in meetings but thereafter they become conspicuous by their silence and inactivity.

I am, however, glad to report that my meetings have had a revival response and our people, despite absurd cowardly reactionary movements by Jack-in-the-Box, supposed to be leaders, are really keen and interested in our struggle for freedom. There is a lot of spade work to be done, but I am optimistic of their support.

I am indeed disappointed to hear that the Coordinating Committee has ceased to function.[42] How can we hope to have the confidence and trust of our people if the leaders betray the people's interest. There are still some who call themselves leaders, but wait and beat around the bush when this leadership should be proved. This is chiefly due to fear and cowardice. They speak big under the United Party regime but become spineless and weakened when the Nationalists – a government of threat – threatens them. Anyway, the challenge to our very existence may produce the leadership which is prepared to suffer imprisonment and persecution. What is Mr. Golding doing?[43]

Well, friend we must watch developments and make our protest vocal even if it means *banning*! You must keep me informed on all developments towards a United Front in Cape Town[44], as well as reactionary tendencies in our own leadership, as I am getting no word from Stoben and Golding.

Your Party is putting up a splendid fight and no matter what may be said against it, it is rallying the people to the call liberty and brotherhood.

I shall indeed deem it a personal favour if you will keep up our correspondence.

Wishing you well,<br>
I am,<br>
Yours faithfully,<br>
C.I.R. FORTEIN

## Document 19
## K. A. Jordaan[45], "The T.A.R.C. Debacle", *Discussion*, 1, 1 [June 1950]

*THE VERDICT*
Having left the public eye ever since the New Year of 1949, barely six months after its inception in the winter of 1948, the Train Apartheid Resistance Movements was suddenly flung into the limelight on the 22nd May of this year. The occasion was the widely-publicised verdict of the Appellate Division of the Supreme Court, the five judges of which unanimously acquitted A.E. Abdurahman, General Secretary of the Train Apartheid Resistance Committee on the charge of inciting the people at a Grand Parade Meeting, to violate the Train Apartheid Regulations. Close on the heels of this judgement, followed the report in a certain non-European weekly – "The Torch" – that the Train Apartheid Resistance Committee had decided to affiliate to the Non-European Unity Movement and wage the struggle under the banner of the general movement for full democratic rights. Concretely stated, there is, in short, no longer a movement the specific task of which is to fight apartheid on the Cape Town-Suburban trains. In point of fact, there has been no sign since May 29th, when this decision was taken, that either the N.E.U.M. or the T.A.R.C. is preparing to deploy its forces in this direction. We have

therefore perforce to conclude that this decision, taken by the remnants of the T.A.R.C. leadership, independent of the affiliated organisations, was the funeral oration of that movement.

## THE POSTMORTEM
The judgement of the Supreme Court engendered a short-lived revival of interest in T.A.R.C. *[....]* Those who stood four-square behind the movement and who were determined to resist in a militant manner, exclaimed that T.A.R.C. should have begun the mass boarding of the trains at the very inception of the movement. "The decision of the court proves that", they insisted. Others – those who spent the greater part of the year in preparing the case of A.E. Abdurahman – shrugged their shoulders, stating that the decision of the Supreme Court was a mere Pyrrhic victory which did not in any way affect the situation. "We cannot expect the Herrenvolk Courts to fight our battles", they blandly asserted, shutting their eyes to the glaring contradiction between the statement and their preparation for the court case. Another small section who had no desire for any struggle – and it is to the point to state here that they demoralised some of the ardent supporters of and fighters for T.A.R.C. – deprecated the establishment of T.A.R.C. which they considered was doomed to failure. Those who were looking for a protective shield placed the responsibility for the failure on the shoulders of the now extinct Communist Party, the departure of which from the Committee they regarded as political treachery. From another quarter – from Anti-CAD No. 176[46] – comes the pedantic assertion that "it was not the leadership that was found wanting, but the people", thereby implying that it was the duty of the people to lead the leadership in better fashion! *[....]*

As an affiliated body to T.A.R.C., the Forum Club formed part of the leadership of that movement. It must therefore also bear its due part of the responsibility for its failure, even though we had conflicting opinions on the paramount tactical question of how and when we should have gone into action.

## WHAT YARDSTICK DO WE USE?
What, in the first instance, do we mean by the T.A.R.C. debacle? Was it a debacle because the train apartheid regulations still stand? Was it a debacle because we did not embark on any action? *[....]*

It is the purpose of this lecture to show that the T.A.R.C. was not an end in itself; that the struggle was a mere phase in the wider movement for full democracy; that T.A.R.C. was therefore a means of bringing wider and wider layers of the oppressed into the orbit of the political movement, of educating and preparing them for the more important political tasks that still lie ahead of us. It is from this point of view that we must discuss the T.A.R.C. debacle. The various leaders went into the struggle with the long perspective and strategy of draining out of this specific struggle those essential gains for the democratic movement: more cadres, a higher political consciousness, more members for the anti-segregatory and anti-colour bar organisations. The fact that we failed to achieve these fundamental aims makes the Train Apartheid Resistance Movement a failure. And the fact that we came out of the struggle with grievous loss – demoralisation in our ranks, apathy among the people and even hostility to T.A.R.C. – makes T.A.R.C. a debacle. *[....]*

## THE INTRODUCTION OF TRAIN APARTHEID
The introduction of train apartheid cannot merely be regarded as a pinprick and a sop

to the white workers. It will be recalled that the proclamation of Minister Sauer allowed a lapse of a month between the introduction of train apartheid and the prosecution of persons who violated the apartheid regulations. This, according to the Proclamation, was to enable persons to accustom themselves to the new scheme of things. But I think that there was a more important reason than this. Consider the position of the government at the inception of its rule: it merely had a bare majority which placed it in a very precarious state. It had therefore to go very carefully with its oppressive laws lest it engender greater hostility to its rule. It was especially in the Cape that the government was forced to go warily. This area of Cape liberalism with a relatively enlightened Coloured population would not simply allow the government to tamper with their traditional small rights with contumely. The lapse of one month before prosecution was in the nature of a test case to enable a weak government to assess the reaction of the Coloureds before it confirmed the regulations and let loose more diabolical measures. The fact that the laws are becoming more demoniac proves that the introduction of train apartheid and the poor resistance put up against it had given the government its green light. It testifies in especially tragic fashion the weakness of the political movement at the time.

## *THE FORMATION OF T.A.R.C.*

The first sign of opposition to train apartheid came from the Central Executive of the African People's Organisation which issued a statement calling for a principled fight of anti-colour bar and anti-segregationist organisations to render the measures ineffectual. Opposition began to grow when the now defunct Communist Party held a meeting on the Grand Parade where speakers in condemning the schemes of the government, called on everyone to defend the Constitution and remove Malan from the political saddle.

The anti-colour bar, anti-segregatory Communist Party was playing a treacherous role at the time. It regarded the victory of Malan at the polls as a disaster of the first order and considered that the main political task of the oppressed was to get back Smuts at all costs. With the liberals, the agents of the ruling class, they were calling on everyone to defend the slave constitution and to prevent the Nationalists from removing the Coloureds from the common voters' roll. The Malanite victory created such panic in the ranks of the C.P. that its leadership was prepared to utilise anything to embarrass a weak government and bring back "the golden age of Smuts". The Communist Party was, in a word, turning its back on the people, and looking to the United Party and the liberals. In its political strategy it was playing a criminal role.

The Non-European Unity Movement was one of the few principled and consistent bodies at the time. With the A.P.O. it also called for a concerted and principled struggle against Train Apartheid and Herrenvolkism in general. But the N.E.U.M. was very weak at the time. It had no contact with the urban population, no roots in the working-class organisations, and in particular, its federal form of organisation did not lend itself to a large mass resistance movement.

The Local Co-ordinating Unity Committee (Western Province) – woe unto this awkward term – called a meeting in the Stakesby Lewis Hostel to which it invited all anti-segregatory organisations. The Communist Party, Teachers' League of South Africa, The A.P.O., and trade unions were among the fifty organisations represented. At the meeting the N.E.U.M. leadership proceeded very carefully. It put out feelers calling for train apartheid resistance under its banner, Non-Collaboration and the 10-point programme. The Communists present then categorically rejected this. Wiser counsels finally prevailed. The N.E.U.M. leadership agreed to enter into a United Front with all the anti-colour bar and anti-segregatory parties. It very wisely did not insist on fighting train apartheid under its own banner.

A Train Apartheid Resistance Committee of 20 members was then formed, on which the N.E.U.M. had the majority.

## THE NATURE OF THE STRUGGLE

The political strategy of the Communist Party and the N.E.U.M. was truly reflected in the views each held on how the struggle was to be conducted. The C.P. advocated the boarding of the trains almost immediately by bands of individuals, similar to the Indian passive resistance movement. It become quite clear, to all, that the C.P. was not prepared for any long intensive struggle. It merely wanted to use T.A.R.C. to embarrass the government. Thus it insisted on immediate action. The N.E.U.M., on the other hand, had the perspective of utilising T.A.R.C. not merely to fight train apartheid but also to build up the wider democratic movement. It wanted mass action to break the train regulation and advocated the intensive organisation of the people for the purpose. It regarded the C.P. insistence on action as a piece of adventurism. From the point of view of general strategy, the N.E.U.M. was therefore pursuing a principled and commendable course of action. In contrast to this correct political orientation, the C.P. was playing its usual characteristic dual role of building up an independent organisation temporarily in order to undermine a section of the ruling class.

The debate on the form the struggle was to assume finally ended in a compromise. To keep the C.P. in the United Front, it was decided to resist train apartheid by means of and through volunteers; when a sufficient number of volunteers had been enroled these would be a mass boarding of the trains.

Theoretically speaking, therefore, the aim of the struggle was to smash the train regulations after which the United Front would be disbanded. In practice, however, wider issues were involved. For train apartheid cannot be cut into a watertight compartment. It is connected up with the whole system of colour oppression in the country. The smashing of the regulations would therefore open up the way for further, more intensive struggles against other aspects of Herrenvolkism. In this sense, the strategy of building through T.A.R.C. the wider democratic movement was of first-rate importance.

The struggle was against a specific measure in a specific area. It affected mainly the Coloured section of the population and was political in character since it involved the tampering of rights which the Non-Europeans had always enjoyed under the traditional Cape Liberalism. It is false to the core to assert that because apartheid was only introduced on first-class coaches, it therefore only affected the better-paid Coloured persons. The overwhelming support the poorest sections of the community gave to the movement and the small number of the better-paid persons in the movement testify to the fact that here we have a political struggle which affected all sections because it involved the question of traditional rights.

## THE RESPONSE OF THE PEOPLE

Without trespassing against the truth, it can be said that at the inception of the movement the people were to the left of the leadership. At the Grand Parade meeting which T.A.R.C. had organised over 8000 people attended. There the speakers stressed the need for intensive organisation as an essential condition for the mass boarding of the trains. The large audience were told not to violate the train apartheid regulations after the meeting. In spite of this warning, however, many people entered the coaches reserved for Europeans. They clearly showed their resentment to and a bitterness against the new train regulations.

Many of us felt that the time that it would be sheer political folly to call upon an unorganised people to board the trains in mass. It was only with difficulty that the leadership managed to restrain the people, appeal to them to reason, and drive home the need for proper organisation and volunteers. The people were, at the time, to the left of the leadership. Their desire for action was proved by the enlistment of 400 volunteers in a short space of time and the collection of hundred of pounds.

*TACTICS AND STRATEGY*

On the Train Apartheid Resistance Committee, the important and tactical question of when we should go into action, brought the clash between the C.P. members and the rest of the leadership to the forefront.

The C.P., to repeat, insisted on immediate action. Were they, therefore, the most militant section of the leadership? In politics we distinguish very carefully between what people say and what they precisely mean. *[....]* If therefore, we understand the strategy of the Communist Party at the time, bent as it was on an unholy alliance with the liberals and the United Party and turning their backs on the people's movement, then we must understand their insistence on action very carefully. It became quite clear that the C.P. was determined to have action so that it could leave the United Front and carry on its wooing of the U.P. and the Liberals. To be sure, its continued presence on the T.A.R.C. was in conflict with its general strategy of using an independent organisation as a mere temporary expedient and them combining with a section of the ruling class to embarrass a weak regime. In short, whether its call for action was a correct tactic or not at the time it flowed out of a criminal political strategy and orientation.

In direct contrast to the C.P., the other section of the leadership considered the time inopportune for action. They considered that it would be politically criminal to throw a mere 400 volunteers into the struggle. The view was held that many thousands of volunteers were necessary to carry on a successful struggle. Until this was attained, so argued the N.E.U.M., there could be no action. They accused the C.P. of sheer adventurism and opportunism. In exposing the C.P. because of their criminal political orientation, the N.E.U.M. was very much in the right. But things stood differently when it came to the important tactical question of action or no action.

*VOLUNTEERS IN COLD STORAGE*

Consider the situation at the inception of the movement: 400 volunteers had enlisted; the people were in a militant mood; they were being restrained; the volunteers were inactive; funds were rolling in.

On the grounds that the majority section of the leadership was not prepared for any struggle, the C.P. pounced on an excellent excuse to leave the T.A.R.C. and break up the United Front. And as we had anticipated, they began to court the liberals quite openly, using all their resources, not to build up any separate resistance movement, but going to the protection of the slave constitution and outshouting the agents of one section of the rulers in their condemnation of the fascistic Malanite government.

After their departure, the policy of the majority section of the leadership became clearer. On the T.A.R.C. idyllic conceptions of train apartheid resistance began to creep in. Speakers began to express the view that 60 years or more might elapse before there could be any effective resistance to train apartheid. According to some, the resistance movement would only get under way with the majority of the population behind it! Others stated that the ranks of the volunteers had not swelled.

And how could it have been otherwise? What incentive is there for the people to join when 400 volunteers were placed in cold storage. What is the final reaction of the people when they see no resistance in concrete form? On this score, part of the leadership blundered badly. They looked upon the presence of 400 volunteers as a static category. They could not or refused to realise that 400 volunteers, like a rolling snowball, increase as a result of their participation in the struggle. The mood of the people at the time proves that more and more people would have been brought in if the position had been kept fluid through continual boarding of the trains.

Looking back I consider that while the C.P., as an anti-colour bar party had a false and criminal political orientation they were, tactfully speaking, correct in their call for action. On the other hand, the N.E.U.M., while it had a correct political orientation in linking up train apartheid resistance with the wider movement for democracy, blundered badly on the tactical question of action.

## THE AFTERMATH

With the rapid decrease in the number of volunteers, with the insistence on the need for careful preparation over years, with a people having heart and interest in the movement, T.A.R.C. then began to decline. Meetings were still held at factories, on fields, in the streets, to explain to the people the political orientation of the leadership.

But a great opportunity had been lost. Towards the end of 1948, T.A.R.C. was beginning to lose many of its followers and fighters.

Its final act was in the nature of the face-saving device. In response to those who still had a keen interest and whose spirits had not yet been dampened, T.A.R.C. decided to board the trains on New Year, 1949, at Kalk Bay. The result was a complete fiasco. The New Year holiday-makers paid little attention to the speeches of the T.A.R.C. leadership. The moment has already been lost six months back.

Since the day, T.A.R.C. gradually left the public eye. Then came the decision of the Supreme Court which acquitted the general secretary of the T.A.R.C. Was that, then, a call for action? Minister Sauer settled this question when he passed a simple resolution in Parliament confirming the train apartheid regulations. T.A.R.C. was done for.

## THE POLITICAL LESSONS

The main reason for the T.A.R.C. debacle lies in the political cowardice of a section of the leadership who refused to go into action merely because they were not convinced that they could win. It was a section of a leadership which had no enthusiasm, no plan of campaign, no creative imagination, no faith or optimism in the struggle. Their idyllic conception of train apartheid resistance was a mere camouflage for their political cowardice and their refusal to embark on any struggle. The record reason for the failure of the T.A.R.C. was the desertion of the Ex-C.P. which I place on record, because this desertion was forced on them by the refusal of the majority of the T.A.R.C. to go into action! The deceptive strategy of that defunct body has always been of grievous harm to the general democratic movement.

To place the responsibility for the failure of the T.A.R.C. on the shoulders of the people is not to justify one as a leader, first of all, and secondly, it ignores the important time factor in the history of the movement which did not provide any campaign for the militancy the people displayed in the beginning.

The experience of T.A.R.C. proves that the general political movement has made little headway, particularly in the urban centres. The N.E.U.M. has no roots in Cape Town no roots in the organised working-class movement. Its federal of organisation militates against the building up of a mass movement, and the organisation of mass resistance. These are the main conclusions one can draw from this analysis.

## Document 20
## F. Carneson[47], "The Franchise Action Committee"[48], Discussion, 1, 3, June 1951

The lecturer prefaced his address by stating that the views he would express were not necessarily the views of F.R.A.C., though many of its members probably shared his point of view.

### WHAT IS F.R.A.C.?

The Committee was formed for the purpose of fighting the Government's decision to deprive the Coloured people of the franchise, narrow and limited as it was. Initially a small group discussed the matter and decided to sound the opinion of a more representative group. The response was so encouraging that it was found possible to convene a Conference which launched the campaign. None of those who initiated the campaign were happy about the form of organisation they were to adopt, *i.e.*, an *ad hoc* Committee, but in view of the complete inactivity of the organisations such as the A.P.O., Anti-C.A.D. and N.E.U.M., there was no alternative. These organisations, which should have roused the people to militant activity, shirked the issue. The A.P.O. which previously had turned down discussions with the S.A. Indian Congress, remained silent; The Anti-C.A.D. and N.E.U.M. had no plans for the present, and attempted to save their faces by talking of making the Act unworkable after its passage.

Admittedly F.R.A.C. is not the best form of organisation to undertake a broad struggle of the people, but at present it is, unfortunately, the only one.

### THE ACHIEVEMENTS OF THE F.R.A.C.

F.R.A.C. has helped to arouse large masses of Coloured people from their apathy, and given them hope that if they stand together, they will be a more effective fighting force. Meetings have been held far and wide, and publicised by the "Guardian."

As the campaign developed, queer things happened. Golding had originally been against any public activity, but suddenly changed and decided to co-operate with F.R.A.C. (It is important to note that the Co-ordinating to which Golding belongs has not affiliated to F.R.A.C.) In joint discussions the Co-ordinating Committee said that they could only go a certain distance with F.R.A.C. One of their spokesmen explained that they couldn't be very militant because of the large number of teachers in their ranks. The Co-ordinating Committee agreed to go as far as the mass demonstration of March 8th.

Some people claim that demonstrations are of no value, but there is nothing more politically demoralising than inaction when danger threatens. Without demonstrations and rallies, no further action is possible. F.R.A.C. starts from the assumption that the Government can be defeated on this measure, whereas the N.E.U.M. adopts the defeatist point of view that nothing can be done at present. Hence their policy to boycott the Act afterwards; for the present, do nothing.

The Government has shown that it will retreat in the face of determined opposition of the people. The Africans defeated the Government by their demonstration against passes for women.

Even those who advocate the boycott of the Act should realise that a boycott can be applied only when the people are already at the point of militancy. Hence they should act now to heighten the political consciousness of the people, as a necessary prerequisite for the boycott.

The lecturer concluded by stating that a great deal depended on the struggle in the Cape Province. He estimated that 90 per cent. of the demonstrators have no vote, but believed that these demonstrators realise that the Coloured vote is symbolic of much more than a limited franchise – it symbolised a certain citizen-status.

QUESTIONS AND ANSWERS

*Q.* – Did the group who initiated F.R.A.C. take any steps to invite the Anti-C.A.D. and N.E.U.M.?

*Answer.* – The lecturer did not know whether a direct invitation had been sent to these organisations. As far as he was aware, invitations were extended to all organisations through the Press. He himself felt that if the C.P.N.U. and N.E.U.M. and Anti-C.A.D. had been invited, these groups would have clashed at a time when the task was to get the struggle going.

*Q.* – After this F.R.A.C. campaign, can the lecturer explain into what precise strategy it fits?

*Answer.* – F.R.A.C. is engaged in a struggle to defeat the Government on this one issue, the disenfranchisement of the Coloured. It is difficult to say whether F.R.A.C. will survive this fight, or whether it will take on another form. A long-term strategy is not sufficient to guarantee success. The failure of the liberatory movement in the past has been the failure to grapple with immediate problems.

*Q.* – How will these separate struggles lead to a consolidation of the liberatory movement?

*Answer.* – The liberatory movement can be built up only in the course of struggle. The masses are usually not conscious of the course of the struggle, but the struggle itself teaches them. We in South Africa must go through much more political oppression and struggle before we awaken. Our greatest enemy is fear – the lack of a tradition of struggle, cost what it may. Unity will arrive in the course of struggle. F.R.A.C. is quite clear that the present struggle will form part of the broader struggle leading to the closer unity of the various national organisations.

*Q.* – We have all gone through the experiences of the T.A.R.C. where different political tendencies worked together. What makes it difficult for different tendencies to work together? What can be done to eradicate this dog-fight attitude from our political life?

*Answer.* – All political tendencies have different social bases, e.g. Golding and the C.P.N.U. represent fairly accurately the political trend amongst the Coloured people to side with the European dominant group against the rest of the Non-Europeans.

The disagreements amongst the various tendencies are not mere surface disagreements. The only way to overcome these divisions is to narrow the field of possible disagreement by coming together on concrete issues, e.g. the fight against the Coloured Franchise Bill.

*Q.* – Would you be willing to accept the United Party into F.R.A.C.?

*Answer.* – This depends on the United Party. The lecturer would co-operate with the devil if necessary. Politics is the search for allies. In deciding on the tactical possibilities of an alliance between the U.P. and F.R.A.C., the primary considerations would be (1) whether the cause of F.R.A.C. would be furthered, and (2) what effect such an alliance would have on the people.

DISCUSSION

*Speaker A:* The fact that the A.P.O., S.A.I.C. negotiations had broken down could not be cited as an example of the refusal of the A.P.O. to build up a United Front, as at the time of the overtures of the S.A.I.C., these were no particular issues confronting the people which necessitated the establishment of a United Front. Co-operation on a specific issue is not the same as achieving programmatic unity. The S.A.I.C. had at its Conference decided to negotiate with other national organisations. The A.P.O. which accepted the 10-point programme of the N.E.U.M., could not countenance a loose, unprincipled and opportunistic "unity."

*Reply.* – Diverse political groups could discuss the 10-point programme and *agree with every one of those points. The disagreement lies in interpretation, particularly in what must be done in a given situation.* It is necessary to discuss what form of action is necessary at present. We must learn to unite with people who are different from us.

*Speaker B:* Was sympathetic towards the F.R.A.C. because it was fighting in a United Front on a specific issue. However, a certain amount of intransigeance in relation to certain fundamental political issues was necessary. F.R.A.C. erred in that it based itself on no principles, hence a racialist like Golding could associate itself with F.R.A.C. Golding's presence discredited F.R.A.C. When Golding was booed at the F.R.A.C. meeting, this reflected the people's hostility towards the state and those who work its oppressive machinery. F.R.A.C. had also erred in not making public Golding's reservations about the C.P.N.U. not being prepared to go all the way with F.R.A.C.

*Reply.* – We should not be interested in what Golding is going to do in the future. While in theory it is easy to expose Golding, in practice this would tend to take the minds of the people away from the main issue – struggle. It is sufficient to draw the lesson of the bankruptcy of a policy of negotiating with the Government. Golding has publicly admitted that his past policy has failed by coming to F.R.A.C. F.R.A.C. cannot have disagreements with Golding because it was understood that the C.P.N.U. would go only for a certain distance with F.R.A.C. The latter body does not dictate what Golding must say neither does Golding dictate what F.R.A.C. must say. F.R.A.C. cannot have a programme because it is not the national liberatory movement.

During the struggle the masses drive the opportunists closer to the militants. If the opportunists break away afterwards, they leave some of their own supporters with the militants. The moderates either lose their moderation or disappear as a political force.

If the present campaign is successful, it will be very difficult for anyone to stand as candidates for the special Coloured representatives.

*Speaker C.* – Politics is the expression of class interests. This is true for F.R.A.C.

also. In a certain sense the Anti-C.A.D. is opportunistic, but one cannot equate the Anti-C.A.D. and C.P.N.U. The former is in the camp of consistent democracy, and, unlike the C.P.N.U., has a definite political ideology. The C.P.N.U. merely represents the small business interests in the Cape.

What will F.R.A.C. do if the people show no sign of boycott? It is the function of the leadership to lead the people. Has Kahn's efforts in Parliament really raised the political understanding of the Africans?[49]

The defence of the Coloured vote should be a point of departure for further struggles, in spite of the Coloured vote being anachronistic and hollow. (Golding merely wants to retain the Coloured vote – for the United Party.) F.R.A.C. will nullify their gains if they should decide to work the Act. This would be a setback for the liberatory movement. The lecturer gives the impression that he is not interested in a long-term view. Must F.R.A.C go the way of T.A.R.C. – into the limbo of forgotten things?

*Reply.* – If we examine the "Torch," "Burger" and Golding's statements, there is often amazing agreement, not in words, but in what is advocated.[50] Both Golding and the "Torch" are against the demonstration. People are judged by their deeds, not their words.

The boycott is not a weapon in itself. Its judicious use can form part of the struggle, but the boycott can never be the main struggle.

In reply to this speaker's statement that Golding wishes to retain the Coloured vote for the United Party, the lecturer said that he gave no thought to Golding's motives. The Coloured franchise is an important citizen-right, and is not anachronistic.

## Document 21
## E. L. Maurice[51], "The Rôle of the Non-European Teacher in the Liberatory Movement", *Discussion*, 1, 5, June 1952

*[....]* It is necessary for me, by way of introduction, to make two reservations with regard to what I am going to say on the subject of my lecture. In the first place, I have to state quite clearly that what I have to say has no relation whatever to any position I may hold in the Teachers' League of South Africa, and my views and opinions must, on no account, be considered in relation to my position in that organization. *[....]* In the second place, I wish to submit that the subject of my lecture is a comparatively new one which has only become the subject of thought and speculation within the last decade or so and, because of events in recent years, has become the subject of much controversy and criticism in the last few years. *[....]*

**The Significance of the Organised Teachers in the Liberatory Movement**
Now, an individual teacher, or teachers as individuals, mean little or nothing in the subject of our discussion. *[....]* It is the teacher in association, in organization which is important for the Liberatory movement. Put in another way it is the "mass movement" of the teachers – if I may employ that term of a small professional group – which is of significance and not the more advanced individuals who would in any case whatever their profession, play a part in the Movement. The question is therefore, can, do, or will the non-European teachers' organizations play a part in the Liberatory Movement?

Quite naturally it must not be thought that I am giving to the teachers' organizations an existence separate from the individuals who compose the organizations – I am merely saying that the corporate nature of the teachers' organizations gives to them – the teachers – their real significance and place in the Liberatory Movement.

**The Non-European Teacher and "The Politics of Education"**

In addition, it must always be remembered that teachers are merely operatives and that the really important thing about them is that they are the means by which the process of education is kept going in society. And there is no doubt that education, as one of the social forces, has an extremely important place in modern society. To us in South Africa the appointment and recent report of the Eiselen Commission in African Education, the new move to harness "Coloured Education" in a similar way through the suggestion of the appointment of a similar commission, the doctrine of Christian National Education[52], as well as the general discriminatory, segregated educational systems of this country, with its more than a million children deliberately kept out of school, not to speak of the thousands inside who receive no more than a mere smattering of schooling and no education – all these must adequately serve to illustrate the importance attached to the educational process in society. No greater proof of its importance could, indeed, be required than its denial of education to the oppressed non-Europeans, and the attempts by the ruling class to twist education to serve their own particular political needs. And it is because the teachers play the chief part in the operation and direction of this important social force that they become significant in society. In a sense, therefore, the rôle of the non-European teacher in the Liberatory Movement means the rôle of education in that movement.

You will have realized by now that I am not circumscribing my definition of education within the narrow limits of the mere acquirements of literacy. [....] For we must all be aware of the intimate relation which exists between the educational system of a country and its political system, for in few places in the world is this relation better exemplified than in South Africa. [....] There are many people who view education merely as a process by which the "cultural heritage" of a group is transmitted from one group to another, and, in that respect give education a completely harmless function in society. Education to them, not being political, must merely perform the task of passing to the rising generation the culture of the older ones and the developments in education must of necessity, wait upon the development of the cultural heritage of the group. Education, therefore, differs according to the cultural heritage which gives it its form and substance and in this way, according to them, each "cultural group" must have its own education in and through that culture which is particularly its own. This view of education, very significantly, in view of the tribal social patterns and organizations which it envisages, has recently been "authoritatively" supported by the Eiselen Report which holds that "In general, the function of education is to transmit the culture of a society from the mature to its immature members, and in so doing to develop their powers." This formulation of the aims of education as the mere transmission of culture is, I submit, merely a reactionary attempt to rob education of its potency and force in the social system and is at complete variance with progressive thought upon the subject. It makes of education a stagnant force, impotent to carry out its real social tasks. And if the teachers were to accept it, their rôle in the Liberatory Movement would be as futile as their philosophy of education would be insane.

Fortunately, *[...]* non-European teachers have increasingly come to accept a view of education which, if not diametrically opposed, is certainly based upon a social evaluation of education quite different from that which, for example, was accepted by Eiselen and his fellow commissioners. Non-European teachers have learned in a variety of ways that they must help to break the prevailing social and political system of this country. Ironically enough, as the group which has made great educational strides, they have learnt that their salvation does not lie in education! There was a time, in the not very distant past, when they believed that the lengthening of their names by the addition of individual letters, usually in pairs placed at the end, would bring liberation to them as a group and that, by begging the authorities for more schools, they could lead others along the same road to salvation. That illusion has been fortunately shattered by the mere course of history. Faced with the task of working a discriminatory and segregatory educational system, in which not the least disturbing feature is the unequal pay for equal qualifications and work, and seeking the cause, the teachers have been forced to the inevitable conclusion that the reason is to be found in the prevailing social and political system, and that educational liberation is related to social liberation. Above all, their theoreticians have shown repeatedly that in all countries, and in South Africa more than in any other, education is the mere handmaid of politics and so "the politics of education" has become a phase of everyday currency with them. This realisation that they must play their part in changing the *status quo* – that education must be for social change – is perhaps the most important lesson the teachers have taught themselves in the whole history of the profession and the nature of the lesson, as well as the extent to which it has been learnt and can, and will be applied, has the deepest meaning for the Liberatory Movement.

**The New Doctrine – "Education for Social Change"**

The new doctrine of education for social change is no mere catchword. In a sense, it is allied to the many other progressive educational movements, such as education for democracy, education for citizenship and the like. But in this country, with its system of Herrenvolk domination whose ramifications are found in every walk of life, education for social change finds very fertile ground. *[....]* The very society in which the education is given provides education with not only the very substance of what requires change but also provides it with the very tools and materials to effect that change. Education can never be for society if the educators and educands are opposed to that society and it is this employment of the educational process to foster opposition to the *status quo* which is the vital force in education for social change. It is some years ago that the Teacher's League, for example, gave concrete expression to this new educational outlook when it passed a motion which called upon the teachers to create in the pupils a desire for democracy; and there are definite indications among both the teachers and the rising generation that this is being done.

It would hardly be correct, of course, to say that all, or even the majority, of non-European teachers have accepted fully, or even partially, the new educational outlook. There are, in the whole of South Africa, approximately twenty-five thousand teachers, and in a total population of about ten million they form a group representing about one four-hundredth of the total population. Numerically, therefore, one may be inclined to minimise their importance within the non-European class but it must be borne in mind that they have their origin in their policy of educational segregation and this is giving them, more and more, a group consciousness which, when added to the intellectual and theoretical advances they have made, adds considerably to their potential of influence in the community. On the other hand, it must also be said that the policy of educational segregation which gave birth to the non-European teaching profession, is of comparatively recent origin and that the profession is only just passing into its second generation, the first of which had a most dissipated life. Moreover, with over a million children still seeking admission to school, the non-European teaching profession, assuming that the present segregatory system is to continue, is only half its potential size. Above all, however, there are good signs that non-European teachers are seeking a closer unity which must inevitably give to the powerful doctrine of education for social change a wider and more purposeful meaning. *[....]*

**The Rôle of Enlightenment the Teacher can Play inside and outside the Classroom**
We are all aware that, despite the advent of the film, radio and even the television, the textbook is still the great instrument of education. And we are also all aware that the textbooks in this country, thus far, have been written by members of the ruling class. I need hardly spend my time explaining that the ideological bases of these books are diametrically opposed to the interests of the Liberatory Movement and that, by and large, they all serve to preserve the *status quo* and further the interests of the ruling class. In general, they are written in word and spirit, to entrench the inferiority of the non-Europeans and to regard the domination and supremacy of the white ruling class as part of the unalienable and divine scheme of things for this country. *[....]*

In these circumstances the non-European teachers have an important contribution to make in nullifying and negativing the effect of these ideas and doctrines upon the minds of their charges and in giving their children an ideological armoury which will later serve them in the adult society in which they will find themselves. There are two related courses open to them. The one is to rewrite the school textbooks and, in particular, the official histories of South Africa, and the other is to equip themselves with correct knowledge and the new idea of the liberatory movement in order to cultivate the proper approach to the teaching of their subjects. The first course naturally bristles with difficulties and all attempts thus far have met with very little success but there is increasing evidence that the teachers are more and more pursuing the second course with much effectiveness. In recent years the discussions among teachers have turned more and more to what they teach and the old slavish servility to the prescribed syllabus has been replaced by the critical approach and the consideration of the mental stock of ideas which the teacher leaves with his pupils. In this respect, I think, the contrast between the teacher of to-day and the teacher of yesterday is more glaring than in any other.

But the school life of the teacher and the pupil is not confined to mere classroom instruction. *[....]* The recent successful boycott of the Van Riebeeck Celebrations may serve as a useful example of the contribution which teachers may make to the struggle, for there is no doubt that its success was, in part, due to the good work done by the teachers.[53] It is true that it was merely a specific and passing phase in the struggle but it would be incorrect to minimise its importance in the relationship between the three points of the eternal triangle – the parent, the pupil and the pedagogue. Each has learnt a useful lesson which will stand him in good stead in the future. Beyond these concrete examples of the text-books and the school activities it must be remembered that the relationship between the pupil and teacher in the classroom situation provides manifold and varied opportunities to the teacher to carry out educational work – apart from the mere preparations for examinations – which is of great importance in fitting the rising generation into the liberatory movement. I take it for granted that we all accept that the liberatory movement, has, and must have, an ideological basis and that these ideas must grow among the people as widely as possible. Whether it be in the selection of reading books, in papers, in the discussion of current affairs and topical events, the teacher is provided with a hundred and one situations which he can usefully employ for the purpose he has in mind. [....]

## The Affiliation of Non-European Teachers' Organizations to the Liberatory Movement

At least two non-European teachers' organizations have come to realize that their own particular educational problems are closely and intimately related to the political and social problems of the non-European people generally, and that, until the latter are solved, the solution of educational problems must remain at the level of mere reformism.[54] This realization has led them to affiliate to and co-operate with the political organizations of the people in the Liberatory Movement, and so place upon the teachers an important duty outside of school, a duty no so much as teachers, but as citizens. Not, of course, that such co-operation and alliance with the Liberatory Movement does not naturally give a definite and clear orientation to their work as teachers in the classroom, but that, in addition, it throws upon them the onus of playing their part directly in the organization of the Movement. Outside of school, therefore, the teachers have infiltrated into the organizations of the people, and in many instances are playing leading rôles in those organizations. This movement of teachers into politics is comparatively recent, but I think there is ample evidence that it has great meaning and significance for the Liberatory Movement. The teachers, considered as a social group, form the only section among the oppressed non-Europeans which has had a measure of education and enlightenment and their active participation in the political movement must bring fresh life and vigour and inspiration to the Movement. Indeed, the fact that, on these grounds, the Cape Education Department has found it necessary to refuse official recognition to two such teacher organizations is in itself a measure of their importance in the struggle for freedom. At the same time, of course, it must not be thought, as seems current in many quarters that, because teachers have been fortunate enough to receive education and enlightenment, they are necessarily destined to lead the Movement, to form the leadership, or as some would have it, that they are THE leaders of the people. That is a matter for History. I think, generally, teachers are sufficiently modest to claim that, because of conditions in this country, they rank among the leaders of the people and that they wish to participate in the Liberatory Movement.

## The Shortcomings of and the Limitations placed upon the Teachers

It must always be borne in mind in considering the rôle of the non-European teachers in the Liberatory Movement that there are many obstacles in their way. [....] it would be fallacious to judge the rôle of teachers' organisations throughout the country by the policies and practices of the one or two progressive ones among the seven or eight that we have in the whole country. So also would it be grossly misleading to believe that the progressive theory of education to which I have referred is generally accepted, even by the majority of teachers in this country. In fact, as a whole, it is a matter of conjecture whether the teachers are really so educated and enlightened as we believe, and whether they really are head and shoulders above the community in this respect. It is too often forgotten that the overwhelmingly majority of them have an academic education of merely a Std. VI or Std. VIII level and that, in addition, the weight of reaction still hangs heavily around their necks. It must not be forgotten, for example, that it was mainly to the teachers, that the ruling class turned for the personnel to work the Coloured Advisory Council, and I am not certain whether they will not again turn in that direction to find some support for the new Coloured Representative Council and the Bantu Local Authorities which are to form the new homes of non-European reactionaries.

In addition, of course, teachers have always held a kind of hybrid position as quasi-civil servants who are paid directly by the government or by some governmental agency, such as the Provincial Councils. Whoever pays the piper generally calls the tune, and the appointment and dismissal of teachers rests with these governmental organs, and, what is more important, their conditions of service are laid down for them by the State. To a great extent, therefore, their activities are controlled by the law; and while in the Cape the teachers do enjoy a relatively large measure of freedom, in other provinces they are almost bound hand and foot. No non-European teacher in Natal, for example, may take any active part in politics nor may he even criticise the educational administration or write a letter to the press. In the Orange Free State, the burning question is still who employs the teacher, and he, therefore finds himself completely at the mercy of whomever happens to control the school. In the Transvaal, where one finds the largest teachers' organization in the country, it is significant that members' subscriptions are collected by the authorities. Above all, non-European schools are dominated by the managers whose powers are wide, evasive and all-pervading. So that, to the legal limitations upon their activities is added a strong administrative straightjacket which often succeeds in holding the teacher in check, and, far worse, often winning him over to the side of reaction. What will happen to the African teachers when the recommendations of the Eiselen Commission are implemented and they become the direct employees of the State, as full-fledged civil servants, may well be imagined.

**Conclusion**
By way of conclusion, I may say that I have attempted to give a balanced picture of the situation as it appears to me. I have no doubt that we all have in our minds imaginary rôles we would like the teachers to play in the Liberatory Movement, and many of us are doubtless severe in our criticisms of the part they have played hitherto. But there are many factors in the situation, and we must take account of all of them. Personally, I see much that is hopeful, but it would be fatal to err on the side of optimism.

**DISCUSSION ON THE RÔLE OF THE NON-EUROPEAN TEACHER IN THE LIBERATORY MOVEMENT**
*Mr. Sisam:* Does the lecturer think that a liberatory movement does in fact exist in South Africa?

*Lecturer:* The beginnings of a liberatory movement do exist. Certain liberatory ideas have grown up, and there is an ideological approach to the political problems of the country which certainly form the basis of such a movement.

*Mr. Sisam:* How would the teacher set about instilling ideas of liberation into the pupil when the subjects to be taught are laid down by the authorities?

*Lecturer:* The curriculum cannot wholly prescribe what is to be taught nor how it is to be taught. How it is to be taught must be determined in the classroom itself by the teacher who has to take into account the situation at the particular time. It is the approach to the syllabus rather than the syllabus itself that is important.

*Mr. Gamiet:* Is the speaker in favour of the policy of the newspaper *"The Torch"*, which from time to time calls for more "coloured schools"?

*Lecturer:* I cannot accept the statement that *"The Torch"* has called for more coloured schools. *"The Torch"* is opposed to educational segregation, and that being the case, a call for more coloured schools would not conform with its policy. The fact remains, however, that whether one calls for more coloured schools or not, one will receive only coloured schools. Non-Europeans realize that they live under the system of segregation, and that they will therefore have to use segregation to fight segregation.

*Mr. Gamiet:* The lecturer's approach is idealistic, and he has not connected it with the rôle of the teacher in the political movement. I agree that the teacher's approach in the classroom should be to instil ideas of democracy as far as this can be done, but it is largely in the political sphere that we must associate the rôle of the teacher. This question the lecturer has not squarely faced and fairly answered. The lecturer propounds the amazing idea that the teachers, because they form only one four-hundredth of the non-European groups, cannot play an important rôle in the emancipatory movement. He makes great play of their numerical inferiority. We should remember that it is not numbers that count but the weight of ideological leadership. The rôle of the teacher should be to help in leading the oppressed peoples, ideologically and politically. The teacher's task is to bring guidance and his function is theoretical and political clarification. By virtue of his education and therefore better understanding of political processes he can play a dynamic rôle in the liberatory movement by helping to forge a link between the comparatively well-educated groups and the workers. Social change cannot come about only by theoretical work but by leading the people politically, and here the teachers can play an important part. If, as the lecturer suggests, the non-European teacher is so restricted in Natal, Transvaal and O.F.S. that he is prepared to accept blindly oppressive measures, then who is going to lead? The teachers in these provinces must themselves first break their chains. The teachers there must also realize that their professional disadvantages cannot be removed in isolation; they must link their struggle with the fight of the people.

The coloured teachers in the Cape as a whole have not only evaded the struggles of the people but have adapted themselves to the system of segregated coloured education. Coloured teachers are well paid compared to other sections of the coloured people. This has partly been done to separate them from the rest of the people and to lead them into thinking that they have a vested interest in our system of segregated education to the extent of even leading them to defending it. Many have even been bribed into abstaining from the struggles of the people. There has been no real leaning to the mass of the African teachers who suffer from more severe disadvantages than the coloured teachers. Coloured teachers in the Cape, as intellectuals, have a certain amount of tradition, but they are not discharging their duties as political leaders.

There is a tendency for coloured teachers to regard themselves as a peculiar social and economic class. There must be a radical change in this attitude to bring about the integration of teachers into the liberatory movement of the oppressed.

*Mr. Clarke:* Unlike Mr. Gamiet, I fail to see that the rôle of the teachers as the spearhead of the liberatory movement has any historical basis. My contention is that the teachers as a group have always been a privileged class. I must also point out that

Mr. Maurice merely quoted the number of teachers in passing and that he did not use that as any indication of their influence and power.

*Mr. Meyer-Fels:* I feel that if any correlation between the militancy of the teacher-organisations and the real wages of teachers were to be made the results would be quite revealing. It would, I imagine, reveal less and less militancy with the increase of wages. Secondly, I feel that both the lecturer and Mr. Gamiet have not considered sufficiently the class position of the teacher. The failure to place them where they belong, that is, with the petty bourgeoisie, has led to a wrong assessment of the rôle of the teacher in the movement. It is true that they will at times, due to their superior education, fulfil the rôle of minor leaders and politicians, but I do not believe that they will play the rôle of leaders in the emancipatory movement.

*Mr. Jordaan:* I have some disagreement with Mr. Gamiet on the rôle he assigns the non-European teacher in the liberatory movement. He invests the teacher with an historic mission which is clearly unhistoric, for never in the history of liberatory movements the world over have the teachers as a professional group either led or played an important part. At most they have as individuals become part of the political leadership.

The leadership of the downtrodden masses is drawn from the bourgeoisie and petty-bourgeoisie because it is precisely intellectuals from this stratum who, by virtue of having a tradition of property ownership and therefore an independent livelihood, have the time, the money and educational equipment to develop an independent ideology of emancipation for the workers and lead them in their struggles. Precisely also because of this advantageous economic position, they remain unaffected in their ideas and *Weltanschauung* by any fluctuation in their economic fortunes. Nor are their ideas affected by and subordinate to their bourgeois origins.

The non-European teachers, on the other hand, have sprung from the ranks of the workers to acquire what amounts to a petty-bourgeois mode of life. They have no tradition of economic independence or ownership and because they are in point of fact tied to the state apparatus as servants, they cannot hammer out an independent ideology for the people nor lead them in their day to day struggles. Furthermore, as dependent beings, they are easily influenced in their ideas by fluctuations in the economic conditions under which they work.

I do not think that Mr. Maurice grasps this peculiar place the teacher occupies in society and the rôle a political leadership is called upon to play in the liberatory movement. His lecture is revealing in as much as it does not reveal the rôle the non-European teacher is playing or can play in the liberatory movement. He conceives of a leadership in terms of a pedagogic intercommunication of a small group of professionals and a distant mass of people, and seems to regard what I would call a mere idealistic enlightenment as a *sine qua non* for liberation. He fails to understand the importance of an independent ideology and the need for a leadership to participate actively in the struggles of the people. It is true that he does not see much the teachers are doing to further the cause of liberation, and, by implication, regards their connections with the political movement as purely *de jure*. But what he considers their contribution to liberation can be, is pure enlightenment which has nothing to do with the political task of transforming this country by active political struggle on the basis of an ideology of liberation into a decisive democratic country.

The history of the T.L.S.A. makes my point clear. In 1942, the Coloured teachers were militant because, as grossly underpaid servants, they regarded themselves as part of the oppressed people and forged political ties with them. But from 1946 a radical change came about. To put in simply: the teachers were bribed off by salary increases. They subsequently lost their former militancy and their ideas of liberation from a colour-bar system and for educational and political democracy. Their tenuous connections with the political movement withered away, and they came to consider themselves as a privileged group concerned with their own peculiar problems as teachers. In point of fact, whereas earlier they wanted to break through a colour-bar system, they are now accommodating themselves to and thriving within the framework of that same system. They feel that by struggling for more now, they have something more to lose than their chains.

This fact comes as a belated warning to that political tendency which has up to now concentrated all its forces on the Coloured teachers. They have been building on shifting sands. Now feeling the effect of a purely privileged milieu, the T.L.S.A. leadership is proposing some sort of union with the less privileged African teachers in C.A.T.A. When this move comes at a time when the Coloured teachers feel themselves to be poles apart from the African teachers and when reaction is rearing its ugly head in the T.L.S.A., one has perforce to conclude that this is an act of desperation, an act that is hyper-revolutionary because the times are not propitious. Because it would mean a Coloured-African teacher unity at the top and not from below, and would drive out the preponderantly conservative section in the T.L.S.A., leaving this body in rags. I would like to know Mr. Maurice's opinion on this proposed federation scheme.

*Mr. Daniels:* I have no doubt that teachers can play an important rôle in the liberatory movement. What Mr. Maurice loses sight of, however, is the fact that education in itself is not the only means for social change. It may be true that pupils take their attitude from teachers, but what will the attitude of pupils amount to if there is no youth movement into which they can be attracted and trained for work in the national movement to provide future cadres for the national movement?

I agree entirely that the existence of a class mentioned by Mr. Jordaan, is necessary, but in South Africa with its peculiar problems the non-European teacher is forced into the position of the intellectual. The conditions under which teachers work, however, where they are in effect doing the work of the rulers means that their work in the national movement is limited. Hence the continuing shelving of important proposals that arise in the T.L.S.A. If teachers were not so limited, that position could not arise.

The rôle of the teacher cannot be considered in abstract. When the proposal was made that the T.L.S.A. should affiliate to the Trade Union movement, a fine opportunity was lost, when the idea of gaining the support of the workers was abandoned, and, as the most advanced of the non-European oppressed, of politicising the Trade Unions. The interests of the teacher class, however, made the T.L.S.A. turn its back on affiliation with the workers. Thus, while I feel that the non-European teacher has a great potential in the task of national liberation, national emancipation will come not because of, but in spite of, the teacher.

### Mr. Maurice's Reply

Mr. Maurice pointed out that Mr. Jordaan had misinterpreted the federation between C.A.T.A. and T.L.S.A. by labelling it as "an act of desperation". This move towards federation was within the League's Constitution and the first attempt to implement it had been made as early as 1946, and was not something new. He also denied that he had assessed the strength of the teachers in terms of numerical strength. He further felt that he was not called upon to answer the references made to the T.L.S.A. in view of his introductory reservations. That being the case, he would therefore not touch the references made to the T.L.S.A.

In view of the limitations placed upon the teachers it was wishful thinking to expect the teacher to play the rôle Mr. Gamiet expected from them. It was clear from what had been said, that the teacher could not be the spearhead of the emancipatory movement. Non-European teachers as a class had only existed for the last 30 years, and the possibilities of the rôle the teacher could play was now only beginning to crystallise.

He agreed that the salaries of teachers were directly related to their militancy. The leadership had pointed out, and was still pointing out, that the monthly green cheque of the teacher had carried him from the path of 1946.

In conclusion the speaker said he was pleased that his lecture had provoked so much discussion. He pointed out that as this was a new subject, he had therefore expected many different points of view.

## Document 22
Report of the first National Conference of Women held in the Trades Hall, Johannesburg, South Africa, 17 April 1954

Coming from many places, large and small, in different parts of South Africa, nearly 150 women attended the first national Conference of women, held in Johannesburg, to fight for women's rights and for full and equal citizenship for all.

The women had responded to an invitation sent to organisations and individuals to attend this Conference. The invitation was the result of the growing need that women felt for a different type of women's organisation – one that would:
- embrace all women, irrespective of race, colour or nationality
- help to stengthen, build, and bring together in joint activity the various women's sections in the liberatory movements, and other women's organisations,
- participate in the struggles of the working and oppressed peoples for the removal of class and race discrimination, and for full and equal citizen rights,
- express the needs and aspirations of the housewives, wage-earners, peasants and professional women of South Africa,
- bring about the emancipation of women from the special disabilities suffered by them under laws, customs and conventions, and strive for a genuine South African democracy based on complete equality and friendship between men and women, and between each section.

While there are in South Africa many different women's organisations – religious, social, or political in character – there was no organisation of women that brought the many sections of women together with these aims. The existence of such women's organisations in other countries, and their co-operation on a world scale through the Women's International Democratic Federation, provided South Africans with inspiration and guidance.[55]

Beginning in 1952, South African women in different towns began discussing the need for and possibilities of such an organisation, and by 1953 it was possible to call the women together at a National Conference.

Speaking in Zulu, Xosa, Sesutho, English and Afrikaans, delegates from all parts of the country welcomed the Conference with joyful enthusiasm, many declaring that they had long awaited such an event. With single-minded determination, the delegates resolved to establish the Federation of South African Women.[56]

This report is compiled from the minutes of that Conference, and contains extracts from the speeches, resolutions and the Charter adopted by the Conference.

The Headquarters of the F.S.A.W. is in Capetown, and all interested in working for the liberation of women in South Africa, should write to the Secretary, P. O. Box 2706, Cape Town.

OPENING OF THE CONFERENCE – Ray Alexander speaks on the Struggles of Women in S. Africa

Mrs. Ida Mntwana in the Chair called on Ray Alexander to open the Conference.[57] Ray Alexander said:

On behalf of those women who helped to prepare this Conference, I bid you all welcome from the depths of my heart.

I greet you all, delegates and visitors who made this a great meeting, which will be of historical importance to our country and to our peoples' struggle for freedom.

All of us are here because we want to find solutions to the problems which mean so much to women: the winning of equality, democratic rights for women and our men, the right of our children to be brought up in decent homes, schools, and with opportunities for a full life.

Our sisters of Russia, Czechoslovakia, China and other countries have won freedom, independence and happiness. They are enjoying full equality with men in all spheres of economic, political, cultural and social life.

What is the position of the African, Coloured and Indian women of this country? They have no political rights, no right to elect or be elected on the governing bodies of the country.

The Government of our country represents a minority of the people. It is a government of the Europeans only, and represents the interests of the landowners, mine-owners and factory-owners. To maintain power it makes laws discriminating against the great majority of the people: the African, Indian and Coloured people.

The Pass Laws, the Native Urban Areas Amendement Act with its vicious Section 10, have been responsible for filling up gaols – nine out of ten gaols in South Africa are overcrowded. Farm gaols are built and filled with men whose lives are wasted away to provide cheap labour for the farmers.

The Riotious Assemblies Act, the Suppression of Communism Act, the Criminal Laws Amendment Act, the Public Safety Act were introduced with the express aim of destroying the peoples' organisations and killing their desire for freedom in the country of their birth.

By means of a great mass of laws, to which new ones are added every year, the rulers of this country are trying desperately to prevent the advance of the people towards full citizenship. These laws divide them according to race; deny the majority freedom of movement, residence, ownership and education, and seek to keep the people in ignorance, poverty and submission, a source of cheap and unskilled labour.

The people will not become submissive slaves. The reply is to organise, men and women, young and old, in a united fight against unjust laws, and for security, peace, friendship and freedom.

In these struggles our women have played an important part. During the Defiance Campaign, hundreds went to gaol, some of them expectant mothers, some with their babies. Our women have come out on strike against the Coloured Voters' Bill, against the banning orders issued to Trade Union leaders under the Suppression of Communism Act.

These struggles have produced many leaders, have made us feel the need for an organisation to embrace still wider sections of women and make them a great force in the struggle for freedom.

We have learned with great satisfaction, and it has inspired us, of the wonderful work done by the Women's International Democratic Federation. It was formed in 1945, to organise and unite all women in defence of their political, economic, legal and socal rights, and to ensure social progress for complete equality between men and women in all spheres.

All over the world women in Europe, in India, in the Middle East, in America, Australia, China, Africa, everywhere – have formed Women's organisations affiliated to the W.I.D.F., which now represents 140 000 000 women.

The women of the whole world, on whom falls the responsibility for the welfare of their homes, are growing more and more aware of the need to participate actively in the struggle for peace, national liberation, and friendship of all people, irrespective of race and colour.

In the last 10 years women in many countries have won democratic rights. We are all proud of the fact that Mrs. Pandit is the President of the United Nations, which shows the shallowness of race prejudice in South Africa where Indian, Coloured and African women do not have the right to vote or sit in Parliament. *[....]*

RESOLUTIONS:
THE FOLLOWING ARE RESOLUTIONS ADOPTED
1) *NATIVE LAND & TRUST ACT AMENDMENT BILL AND THE NATIVES RESETTLEMENT BILL*
   RESOLVED: That this Conference condmens the immoral and unjust principles contained in:
a) The Natives Resettlement Bill, which seeks to deprive all Africans of freehold rights in urban areas; to remove many thousands from their homes; and to deny to Africans the right to become a permanent part of the urban population;
b) The Native Land & Trust Amendment Bill, the provisions of which would cause misery to thousands of rural Africans, and which seeks to render over a million farm labourers homeless and landless, and to legalise slave labour.
   This Conference urges the Government to withdraw these infamous Bill, as being in conflict with the basic human rights of all men and women to live freely, to work freely, and to own their own homes.
2) *BANTU EDUCATION ACT*[58]
   RESOLVED: That this Conference condemns:
a) The Bantu Education Act as a vicious attack on the development of the African people, which divides and restricts the education which is the right of all people, and thus seeks to depress the African people to a condition of perpetual serfdom.

b) The move by the Government to control the education of half a million children in Mission schools by the forced sale or lease of school buildings against the threat of loss of subsidy.

3) *SEPARATE REPRESENTATION OF VOTERS ACT*

RESOLVED: That this Conference opposes utterly the Separate Representation of Voters Bill, which seeks to deprive the Coloured people of democratic rights, by removing them from the Common Roll and substituting the limited and undemocratic form of representation to which the rights of African people have already been limited.

That this Conference urges that the franchise be extended to all men and women over eighteen years of age, irrespective of colour or race.

4) *PEACE*

RESOLVED: That this first National Conference of Women delegates, representing 230 000 women, sends greetings to women throughout the world. We pledge ourselves to work with women everywhere for our rights as women, for protection of all children, for freedom for all human beings, for peace.

5) *NATIVE LABOUR SETTLEMENT OF DISPUTES ACT*

RESOLVED: That this Conference condemns the Native Labour Settlement of Disputes Act, and the Industrial Conciliation Bill, as slave labour laws, and undertakes to fight against these Acts.

6) *KENYA*

RESOLVED: That this Conference of 150 delegates, representing 230 000 people, protests against the brutal acts committed against the innocent women and children of Kenya. We demand the withdrawal of troops, and hands off Kenya![59]

7) *FREEDOM CONGRESS*

RESOLVED: This National Conference of Women pledges its support for the Congress of the Peoples. It pledges to work actively to organise women from all walks of life, housewives, domestic workers, factory workers, women from the reserves and on the farms, to ensure that women shall be directly represented at the Congress.

## WOMEN'S CHARTER
### PREAMBLE

We, the women of South Africa, wives and mothers, working women and housewives, Africans, Indians, European and Coloured, hereby declare our aim of striving for the removal of all laws, regulations, conventions and customs that discriminate against us as women, and that deprive us in any way of our inherent right to the advantages, responsibilites and opportunities that society offers to any one section of the population.

### A SINGLE SOCIETY

We women do not form a society separate from the men. There is only one society, and it is made up of both women and men. As women we share the problems and anxieties of our men, and join hands with them to remove social evils and obstacles to progress.

Within this common society, however, are laws and practices that discriminate against women. While we struggle against the social evils that affect men and women alike, we are determined to struggle no less purposefully against the things that work to the disadvantage of our sex.

## TEST OF CIVILISATION

The level of civilisation which any society has reached can be measured by the degree of freedom that its members enjoy. The status of women is a test of civilisation. Measure by that standard, South Africa must be considered low in the scale of civilised nations.

## WOMEN'S LOT

We women share with our menfold the cares and anxieties imposed by poverty and its evils. As wives and mothers, it falls upon us to make small wages stretch a long way. It is we who feel the cries of our children when they are hungry and sick. It is our lot to keep and care for homes that are too small, broken and dirty to be kept clean. We know the burden of looking after children and land when our husbands are away in the mines, on the farms, and in the towns earning our daily bread.

We know what it is to keep family life going in pondokkies and shanties, or in over-crowded one-room apartments. We know the bitterness of children taken to lawless ways, of daughters becoming unmarried mothers whilst still at school, of boys and girls growing up without education, training or jobs at a living wage.

## POOR AND RICH

These are evils that need not exist. They exist because the society in which we live is divided into poor and rich, into non-European and European. They exist because there are privileges for the few, discrimination and harsh treatment for the many. We women have stood and will stand shoulder to shoulder with our menfolk in a common struggle against poverty, race and class discrimination, and the evils of the colour-bar.

## NATIONAL LIBERATION

As members of the National Liberatory movements and Trade Unions, in and through our various organisations, we march forward with our men in the struggle for liberation and the defence of the working people. We pledge ourselves to keep high the banner of equality, fraternity and liberty. As women there rests upon us also the burden of removing from our society all the social differences developed in past times between men and women, which have the effect of keeping our sex in a position of inferiority and subordination.

## EQUALITY FOR WOMEN

We resolve to struggle for the removal of laws and customs that deny African women the right to own, inherit or alienate property. We resolve to work for a change in the laws of marriage such as are found amongst our African, Malay and Indian people, which have the effect of placing wives in the position of legal subjection to husbands, and giving husbands the power to dispose of wives' property and earnings, and dictate to them in all matters affecting them and their children.

We recognise that women are treated as minors by these marriage and property laws because of ancient and revered traditions and customs which had their origin in the antiquity of the people and no doubt served purposes of great value in bygone times.

There was a time in the African society when every woman reaching marriageable stage was assured of a husband, home, land and security.

Then husbands and wives with their children belonged to families and clans that supplied most of their own material needs and were largely self-sufficient. Men and women were partners in a compact and closely-integrated family unit.

## WOMEN WHO LABOUR

Those conditions have gone. The tribal and kinship society to which they belonged has been destroyed as a result of the loss of tribal lands, migration of men away from their tribal home, the growth of towns and industries and the rise of a great body of wage-earners on the farms and in the urban areas, who depend wholly or mainly on wages for a livelihood.

Thousands of African women, like Indian, Coloured and European women, are employed today in factories, homes, shops, offices; on farms and in professions as nurses, teachers and the like. As unmarried women, widows or divorcees they have to fend for themselves, often without the assistance of a male relative. Many of them are responsible not only for their own livelihood but also that of their children.

Large numbers of women today are in fact the sole breadwinners and heads of their families.

## FOREVER MINORS

Nevertheless, the laws and practices derived from an earlier and different state of society are still applied to them. They are responsible for their own person and their children. Yet the law seeks to enforce upon them the status of a minor.

Not only are African, Coloured and Indian women denied political rights, but they are also in many parts of the Union denied the same status as men in such matters as the right to enter into contracts, to own and dispose of property, and to exercise guardianship over their children.

## OBSTACLE TO PROGRESS

The law has lagged behind the development of society; it no longer corresponds to the actual social and economic position of women. The law has become an obstacle to progress of the women, and therefore a brake on the whole of society.

This intolerable condition would not be allowed to continue were it not for the refusal of a large section of our menfolk to concede to us women the rights and privileges which they demand for themselves.

We shall teach the men that they cannot hope to liberate themselves from the evils of discrimination and prejudice as long as they fail to extend to women complete and unqualified equality in law and in practice.

## NEED for EDUCATION

We also recognise that large numbers of our womenfolk continue to be bound by traditional practices and conventions, and fail to realise that these have become obsolete and a brake on progress. It is our duty and privilege to enlist all women in our struggle for emancipation and bring to them all realisation of the intimate relationship that exists between their status of inferiority as women and the inferior status to which their people are subjected by discriminatory laws and colour prejudices.

It is our intention to carry out a nation-wide programme of education that will bring home to the men and women of all national groups the realisation that freedom cannot be won for any section or for the people as a whole as long as we women are kept in bondage.

## AN APPEAL

We appeal to all progressive organisations, to members of the great National liberatory movements, to the trade unions and working class organisations, to the churches, educational and welfare organisations, to all progressive men and women who have the interests of the people at heart, to join with us in this great and noble endeavour.

OUR AIMS

We declare the following aims:–

This organisation is formed for the purpose of uniting women in common action for the removal of all political, legal, economic and social disabilities. We shall strive for women to obtain:

1) The right to vote and to be elected to all State bodies, without restriction or discrimination.
2) The right to full opportunities for employment with equal pay and possibilities of promotion in all spheres of work.
3) Equal rights with men in relation to property, marriage and children, and for the removal of all laws and customs that deny women such equal rights.
4) For the development of every child through free compulsory education for all; for the protection of mother and child through maternity homes, welfare clinics, creches and nursery schools, in countryside and towns; through proper homes for all; and through the provision of water, light, transport, sanitation and other amenities of modern civilisation.
5) For the removal of all laws that restrict free movement, that prevent or hinder the right of free association and activity in democratic organisations, and the right to participate in the work of these organisations.
6) To build and strengthen women's sections in the National liberatory movements, the organisation of women in trade unions, and through the peoples' varied organisations.
7) To co-operate with all other organisations that have similar aims in South Africa as well as throughout the world.
8) To strive for permanent peace throughout the world.

## Document 23
## The Freedom Charter adopted at the Congress of the People at Kliptown, Johannesburg on 25 and 26 June 1955[60]

**WE,** the People of South Africa, declare for all our country and the world to know:

that South Africa belongs to all who live in it, black and white, and that no government can justly claim authority unless it is based on the will of all the people;

that our people have been robbed of their birthright to land, liberty and peace by a form of government founded on injustice and inequality;

that our country will never be prosperous or free until all our people live in brotherhood, enjoying equal rights and opportunities;

that only a democratic state, based on the will of all the people, can secure to all their birthright without distinction of colour, race, sex or belief;

And therefore we, the People of South Africa, black and white together – equals, countrymen and brothers – adopt this Freedom Charter. And we pledge ourselves to strive together sparing neither strength nor courage, until the democratic changes set out here have been won.

## THE PEOPLE SHALL GOVERN!
Every man and woman shall have the right to vote for and stand as a candidate for all bodies which make laws;

All the people shall be entitled to take part in the administration of the country;

The rights of the people shall be the same regardless of race, colour or sex;

All bodies of minority rule, advisory boards, councils and authorities shall be replaced by democratic organs of self-government.

## ALL NATIONAL GROUPS SHALL HAVE EQUAL RIGHTS!
There shall be equal status in the bodies of the state, in the courts and in the schools for all national groups and races;

All people shall have equal right to use their own languages and to develop their own folk culture and customs;

All national groups shall be protected by law against insults to their race and national pride;

The preaching and practice of national, race or colour discrimination and contempt shall be a punishable crime;

All apartheid laws and practices shall be set aside.

## THE PEOPLE SHALL SHARE IN THE COUNTRY'S WEALTH!
The national wealth of our country, the heritage of all South Africans, shall be restored to the people;

The mineral wealth beneath the soil, the Banks and monopoly industry, shall be transferred to the ownership of the people as a whole;

All other industry and trade shall be controlled to assist the well-being of the people;

All people shall have equal rights to trade where they choose, to manufacture and to enter all trades, crafts and professions.

## THE LAND SHALL BE SHARED AMONG THOSE WHO WORK IT!
Restriction of land ownership on a racial basis shall be ended, and all the land redivided among those who work it, to banish famine and land hunger;

The state shall help the peasants with implements, seeds, tractors and dams to save the soil and assist the tillers;

Freedom of movement shall be guaranteed to all who work on the land;

All shall have the right to occupy land wherever they choose;

People shall not be robbed of their cattle, and forced labour and farm prisons shall be abolished.

## ALL SHALL BE EQUAL BEFORE THE LAW!
No-one shall be imprisoned, deported or restricted without a fair trial;

No-one shall be condemned by the order of any government official;

The courts shall be representative of all the people;

Imprisonment shall be only for serious crimes against the people and shall aim at re-education, not vengeance;

The police force and army shall be open to all on an equal basis and shall be the helpers and protectors of the people;

All laws which discriminate on grounds of race, colour or belief shall be repealed.

## ALL SHALL ENJOY EQUAL HUMAN RIGHTS!
The law shall guarantee to all their right to speak, to organise, to meet together, to publish, to preach, to worship and to educate their children;

The privacy of the house from police raids shall be protected by law;

All shall be free to travel without restriction from countryside to town, from province to province, and from South Africa abroad;

Pass laws, permits and all other laws restricting these freedoms shall be abolished.

## THERE SHALL BE WORK AND SECURITY!
All who work shall be free to form trade unions, to elect their officers and to make wage agreements with their employers;

The state shall recognise the right and duty of all to work and to draw full unemployment benefits;

Men and women of all races shall receive equal pay for equal work;

There shall be a forty hour working week, a national minimum wage, paid annual leave, and sick leave for all workers, and maternity leave on full pay for all working mothers;

Miners, domestic workers, farm workers and civil servants shall have the same rights as all others who work;

Child labour, compound labour, the tot system and contract labour shall be abolished.

## THE DOORS OF LEARNING AND CULTURE SHALL BE OPENED!
The government shall discover, develop and encourage national talent for the enhancement of our cultural life;

All the cultural treasures of mankind shall be open to all, by free exchange of books, ideas and contacts with other lands;

The aim of education shall be to teach the youth to love their people and their culture, to honour human brotherhood, liberty and peace;

Education shall be free, compulsory, universal and equal for all children;

Higher education and technical training shall be opened to all by means of state allowances and scholarships awarded on the basis of merit;

Adult illiteracy shall be ended by a mass state education plan;

Teachers shall have all the rights of other citizens;

The colour bar in cultural life, in sport and in education shall be abolished.

## THERE SHALL BE HOUSES, SECURITY AND COMFORT!
All people shall have the right to live where they choose, to be decently housed, and to bring up their families in comfort and security;

Unused housing space shall be made available to the people;

Rent and prices shall be lowered, food plentiful and no one shall go hungry;

A preventative health scheme shall be run by the state;

Free medical care and hospitalisation shall be provided for all, with special care for mothers and young children;

Slums shall be demolished and new suburbs built where all shall have transport, roads, lighting, playing fields, creches and social centres;

The aged, the orphans, the disabled and the sick shall be cared for by the state;

Rest, leisure and recreation shall be the right of all;

Fenced locations and ghettoes shall be abolished and laws which break up families shall be repealed.

**THERE SHALL BE PEACE AND FRIENDSHIP!**
South Africa shall be a fully independent state, which respects the rights and sovereignty of all nations;

South Africa shall strive to maintain world peace and the settlement of all international disputes by negotiation – not war;

Peace and friendship among our people shall be secured by upholding the equal rights, opportunities and status of all;

The people of the protectorates – Basutoland, Bechuanaland and Swaziland – shall be free to decide for themselves their own future;

The rights of all the peoples of Africa to independence and self-government shall be recognised and shall be the basis of close co-operation.

**Let all who love their people and their country now say, as we say here: "THESE FREEDOMS WE WILL FIGHT FOR, SIDE BY SIDE, THROUGHOUT OUR LIVES, UNTIL WE HAVE WON OUR LIBERTY."**

Issued by the Congress of the People, Box 11045, Joh'burg, and printed by Pacific Press (Pty.) Ltd., Jeppe.

---

Document 24
"Wreckers at Work", (Editorial), *Liberation*, 18, April 1956

> "People seem to be alarmed at the fact that there may be a so-called Right wing, Centre and Left wing in the Congress. To me it is a healthy sign in any organisation when people freely express their point of view."
>
> –President A. J. Luthuli.[61]

It is always necessary to distinguish between constructive criticism of a movement, the criticism of those who wish to help it, and the attacks and criticisms of those who wish to disrupt the movement. The African National Congress, like any other serious political movement, should and we believe does welcome the first sort of criticism whether coming from its own members or from well-disposed observers, for only by coolly analysing its work and heeding useful suggestions can a movement become strong.

When, however, the police or the Native Affairs Department attack the Congress, all politically conscious people are well aware that they do not wish, by their criticism, to improve Congress but to weaken or destroy it. Similarly, all are aware that organisations of the type of the "Bantu National Congress" or the "National-Minded Bloc" are not on the side of Congress in its struggle against apartheid and inequality.[62] On the contrary, they are on the side of the Government, and they seek to gain the favour of the Nationalists in their fight against Congress. Knowing who such critics are and what they want, we shall be on our guard against distortion, lies and slander, for these are the weapons that are customarily used against the leaders of the people's struggle for liberation.

## "New" Critics of Congress

Recently, a whole chorus of critics of Congress has arisen. These critics claim to be friends, or even members of Congress. Their methods however, as we shall see, are far from friendly. Their methods reveal their real aims.

Let us begin with the letter sent to the annual conference of A.N.C. in December by Dr. A.B. Xuma, a former Congress President.[63] It is rather remarkable that Dr. Xuma should have sent such a letter. Since the end of his term as President he has shown no interest in Congress at all. During all the bitter years of the Nationalists, in which the movement has gone through one hard struggle after another, in which scores of the most active and experienced leaders have been victimised by the Government, he has maintained inactivity and silence. In the Western Areas campaign, the Doctor, who is a Sophiatown land-owner, maintained his own separate landowners' organisation, separate from Congress and not at all co-operative. It is doubtful whether he attended a single A.N.C. meeting in the past five years, or whether he is even a member of the A.N.C. in good standing any more. We mention these facts not in order to belittle Dr. Xuma's past services to Congress, but in order to show how little qualified he is to comment on Congress **now**, his utter isolation from and ignorance of the movement as it is today. When he writes that he is "alarmed and distressed at certain tendencies that have developed in Congress in recent years," he is speaking not of what he knows, but of what someone else has told him.

### The Congress Alliance

Dr. Xuma writes that the A.N.C. has "lost its identity as a national liberation movement with a policy of its own and a distinctly African leadership." "One hears or reads," he adds, "of statements by the Congresses and hardly ever gets the statement of the A.N.C." The suggestion, obviously, is that because Congress has entered into an alliance with other organisations having similar aims, it has somehow "lost its identity." Does Dr. Xuma disapprove of the alliance with the S.A.I.C., the C.O.D., the S.A.C.P.O. and the S.A.C.T.U.? He does not say so. In fact, the beginnings of that alliance date back to the period of his own Presidency. The famous "Xuma-Dadoo Agreement" of the 'forties began that friendly association of the two Congresses which – cemented by the joint struggles of the defiance campaign and other common struggles, and reinforced by the new organisations of democratic Europeans, Coloured people and trade unionists which were stimulated and inspired by those struggles – has developed into the firm comradeship of the present Congress movement. It would be strange if Dr. Xuma would now advocate the breaking up of that alliance.

Is it true that only statements from "the Congresses" are now issued and none from the A.N.C.? Certainly not. Naturally, when it is necessary and appropriate, joint statements are issued. But the A.N.C. as such continues to issue public statements on a wide variety of subjects. In fact we doubt whether the A.N.C. has ever in its history issued more statements on all sorts of current events than during the past few years. It has its own Bulletin now, and is planning a newspaper of its own.

So, if you examine this charge of Dr. Xuma's carefully, you find that it is vague. He does not say exactly what he is criticising, or what he wants. His allegation about insufficient statements being issued is not very sound, either. He does not specify any issue on which he thinks Congress was at fault in not issuing a statement.

### *"Disintegrating into Splinters"*

Dr. Xuma's next criticism is that the movement is "disintegrating into splinters." In support of this statement, he points to the so-called National-minded Bloc" and to the "Bantu National Congress." But surely Dr. Xuma knows that both of these organisations are insignificant, tiny groups, separate from and openly hostile to Congress? What have such pro-apartheid groups as the Bhengu-ites, sponsored by the Government, to do with the Congress?[64] Congress is fighting a life-and-death struggle against the tyranny of apartheid. It can have no place for those who, whether for Judas-money or out of ignorance, support the Government. It is not true that Congress is "disintegrating." Dr. Xuma's statement is based on wrong information.

Dr. Xuma goes on to make a third allegation: fear of criticism and lack of internal democracy. He says: "Many who have dared to criticise the hierarchy have been expelled ... without a democratic hearing." That is a serious charge. Who has been expelled for criticising the "hierarchy?" Who was denied a hearing? Dr. Xuma does not give a single example. When making serious charges it is better to substantiate them with facts. Otherwise you may be accused of malice and mischief-making.

We have said enough of Dr. Xuma's attack to indicate his methods. He attacks the Freedom Charter without indicating a single clause or phrase with which he disagrees. He attacks the defiance campaign, the Congress campaigns against the Western Areas scheme and the Bantu Education Act. We cannot remember any alternative policies put forward by him at any time, nor does he do so in this letter. It is difficult to avoid the conclusion that he is "looking for points" in order to attack the present leadership of Congress. The conference did not take his letter very seriously, and quite rightly so. It only becomes important and significant in the light of other things that are being said.

### *"The World"*

"The World" is the new name of the newspaper that was formerly known as the "Bantu World," and which was expelled from the A.N.C. conference in December. Its editor, Dr. Nhlapo, claims to be guided by the principle of "absolute truth." Since December, however, "The World" has been caught red-handed in quite a number of departures from the truth. During the months of February and March alone it had to publish the following repudiations of its own lies:–

— A letter from Mr. J. B. Mafora, President of the O.F.S. province of the A.N.C. denying the "disgusting" report in the "World" that the Free State A.N.C. had opposed the Freedom Charter. "For the Free State, the Freedom Charter is a lead – we accepted it at the historical Congress of the People which was held at Kliptown."

— A letter from Dr. A. E. Letele, Treasurer-General of the A.N.C. refuting the "World" allegation that he had said there were things in the Xuma letter "best left for the ears of the Executive Committee alone." Wrote Dr. Letele: "One can overlook (sometimes) a misquotation of one's speech, but the appending of a downright fabrication of one's speech is malicious ... Neither the outrageous statement quoted nor anything even resembling it was at any time made by me."

— A letter from Mr. A. Gumede, Assistant Secretary of the Natal A.N.C. "categorically denying" a statement in the "World" "that Natal would secede from the A.N.C. if Chief Luthuli were not elected as President." The Natal delegation, and President Luthuli himself, were "much aggrieved and damaged" by this statement, wrote Mr. Gumede.

— A letter from Mr. A. P. Mda, refuting a statement in the "World" that he belonged to a "nationalist group" in the A.N.C. "In any event your paper appears to me to be more than just interested in factional groupings in Congress. Why?" shrewdly asks Mr. Mda.

Thus each of the excellent writers of the above letters have stuffed "The World's" lies down its own throat. But the paper did not comment on any of the letters we have quoted. It did not apologise for misinforming its readers. It did not promise not to lie any more. In this, "The World" shows contempt for its readers.

Why did "The World" publish this misinformation? Each and every one of its lies implies that there were "splits" which do not in fact exist. We can only conclude that the newspaper reports non-existent splits because it hopes thus to encourage real ones, and to discredit the A.N.C.

### Mr. Ngubane[65]

We now come to Mr. Jordan K. Ngubane, who writes a column entitled "African Viewpoint" in the Natal paper "Indian Opinion." It is difficult to write at all temperately about Mr. Ngubane. His weekly outpourings show a reckless disregard not only for facts but also for the principles of journalistic ethics. He has recently announced his conversion to the Liberal Party, but it would be hard to find anything more illiberal than his methods and views – prejudices would be a better word. He surpasses Dr. Xuma and even "The World" in the irresponsibility of his allegations, the venom of his insinuations, and the obvious malice which he displays towards the A.N.C.

Here is a sample of Mr. Ngubane's technique. He wants to "prove" that Congress is "split" (his favourite theme) between the "Centre" and the "Left," and he takes as an example of the Centre the President-General of the African National Congress. We should remark here that – we are sure without permission – Mr. Ngubane constantly makes free with the name and the alleged opinions of Mr. Luthuli.

Now, Mr. Ngubane speculates that "if he got a passport and an invitation" to go to Britain, Mr. Luthuli would accept and go. Then he goes on to speculate that "the Sisulu wing" would **most probably** decline an invitation from the West." It is "**quite possible**," he writes, that "they" would "turn down an invitation to visit India." "I think," he continues, "they would go to Bucharest, Moscow and Peking." Then, in the next sentence, this extraordinary journalist goes straight on, after this series of guesses and speculations **of his own creation**:

"**That shows** how divided Congress is at the moment." (Our emphasis throughout.)

On the contrary, all it **shows** is how illogical and confused Mr. Ngubane is "at the moment"; how this new recruit to the Liberal Party mistakes his own sick fancies for real facts. Nor is this untypical of Mr. Ngubane's methods.

### Red-Baiting

He keeps repeating and insinuating that the African National Congress is "dominated by the Left," and moreover by unspecified persons or organisations outside Congress. In "Indian Opinion" of February 17, he wrote: "My own view is that Dr. Xuma's letter was treated with contempt because the leaders of the African National Congress and their followers are no longer the real masters of the movement."

This is an extremely grave allegation, as injurious as it is insulting to the leaders of Congress, and not least to the President, of whom Mr. Ngubane affects to be so great an admirer. What proofs, what revelations, what facts has he in support of this grave charge? Not one. It is "my view." That is all.

And he repeats it again and again. The A.N.C. he writes, in the same article, "is not controlled by the African people." It is "little more than a front serving the aim of its temporary masters." Who are then in control of the A.N.C.? Mr. Ngubane's answer will not surprise those who know the technique of the smearing red-baiter. "The direction Congress is taking will lead straight to Moscow."

Of course, we have heard this before. General Rademeyer, in spite of the fact that his special branch of the police have taken drastic steps to ban alleged Communists from the Congresses and from all political activity, last year accused the Congress of the People organisers – that is, the leaders of the Congresses – of running a "Communist plot". Having made the allegation, he sought to produce evidence to prove it by means of constant raids and other police activities, before, during and after the Congress of the People. So far the lack of any prosecution would indicate that they failed to find any such evidence. Yet Ngubane continues to parrot these allegations – which if they were true, would in this unhappy South Africa of ours be matters not for debate in the "Indian Opinion" but for suppression by the police.

When a man starts writing in this unbalanced way, flinging around the gravest allegations without a jot or tittle of evidence, then you must know he is not out for serious discussion or constructive criticism, but purely and simply to make mischief.

### *Driving a Wedge*

Mr. Ngubane never tires of trying to drive a wedge between President Luthuli and his colleagues in the National Executive of the African National Congress, and there is no mean insinuation to which he is not prepared to stoop in these endeavours. Perhaps the lowest depths were reached in an article in the "Indian Views" of February 3, in which he wrote that the Congress leaders had deliberately sabotaged the campaign against the Western Areas removal in order to discredit the President!

> The whole campaign (against Western Areas Removal) was a cynical move to make Mr. Luthuli's leadership of the A.N.C. look ridiculous in the eyes of the world ... the whole thing was a Leftist trick to undermine Mr. Luthuli's hold on the movement.

Just think what he is saying. That the leaders of a great people's movement like the African National Congress, of set purpose, went and caused the failure of an important campaign. That their purpose was to discredit themselves, because by so doing they would at the same time discredit their own President, whom, says Mr. Ngubane – and nobody else but Mr. Ngubane – they want to get rid of. Have you heard anything like it? No sane and rational person could believe such stuff: it is the raving of a mind clouded by prejudice.

Does Mr. Ngubane himself solemnly believe this fantastic rubbish? If he does, then it is a pitiful example of what anti-Communist prejudice and red-baiting can do to the mind of one who has shown himself on other occasions to be an intelligent man and an able writer. We wonder whether "Indian Opinion" imagines it is furthering the cause of Indian-African unity by giving currency to this type of baseless slander against the elected leadership of the A.N.C. [....]

### *What Are They After?*

The methods of these "new" critics of Congress preclude any sort of reasoned discussion with them at present. For they never commit themselves to criticising a single decision, statement or action on its merits. They never quote a Congress document, statement or resolution. Instead, they spread wild, airy generalisations, they invent fantastic plots and conspiracies, they make irresponsible statements.

This sort of "criticism" does not aim at honest discussion. Its real aims are clear enough. They are:

> Firstly, to create disunity and dissension in the ranks of the African National Congress, and to isolate the left-wing working-class element in Congress;
> Secondly, to separate the African National Congress from its allies – the Indian Congress, the Coloured People's Organisation, the Congress of Democrats and the Congress of Trade Unions;
> Thirdly, to oppose and belittle the Freedom Charter as the common programme of all these organisations.

The main weapons on which the critics rely are also very clear.

They rely on African chauvinism and the spirit of racial exclusiveness. They rely on red-baiting and anti-Communist prejudice. Is it a coincidence that these are also the favourite weapons of the Nationalist Party?

We believe that these efforts at disruption will fail, and that the unity of the African National Congress and the Congress movement is more firmly based today than it has ever been.

### *The Struggle for Unity*

But that unity has only been achieved in the process of constant struggle and it can only be maintained and strengthened by means of continued struggle against all, whether inside or outside the Congress, who seek to wreck and disrupt it.

What do we mean by Congress unity? Do we mean that a single Philosophy and outlook should be imposed on the whole movement? No: as a national liberation movement there is room within the A.N.C. and its sister organisations for men and women of all shades of political and religious belief. We are in full agreement with the statesmanlike and broadminded view expressed by Congress' President in the quotation that stands at the head of this article.

Does Congress unity imply that the A.N.C., for example, should become a political party composed of and representing a single class? No: the struggle for national emancipation brings together many classes: workers, peasants, business and professional men – despite the deep cleavages between them.

Congress unity, then, does not imply a uniform ideology, or a homogeneous class composition. But it **does** mean the subordination of differences in the common struggle. The alliance of the Congresses does not mean their merging into one, or the loss of their separate identities. But it does mean their close brotherly association against the common enemy: monstrous White domination, and for the achievement of a common programme: the grand, inspiring Freedom Charter.

The people's alliance which has grown up in our country has an extraordinarily difficult and dangerous task before it. Its adversary, the South African ruling class, is a formidable one. It is backed by and closely linked with foreign imperialism. It is armed and ready to use violence, and it will stop at nothing to retain its oppressive and unjust rule. It is ruthless, cunning and desperate. This dangerous adversary will be defeated, and the people shall govern, for the tide of history is running for freedom. But how soon that victory will be won, and how costly it will prove will depend largely upon how speedily and effectively the Congress movement, at the head of the freedom-fighters of South Africa can accomplish their great tasks:– to rally and organise the overwhelming majority of the people, African, Indian, Coloured and European; to spread clear thinking, unity and courage among the masses; to win the people's understanding of and devotion to the common aims and aspirations emblazoned in the Charter; to inspire the masses with determination to win the Charter.

Those who seek to divide the ranks of the people, to sow discord and to spread confusion, are – whether or not they realise it – holding back the advance of freedom and helping the enemies of the people to perpetuate apartheid and minority domination. The so-called "Africanists," the Xumas and the Ngubanes, should honestly and self-critically re-examine their position in the light of the endorsement of the Freedom Charter by the African National Congress in special conference at Easter. The struggle for freedom is on. Now is the time for all good men to come to the aid of the Congress – and we are sure a friendly welcome awaits all who now come forward to help, whatever their position might have been before the Easter Conference. We are sure, too, that the movement will know in what light to regard those who, despite the overwhelming majority decision at Conference, call themselves Congressmen yet continue to belittle the Charter and try to split the people's alliance.


## Document 25[66]
## Letter from E. R. Roux[67] to John Gomas, 23 July 1956

Botany Dept.
University
Johannesburg
23 July 1956

Dear John,

It would be peculiar if I had the same point of view to-day as I had in Moscow in 1928. I was a loyal Party member then – I left the Party in 1936. Surely I must have changed my viewpoint in the interval.

I am sorry that *Time Longer than Rope* is out of print. I have only my own annotated copy which I don't want to part with. If you try Foyle's bookshop, Church St., Cape Town, they may be able to get you a second-hand copy; failing which somebody ought to be able to lend you one. Try Brian Bunting.

I think you are mistaken in suggesting that the whites in the movement generally speaking used it for their own personal aggrandisement. As good Stalinists they used it for the greater glory of the Soviet – everything else came second. I left the C.P. because I did not approve of the Moscow line. You stayed in a long time after I got out.

In spite of criticism I admit that the best African leaders – as the defiance campaign showed – were those trained by the Party.

Solly and his aides were never really good interracialists.[68] Trade unionism often corrupts.

I don't think there is any particular virtue in a black skin or a white one. But a white one exempts you from racial oppression in this country. I have usually kept out of black organisations myself because a white skin gives one an unfair influence.

Nevertheless I do feel that there is a place for an organisation without colour bar in which all races can meet on equal terms. That was the ideal of the C.P. Unfortunately the Party had ideas and practices in other respects, of which one did not approve.

I do not think democracy, progress and peace will inevitably come into being when the blacks achieve power. Corruption, reaction and oppression will not necessarily evaporate. Nevertheless, one must work for a black government, for until that is achieved the evils mentioned will be inevitable. A black government could not racially oppress a black majority.

Apart from these reservations I think I have for a long time followed the advice set forth in your letter to the G.C.P.

With kind regards<br>
Yours sincerely<br>
Eddie

P.S. Sorry I was too busy to post this last week. My best wishes. ER.
P.S. I still wear the suit you made me. Still my "best" suit.

## Document 26
## Letter from Patrick Duncan[69] to John Gomas, 3 October 1956

In the train<br>
Patrick Duncan<br>
3 October 1956

Dear Sir,

I very much appreciate your sending me a copy of yr ltr of 1 Sept.

I endorse much of what you say, particularly about hatred. I agree with your views on honour and respect. At the same time I do not quite accept your paragraphs 2 and 3. They imply that in politics white and non-white must be eternally and irrevocably separated. Thus, to me, they share something of the philosophy of the present government. I believe that *all* persons in this country should be equal and that race-barriers should come down, not only in the future South African state, but also in the struggle that is going to produce that State. If you have struggled for 37 years against white domination you have my admiration and respect. Keep it up!

Yours Sincerely<br>
Patrick Duncan

## Document 27
## Letter from John Gomas to The Editor,
## *New Age*[70], 15 October 1956

The Editor,
New Age,
6 Barrack St.,
*Cape Town,*

Sir,

To my letter of advice to any whiteman in South Africa, you put three questions to me.

Your 1st question: Am I in favour of a colour-bar?

This question reminds me what I have seen how white foremen kick non-white workers under the seat of their pants than ask "how do you like it?" I have personally experienced such kicks, too. It hurts and is most undignified.

For 55 years I have suffered as a non-white under the oppression of the colour-bar and for 37 years openly fought against it, now a white man who benefits from the opperation of the colour-bar against the millions of non-whites, ask me, "do you like it?"

I would not be so stupid to ask even a white-man whether he likes the colour-bar, because, obviously he enjoys the benefits derived from the effects of the colour-bar and do his utmost to maintain it and extend its scope.

Of course, only a South African white man, *[blinded]* racial prejudice, would dare to ask such a ridiculous question to a person like myself, most of all.

Your 2nd question: Should there be no organisation to which white and non-white can belong in a basis of equality?

I said NO in paragraph (3) of my letter, for the reason that white men only associate with non-whites to secure and further their interests of white domination.

For what purpose would white men otherwise join in the organisation with non-whites in this country? To fight for democracy for the whites? But that they have.

Do they want to help the non-whites to progress and attain democracy? Then they must work to pursuade their white kith and kin to become decent human beings and as I advised in my letter. Such white men, yes, would earn by their deeds our respect and friendship. But I have never met such white men.

Your 3rd question: Am I in favour of the I.C. Act which forbids white and non-white to belong to the same trade union?[71]

It has proved disastrous for the non-white workers to belong to the same trade union with white racialists who have persistently and violently opposed the advancement of the non-white workers.

The white garment workers of Johannesburg practiced apartheid in their union long years before the existence of the said I.C. Act. Why did you not expose and oppose them? Such in fact is the actions of enemies rather than friends, comrades or brothers.

John Gomas
24 Sterling St.,
Cape Town
15/10/56

## Document 28
## Brian Bunting[72], "Problems of the Multi-Racial Conference"[73], *Liberation*, 28, November 1957

THE decision of the Congresses to take part in the forthcoming multi-racial conference has naturally aroused a great deal of discussion in democratic circles in South Africa. There have been those who have welcomed the multi-racial conference as a beacon marking out the road to a united anti-Nationalist front in which all sections of progressive opinion could participate and which could generate the strength to bring the Government to its knees. On the other hand, there have been those who look upon the multi-racial conference with suspicion, fearing that it will prove merely a trap for the unwary, and the militancy of the masses will be drowned beneath the calm waters of liberal complacency.

Contradictory though it may seem, both views of the conference are correct. The conference possesses great possibilities, but also great dangers. To ensure that the democratic cause achieves the greatest possible impetus from the conference, it is essential that all Congressmen and progressives who take part in it should be absolutely clear about what they are doing, and about the tactics of the united front.

Let us first make it clear that in the struggle against the Nationalists a united front is absolutely necessary. For what is the purpose of the united front? It is the mobilisation of the masses of the people in active struggle against the apartheid tyranny. What do we mean by the masses of the people? We mean in the first place all the millions of Non-European oppressed who suffer under the lash of the colour bar who are hounded by the pass laws, deprived of the deprived of the right to live a normal life by section 10, the victims of the police terror, the disfranchised – in fact, the majority of the South African people. But side by side with them we must aim to mobilise all other sections of the people, European and Non-European, who are prepared today, for a variety of reasons to oppose particular aspects of Nationalist policy. Why do we emphasise the mobilisation of the masses of the people? Because it is only when the masses of the people are mobilised and organised that a weapon will be forged in South Africa which is strong enough to defend the people against the attacks of the Government, to win for them the rights enshrined in the Freedom Charter.

The Europeans alone cannot put things right. Those Europeans who are opposed to the policies of the Nationalist Government, and who yet restrict their political activity to taking part in and preparing for elections, have become the prisoners of the Nationalists just as much as the Non-Europeans. The restriction of the franchise to "Europeans only" is the basic reason for the United Party's ideological capitulation to apartheid. Therefore the solution must be sought outside Parliament and outside the electoral system, because it is only through extra-Parliamentary struggle that the mass of the people can make their voices heard.

Spearheading the extra-Parliamentary struggle **against** the Nationalist Government and **for** equal rights for all is the Congress movement – the alliance of the national organisations of the African, Indian and Coloured people with European progressives and trade unionists who have identified themselves completely with the Congress movement. Those who decry the need for a united front should recognise that the Congress movement itself is a united front. It is also instructive to remember that this united front was born of the great Defiance Campaign, where it proved itself as the only effective vehicle by which the protest of all sections of the people against the unjust laws could be organised. No united front, no defiance campaign – and the defiance campaign was perhaps the greatest organised demonstration of the people against the tyranny of white supremacy that this country has ever seen. The unity built up in the defiance campaign was strengthened during the campaign for the Congress of the People in 1955, at which the Freedom Charter was adopted, and was sealed by the treason arrests of December 1956.

## THE BEDROCK

The unshakeable unity of the Congress movement, all should realise, is the bedrock on which all effective opposition to the policies of the Government is based. It was the foundation of the bus boycott and one of the factors which guaranteed the victory of the thousands who marched 20 miles a day rather than pay the fares increase. It is the foundation of all organised political activity by other sections of the population as well. Had it not been for the defiance campaign and the coming into existence of the united front, the Liberal Party would never have been born. Had it not been for the unity of the accused in the treason trial, the massive national and international support for the Treason Trial Defence Fund would never have materialised – and it is essential to appreciate that the Fund has not won support on this scale merely because it is a worthy charity, but mainly because it has provided an opportunity for thousands of people to do something concrete to express their hatred of the Nationalist Government and their fellow-feeling for the accused and the cause they stand for. The courage and spirit of the treason accused has not only inspired the thousands of rank-and-file Congressites to reach new heights of militancy in political action (against passes for women, the Mamathola removal etc.), but has also been the underlying factor which induced the clergy to protest against the Church Clause, the nurses against apartheid, the press against the threat of censorship, and even the United Party to come forward with its new Senate plan, feeble though it is.

Maybe not all those who are emboldened to speak their minds against the Government are conscious of this, but it is a fact all the same. What would be the picture in the country if the Congress movement did not exist, if the people simply accepted their fate without protest, took out passes, moved at the crack of Verwoerd's whip, were subservient and demoralised and made no claim for equal citizenship rights? Who then would dare to criticise apartheid? It is precisely the resistance of the mass of the people which is the basis of almost all opposition to the Government.

The Congress movement is an alliance of all sections of the people in the liberatory movement. At the moment, for historical reasons, each national group is organised in its separate national organisation, but there can be no doubt that with the passage of time and ever-closer co-operation in active political struggle, with the growth to political and organisational maturity of each group, the tendency will be for the barriers to break down and ultimately for full political and organisational cohesion to be brought about. Each group at the moment still fears to abandon the protection of its own organisation, and, in view of the special situation facing each group it would be wrong to do so.

Not only inside the organisations themselves, but also among the masses of the people who are not yet organised there are still feelings of racial exclusiveness and antagonism which hinder the fullest and freest co-operation, and which make impossible the creation of one, united, all-in Congress body as is advocated in some quarters. To deny this is to fly in the face of the facts. The existence of Africanists inside the A.N.C., the recent tribal clashes in Johannesburg and elsewhere, the separation in the trade union movement – these and many other proofs of surviving disunity can be adduced.

But the time will undoubtedly come – the sooner with each joint campaign, with each shared disaster or united victory – when the fullest possible unity, inside the Congress movement will become a reality.

But the Congress movement is not only in process of building unity between people of different races. It is also a uniting of people belonging to different political and class groups within each national group. Inside the premier national organisation, the African National Congress, for example, we find working together for the achievement of common aims the worker and the businessman, the lawyer and the intellectual, the communist and the nationalist. They do not see eye to eye on all issues, but they do agree to work together in defence of their rights as Africans against the oppressive policies of the Nationalist Government, and for the achievement of the aims of the Freedom Charter. What unites them most strongly at the moment is their participation in the work of their national organisations.

But what gives the A.N.C. its distinctive and almost unique militancy in the present situation is its overwhelmingly working-class character, in the sense that the workers make up the bulk of its membership and are in a position to determine the nature of its policies to a far greater extent than was the case (and still is) with, say, Gandhi's Congress in India, or the national liberatory movements in most other countries (Ghana, Egypt, Indonesia the Sudan etc.), where the rising national bourgeoisie were (and still are) the dominant factor.

The position is different with the Indian Congress in South Africa, for example, which has a larger middle-class element, and again with the Coloured Peoples' organisations, many of which are entirely dominated by intellectuals (though SACPO has made a conscious effort to base its activities on the organised strength of the working class). But it is the A.N.C. which, by virtue of its leadership and initiative and its greater membership, sets the tone and the pace for the whole Congress alliance, and it is the unique role of the A.N.C. to demonstrate that the national struggle in South Africa is inextricably bound up with the class struggle.

## FIRST PRIORITY

The unity which has already been achieved within the Congress alliance, then, based on the Freedom Charter, must be seen as the first priority in all our political efforts in the immediate future. Why? Because it is this alliance, and only this alliance, which has shown itself capable of mobilising the widest section of the oppressed peoples in effective political action.

No single one of the organisations could have achieved so much by itself, nor even attempted it. For it is precisely the spectacle of the growing unity between the different national groups which has been the most inspiring feature of the political scene during the last few years.

It is necessary to emphasise the word "growing", for the whole Congress alliance is all the time in process of developing – the ties become stronger, the unity deeper, the separatist tendencies weaker with each campaign in which they participate together. But the unity is not complete and will not come to fruition by itself. It must all the time be fought for consciously and with determination. The need to deepen the unity between the Congresses must always be in the forefront of our political calculations.

In view of the fact that the Congress alliance exists, is growing stronger and has already achieved country-wide recognition as the leader of the mass opposition to the Government, what is the need, many people ask, to broaden the front? Why should we work with the liberals and the bishops ? How can they help us? Will we not merely be forced to water down our policy and capitulate to their opportunism? Most of those who will be attending the multi-racial conference cannot be expected to agree with or accept the Freedom Charter as a basis for action. What, then, can be hoped for from this conference and from working with these people?

To answer these questions correctly, we must take another look at the general political situation in the country. The Nationalist Government is in power and, as far as can be judged, still firmly in the saddle. Many people are predicting that in the elections next year they will win with an even greater majority than ever before. But, win or lose, Nationalist Party or United Party, the plain fact is that the forces behind the maintenance of colour-bar policies in this country are still strong, while the forces behind the Congress alliance are still comparatively weak. Great though are the achievements which stand to its credit, the Congress alliance is still not in a position to draw into political action the vast majority of the Non-European peoples, let alone the Europeans. The Freedom Charter lays down a very fine programme of principles to fight for, but the Congress organisations, while potentially capable of achieving them, have actually not quite measured up to them. There is a long way to go before we can say we are in sight of our goal.

Meanwhile the Government continues with its ruthless and inhuman attacks on the people. Daily people are suffering, homes are broken up, men and women endorsed out of town, beaten up by the police. New and more vicious legislation is promised for the next session of Parliament. With the growth of opposition against it, the Government is driven to adopt ever more drastic means of maintaining itself in power. As more and more people are drawn into the fight against it, the Government responds by widening still more the area of the conflict. Where, in 1950, it was the Communists and the Congress leaders who were their main target, today the ranks of the victims have been swollen to include members of the Liberal and Labour parties, non-conformists of all types, the Anglican clergy and many others.

**NATIONALIST FAILURE**
In fact, one of the most convincing portents of the coming Nationalist defeat is their complete failure either to isolate and destroy their enemies or to win friends and influence people outside the ranks of the "bittereinders". It is stock Nazi technique to pick off your opponents one by one and, while the bystanders hold their breath and hope they won't be touched this time, wipe them out. Ever since they came to power the Nationalists have been trying to do the same thing, but all they have succeeded in doing has been promoting ever-deeper unity in the ranks of the opposition against them. Meanwhile their own failure to win adherents to their cause from the other sections of the population has been startling. Today it is the Nationalist Government and its apartheid policy which are execrated not only in this country but throughout the world.

At the same time, though there is widespread opposition to Nationalist policies amongst both Europeans and Non-Europeans in South Africa, the Nationalists remain in power for the sole reason that their opponents are disunited. Outside of the Congresses, there is no agreement as to what should be done and how it should be done. As between the bishops and the Liberals and the Labour Party and the Unity Movement and the various organisations and individuals who profess to abominate Nationalist policies (not to mention the United Party, which is almost unmentionable) there are few points of contact and almost no measure of understanding. That is precisely why the multi-racial conference is so important.

At the multi-racial conference there will be gathered together for the first time practically all shades of anti-Nationalist opinion – for though the formality has been gone through of inviting Nationalists to attend, it is doubtful if any will, apart from the Special Branch.

Congressmen will be able to mix with men and women belonging to other groups, many of whom have in the past been their political opponents, but all of whom are now brought together because they face a common danger "But" it is objected by some, "the Congresses share a common programme the Freedom Charter. Those who will be attending the multiracial conference with them do not accept the Charter, cannot be expected to accept the Charter as the basis for unity. Many of them have not even abandoned the last traces of white chauvinism, and speak of giving us rights 'when the time is ripe'. Many of them are our class enemies, whose real motive is to perpetuate the power of the ruling class by buying us off with a few concessions. We should go to the conference only if others accept our programme, otherwise we will have betrayed our cause."

Others ask: "How can you expect the lion to lie down with the lamb? The Liberal Party is merely the new face which is being presented to the people by the more enlightened wing of the industrial and finance capitalists. If we co-operate with them, do we not merely help to strengthen our enemies, lend them our mass backing to strengthen the institutions of the ruling class? Should we not rather concentrate our attention on destroying the whole capitalist system which is the root of all the evils from which we suffer? At what point can it be said that our interests coincide with theirs?"

There are several points to be made here. First of all, there is no ideological unity in the Liberal Party, there are only Liberals and Liberals. One wing of the Liberal Party can almost be described as reactionary; but another wing is moving ever-closer to the Congress point of view, and already works closely with the Congresses in some centres.

Secondly, may not co-operation with others also help to strengthen us? Given a correct approach, there is no reason to fear that we must necessarily get the worst of the bargain. Thirdly, it is not true to say that we and they have no interests in common. Granted, the time may come in future when our policies and interests may conflict with theirs; and of course our long-term perspective is quite different from theirs. But meanwhile, now, if the industrialists and finance capitalists are against the pass laws, should we not welcome their co-operation in a campaign to abolish them?

It may be true that their motives in wanting the pass laws to go are different from ours, but let us ask: would we rather have them with us or against us on this issue? If there is division in the ranks of the ruling class over things like these, why should we not take advantage of such divisions? Is it good tactics to help unite the ruling class, and bring about a united front against us?

## SECTARIANISM
To adopt such an attitude is to misread the possibilities of the present situation in South

Africa, and to betray sectarianism of the worst order at a time when the needs of the struggle demand the creation of the broadest unity amongst anti-Nationalists. Granted many people cannot accept the Freedom Charter. We don't ask them to. Did Stalin insist that Churchill and Roosevelt accept Communism before he accepted their help during the last war? Did he refuse their co-operation because he was afraid of what they would do to him after the war? Of course not. The first principle of the unity of the Allies in the war was united struggle against the monster of Hitler Germany, which threatened equally capitalist Britain and America and Communist Russia, and indeed the whole world. In the same way, the first principle which should be put forward and accepted at the multi-racial conference is condemnation of the apartheid policy of the present Government, and the need to forge some sort of unity in action against it. Not all who are present at the conference may even accept this, but it is likely the majority will.

However, it would be unwise to hope for too much. The conference is a first attempt. Many of the participants will be meeting one another, hearing one another's point of view for the first time. It is even a triumph in itself that in the year of the law designed to end all contact between Black and White except on the basis of master and servant, such a conference is being held at all. We shouldn't risk ruining the conference by demanding a fully-fledged united front at the end of it. Many more meetings and many more shared political experiences will be required before that becomes a possibility.

Yet great opportunities will still exist and must be fought for at the conference. During the last year we have already seen both Congressmen and others shedding their prejudices to work together for a common objective. Congressmen, Liberals, Labourites, Black Sash and others have taken part in joint demonstrations against the Group Areas Act in Johannesburg. Congressmen (including COD, against whom many liberals seem to have a particularly violent and unreasonable prejudice), Liberals and others have appeared on united platforms in many centres in Natal in protest against the Group Areas Act and the pass laws. The CATAPAW demonstration against passes for women in Cape Town also succeeded in bringing together for the first time a wide range of opinion, from the A.N.C. to the Mothers' Union.[74] Did the Congresses suffer by securing the co-operation of others in these protests? They didn't ask us to give up the Freedom Charter. We didn't ask them to give up their principles. Yet both sides found they could work together and thereby mobilise wider mass support for the struggle against Nationalist policies.

The great possibilities opened up by this sort of co-operation must be placed before the conference. Others may dither and philosophise, but Congress should indicate, at least, that it hopes to see some sort of action flow from the multi-racial conference. It is time to talk, yes, because we must understand one another; but it is also a time to act, before we are all destroyed by the common enemy.

Mao Tse-Tung once remarked that "the tactic of the united front and the tactic of closed door sectarianism are tactics diametrically opposed to one another.

> **The one is to accumulate large forces so as to surround our enemies and annihilate them. The other is to rely on a single horseman to wage a desperate fight with a formidable enemy.**[75]

The purpose of a united front, he said, is to mobilise million and millions of people and all potential friendly forces to advance and attack the centre-most objective. Failure to build a united front, insistence on keeping our principles pure and not defiling them by contact with others, means that we shall set up diverse objectives and consequently our bullets would hit the lesser enemies or even our allies rather than the principal enemy. This means that we shall be unable to pick out the right enemy and shall waste our ammunition. In this manner we shall be unable to drive the enemy into a narrow isolated position. In this manner we shall be unable to draw over from the enemy's camp and his front all those who have joined them under compulsion, those who were our enemies yesterday but may become our friends today. In this way we shall be actually helping the enemy, retarding and isolating our own movement, causing it to dwindle and decline, and even to take the road to defeat.

## THE STRAIGHT AND NARROW

The other would say: "all such arguments are erroneous. Our force must be pure and absolutely pure and our road must be straight and absolutely straight. Only what is recorded in the 'Bible' is correct. The national bourgeoisie is destined to be entirely and eternally counter-revolutionary. Not a single inch must be yielded to the rich peasants. As regards the yellow trade unions, we should fight them tooth and nail. Has there ever been a cat that does not love meat or a war-lord who is not counter-revolutionary ? The intellectual can remain revolutionary only for a day or two, and it is dangerous to recruit them. Hence the conclusion: closed-door sectarianism is the only magic wand, and the united front is the tactic of opportunism." [....]

In conclusion, it should be emphasised that all political movements, while in the course of their development, are in the process of changing. As they grow stronger, their character alters, their power of attraction increases, their responsibilities become more heavy. Only those do not change who are isolated from the main stream of political development, like the Trotskyites and our own Unity Movement, who are being left behind by history. As we enter the door of the multi-racial conference, let us be prepared to discuss with those who think differently from us, let us try to win them to our point of view, let us by all means canvass the virtues of the Freedom Charter and never betray a single clause of it; but let us not be rigid and unbending, or unwilling to meet others half-way if by doing so we can advance our cause. Without losing sight of our goal, let us realise it may not be possible to reach it at the first attempt. Let us be determined to register some progress, rather than retire empty-handed and frustrated. Let us, above all, recognise that if we are true to our principles, we cannot fail to make an impact on those who meet with us. Out of the war-time co-operation of the great powers emerged the Atlantic Charter, the United Nations Charter and the Charter of Human Rights, which are the foundations of our own Freedom Charter, and the goal of millions of people throughout the world fighting for their freedom.[76] We too live in a period of history in which the minds of men are open to new influences on a scale that was never before possible.

**Already new political currents are flowing in South Africa whose direction and ultimate destination we can only guess at. Within the last year great cracks have appeared in the Nationalist facade, while strong new bonds of friendship have grown up between some sections of the opposition. By taking part in the multi-racial conference with goodwill and good faith, we can help to usher in a new era in South African politics, break down the barriers which divide our peoples, win new recruits to our own army, and bring closer the reality which is embodied in the slogan "Freedom in our lifetime."**

## Document 29
## Kenneth Hendrickse, "The Opposition in Congress",
## *The Citizen*[77], 3, 3, 4 March 1958

WHAT EVERY INTELLIGENT DEMOCRAT HAS BEEN EXPECTING HAS HAPPENED. AN OPPOSITION GROUPING HAS PRECIPITATED OUT IN THE "MULTI-RACIAL" CONGRESS MOVEMENT. THEIR BULLETIN "ANALYSIS" IS SHARPLY CRITICAL OF THE CONGRESS PATRONS WHO DOMINATE THE CONGRESS MOVEMENT.[78]

Here, however, I wish less to add my voice to their criticisms than to deal with some of the ideas of the oppositionists themselves.

BLIND TO CONGRESS RACIALISM

On the question of the elections their attitude is largely correct: they reject both separate representation and the "minority" parliament. While their support of the demand for a boycott of all the elections to the bogus parliament is implicit, they do not, however, come out forthrightly in support of it.

Their demand that the whole people be organised "across the length and breadth of South Africa" is also an obviously correct demand. But they imagine, however, that it is into the Congress movement that the whole people can be organised and united. Leaving aside now the implicit sectarianism of this approach their major fault is that they are completely blind to the Congress movement's racialism.

The Congress "alliance" is made up of various "racial" organisations in which people are divided according to the way they have been "racially" classified by the oppressive South African ruling class, that is, as so-called "Africans", "Coloureds", "Indians" and "Whites". And unless this matter is dealt with first the oppositionists' attack on the Congress regime will remain superficial and therefore meaningless. It is multi-racialism – a gratuitous concession to apartheid – which is at the root of all other evils in Congress.

PATRONS DOMINATE "ALLIANCE"

Multi-racialism like Non-Europeanism serves only one purpose: to conserve and entrench the apartheid consciousness of the people with its concommitant feelings of "racial" inferiority and superiority corresponding to the position accorded them on the scale of "racial status". And it is precisely the multi-racialism of Congress which enables the "Whites only" Congress of Democrats to dominate the Congress "racial" alliance and to subordinate its struggle against oppression to the interests of "sympathetic", "White" patronage. For as long as the people are organised according to their acceptance of an inferior "racial" or more correctly aparte socio-political status they will tend to look for leadership not to those who have the right ideas and the courage of their convictions but to the "sympathetic" patrons who enjoy a superior aparte status.

The people in South Africa will be united in non-racial, democratic, anti-apartheid political, labour, district and cultural organisations according to their level of political consciousness and understanding, not in racial organisations according to their "race" classification. Where there is any acceptance, whatsoever, of apartheid, colour bar or segregation whether voluntary or enforced there can only be division and paralysing weakness. The people cannot be united in the multi-racial Congress "alliance".

## THE "CLASS APPROACH"

The oppositionists in Congress suffer from another serious blind spot. Because they feel themselves socialists whose "only goal" is the "break down of exploitation" the Colour Bar in their eyes tends to become just one of those irritating tertiary phenomena which the South African proletariat will simply brush away in their march towards a new and glorious Socialist South Africa. But the reality of the situation is that the South African worker is not even in a position to accomplish the comparatively simple and immediate task: the shaking off of the Colour Bar yoke from his shoulders!

Our oppositionists friends in Congress pride themselves on their "class approach". But a class approach is a scientific method of analysing social problems and phenomena: an interpretive instrument and guide to action not a magic wand which enables one to escape the obligations of immediate historic tasks.

Everything else in South Africa, today, must be subordinated to the task of transforming the consciousness of the whole nation from a racialist acceptance of apartheid consciousness to a democratic non-racial South African national consciousness. For the task before the people is the total abolition of the Colour Bar. It is South Africa's burning need. She requires it for her further economic, social, political and cultural development.

Those who belittle the struggle of the Colour Bar or give it a position of secondary historical importance because they are "socialists" are making a very serious mistake. This attitude inevitably aids the reaction.

As to ANALYSIS's attitude to the Liberals, the Multi-racial Conference and the Congress "United Fronts", its wrong approach to these questions is at root the oppositionists' failure to grasp the idea that I have put forward in this article: Namely, that the total elimination of the Colour Bar is an inescapable historic task if we are to create the conditions for a modern social struggle in modern South Africa.


## Document 30
## W. M. Tsotsi, "Presidential Address to the All-African Convention Conference", Edendale, 14 to 16 December 1958[79]

It is once more my pleasant duty to address the delegates and visitors to the Conference of the All African Convention, 1958. When at our last Conference in December, 1956, I suggested that we might not be able to meet in conference again, some people might have thought that I was a pessimist. The failure of the All African Convention to hold it Annual Conference last year, owing to Herrenvolk interference, must indicate to us that we shall not always be able to meet as we like. There is no reason to hope that the virtual ban on meetings imposed by the ruling class on the majority section of the population in the rural areas, will not eventually be extended to the organisation which is representative of that section. The awareness of this fact must surely impress on us the urgent necessity of using the vital opportunity afforded us by this Conference as profitably as we can, bearing in mind that we must never forget that the whole African, indeed the whole Non-European population of this country looks to this Conference of the A.A.C. for leadership and guidance in the period of crisis immediately ahead of us.

I would appeal to all the delegates here to conduct themselves in the deliberations at this Conference with the grave seriousness and restraint consistent with the dignified status of the All African Conference.

The two years which have passed since our last Conference have seen the rapid implementation of recommendations of the Tomlinson Report, that blue-print of the preservation of the so called "Christian Capitalist Civilization" for the Herrenvolk, and the prevention of the development and extension of a free modern capitalist economy amongst the Non-Europeans by placing them in a Procrustean bed of tribal backwardness. In order to fill up the yawning gap which is thus being created in the country's economy, the ruling class has embarked on a form of state Capitalism for Non-Europeans only.

*[....]* the Government through the South African Native Trust is by far the largest private owner of Non-European occupied land; through its labour bureaux the largest recruitment and controller of Non-European labour and one of its largest employers. Very soon through its projected Development Coordination the Government will be the largest financier of African enterprises. This Development Corporation will be a huge concern "for promoting capital formation through commercial institutions". It will establish a "Bantu Commercial Bank" a "Bantu Savings and Credit Bank", a "Bantu Insurance Company", a "Bantu Building Society" etc. And all this under the shameful pretence of a new economic trusteeship which asserts that "the Bantu must be guided to construct their own economy in their own soil, in their own milieu and out of their own spirit and energy and to move forward along the path of their own civilization according to the tempo of their own ability to develop".

The *deux ex machina* which has been set up to convert the African section of the Non-Europeans into a valuable asset in the Verwoed & Co. Development Corporation (Pty) Ltd is the Bantu Authorities. It will be one of the functions of these Authorities to crush the rising African professional and business class which demands a share in the economic power based on capitalist democratic rights, and to create a new African intellectual and business man who will submit to "traditional Bantu Principles" in all his professional and commercial dealings. In other words a Quisling type of African teacher and trader will be mass-produced through the Bantuised Schools which will be strictly controlled by the Government through its Native Commissioners, policemen-intellectuals, policemen-chiefs and headmen etc. The stage has been set for a vital clash between a Herrenvolk-tribalist bureaucracy on the one hand and representatives and organisations of the people on the other. *[....]*

The basic reason why the ruling class is determined to exclude the Non-Europeans from sharing in the economic wealth of the country is that the non-Europeans as a section must be made to produce that wealth for the Herrenvolk. *[....]* The poverty of the people is a necessary instrument of the Herrenvolk policy; for rather than starve to death the people will go out to seek work and will accept a mere pittance for wages in order to preserve life.

Let us consider briefly the methods and extent of this impoverishment. I shall refer only to the more glaring instances. It is generally known that the creation of land hunger is one of the chief methods employed by the Herrenvolk for the exploitation of Non-European labour. *[....]*

By far the largest extent of land in the "Reserves" is Crown land and the African people who occupy it are Government tenants subject to payment of an annual rental.

Less than 50% of the African males in the reserves have been allocated small residential sites (and some of these arable land) with little or no security of tenure. The vast majority of the men and practically all the women have no land which they can own or occupy except as dependants or subtenants. By means of the Betterment Areas Proclamation which is being applied piecemeal the Government has terminated all rights of occupation of Crown land including the grazing of stock except on approval by South African Native Trust Officials. The Trust has virtually seized the people's land and is busy redividing it. In terms of the Tomlinson Report, "a revision of the system of land tenure is regarded as one of the pre-requisites of the stabilisation of the land in the Bantu areas and the full economic development of their potential".[80] To achieve this aim the land in the reserves is being redivided. The vast majority of those comparatively few peasants who occupy any land at all are being deprived of their land which is to be re-allocated as "economic units" under conditional title to a few African farmers on a full-time basis. The vast majority who constitute a landless population are to be shifted to so-called rural villages which will have all the evils of urban locations with respect of a living wage to off-set them. In the meantime the landless are not even allowed to keep stock in the "Betterment Areas". [....]

It must be observed here that in terms of the white paper on the Tomlinson Report, "The Government is not prepared to do away with tribal tenure of rural land and to substitute individual tenure based on purchase nor does it propose to give preference to individual acquisition of land above tribal and Trust purchase in the released areas."

The landlessness and homelessness of the African population is no better in the urban areas than it is in the rural areas. The ruling class has steadfastly set itself against this permanent urbanisation of the Africans in the industrial and mining areas the so-called European areas – even though the economic interests of the country demand it. The result is that the African in these Urban areas is not made to feel at home. A large proportion of the African workers is migratory. [....]

We must realise that all the landlessness, poverty and homelessness of the African people which I have described above has been possible because of the exclusion of the Non-Europeans from the Government of the country. Because of their lack of political rights because of their non-citizen status, the majority section of the population has been outlawed and foredoomed to a life of perpetual servitude. It is for this reason that the fight for full equality occupies a central position in the 10-Point Programme of the N.E.U.M.

It is therefore much to be regretted that there has arisen of late within the Unity Movement a tendency to minimise the importance of the demand for the full franchise. This tendency has been the chief cause of the development of internal theoretical differences within the Movement, differences which have now reached a climax and can no longer be concealed. As early as 1954 in my Presidential address to the A.A.C. I warned the Movement against this development in the following words:- "In such periods of comparative inactivity that solidarity within the ranks which is engendered by the prospects of immediate battle is often lacking. Differences of opinion assert themselves and temporary ideological groupings begin to appear. Although such differences and groupings are unfortunate, and sometimes undesirable, they are as inevitable to the growth of a healthy political movement as toxins in the life of the human organism. The transformation of the groupings into organised and closed factions is an evil which must be avoided at all costs. The art of leadership consist precisely in preventing such a development.

Ideological differences within the movement may be inevitable and may even constitute a necessary part of its dialectic, but petty jealousies and rivalries for power and positions are quite unnecessary and intolerable and those who indulge in such mean practices do not deserve a place in our leadership and must be ruthlessly cast out of it. It is the duty of all of us in the liberatory movement to refuse to be party to the squabbling of rival groups and to expose those who do not scruple to indulge in personalities and cheap gossip in order to feather their own nests. Unless we perform our duty in this regard the movement is bound to suffer. [....]

First of all I wish to state that the division has arisen as the result of the fact that certain individuals and groups within the movement are dissatisfied with the 10-Point programme of the N.E.U.M. They consider that this programme is very inadequate for the solution of our political and social problems in South Africa. What creates confusion is that these opponents of the 10-Point Programme instead of condemning the programme outright pretend that their views are consistent with it. To denounce the 10-Point Programme would put them beyond the pale of the N.E.U.M. and render them without a political home.

[....] In order to underline the fundamental implications of this tendency I shall quote extensively from a remarkable pamphlet written by a spiritual member of the group who is an avowed enemy of the N.E.U.M. There is this added advantage in quoting from this publication, namely that it is written under a pen name. The identity of the author is therefore presumably unknown to all of us and there is less danger of the cry of "Informer" being raised by those who are richly endowed with a persecution complex. I refer to the roneoed pamphlet "It is time to awake" by R. Mettler which purports to be a criticism of I.B. Tabata's "The Awakening of a People", a book that is recognised by us in the Unity Movement as correctly setting out our political ideas.[81]

R. Mettler makes no bones about attacking the 10-Point Programme from many angles. Basically his criticism is that *"The existing programme of the N.E.U.M. exposes the aspirations of the African Middle Class."* He criticises the resolution on the programme passed at the 1943 N.E.U.M. Conference to the effect that all our disabilities economic, educational, social, cultural flow from the lack of political rights and that our struggle is therefore chiefly political. R. Mettler asserts that this attempt to separate political subjugation from economic exploitation "runs throughout the documents of this movement and leads eventually to the false positioning they take up in all situations. Surely our lack of political rights flows from our separation from the ownership of the means of production" he profoundly concludes. Then again Mettler states: "[....] In so far as the N.E.U.M. is not firmly based on the working class its ideology must lead it into the political emptiness that characterises its past history." It will be observed that Mettler's strictures as quoted are identical with those of the revisionists within our ranks except that the latter substitute the "existing leadership" for the former's "existing programme" of the N.E.U.M. Another fact which must be noted is the belittling of the demand for political rights which the N.E.U.M. regards as pivotal in its programme.

R. Mettler is very outspoken in his condemnation of the demand for the Franchise which we consider to be the most important of the 10-Points of our programme. He says, "We must state without equivocation that in the alliance between the middle class and the workers in the liberatory movement a programme that is based on the vote as the first point denotes the ideological hegemony of the petty bourgeois politicians [....] Mettler again states "It is a fact that the National Movements throughout Africa are stressing these political claims. Kwame Nkrumah of Ghana was fond of saying "seek ye first the political kingdom and all things shall be added to you."[82] The people of India, Indonesia, Ghana and others have been given the vote and yet these countries are still based on exploitation and the basic struggles continue." *[....]*

The revisionists within our ranks consider that the 7th Point justifies this so-called leftist interpretation of the 10-Point Programme. On the other hand R. Mettler finds this point equally obnoxious. "It is also no accident that the N.E.U.M. proposes the re-distribution of the land (even if by vote in Parliament) and yet will not dare to mention the factories and the mines. The former, radical as it is, is still consistent with the building up of a capitalist country while the latter would imply a conflict with Capitalism ... The authors of the 10-Point Programme have not told us how they will achieve this democracy if the rural workers do not first seize the land ... There has been no clear cut programme put forward that demands without equivocation the re-allocation of land. To talk about the vote when the problem is the redivision of land is futile."

Even at the risk of being called names such as "Herrenvolk hirelings" we have to point out to our enemies whether within or without the Unity Movement that the seizure of land and its redivision is not part of the 10-Point Programme. When we talk of "acquiring" land in Point 7 we mean and have always meant lawful acquisition within the framework of the capitalist society of which we are part.

The whole basis of the attack on the 10-Point Programme is the denial of the reality of colour oppression in South Africa and consequently the denial of the necessity for a National liberatory movement. On the contrary the National problem is viewed as simply a class problem thinly covered over with colour wash designed to conceal its identity. The expressed aim of the N.E.U.M. is to liquidate the National oppression of the Non-European in South Africa *[....]*

The implication of the identification of Herrenvolkism with capitalism cannot be fully understood except in the light of the liberal concept of "White capital and Coloured labour". Expressed in other words the idea is that in South Africa the Whites are the capitalists and the non-Whites the workers. R. Mettler states this idea as follows:– "The ruling class resident in South Africa is generally speaking white. Equally in broad outline the non-white people are predominantly workers. The exploitation of the working class has been covered up by colour oppression". Although Mettler does say that "There is an overlap of classes which transcends the racial barriers" it is clear that his whole outlook on the class struggle in South Africa is not free of racialism particularly in the light of his other allegation that in isolated cases the worker (read: the Black) can support the right instead of the left and the capitalist (read: the White) can support the left. Mettler lends support to this contention by the following statement "The white intellectuals are completely isolated from the working class by both class and colour differences and thus tend to lean over heavily towards the ruling class. The non-white intellectual on the other hand is in close physical contact with the worker and feels the brunt of oppression himself. He thus leans more towards the people". In other words Mettler sees the class struggle in South Africa as the struggle between Black and White. The same attitude of damning the White working class as Herrenvolk and therefore capitalist is apparent in the statements of the young so-called leftists in our movement. Basically this idea springs from the influence of African nationalism. This theoretical mistake is inevitable if we seek to deny the bourgeois character of our national liberatory movement on the fatuous ground that "We already have a capitalist society and thus are not struggling to make a new capitalist society".

The correct theoretical analysis of the position is set out on page 5 of "The Awakening" as follows:– "But in the conditions obtaining in South Africa the clear-cut class divisions have been obscured. The Herrenvolk have elaborated a means of re-enforcing economic exploitation with all the vicious machinery of racial oppression". The correct deduction from this statement is not that we should ignore racial oppression because it is an instrument of oppression. That would be as foolish as to say in warfare we must ignore the bomber and concentrate on the bomb. Rather must we fight racial oppression and strive for political equality for, to quote from the Awakening once more, "Without political equality it will never be possible to speak of working class unity, and without working class unity it will never be possible to fight exploitation....The trade Union question in South Africa presents itself primarily as a national (political) question and only secondarily as a class question. The second cannot be evolved independently of the first".

We have to accept the concept of stages in the liberatory movement otherwise we will continue to confuse Herrenvolkism with capitalism and thereby create unnecessary theoretical misunderstanding. But R. Mettler is so hostile to this idea that he does not scruple to distort it. He says, "our perspective is not the mechanical one of stages in which we will first achieve the 10-point programme and build up a state wherein we can start a new struggle based on a new Trade Union Movement". We need only state that there is nothing mechanical about the concept of stages. We have to view the struggle in motion and where and how one stage ends and another begins cannot be predetermined in a mathematical fashion. It will depend on the dynamic of the situation and the relationship of forces.

Our view of the trade Union question as primarily a national political question has already been stated. The revisionists have attempted to confuse the issue by falsely stating that we do not want to see the trade Union Movement built up and strengthened. It is certainly not our task as a political movement to form trade Unions. This would be sheer economism. After all even Mettler realises the true function of trade Unions because he says: "The trade Union Movement will have to be built up in the coming period..We must clearly state that the *trade Union's primary purpose is to fight the economic struggle* (our emphasis). That is, it has to fight for improved conditions in the factory ... But the trade Unions are not a substitute for a political movement and as the workers need a political party to serve their own interests to put forward their aspirations, a mass worker's party must be formed." If this is what the revisionist want, let them say so openly. A workers' political party will be welcome to affiliate to the liberatory movement just as the ex-communist party was, provided that it accepts the 10-Point Programme and all that it stands for.

Mettler is very forthright in his attack on the federal structure of the N.E.U.M. "When the N.E.U.M. called for interracial Unity" he says "the slogan was progressive. Today the needs are for a movement without racial barriers and a name such as 'Non-European Unity' no longer serves the needs of the liberatory movement. A movement that ties itself in advance to a specific organisational form runs the risk of ossification and to have made the federal structure as constituted today an article of faith in the N.E.U.M. is a sign that ossification has indeed set in." Mettler adds that "the federal structure would be permissible if it allowed for a federation on class grounds but in actual fact it has become a federal body first on racial grounds which must today be rejected." Mettler then goes on to advocate the formation of a unitary organisation "in so far as it is opposed to the current cumbersome racial division."

I have quoted extensively from R.Mettler not because I consider that his views are in themselves worthy of consideration but firstly because he is obviously hostile to the N.E.U.M. and its 10-Point Programme and secondly because his views are identical with those expressed by certain individuals and groups within the movement. The inference which I seek to be drawn is that these individuals and groups are also enemies of the N.E.U.M. If they deny this accusation the onus is on them to show how their views differ from those of Mettler.

[....] We have to appreciate the danger to the movement of giving the revisionists free hand to propagate their views from our platforms and our organs. It is not merely a question of creating division and strife within our organisations, bad enough though that is. Much more serious is the betrayal of the organisation to the Herrenvolk fascists. To give the 10-Point Programme a leftist interpretation, no matter how cockeyed is to bring the whole movement within the definition of statutory communism and to run the risk of it being made an unlawful organisation within the meaning of the Suppression of Communism Act. It is difficult to resist the inference that this is a consummation which many of the revisionists would devoutly wish as offering an easy method of escape from the hazardous tasks which presently devolve on them as members of the liberatory movement.

The lessons of the Treason Trials do not appear to have been sufficiently learnt by some of us. It is well known in liberatory movement circles that the majority of the persons who are members of the organisations involved in the Treason Trials are simple workers or peasants to whom the idea of mock elections could never have appeared subversive. Yet a few of these people have to stand their trial on a charge of High Treason precisely because a false coloration of leftism was imparted to their organisation by a few politically advanced petit-bourgeois intellectuals. All of us know that the tribalists of A.N.C. and the merchants of the S.A.I.C. are incapable of demanding the "liquidation of capitalism, equal distribution of wealth, common ownership of the means of production, land mines and factories," and yet the record would appear to indicate that that this was part of the programme of these organisations. This sort of thing inevitably happens when a few so-called "leftist" theoreticians seize control and leadership of the people's organizations and proceed to impose on them ideas which are inconsistent with the aims and objects of the organisations and are in advance of the standard of political consciousness reached by the generality of the membership. The result is that in time of crisis the progressive facade breaks down and the political fraud is exposed. Then begins the splitting up of the organisations into the respective political groupings of its membership from the extreme right to the extreme left.

It was in order to avoid such an eventuality that the N.E.U.M. adopted a minimum programme and a federal structure. Mr. I.B. Tabata correctly states the position on page 46 of "The Awakening of a people" when he says:– "The Problem was to create a mouthpiece of the whole of the African People, a forum from which their voice could be heard. It was obvious that no single party could fulfil this task. A single political party cannot represent a whole community or race, for the mere fact of belonging to the same race has nothing to do with a man's political affiliations. In any given community people share different political ideas ranging from the extreme left to the extreme right – Any attempt therefore to form a unitary political organisation or party was doomed to fail. Further no one party could claim to represent tribalists, nationalists, internationalist and liberals and at the same time integrate and attend to the specific tasks of industrial workers, farm labourers, peasants, professional classes etc. Yet the very crux of the problem was to find a form of organisation which would meet the demands arising out of twofold oppression – National oppression and class exploitation". The tragedy of the situation is that the internal differences should arise at a time when the need for the unity of the oppressed is greater than ever. At this very moment when the rest of Africa is beginning to awake and cast away the imperialism and colonialism which has held it in thrall for centuries, when the cry for independence and self-determination is ringing with ever-growing insistence throughout the length and breadth of the "dark continent". At this time, moreover when in our own country the most down-trodden of all, the African peasants and workers are beginning to show fight. Just at the moment, I say, when the influence of its leadership should be felt throughout the continent of Africa, the N.E.U.M. must be rent asunder by divisions inspired by a few ambitious people in and around its leadership. This is a situation which we must try to remedy at all costs. If at this conference we cannot achieve a unity of ideas we must achieve at least a clear demarcation of differences.

Those whose politics consist of stereotyped slogans and cliches will no doubt raise their eyebrows when I say it is our duty to guide and not to condemn categorically the emergent African nationalism. We have to recognise that in so far as it is genuinely anti-imperialism and anti-colonialism, African Nationalism is a progressive political force. It is only when African Nationalism degenerates into racialism i.e. is anti-white, anti-Coloured, anti-Indian and when it is tied to the apron strings of imperialism and is the latter's agent for the economic exploitation of the colonial peoples that it has to be condemned and fought. [....] To safeguard against such a development we have to implant in the minds of the poor peasants and workers who constitute the majority, the desire for an effective say in the control and direction of the destinies of the countries which can only come about as the result of the extension of full political equality to all. Political history has shown no other method of ending economic exploitation except through political control by the majority section of the population who, in a capitalist society are inevitably the workers and the poor peasants. Once the importance of political rights has been driven home to the common man he will take the necessary steps to achieve these rights, and, armed with this new power he will proceed to put an end to exploitive relationships in society. [....]

In conclusion let me express the hope that theoretical discussions, important though they are will not take up too much of the Conference's time. The more vital questions affecting the practical struggles of the people against political emasculation and economic ruin must take precedence. The large delegation of peasants present at this conference must not be allowed to go away feeling that their attendance has not been worth the trouble and expense which it has entailed. Let us therefore settle down to the business of this conference namely to build up a movement which will be resilient and powerful enough to withstand and finally overcome Herrenvolk oppression, and so change this beautiful land or ours from a prison camp to a free society where all may live with dignity and justice.

(Issued by the Lady Frere Soya, Secy. J. B. Vusani Box 40, Lady Frere).

## Document 31
## S.O.Y.A. National Executive Committee[83], The Maritzburg Conferences and the Tasks of the Immediate Future, 31 May 1959

*[....]* We must proceed to consider the basic general ideological concepts of the Unity Movement, on which we impeach and indite this defected clique with treachery and desertion before the toiling masses of the Non-European oppressed. Reduced to their essence these major general concepts, by which the N.E. Unity Movement has always stood before the oppressed people of S.Africa, and which today are being betrayed by the defected clique are:–
1. Our concept of building Non-European Unity and National Unity by which alone liberation can be achieved in this country, and the foundation of a true S.Africa Nation laid; the truly united nation of a future liberated S.Africa which should no longer be cursed with and viciated by artificially fostered racial prejudices, sectarianism, and an anarchical exploitative social order where man lives off man.
2. Our Land Demand by which we certainly demand no "free right to buy the land", where the African peasantry kraaled off in the Land Reserves, is so obviously poverty stricken, but by which we specifically demand "a new division of the land in accordance with the whole population that lives on and works the land"; and implied in which demand is a categorical rejection of both the system of Land Reserves and the socalled White Areas out of the rest of the land surface of S.Africa.
3. Our Workers' Demand, by which we certainly cannot mean that the exploited segregated non-white workers can end their particularly intensified exploitation through the colour bar, by having to buy and own industry too through "a free right to buy"; but by which we definitely demand the ending of all labour segregation, a free right to seek work, to acquire skills, equal opportunity, equal pay for equal work, to be protected by labour legislation in all industries, and to form trade unions; all these as minimum demands towards the establishment of complete equality between the buyer and seller of labour, and towards "the ending of all oppression and all exploitation".
4. Our Full Vision of the Ten-Point Programme, by which the Ten-Point Programme is certainly no maximum programme or the very end of our liberation; but a minimum programme to build up a National Movement in S.Africa, with all the social groups to be found among the Non-European oppressed brought together in a common struggle against Herrenvolkism and imperialism for true liberation; and a minimum programme which stakes the basic minimum demands to which we the Non-European oppressed pledge ourselves for the only true foundation or starting point to build up a future democratic society in S.Africa, towards the fullest or the very maximum conditions of a really liberated people in this country. We accept no other basic or foundational starting point as a true one less than this minimum programme.

*[....]* in the course of the last two years, the defected A.A.C. leadership has skilfully sought to build up certain new and alien concepts of mental enslavement which have been particularly against the youth intelligentsia, out of whom, it has been clear, that the intention had always been to turn out permanent nodding-shadows who were for ever to hero-worship the defectors. Thus in these last two years this clique of the

defected A.A.C. leadership has built up the whole mumbo-jumbo of "the wise and revered parentage of the movement," "the unquestionable age-seniors," the repulsive nausea of "the humble and ever unquestioning youth." This new religion has been built up very ruthlessly and has been particulary directed against the youth intelligentsia in the S.O.Y.A. The purpose was clear, that it was to break the intellectual development of the S.O.Y.A. once and for all, and thus possibly secure the permanent grip of the defectors over the All-African Convention. As a whole National organisation of intellectuals and organisers the S.O.Y.A. has been a special threat to the defecting A.A.C. leadership, for indeed it has been the desperate purpose of these defectors possibly to desert with the name of some organisation as an historical cloak for ever to cover up their treachery before the eyes of the masses of the oppressed people.

On finally reaching their bogus 1958 Maritzburg Conference, the defected A.A.C. leadership fashioned out a special fascist committee called a credentials' committee. This committee was never a creature of a free decision of genuine delegations to an All-African Convention Conference. But to all wonder, it was a product of the socalled Executive of the Convention. Right at what should have been a Conference, the highest deciding body of a political organisation, we thus found a degenerated bureaucratic Executive who now hence-forth meant to decide for the very Conference itself. Then the alien fascist committee was given all the ruthless functions to judge upon and refuse credentials of the very people's organisations themselves which came to Conference, and as it was later to be seen, this fascist screening was to be applied against the very old affiliated organisations of the Convention. [....]

The bogus Conference was further packed in every possible unscrupulous manner. The mean and base connections and deception exploited to bring many of the unknowing peasantry as a socalled delegation to this sham Conference, have since been uncovered. [....]

In the deliberations themselves shamless bureaucracy was used by those in the chair to muzzle and gag all free discussion by the progressives, while the defectors gave themselves all the time not even to contribute but to lecture their special diatribes onto the fettered delegations. All the progressives who meant to uncover the betrayal and desertion of the defected leadership were rigidly muzzled in the course of all the discussions.

Then came the final attempt to begin sacking certain active progressive organisations from the Convention. Once more decision was taken and announced from above by the ruthless fascist junta who continued to mask themselves behind the name of an Executive of the Convention, that this clique of a defected official leadership of the All-African Convention, was, on the basis of evidence manufactured by its socalled credentials committee, hence-forth expelling the following organisations from the All-African Convention:– The New Era Fellowship, the Cape Flats Educational Fellowship, the Langa Educational Fellowship, and the Wits branch of the S.O.Y.A.[84] Like the so many other decrees of the bogus gathering these socalled expulsions from the Convention were also decided from above [....] In particular not definite ideological questions were ever tabled before a full open discussion of a genuine free Conference of the Convention against these organisations. Thus no genuine and free Convention of the All-African Convention was ever constituted to consider and decide on a full discussion on definite ideological questions tabled against these organisations. [....]

The defected leadership of the A.A. Convention has gradually lost vision and perspectives in a developing dark future, until they have ultimately seen their only hope in a capitulation to the threatening ruling Herrenvolk. First this leadership gradually broke down and became reconcilable to the Liberal wing of the Herrenvolk. Thus their personalities began to be found in the new Liberal publications like "Africa South"; they were found coming out to march with the Liberals in such demonstrations as those against University Apartheid; they were found addressing Black Sash meetings; in the leadership of the C.A.T.A. they have sought to be recognised by the Native Affairs Department, and finally expelled the general Secretary of the C.A.T.A. who would not open such collaborationist and sell-out negotiations with the Herrenvolk; and in their press they have sought advertisement even from the Verwoerd Apartheid Industries on the borders of the Reserves which they have openly accepted as bringing some opportunity to their group of "the incipient non-white apartheid traitors". In all, all this has been an abandonment of the traditional defined relations with the Herrenvolk, and collaborating fraternization was gradually taking the place of principles. If only individuals were to be found in these transgressions, the acts were however readily defended by the whole clique of this defected leadership. Indeed they have not lacked their own plagued and unimaginative black sheep who have idiotically committed the regular blunders for the whole crowd to defend everyday.

Then the developing collaboration and fraternization was soon followed by an expressed attitude against the role of the masses in the National Movement. Hence A.C. Jordan recorded their harm and undesirability as they might soon invite serious persecution and prosecutions from the ruling Herrenvolk;[85] and since the 1956 A.A.C. Conference the whole clique began to set itself against the role of the workers in the National Movement. In the course of the last two years L. Sihlali was to betray the motives of this enemity in the typical naive fashion that "the workers were of too radical an outlook" to be allowed their due class significance in the National Movement,[86] and Jane Gool was also to play her own role when she blurted out in Natal that "those who want to organise a class-conscious urban working class have no place in the National Movement". [....]

With the interests of the masses thus renounced in the struggle, then nationalism or colour-group politics becomes the convenient opium of the Middle Classes with which to rally the ignorant masses onto behind their colour-leadership, irrespective of the class material interests of that leadership. Nationalism is therefore a convenient ideology of the Middle Classes, by which these classes always blur off class material interests and thus hope to deceive the toiling masses of the people to rally onto their cause, without ever making class material interests an issue. Tsotsi has already announced that, "like" all Middle Classes, their Revisionist group are prepared to exploit the popular sentiment of nationalism, provided they will always be strong enough to control it not to assume an "Anti-White" character – apparently against their senior Herrenvolk class colleagues, and the condition he thus lays down is only logical for a political band who mean particularly to go out of all their way to allay the suspicions of the ruling Herrenvolk, in order ultimately to reconcile it with surity of common material interests onto a common multi-racial society. We here wish to restate the traditional outlook of the Unity Movement, that nationalism forever remains the deceptive ideology of the Middle Classes, for masquerading for a following of the masses for the people, without ever allowing class material interests to come to the foreground of our politics. The masses of the people have no need for nationalist politics. Their material conditions of exploitation are always self-evident enough as never to require any extra sentiments of colour-sensation and chauvinism, in order to bring forward the grim lesson of building up a political struggle. *[....]*

It is obvious that the more acute grows the struggle of the colonial people in both Africa and Asia, Imperialism too will constantly try to perfect this own counter methods to save its world stake. The system of prefect independencies began with India, was extended to Egypt, and now lately it has reached Ghana. Already in its days of West Africa, it has given birth to it s other offshoots of "partnership" and "multi-racialism", for application in those countries where the imperialist population cannot possibly be withdrawn anymore for some groomed colonial prefectships; and in all these tactics of imperialism the colonial Middle Classes, trading under the banner of popular nationalism, are the special target to groom out for a compromise. It is therefore clear that in the circumstances of that kind of future, the colonial national movement can only save themselves for true liberation by elaborating our ideology clearer and clearer in the dominant and decisive interests of the masses of the oppressed people. In the general perspectives of a whole continent where the colonial Middle Classes are coming forward under the banner of popular nationalism for a decisive deal with imperialism, then the progressive movements can only save themselves by building a clearer and clearer position amongst the masses of the oppressed peoples. *[....]*

The modern world urban working class occupies the position of the basic social however on which is directly supported the whole modern world economy built up by capitalism-imperialism. This is a completely dispossessed class; no longer bluffed by any proprietorship however meagre or token; but who specifically have to live by the daily marketing of their labour power to the private owners of present social industries. They are the very life blood of the present world capitalist industry, and the producers of the daily bill of profits of the private owners of that industry. If a peasantry still exists in the colonial countries for exploitation too, it has to be appreciated that it can also be exploited only via the position of the urban working class through a migratory labour system. Hence the land policy of the colonial Herrenvolk which is specifically designed in order to smoke out regular migratory labour out of the colonial peasantry. *[....]*

In this particular position, the world urban working class logically takes the leadership of the whole world struggle against present oppressive and exploitative society. It is the ideology of this class which becomes the only true ideology of social change in the modern world. Having lived the life of daily exploitation, its interests immediately correspond with that radical demand "to end all oppression and all exploitation," and it becomes a champion of the interests of all the toiling masses against oppression and exploitation. It is therefore the ideology of the world urban working class truly representing the interest of all the toiling masses which alone we allow to interpret, elaborate and develop the Ten-Point Programme of the N.E. Unity, and build up a national struggle in S.Africa. This is the programme of a definite progressive movement which, however, is not presented for a single-class struggle such as a labour movement, but for "a national struggle" in colonial South Africa. Its full vision is to bring together all the social groups to be found amongst the Non-European oppressed, but for true liberation. Members of the Non-European Middle Classes are obliged to the national movement, because in any case they are an oppressed social group too like the whole non-white population, but they have to be pledged to true liberation and the ending of all oppression and all exploitation. In particular they cannot still aspire for a repeat or continued exploitative society. Like all the other social groups they too are acceptable on definite ideological conditions to the national movement, and those conditions are those which should forever flow from our uncompromiseable demand to end all oppression and all exploitation for true liberation in South Africa. In conclusion we would therefore like at establish that the interests of the toiling masses are the dominant ones in the national movement. *[....]*

We would like to end up this statement with a certain commentary and suggestions on practical organisational tasks. *[....]*

In the urban centres we shall expect all organisational tasks immediately to follow the pattern of the Vigilance Associations, while in the rural villages they should take that of Village Associations.

The concept of Village Associations amongst the peasantry should be able immediately to bring forward the lesson, in the mind of the peasant, that the rural village is a single unit even though so scattered. It is capable of wielding a single independent organisation of the whole village just as the traditional village assembly or the present church have always done. Needless, of course, to say that in the vernaculars the Village Association will carry exactly the same concept of Iso-lomZi as the urban vigilances.

With particular regard to the organisational tasks amongst the rural population we must here reject a certain bankrupt and dead idea which, however unenunciated all along, has succeeded to make itself the practised official policy in this section of the population. In the 1958 A.A.C. conference some of the delegates from the towns took particular trouble to discuss some of the observable questions at present in the organisation of the peasantry. In the course of 1958 it had come to our notice that a socalled A.A.C. Regional Conference had been convened in Lady Frere. Many people came from various villages in a side area of the Transkei. It did become clear that nearly all those socalled delegates to the socalled regional conference under the name of the A.A.C., had come either as individuals representing the mere unorganized rural village or as representatives of some committee which had been established as the permanent standing political committee of some village. An attempt was therefore made in the socalled 1958 Conference to bring up the question of peasant organisation. An effort was particularly made to bring it to the notice of the peasantry themselves at conference, that however political work was begun in the peasant villages as in the urban communities the clear purpose must always be ultimately to found standing mass people's organisations. It is not just the unorganised village or some small committee of select men which should be the final and lasting basis of our political struggle in a village, but a definite mass people's organisation. *[....]*

Only the direct purpose of founding mass people's organisations in the peasant villages has all the dynamics immediately to bring the whole population of the village into the political struggle. Then and then alone is a real democratic organisation of the people brought into being. Its standing Village Committee then becomes a duly elected democratic committee with an actual organisation of the people behind it. It avoids becoming leader-cult, self-conscious, itinerant bureaucrats who feel themselves to have undertaken to preach a salvation cause onto a passive village mass, but becomes a real working institution of the village people. Finally such people's organisation can always bring up successive generations of its own leadership, and make the struggle ever acquire greater and greater momentum in the village. That is how we mean the Soya to undertake organisational work amongst the peasantry in the new period.

In general there is no need to expect some favourable previous influence of the ideas of the Unity Movement in an area before a Vigilance Association or Village Association can be instigated with confidence. An organizing committee of some few initial recruits made out through personal contact, is the first step towards the founding of a mass people's organisation in any village, whether urban or rural. Once collected this committee immediately proclaims itself a Vigilance or Village Association organizing committee and begins regular theoretical and organisational work towards the foundation of the actual mass people's organisation of the whole village. It holds regular study groups on topical and relevant matters, does active recruiting to swell up its own numbers, and already begins issuing agitational leaflets on arising issues to the whole village. As all the work of this committee gains momentum then the organisers can see when they can successfully attempt a fair public meeting to establish the actual people's organisation of the whole village. Even this actual people's organisation of the whole village may not initially have any impressive numbers. A real mass following is always the product of time and much patient work, and the start is always a humble one. But the secret of initiative is precisely that this start must be made however humble. [....]

It is therefore against the full background of this leaflet that we expect the whole Soya and all the progressives in the A.A. Convention to work in the new period. We have completely rejected and disowned the whole hitherto official A.A.C. leadership as deserters from the Non-European Unity Movement and capitulators to the Herrenvolk. [....] We categorically say to all the masses of the African people and all the Non-European oppressed that this clique no longer represents the All-African Convention anywhere in South Africa [....] We of the Soya therefore here and now pledge ourselves to the work for "a reassembly and to rebuild the All-African Convention."

ISSUED BY:
THE NATIONAL EXECUTIVE COMMITTEE     General Secretary
OF     S. VUTELA[87],
*THE SOCIETY OF YOUNG AFRICA.*     775 MOFOLO, *JOHANNESBURG.*

**NOTES**

1. Harry Snitcher was an advocate and Chair of the Cape Town District Committee of the CPSA. In 1938 he ran for Parliament on a Socialist Party platform. He was one of the eight members of the CPSA Central Executive charged with sedition following the 1946 African Mineworkers' strike.
2. Daniel Francois Malan (1874-1959), politician and theologian, became an M.P. for the NP in 1918, joined the Pact Government in 1924, and after the election of the Fusion Government in 1934 led the opposition Purified National Party. Following the 1948 electoral victory of a reunited NP, Malan became Prime Minister. Oswald Pirow (1890-1959) was a lawyer and politician who became Minister of Justice in 1929. The next year he helped pass the Riotous Assemblies Amendment Act through Parliament. A supporter of Adolf Hitler, Pirow opposed South Africa's entry into World War Two and founded a New Order to create an Afrikaner socialist state in South Africa. He withdrew from politics after failing to promote unity of the far right. Eric Louw, an advocate of the removal of blacks from the common voters' roll, became Minister of Economic Affairs and, later, of Foreign Affairs during the apartheid era. J. F. J. van Rensburg was a leader of the *Ossewabrandwa*g (Oxwaggon Sentinels), formed in 1939. Under Van Rensburg's leadership, this became a national socialist paramilitary organisation during World War Two, engaging in anti-war sabotage. By 1943 the *Ossewabrandwag* was finished, as the NP became the dominant voice of Afrikaner nationalism.
3. Hawa H. Ahmed was the pseudonym of Halima Gool (d. 1993), active in Cape Town radical politics in the 1930s and '40s and married to Goolam Gool. She was Secretary of the NLL and the Anti-CAD, was a speaker at the Non-European Women's Suffrage League in August 1938, and organised a Laundry Workers' Union which she represented at the 1939 NEUF conference. Her notebooks contain one lecture

on "The Evolution of Society: the Epoch of Barbarism", and another on the "History of Women", which examines the basis of matriarchy in the ancient world through a consideration of the writings of Engels, Darwin, Briffault and Lafargue. In 1941 she addressed the Durban-based Liberal Study Group, attended by NIC radicals, on the status of women; the following year the group formed a Women's Class, possibly inspired by Gool's talk.

4   Dr Goolam H. Gool (1905-62) was a British-trained physician who joined the Lenin Club in the early 1930s and initially supported the minority CLSA faction but later moved to the WPSA. He formed the NEF in 1937 and was briefly President of the NLL. He was a founding member and on the Executive of the AAC and the Anti-CAD and Vice-Chair of the NEUM but became profoundly disillusioned with NEUM politics in the 1950s. He was married to Halima Gool.

5   Benjamin M. Kies (1917-79) was a prominent Cape Town-based intellectual, active in the NEF and a leader in the TLSA, Anti-CAD movement and NEUM. Kies had a profound influence on several generations of political activists in the Western Cape, which reached a cult status despite verbal opposition to personality cults. In 1937 he was one of a younger generation of radicals who ousted the old-guard APO-supporting leadership of the TLSA, moving the organisation in a more radical direction. For many years a teacher at Trafalgar High School, in 1956 he was banned from teaching because of his political views and subsequently became an advocate. He edited the TLSA organ, *The Educational Journal*, as well as *The Torch*. His ideas on the origins of segregation and his thesis of "teachers as a vanguard" who could disseminate political ideas amongst the oppressed were extremely influential within NEUM circles. He presented the second A. J. Abrahamse Memorial Lecture, a triennial lecture delivered under the auspices of the TLSA, on 29 September 1953. His lecture, entitled *The Contribution of the Non-European Peoples to World Civilisation*, was published as a pamphlet. In the late 1950s he and Hosea Jaffe led an Anti-CAD faction within the NEUM which argued that many AAC leaders were moving towards bourgeois African nationalism. Although often associated in the public eye with Trotskyism, used as a pejorative label, Kies, like I. B. Tabata, put forward a left political alternative to Communist-Party orthodoxy and to black nationalism. Kies and his comrades created a critical intellectual climate around Cape Town that existed nowhere else in South Africa and has not existed since. However, their conception of politics excluded popular agitation and their scepticism about mass action eventually led to their political marginalisation.

6   *Herrenvolk* – German for "master race". The term carried connotations of Nazi Germany and could therefore be used to characterise the politics of the South African regime. This term was frequently used in NEUM discourse, along with the expression "quisling". Widkun Quisling was a Norwegian politician who collaborated with the German occupation forces during World War Two. The term was subsequently used to identify any collaborator with an alien and illegitimate regime. The NEUM's use of these terms arguably deflected from an explicit focus on class analysis and reinforced nationalist sentiments.

7   John Tengo Jabavu (1859-1921) was a teacher and editor of the influential Xhosa Eastern Cape weekly, *Imvo Zabantsundu* (Black Opinion), which expressed the aspirations of the emergent black petty bourgeoisie. Abdullah Abdurahman (1872-1940), a doctor who received his medical degree from Glasgow University in 1893, was President of the APO from 1905 to 1940. For many years he was a member of the Cape Town City Council. He was opposed in later years by a more militant younger generation of political activists, which included his daughter Cissie Gool. Francis Herman Gow (b. 1890), an educator and religious leader in the African Methodist Episcopal Church, served on the CAC. Pixley ka Izaka Seme (1881-1951), a lawyer by profession, was a principal founder of the ANC and a proponent of the notion of black economic self-help. He proposed the idea of upper and lower houses to represent chiefs and commoners in the ANC, based on the British bicameral system. Under his Presidency from 1930 to 1937, the ANC became increasingly conservative and inactive as he promoted the interests of the aspirant African commercial class and sought closer ties with chiefs. Abdulla Ismail Kajee (1898-1947) was a moderate Moslem businessmen who led the NIC from the mid-1930s until 1945, when he was sidelined by a more militant group led by G. M. Naicker. John Langalibelele Dube (1871-1946) was first President-General of the ANC until 1917 and remained President of the Natal ANC until 1945. He launched the *Ilanga lase Natal* (Natal Sun), Natal's first African paper, in 1903. Like Seme, he was an advocate of black self-help, yet their political relationship was marked by personal rivalry. Dube successfully fought the challenges of younger and more radical leaders in Natal, such as A. W. G. Champion and J. T. Gumede.

8   The SALP was formed in 1910 under the leadership of Colonel F. H. P. Cresswell on a white labour protectionist platform. It peaked in popularity around 1920 and thereafter declined. In 1924 it formed the Pact Government with the NP, and it split in 1928. From 1943 to 1958 it formed electoral pacts with the UP, and it finally ceased in 1958, when it lost all its Parliamentary seats.

9   In 1919 Clements Kadalie founded the ICU as a trade union of dockworkers in Cape Town, and that year

it successfully fought its first strike. In the 1920s it became less concerned with urban trade-union work and turned to organising in the rural areas. Its members included both Africans and coloureds.
10. By the late 1920s the ICU was weakened by state repression and by the personal rivalries and financial corruption of its leadership. William G. Ballinger (1894-1974) came to South Africa in 1928 as an advisor to the ICU but was unable to prevent its disintegration into hostile factions. In 1930-31 he represented the ICU at the Non-European Conferences. He was a member of the Joint Council movement, and from 1948 to 1960 he was a Natives' Representative in Senate for the Transvaal and Orange Free State. He helped found the Liberal Party but later lost sympathy with it. He was married to Margaret Ballinger.
11. In the 1930s the government restricted Indian occupancy of land in the Transvaal, and in 1943 the Pegging Act prohibited the transfer of property between whites and Indians in Durban for three years, closing off the main avenue of investment still available to Indians in Natal and the Transvaal. In 1946 the Pegging Act was extended throughout Natal and the Transvaal by the Asiatic Land Tenure and Indian Representation Bill, known as the Ghetto Act. This prohibited, with few exceptions, the further sale of property within Natal to Indians and introduced the notion of Indian communal political rights.
12. Daniel R. Koza (d. 1964) was a leading trade unionist in the 1930s and '40s. He worked with Max Gordon in the ACDWU and became its Secretary after Gordon's internment until his resignation in 1948. He was a member of the PTU in CNETU. He was involved with the AAC, attending its 1943, '44 and '48 conferences, and he was a founder of the ADP. At the AAC's December 1944 conference he represented the FIOSA and argued for the full recognition of African trade unions, including the right to strike. This became PTU policy. In the 1950s he was involved with the Johannesburg PF but grew more distant from the AAC and the NEUM and went to England to study. Isaac B. Tabata (1909-90), political activist and author and pre-eminent figure in the NEUM, was born near Queenstown in the Cape and educated at Lovedale and Fort Hare. In 1931 he left university and moved to Cape Town, where he worked as a truck driver, joined the Lorry Drivers' Union and became a member of its executive. He also joined the Cape African Voters' Association. In 1933 he began attending meetings of the Lenin Club with Goolam Gool and joined the WPSA. In the early 1940s he was one of a group of radicals who took over the leadership of the AAC, arguing for a boycott of all racial structures proposed by the government, and he was a founder of the NEUM. As an organiser for the AAC he made yearly trips to Transkei in the late 1940s and early '50s. He was banned in 1956. In 1961 he established and became president of APDUSA. Tabata was married to Jane Gool, sister of Goolam Gool, and an activist in the Anti-CAD, AAC and NEUM. They left South Africa in 1963 and lived in Tanzania, Zambia and Zimbabwe.
13. When the draft declaration was prepared, it was expected that the SAIC would be attending the Unity Conference, along with the AAC and Anti-CAD. Thus the original draft, reprinted in Karis and Carter (1973: 352-7), begins: "These three organisations ..."
14. Mrs Zainunnissa "Cissie" Gool (1900-63) was the charismatic daughter of Abdullah Abdurahman, sister-in-law of Goolam Gool and a prominent Cape Town political leader. In the early 1930s she unsuccessfully challenged her father's leadership of the staid APO; then, with James La Guma and John Gomas founded the NLL in December 1935, serving as its first President. She was a founder and first President of the NEUF, a member of the short-lived SASP and served on the CPSA's Political Bureau. From 1938 to the 1950s she represented District Six on the Cape Town City Council and for many years was the only woman on the Council. She was restricted under the Suppression of Communism Act. See Everett (1978).
15. Founded in 1902, the African Political Organisation – later renamed African People's Organisation – sought to extend the legal and political rights held by coloureds in the Cape Colony to those in the northern colonies. Led by Dr Abdullah Abdurahman, who was president from 1905 until his death in 1940, the APO was a significant political force until the mid-1920s, at its peak counting 20 000 members in 111 branches throughout southern Africa. It made overtures towards co-operation with Africans in the ANC. Later it became more of a mutual-benefit, burial and building society, and an object of scorn to the generation of coloured radicals entering politics in the 1930s.
16. Janub "Jane" Gool (1902-96) graduated from Fort Hare and became a teacher in Cape Town's District Six. In 1935 she, her brother Goolam Gool, and I. B. Tabata attended the inaugural meeting of the AAC, and from that time she became "part and parcel of African politics". She joined the Cape Town WPSA in the 1930s, was a founding member of the Anti-CAD, a leading activist in the AAC and NEUM and co-founder of APDUSA; she frequently spoke on international events. She was married to I. B. Tabata. Banned in 1961, two years later she and Tabata went into exile and lived in Tanzania, Zambia and Zimbabwe. In exile she represented the UMSA. She authored the pamphlet *The Crimes of Bantu Education*.
17. Dr Yusuf Mohammed Dadoo (1909-83) trained as a medical doctor in Britain, where he joined the ILP in Edinburgh and became involved in Indian anti-colonial agitation. On his return to South Africa, he became an activist in the TIC. His politics were influenced by Gandhi's notion of *satyagraha* and by an

advocacy of Non-European unity, and he was a founder of the NEUF in 1938. The next year he joined the CPSA. He was jailed in early 1941 for leading anti-war protests but, following the CPSA, reversed his position on the war once Germany invaded the Soviet Union. He became President of the TIC in 1945, moving it away from the politics of the Indian merchant class and giving it a more confrontationist style. He and other Communists were charged and tried for allegedly organising the 1946 African mineworkers' strike. In 1947 Dadoo, Dr A. B. Xuma and Dr G. M. Naicker signed the "Doctor's Pact" with the aim of promoting joint African-Indian action. This paved the way for the Defiance Campaign; Dadoo and Yusuf Cachalia represented the SAIC on the Campaign's Joint Planning Council. Dadoo was President of the SAIC in the early 1950s, and when the SACP was reconstituted as an underground organisation in 1953, he was on the Party's Central Committee. He was banned during the Defiance Campaign and left South Africa in 1960. In 1972 he became Chair of the SACP.

18 *Workers' Voice* was published by the Trotskyist CLSA 1935-6. In the 1940s the CLSA's successor, FIOSA, published both a newspaper and a theoretical organ by that name.
19 Archibald Percival Wavell, 1st Earl (1883-1950), was a professional soldier who attained the rank of Field Marshall. In June 1943 he was appointed Viceroy of India and was involved in continuing political negotiations about its future constitutional status. He released the Indian Congress leaders from prison in the summer of 1945. He was replaced as Viceroy by Earl Mountbatten in February 1947.
20 Leon Trotsky (1879-1940) was a Russian revolutionary and a leader of the October 1917 revolution. He founded the Red Army during the Russian Civil War. After Lenin's death in 1924 he was ousted from the Communist Party of the Soviet Union and exiled by Stalin. He was assassinated in Mexico by an agent of Stalin. The reference is to Trotsky's 1935 letter to the South African comrades, written in response to the draft theses of the Lenin Club's majority tendency, which became the WPSA. It was published in *Workers' Voice: Theoretical Supplement*, November 1944, and is reprinted in *South Africa's Radical Tradition*, Volume One.
21 The French Communist Party participated in the post-war French government. They had acquired legitimacy on account of their involvement in the resistance movement, but with the intensification of the Cold War they withdrew from the government in 1947. Post-war French governments were concerned to re-establish control over their overseas empire and many on the Left agreed with this policy.
22 Ernest Bevin (1881-1951) was a trade-union leader, a critic of the orthodoxy of interwar British economic policy and, from May 1940 to May 1945, Minister of Labour in the Churchill Coalition Government. He then served as Foreign Secretary in the post-war Labour administration and is generally regarded as one of the architects of Cold War diplomacy. His attitude towards Africa was essentially that it should provide primary materials for the industrial economies.
23 The 1924 Industrial Conciliation Act introduced a system of collective bargaining between employers and employees which effectively gave trade unions their long-pursued objective of legal protection. The system of industrial relations was criticised by the left as enshrining a principle of class collaboration but the legislation arguably facilitated the growth of white trade unions. Essentially, the Act was discriminatory on racial grounds. It excluded the agricultural, domestic and government sectors. Moreover, it did not incorporate pass-bearing Africans and indentured Indians. This was achieved by a narrow definition of "employee" so that exclusions included anyone whose contract of service came under the Native Labour Regulation Act of 1911, provincial pass laws and the Indian labour statutes of Natal. In the 1940s, political agitation aimed at winning recognition as employees for groups excluded under the Act. In 1947 the government presented the Industrial Conciliation ("Native") Bill which, with some support from secondary industry, gave some degree of recognition to African trade unions.
24 *Majority Rule: Some Notes* was originally serialised in the TLSA's organ, *The Educational Journal* (1929-79), and published by the TLSA as a pamphlet in 1982. This document gives the NEUM interpretation of the TARC episode. Victor Wessels (1929-79), considered to be the leading intellectual in the NEUM in the 1970s, was the son of Reverend Dan Wessels, a Moravian Minister in Hernandal. A graduate of Livingstone High School and of UCT, he later returned to teach at Livingstone, where he became renowned as a teacher. He was on the Executive of the TLSA and the Anti-CAD and a leading figure in the Unity Movement's educational fellowships. In 1968 he was transferred to Upington but was driven out of town two years later with the support of the security police and returned to Cape Town. He was banned from teaching in 1969 and subsequently ran a garage. He worked with the Municipal Workers' Association in Cape Town. A. E. "Sonny" Abdurahman, the TARC Secretary, was the nephew of Dr Abdullah Abdurahman.
25 *Freedom* was a publication of the CPSA.
26 Ruth First (1925-82), political activist, journalist and scholar, was the daughter of Baltic immigrants. First joined the CPSA while a student at the University of the Witwatersrand and was secretary of the Young Communist League and the Progressive Youth Council. When the CPSA leadership was arrested

following the 1946 African Mineworkers' Strike, she became temporary secretary of the Johannesburg CPSA office. Later, she became Johannesburg editor of *The Guardian* and editor of *Fighting Talk*. In the late 1950s she was a defendant in the Treason Trial, and she was detained in 1963. Through her journalistic work she illuminated the conditions of black farmworkers in Bethal. She published a number of monographs on southern African labour and politics and developed a reputation for being more intellectually tolerant of other Left perspectives than some of her more orthodox Party comrades. She was married to Joe Slovo. She was assassinated in Mozambique.

27 *The Guardian* was a weekly CPSA-aligned newspaper which began publication in February 1937 and was banned in May 1952, reappearing as *The Clarion*, then, due to successive bannings, as *People's World*, *Advance*, *New Age*, and *Spark*.

28 Davidson Don Tengo Jabavu (1885-1959), oldest son of J. T. Jabavu, studied at Lovedale and Morija Institution in Basutoland, received a bachelor's degree from the University of London and a diploma of Education from the University of Birmingham. On his return to South Africa in 1915, he was the first faculty appointment at Fort Hare, rising to become Professor of Bantu Languages. He was President of the AAC from its founding until 1948, preferring persuasion and gradualism to mass action. Alfred Bitini Xuma (c. 1893-1962) was a medical doctor and the first black person to get a Ph.D. from the London School of Tropical Medicine and Hygiene. In 1935 he became Vice-President of the AAC, and in 1939, President-General of the ANC, which he reorganised and rebuilt in the 1940s. In 1949 he was unseated by the more radical ANC Youth League.

29 This refers to "A Call for African Unity", which was signed by Xuma, Jabavu, Moroka, Matthews, Bokwe, Godlo, Mosaka, Baloyi, Champion, Selope Thema, Ntlabati and Mahabane, in Karis and Carter (1973:368-9).

30 Professor Z. K. Matthews (1901-68), educationist and political activist, studied at Lovedale College and at Fort Hare, and in 1923 became the first African to obtain a B.A. in South Africa. He became head of Adams College, and with Albert Luthuli attended the Durban Joint Council. In 1930 he became the first African to earn an LL.B. in South Africa and was admitted to the Johannesburg bar and the Transvaal division of the Supreme Court. In 1934 he obtained an M.A. from Yale University and then studied at the London School of Economics. In 1936 he became a lecturer at Fort Hare and in 1944, professor and head of the African Studies department. He served on numerous educational and political bodies, including the SAIRR. Matthews launched the AAC in 1935 with D. D. T. Jabavu. However, his loyalty lay with the ANC; he supported the ANC Youth League Programme of Action in 1949 and proposed the idea of a Freedom Charter in 1953. From 1942 to 1950 he was a member of the NRC.

31 Moses M. Kotane (1905-78) was a leading Communist and prominent member of the ANC. Having worked in various jobs, he joined the ANC in 1928 and the CPSA in 1929. He quickly became a full-time CPSA organiser and worked on *Umsebenzi*. From 1931 to 1932, he attended the Lenin School in Moscow. In the mid-1930s, coinciding with the Comintern's Peoples' Front period, he helped steer the Party away from the New Line. In 1935 he was removed from the CPSA political bureau because of a dispute with Lazar Bach, but with Bach's marginalisation, Kotane was reinstated. In 1939 he became CPSA General-Secretary, a post which he held until his death. He was banned in 1950, prosecuted for his participation in the Defiance Campaign in 1952 and was a Treason Trial defendant from 1956 to '58. In 1963 he went into exile. For his biography see Bunting (1975).

32 John B. Marks (1903-72) joined the CPSA in 1928, studied at the Lenin School in Moscow and became a full-time Party organiser and trade unionist upon his return. He was a member of the Party Politburo from 1930 to 1937 when he was temporarily expelled. In 1946 he was elected to the Party's Johannesburg District Committee and, shortly before its dissolution, to its Central Committee. He helped revive the ANC in the late 1930s, becoming a member of the Transvaal ANC Executive in the early 1940s. He helped form the AMWU in 1941 and was President of CNETU in 1945. In 1946 he was elected to the ANC National Executive. He was banned in 1952, left South Africa in 1963 and in 1969 became Chair of the SACP in exile.

33 The *Bunga* – literally council – refers to the United Transkeian Territories General Council, an African mock parliament controlled by white officials.

34 Gana Makabeni (d. 1955) was a Transkeian-born trade unionist, an ANC activist and a member of its National Executive Committee in the 1940s. He was elected to the CPSA Central Committee in 1926 but expelled in 1932 for supporting S. P. Bunting. Although he worked with Communists, he was concerned to build trade unions that were independent of both white and Communist domination. He was Secretary of the ACWU from 1928 to 1955 and helped found the CNETU in 1942 and became its President, to be replaced by J. B. Marks in 1945. Following the CPSA's banning in 1950, the balance of power shifted and he regained control of the Transvaal CNETU.

35 A. P. Mda (1916-93) was educated and began his teaching career in Catholic schools. His political career

began in the late 1930s as an ANC organiser in Orlando. He was a member of the ANC national executive, one of the founders of the ANC Youth League in 1944, and in 1947 became head of the Youth League. From 1949 he never held political office but he continued to be extremely influential in Africanist circles although he did not support the PAC's break with the ANC. Although socialist in outlook, he believed that Communists in the ANC were weakening African nationalism. In 1963 he went to Basutoland.
36 Oliver Tambo was born 1917 in Bizana, East Pondoland and received a B.Sc. at Fort Hare in 1941. He was a founder and leader of the ANC Youth League and, with Nelson Mandela, opened the first African law partnership in South Africa. He was banned in 1954 and '59 and went into exile. In the early 1960s he helped establish the short-lived united front of the ANC, SAIC and PAC. From 1967 to '77 he was ANC Acting President and in 1977 became its President-General, retiring due to ill health. His leadership was pragmatic and accommodationist, enabling the ANC to reign in its factions and present a unified face to the international community, unlike the strife-ridden PAC.
37 Robert Mangaliso Sobukwe (1924-78) was the pre-eminent intellectual and leader of the Pan-Africanist Congress. Sobukwe entered Fort Hare in 1947, where he became a leader of the ANC Youth League and a staunch supporter of the Programme of Action adopted in 1949. After his graduation in 1949, he worked as a teacher. He supported the Defiance Campaign but had minimal interaction with national ANC politics. In 1954 Sobukwe began teaching language at the University of the Witwatersrand and became involved with Africanist politics, editing *The Africanist*, but maintaining a behind-the-scenes profile. He advocated the Africanist breakaway from the ANC in November 1958 and became President of the PAC at its founding in 1959. Following his participation in the PAC's anti-pass campaign in March 1960, and the Sharpeville-Langa massacres, he was sentenced to three years' imprisonment. His sentence was extended by a special act known as the Sobukwe Clause, and he was released in 1969, subject to house arrest. In late 1975 he opened a law practice. For his biography see Pogrund (1990).
38 See Documents 13, 14 and 19. According to a report in *The Citizen Annual 1958*, the funds collected during the TARC campaign were never accounted for after the campaign's collapse.
39 Through the inspiration and campaigning of Eastern Cape political leader John Tengo Jabavu and the impetus of James Stewart, principal of the Lovedale Missionary Institute, the South African Native College opened in 1916 on land provided by the United Free Church of Scotland at the site of the Fort Hare military post. To many in the Eastern Cape it was *i koliji ka Jabavu*, Jabavu's College; it later became known as Fort Hare College. Initially, students studied matriculation subjects; later Unisa degree courses were added. Its students included Nelson Mandela, Oliver Tambo, Robert Mugabe and other future African leaders. In 1949 it affiliated with Rhodes University but in 1959 it came under the control of the Department of Bantu Education which redefined it as a university for Xhosa-speaking students only. In the 1960s it was a centre for the black consciousness movement and the site of student agitation in the 1970s and '80s.
40 This is most likely a reference to Tabata's letter to Nelson Mandela of 16 June 1948 which concerned the organisational question. Tabata argued that the ANC was a backward-looking and unprincipled organisation and thus that there was a contradiction between the parent body and the ANC Youth League which rejected inferior status and supported the boycott of racial structures. See Karis and Carter (1973:362-8).
41 John Gomas (1901-1979) joined the ANC, ISL and ICU in 1919. By 1923 he was a full-time ICU organiser, and in 1925 he joined the CPSA. His political development shows several turning points. In the 1930s he supported Comintern directives to form a popular front with white labour. By the 1940s he was alienated from the CPSA's increasing orientation to white labour and white parliamentary politics and was increasingly in agreement with Trotskyists, while attacking them for their practical inactivity. In the late 1940s Gomas was removed from the CPSA hierarchy but despite his declining role in the Party, he endorsed its electoral candidates and remained a member until it disbanded in 1950. In the early 1950s he tried to organise united fronts against apartheid in the Cape Peninsula. Gomas came to identify with the views expressed by disillusioned Communist George Padmore in *Pan-Africanism or Communism? The coming struggle for Africa*, ascribing the failure of black organisations to their attempts to please whites. In 1959 he joined the PAC. For his biography see Musson (1989).
42 This is probably a reference to the Anti-CAD. According to I. B. Tabata, Goolam Gool, who headed the Anti-CAD, was unable to call a meeting of its Executive because its members felt unable to discuss politics in the repressive atmosphere of the post-1948 apartheid era. The Anti-CAD failed to hold a conference for seven years (interview with Tabata and Jane Gool, Harare, 17 December 1987).
43 George John Golding (1906-60s) attended Zonnebloem College and became a teacher and principal in Cape Town. He became Chair of the CAC in 1943 and in 1944 founded and became President of the CPNU, a body which superseded the APO and later rivalled the SACPO which became part of the Congress Alliance. In the 1950s he attempted to challenge the government's removal of coloured voters from the common voters'

roll. He co-operated at various times with the opposition UP and with the government.
44 After the breakdown of the TARC, efforts to build united fronts in the Western Cape led to the formation of the FRAC in 1951. See Document 20.
45 Kenneth A. Jordaan (d. 1988), a teacher by profession, was a Cape Town-based socialist who worked in the FIOSA in the 1940s, the Forum Club in the 1950s and, with Hassan Bavassah, in the tiny, ephemeral Workers' Democratic League around 1960. Jordaan was highly respected by both Trotskyists and Communists for his theoretical writings of the 1940s and '50s. He went into exile in the early 1960s and was associated for a time with the PAC. He was a contributor to *Race and Class* but many of his writings remain unpublished. He died in Zimbabwe. *Discussion* was the organ of the Cape Town Forum Club, a discussion club of the early 1950s which represented the remnants of the FIOSA. In the late 1940s, the Fourth International advised South African Trotskyists in the FIOSA and WPSA to merge. Some of those in the smaller FIOSA, such as Hosea Jaffe and W. P. van Schoor, chose to join the NEUM, where the WPSA worked underground. Those who chose not to, including Jordaan, Arthur Davids, Eric Ernstzen and Zayed Gamiet, formed the Forum Club. On the Workers' Democratic League see *Lessons of the March Days*, Bulletin no. 1, September 1960, Mr. P. Duncan Papers, folder 8.71, Borthwick Institute, University of York.
46 The Anti-CAD movement published a series of bulletins with frequently acerbic commentary on a variety of political topics in the 1940s and '50s.
47 Fred Carneson (b. 1920) was from a white working-class family. During World War Two he fought in North Africa. He was Secretary of the CPSA Cape Town District Committee from 1945 to 1947 and joined the Central Committee in 1947. In 1949 he was elected to represent Africans in the Cape Provincial Council but was expelled because of his Party affiliation in 1952. He was a Treason Trial defendant and was jailed for over five years in the 1960s on the charge of organising for the underground SACP. After his release in 1972 he went into exile for a number of years.
48 The FRAC was formed in 1951 as an *ad hoc* alliance to contest the Separate Representation of Voters Bill, whose purpose was to whittle away the remnants of the coloured franchise. The Bill was placed before Parliament in March 1951. FRAC organised a political strike in Cape Town on 11 March 1951, with 15 000 marching through the city, and a similar event in Port Elizabeth on 7 May. The FRAC alliance did not include the NEUM, and the Anti-CAD opposed these events. For its viewpoint see *National Anti-CAD Statement on the Proposed "Political Strike" on 7th May, 1951*, 19 April 1951. This criticised the Franchise Action Council – said to comprise the Coloured People's National Convention and the former Franchise Action Committee – for its decision to call a political strike to defeat the Separate Representation of Voters' Bill and to defend the Non-European franchise. The Anti-CAD argued firstly, that the proposed strike was not a proper strike because it exempted certain "essential" workers in advance, thus dividing the workers; secondly, that the black people were not prepared for a strike because they were not organised in trade unions; and thirdly, that the people calling the strike were themselves supporting or working discriminatory institutions such as the CAC, which was a forerunner of the Separate Representation of Voters' Bill. The Bill was passed into law in June.
49 Sam Kahn, a lawyer by profession, joined the CPSA in 1930 and became a member of its Central Executive in 1938. He organised several trade unions, was active in the NLL, served on the Cape Town City Council from 1943 to 1952 and from 1949 to 1952 represented Africans of the Cape Western district in Parliament before his expulsion for being a Communist. He was banned in the mid-1950s and left South Africa in 1960.
50 *The Torch* was a newspaper of the NEUM edited by B. M. Kies. It was published in Cape Town from 1946 until 1962 and produced a Northern edition.
51 Edgar L. Maurice, the first Principal of the Harold Cressy High School established in 1950 in District Six, was for many years a leading figure on the TLSA Executive.
52 The Native Education (Eiselen) Commission of 1949 was chaired by Werner W. M. Eiselen, Professor of Bantu Studies at the University of Stellenbosch, who was Secretary of Native Affairs from 1949. It recommended separate education and mother-tongue instruction for Africans. These recommendations were implemented with the Bantu Education Act of 1953. The recommendations reflected the doctrine of Christian National Education, which was derived from Calvinist ideas and linked with the development of Afrikaner nationalism. The goal of Christian National Education was to prepare children to occupy their respective social positions in segregated society. It evolved in the 1870s in the Transvaal and the Orange Free State when the Dutch language and religion were reinstated in schools. After the Anglo-Boer War Christian National Education schools were established to oppose Lord Milner's policy of Anglicisation. It later became official NP policy.
53 Jan van Riebeeck (1619-77), a representative of the Dutch East-India Company, landed at the Cape on 6 April 1652 and founded the first white settlement. He was Commander of the Cape from 1652 to '62.

He imported slaves and fought the first war against Khoi pastoralists from 1659 to '60. In the early 1950s the planned countrywide Tercentenary Van Riebeeck Festival generated much political activity amongst black South Africans to promote a boycott of the celebrations, especially in the Cape Peninsula. K. A. Jordaan lectured a branch meeting of a teachers' union on Van Riebeeck's historical significance in early 1950, and in late 1951 he addressed a symposium sponsored by the Modern Youth Society on the subject. See Jordaan (1952). The NEUM successfully planned and promoted a boycott of the celebrations. Phyllis Ntantala (1992:149-52) recounts the work of the CATA, TLSA, SOYA and Anti-CAD in holding numerous local meetings on the need for a boycott, using the slogan "We Have Nothing to Celebrate". The NEUM's "Boycott the Van Riebeeck Celebrations" rally took place at the Grand Parade, Cape Town on 4 April. At the climax of the celebrations, 6 April 1952, the Transvaal ANC and TIC called for a "People's Protest Day", arguing that "This Van Riebeeck celebration cannot be a time for rejoicing for the Non-Europeans" (Karis and Carter 1973: 482-3).

54 This refers to the TLSA and the CATA. The union of the TLSA and CATA mentioned in the Discussion presumably refers to the Cape Teachers' Federal Council, founded by W. P. van Schoor of the TLSA and Leo Sihlali of CATA.
55 The Women's International Democratic Federation was a left-wing organisation aligned with the international Communist movement, with which FEDSAW was in contact but not formally affiliated.
56 FEDSAW was formed in 1954 by women leaders from the Congress movement, including Ray Alexander, Marcelle Goldberg, Helen Joseph, Florence Mkhize, Lillian Ngoyi, with a goal of uniting women across sectional lines. In 1955 and '56 the ANC Women's League and FEDSAW led several mass demonstrations against the extension of passes to African women (Karis and Carter 1973: 403-5). FEDSAW's history in the 1950s and '60s illustrates both the problems of subordination to a male-determined agenda and of political sectarianism. FEDSAW's decision to structure itself as a federated body aligned with the Congress movement rather than as an organisation based on individual membership cut it off from women who were outside that political tradition. Although Ray Alexander, for one, had favoured individual membership, after she was banned FEDSAW's national executive moved to the Rand, where the ANC and the Transvaal ANC Women's League were able to ensure a federal structure. Within the Congress movement, FEDSAW had second-class status, being refused official representation on the Congress Alliance.
57 Ray Alexander (b. 1913) immigrated to South Africa from Latvia in 1929, joined the CPSA and became a trade-union activist, noted particularly for her work in the FCWU. From 1938 to '50 she was on the CPSA's Political Bureau. In 1954 she was banned from labour activities. That year she was elected to represent Africans in the Western Cape in Parliament, following Sam Kahn and Brian Bunting, but was prevented from taking the seat. In 1965 she and her husband, H. J. Simons, went into exile for many years. They co-authored the seminal study, *Class and Colour in South Africa, 1850-1950*. Ida Fiye Mntwana (1903-60) was a women's leader and ANC activist. She joined the ICU in 1927, was the first President of the Transvaal ANC Women's League, was elected to the Transvaal ANC Executive in 1953 and became National President of FEDSAW in 1954. She was a leader in the women's anti-pass demonstrations in the 1950s. She was an organiser for the Congress of the People and a Treason Trial defendant from 1956 to '57.
58 The Bantu Education Act of 1953 implemented the recommendations of the Native Education (Eiselen) Commission of 1949. The Act removed African education from the Christian missions and placed it under the Department of Native (Bantu) Affairs. It specified that African students should study a special syllabus to prepare them for their inferior social position. In the words of Hendrik F. Verwoerd, Minister of Native Affairs from 1950 and later Prime Minister: "There is no place for [the Native] in the European community above the level of certain forms of labour. ... for that reason it is of no avail for him to receive a training which has as its main aim absorption in the European community". For a NEUM analysis, see Tabata's (1980) *Education for Barbarism: Bantu (apartheid) education in South Africa*, originally published in 1959. Ntantala (1992: 153-63) discusses NEUM/ANC/COD tensions in the struggle against Bantu Education, from a perspective sympathetic to the NEUM. The COD produced a pamphlet called *Educating for Ignorance*.
59 This refers to a popular anti-colonial uprising in Kenya, called "Mau Mau" by the British colonial authorities, which led to the imposition of a State of Emergency in the early 1950s.
60 Following the Defiance Campaign, the ANC faced criticisms for its lack of ideological clarity, both from the ANC Youth League and from the NEUM, which had its own Ten-Point Programme, and in August 1953 Professor Z. K. Matthews called for "... a Freedom Charter for the Democratic South Africa of the Future". The drafting of the Charter was conceived as a three-stage process attracting "Freedom Volunteers" throughout the country and linking up with the ANC's Western Areas and Bantu Education campaigns. Provincial committees were to establish local committees to elect delegates to draft the

Charter, however the local committees were largely stillborn. Initially, neither the COD nor SAIC were enthusiastic about the call for a Freedom Charter. However, as the campaign went on, Africanists criticised the high-profile role of COD whites. The seemingly disproportionate influence of COD whites, coupled with the Charter's multinational conception of the South African nation, which to Africanists denied the African majority their rightful possession of the land, exacerbated tensions between them and the rest of the ANC. The Charter's adoption at the Congress of the People in June 1955, before its acceptance by the ANC, intensified tensions in the ANC: Once the Congress of the People began to publicise the Charter, it became difficult for the ANC to amend it, despite pressure to do so. For instance, in October 1955 the Natal ANC Provincial Council passed a number of resolutions which they hoped to incorporate in the Charter, and which foreshadowed criticism by Africanists and others. The Natal amendments called for careful review before the ANC's endorsement, arguing, among other things, that its national clause emphasised racial distinctions rather than nation-building. Yet, when the ANC finally ratified the Charter in 1956, despite reservations by both Africanists and Natal delegates, the Natal amendments were not incorporated.

61 *Liberation* was a journal of the Congress Alliance. Albert John Luthuli (c. 1898-1967) was a Zulu chief and teacher who studied at and later became head of Adams College high school and was President-General of the ANC from 1952 to '67. He was subjected to a series of banning orders in the 1950s. In 1960 he was awarded the Nobel Peace Prize for his committed leadership of non-violent struggle against apartheid. His autobiography is entitled *Let My People Go*. He died under mysterious circumstances.

62 The Bantu National Congress was formed by S. S. Bhengu in early 1952. It was pro-apartheid and financed by Afrikaner nationalists and failed to gain any popular following, except among certain chiefs. In April 1954 Bhengu was convicted of theft and fraud and sentenced to prison. The National-Minded Bloc was led by R. V. Selope Thema and was concerned that whites and Indians were exerting undue influence on the ANC.

63 Xuma's letter was published as "Dr Xuma's Letter Congress Would not Read", *The World* (Johannesburg), Saturday, 28 January 1956. See Karis and Carter (1977: 242-5).

64 This refers to the followers of S. S. Bhengu, founder of the pro-apartheid Bantu National Congress.

65 Jordan K. Ngubane, a politician and journalist, was educated at Adams College, became assistant editor of *Ilanga lase Natal*, worked on the *Bantu World* and in 1944 became editor of *Inkundla ya Bantu*. He helped found the ANC Youth League in the early 1940s and, using his newspaper, assisted Albert Luthuli's rise to prominence. Ngubane was deeply critical of Communist influence in the ANC and moved to the Liberal Party in the 1950s, becoming its National Vice-Chair. He later became sympathetic to the PAC. He was banned in 1963 and went into exile. He later joined Inkatha. He is the author of several books, including *An African Explains Apartheid*.

66 Documents 25, 26 and 27 reflect Johnny Gomas' increasing disillusionment about the possibility of working with whites on an equal basis, a view which led him to join the PAC in 1959.

67 Edward R. Roux (1903-66), a botanist by profession, was one of the first South African-born white Communists. He helped establish the YCL as a student and, with Willie Kalk, pushed it to recruit blacks. He joined the CPSA in 1923 and was profoundly influenced by S. P. Bunting. He was elected Vice-Chair in December 1924. Along with Bunting, he fought for greater interaction with black workers. He attended the Sixth Comintern Congress in 1928 and became a supporter of the Native Republic thesis despite initial opposition. In the 1930s, increasingly critical of Comintern intervention, he was marginalised within the Party and left in 1936. In 1944 he wrote a biography of Bunting, and in 1948, *Time Longer than Rope*, the first major and still indispensable study of the liberation struggle. He pioneered Easy English, a technique for teaching English as a second language. From 1957 to 1963 he was a member of the Liberal Party, and he was banned in 1964. For his autobiography see Roux (1972).

68 This refers to E. S. "Solly" Sachs (1901-76), born in Lithuania and described by his brother, Bernard Sachs (1959: 44-59), as a "Talmudist and rebel", a political pragmatist who was "the perfect apparatus man" and an admirer of Stalin's political realism. Solly Sachs was expelled from the CPSA in September 1931. His life's work was the predominantly Afrikaner and female Garment Workers' Union, to which he was elected Secretary in November 1928, and which was the subject of his book, *Rebels' Daughters* (1957). Sachs believed in the progressive potential of white workers. Disillusioned with the SALP, he launched the ILP in 1943, which proved an immediate non-starter, but in the 1950s he still hoped to build a strong Labour Party. He was forced to resign from the GWU in 1952 under the Suppression of Communism Act and later went into exile in Britain.

69 Patrick Duncan (1918-67) was the son of Sir Patrick Duncan, former Governor-General of South Africa. Through the course of his life, he became increasingly radicalised. From 1941 to '52 he was in the British colonial service in Basutoland, where he became fluent in Sesotho. He resigned his post in 1952 to participate in the Defiance Campaign. Passionately anti-Communist, he joined the Liberal Party in 1955,

became its National Organiser and edited *Contact*. He resigned from the Liberal Party in 1963 in opposition to its non-violent stance and joined the PAC, which he represented in exile. His papers are in the Southern African Archives, Borthwick Institute, University of York.
70 *New Age* was a newspaper aligned with the Congress Alliance and run by a collective of Communists, including Lionel Forman, Brian Bunting, Sonia Bunting, Fred Carneson and Alex La Guma in Cape Town, Govan Mbeki in the Eastern Cape, M. P. Naicker in Durban and Ruth First, Michael Harmel and Ivan Schermbrucker in Johannesburg. Forman and Odendaal (1992: xxiii) write: "... these few individuals largely shaped the policy of the paper. Their world view and politics to a large extent became those of the liberation movement."
71 In 1956 the Industrial Conciliation Amendment Act required "mixed" unions – those with white and coloured or Indian members – to split into racially-divided unions or form separate racial branches controlled by white executives, and it ended future recognition of such "mixed" unions. The Act authorised the government to declare strikes in essential industries illegal and facilitated job reservation for whites.
72 Brian Bunting (b. 1920) – a Communist, journalist and author and the son of S. P. Bunting. He worked on the *Rand Daily Mail*, *Sunday Times* and after World War Two edited a number of newspapers, including *The Guardian* and its successors, *Advance*, *Clarion*, *Peoples' World* and *New Age*. In 1946 he was elected to the CPSA's Johannesburg District Committee, and he later became a member of the CPSA Central Committee. From 1952 to '53 he was a Natives' Representative in the House of Assembly but was expelled because of his CPSA membership. He was banned and detained, and in 1963 went into exile, where he was an editor of *The African Communist*.
73 The Multi-Racial Conference was held at the University of the Witwatersrand, 3 to 5 December 1957. The idea came from the Conference of the Interdenominational African Ministers' Federation, which was held in October 1956 to consider the Tomlinson Report. At the time, most of the ANC leadership was involved in the Treason Trial, and neither the ANC nor the SACP wanted to convene the conference on their own initiative. Alan Paton played a key role in organising the conference. Attendance was diverse and included representatives from IDAMF, SAIRR, ANC, the Black Sash, SAIC, SALP and individuals such as the flamboyant Alexandra Africanist Josias Madzunya, Vic Goldberg, who represented the COD, and Baruch Hirson. The NEUM and its affiliates did not attend. The conference called for the creation of a common society, for universal adult suffrage on a common voters' roll (despite different views on how to achieve that goal) and for a constitutional Bill of Rights. The Communist M. D. Naidoo's call to carry the struggle to the masses was withdrawn in favour of Archbishop Hurley's more moderate proposal for a continuing body to carry out the conference resolutions.
74 The 1950s saw the formation and development of a number of women's organisations and movements. The Black Sash was formed in 1955 as the Women's Defence of the Constitution League but it became known for the sashes worn by its members to symbolise their mourning for attacks on the constitution. Although membership was open to all women residents of South Africa, in practice it was a white organisation. The Mothers' Union was an organisation linked to the Anglican Church and concerned to uphold traditional values of motherhood and family. Its members' participation in the struggles against the extension of passes to African women is detailed in Hooper (1989).
75 Mao Zedong (Mao Tse-tung) (1893-1976) was the leader of the Chinese Communist Party from 1935 and developed a political strategy influenced heavily by the specific circumstances of Chinese society, particularly the place of the peasantry. From 1949 he was the leader of the People's Republic of China. He identified increasingly with a socialist strategy distinct from that of the Soviet Union, culminating in the Sino-Soviet rift of 1960.
76 The Atlantic Charter was drawn up by British Prime Minister Winston Churchill and U. S. President F. D. Roosevelt in August 1941. The Charter's emphasis on human rights was seized upon by black South African activists. They argued that South Africa, as a wartime ally of the anti-fascist Allies, had a moral obligation to apply the Charter to its own affairs. At its annual conference in December 1943, the ANC adopted a charter of rights entitled *Africans' Claims in South Africa* (Karis and Carter 1973: 209-23), which was modelled on the Atlantic Charter. The demands included the abolition of racial discrimination, an equal franchise, no restrictions on movement and residence, and a range of egalitarian economic and social reforms. The agenda subsequently made an impact at the UN and at congresses of the Pan-Africanist movement. The UN Charter was drafted during the war and the UN formally established in October 1945. In December 1948 the UN General Assembly adopted the Universal Declaration of Human Rights, which entailed a pledge by UN member states to guarantee both civil and social rights.
77 *The Citizen*, published in the late 1950s, represented the views of a number of Cape Town-based individuals disillusioned both with the NEUM and with the Congress Alliance. Many of the group later joined the Liberal Party.
78 *Analysis* was an ephemeral publication of the Socialist League of Africa.

79 Wycliffe Mlungisi Tsotsi was born in Transkei and educated at Fort Hare. He was principal of Freemantle School for Boys and later became a lawyer. He was a member of the Transkei Teachers' Association until its merger with the CATA, and he helped to politicise CATA and pushed for its affiliation to the AAC. He was a leading figure in the AAC and its President from 1948 to '59, coming under increasing attack from its left-wing. In the 1960s he moved to Basutoland and then to Zambia, where he worked as a lawyer for the Zambian government. *Ikwezi Lomso* (Morning Star), edited by Livingstone Mqotsi in the late 1950s, details the activities of the AAC and the TOB in Transkei. It discusses the tensions and split in the AAC and other NEUM affiliates from the point of view of the AAC leadership.

80 In 1954 the government-appointed Tomlinson Commission outlined a programme for the rehabilitation of the African reserves premised on the assumption that South Africa would never become a unified society. Although its proposals for extensive investment to stabilise the reserves were not followed through by the government, its Report served as the basis for the policy of separate development adopted by the government of H. F. Verwoerd.

81 R. Mettler was a pseudonym of Baruch Hirson. Hirson, a physicist by profession who taught at the University of the Witwatersrand, was a Johannesburg-based socialist who entered politics through the Hashomer Hatzair, a Jewish youth group, worked in the Trotskyist WIL in the 1940s, and in the 1950s, with the PF, a NEUM affiliate. He broke with the NEUM over the issue of how to fight the extension of apartheid to universities. He later worked in the COD and in the tiny Socialist League of Africa, which criticised the COD from the left. In the early 1960s he became involved with the NCL/ARM, was imprisoned for nine years and upon release went into exile in England, becoming a historian. For his autobiography see Hirson (1995). *It is time to awake* was a critique of Tabata's *The All-African Convention: The awakening of a people*, which Hirson himself had published in 1950 under the name of "People's Press". A copy of *It is time to awake* is at the Borthwick Institute, University of York, and in the Karis-Carter microfilm collection. For another Trotskyist perspective of Tabata's book see Arthur Davids, "A Critical Analysis of I. B. Tabata's Book – *The All-African Convention*", Cape Town: Forum Club, reprint, *Discussion*, 1, 2 [c. December 1950].

82 Kwame Nkrumah (1909-71) was a Ghanaian politician and proponent of Pan-African unity. He was educated in the U.S. and Britain and in 1945, co-chaired the Fifth Pan-African Congress in Manchester. On returning to the Gold Coast, he became Secretary-General of the United Gold Coast Convention but subsequently formed the Convention People's Party. He was Prime Minister from 1952 to '57, when Ghana became independent, and he continued in that post until 1960, when Ghana became a republic and he became President. His domestic policies became increasingly repressive, and he was later deposed by a military coup and exiled.

83 SOYA's formation in 1951, largely at the direction of I. B. Tabata, was a response to the increasing numbers of African workers in towns and mounting pressure from NEUM youth for more township activity. It was also an attempt to counter the growing influence of the ANC amongst students and urban youth. To compete with the ANC Youth League, SOYA began as an African-only youth grouping geared especially to the political education of working-class Africans. Its membership became non-racial in the mid-1950s, including coloureds and Indians, yet many members maintained an Africanist orientation. It had branches in the Transvaal, Western and Eastern Cape and Natal, and at Fort Hare, virtually all those connected with it were blacklisted in 1954. The formation of and opposition to SOYA within the NEUM reflected mounting tensions and rivalry, indicated by SOYA's affiliation to the AAC, rather than directly to the NEUM. Hosea Jaffe, who played a central role in the Cape Peninsula educational fellowships, vigorously opposed SOYA's formation. This pamphlet represents the views of the Wits SOYA. Possibly because of geographic proximity to those AAC officials who lived around Johannesburg, the Wits SOYA was particularly subject to pressure and criticism by the AAC leadership and, due to its more explicitly socialist line, it was expelled in the late 1950s, in contrast to the Cape Town SOYA which followed Tabata.

84 The New Era Fellowship was a radical discussion and debating society which was formed by Goolam Gool in 1937 and which ran until the late 1960s. It met at the Stakesby Lewis Hostel and in the Fidelity Hall on the edge of District Six in Cape Town. W. P. van Schoor addressed its first meeting with a lecture on "Imperialism". It provided a forum for black students at UCT who were isolated from the university's all-white intellectual life. Its speakers included UCT lecturers, such as Lancelot Hogben and Frederick Bodmer, as well as foreign visitors, and it attracted political activists and people outside the university. It initiated the campaign against the CAC, launching the Anti-CAD on 28 February 1943. The views of some of its leading members are found in *Trek*, published in Cape Town. The NEF's success led to the formation of a network of fellowships throughout the Cape Peninsula, a venture in which Hosea Jaffe was centrally involved. Fellowships were set up in the Cape Flats, South Peninsula, Southern suburbs, Northern areas, Langa and Paarl and eventually in Port Elizabeth and Kimberley. Their audience was often mainly coloured and middle-class.

85 A. C. Jordan (1906-68), a leading African literary writer and intellectual, was born in Transkei and educated at St John's College, Lovedale and Fort Hare. In 1956 he received a Ph.D. from UCT, where he lectured in African languages. He was a prominent member of the AAC and NEUM but was ostracised over disagreements about how to fight the extension of apartheid to universities. He was married to Phyllis Ntantala. In the early 1960s he and his family went into exile. From 1964 he was a professor of African Studies at the University of Wisconsin, Madison.
86 Leo Linda Sihlali (1915-89) studied at Lovedale Missionary Institution and Fort Hare and later received a B.A. from Unisa. A teacher by profession, he was a leading figure in the CATA, AAC and NEUM. In the 1940s he was involved in the struggle against Rehabilitation in Transkei, and he successfully pushed for CATA's affiliation to the AAC. From 1951 to '53 he was President of CATA and from 1953 to '55, editor of its organ, *The Teacher's Vision*. In 1951, along with W. P. van Schoor, he formed the Cape Teachers' Federal Council, an umbrella organisation linking CATA and TLSA, and became its first President. In 1955 he and the entire CATA Executive were dismissed from their teaching positions because of their opposition to Bantu Education; Sihlali subsequently worked as a shop assistant. CATA successfully sued the government for wrongful dismissal using Sihlali's appeal as a test case. In 1956 he became General-Secretary of the AAC and in 1960 was a founding member of the APDUSA. In the 1960s he was banned, house-arrested and imprisoned for three years on Robben Island. He spent his last years in Mount Frere, and in the 1980s supported the New Unity Movement.
87 Sefton Vutela, Secretary of the Wits SOYA, was expelled from Fort Hare in the late 1950s for leading student protests. He moved to the Johannesburg area where he and several other CATA members tried to push the SOYA and the NEUM to engage with mass politics, through their leadership of residents' associations and of protests against advisory boards. At the time, Vutela and his circle were committed to Tabata and thought that in pushing for the NEUM's involvement in mass politics they were implementing his ideas. Thus, they did not align themselves with left critics of the NEUM, such as Baruch Hirson, on the one hand, and Austin Lepolesa, Ismail Mohamed and Roseinnes Phahle, on the other. However, Vutela's circle was opposed in its initiatives by other supporters of Tabata, who included Jennifer Davis, Andrew Lukele, Dr Saloojee and Edna Wilcox, Victor Sondlo and Norman Traub, on the grounds that they were winning the "heads" – i.e. the leading positions – but not the "bodies" of popular organisations. Both the Vutela circle and the Lepolesa circle were later expelled from the SOYA and the AAC. Lepolesa subsequently joined the ANC Youth League.

# Part One

## Building the national movement

*Uses of the boycott*

***EDITOR'S NOTE***
*South Africa's racially exclusive political system led popular movements to consider the tactic of boycotting racial institutions. For many on the Left, the issue was not simply that the South African Parliament was a reformist institution but that it was a racist institution. In comparative perspective, the boycott has taken both economic and political forms, with the former exemplified by the Irish peasantry's rent withholding campaigns of the 1870s to the 1880s, and the latter, by the responses of socialists and nationalists to cosmetic political institutions such as the Russian Duma of 1906 or the limited political openings available to colonised peoples. South African progressives interpreted these traditions in various ways in light of their own immediate circumstances.*

## Document 32
## Babeuf [K. A. Jordaan], "A History of the Franchise in S. Africa", *Workers' Voice*, 5, 5, September 1946

In the course of 36 years since the establishment of Union, the Africans, the Coloureds and the Indians have gradually been deprived of their franchise rights, rights which constitute the most elementary features of political democracy. The last decade has witnessed the reduction of the African vote to an empty system of representation, the attempt to put the Coloureds on a separate voters' roll and the reduction of the Indian franchise to a communal vote and separate representation. This year, thousands of Non-Europeans, constituting over 80 per cent of the total population, number less than 3 per cent of the total electorate. It is therefore clear that as far as the franchise is concerned, the Non-Europeans have ceased to be of any political force in the country, and thus they have ceased, by legal and constitutional means, to have a hand in the shaping of their own destiny.

Parallel with the dwindling of political rights has gone the tightening up of the colour bar system, of segregation, of discriminatory legislation – in short, of the development to perfection of the system of exploitation and oppression.

In the struggle for national liberation from oppression and the attainment of full democratic rights, it is necessary that we formulate a thorough and consistent attitude to the franchise and assess its place in the liberatory movement. And this means nothing more than that we have first of all to understand the franchise today not only in its social and economic setting, but in the light of the historical forces which have moulded it and made it what it is to-day; and what these forces will make of it in the future unless new forces intervene.

The complexity of the franchise system in South Africa is the mirror of the complex social and economic structure of this country – a structure which has baffled even the most tried foreign revolutionaries, a structure which the leadership of the national liberatory forces must learn to understand and master in the task of building up a revolutionary movement. No apology is, therefore, needed for this historical analysis of the franchise.

One of the most fundamental features of the history of South Africa is the slow tempo of her development. Regarded for almost [-] years by Dutch and British commercial capitalism as a half-way house, as a refreshment station, and finally as a military outpost to serve the interests of distant lands and a foreign merchant class, this vast sub-continent was condemned to a long and dreary backwardness. Up to 1815 the Cape was not regarded as a colony in the normal sense of the term. There was no large-scale colonization of the Cape during this period; nor did the Company encourage wide-scale expansion into the interior.[1] The duty of the Company's officials was to enforce and protect the Company's monopoly and further in every conceivable way the interests of the foreign merchants. The officials were the government of the Cape. Since they had to further the interests of a class which was not inside but outside the Colony, and since the few colonists here were in a position of subservience, there was no need for representative or electoral institutions; there was no need for a franchise. The economy of the Cape was based, during this period, on slave-labour and the labour of the Hottentots, whose tribal life was disintegrating, and who were transformed into semi-serfs; because of their economic status the latter had no hope of having a voice in the government or any government based on property qualifications in the near future.

The Congress of Vienna, 1815, gave the Cape permanently to Britain[2] *[....]* The Cape now came to be regarded as a potential colony; immigration was encouraged, expansion into the interior and colonization took place rapidly, and commercial and industrial activities on the part of the rising burgher class were allowed to develop. Britain decided to give the Cape electoral institutions in order to further the interests of these colonists. But these electoral institutions were strictly subordinated to the Imperial Government, so that the imperialist could gain a strong foothold here and with the help of the colonists exploit the new Colony under the cloak of representative institutions. *[....]*

**Babeuf, "A History of the Franchise in S. A.", *Workers Voice*, 6, 1, July 1947**
(Continued from last issue.)
THE FRANCHISE IN BRITISH COLONIES
Having obtained a strong foothold in the country, Britain was able to grant the Cape and Natal Responsible Government, whereby the executive became responsible to an elected legislature, a government which was strengthened to further the interests of the rising bourgeoisie and to pass legislation for the further subjection and exploitation of the Non-Europeans. The vote, with the same qualification, was extended to the Indians who came to Natal from 1860 onwards to serve as cheap labour on the sugar plantations. So very few Non-Europeans could qualify for the vote that the government was prepared to allow political equality for the time being. The franchise in the Cape Colony remained the same until 1892, when the qualifications were raised because a cry arose that "blanket kaffirs" were getting on the register. *[....]* We must regard the reduction of the non-European vote from this period as part of the general plan of the imperialists to deprive the black population of a voice in the affairs of the country so that the imperialists could perfect, unhindered, the system of race oppression and exploitation as it is known to the bulk of the population today. The political status of a people is a reflection of their economic status and a change in the former is fundamentally dependent upon a change in the latter. *[....]*

THE BOER WAR AND THE UNION
In 1899 the Boer War broke out, a war fought for the control of the gold and other

mineral fields in the north and thus, indubitably, for the control of the economic and political life of the country.[3] And Union can be regarded as a conciliation when Britain decided to enlist the support of the weakened Boers and the white population in general to act as her hangman in the exploitation of the country which very fittingly was incorporated into the British Commonwealth with full self-government. Full self-government for South Africa within the Empire was given after the complete economic and political triumph of the imperialists. This self-government was to act as an effective means for furthering the total subjection of the black population. With the widening of political democracy for the whites and the furtherance of their economic interests, on the one hand, have gone the tightening up of the colour-bar and segregation and exploitation of the blacks and the seizure of their political rights, on the other.

The franchise systems of the four different colonies differed radically in many respects and it is clear that the Union of the colonies could only have been accomplished if a more or less uniform system was adopted for the whole country. [....]

The result was a compromise. The Cape had to give up the right of Non-Europeans to sit in Parliament, a right which had, however, never been exercised because of the high wage and property qualifications. By entrenching the franchise clause in the South African Constitution, dealing with the Cape Non-European vote, the National Convention decided to play up to the backwardness of the old "Cape liberal" policy, a policy which was, however, becoming more and more doomed to death in the face of the supreme legislative body representing all the provinces. The legislative supremacy of Parliament left the door wide open for further inroads on Non-European political rights. [....]

## THE FRANCHISE SINCE UNION

[....] We have to consider and explain the development of the franchise out of the whole social and economic system of the country, a system which relegates the Non-Europeans to the position of wage slaves. The tightening up of the colour bar, of segregation, the lowering of the wages of African mine and farm workers were done not only for the super-exploitation of the blacks, but also so that the whites might be able to live better, to get the best jobs and prosper economically. The formal democracy and economic prosperity of the whites were achieved only at the expense of the Non-Whites. Imperialism uses its 10% democracy of the whites as the instrument for the total subjection of over 80% of the population. The reduction of the Non-White vote was meant to give the ruling class a free hand in the exploitation of the country, unhindered by the desires, the representations of the vast bulk of the population. To the white population South Africa is a formal democracy; to the black population South Africa is the dictatorship of imperialism. [....]

## REPRESENTATION

In the system of representation a similar policy is followed to reduce the political influence of the Non-Europeans. [....]

The policy of separate voters' rolls and separate representation has gone hand in hand with the policy of segregation and the colour bar. It reduces the African vote to a barest minimum. It also means that the Africans cannot elect even one militant member to Parliament.

An attempt was made in 1943 and is still continuing to place the Coloured on a separate voters' roll by the creation of the Coloured Advisory Council. To help prevent real Non-European unity the Government has preserved the small number of Coloured voters on the White electoral roll. In any case this vote is insignificant, and to date the Government has thought it unnecessary to put them on a separate roll.

To round out its system of separate "representation" and hamper the building of Non-European unity, the Government suddenly, in 1946, put the Indians on a separate roll, granted them a communal franchise and European representation in Parliament akin to that of the Africans.

It is clear that, with the ever increasing exploitation of the black population by colour bar laws, segregation, wage-cuts and a cheap labour policy, imperialism was able to achieve and maintain its unique position, both with regard to itself and the white population. With extra pay for whites, a white labour aristocracy, privileged jobs and full democracy, imperialism has rewarded the Herrenvolk to act as their instruments of oppression. The basis for the white political democracy is, in short, the complete subjugation of the blacks. It is impossible for any Nationalist Party or a party with strong fascist tendencies to rule without the help of the imperialists, for the latter alone have the wealth, the power, to maintain the privileged position of the Whites and the subjection of the Non-Europeans.

Our struggle for national liberation from imperialist oppression is the struggle for full democratic rights, for all races. This struggle is inextricably bound up with a change in the economic and social system of the country. For the franchise is the reflection of the economic supremacy of the Whites and the oppression of the Blacks. And this change can only come about by the relegation of imperialism to the rubbish heap of history, for it has built up the social, economic and political system in this country with the help of its hangers-on, the Herrenvolk. We thus co-ordinate the struggle for full political rights with a social and economic reconstruction and a successful struggle against imperialism. Only petty bourgeois nationalists can imagine that full democracy can be achieved without an anti-imperialist struggle and programme.

And how is full democracy to be achieved? Many legalists say that the Non-Europeans will never get full democracy for the Government will never grant them that. In its essentials legalist reformism implies the submission of the oppressed to the laws and institutions of the oppressor. The imperialists and their hanger-on have "legalised" and "constitutionalised" their dictatorship over the Non- Europeans after the use of brute force. We can only achieve full democracy after the use of mass organised methods of struggle, achieving out goal "peacefully if possible, through force if necessary." The transfer from capitalism to socialism will result not at all from formal democratic principles [-] above society, but from the material conditions of development of society itself. We consider it as reactionary to judge the movement from the point of view of the judicial principles of legality. No slave parliament, no government which maintains its constitution and economic and political structure and dictatorship by force will ever dream of making or allowing a peaceful transfer to socialism. "Not believing in force," says Trotsky "is the same as not believing in gravitation." Our road to universal suffrage and therefore a free entrance into the historical processes at work in society lies through social revolution. Class force in the struggle for liberation and democracy lies not in parliament but outside parliament, in the revolutionary working class. But, while we aim at the complete overthrow of bourgeois institutions, we must temporarily avail ourselves of them in our fight for liberation, for this would prove a real education for the workers. Despite and because of the totally reactionary nature of the Government and Parliament of this country, we are not prepared, like many abstentionist petty bourgeois nationalists have done, to turn our backs on Parliament. Our policy has always been to give our critical support for working-class candidates, and to strengthen the development of independent labour political forces. That is why the American Trotskyists, the Socialist Workers' Party, call for a labour party, why the British Trotskyists said "Labour to power" in the 1945 general election; why F.I.O.S.A. has supported Communist Party candidates in elections in South Africa, why we put up a condidate for municipal elections in 1945. Both the boycotting of institutions (C.A.C., N.R.C., etc.), and making use of elections, serve to educate the working class if they form part of the class struggle and the struggle for democracy.

We stand for the education of the revolutionary class, the working class in its struggle against the rulers; and for the social revolution and the reconstruction of society which will reduce the Union slave-parliament, and all bourgeois organs and imperialism to dust and bring equal rights to all.

**Published in the interests of the 4th International Organisation of S. Africa**

## Document 33
"Views on Boycott: Majority Support at Emergency Conference", *The Guardian*, 12 June 1947

**Johannesburg**, – Mr. William Ballinger told the emergency conference of the Transvaal African National Congress held in Johannesburg last week-end that he was still not certain whether he would stand as a candidate in the Transkei by-election.

The Conference passed a resolution calling on all native urban and other advisory boards to adjourn indefinitely in support of the adjournment of the Native Representative Council.

During a stormy session of the conference, a small group of delegates led by Councillor P. Mosaka, and supported by Senator Basner, Mrs. Ballinger, M.P., and Mr. Ballinger, spoke against the Congress decision to boycott elections under the 1936 Native Representation Act.[4]

A motion calling for a national conference to rescind this decision was defeated by 42 votes to 14.

CONFERENCE DECISIONS
The Conference decided the Smuts proposals to members of the N.R.C. should be completely rejected; a campaign for full franchise and citizenship for the African people be embarked upon; the Industrial Conciliation (Natives) Bill uncompromisingly opposed; and the Congress decision to boycott elections under the 1936 Act immediately implemented by a country-wide campaign.

Opening the conference, the Transvaal president, Mr. C. Ramahanoe, spoke of the deadlock between the Government and the native Representative Council. "One section of the representatives of the African people are on strike," he said, "but the other section continues as if nothing has happened.

"Mr. Ballinger is the very man we are glad to see at this conference. The people of the Transkei have decided to boycott the by-election but in spite of this Mr. Ballinger says he will continue to contest the seat."

## XUMA SPEAKS OUT

Dr. A.B. Xuma made a strong attack against the executive committee of the Bantu Men's Social Centre which had refused the use of the centre hall to the Congress, the Council of Non-European Trade Unions, and the African Democratic Party. "If this is to be the policy of the centre we must pray to be saved from our friends."

Mrs. Ballinger told the conference she had taken every opportunity to tell the Prime Minister that the Government is allowing a dangerous and unhealthy situation to develop. She had told him it was no use saying the country's Native policy was working well. "Since Smuts' Government came into power there has been a conspicuous narrowing of the liberties of the African people," she said.

## "IMPRACTICABLE"

During the afternoon Councillor Mosaka bitterly criticized Congress leadership. When it was suggested he was not talking to the point Mr. Mosaka retorted: "I adjourned the N.R.C. Listen to the man who adjourns the Council."

Mr. Mosaka then said the boycott is impracticable. "If the anti-C.A.D. people had stood for the C.A.C. it would have embarrassed the Government as completely as the adjournment of the N.R.C. has today...We have a choice of killing the N.R.C. from within or without. We should choose our men and kill this animal from within...I want a clear lead."

Senator Basner said he thought the boycott resolution so silly that he did not think grown men would waste a whole day talking about it. He gave his assurance that if the boycott were carried through he would not stand for re-election. "But before you carry it out you will have the fight of your lives from me and from others."

Mr. Edwin Mofutsanyana pointed out that the conference was not competent to discuss the boycott as though a resolution on it had never been taken by the Congress. "We need discussion on the practical ways of carrying out the decision. The people of Jabavu and Moroka are facing an advisory board election. We must tell them to boycott these elections."

Miss Josie Palmer said: "Give the people a lead and they will act."[5]

Mr. A.M. Lembede said his advice to Senator Basner and Mr. and Mrs. Ballinger was that they should not stand for any further elections under the 1936 Act.[6]

Large numbers of delegates from Congress branches and other organizations attended this all-day conference.

---

## Document 34
Moses M. Kotane, "Boycott of Elections under the 'Representation of Native Act'", *Freedom*, 6, 5, September–October 1947

**A BLOW FOR DEMOCRACY**

When at the Emergency Conference of Africans, on October 7, 1946, the delegates by 495 votes to 16 decided to boycott all elections under the Representation of Natives

Act of 1936, they took one of the most important decisions in the struggle for democracy in South Africa.

The importance of the boycott decision lies in the fact that it is a practical effort to remove the veil behind which the political enslavement, economic strangulation and social degradation of the African people are perpetrated and perpetuated.

The decision has riled and infuriated the ruling class and its press, shown up the "Native Representatives" and many of the so-called friends of the Native, and has embarrassed some of the African leaders. But it enjoys the full and wholehearted support of the overwhelming majority of politically minded Africans.

## HOW IT STARTED

The adjournment of the Native Representative Council set the ball rolling. It will be remembered that the Native Representative Council adjourned its session indefinitely in August, 1946, as a protest against the reactionary Native policy of the Government. The legislation affecting the Non-European in South Africa.

## BOYCOTT DECISIONS

Following the adjournment of the Native Representative Council, the Transkei Organised Bodies in conference at Umtata on the 29th September, 1946, unanimously decided:–

(a) "that this conference of the Transkei Organised Bodies endorses the step taken by the Native Representative Council to adjourn its session and in calling upon the Government forthwith to abolish all discriminatory legislation affecting Non-Europeans in this country;

(b) "that this conference unconditionally rejects the policy of racial discrimination embodied in the 1936 legislation and allied discriminatory laws ...." It called "upon the members of the N.R.C. forthwith to discontinue their service in that Council."

Decision (a) above was telegraphed to the Emergency Conference of Africans held at Bloemfontein on the 6th and 7th October, 1946.

The Emergency Conference was attended by 511 delegates. After debating for two days the line to be adopted in the situation which has arisen, the delegates by 495 votes to 16:

(a) endorsed in full the action taken by the Native Representative Council;

(b) called upon all Councillors to attend the meeting convened for the 20th November, or any other meeting called for the purpose of hearing the reply of the Government to their demands;

(c) declared the Representation of Natives Act of 1936 to be a fraud and means to perpetuate the policy of segregation, oppression and humiliation; and

(d) called upon the African people as a whole to boycott all elections under the Act, and to struggle for full citizenship rights.

As has already been stated the resolution was passed by an overwhelming majority, but no machinery to implement decision (d) was set up.

At its annual conference at Bloemfontein in December, 1946, the African National Congress instructed the incoming N.E.C. to conduct a powerful nation-wide campaign for:–

> A boycott of all elections under the 1936 Act and a demand for representation on Municipal Councils, Provincial Councils and Parliament through a common franchise.

The National Executive Committee of the Congress was instructed to provide "a machinery for the carrying out of and speeding up of the realisation of the programme of action," a programme which had as its number one, two and three the following important demands: Boycott of elections under Act No. 12 of 1936, abolition of Pass Laws and recognition of African trade unions under the Industrial Conciliation Act of 1937.

The Communist Party National Conference in January this year endorsed "the decision of the Bloemfontein Conference to boycott completely the farcical representations granted 'under the Representation of Natives Act'", and expressed "the readiness of the Communist Party to participate in any active campaign to make this decision effective."

It will be seen here that it was only in January, 1947, that the Communist Party of South Africa took a decision on the boycott issue, and that its decision was one of supporting a decision taken by various representative African organisations.

## EFFORTS TO BOYCOTT

When we came back from the Emergency Conference we reported its decisions to the local Committee of the African National Congress and to the Anti-Pass Committee. It was then decided to call a conference of African organisations in the Peninsula to discuss how the decision to boycott can be made known to the African people.

A Conference was then called by the Congress for November 30, 1946. It was held at the Bethel Institution, Blythe Street, Cape Town. At this conference there were 31 delegates representing 14 organisations and societies. After a long debate it was agreed to set up a machinery to conduct the campaign for boycott. This committee was to meet on the 14th December, 1946. I understand that on that day it was agreed to start work after the holidays.

In the meantime the Annual Conference of the African National Congress expressed strong views in favour of the Congress assuming the leadership without having to rely upon other organisations. Because of these feelings and because of what happened with the Anti-Pass Council, the suggestion that Congress should take over the leadership was unanimously agreed by the delegates.

When the General Secretary of Congress was in Cape Town towards the end of April we discussed with him ways and means of making the boycott a success. But up to the time of writing we have not yet heard of what is being done about the campaign.

In the Transkei they worked hard to popularise the decision, and it is public knowledge that at a meeting held at Umtata on the 23rd May, 1947, and attended by 200 voters representing 22 of the 27 magisterial districts in the territory it was resolved, by a majority of 3 to 1, to boycott the by-election caused by the death of Mr. G.K. Hemming, M.P.

The stand of the Transkei African Voters is very important indeed. It is important as a clear demonstration and protest against the policy of segregation and discrimination, and also as a reminder to opportunists that resolutions are passes in order to be carried out.

It is my view that the boycott can be made a success if the leaders of the African people will honour their decision and campaign for it. The majority of the African people are in a mood for some action. They have tasted the fruits of segregation, and what General Smuts said to the leaders recently will not set their minds at rest.

## ARGUMENTS AGAINST THE BOYCOTT
Arguments against the boycott come from two sources:–
(a) Those to whom representation of "Natives" has become a paying proposition – £1 000 a year; free travelling pass, plus the honour which accompanies the letters M.P.
(b) Those who are not against the boycott in principle but regard it as a bad political tactic; those who fear that to boycott at this stage would be letting in reactionaries unopposed.

To the first-mentioned group, getting into Parliament is more important than the views of the electorate. They will stand as long as they can find one misguided person or a stooge to nominate them and two others to second and support the nomination. They will say that the meeting of the Transkei voters which decided to boycott was attended by only 200 voters out of 2 372 voters on the Roll.

Looked at from that angle, then those who took the decision were in a minority of 12 to 1. But the meeting was one for representatives of districts, and 22 out of 27 districts took the momentous decision. But they will insist that it was not a matter of representatives but one that concerned individual voters.

They will try to score a debating point, conveniently forgetting that it had to be and could not be a meeting of representatives of magisterial districts. Let it be remembered that the Transkei is not a Johannesburg or a Cape Town, but a huge area which stretches from Kentani to Bizana, from Bizana to Umzimkulu, from Umzimkulu to Matatiele, from Matatiele to Cala and from Cala to Butterworth. In this territory transport is not very well developed, money is scarce, and very few Africans possess cars. It is therefore obvious that it is an impossible task to get 2 372 voters to assemble at Umtata, in some cases coming from a distance of over 100 miles.

To the second group, the fear is that undesirable elements will get into Parliament through negligence on the part of the electorate. They overlook the fact that such "representatives," who got into their positions against the views and interest of the people they claim to represent, are no representatives at all. Though their fear cannot and should not be treated or discarded lightly, it is dangerous if carried to extremes.

If we are to be dominated by fear of stooges and reactionaries, and if we are to allow our actions to be conditioned by the attitudes of such persons, then it means that we can never agree to Africans embarking on a boycott. Whether in that case we would then be against the boycott in principle or as tactic it is difficult to say. The best way to deal with "representatives" who get into Parliament against the views and interests of the people they claim to represent, is to repudiate them publicly.

For ten years we opposed the boycott and during that period we supported members of the Natives Representative Council and the Representatives of the Africans in Parliament and the Cape Provincial Council. We supported them not because we thought the form of representation was good and useful, but because we feared that the Africans were not organised and united to be able to carry out a successful boycott, and because we thought that the three institutions could be used to destroy the system from within. Except for the adjournment of the Natives Representative Council none of the two aims has been achieved.

But all Africans, even those who are against the boycott, are agreed that the present system of representation is bad and ineffective. We are aware of the fact that the system is designed to safeguard and ensure white domination in this country. Even the "Bantu World" says:–

"We are all agreed that the present system of African representation in the councils of the State is inadequate and ineffective," (August 16, 1947.)

If therefore we are agreed that the system of representation is bad and ineffective, why should we be afraid of people who will take advantage of the loopholes in the law to get into Parliament? Those European "friends of the Africans" who, while they themselves enjoy full democracy and citizenship are opposed to the boycott and are consequently against the Africans ridding themselves of something deceptive and achieving for themselves the full franchise which these Europeans enjoy, cannot escape from being looked upon by the Africans as representatives of white supremacy.

Our new M.P., Advocate Buchanan, will also be characterised thus. It will always be remembered – in spite of the propaganda to the contrary and despite the confusion which he and the press have created – that he has flouted the decision of the Transkei African voters.

It is all very nice and consoling for him to say that only 190 voters out of 2 372 on the roll were for the boycott and wanted him to resign, and that therefore 2 182 were against the boycott and did not want him to resign. The question is, how did all these positively indicate their approval of his tactics and his standing for Parliament?

**THE COMMUNIST PARTY AND THE BOYCOTT**
In spite of the nonsensical ravings and lies of the Capitalist daily press and its satellite "Bantu Press" that the movement is instigated and controlled by the Communist Party, the fact remains that this is not the case. The Party cannot by itself conduct a campaign in favour of the boycott. The initiation came from and will in future have to come from African organisations.

But the Party, recognising the boycott as a struggle for democratic rights, will give it its full support. It was the African organisations and conferences which adopted the decision to refuse to co-operate with the authorities in perpetuating a fraud, oppression and humiliation, and instead "to struggle for full citizenship rights." The responsibility for the success of the campaign, therefore, rests upon them.

Issued by the Communist Party of South Africa, 58, Burg Street, Cape Town.

Document 35
"New Tactics Proposed for N.R.C. Boycott: Xuma's Address to African Congress", *The Guardian*, 18 December 1947

**BLOEMFONTEIN.** – In his presidential address to the annual conference of the African National Congress over the week-end, Dr. A.B. Xuma urged the African people to re-elect the present members of the Natives' Representative Council on a boycott ticket.

Tracing the history of the N.R.C. over recent months, Dr. Xuma referred to General Smuts' promise to place more concrete proposals before the whole N.R.C.

"However, before long we heard it rumoured that it was Government strategy not to call a statutory meeting of the present N.R.C. in the hope that they will present the concrete proposals before a new Council to be composed of untutored representatives.

> "The proposals, vague as they are, have been published, and the present councillors completely ignored. This is not calculated to win the faith and confidence of the African people."

Dr. Xuma said the Government's act in side-stepping the present councillors had influenced the congress to change its strategy in implementing the resolution to boycott the Natives' Representation Act of 1936.

### GIVING SMUTS A CHANCE

"We urge the African people to send back the present N.R.C. members to give General Smuts another opportunity to keep the engagement he promised to have with all the present members of the Council."

> "We must not abandon the boycott as an ideal; but we must return the present councillors as a second step in our strategy to organize our people for the final state – the complete boycott of elections.

"We are not abandoning the field. We are merely withdrawing for the time being to regroup and change our tactics for a final blow."

It is understood a meeting of the national executive confirmed a recent decision of the working committee to contest the elections on the boycott ticket as a positive method of carrying out the boycott decision. *[....]*

---

## Document 36
## "N.R.C. Boycott Campaign to be Intensified",
*The Guardian*, 18 December 1947

JOHANNESBURG. – Chief topic debated at the annual conference of the African National Congress in Bloemfontein last week was the boycott of the 1936 Native Representation Act. One and a half days of the last two days' continuous discussion at the conference was devoted to this question.

> By 67 votes to seven, conference adopted the resolution of the national executive which pledged the Congress to intensify the campaign and get African public opinion mobilized behind the boycott resolution of the 1946 conferences.

"The best and most effective way of attaining this objective is to help in a campaign to return the Native Representative Council, as far as possible, and for Congress to elect others on a boycott ticket, to continue the work begun by this council, and to make it possible for General Smuts to keep his appointment promised in May last with this Council, and for the government to meet them once more at the usual statutory session of the council which for tactical reasons, has been abandoned this year.

"To advise the electorate to abstain from voting at this stage will merely leave the field clear for collaborators who will be used to undermine and nullify our campaign.

Besides, instructions for non-participation in these elections will cause great confusion and division among our people, the Council, the electorate and among the rank and file".

**This must be avoided and everything done to consolidate our forces behind a definite campaign by electing trusted and tried men to carry out our policy in the Council.**

The position of advisory boards and the European senators and members of Parliament – the latter also elected under the 1936 Act – was not clarified by this conference. A few delegates referred to them in passing in their speeches, but Congress policy was not elucidated in any conference resolution.

Here are a few points made by some of the speakers during this debate:

**Dr. R. T. Bokwe** – Cape: "'Boycott' is a nice word. But putting it into effect is another matter. Few of you know what work lay behind the resolution of the Native Representative Council when it adjourned en bloc. It was not a spontaneous action."

**E. Mofutsanyana** – Transvaal: "Everything possible has been done to violate last year's decision. As long as no attempt is made to make Congress decisions respected by the people, we shall remain where we are. There is no discipline in this organization. A positive boycott must be one in which the leaders go to the people in town and country."

**O. Thambo – Transvaal: "Confusion about this resolution flows not from the resolution itself, but from opposition to it. One leader of Congress speaks for the boycott; and another speaks against it."**

**R. G. Baloyi** – Transvaal: "There has been no answer to Mrs. Ballinger's query: "What is to happen to us? I say we must boycott. If Congress members contest, we must expel them. You must be disciplined."

**S. P. Sesedi** – Cape: "The considered opinion of the Cape is that now is not the time to boycott."

## PEOPLE MISLED

**G. Makabeni** – Transvaal: "The people who were so eloquent for the boycott last year are fighting it as eloquently this year. The people are being deliberately misled."

**Dr. Xuma** – president-general: "Unfortunately when you took this decision I was at Lake Success. I would have warned you against plunging into this thing.

**Prof. Z. K. Mathews** – Cape: "Much as we would like to have the boycott paralyse all the machinery of the government, we will not do so by speeches here. We can admit all the strictures against Congress: but the fact remains we have not done the work for the boycott."

**S. Msimang** – Natal: "We understood from the boycott resolution our job was not to go out and declare a boycott, but to intensify the campaign. We are organising the advisory boards in Natal to be in readiness for the time when Congress will say: 'Now is the time to boycott.' We are telling our chiefs they must not boycott until we have a united front. Then we can meet any obstacle."

## NO AMENDMENTS

When the time came to vote on the boycott, Mr. A.W.G. Champion who was the speaker in the absence of Mr. S. Thema, said he would not allow any amendments: "You vote for or against this resolution of the national executive." A number of delegates felt the resolution had many loopholes, and should be amended. This they were not permitted to do.

Other resolutions passed by the conference registered strong protests against the order given to the South African police to fire when they consider themselves to be in danger; called on the Government to declare all Fascist and Nazi organizations illegal; pledged full support of the Congress to the people of Moroka and elsewhere in their struggle against high rents; and demanded the recognition of African trade unions under the 1937 Industrial Conciliation Act. The proposed Industrial Conciliation (Natives) Bill was roundly condemned.

## Document 37
"Communist Election Policy Defined: National Conference Decision", *The Guardian*, 8 January 1948

**JOHANNESBURG. – Everything possible will be done by the Communist Party in the forthcoming general elections to work for the defeat of the extreme reactionary and pro-Fascist forces represented in the Nationalist Party.**

This is the decision on general election policy arrived at by the National Conference of the Communist Party, held in Johannesburg on January 2, 3 and 4. The conference was attended by over 50 delegates from all parts of the country.

> **The resolution on the general elections points out that the conference recognised that as long as the vote is denied to the African, Coloured and Indian peoples, Parliament cannot be representative of the great bulk of the population, but must perpetuate the present backward and oppressive system of society.**

"Conference regards the primary task of the Party in the forthcoming general elections as that of advancing the struggle for the universal franchise, and for a Socialist Democracy, and of rallying the people against Imperialism."

### SEDITION CASE

Conference passed a unanimous resolution, recording its strongest protest against the continued prosecution of members of the central executive of the Party and others.

> **The Government's conduct in this case constitutes a grave attack on civil liberties and deserves the universal condemnation of all liberty-loving peoples.**

"Conference calls upon all workers and democrats to unite in protesting against the Government's action and to demand the immediate withdrawal of the prosecution."

The Native Representation Act of 1936 was condemned as a vicious measure of racial discrimination, intended to defeat the demands of the African people for their direct representation in Parliament and to cloak the undemocratic structure of South African society.

The resolution on this subject, reads:

"Conference recognises that the stand taken by the members of the Native Representative Council has forced the Government to make concessions, but denounces these concessions as useless and a further attempt to deceive the African people as to the real character of the segregation system.

> **The N.R.C. cannot achieve any useful purpose and the African people's efforts must be directed towards its abolition. In the forthcoming elections to council, Conference resolves to work for the election of a bloc of candidates pledged to repeal the Act, the introduction of a universal franchise and the recognition of the right of all Africans to sit in Parliament.**

Questions of the forthcoming nominations for the Native Representative Council, and the matter of African representation in the House of Assembly and the Senate, were referred to the Central Committee of the Party for further discussion.

## BAN THE FASCISTS

Other resolutions demanded the outlawing of open Fascist organisations such as the Ossewa Brandwag, the Greyshirts and the Pirow New Order Group; condemned mass police raids on African locations, and cases of police brutality against Non-Europeans; and demanded the immediate introduction of the National Health Services plan.

> **The conference was characterised by the great amount of attention paid in commission to work in the rural areas, and by the greater representation and high standard of debate of African delegates from centres such as the East Rand.**

The proposed Industrial Conciliation (Natives) Bill was vigorously condemned, and the Central Committee was instructed to concentrate its full energy upon the carrying out of a broad and intensive campaign among all workers and friends of Labour to secure the rejection of the Bill and the amendment of the Industrial Conciliation Act of 1937 so as to include on an equal basis all workers without discrimination.

## REACTIONARY CAMPAIGN

Delivering his opening address to the Conference, Bill Andrews referred to the attempt of international Capitalism, allied with the forces of Reaction, including the survivals of Fascism and Nazism, to rally to a general counter-attack on all progressive forces, whose spearhead is the Communist movement.[7]

> **We note the increasing truculence of governments which are controlled by big business, land monopolists and other vested interests; the alliance, open or concealed, between these governments and the dregs of Fascism, and the threat of a Third World War, with the atomic bomb waved threateningly in the face of the U.S.S.R. and its Democratic and Socialist allies.**

Bill Andrews said the forces of liberty and progress were immeasurably stronger really and potentially than the dark forces of Reactionary Capitalism.

"Our part in South Africa may seem a small one, but remember that a hundred and fifty million or more of our fellow men and women in this great Continent of Africa have started on the road to liberty. Do not forget Molotov's clarion cry on the thirtieth anniversary of the glorious Soviet Revolution: 'We are living in an age when all roads lead to Communism'."[8]

## Document 38
## I. B. Tabata, *The Boycott as Weapon of Struggle*, June 1952

Since the first days, in 1943-44, when the All-African Convention, the National Anti-C.A.D. and the Non-European Unity Movement adopted the Boycott slogan, the enemies of the Movement have alternatively sneered at it, pretended to adopt it in order more effectively to debase it and render it ineffectual, and, finally, they have misrepresented it to the people with the express purpose of making it appear meaningless and ridiculous.

This vicious attack upon one of the most potent weapons in the armoury of the people struggling for liberation came from the intellectuals. The most interesting feature in this "struggle" of the intellectuals against the people's Boycott weapon is that it has thrown into one camp elements of the most diversified political outlooks: intellectuals who proclaim themselves as internationalists; rapid African nationalists, or more simply, ardent tribalists; doctors and professors who mouth democratic phraseology but secretly harbour a nostalgic hankering for the return of the idyllic days of barbarism; Gandhi-ists, and now the latest adherents of Gandhi-ism in its grotesque cubistic or (is it) dadaistic form, called Dadoo-ism – all of them have formed a tacit united front in their self-appointed task of not only besmirching the people's Boycott slogan and laughing it out of court, but rendering its application impossible. Be it noted that, while all of them are opposed to the Unity of all Non-Europeans, preferring to remain in their respective racial pens, they are nevertheless united on this issue. Their common hostility to the people's weapon is so strong that it cuts across the artificially-created racial barriers and brings them together.

This situation makes it necessary to explain the meaning of the Boycott weapon, its effectiveness and its proper use. It is also incumbent on us to show why the intellectuals are mortally afraid of it. For their attitude towards it has its roots in the historical setting of the political and social structure of South Africa. *[....]*

### PROBLEM OF GOVERNMENT
As capitalism won the battle over tribalism, as the whole of the Non-Europeans were becoming encompassed by the new social system, the problem of government became more acute. Capitalism had taken over the territory, but the people have not yet been integrated into this system, which has its own logic in the regulation of relations between man and man. Before the Whites had arrived in this country there had been orderly government within the respective tribes. The central authority was invested in the chief and his councillors, who derived it from the sanction of the people. But now the old forms of governing, to which the people were accustomed, had been destroyed and the tribal bonds broken. This had been dictated by military needs; during the period of military conquest it had been a matter of prime importance to break the power of the chief, who was the rallying-point of resistance. But the very efficiency with which the military machine had smashed the chieftainship and the authority of the chiefs presented the Whites with the problem of governing the people they had conquered. The lack of cohesion made government well-nigh impossible and anarchy threatened to become the order of the day.

The rulers were faced with a problem which was all the greatr because they had decided to keep the power of government exclusively within their own hands. This very exclusiveness, however, separated the governors from the governed. It drew a line of demarcation between them, which was reinforced by the natural antipathy between conqueror and conquered and the difference in language and outlook. Between the White ruler and the ruled there existed a yawning gap. Obviously some channels of communication had to be established in order to maintain control. But how could they control a people if they had no channels of contact? The only centres of authority that the people knew were the chiefs and councils familiar to them in their tribal life.

Failing the only sane policy – to the rulers' anathema – of integrating the people into the new system of government on an equal footing, they were left with only one alternative, namely, to create chiefs who would constitute the channels of contact they needed. This placed the rulers on the horns of a dilemma. For to resuscitate chieftainship was to run the danger of summoning up the memory of the heroic resistance of the recent past and provide the vanquished with a new rallying-point.

## POLICEMEN-CHIEFS

The dilemma was resolved by the creation of Policemen-Chiefs. *[....]*

*[...]* a system of headmanship was carefully worked out. Each Policeman-Chief was surrounded by a troupe of headmen, each of whom was responsible, not to the Policeman-Chief, but to the Government. In this way the whole of the so-called Reserves was infested with an army of these Government creatures who vied with one another in serving their masters. In them the Government had a band of willing and efficient agents for controlling the African masses. All the laws and regulations which it pleased a tyrannical Government to make, were energetically carried to the people through the channel of these agencies. The Policemen-Chiefs and headmen were the first effective instruments for the domination of the African people. *[....]*

## INTELLECTUALS AS SECOND AGENTS

As the country developed, capitalism disrupted tribalism and swallowed up feudalism, industry grew and towns sprang up all over the country. *[....]*

This colossal expansion could only be done by harnessing a vast army of the dispossessed. It could not be carried out without the cheap labour of the conquered Non-Europeans. All this reinforced the disruption of tribalism and shattered the last remnants of the tribal unit.

As the people became absorbed into the new system, the hold of the Policemen-Chiefs over them was necessarily loosened. Even the migrant labourer who returned home from time to time came back with a new outlook. He no longer accepted the old traditions that gave the chief power over him. During his sojourn in the mines, the towns and the White man's farms he had learned to fend for himself as an individual. He no longer thought in terms of the tribe, but of the welfare of himself and his family. Large numbers severed the tribal bonds and settled in towns and peri-urban areas, while new generations grew up without any knoweldge of the tribal life. Once more a new problem of maintaining control over the Africans arose. *[....]*

As the system of capitalism unfolded, however, it became abundantly clear that the promises were a delusion and a snare. The educational system itself was not designed to liberate the people, but to enslave them. Now a new crop of intellectuals sprang up, with a totally different outlook, and corruption set in. If the old African intellectuals who collaborated with the missionaries can be excused because they were unaware of the pitfalls involved, the same cannot be said of their successors. This new generation was fully aware that the few privileges they enjoyed were offered to them as bribes in order to separate them from their people. By this time a pattern of racial discrimination had clearly emerged and was crystallised in the so-called Act of Union, which glorifies herrenvolkism and extols racialism as the very foundation-stone of the South African State. All the Acts that reached the statute book thereafter were simply the working out of a clearly evolved plan. Year after year the African intellectuals could see unfolding before their very eyes a whole series of legislative measures that were grinding their people ever more ruthlessly and reducing them to a state of unmitigated servitude.

The new generation of African intellectuals were self-seeking imposters who inherited the prestige and traded on the good name of their predecessors. They knew that the narrow margin of privilege separating them from their more unfortunate brothers was granted them at the price of collaboration with the White agents of oppression. The whole process of reducing the Black man to his present position would have been impossible without the help of these intellectuals. It was they who shackled the mind of the people and led them into bondage. [....]

For them the prime motive was the desire to escape, as a privileged few, from the rigours of oppression. Although segregation spelt frustration and stagnation for the rest of their people, it offered the so-called "elite" the possibility of fat jobs – jobs that would only be open to them in segregated spheres. They had visions of themselves in the sphere of education, for instance, receiving professorships and inspectorships in "Native" colleges and schools; in segregated areas they visualised themselves as running big businesses, freed from White competition; there would also be plenty of jobs for them as petty officials. In short, this small "elite" would be free, like their masters, to batten on the masses. It was the dangling of this miserable bribe before their eyes that set the intellectuals along the tortuous road of collaboration, the road that led the African people into a political desert. [....]

To get an idea of the police-function of the intellectuals, we have only to visualise what takes place to this day. Dotted all over the country in the so-called "Native Reserves" are the Resident "Native" Commisioners' offices. These are the centres of administration. It is here that the people have to come for their allotments of land and get permission to buy cattle; it is from here that they have to get their passes to go and seek work; it is also here that they have to pay their taxes and the inevitable fines. In short, these offices are the centres of control over the lives of the people. If you have the time to spare, if you have a heart of stone and nerves of steel, go one day and stand at the entrance of any of these offices. There you will see how these Black pseudo-intellectuals behave towards their own people. There you will see the powerful combination of the policeman-chief and headman and the policeman-intellectual at work. All day long the impoverished peasants stream in to settle their many problems. The headmen bring in from the villages men and women charged with breaking one or other of the many regulations. As they enter, the clerks and interpreters bark their orders. All day long you hear the voice of the White master issuing through the Black mouth. How enthusiastically these pseudo-intellectuals bully and badger the people has to be seen to be believed. To the people the administrative offices become a symbol of tyranny before which they tremble in fear, filled with a sense of their own inferiority. There is no need for the White master to assert his authority; these Black agents before whom the people cower, do the job all too well.

But that is not all. A fuller picture of the function of the policeman-intellectual emerges when we depict the structure of South African society. On top sits the White ruling minority:

at the base is the vast majority of the Non-European masses and sandwiched in between is a thin layer of intellectuals, who are the purveyors and transmitters of herrenvolk ideas to the people. They are the connecting link between the ruler and the ruled. In fact, they are the most useful instruments of ruling. Consider what a problem any Government would have to rule the people without their assistance. Language alone stands as a barrier between the Government and the people. Any law in any society is a law because of the consent of the people. Without their consent the law is not worth the scrap of paper it is written on. [....] Here in South Africa the task of procuring this consent, even though given grudgingly, is the function of the literate and therefore a vocal section of the Non-Europeans. The various Governments in this country have been able to rule the Non-Europeans largely by virtue of the co-operation of the intellectuals, who have to make the most obnoxious laws palatable to the people. In this way the intellectuals stand guard over the population as policemen in the interests of their masters.

## THE BOYCOTT AND THE INTELLECTUALS

From the above analysis it becomes clear that the intellectuals have now a stake in the present set-up of South African society. [....] In this scheme of things they play the rôle of collaborating with the oppressor in working the machinery of oppression. It is their acceptance of this function that determines their attitude to the Boycott weapon of the people. If they intend to continue collaborating with the oppressor they must view the people's Boycott with alarm. For it hits at the root of their fundamental position: it threatens their very existence as collaborators.

The Boycott is not in itself a policy. It is a specific application of the policy of Non-collaboration. It is this policy that the enemies of the Boycott slogan are mortally afraid of. [....]

When they try to distort the meaning of the Boycott slogan, when they shout: "The boycotters, to be logical, should also boycott the segregated schools, education, etc.", it is not because they are ignorant of the true meaning of the Boycott; it is precisely because they understand it all too well. They would like to throw dust in the eyes of the people by reducing it to absurdity. Let us state again: the Boycott is directed against those political institutions that are created for our own enslavement. Nobody in his senses would advocate taking our children away from the present segregated schools, since there are no other schools they can attend. This would be worse than cutting off our noses to spite our faces. In the one instance we have no choice in the matter. We must educate our children in the cause of liberation itself: they must acquire the intellectual equipment, even though only segregated schools are open to them. But in the case of the political institutions, there is nothing to force us to operate the machinery, if we don't choose to do so. Those who operate it do so of their own free will. It is because the Boycott exposes this voluntary acquiescence on the part of the quisling-intellectuals that they direct their venom against it. [....]

## IS THE BOYCOTT NEGATIVE?

We have said that the Boycott is not in itself a policy but a practical application of the policy of Non-collaboration at a specific time. It is particularly applicable at those moments when the quislings are engaged in the very act of luring the people into putting the noose round their neck. The boycott has the effect of not only arresting the hand that carries the rope, but of holding it aloft for all to see. The quisling is, as it were, caught in the act, red-handed. In his fury he slanders the Boycott, pours scorn upon it, reviles it. But all this vituperation hasn't worked. The people stubbornly continue to use the Boycott, for they have discovered it to be an effective weapon.

The quislings have been forced to yield ground. While refraining from openly attacking it, they now resort to sniping tactics. Their latest distortion is that the Boycott is negative. They argue that it calls upon the people to sit down and fold their arms, that it bids them refrain from action. Nothing could be further from the truth. *[....]*

When an organisation, for instance, advocates boycott, it cannot just pass a resolution to that effect and merely announce the fact to the masses. That would be meaningless. It takes upon itself the duty of going out to the people and carefully explaining to them why they must boycott a particular institution or elections to it. In this way it engages in political activity of the highest order. And this is not all. It calls upon the people to bestir themselves, throw off their lassitude and intervene in their own fate. With a consciousness arising out of a clear understanding of the issues involved, the masses take the positive step of boycotting. This is action. It is action of first-rate importance. Deliberately and with a full sense of responsibility, they do two things: they cut the strings that bind them to the quislings and secondly they intervene in the plans of the rulers. By withholding their consent they frustrate these plans, which cannot work without their co-operation.

The ability to defeat the plans of the rulers in this way has in turn a further effect on the masses. It reinforces their rejection of inferiority; it restores their self-respect and gives them a sense of their own importance; it reveals to them their own strength born of unity in action.

Another important aspect of the use of the boycott is that it is a weapon against which the rulers have no defence. If the people refuse to take part in elections to dummy councils, they can snuff out these agencies of domination, and the rulers can't do anything about it, because they can't prosecute. Let us take as an example the latest occasion on which the boycott weapon was used. When the herrenvolk took it into their heads to celebrate the Van Riebeeck Tercentenary, the Non-European Unity Movement decided to boycott it. The local Co-ordinating Unity Committee (in the Cape) launched an intensive campaign of boycott. Innumerable meetings were held all over the Cape Peninsula. The people were told the real significance of the celebrations, namely, the conquest of the inhabitants, the confiscation of their land and their economic enslavement: the rise of the herrenvolk to a position of domination with all the political power exclusively in their hands and a corresponding deterioration in the condition of the Non-Europeans. The Committee took the opportunity of reviewing the past and explaining to the people how their present plight came about; step by step it unfolded the machinations of the rulers, the methods they adopted and the agents they employed for their deception. As some of these worthies were busy trying to entice the Non-Europeans to join the herrenvolk celebrations, the Unity Committee found it easy to show up the rôle of such agents and it demonstrated how the people themselves, by their very acquiescence, are to a large extent responsible for their present position. It called upon the Non-Europeans to refuse to be a party to the celebration of their own enslavement and, by boycotting the festival, to register their protest against the whole herrenvolk policy that has denied them human rights. *[....]*

It was in this way that the Unity Committee for the first time penetrated all layers of the population. The boycott had become a live issue discussed in the streets, the trains and the buses; in the classrooms and playgrounds; in the factories and the very homes of the people. *[....]* Thus within a short space of time the boycott campaign brought political education to the people and lifted them out of their lethargy. It is now history that the Non-Europeans boycotted the Van Riebeeck celebrations almost completely, a fact which was a source of surprise and alarm to the herrenvolk. *[....]*

## WHY THE BOYCOTT?

We have said that we do not choose at random our weapons of struggle. Each situation demands the use of a particular weapon according to the conditions prevailing at the time. Now we have shown that the herrenvolk in solving the problem of controlling a conquered people and also arresting their development within the present system, employed two highly successful methods. First, "divide and rule": they erected barriers between the various sections and used the intellectuals to maintain these barriers. At the same time, within each section, they drove a wedge between the people and the intellectuals, who served the interests of the rulers to the great detriment of their people. Secondly, the rulers made use of the intellectuals to persuade the rest of the people to operate the machinery of their own enslavement. We have unfolded how the intellectuals were turned into effective agents for dragooning and policing their people into the acceptance of inferiority; how a chain of collaboration was started between the liberals and the intellectuals and led the people down the disastrous road of "developing along their own lines".

At the end of that road they found themselves in a state of complete disorganisation and demoralisation. There was a mass of unorganised landless peasantry who fell easy prey to recruiting agents for the mines and White farms; there was a mass of agricultural labourers living under conditions of serfdom; in the towns were hundreds of thousands of unorganised workers who had no defence against exploitation. Those few – very few – who were organised into trade unions (illegal) could not even carry out their proper trade union function. They were stifled by the encrustation of a top layer of bureaucrats. In the political field rank opportunism had shattered and almost annihilated the organisations of the people. The few militants had become disillusioned by the irresponsible ventures of stunt-addicted opportunists. The people were left without hope. They had lost faith in leaders, and what is more, they had lost faith in themselves, in their ability to put up a struggle. This is the morass to which "developing along their own lines" had brought them. To this desert collaboration had brought them.

To get the people out of the morass it was necessary to sever the link that bound them through their leaders to their oppressors. It was necessary to cut the chain of collaboration.

Here is where the Boycott proves itself a most effective weapon. It is the hammer and chisel that snaps the chain. It is in this sense that we say the Boycott is necessitated by the objective conditions in this country, that the need for the use of the Boycott weapon arises out of the living realities of a whole system of racial oppression in the so-called Union of South Africa.

Once the stranglehold is loosened and the people are free to think for themselves they can examine their position, review their past mistakes and on the basis of this choose the proper course to follow. The successful use of the Boycott weapon gives them the necessary confidence and builds up their morale. If it is used simultaneously by all sections of the oppressed – as we have depicted above – it has a unifying force. *[....]*

United action at this stage is directed simply at defeating the plans of the rulers. But the policy of Non-collaboration – of which the boycott is one application in specific circumstances – implies much more than this. In its larger aspect it means not only rejecting and defeating the rulers' plans for their oppression, but directing the people towards organising their own forces for a concerted struggle for liberty. In place of the herrenvolkism of the rulers they counterpose the conception of the equality of all men. At that stage their united forces will be directed towards building a society in South Africa in which all men and women, irrespective of colour and creed, shall have equal rights and opportunities. Then only will the true Union of South African begin to take form. This will be the Nation of South Africa.

The Boycott weapon, then, has a very positive part in Building the Nation. And all who oppose the Boycott stand condemned before the people as the defenders of herrenvolkism, with all the destruction that it brings in its train. The intellectuals have to make their choice: either to continue as collaborators or take their place alongside their people, and together with them go forward to the task of Building the Nation, a Nation free from race hatred and oppression.

## Document 39
## Walter Sisulu, "Boycott as a Political Weapon", *Liberation*, 23, February 1957

**A timely article by the banned ex-Secretary of the African National Congress, now on trial for treason.**

Boycott has been used as an effective political weapon in different countries ever since it came into use as a recognised method of struggle against the Irish Land Act of 1880.[10]

There are outstanding examples from all over the world of the effectiveness of boycott in political struggle: the boycott of the Duma in Russia during the struggle against the Czarist regime;[11] the boycott against the British Legislative Council in India by the Indian Congress. And we in this country are in a particularly good position to understand fully how effective the boycott weapon can be, both as an economic and political weapon. It is still one of the few methods of struggle which are not illegal in South Africa today.

Since the end of the last war, we have seen outstanding examples of successful boycotts: the Alexandra bus boycott of 1944; the Western Native Township Tram boycott; the Port Elizabeth bus boycott; the Cape Town bus boycott; the unique Evaton bus boycott which continued for more than a year, and finally brought down the bus owners to their knees. No less remarkable is the bus boycott on the Rand and Pretoria at the time of writing this article. The fact that people can walk for twenty miles a day, week in, week out, in a 100% effective boycott, organised in less than two weeks; and in such diverse areas as Sophiatown, and W.N.T. in less than two days – this is a tribute to the determination of the people in utilising this form of struggle.

Tens of thousands of Africans have participated in these boycotts, and even more compelling is the fact that 20 000 Africans in the Moroka-Jabavu areas have carried on a boycott in sympathy, in support of their brothers who are struggling against higher fares.

In these boycotts our experience is that each time they have raised the political consciousness of the people, brought about a greater solidarity and unity among the masses. In this way they have raised the peoples' organisations to a higher level, demonstrating the correctness of the action.

However, inevitably people with limited democratic rights and few means of expressing their grievances begin to think of boycotts as a means to demand political rights. And it is our main concern in this article to discuss boycott as a political rather than a purely economic weapon.

## WHEN TO BOYCOTT?

There has been controversy over the correctness of the timing of various boycotts against existing institutions and Parliamentary bodies. Such controversies existed in the left movements in Europe, in Germany, Austria, Hungary, and to a lesser extent in England; the issue being whether or not it is correct for members of progressive parties to participate in parliamentary elections and other reactionary institutions. In our own country this controversy has existed for more than ten years. This is a question on which we must have a clear decision. Taking the history of these countries, learning from their experience, we may be able to understand our own problem more easily. For although conditions differ from one country to another, yet the principle is much the same.

During and after the war the national liberatory movement took a greater interest in the boycott weapon; the Unity Movement, the Communist Party of South Africa, and the African National Congress all decided at different times on the boycott of the different political institutions, such as parliament, Advisory Boards and Bungas. Even during this period the issue was a highly controversial one within the organisations concerned. It was during this period that the political consciousness of the people began to emerge, and the militant spirit of the masses was felt. It was also a period of industrial development, of historic strikes and protests of the people; the Squatters movement of 1944-43; the Mine Strike of 1946 in which many Africans were killed. All these things raised the greatest indignation among the people. This was, therefore, correctly regarded as the best time to build the national movements and to force the powers by mass action instead of by petitions or deputations. This also made people naturally regard government institutions with contempt.

It was also argued that people did not distinguish clearly between their own organisations and reactionary bodies; and that there was a need of making people adopt an attitude of contempt to the Advisory Boards and Councils and to understand their functions and limitations. To work within these bodies and at the same time to condemn them unreservedly would have led to confusion. Therefore the best approach seemed to be an active boycott of such institutions.

There were, however, some who chose the weapon of boycott because it seemed an "easy" course, one which would not expose either the people or their leaders to any hardships. This school of thought is found even today amongst those who shout the loudest and become more militant when they talk of boycott. They see no other suitable form of struggle save boycott. That explains also why some of those who favour boycott are so strongly opposed to any other form of struggle, under the pretext that the people are not yet trained and ready.

Since the decision of the A.N.C. in 1919, this issue has come up for discussion at almost every conference. There are differences of approach. As far as the Unity Movement is concerned, anyone who participates in any of the elections of various political institutions are collaborators of the government; that whoever so participates, even when fighting for the destruction of such institutions, betrays the struggle. It sounds very militant, of course, to talk about positive boycott, about collaborationists and non-collaborationists. This tendency is confined not only to the non-European Unity Movement, but has penetrated the ranks of the A.N.C.

This surely is being dogmatic. It is a serious political mistake of confusing the tactics with the principle; which means that the decision to boycott is not subject to any changes.

Let us examine the arguments advanced by both sides, those who believe that boycott is the best possible weapon with which to oppose these inferior political institutions, and those who believe that boycott is not necessarily the best or only method.

## MILITANT OR EXTREME?
From the first point of view, the argument is advanced that these institutions were created to serve the interests of the oppressors and to deceive the oppressed and fool them into believing that they have some poplitical rights. It is argued that the effect of this is to retard the progress of the oppressed people. That to participate, therefore, in these institutions amounts to collaborating with the oppressors, confusing and bluffing the masses; and that the correct thing to do is to have nothing at all to do with these institutions at any time, under any circumstances.

This, indeed, sounds very militant and uncompromising, and it is this approach which raises a tactic into a principle. On the other hand, it is argued that boycotting of these institutions may not necessarily be the best and correct method to fight against their existence. But on the contrary, participation in these institutions may at certain times be the most effective and correct method of exposing them and struggling for more effective representation.

This approach clearly recognises the fact that these institutions exist not because of our wishes, nor are they due to our making; that the people may participate in them for various reasons, and that the correct thing to do is to educate the masses about the purpose of these institutions, thus making them have no confidence in them as such. This approach recognises the fact that the principle is not the boycott of the institutions, but the principle is the rejection of differential political institutions.

## CONDITIONS CHANGE
**The failure on the part of many people to realise the seriousness of elevating a tactic of struggle into a fundamental principle could do irreparable harm to the movement.** Take, for instance, this decision to boycott taken several years ago. Does it follow that because it was correct then it is correct today? Have conditions not changed at all since the decision was taken? They certainly have. Many forms of struggle which were legal then are illegal today. Organisations and leaders have been banned. Almost all forms of protest have been outlawed. Holding meetings has become almost impossible. Surely the wisdom of leadership lies in knowing what tactics to apply at a given time, dictated to leadership by the prevailing conditions. The correctness of such tactics must be judged from their effect on the movement. The primary thing is that such tactics raise the standards of the organisation higher and higher. Once we differentiate between the principle and the tactic, in other words in this case to know that the boycott is a tactic and the rejection of reactionary political institutions is the principle, then the fight against such institutions can include participation in them with a view to rendering important the system that gives rise to them.

The A.N.C. resolution for the boycotting of these institutions also made provision for the establishment of the Council of Action, whose function was to decide upon the institution to be boycotted. It was realised that it was not sufficient to say that we boycott these institutions, when people may not be ready for it. There are people even within the A.N.C. who do not realise that boycott is a tactic and only one of the methods to be used for the struggle for national independence and against white domination and discriminatory laws. The fact, some of them argued at the Queenstown National Conference in 1953 that they regarded the decision to boycott not just as a tactic.

They were wrong, and Congress should rediscuss the whole matter now with a view to reviewing the unclear and unsatisfactory 1949 resolution, which no longer reflects a greatly changed situation.

## Document 40
## Anti-CAD, *Why You Should Not Vote!* [1958][12]

The Anti-C.A.D. Movement was formed in 1943 to fight the Coloured Advisory Council and the beginnings of a Coloured Affairs Department. The Anti-C.A.D. smashed the C.A.C. by using the boycott weapon: no organisations of the people went near to it; the people would have nothing to do with the C.A.C.-men or Quislings. For 15 years the Government has not been able to set up a Coloured Affairs Department to act as policeman over the Coloured people in the same way as the Native Affairs Department controls the African people.

The Anti-C.A.D Movement is calling upon all Coloured voters *NOT* to vote in this dummy election. Here are some of the reasons why you should *BOYCOTT* this fraud of *apartheid* and to help in your own political enslavement.

*YOU SHOULD BOYCOTT:–*
  I. BECAUSE to vote on an *aparte* voters' roll for White "Coloured Representatives" means to accept political inferiority, to work a political fraud, and to give up your right to a franchise, that is, the right of anyone of any colour or sex or religion to sit in parliament and provincial council as well as to vote for anyone of any colour or sex or religion.
  II. BECAUSE voting in this dummy election means taking yourself and the WHOLE of the Coloured people, men and women, a step backward, AWAY from full franchise and citizenship rights.
  III. BECAUSE the Coloured people in meetings not only in the Cape Province, but also in the O.F.S., Transvaal and Natal have called upon you not to betray them by voting. There are about 1 1/2 million Coloured people: there are only about 29 000 Coloured voters. The voters must not put the *Herrenvolk* in a position to say that they, the voters, accepted political *apartheid* and therefore every form of *apartheid* on behalf of the whole 1 1/2 million Coloured people.
  IV. BECAUSE a vote for any candidate – U.P., Nat., Independent or Treason trialist – means a vote for *Herrenvolkism*, for *apartheid*, for segregation. Every candidate BY THE ACT of trying to get into parliament through this *aparte* voting fraud ACCEPTS *apartheid* for the Coloured people – although he rejects it for himself.

V. BECAUSE voting for dummy representation means voting for job *apartheid*, Group Area *apartheid* or locations, "race" classification and re-classification, segregated schooling and the doping of the children by Eiselen-de Vos Malan schooling, bus and train *apartheid*, hospital and bioscope and sports *apartheid*, and every other form of *apartheid*, past, present or to come.

VI. BECAUSE voting for dummy representation means accepting the COLOURED AFFAIRS DEPARTMENT which seeks to control and police the lives of the Coloured people in the same way as the Native Affairs Department regiments the African people.

VII. BECAUSE accepting dummy representation means accepting the lie that *every* Coloured woman and *every* Coloured man (yourselves included) is unfit for the franchise.

VIII. BECAUSE working this *Herrenvolk* fraud brands you as a voluntary slave in the eyes of the world, that is, as a slave voting to keep himself and others in slavery.

IX. BECAUSE YOU MUST TURN YOUR BACK ON DUMMY REPRESENTATION; YOUR TASK IS TO BUILD THE LIBERATORY MOVEMENT FOR FULL CITIZENSHIP RIGHTS. YOUR TASK IS TO ORGANISE THE PEOPLE IN THE ANTI-C.A.D. MOVEMENT, WHICH IS PART OF THE NON-EUROPEAN UNITY MOVEMENT.

NO ONE CAN FORCE YOU TO VOTE.<br>
THERE IS NO FINE OR PENALTY IF YOU DO NOT VOTE.<br>
DO NOT BETRAY YOUR PEOPLE BY VOTING.<br>
BOYCOTT ALL CANDIDATES.<br>
STRUGGLE FOR FULL CITIZENSHIP RIGHTS!!!

## Document 41
### John Gomas, *Seperate Representation ----- Our Damnation* [1958]

27 Sterling Street,<br>
*Cape Town.*

Since Union –1910– the franchise rights of the non-white people in the Cape have been cut and trimmed to secure white supremacy and thereby has created a custom that the white man must represent, guide and lead non-whites in all spheres of public activity. The Africans endured separate representation by whites for 21 years in Parliament and Provincial Council (let us not forget, this was the work of the U.P.). To conform to this pattern, the Coloured man was removed from the common roll and white domination widened.

Now, as with the Africans, every white Tom, Dick and Harry comes forward and swears to all that is sacred that he is a true "friend" or "comrade" of the coloured people and will fight with all his might for their rights.

Apart from the profit, prestige and privileges a white representative enjoy among his white community he will also be only another big boss to the non-whites. For, irrespective whether such a white candidate was a so-called fighter for non-whites' rights or not, the fact remains, by offering to represent non-whites in the present set-up, ipso facto, supports the system of white supremacy, apartheid, etc.

In this way the white man who volunteer to "sacrifice" himself to represent non-whites, is either stupidly blind to the degradation he inflicts on non-whites or he deliberately accepts the opportunity to enhance his personal interests and to perpetuate white domination. This state of relationship causes the white people to be utterly callous and inhuman to the non-whites.

I believe that when the non-whites accept and support white representation and leadership, they doom their own future for advancement. For by so doing, they reject the possibility of ever being qualified to represent their own interests. And since non-whites have elected whites to represent them, the white representatives are looked upon and respected as saviours even greater than their own non-white leaders.

The whites compete with the non-white leaders for leadership over the non-white masses but the whites would not dream to have this position reversed.

In the course of the last 300 years, the policy of white trusteeship has proved to be the greatest farce to the non-whites and most profitable boon to the white man, be he busdriver, lawyer, shopkeeper, professor, priest, M.P. or others. Therefore faith in white leadership and representation is the greatest stumbling block to non-white progress, self-assertion and independent leadership.

Because of this, the coloured people particularly to a considerable extent, dislike black people, to say the least and hold those who are white in the highest esteem.

If there is to be progress and democracy for the non-white people then this worship and acceptance of white superiority must be destroyed in the minds of the non-white people and to build up confidence in their own ability to overcome the problems of this land which is not of their making.

The non-white people have suffered long and patiently so that it is time that there can be no halfways about this. However, the "friends" and "comrades" say it is better to vote for a U.P Liberal or treason trialist that allow a Nat. to be elected.

But the non-white people generally did follow such a policy of the lesser evil and in consequence got the worst racialist government and oppression second to none in the world. Although, the Englishman, Prof. Haldane already said in (I think) 1938 that he would rather be a Jew in Berlin (under Hitler) than a black man in Johannesburg.

Therefore should the coloured people operate and support the Separate Representation Act for Coloured people to vote for white candidates, it will only mean setting in motion a process for *further self abasement*. No where else in the world are there people called upon to besmirch themselves as our "friends" and "comrades" are doing to us. Search all over the world and you will not find the like of a George Golding.

Should we reject the separate representation of candidates and *boycott* all elections run on the basis of a separate Coloured Voters' roll for Parliament, Provincial Council and Union Council for Coloured Affairs, we will gain our own self respect and win the respect of decent people in South Africa and throughout the world and strengthen our morale in the fight for full democratic rights.

J. GOMAS.

## Document 42
"Boycott the Dummy Elections: 2 000 Demonstrate At Mass Rally", *The Torch*, National Edition, 1 April 1958

HISTORY-MAKING CLIMAX TO ANTI-C.A.D. BOYCOTT CAMPAIGN
**The Mass Anti-C.A.D. Boycott Rally filled the old Drill Hall on Sunday, March 30th, and overflowed on to the pavements at the greatest political rally on the franchise in the history of the Coloured people. It is conservatively estimated that at least 2,000 people were present.**

At 2.30 p.m. already three-quarters of the 1,100 seats provided were filled. Lorries and buses, specially organised, brought people from various parts of the Peninsula. With them they brought their banners carrying boycott slogans. These were placed inside the hall, which was already lined with posters and placards. At intervals throughout the meeting the Secretary, Dr. N. Murison, read telegrams and other messages of solidarity from 43 organisations or communities in the Cape Province.

**PURPOSE OF CAMPAIGN**
In his opening address the Chairman, Councillor R.E. Viljoen, said that the purpose of the boycott campaign had been not only to get a boycott of this dummy election and to oppose the Coloured Affairs Department, but to build the Anti-C.A.D. Movement of the people in the struggle for full citizenship rights. The campaign, which would continue after the "elections", was on the basis of the 10-point programme of the Non-European Unity Movement.

He said that the Anti-C.A.D. had held over 90 meetings throughout the Union since the opening of the campaign in the Banqueting Hall on February 2nd, and everywhere the boycott had been acclaimed. The meeting that had impressed him most of all, he said, was one held in the relatively small township of Heatherdale, Bloemfontein, O.F.S., where a crowded gathering of people who had never had any shadow of a franchise or a vote called upon the people of the Cape not to betray them by accepting dummy representation and taking part in dummy elections.

**NOT FOR ANY SECTION**
The first speaker, Mr. A. Omar, said that the Anti-C.A.D., as a section of the N.E.U.M., was opposed to dummy representation for any section of the population.[13] He condemned those who accepted dummy representation as being good enough for one section. In particular, he exposed those who are now trying to get the Coloured people to work separate representation but who rejected it for Indians in 1948.

Mr. Ismail Abdurahman, speaking on the C.A.D., ridiculed and rejected the claim that the Commissioner for Coloured Affairs, I.D. du Plessis, had the so-called "Cape Malays" in his pocket. Mr. Abdurahman said the so-called "Cape Malays" regard themselves as Moslems and a section of the Coloured people. Together with the rest they reject the C.A.D. and dummy representation. He particularly exposed the role of "Malay" Quislings seeking to divide the people in order to betray.

**"FRAUD, LIE, HYPOCRISY, DANGER"**
Mr. W.P. van Schoor, President of the Teachers' League of South Africa, said that one of the most fundamental tasks of the campaign had been to expose the "fraud, the lie, the hypocrisy and the danger" of separate representation. He then dealt with the N.A.D.

and C.A.D. in order to dispel any illusions people might still harbour about a C.A.D. or separate representation being somehow "different" for Coloured people. Referring to "friends" such as Huddleston and Dadoo who are supporting dummy representation for Coloureds, he said we would have to be firm when dealing with those who betray.

Mr. C.M. Kobus dealt with the history of those who, for 21 years, have claimed to be "fighting from within". He demonstrated how the period of "Native representation" had seen an even greater load of anti-African legislation. It was an insult to the intelligence of the Non-Europeans to expect that after 21 years' experience of "separate representation" for Africans they should continue to work the fraud, let alone extend it to the Coloured section.

### "I SHALL NOT VOTE UNTIL.."

Mr. R.O. Dudley concluded his analysis of the reasons for dummy representation and his exposure of the trickery connected with sending the "best man" as dummies to Parliament, with the enthusiastically received suggestion that every one should pledge that "I shall not vote until every person, every mother and father, sister and brother, son and daughter, has the full franchise on the common roll."[14]

Dealing with the "best men" fraud, Mr. Dudley showed how the dummy "Coloured Reps." cannot vote on such fundamental things as Constitutional changes, and motion of "no confidence" – and every honest Non-White has no confidence in **Herrenvolk** Government – or the budget. The place of every honest "best man", he said, is with the people in the struggle.

### HEILIGE BELOFTE

The Rev. Dan M. Wessels, coming straight from his duties in connection with Palm Sunday, reminded the gathering of the "heilige belofte" made in the City Hall 15 years ago, that the Anti-C.A.D. Movement would not rest until all had obtained full citizenship rights. He said it was a great tribute to the strength of the Anti-C.A.D. Movement's principles that although many so-called "volksleiers" had fallen by the wayside, the Movement was to-day stronger than it had ever been.

He said it was not without significance that the **Herrenvolk**, while declaring an internal political truce over Easter, nevertheless chose the day before Good Friday, the day on which Judas betrayed Christ for thirty pieces of silver, as the day on which the Coloured voters should make a X to sign away the rights of the people. He then affirmed the great democratic principle which has come down to us from America: "No taxation without representation".

### A MIGHTY POLITICAL WEAPON

The final speaker, Mr. B. M. Kies, said that no matter how many "slaves, scabs or political scoundrels" the **Herrenvolk** managed to persuade or seduce into voting for them on April 3rd, the campaign had made it absolutely clear that **Herrenvolkism** has lost forever all claims it had, or imagined it had, to a Coloured appendix. The Coloured people had matured politically during the past 15 years and the campaign had showed dramatically how they have come to realise themselves as a section of the Non-White oppressed. Every voter knows that it is the "expressed will" of the Coloured people as a whole that the dummy elections be boycotted. Through the correct wielding of the mighty political weapon of the boycott in this dummy election, he continued, the Coloured people could: (1) Smash dummy representation for Coloureds; (2) Give a vital or finishing blow to dummy representation for Africans; (3) Make it doubly difficult for the **Herrenvolk** to start with dummy representation for Indians; (4) Strike the **Herrenvolk**, already in a difficult internal and external economic and political position, a mighty blow at a time when it could least afford it.

Time was allowed for questions. These were quickly dealt with by Mr. Kies. In answering two on the Anti-C.A.D. attitude to the treason trial and treason trial candidates, he said that the Anti-C.A.D. holds that anyone accused of a political crime has the right to the best possible defence and to this the Anti-C.A.D. has subscribed and will subscribe. But it regarded it as a contemptible and despicable piece of opportunism to seek to exploit people's political sympathy for one facing a political trial in order to betray them by working the fascist machinery of political enslavement. The treason trial candidate was not different from any other, Nat., Sap., or otherwise.

**ONE VOICE**
The resolution – the one used throughout the campaign – was read by Dr. Murison. In proposing its adoption, Mr. Y. Abader added a rider repudiating the collaborationist "Malay" so-called leaders who supported the C.A.D. and dummy representation. Mr. Ajam seconded the resolution. It was carried unanimously and acclaimed.

## Document 43
"Oppositionists in Congress Attack C.O.D. Against Participation in Racial Elections", *The Citizen*, 3, 3, 4 March 1958

"WE REJECT THE SLOGAN 'THE NATS MUST GO!' THE ONLY SLOGAN WE KNOW IN ELECTION TIME IS 'THE FULL UNFETTERED FRANCHISE'" SAYS "ANALYSIS" THE ORGAN OF A GROUP IN THE CONGRESS MOVEMENT WHO ARE OPPOSED TO THE PRESENT LEADERSHIP.

It is sharply critical of the Congress of Democrats: "Without abiding by a democratic decision, a small set of leaders are set on subverting the interests of the whole liberatory movement to their own ends".

TREACHEROUS MANOEUVRE
"The decision to boycott elections goes back to the 1949 conference of the ANC, but this resolution has never been put into operation. In Easter, 1957, the SACPO conference passed a resolution to boycott "Coloured Representation" in Parliament ...[15] But there was a group of Congress leaders centred mainly in COD who were determined to reverse the decision. They did, in fact, succeed in obtaining a reversal in December .... in what can only be described as a teacherous manoeuvre ..."

BOYCOTT SABOTAGED
ANALYSIS makes it clear that the COD-controlled papers FIGHTING TALK, LIBERATION and NEW AGE were all party to the sabotage of boycott.

It is pointed out also that instead of a "militant" rejection of Separate Representation and the "minority" Parliament the people are going to be "served up" with a horse-deal by the "Congress and Liberals" agreed to behind the scenes without the consent of the "Congress rank and file".

CONGRESS WEAK

The weakness of Congress is emphasised: "As long as Congress cannot intervene to help the people of Zeerust, of Tzaneen, of the Transkei etc. it cannot claim to be the leading voice of the oppressed people of South Africa".[16]

It is explained that "Congress is organisationally weak" because "its resources are squandered through inefficiency, bureaucratic control" and because "its leadership is divorced from the rank-and-file as the current discontent in the Transvaal ANC amply testifies".

RELIES ON "WHITE" POLITICS

The COD-dominated Congress is accused of "placing their reliance" on "white politics": "... Congress always turns towards the Liberals in attempting an United Front and never to potential allies that arise from amongst the ranks of the mass of the exploited people".

As to the Multi-Racial Conference it is declared that "the deliberations veered heavily to the right and leftist ideas were smothered in the atmosphere of concession and temperance. Unfortunately, Congress contributed its mite to the sterility of thought at most sessions....the liberal ideology prevailed at the Congress."

ANALYSIS does not attack the multi-racialism of the 'Multi-Racial Conference' or the 'multi-racial' apartheid structure of the Congress movement.


Document 44
"The Revolt of the Women", *The Soyan*, December 1959[17]

Early in June the African women of Durban set in motion a process that was to have far-reaching effects in the whole of Natal. What started off simply (so it appeared), as the call for the boycott of the beer-halls was to become the beginning of the upsurge of the women of Natal against oppression. There are a complicity of reasons responsible for what became the successful boycott of the beer-halls. (a) the resentment of the people against restrictions on home-brewing; (b) The complaint that the men spent much needed money for the maintenance of their families, on alcoholic drinks and (c) by far the most important, the dissatisfaction flowing from the fact that restrictions were placed on the home brewing of such beverages, whilst the local authorities, the Durban Corporation, could brew and sell *and* make enormous profits. The boycott of the beer-halls was only one symptom of the growing discontent of the people against all oppressive measures. For the women extended their struggle to an attack on and destruction of Durban Corporation property, the Bantu Affairs Administration buildings, other properties, buses etc. And significantly for us, their wrath was also directed against the local collaborators, not only was their property destroyed but they had to flee for their lives. It soon became clear that the fight of the women of Durban and its immediate surrounds was directed against the Local Authorities. The significance of this will be discussed later. Several deputations were led where the women attempted to put forward their grievances and demands, particularly with regard to influx control, passes for women, permits to seek work etc. The Herrenvolk were not slow to take reprisals and one form these reprisals took was the mass arrests of women. Early in July

23 women were found guilty for damaging a Corporation bus and 20 were sentenced to 3 months imprisonment with a further 3 months suspended and £15.2.6., to be paid for damage to the bus. In July 111 women all told were convicted for public disturbances. In the towns then, the protests were in the form of the boycott of beer-halls, attacks on Corporation property and on collaborators, passes for women, influx control, shack demolition, Higher wages and Bantu Education.

From then on the unrest spreads to the Rural Areas and it is the women who are in the forefront of the struggle. A rough estimate reveals that over 20 000 women from 30 areas participated in the struggle and the main rural areas involved were on the South Coast and Inland. In the Rural areas the attack was directed against the dipping tanks, the Pass Laws, the Rehabilitation and Tribalisation schemes, Poll Tax, Influx Control and Bantu Education. Only in Harding, did both men and women demonstrate their opposition to the Rehabilitation Scheme etc. By the 23 August, 1959, 1 200 people had been jailed. The Daily News of the 22nd August, 1959 stated that, 1 100 people had been arrested in 10 days and 877 were sentenced. The total years of imprisonment of all those found guilty came to 228 years and or fines totalling £13,00. Magistrates warned that compensatory fines will be imposed on tribes for damage to property.

In the last two years, we have found that the unrest and the resistance to oppression has been growing. This is directly related to the Implementation of the Rehabilitation and Stabilisation Schemes, to Verwoerd's redivision of the land and the attempt to create a Kulak class among the peasantry, to Bantu Authorities, Bantu Education, to increase taxation and to the forced removal of large groups of settled communities, together with Passes for women.

We know of Sekukuniland and the arrest of 200 women and man, who were opposed to Bantu Authorities and Bantu Education, and the banishment of the chief who was with the people.

In Zeerust the same things has occurred with the attempted removal of the Township and the sympathy boycotts of the people in other areas.

In the Cape, the unrest and the agitation, attended by arson and violence has been the order of the day, for a long period, Particularly in the Transkei, the Ciskei and tembuland. Banishments too, are a common occurrence and as was predicted at the 1958 Conference of the A.A.C. in the address on the National Situation, mass trials are an everyday occurrence.

It is against this background, schematic though it may be, that we must view the present unrest in Natal. I am not suggesting that all these events are directly connected, for that in fact is one of the problems we have to discuss, viz., the question of co-ordinating the struggle of all the oppressed in South Africa.

In discussing the nature of the unrest in Natal, two other events must be mentioned. Firstly, the dockworkers strike in January and February of this year, when hundreds of African dockworkers demanded increased pay and were eventually replaced by other migrant labourers, brought in from the rural areas. Inspite of the militancy and solidarity of the dockworkers, their strike failed because they have no proper trade unions.

And secondly, the demonstration of the women of Cato Manor against the destruction of their homes in the name of slum clearance. The women by squatting with all their possessions on the City Hall steps forced the Herrenvolk to deal directly with them and to consider their protests against the destruction of the only homes they have. These two events then, were indications early in this year, of the growing militancy of the people in the face of inhuman conditions of life.

Certain features characterise all the demonstrations and these we must discuss.

### 1) *THE SPONTANIETY OF THE PROTESTS*

Spontaniety is generally regarded as the index of the militancy of the people which militancy has been engendered by the pressure and intensification of oppression which results only in starvation and death. The African women in Natal were in revolt and this whole revolt was sparked off by the demonstrations in Durban early in June. Desperation caused by poverty had driven the women to registering their vehement rejection of all oppressive measures and into trying to obtain redress to their grievances. We did not need to read the ANC denials of being responsible for the unrest, to know that in fact, no political organisations have been behind the protests. An outlet for the militancy of the people had be found, particularly in the absence of political leadership, which accounts for the diverse forms of protest adopted by the people.

In passing mention must be made of the courage of the women in the face of the Saracens, police and guns of the Herrenvolk.

### 2) *HEIGHTENING OF POLITICAL CONSCIOUSNESS AS SHOWN BY THE NATURE OF THE PROTESTS*

Durban SOYA in a bulletin on the local unrest in June said that political consciousness had heightened since the tragic Race Riots of 1949, because there had been no evidence of racialism.[18] Instead the wrath of the people had been directed against the Corporation, N.A.D., the Government and the officials, collaborators, etc., which to the people symbolise oppression. But it was pointed out then, that the Corporation etc., are only sub-agents, who carry out the master plans worked out in Parliament, and that the real struggle is for the franchise. We must once more record the complete absence of racialism in the whole of Natal, inspite of all the attempts of the Herrenvolk to stir up racial antagonisms and provoke a racial progrom. In the rural areas, we find the wrath of the people directed against the Bantu Administration Department, dipping tanks, dipping inspectors, etc., who are there to work the machinery of oppression. The struggle has been directly against Bantu Authorities, Taxation, Influx Control etc., and both what has happened in town and country in Natal further justifies our standpoint that the political consciousness of the people has heightened. In fact, Natal has been considered the most backward part of South Africa where racialism abounds, yet the struggle of the people today give us reason to be happy, because almost overnight the whole political clime in Natal, had undergone a revolutionary change. In fact overnight Natal has caught up with the rest of South Africa.

It is true that the most striking characteristic of the unrest was the fact that only the women participated in the struggle and that they were concerned primarily with wrenching concessions and reforms from the ruling powers. But this was the awakening of the people of Natal and as one person said "the tearing asunder of the whole tribal integument."

What effect did this awakening of the people have on the various sections of South African Society and what is our attitude to the struggles of the people.

### 1) *THE HERRENVOLK*

It was to be expected that the Herrenvolk would retaliate with a show of brute force and have employed every weapon in their general armamentatarium. Baton charges,

Saracens, threats and reprisals, shootings and all night police vigils, with the hills of Cato Manor armed with machine guns. Inspite of all this the unrest continues.

Generally amongst the whites there was panic and fear. Vigilantes were formed and some amongst the intellectuals gave South Africa only 5 years more under the present regime. They realise the significance of these demonstrations and because they cannot ally themselves with the people, desire to leave the country in the name of seeking security for their children.

It is interesting to recall what individual "white" leaders have said as regards the unrest.

Mr. Mitchell: Leader of the U.P. in Natal, wired Verwoerd for greater intervention on the part of the Herrenvolk to quell what he termed "open Rebellion".

The Police Chief: lays the blame for the unrest on the ANC and the agitation dome by them.

Eiselen: Secretary for Bantu Administration and Development condemned the people for the lawlessness and threatened dire measures against them. He maintains that the senseless destruction of property should be seen against the background of exaggerated criticism of everything the State did for the benefit of the people, by subversive organisations viz., the ANC. He also paid tribute to the police, just as Luthuli did.

Eiselen also said on the 18th August, 1959 that he deplores the fact that certain classes of people and some town councils and officials are branding as unfair and unreasonable certain legislation introduced since 1923.

*The Durban City Council* being affected by the pressure from the people by their demands for human rights, were forced, at the height of the struggle of the African women, to discuss the granting of some form of municipal representation to the Indian people. This proposal came from the Mayor of Durban and was clearly a further application of their policy of divide and rule and an attempt to destroy the growing unity of the Indian and African people, particularly because all attempts at pogrom-mongering had failed. While on the one hand then we have proposals for some form of Municipal representation to the Indian people, the African people who were actually in a process of a struggle for rights were subjected to an intensification of pass raids, "beer" raids, etc. But the leadership of the Natal Indian Congresses once more demonstrated their political opportunism when they at once started sending petitions, deputations, appeals etc to the local authorities appealing for such municipal representation. Inspite of all their talk of unity with the African people, they are quite willing to wrench concessions for themselves from the rulers, at the expense of the African people.

*The Natal Indian and African Congresses*
Lacking a principled political approach to the problems of the oppressed in South Africa and because neither the ANC not the NIC can any longer claim to represent the aspirations of the workers and peasants, it is not unexpected that the women who took part in the demonstrations were condemned by these organisations and in particular, by the great Christian, moderate, non-violent collaborator Luthuli. The Congresses deny responsibility for the unrest and we have no reason to disbelieve their vehement denial. For we know that they are not at all interested in the struggle of the people for a democratic South Africa. They are afraid of the real struggles of the people, which will put an end to their collaborationist, concessions-seeking politics. They are content

with sham struggles and the Misuse of the boycott (as a weapon of struggle) in the form of cigarette and potato boycotts.

They called for an end to the demonstrations and for a judicial enquiry into the causes of the unrest and also for negotiations between the Authorities and the people. They have refused to support the struggles of the African women and in fact condemned the peasants for irrationally destroying amenities, which have become a symbol of authority. There has been no attempt to channelise the militancy of the people or to give them a lead. Their praise is reserved for the police for their handling of the situation. We see the complete lack of understanding of the mood of the people and the significance of their struggle but this is in keeping with the collaborationist-opportunistic politics of the Congresses who are interested only in the maintenance of the status quo.

*The Attitude of those of us in the Movement* is determined by our understanding of objective socio-economic and political conditions in South Africa. We realise fully that this unrest has been precipitated by the intensification of Bantu Authorities and Bantu Education and increased taxation. We support the people in their struggles with this understanding that we are quite aware that the unrest is spontaneous and isolated. BUT it is our duty as politicos to take advantage of the militancy, in order to put forward our ideas.

(i) We must channelise this militancy and try to give it organised form in *permanent organisations* of the people.
(ii) But this we can only do if we see to it that we use every opportunity in order to spread political education. Education which must centre around the need for principled Unity and the struggle for the full franchise and the rest of the Ten Point Programme i.e. on the basis of equality.
(iii) Only if we can disseminate our ideas, will we get the development of political consciousness which will lead to the formation of the people's organisations which must be brought into the A.A.C. Only in this way can the struggle throughout the country be co-ordinated.

**NOTES**
1  The Company refers to the Dutch East India Company, formed in 1602 to co-ordinate Dutch trading ventures in the East Indies on behalf of both Dutch merchants and the Dutch government. In 1652 it established a settlement at the Cape under the leadership of Jan van Riebeeck. Company officials ruled and administered the settlement for the Company's benefit with extreme corruption and inefficiency. British forces conquered the Cape in 1795, and in 1804 the Dutch government allowed the Company's charter to lapse.
2  The Congress of Vienna (1814-15) was a European assembly convened to redraw the map of Europe after the initial defeat of Napoleon I by Russia, Prussia, Austria and Britain. Its aim was to create a balance of power in Europe, to preserve the European monarchies and to contain liberal and nationalist forces.
3  The Anglo-Boer or South African War (1899-1902) was fought between Britain and the two Boer Republics. The roots of the conflict were complex but a critical factor was the discovery of gold on the Rand in the 1880s. Some British politicians, together with Lord Milner, had the agenda of British dominance over southern Africa. Early Boer victories were followed by British successes as their forces increased in strength. By mid-1900 the Boer army seemed defeated but their guerrilla forces continued the struggle into 1902, and their tactics were later studied by groups planning armed struggle in the 1960s. British supremacy was eventually enforced through a scorched-earth policy complemented by concentration camps for Boer women and children.
4  Paul Mosaka (c. 1911-63) was a successful businessman with political ambitions who, in the mid-1950s, took over and developed the Johannesburg African Chamber of Commerce. In 1942 he was elected to the NRC to represent Transvaal and the Orange Free State, and in 1942 he, along with Hyman Basner, Self Mampuru, Daniel Koza and others, launched the ADP, which survived about five years. Basner (1905-77), a Johannesburg lawyer and vigorous defender of African rights, particularly in rural areas, emigrated from Latvia and joined the CPSA as a young man but left it in 1938. From 1943 to 1947 he

was a Natives' Senator for the Transvaal and Orange Free State. He left South Africa in 1962. For his memoirs see Basner (1993). Margaret Ballinger (born Hodgson) emigrated to South Africa from Scotland in 1904. She was Natives' Representative for Eastern Cape from 1938 to 1960. She and her husband, William G. Ballinger, helped found the Liberal Party, and she was its first President from 1953 to '55. The Ballingers both grew disenchanted with the Liberal Party's advocacy of universal rather than qualified franchise and its acceptance of extraparliamentary activity.

5   Edwin Thabo Mofutsanyana (1899-1995), born in Witzieshoek, joined the ANC in 1923 and the CPSA several years later, and attended the Lenin School in Moscow in the early 1930s. For most of the 1930s he was a member of the CPSA's Politburo and in the 1940s Chair of its Johannesburg District Committee, member of its Central Committee and editor of its newspaper, *Inkululeko* (*Freedom*). He was one of the people charged with inciting the African Mineworkers' Strike of 1946. He ran, unsuccessfuly, as a Communist candidate for the NRC in 1937, '42 and '48. He was elected to the AAC's Executive Committee in the late 1930s but put his energies into rebuilding the ANC. After being banned, he moved to Basutoland (Lesotho). He was married to Josie Mpama (or Palmer), for many years the only African woman leader in the CPSA. Mpama was CPSA branch secretary in Potchefstroom in the 1920s and attended the Seventh Comintern Congress in 1935, planning to present a paper on South African women. Instead, she was given a pre-prepared speech which she presented under the pseudonym Henderson. See *International Press Correspondence*, 15, 60, 1935, pp. 1 474-5. She helped to revive the ANC in the late 1930s, was a leading figure in anti-pass struggles and was Transvaal President of Fedsaw. She was banned in 1955 and detained in 1960.

6   Anton M. Lembede (1914-47), a key figure in the intellectual development of African nationalism, attended Adams College and received B.A., LL.B. and M.A. degrees from Unisa. He helped found and was the first President of the ANC Youth League and was a strong proponent of the boycott of racial political institutions, such as the NRC. He was highly critical of and tried, unsuccessfully, to exclude Communists from the ANC.

7   William H. Andrews (1870-1950) emigrated to South Africa from England in 1893 and organised for the Amalgamated Society of Engineers (later Amalgamated Engineering Union). In 1902 he helped form the first TLC. In 1909 he became the first Chair of the SALP and was elected as M.P. in 1912. During World War One he led the anti-war faction in the SALP and chaired the ISL upon its secession from the SALP in September 1915. With the formation of the CPSA, Andrews became its Secretary and editor of *The International* and in November 1922 was elected to the ECCI. He resigned as CPSA Secretary and became inactive in Party affairs following its December 1924 resolution not to apply for affiliation to the SALP. He was Secretary of the SATUC and later the SATLC from 1925 to '32. He was formally expelled from the CPSA in September 1931 but reinstated in 1938 and chaired its Central Committee in the 1940s.

8   Vyacheslav Molotov was a leading figure in the Soviet administration for several decades, serving under both Stalin and Kruschev. He was head of the Comintern during the New Line period and was Foreign Minister in the 1940s. To many, he epitomised the character of the Soviet regime during the Cold War. He was deposed as a member of the alleged "anti-Party" group in 1958.

9   This pamphlet was translated into Xhosa as *uKwayo: isiKrweqe ne Khaka* by Phyllis Ntantala and distributed in Transkei, chiefly by SOYA members. Ntantala (1992:167) states that during the enquiries into the causes of the 1960 Pondoland uprising, rural people at a meeting in Bizana chaired by the Chief Native Commissioner of Ciskei quoted concepts from the Xhosa translation.

10  This refers presumably to the Irish Land Act of 1881, introduced by the Gladstone Liberal Government. The measure was a response to the agitation mounted by the Land League against evictions in Ireland. It introduced the so-called "three Fs" – fair rents, free sale and fixity of tenure. This response is perhaps best seen as a political gesture rather than a considered economic agenda for the Irish rural economy.

11  The Duma was the Russian Parliament introduced as a reforming measure after the Revolution of 1905. This limited liberalisation raised for left-wing parties the question of whether to participate. The Social Democratic Party (in the pre-1914 sense of the term) at that time included both Mensheviks and Bolsheviks. They agreed on a general policy of boycott on two grounds. Firstly, the Social Democrats remained optimistic about the possibility of successful armed revolution; secondly, they saw the reform as cosmetic and not involving any significant transfer of power from the autocracy. In subsequent years the limited powers of the Duma were further reduced as the autocracy regained more self-confidence.

12  Documents 40 to 43 refer to the first elections of white Coloured Representatives, which took place in 1958. The NEUM organised a successful boycott supported by 80 per cent of the eligible voters. SACPO's decision to run candidates resulted in a stunning defeat. In Cape Town its candidate, Piet Beyleveld, was overwhelmingly defeated by the UP.

13  This is probably Abdullah Omar, who was profoundly influenced by Benjamin Kies while a student at Trafalgar High School, joined the NEF and became Secretary of the Cape Anti-CAD. He received a law

degree from UCT in 1957, subsequently opened a law practice with Cadoc M. Kobus of the AAC, then practicing in Langa, and defended numerous political prisoners. By the early 1980s he thought the Unity Movement too passive, and he joined the UDF, becoming a leading activist. He became Minister of Justice in the first democratic Parliament.

14 R. O. Dudley, a Deputy Principal of Livingstone High School, was involved in the NEF in the 1940s and was a leading member of the TLSA, Anti-CAD and NEUM and a founding member of the New Unity Movement.

15 SACPO, later renamed the CPC, was formed in September 1953, largely from members of the FRAC.

16 This refers to the series of rural protests and uprisings that shook South Africa in the late 1940s and '50s.

17 *The Soyan* was to organ of SOYA, an AAC affiliate. For other accounts of the 1959 Natal women's protests see Yawich (1977) and Lodge (1983:147-51).

18 In January 1949 an altercation in Durban between an African customer and an Indian shop assistant during a crowded rush hour led to several nights of violence which included physical assaults and arson and looting of factories, stores and dwellings. Of the 142 deaths officially recorded, 50 were Indians and 87 Africans; of the 1 087 injured, 503 were Indians and 541 Africans. Dismal economic conditions fuelled the tension which led to the 1949 Durban Riots. By the mid-1940s about one-half of Durban's African population lived in Indian-owned slums, and Indians controlled the bus service and retail outlets. The Pegging Act and the Ghetto Act caused property prices and rents to soar while Indian-owned slums became increasingly overcrowded.

# Part One

## Building the national movement

### National liberation and trade-union organisation

***EDITOR'S NOTE***
*The black trade union movement reached an apex during World War Two. But the squashing of the 1946 African Mineworkers' Strike and the ensuing repression faced by its leaders left the black labour movement severely weakened on the eve of apartheid. Both the leadership of the Congress movement and of the NEUM believed that trade unions should be integrated into the national liberation movement through affiliation to particular organisations; however, activists in the Congress movement far outstripped those in the NEUM in terms of practical trade-union work. In the early 1950s, left-wing debates about trade-union organisation concerned the question of whether to build trade-union unity across the colour bar or to build the black trade-union movement. However, as the state restricted the possibility of the former through racist legislation, political and trade-union activists followed the strategy of attempting to integrate the black trade-union movement into the national liberation movement – for example, through the affiliation of SACTU to the Congress Alliance.*

Document 45
Ray Alexander, "Trade Unionism in South Africa",
*Discussion*, 1, 6, 1952

*[....]* The first Trade Unions were organised by British immigrants who came to South Africa in the 1880's, with trade union experience. They formed local branches of British Trade Unions. The Amalgamated Engineering Union is still a part of the British union.

In 1902 the Transvaal Miners' Association was formed, which later became the S.A. Mine Workers' Union.

**Fight for Trade Union Recognition**
From the very outset and for many years afterwards, these unions met with hostility on the part of employers and State authorities, as a result of which conflicts broke out between employers and workers on the Diamond Mines of Kimberley and later the disputes shifted to the Witwatersrand.

In 1907, the mining companies proposed to increase the proportion of African miners employed and the Transvaal Miners' Association was not prepared to accept it and so they came out on strike. Thereupon, the State introduced the Transvaal Industrial Disputes Prevention Act of 1907, but despite this, the most serious dispute in South African history took place in 1913. The miners all along the Reef struck for Trade Union recognition.

A judicial Commission was appointed after the termination of the strike, which recommended recognition of the Miners' Union by both the Government and the Chamber of Miners, and rules dealing with future industrial disputes.

At the end of December, 1913, the European Coal Miners of Natal struck, and the Transvaal Federation of Trades, the co-ordinating body, established in 1911, brought the Gold Miners in the strike, as well as the workers engaged on the State-owned railways. Thus there was the general strike of 1913.[1]

The Government, alarmed at these developments, declared Martial Law, brought in

Commandos and the Defence Force, arrested trade union leaders and Labour Party members, and deported nine trade union leaders without trial. The action of the Government was criticised by judges, Parliament and Imperial authorities. The Government, therefore, introduced the Indemnity and Riotous Assemblies Acts – the Indemnity Act to give them indemnity of all the brutal action against the workers; and the Riotous Assemblies Act to prohibit strikes in public services and to illegalise strikes so as to prevent other workers from coming out on strike.

**World War No. 1**
In 1914 World War I broke out and the Government of the day was forced to give certain concessions to the workers in order to gain their support. During the war period, industry advanced and the bargaining power of the workers was strengthened. By 1915, the Chamber of Miners, Municipalities and some employers accepted and Closed Shop principle, recognised trade unions and the Unions obtained wage increases for the workers. These victories for unions resulted in a tremendous growth of the Trade Union Movement. Whilst in 1915 there were only 10 538 organised workers, by 1918 the number of organised workers totalled 77 819.

By the end of the War and the Declaration of Peace, the cost of living rose and again unrest arose among the workers who had learned to be organised and struggle for improvements in wages, as is shown by the number of strikes – 1916 – 10, 1919 – 47, and 1920 – 66 strikes. In these disputes, not only European workers took part, but also Coloured, African and Indian workers.

The war had also forced large numbers of non-Europeans into industry, and gave rise to the formation of non-European trade unions, which opened an important chapter in Trade Union history. The Industrial Commercial Workers' Union was the first wholly non European Trade Union organised, and was formed in Cape Town in 1919. This Union, organised by the late Mr. Clements Kadalie, covered farm workers, domestic employees, as well as African, Indian and Coloured Industrial workers. There was great enthusiasm for this mighty, new union, and its membership soon rose to over 100 000 paid up members. The first successful strike led by the I.C.U., as the Union was known, was the strike of the Cape Town Dockers in 1919. These workers won themselves 8/- per day whereas before they received 4/- per day.

The end of the boom period marked a period of wage cuts, unemployment and strikes. Strikes took place of the African Gold Miners, European Engineers in Johannesburg, Tramway workers in East London, Railway and Engineering Workers in Durban. The climax was reached in 1922 in the great Rand strike.[2] The main issue was the decision of the Chamber of Mines to modify the colour bar, employ non-Europeans in skilled jobs, and increase the ratio of Africans to Europeans. After 76 days the strike ended with 320 persons dead. The strike was called off by the Federation of Trades, and the Mines took back such men as they required, on their own terms.

The Government appointed a Commission and a Mining Industry Board to consider future mining policy. The Mining Industry Board advised the repeal of the colour bar imposed in the Mines and Workers Act of 1911, and proposed a conciliation scheme to settle disputes at joint conferences between the mine owners and miners. A permanent Conciliation Board with an equal number of representatives from both sides, came into operation in 1922. The Government introduced the Industrial Conciliation Bill, which subsequently became the Industrial Conciliation Act of 1924, and was amended in 1937.

## Industrial Legislation

Although Trade Unionism declined after the 1922 Rand strike there were other consequences favourable to labour, i.e. the enactment of industrial legislation such as the Wage Act and Industrial Conciliation Act. There were already industrial laws such as the Workmen's Compensation Act (1914), the Miners' Phthisis Act (1912), the Workmen's Wages Protection Act (1914), the Factories Act 1918, the Juveniles Act (1922) and the Apprenticeship Act (1918).

The Industrial Conciliation Act mainly aimed at the prevention of strikes, i.e. "peace in industry" by negotiation, conciliation and arbitration, but by the definition of "employee" in the Act, Africans are excluded – the golden rule of the boss class "divide and rule policy."

In addition, workers employed in Agriculture, Government service and by the Railways are excluded.

From the very introduction of the Industrial Conciliation Act, the Trade Union Movement urged the deletion of the colour bar clause and its extension to all workers. Many argue that workers would be able to improve their conditions to the same extent and even more, if the Industrial Conciliation Act and Wage Act were not in existence. They point out that the prohibition of strikes in whole or in part by the existence of the Industrial Conciliation Act, deprives the workers of their only strong weapon; and that the existence of Industrial Council Agreements or Determinations tend to bring about a spirit of collaboration between employers and workers, which hinders the growth of class consciousness among workers. Above all, this machinery divides into racial groups and prevents the achievement of unity against the employers. Yes, these view points are true!

After 30 years of experience of these laws we cannot but see that the boss class have largely succeeded in achieving the aims which they had in view when they introduced the Industrial Conciliation and Wage Acts. A large number of workers have improved their conditions, but at the expense of the independence of the working class. A great responsibility rests upon the Trade Union leaders and members who have accepted this position of conciliation and compromise with the bosses and the Government. Yet, it is possible for a Union to use these laws in such a way that not only are conditions improved, but the militancy and unity of the workers are raised to higher levels. These laws like other things should be used as weapons with which to improve the workers' conditions of life, build their trade unions and through organisation develop their understanding of political and economic problems.

## The Formation of a National Trade Union Organisation

Colonel Creswell, leader of the Labour Party and Minister of the newly formed Labour Department, convened a conference of trade union representatives to consider the operation of the Industrial Conciliation and Wage Acts, and the formation of one National Trade Union Centre.[3] From this gathering the S.A. Association of Employees' Organisation, later known as the S.A. Trade Union Congress, was established, and reformed in October, 1931, as the S.A. Trades and Labour Council.

In the S.A. Trade Union Congress there were Trade union leaders with different points of view. The reactionary type that were against accepting the applied affiliation of the Industrial Commercial Workers' Union, on the grounds that the Congress would be dominated by non-European Trade unions, and the progressive leaders (called the

Left's) who fought for one trade union centre irrespective of colour, urged the acceptance of the I.C.U. and generally denounced colour-bar policies of European Trade Unionists. The "Left" group pressed for unity of the working class, for the amendment of the Industrial Conciliation Act to include in the definition "employee" all workers, *i.e.*, Africans, and that anti-strike clauses in the Act be repealed. Our late comrade, Bill Andrews, was the leader of this group.[4]

These differences of opinions and the existence of the Cape Federation of Labour Unions (an organisation created in 1913 and supported mainly by Cape unions) was a serious obstacle in the establishment of one National Trade Union Centre.

## The Organisation of Non-European Workers in Trade Unions

Except in the Cape, where the Cape Federation of Trade Unions from their inception included coloured artisans, the organisation of non European workers was done by the I.C.U. The successful strike of the Cape Town dockers gave impetus to other workers. 11 Unions moved their Head offices to Johannesburg, from where they issued a monthly journal called the *Workers' Herald*, and, in general established an elaborate machine with many paid organisers. These thousands of members, mainly Africans, supported the I.C.U. with great enthusiasm and sacrifice. The loose grouping of workers of different industries within one organisation instead of one Union for one industry, lack of experience, the scarcity of competent leaders, insufficient accounting of the funds, were some of the factors which prevented it from becoming an effective organisation. By the onset of the big depression in 1930, it had virtually ceased to function. Sections of the I.C.U. are still in existence in East London, Bloemfontein and Natal.

The hopes, enthusiasm and imagination which fired the non-European workers, particularly the Africans, were lost, and left many workers bitterly disappointed. Nevertheless, the I.C.U. left an everlasting impression. The Government was worried, and was actually plunged into a Cabinet crisis in 1928, when Madeley, then Minister of Posts and Telegraphs, and also a leader of the Labour Party, received an I.C.U. deputation.[5]

The European Trade Unions began to realise the strength of the African workers, and the S.A. Trade Union Congress had a number of conferences with the I.C.U. and recommended their affiliated unions to enrol all workers irrespective of race into their unions. Most important of all, the non-European workers learnt the possibilities of being organised, and the advantages of organisation.

In 1936, the Union started upon an era of industrial expansion and non-European workers entered industries in large numbers. New enthusiasm swept through all workers, particularly the non-Europeans, for trade union organisation. The growth in Trade Unionism is shown by the increase in the number of registered Trade Unions. In 1929 there were 101 unions with a membership of 69 882, and 1946 – 203 unions with a membership of 346 509. These figures do not include African trade unions as they are not allowed to be registered. Of the 203 Unions, no less than 115 unions were affiliated to the S.A. Trades and Labour Council. These Unions had a mixed membership of Europeans, Coloured and Indian workers, and a small number of African unions were also affiliated to the S.A. Trades and Labour Council. Only one Union maintained a colour bar clause in its constitution, and it was the S.A. Mine Workers Union. The majority of African unions in the Transvaal were affiliated to the Transvaal Council of Non-European Trade Unions, which was formed in 1938.[6] Many efforts have been made to convert this council into an organisation of all non-European trade unions throughout the country, but it met with little success. In all other provinces, the Non-European Unions are affiliated to the S.A. Trades and Labour Council or to the Western Province Federation of Labour Unions. Despite many attempts by the reactionary racialist leaders, the S. A. Trades and Labour Council has no colour bar in its constitution, and is open to all Unions, registered and non-registered. It is important to organise all workers who are mainly African into unions, and these unions and others should affiliate to the S.A. Trades and Labour Council. This is the only way the non-European workers will be able to exercise influence on the policy of the Council. The division in the ranks of the workers can only be of help to the bosses and the Government.

Unity of the working class can only be achieved by all workers irrespective of colour, being organised and affiliated to one body. The S.A. Trades and Labour Council and the Council for Non-European Trade Unions have at every Conference passed resolutions for the amendment of the I.C. Act to include African workers. However, despite these resolutions the Act has not been amended, which was mainly due to
(a) because European reactionary Trade Union leaders opposed it, and
(b) the N.E. Trade Unions, in fact, the whole of the Trade Union Movement did not press hard enough for this amendment.

**Racialism in Trade Union Movement**
During 1947 and 1948, "pure" white Trade Unions such as the S.A. Mine Workers' Union and the Iron and Steel workers with their Secretary, Mr. van der Bergh, led a group of unions affiliated to the S.A. Trades and Labour Council for the introduction of "apartheid" in the S.A. Trades and Labour Council conferences, and tried to amend the S.A.T.L.C.'s Constitution by introducing a colour-bar clause. This attempt was defeated by the efforts of the progressive Trade Unions affiliated to the S.A.T.L.C. with little help of African trade unions, who are not affiliated to the S.A.T.L.C., and therefore, do not attend Conferences to help in the making of progressive Trade Union policies.

With the coming into power of the Nationalist Party Government in 1948, and the introduction of their apartheid policy in the Trade Union Movement, a number of "white" unions broke away and formed the Co-ordinating Council in Pretoria (which consists of European unions only); the Blankewerkers Federasie formed and financed by Nationalist Party supporters prior to the 1948 election, claims to have two unions such as shop assistants in country towns and wine workers – but has been useful to the Nationalist Government as a mouthpiece of reaction when it gave evidence to the Commission on the Unemployment Insurance Act and the Industrial Legislation Commission. The S.A. Federation of Trade Unions is a body that only accepts the affiliation of registered Trade Unions – African Unions are debarred.

The Trade Union Movement is very divided now. In addition to the above mentioned bodies, there are the Transvaal Council for Non-European Trade Unions, the Western Province Federation of Labour Unions and the S.A. Trades and Labour Council. The S.A. Trades and Labour Council is the most representative body of workers. It is the duty of every sincere Trade Unionist and every sincere worker who believes in the unity of the working class, to see that all unions, particularly the Non-European Unions, affiliate to the S.A.T.L.C., not to splinter bodies like the Western Province Federation of Labour Unions and the S.A. Federation of Trade Unions with their colour bar. Let us make no mistake, there are a number of Trade Unions with a majority of Coloured members in its membership, who are affiliated to the S.A. Federation of Trade Unions. *Unity of the working class must be brought about, and this unity will become a reality only when the thousands of non-European and African workers engaged in semi-skilled and unskilled work have been organised, have raised their wage standards, have secured themselves the right to enter in every skilled trade and occupation and have made the European workers behave like fellow workers – not like a "white baas"!*

It is, therefore, necessary to give to the worker an understanding of the aims of Trade Unionism, its history, its record of working class struggle for democratic rights, like the part played by the British Trade Unions in the Chartist Movement, and the struggle of other workers in other countries who succeeded in bringing about a state of affairs where the workers are governing.[7] Yes, the workers by accepting responsibility of leadership in Trade Unions, responsibilities as Treasurers and shop stewards, etc., receive the first lessons in how to administer their country.

In the Trade Union Movement we are often confronted with people who say Trade Unions should not be concerned with politics. I do not agree with this point of view. A Trade Union is an organisation of workers and has a duty to take an interest in all matters that affect the working class. Economics cannot be separated from Politics. The colour bar system, whilst it is political in the first place, directly affects the rights of the European to work, his wages and his general condition of life.

Some Trade Unions believe that only the industrial laws are their concern. Who makes the industrial laws in our country? – a parliament that is not elected by the majority of the working class. The majority of the working class are Africans, and all non-European women, who are factory workers and have not got the right to vote, to be elected to Parliament and make the laws affecting them. Politics concern the workers' bread and their rights as citizens. It is, therefore, no accident that some unions in Port Elizabeth, Worcester and other towns are whole-heartedly supporting the Campaign of Defiance of Unjust Laws.

The Trade Union Movement in South Africa is destined to play an important part in the fight for democratic rights, and for a free, happy and prosperous South Africa.

## DISCUSSION AND QUESTIONS

*Miss Butcher:* If the European workers refuse to be organised in mixed unions, is there any justification for separate trade unions?

*Lecturer:* There is no justification for organisation in separate unions. All workers irrespective of colour should organise in the same unions.

*Mr. Meltzer:* What is the lecturer's attitude towards the Non-European Trade Union Council?

*Lecturer:* I have no disagreement with the formation of this Council, but I feel that it should urge its unions to affiliate to the South African Trades and Labour Council. This is necessary to obtain unity of all workers and will help in the formulating of a progressive policy in the S.A.T.L.C. The organisation of the whole working class is necessary, not only for the day to day struggles of the workers, but for political purposes as well. If the unity of the working class is to be achieved, we must firstly strive for the unity of all trade unions.

*Mr. Cohen:* Could the lecturer tell us why the Furniture Workers' Union are considering withdrawing from the S.A.T.L.C. and why the Cape Garment Workers'

Union and Building Workers' Union are not affiliated to the S.A.T.L.C.?

*Lecturer:* These unions lack progressive leadership.

*Mr. Marney:* Achieving the unity of the non-European workers in South Africa is more important than the unity of the working class. If the non-European workers think they can achieve their ends by remaining out of the S.A.T.L.C., therefore, the formation of a non-European Trade Union Council is of the utmost importance. The white workers are opposed to non-European workers. The S.A.T.L.C. therefore loses its importance in connection with the abolition of the colour bar. Trade Union organisers should rather concentrate upon the organisation of the non-European workers than the achievement of black and white working class unity.

Striving to achieve unity of black and white workers becomes reactionary, because the unity will be at the expense of the black workers. The only way in which we can achieve progressive unity is through the proper organisation of independent non-European trade unions. It must be clearly understood that the class interests of the black workers and the white workers are not identical. The whites are interested in maintaining the *status quo* and defending their privileged position. The South African Trades and Labour Council is a product of the history of European Trade Union movement and is closely associated with the perpetuation of the colour bar. The struggle for the existence of the S.A.T.L.C. is a lost cause. Furthermore the leaders of the non-European Trade Union Council have probably realised the futility of striving for the unity of black and white workers; therefore they have refused to affiliate to S.A.T.L.C.

*Lecturer:* I believe in the unity of the working class, not at the expense of the non-European workers – that is not unity. In spite of the many defeats the progressive trade unions in S.A.T.L.C. have suffered, and in spite of the attack on the S.A.T.L.C. by the Government and its demand to introduce segregation, we can be proud of the fact, that the S.A.T.L.C. has no colour bar. To do what you suggest – resign from the S.A.T.L.C. and affiliate to the Non-European Trade Union Council, will leave the T.L.C. to some trade union leaders who might agree to the government's pressure and thus give them victory over the Trade Union Movement. Our job is to strengthen the S.A.T.L.C. and make it an important organisation to work for the interests of the worker, i.e., non-European workers and others.

*Mr. Meltzer:* I feel that the lecturer has no real perspective of the fundamental issues at stake. She has dealt with the subject from a narrow organisational and administrative point of view and so failed to assess the real social forces. Moreover, she has failed to point out the decisive changes that came about as the direct result of the 1922 Rand Strike, by which the white workers gained a new status, politically, economically and socially. As a result of the 1922 strike the white workers were integrated in the State and thereafter became more and more reactionary.

Miss Alexander by keeping her eyes fixed on the S.A.T.L.C. and trying to create unity among non-European and European working class through its agency, has failed to offer a basis for the building up of non-European trade unions. A mechanical view of unity such as she envisaged through S.A.T.L.C. merely means that non-Europeans must tail behind. Miss Alexander's attitude towards the Non-European Council of Trade Unions implied that she was merely using it as a bargaining lever.

*Lecturer:* The remarks by Mr. Meltzer are unfounded and a slander on the work I do in the trade union movement and the ideas I put forward here. Obviously Mr. Meltzer did not listen to what I said.

Document 46
D. Tloome[8], "The Origin and Development of Non-European Trade Unions", lecture delivered to the
Johannesburg Discussion Club on 27 February 1953,
*Viewpoints and Perspectives,*[9] 1, 1, 21 February 1953

*[....] Current Position of Non-European Trade Unions*
A survey of Non-European Trade Unions discloses that a period of decline is overtaking these Trade Unions. And, in my opinion, this is due to the fact that the entire trade union movement has failed to come out as a militant movement capable of giving the workers hope for the future. The tendency among some trade unions, of both black and white workers, is to keep exclusively to economic demands of the workers and leave their political ignorance to unscrupulous politicians. This tendency has led the workers to believe and regard the trade unions as instruments for taking up complaints and preparing workers demands for the next sitting of the Industrial Council of the Wage Board. The fact that a militant trade union movement, fearlessly taking up those issues, both economic and political, which are keeping down the workers in political ignorance and by exploitation, can become the vanguard and the hope for a better life for all workers, is not imagined by some trade unionists.

According to information available, Non-European trade unions fall under four heads, namely, (a) Non-European Trade Unions independent of unions of other races. (b) Non-European Trade Unions under the supervision of registered Trade Unions. (c) Unions supervised by the S.A. Railways & Harbours Administration. (d) Non-Europeans who are members of inter-racial Unions.

*Non-European Trade Unions Independent of Unions of Other Race*
32 African Trade Unions fall within this group, the geographical distribution being as follows:–
Johannesburg 21 Pretoria 1. Durban 4.
Cape Town 2 Port Elizabeth 3. East London 1.
It is clear from these facts that a good number of unions have gone out of existence since 1942, which in effect means that many industries still remain unorganised.

*Non-European Trade Unions Under the Supervision of Registered Unions*
Quite a good few Non-European Trade Unions are operating under the supervision of Registered Unions. Such unions are found in industries like Printing, Clothing, Furniture, Sweet, Textile and Laundry industries. Unfortunately figures for geographical distribution are not readily available.

*Union Supervised by the S.A. Railways & Harbours Administration*
There is an Association of Non-European staff of the S.A. Railways & Harbours Administration in existence, with branches in Pretoria, Durban, Johannesburg, Cape Town, Port Elizabeth, East London, Kimberley and Bloemfontein. This association was established by the administration as a counter to the independent and militant union known as the S.A. Railways Harbours and Airport workers Union, with Head Quarters in Cape Town. At best it can be said that this association is nothing more than a Company Union.

*Non-Europeans Who are Members of Inter-Racial Unions*
The Industrial Legislation Commission's investigations disclosed that there were

twelve such African Trade Unions, seven of which were situated in Port Elizabeth, four in Cape Town and one in Johannesburg. Those in Port Elizabeth were affiliated to the one federation and had the same secretary. Although the Department of Labour took steps to see that African Members were separated from the entire membership of the other races, it is claimed that the four Cape Town unions took no such steps to have the Africans removed from their membership rolls. The Johannesburg one is the Garment Workers' Union which has a branch including approximately 1 600 African women members who, in terms of the judgement of the Supreme Court fall within the meaning of the term "employee" in the Industrial Conciliation Act.

The position of African Trade Unions is summarised in the Industrial Legislation Commission's investigations as follows: There are at least 52 African Trade Unions in existence with a total paid up membership of approximately 34 551. If the Railway Staff Association is excluded, the membership of the remaining Unions is approximately 17 296. In addition there are twelve mixed Trade Unions of which the African paid up membership totalled approximately 3 700.

*Unity of All Workers in Trade Unions*

The most significant question that constantly comes to the fore in the South African Trade Union movement, is the unity of all sections of the working class. This is the basic principle which underlies a successful trade union movement. It is common knowledge that in South Africa labour is not considered according to its value, but according to the colour of its skin. The effect of this theory on the living and working conditions of the workers of South Africa constitues one of the problems of disunity in the trade union movement.

There is a vast difference in the status between the European and Non-European workers. The European workers are accorded every protection, under the industrial legislation of the country, to make the fullest use of the machinery of collective bargaining, in order to improve their economic position. Besides, it is the technique of the ruling class to accord citizenship and political rights to the European workers, so as to ensure that they will always consider themselves an integral part of the exploiting class, ready to resist any attempt to bring about unity between them and their less privileged fellow workers.

The Non-European workers, on the other hand, are denied all claims to citizenship and political rights. They are ruled under a system which has been systematically designed to keep them under conditions of poverty, ignorance and disease in perpertuity; They are kept out of the skilled jobs, which are preserved as the sole monopoly of the European workers; They are not permitted to enter into any trade as apprentices, above all, they have no citzenship rights to use as a pressure to improve their conditions. Their oppression, therefore, under such conditions is twofold: They suffer both national, and economic disabilities, and their destiny is left in the hands of people who regard them as floating cheap labour awaiting exploitation.

Under these circumstances, it is quite obvious that the unity of all sections of the workers requires a clearsighted and resolute policy, designed to uphold the basic principles of trade unionism, namely to develope and maintain maximum unity of all workers. Perhaps one might be led to believe that the persistent racialist propaganda by the ruling class and the influence of Apartheid policies of the Government is at the bottom of failure to secure workers unity in the trade unions, but that argument cannot be basically the cause. The realities of what is to be done are not far-fetched. The first task that is facing the Non-European workers is unity of the Non-European workers themselves in their trade unions. Then there is the need to join their national liberation movement which is engaged in a struggle to remove the very disabilities which are the cause of non-recognition of African Trade Unions and the inferior status attached to Africans by a host of discriminatory legislation. Once all the workers enjoy the fullest democratic rights, the struggle for unity will have been brought nearer home, and an independent and vigorous trade union movement, fighting fearlessly and without hesitation will find a place in the hearts of thousands of workers who are engaged in a bitter struggle for full democracy.

## DISCUSSION

*Mrs. Lipman.* If it is a fact that the organisation of Non-European Trade Unions will never really be possible until the National Liberatory struggle is successful, shouldn't the existing Non-European Trade Unions be more active in the Liberatory struggle.

*Lecturer.* The trade Unions must be built up at the same time as the Liberatory movement is being built up. It must be remembered that the factory workers are the backbone of the Liberatory movment. Unfortunately many of the existing Trade Unions are not interested in anything but wage demands. There is a strong feeling that politics should be left out.

*Mrs. Berman.* At a previous meeting of the Club, the view was put forward that it was the political disabilities such as the Pass Laws, restriction of movement etc, rather than economic disabilities of low wages etc, which affected the Africans most. This being the case, Africans would be more likely to support the Liberatory movement rather than the Trade Unions which in any case, were becoming increasingly difficult to organise. In other words, Africans were not yet class conscious and this fact must affect the successful organisation of African Trade Unions.

*Mr. O'Dowd.* I disagree with the last staement. The ecnomic struggle is something very positive for the Africans. On the whole there is a homogeneity of class interests and I believe that Africans are learning techniques of class struggle – in fact more rapidly than an African bourgeoisie is developing. The African people are liberating themselves not from a foreign oppression but from an oppressive capitalist economic system and the Non-European Trade Unions have therefore a most important role to play.

*Mrs. Berman.* Are those Non-European Trade Unions that are affiliated to European Trade Unions, for example the Laundry Trade Union, more successful in their economic demands?

*Lecturer.* Yes, because in those cases there is no economic rivalry and therefore no antagonisms. It also depends on the Trade Union officals. In the case of the Laundry Workers Union, the organiser has always put up a strong fight on behalf of the Non-European workers.

*Mrs. Berman.* Many of the so-called European workers in this country should not really be classified as workers. In the early days of industrial development, when there was a shortage of technicians and artisans, skilled workers had to be enticed from overseas at high rates of pay. In the course of years, these men formed themselves into Trade Unions to protect their privileges and these Trade Unions are today only interested in maintaining a status quo. So today we have the artificial position of a group of protected European "workers" earning wages which are uneconomic to industry as a whole, and which are high at the expense of the poorly paid unskilled African worker. Their wages are uneconomic because the work they do does not in most cases warrant the wages they earn and serves only to send up production costs. Were the position to be rationalized the unskilled workers would be trained to do most of the skilled and semi-skilled work at economic rates of pay, and this particular group of European workers would lose their privileged position. It is doubtful whether even a greatly expanding secondary industry could absorb them at their existing rates of pay. Their wages would have to come down accordingly. It seems obvious to me that the Non-European Trade Unions must expect no assistance from this particular group of European Trade Unions who can only view the success of the demands of Non-European Trade Unions as a threat to themselves.

The position of the lower paid European worker is quite different. Once Non-European skilled and semi skilled workers are admitted freely into Industry, the South African economy as a whole must benefit. Africans earning more money represent a greater purchasing power. Industry can then produce in greater and therefore more economic quantities, and on a more rational basis, where the wages earned are related to work performed and not to historical privileges. The lower paid European workers have therefore to gain by allying themselves with the work and demands of the Non-European Trade Unions.

*Dr. Hathorn.* Would the lecturer tell us something about Trade Union organisation in Port Elizabeth.

*Lecturer.* They are well organised. One does not find the same distinction between political and economic demands. The Trade Union leaders were in the vanguard of the Liberatory struggle.

*Mr. Lipman.* In the Transvaal, the leadership at the moment is in the hands of the petty-bourgeoisie. In order to preserve some sort of unity, has not this leadership sacrificed the interests of the workers and the Trade Unions. And have not the Trade Unions put up an active fight.

*Lecturer.* They have recently and large number of Trade Unionists are now to be found amongst the leaders of the Liberatory movement.

*Mrs. Berman.* In the classic National Liberatory Struggle the differing class interests are subordinate to the interests of the National Struggle as a whole. The working class and the bourgeoisie work together to throw off colonial oppression. South Africa however is in a unique position. Due to her peculiar historical circumstances we find neither a well developed Non-European bourgeoisie nor a class conscious Non-European proletariat. This fact has led to differing views on the nature and course of the National Liberatory Struggle in South Africa. The one view holds that in the course and realisation of the National Liberatory Struggle an African bourgeoisie will develope, and the classic pattern will follow from then onwards. The proletariat will have gained certain political freedoms but not its economic freedom. Holders of this view claim that only when this political freedom has been achieved, will the proletariate become truly aware of the nature of their still present economic disabilities and develop a class consciousness. If this is the pattern then one must expect the greater part of the leadership of the National Liberatory movement to be in the hands of the bourgeoisie and one must expect the situation that Mr. Lipman mentioned. On the other hand, just because there is no well developed bourgeoisie it is just as likely that the class conscious elements will assume leadership and that the interests of the bourgeoisic will be pushed aside. In this case, the nature of the struggle will broaden to include economic demands, ie, the demands will be not only for the extension of existing freedoms and privileges to all, but a fundamental change in economic relationships. If as Mr. Tloome says more militant Trade Unionists are coming into the leadership – which has already happened in Port Elizabeth, where one does not see the same distinction made between political and economic demands – this may be a pointer to the way in which the struggle is developing.

Document 47
"Answer to Government's Apartheid Unions",
*The Citizen*, 1, 3, 30 April 1956

"THE LABOUR MOVEMENT MUST FIGHT ALL ATTEMPTS ON THE PART OF THE GOVERNMENT TO CONTROL THE FREE ASSOCIATION OF WORKERS IN TRADE UNION ORGANISATIONS. IT IS THE UNCHALLENGEABLE RIGHT OF WORKERS TO MAKE THEIR VOICES HEARD AND THEIR ORGANISED STRENGTH FELT IN BOTH THE ECONOMIC AND POLITICAL FIELDS" SAID MR. JOHN GOMAS WHEN INTERVIEWED BY OUR REPORTER ON THE INDUSTRIAL CONCILIATION BILL.

Mr. Gomas, well known over the last 30 years as a militant trade unionist, rejected the whole idea of "racial" kraaling of workers. "Racialism had greatly weakened the workers' struggle. Separate "racial" trade unions, as provided under the I.C. Bill, will cripple the labour movement he said.

### WORKER INTERESTS OVERLOOKED

"My attitude is simple. If the Government refuses to register non-racial unions, the labour movement must organise the workers in unrecognised, unregistered trade unions, or in other forms of worker association.

"The Government is dominated by the bosses, especially the Chamber of Mines bosses. It is wrong to think that a state, which entirely overlooks the interests of the majority of workers, should be permitted to decide whether a workers' organisation is to be registered or not, or even arbitrate between employer and employee.

### ATTEMPT TO PARALYSE

"Registration of trade unions, and Government arbitration, are the means by which the Government has attempted to paralyse the labour movement and whereby it has bribed off a section of the more privileged workers, especially the so-called white 'aristocrats' of labour.

### WORKERS STRENGTH

"The strength of the worker lies in his unity and discipline, in non-racial, democratic worker organisations. It does not lie in Government registration, recognition, or arbitration. Their organised strength should be the workers' final court of appeal in the struggle between worker and employer, worker and apartheid industrial legislation and even between workers and the bribed, reactionary and privileged unions begging apartheid protection.

## THE I.C.U.

"I have been associated with the trade union movement since 1919 and during that year, both the Tailors' Union in Kimberley and the I.C.U. in Cape Town – both unregistered, without industrial legislation or arbitration – organised and successfully fought for higher wages. The wages of I.C.U. workers were doubled from 4/- to 8/- per day.

"It is widely known that most of the recent wave of strikes in England are not 'official' but 'unofficial' strikes.

## MAJORITY NOT "EMPLOYEES"

"Those who cling so dearly to 'official recognition' must never forget that most South African workers, so-called 'Africans', are not even recognised as employees and are therefore never registered when organised into trade unions.

"It is the organised unity of the whole of the workers and not registration which will strengthen the labour movement.

"Had the workers of South Africa been organised and united in non-racial trade unions, they would easily have dealt with such legislation as the I.C. Bill. And more than that, in the face of a united labour movement, the apartheid system as a whole could hardly survive", said Mr. Gomas.

## Document 48
"The Anti-C.A.D. and the Trade Unions", *The Torch*, 1 April 1958

**From the very beginning the Anti-C.A.D. Movement has been very concerned to get the organised workers to take their proper place and to play a full part in the national liberatory movement. This will be seen already from the discussions and resolutions of the Second Conference, held in 1944.**[10]

Reporting on the Conference, Bulletin No. 30 January 19th, 1944, said: "In view of the growing, unemployment (see "Cape Argus", Jan. 11th), particularly amongst Non-Europeans, artisans as well as unskilled and semi-skilled workers, the Conference decisions with regard to the Trade Unions and the Anti-C.A.D. Movement must be given great attention. The role that the C.A.C. plays in trying to set one section of the workers against another, has already been demonstrated in their attempt to stir up Coloured against African workers in Cape Town. As the unemployment position worsens still more, the C.A.C. will be still further used by the Government and the employers to continue this foul task of deceiving the workers in order to protect the employers. Conference passed two resolutions on the Trade Union question:

(1) "This Conference instructs all local committees and Individual organisations to make every endeavour to enrol the organised workers, the Trade Unions, into the Anti-C.A.D. Movement, and calls upon all trade unionists to assist in this task".

(2) "This Conference urges the organised Trade Union Movement as represented by the Cape Federation of Labour Unions, the S.A. Trades and Labour Council, the Non-European Councils of Trade Unions (Pretoria, Port Elizabeth and Johannesburg) to call a special Conference to consider the disastrous effect of a C.A.C. and C.A.D. upon the status of Coloured workers in trade unions and thus upon the trade union movement as a whole".

"It is now for every individual worker and workers' organisations to take up this matter anew, and to impress upon the trade unions that the Anti-C.A.D. Movement is not attempting to interfere with their domestic affairs, but is trying to obtain their active co-operation against the C.A.C. which is a direct and immediate threat to the status of the Coloured worker and thus to the standard of the whole working class".

That was 1944. And in 1954, at its 5th National Conference, held in Cape Town on January 7th-8th, the Anti-C.A.D. re-affirmed its stand and urged the workers to fight against the policy of collaboration which was destroying them. The resolution on this declared:

"That this Conference:
(i) Condemns and rejects the increasingly fascistic legislation used or directed against the Trade Union Movement in South Africa, as evidenced by the Native Labour Settlement of Disputes Act of 1953, which destroys the right to strike, places the African workers under the Native Affairs Department, and extends the machinery of industrial oppression; by the Native Building Workers Act, which extend inferiority and segregation in work and wages; by the Suppression of Communism Act, which is used to decapitate the trade unions; by the proposed Schoeman Bill to divide the unions still further on racial lines, to increase competition and race-hatred among the workers; and by the threat to place the Coloured workers and their "Unions" under the Coloured Affairs Department;
(ii) Views these measures as the continuation and intensification of previous oppressive legislation introduced and applied by all **Herrenvolk** parties especially since the Act of Union, and as the inevitable consequence of denying citizenship to the Non-Europeans of South Africa;
(iii) Calls upon the workers to boycott the machinery of industrial collaboration, i.e. as in the Native Labour Settlement of Disputes Act;
(iv) Deplores and warns against the policy of adaptation, capitulation, collaboration, and of isolation from the National Liberatory Movement, preached and practised by the trade union bureaucracy, both White and Non-White, against the interests of the workers, both White and Non-White;
(v) Declares that without a consistent, principled struggle against trade union collaborationism the trade unions will be utterly destroyed and replaced by company and State unions unreservedly controlled by the Native Affairs Department and the Coloured Affairs Department;
(vi) Reaffirms the resolutions adopted during the past eleven years of the Anti-C.A.D. and N.E.U.M. on the necessity for Trade Union participation in the National Liberatory Movement in order to create free, unfettered, democratic, non-racial unions, and declares that the very life and future of the unions as well as the full development of the liberatory movement depends upon the struggle of the workers in their unions against the **Herrenvolk** and bureacrat-collaborators, so that the trade unions may take their rightful place in the Anti-C.A.D. and the Non-European Unity Movement'."

## Document 49
"The Stay-Home Call: Why did it fail?", *Congress Voice*, issued by the Emergency Committee of the A.N.C., 2, 2, May 1960

There was great disappointment among Congressmen and progressives throughout the country when the one week strike called for the 18th to the 25th April, 1960, failed to materialise. Many supporters of the Congress movement – especially those selfless activists and field-workers who, regardless of the personal dangers and risks involved, did such wonderful work during the campaign – would like to know the reasons why the strike failed.

The movement must learn from the achievements, as well as from the mistakes and shortcomings of each campaign. It is therefore the duty of the Emergency Committee to examine the whole campaign thoroughly to find out what really caused the people to disregard such an important political call.

Various reasons have been given for this. It has been suggested that the causes of the failure were that:
- "People were in no mood to have stay-home campaigns in close succession."
- It was "called after a week of heavy holiday spending."
- Because the call was "for a week instead of a day or two."
- The employers had threatened the workers that those who stayed home would lose their jobs, and that "the authorities warned that people who lost their jobs through staying away from work would be sent back to the reserves."
- The street-to-street police broadcast to the people telling them to go to work and promising protection was another important factor.
- "Almost all the recognised leaders" were in jail.

While these and other factors may, in one way or another, have contributed to the non-response to the call, the main reason for the failure was the ruthless and savage action of the Government. The daily house-to-house raids carried out in African townships by the police and the Army; the arrests, terrorising and imprisonment of thousands of people, were the major factors that prevented people from responding to the call. On this point even the "Golden City Post" of the 24/4/60 had this to say: "The massive police raids carried on throughout the week preceding the abortive stay-away, had the double effect of not only removing many tsotsis and potential trouble makers but of making people nervous about the consequences of resistance to authority."

But perhaps it will be easier to understand if we asked ourselves and answered these questions:

\* Were the demands and slogans put forward in the campaign wrong? Certainly not. They were and still are correct.

\* Were people taken in by police promises made in street to street broadcasts, or were they intimidated by the threats of the employers, or of the Government? – Not at all. Past experience has shown that people always ignore threats from those quarters.

\* Was the fact that the call was made "in close succession" to the previous one a deterrent? – This is doubtful. It may have been to a certain extent, but not much.

\* Was the period of the intended action too long? – In the situation it was not.

While insisting that police terror and ruthlessness were responsible for the failure, we nevertheless have to recognise some fatal weaknesses which gave the authorities time to mobilise their forces, the excitement and confusion that followed the nation-wide arrests and the declaration of the state of emergency.

It will be remembered that there was a very successful stay-at-home strike on the 28.3.60. This was followed by mass arrests in the early morning of the 30.3.60. On the recommendation of some excited and over-enthusiastic activists who urged for a strike on the 31.3.60, and who swore that the people were ready and just waiting for the word, a call was made for that date.

Yet elsewhere that very evening, unaware of the meeting that took the decision for a strike on the 31st, another group of activists was meeting and decided on, and announced other dates! As a result the confusion was confounded. But eventually order was restored, and once this was done, all concerned worked enthusiastically for the stay-at-home from the 18th to the 25th.

It will be seen therefore, that in addition to the difficulties imposed by the state of emergency, the wholesale arrests of leaders and disruption of the leadership on all levels did in fact seriously affect the campaign.

The significant and interesting thing to note is that there has been no suggestion, except from ministers and police authorities, that the people were not interested in the political objectives and demands put forward by the Emergency Committee. Even enemies of the A.N.C. like Mr. B. M. Legwate had to concede that: "The people, though most support the struggle for greater rights, saw that this call was ill-timed and too extended." – "The Star" 22/4/60.

## NEW TASKS

What we have said above are matters of opinion and past history. The question facing us now is: What next? Before dealing with the problems which must be attended to immediately, we should remind ourselves of what Mr. Erasmus, when Minister of Defence, said some time ago. He told the country that as a result of the experience of the civil war in Algeria, the South African army had been reorganised to deal with any threat to internal security.

The employment of the army to surround African townships, and in house to house raids for the arrest of thousands of people protesting against injustices and demanding equality of opportunities and justice, must be what the Minister meant. Now that this barbaric method of suppression has proved effective we may take it that it is going to form South Africa's new basis for relations between the Government and the African people. That is what we are against today.

It is therefore absolutely essential that we should work out organisational methods to meet this new technique. What is needed is a live and efficient organisation which must set itself the task of raising the political consciousness of the masses; a disciplined and active organisation. We must set ourselves the following immediate tasks:

* To organise the Congress on the basis of the M-Plan.[11]

* To make all members aware of the immense task facing them and the grave responsibilities resting upon them.

* To start a house to house propoganda and agitational campaign for the purpose of raising the political consciousness and understanding of the masses, and to stir up hatred and indignation amongst them against oppression.

* To get the people in a state of permanent readiness so that we can always act swiftly to forestall the enemy.

* To impress upon the people the importance of relying on message conveyed by

word of mouth.

\* To see to it that every member is disciplined, punctual and always alert.

Let us all remember that we have reached a point of no return. To survive we must fight on till freedom has been won and the African people are treated as human beings.

## Document 50
## Socialist League of Africa[12], "South Africa: Ten Years of the Stay-at-Home", *International Socialism*, 5, Summer 1961

*[....]* In March and April 1960, the African population staged a series of demonstrations, marches and stay-at-homes in all the large towns of South Africa. In the month of action that followed the shootings at Langa and Sharpeville, the African working class emerged as the only force capable of leading the fight against oppression in this country, and showed that it was capable of paralysing the economy of South Africa by withdrawing its labour.

The one dominant feature that emerges from these happenings is that it was the worker who stood at the head of events; also a specific working class method (the withdrawal of labour) was used, and the action was confined to the large industrial centres of South Africa.

And yet the events centred around an anti-pass campaign and drew in the entire African township population, so that it would appear that this was a national fight rather than a working class struggle.

Because of this there has been endless confusion in the ranks of the liberation movement. To some the fight has appeared to be simply that of African versus White. To others who have tried to examine events more deeply, the events seem to show that the fight is a broad liberation struggle of the whole African people. Because the pass laws are the symbol of colour oppression, it has been argued that the people as a whole are fighting a nationalist cause. And of course there is truth in this argument. The entire African population – every single African man and woman feels the burden of the pass laws above every other colour bar law. It is no accident that every major fight since 1919 has been against the pass laws. This piece of paper has stood as the greatest single barrier against the advancement of the whole people – and it has been the greatest source of bitterness throughout the country.

Nevertheless we want to say that the nature of our struggle goes even deeper. In our fight for democracy and for full equality, in our demand that the people shall govern, we believe that the basic clash is between the working class and the governing capitalist class. At the present stage, the specific working class aspect of the struggle is hidden by the apparent clash of colour. The dominant note in all our struggles seems to be that of an oppressed people against a white minority. But we must beware of so simple an explanation. The first stages of political struggle in any country are always based on the broadest democratic demands and give no indication of the way events will move. To examine the course that events will take in any political struggle we must show clearly what class forces exist and examine their strength, for only then will we understand their direction. The nature of any struggle depends on the relative class strengths in society and in South Africa the major force is the working class of the towns and the farms. This group, when it draws closer to the people of the reserves, will act as the natural leaders of the struggle for liberation.

Already in South Africa the methods used in the struggle are those of the working class and as the struggle develops it will become clear to all that it is only the worker that can give the lead to our fight for democracy.

We also believe that, as it will be predominantly a working class struggle, the aims of this struggle must be for the realisation of working class demands. This must be *socialism*, and at no time can we allow this aim to be obscured. *[....]*

**The first beginnings**

The struggle in South Africa has a long history, but there can be little doubt that an entirely new phase opened up as a result of the second world war.

The war of 1939-45 led to a remarkable change in the economy of the Union of South Africa, and in the process there was an equally remarkable development of the African urban working class. The restrictions on entering the towns were partially lifted by Smuts in order to supply the labour force that was needed to man the ever-growing industries. The main industrial centres grew at a greatly accelerated pace and thousands of workers were needed to man the machines. The townships and locations grew at a fantastic rate, as more and more workers came into the towns. Semi-skilled jobs were opened to Africans and the black proletariat became a force in the economy.

The overcrowding of the townships (and the complete lack of new houses) erupted into the shanty towns movement started by Sofosonko Mpanza; the problems of transport led to the first great bus boycott in Alexandra; the new political awareness was expressed by the formation of the African National Congress Youth League under Lembedi; the starvation wages led to the series of illegal strikes among the VFP (power) workers, the milling workers, the coal distributive workers, the timber workers, and the building of the powerful Non-European council of Trade Unions under Makabeni, Tloome, Marks and others. These wage struggles culminated in the great Mine-workers' Strike in 1946 and tentative plans for a general strike in sympathy.

The workers of the post-war period were building a new tradition of industrial action, and although they drew strength from the earlier struggles in the 1930's, an entirely new generation of workers were being drawn into Trade Union action.

The overall inexperience and the rootlessness of the young working class was not able to sustain this rapid growth of Trade Unionism; and, weakened as they were by the anti-strike laws of Smuts, the movement went into decline after 1946. This partial decline can only be explained if we take into account the fact that the worker was preoccupied with the sheer problem of living, which was so overwhelming. He lacked transport, houses and food. His daily struggle to exist in the squalor of the war-time locations exhausted him, and his immediate needs led him to embark on struggles over rent, houses, busfares, etc. In the process, the trade union struggle was overshadowed and tended to decline in relative importance. *[....]*

In this climate the young students of Fort Hare gathered around the radical solutions offered by the Youth League: many of the town workers were attracted not only by the Trade Unions, but also by the radical program of the Communist Party. There was also general discontent with the backwardness of the ANC leaders like Dr Xuma, Thema, Vundla, and several splinter movements arose as an expression of the radical mood.

It was the 1946 mine workers strike that led to a radical change in the political scene. The brutal violence of the Smuts government led to the permanent adjournment of the Native Representative Council; led to the first of the series of political trials (when the Transvaal executive of the Communist Party was arrested); and led to the growth of a new spirit inside the ANC – most particularly inside the young Youth League.

At the 1949 conference of the ANC this new spirit came to the fore. Led by the Youth Leaguers, the movement adopted a program of action aimed at non-collaboration, disobedience campaign and a general withdrawal of labour. The old leadership was replaced; Dr Moroka took the place of Dr Xuma; a plan was proposed for revitalizing Congress after years of inactivity; and Congress said boldly that it "demanded control of the government by Africans themselves". [....]

**The new spirit and the Nationalist government**

[....] The ANC, now under new, even if vacillating, leadership, called on the people of Johannesburg to observe 1 May 1950 as a day of protest and stay-at-home. The response was immediate – the new urban proletariat was ready for a call to action and the result was overwhelming. Many areas (Sophiatown in particular) stayed home in large numbers and the day appeared to pass peacefully. In the evening crowds collected at street corners in Sophiatown and the police appeared and started firing. 18 people were killed, and many more injured. The government followed with drastic action and declared a ban on all meetings in order to clamp down on the anger that resulted. A pattern was established that was to be enacted on a larger scale ten years later.

The ANC called for a new protest and 26 June 1950 was set aside as a day of mourning for the dead. Once again the people of Witwatersrand responded, and on the day there was a large-scale stoppage of work. However, the response was uneven and demonstrated that Congress was organized only in isolated towns. There was certainly no possibility of moving all the urban centres, and the vast rural hinterland was unaffected by the emerging struggle.

There could be little doubt that in the stay-at-home the Congress movement had forged a new and powerful weapon. It was easy to organise such a campaign in the compact crowded townships where thousands of workers were concentrated. By closing a few entrances (or stationing pickets appropriately) an entire town's working population could be organized into mass defiance. The working force of a town could be withheld by stopping labour at its very source.

The compactness of the townships made contact easy; organizational work which was primitive (and unfortunately still is primitive) was overcome by the solidarity of these vast working class slums. A new-found strength was discovered, and an effective stoppage of industrial and commercial work had become possible.

Even more particularly, as Trade Unions were weak (and often non-existent) and as industrial strikes were illegal under the old war measure 1425, this new Industrial action in the residential areas seemed to offer a solution to the problem of effective working class action.

This was the second successive use of 26 June as a day of protest, and it now became established as a national day of struggle (later to be called Freedom Day). It also established the tradition of the stay-at-home as a weapon of the struggle. Since 1950 the African worker has come to look upon the stay-at-home as the possible answer to government oppression.

Whereas previous strike action had been brutally suppressed (Mine workers and VFP), or had failed through mass arrests, this new method seemed to provide the answer. That it was indeed a powerful weapon is beyond question and it was to be used more and more in the years to cone. However, we will come back to the question of this tactic below, and discuss its use more fully.

**The Defiance campaign**

For the past ten years two main methods of struggle have been used in South Africa. The first is the stay-at-home (or political strike), and the second is the method of passive resistance (or defiance campaign).

The first passive resistance campaign took place against the United Party pegging act. Indians in Natal opposed the UP legislation which denied them land outside certain areas, and organized a campaign of defiance. They occupied land illegally and offered themselves for arrest. The campaign failed against a government that was arrogantly determined to force the legislation through. However this tradition of non-violent defiance was to be taken up again by the ANC, in co-operation with the Indian Congress in 1952.

Congress singled out for attack seven unjust laws that included the Group Areas Act and the Suppression of Communism Act of 1950. The latter having defined communism in such a way as to effectively outlaw any movement that proposed change in the form of government in South Africa.

Passive resistance is open to criticism on many fronts, and particularly as it was to be used again in 1960 by the PAC, an understanding of this tactic is necessary. For the record it must be stated that there is no instance in the history of struggle where this tactic has succeeded. In India, where it was used on a large scale by Gandhi, it did not by itself win freedom, and in fact, as Palme Dutt points out in his *"India Today"*, it served as means of tying down or restraining the mass movement of workers and peasants.

The philosophy of passive resistance is one that flows from a middle class leadership which places no reliance on the masses and their ability to pursue militant tactics. It is a glorification of the leaders and elevates them as political martyrs. Its stress is on the leaders surrendering themselves to the police in protest against bad laws, without at the same time calling for mass action in support of the campaign, for in this way the tactic assumes that it can lead to a change of heart on the part of the ruling class. *[....]*

The campaign to end the seven unjust laws thus failed in its objective, and for several years there was a depressing quiet on the African political front. It was a time of retreat while the people sought to regain their confidence and establish their organizational strength.

**The Freedom Charter**

In 1954 there was a call for a people's convention to draw up a charter of rights. The declared aim was to elect representatives from every district who would come together as a true convention of the people. This was an excellent project, but it never came to fruition. As the day of the meeting drew close, the nature of the project was changed, and on 26 and 27 June several thousand Congress supporters met at Kliptown (Johannesburg). At this rally the *"Freedom Charter"* was presented and enthusiastically received. *[....]*

However it was stated subsequently, after the ANC had accepted the *Charter* as its own program, that this replaced the Programme of Action of 1949. In many ways tactics must be elastic, and must be chosen to suit the needs and conditions of the time. But the Congress movement needs guidance in the methods of struggle. The 1949 program offered civil disobedience, boycotts and general strikes as the method of campaigning. There has been no word since 1952 to suggest that this remains the policy of the movement, and in fact we have indication that passive resistance is to become the main method and that the stay-at-home will be employed as a demonstration of protest. *[....]*

**The bus boycott**

Since 1953, when the defiance campaign collapsed, there has been no struggle that captured the popular imagination as much as the bus boycotts.

The first took place in Evaton in 1956. The people of Evaton boycotted the buses for months, but unfortunately never received the support they needed from the rest of the country. That they won their demands is a tribute to their resolution, their courage and their discipline. However, their isolation and the failure of the national Congress movement to come to their aid are contributory factors that led this corner of the Transvaal (Vereeniging – v.d. Bijl Park – Evaton) to turn most readily to the PAC at a later date.

The people were now emerging from the lethargy that followed the previous defeats, and full emergence was to come from some bold campaign. The people of Alexandra were to provide the basis for the resurgence of confidence.

The issue of struggle in Alexandra itself was the attempt at the beginning of 1957 to raise the bus fare from Alexandra to Johannesburg central (a distance of nine miles) from four pence to five pence. A united front committee composed of representatives of every organization in the township called for a boycott of the buses and received a unanimous response. For the next three months the township population walked 18 miles a day to prevent this rise in fares. The issue was the penny fare, and the people stood determinedly together to fight this issue.

To understand this determination we would have to look at the mood in South Africa at this time. Wages had lagged severely behind the rising cost of living, and averaged £10 per month. Whole families depended on this paltry sum for survival. The penny rise was the bitter end for the worker who was unable to provide sufficient food for his family. There was one place where he knew, from his efforts in the earlier boycott, he could fight with some chance of success. Furthermore, there was the example of Evaton to support the worker in his determination. But perhaps more than this there was the obvious turbulence throughout the country that followed the stories of both Suez and Hungary.[13] Also there was the arrest of 156 Congress men on charges of High Treason followed by the mass demonstrations in Johannesburg when the preparatory examination started.

There was a feeling of disturbance in Johannesburg and this mood must have affected the population of 80 000 in Alexandra as well as the rest of the country which came to the assistance of the marchers. Lady Selbourne residents in Pretoria joined the boycott marchers in a similar protest against an increase in their bus fares, and people as far away as Bloemfontein and Port Elisabeth staged sympathy boycotts.

The committee that led the Alexandra boycott was, as we said above, a united front of all political groups in the township. But the ANC had the largest single group of delegates and at first played the dominant role in policy formulation. Due to the treason arrests the ANC leadership was composed of relatively inexperienced men and women. They looked to the national leadership, concentrated in Johannesburg at the trial, for guidance.

The national leadership showed itself to be out of contact with the new mood in Johannesburg. They failed to give any real guidance, and at a very early stage pressed for negotiations and an early end to the boycott. So eager were they to compromise that they supported the bus company's phoney solution of paying the full fare and later refunding the extra penny.

This was indignantly rejected by a mass meeting in the township, and the leadership passed to a small group of militants who came from small political groupings inside the township.

The ANC leadership did not seem to grasp the significance of this development. They were unable to respond to the new militancy, to the new determination that defied the government (who had threatened to smash the boycott with all their power) and the police (who used every tactic of provocation).

In the end the people of Alexandra won their demand, but instead of concluding on the triumphant note of victory, there were overtones of defeat. Lady Selbourne residents were left out of the unilateral settlement, and to this day the people of Pretoria feel that they were deserted. The buses were boarded in Alexandra itself in a state of confusion instead of in a spirit of victory.

Nonetheless, here was a victory, and throughout the country the people were heartened. The mood in Johannesburg itself was high and when a stay-at-home was called for 26 June, as a day of freedom, there was an 80 percent response. *[....]*

**The £1 a day campaign**
Despite the success of 26 June 1957, Congress as a whole made little organizational headway, and there was a complete lack in initiative in providing a lead to the discontent that was evident everywhere.

The Transvaal ANC was split internally, and the ANC Conference in the Transvaal ended in confusion with rival groups hurling abuse at each other. Strife had emerged internally for a number of reasons. On the one hand there was genuine resentment at the bureaucratic mismanagement of the movement. On the other hand Africanism was emerging again to demand an African ANC free of all inter-racial co-operation. In the Western Cape the Africanist grouping was even able to take over the machinery of the Congress for a short time. *[....]*

The struggle between rival factions brought all Congress work to a standstill and the national leadership was unable to offer a solution and direction out of this factional bickering.

Yet the militancy in the country was high, and the people were in every respect way ahead of their leaders. This was borne out by the one Congress campaign of the time. The attempt of the government to force the women to take the pass was opposed vigorously by the militant women's organization. In the course of a determined struggle 20 000 women converged on Pretoria in convoy to voice their protest.

And yet here too, when the women showed the greatest militancy and organized demonstrations in Johannesburg the campaign was suddenly called off by the national leadership. There is no document explaining this miserable ending to the heroic women's struggle, and so we can only assume on the basis of the talk of the time that

Congress was not prepared to embark on a militant struggle over this issue.

At this time the South African Congress of Trade Unions was organizing the workers, and definite progress was being recorded. At the end of 1959 SACTU launched a new organizing campaign under the slogan £1 a day.[14] This wage demand was modest enough and yet it was not even realisable at the time on a large scale. To achieve this wage would have meant a 50 percent or greater increase for many workers, but the growing militancy of the workers called for a bold imaginative slogan and "£1 a day" caught on as an immediate demand.

SACTU was enthusiastic and at the December 1957 conference there was talk of strike action to achieve this demand. A mass national conference of workers was called for in Johannesburg in March 1958 to start a general campaign for this minimum wage demand.

However, what started out as a Trade Union matter was soon extended to become a united Congress campaign. And with this also came new slogans. At first £1 a day headed the demands and to it were added demands against Group Areas, and the slogan "The Nats must go". By April 1958, however "The Nats must go" had become the major slogan and £1 a day took second place.

The leadership of Congress had transformed an essentially working class campaign into a broad political front and placed at the fore a false slogan which related to the coming general election. And yet the ANC itself refused to put its name to the call for a stay-at-home. Confusion reigned throughout the preparation for 15 April. In Natal the Congress movement was completely divided over the decision and there was no united preparation for the campaign. Yet the national leadership did not intervene. In other provinces organization was half-hearted and, except for isolated areas, no directives were even given.

15 April was a complete fiasco. Except for Sophiatown and a few other areas the response was poor. Leading Congress officials in many Rand towns openly broke the call, and the workers were left in confusion. At the end of that day, however, and ANC top official called off the whole campaign which was scheduled for 3 days, thus raising the question – was it, or was it not a Congress campaign?

Why did this campaign fail after the obvious enthusiasm of the workers' conference? The Congress never offered an analysis of those days, and the workers were to pay for this failure to learn the lesson just two years later.

We cannot say definitely that the campaign would have succeeded – that must remain unanswered because that would take us into the realm of speculation. But there could have been a greater response if the slogan had been confined to "£1 a day" – a slogan which had the support of the entire urban working class. It could have been more successful if the trade union movement had been the centre of the campaign and if the appeal had been directed mainly to the industrial worker.

Whereas an economic struggle can get a response when the demand has the support of the workers, a political strike, directed at affecting an all-white election cannot get the response that was needed to keep the workers at home. And the workers said quite openly that they failed to see how a strike called for one day, or even three days, could win them their wage demands.

We cannot overlook the intense intimidation by the police and army during the week that preceded 15 April. This large-scale show of armed force by the state certainly played a part in influencing the people. But we cannot accept the Congress statements that ascribed most of the failure to this police action. However, as we will show below, this force is a factor we will have to come to grips with, and we dare not overlook the power of the state in preparing our fight.

The result of this defeat was to act as a check in the growth of the liberation movement, and SACTU suffered as well. This body made little effort to explain the reasons for failure to their workers, and the working class never learned the reasons.

We cannot leave this episode without placing a share of the blame for the confusion of these events on a group inside Congress who professed to be Marxists. They kept discreetly silent, stifled open criticism, and never explained the importance of independent working class action.

This group of people have concealed all their ideas behind the front of democratic demands. They have never played an independent role, and have opportunistically shielded their ideas behind talk of national unity, of broad democratic struggles etc. They have surrendered the working class to the mercy of a middle class leadership and abdicated the right of the worker to his own independent organization. The worker will still pay dearly for this class negation in the interests of a clique of careerists, who sully the name of Communism, unless a clear working class party comes forward and gives a lead for independent class action.

**The rural struggle**
Throughout the long history in South Africa, there have been two parallel sets of activity – in the rural areas and in the towns. To date, they have remained largely separate. The fight has flared up in the reserves over the rehabilitation scheme, the culling of cattle, the dipping tanks, and, more recently, over the Bantu Authorities and the issue of passes to women. It is not our purpose to investigate the specific campaigns here. The more recent, in Zeerust and Sekhukhuneland have been discussed fully in *Fighting Talk*, *Africa South*, and elsewhere.

We mention them here because the struggles of Zeerust and Sekhukhuneland took place while the urban areas were quiet and helped restore confidence to the working class. But we must state explicitly that they have never been organized by Congress (or any other political group), and these events took the ANC by surprise. It will be essential, if our struggle is to succeed, to draw closer to the reserves, to organize these areas, to plan joint campaigns of town and country, and to direct the militancy of the reserve areas so that the struggle advances more uniformly in the future.

In many ways, the reserves offer us a base for activity that might become impossible in the towns. The solidarity of the people, their desire for fight, their obvious capacity for resourcefulness, together with their desperate need to break down the reserve system and the restrictions on movement will make this section of the population fighters of the utmost importance. *[....]*

**March 1960**
The ANC declared 1959 an anti-pass year. From the beginning this campaign can only be called phoney – because there was no campaign. At first a scheme was produced that called for the boycott of beer-halls, the holding of several mass-meetings, the summoning of regional and national conferences etc. Either they were irrelevant or, as in the case of the national conference, they produced nothing. The only positive step – the calling of the potato boycott – emerged from a set of legal cases against enforced farm labour for pass offenses. The credit for this was undoubtedly due to the zeal of a Johannesburg attorney not connected with Congress. The revelations which aroused such widespread publicity rallied the man-in-the-street as never before against this

convict labour. Congress, sensing this, was able to offer the one and only positive lead in the whole year of so-called anti-pass campaigning.

When pressed, the ANC leadership said that this was a year of propaganda and education. We must say with all honesty that there was little evidence of education, but propaganda did lead to a positive response. The people at all conferences grew impatient and demanded a lead. By December there were again calls from the rank and file for a general strike against the passes. This demand became pressing and at a workers' conference early in 1960 there was again talk from the delegates of a national stay-at-home.

The Africanists – organised as the Pan-African Congress – had till now concentrated on a campaign known as the "status campaign", and had announced its intention of organizing economic boycotts against firms that discriminated against Africans. This was their answer to the ANC boycott of Nationalist products.

However, the status campaign never eventuated, and early in 1960 they suddenly announced their own anti-pass campaign. They offered a strictly Gandhi-ist campaign of voluntary invitation to arrest for non-possession of passes, and declared 21 March 1960 as the opening date.

By this new move the PAC scored a notable victory psychologically. As a movement they were unprepared for a national campaign of such magnitude, and in fact on a national scale they failed miserably. In Johannesburg a small handful of PAC members responded. Only in the Vereeniging complex did they get a response in the Transvaal. In Natal just less than 150 responded. But in Cape Town the two major African townships did rally to PAC organization and these areas were to become for the coming weeks the centre of the new struggle.

Even then it was police provocation that produced the events which followed 21 March. At Sharpeville a trigger-happy police force, backed by Saracen armoured cars, shot down hundreds of peacefully demonstrating Africans. 87 were killed. In Langa (Cape Town) further shooting accounted for some 17 dead.

The revulsion, both in South Africa and externally, is too well known to be discussed here. The ANC which had stood aside before 21 March, now called for a national day of mourning on the following Monday 28 March and the national stay-at-home followed. In most large industrial areas the workers stayed at home and in most areas where this occurred there was a 90 percent response. In Sharpeville and Langa themselves the stay-at-home was not for a day, but over an extended period, and lasted for more than a week.

At first the government seemed to waver – the pass laws were even suspended – and ANC president Luthuli called for the burning of all passes.

On 30 March the police swooped and detained hundreds of men and women. Events followed rapidly. A young PAC organizer in Cape Town led 30 000 men and women in a march into the centre of Cape Town. Durban followed and there were soon 1 700 detainees in jail and a total of 18 000 arrested in the countryside. At the same time the PAC and ANC were outlawed.

The army was mobilized; the active citizen force kept the alert; all police leave was cancelled. The authorities moved to break the strike and were soon able to do so. They regained their old arrogant confidence and the struggle gradually died down. Once again the authorities had shown their obvious superiority – but not before admitting to indecision and a marked nervousness.

However, the overall result of this campaign was a failure despite the great lifting of morale in the earlier stages. It is to this failure that we must direct our attention.

**Why did we fail?**

*[....]* Firstly, no organization was prepared for a full-scale attack on the government – not on the pass issue or any other of the *apartheid* laws. The way in which the organizations collapsed when the government swooped is an indication of the lack of preparation. Only in Cape Town did the townships stand firm and then only for a short time, and without the necessary support from the surrounding districts. When an important bastion of the colour bar like the passes is at stake, the government will always bring out its entire forces – and, unless we can meet their attack we cannot expect success. The fight against the pass laws is something which must continue; we must never stop until they are gone, but we must choose our timing and methods more carefully in the future.

Secondly we face a strong, arrogant and confident ruling class. It is fortified by a state machine on which it can rely. Above all else it has an army, a police force and auxiliaries like the *skiet commandos* upon which it can rely at all times. The present government and its supporters are also not immediately hit by the withdrawal of labour, because they are not the direct owners of the mines, or the factories, or the large commercial houses. As the Nationalist party's financial bases are the farms and the finance houses, they do not look upon the labour force in the same way as the Chamber of Mines, Commerce and Industries. They are intent on controlling the labour force, but the effects of strike action act as a secondary factor in their own profit structure. This is another reason for urging that farm labour be organized so that the Nationalists feel more directly any action of ours in the future.

**On tactics**

Both ANC and PAC call for methods of non-violence and passive resistance. But the way they make this claim can only lead to confusion. The people as a whole never urge violence. For the most part they are peaceful. They are aware of the dangers of violence and do not wish to initiate it. They do not have arms, and do not think in these terms. However the police and the army are ever ready to use violence in order to protect the government. Once violence is introduced by the authorities – and it invariably is – the workers can not sit by passively. They have to move in some way to protect themselves. And when they do so non-violence ceases to have meaning.

Nor can there be passive resistance in the Gandhi-ist form. When the people of Sharpeville offered themselves up for arrest the answer was spelt out in bullets. But even if this could be avoided we have no confidence in this limited kind of action. Sooner or later the masses must be called on to demonstrate their demands, and this means that they must come into action. This is alien to Gandhi's methods.

The National movement thought it had the reply to the problem by calling on the people to stay peacefully at home. But even this cannot work and the events of April amply demonstrate this. Firstly, the people of the townships cannot stay home indefinitely. To do so is to starve. Even if food is stored in advance the families cannot hold out for long because of the presence of the children, the sick and the aged. The townships can be sealed off and starved out only too effectively by small detachments of the army and the police. But, far worse, the army and police showed in Langa and Nyanga that they could go from house to house, drag the inhabitants out, beat them up and force them to work. Our basic weaknesses, which have led to our present tactics, cannot be turned into strength merely by a movement claiming that it is strong.

Secondly, by staying in the townships, the worker surrenders all initiative. He cuts himself off from his fellow-workers in other townships. He divides himself from his allies in the rural areas, and he surrenders the entire economic centre to his enemies. It was this realisation, whether consciously stated or not, that led to the mass protest marches in Cape Town and Durban. Once we leave the townships, then there must be clearly stated objectives, or else the demonstrations are empty of meaning, and once we march out of the townships, talk of peacefully remaining at home ceases to have meaning!

By using the stay-at-home and by claiming as they do that we can bring the country to a halt by withdrawing our labour both the ANC and the PAC have called for the use of the traditional workers' weapon. This follows from the general recognition that the largest and most capable force ready for struggle in the country is the working class. But there is no analysis of the consequences of this recognition. It is vital that we accept once and for all the fact that future of the struggle rests on the organization of the worker as a class; that it will be this body of men and women in alliance with the rural worker that will lead to eventual victory.

In that case it is urgent that the workers be organized into their own party, with their own aims, and with their own methods of struggle. The Trade Unions must organize the industrial worker, and the strike weapon must be used to secure higher wages and better living conditions. Industrial action must be centred on the factories rather than on the townships – as distinct from the National Liberatory movement itself which has its base in the townships.

A close co-ordination of the two movements can lead the township organization into support of any future industrial action either by picketing or by introducing subsidiary campaigns, such as boycott action against factory produce etc.

The strike is one of our most powerful weapons. Its first use is in the field of economic struggle. Its use as a political weapon is very much more difficult and must be reserved for special periods. We must stop believing that the workers can be called out for each and every political occasion. And when we do in the future wish to employ the general strike, it must be supplemented by other methods of struggle or else we will find that a trigger-happy police force will be able to break it up far too easily. [....]

Once the worker is organized as an independent force, he will be in the forefront of the struggle for freedom, and there will be no clash of interests between his first loyalty to the socialist movement and his work inside the national movement. By knowing his own strength, he will be able to lead the whole population through to democracy and be able to show that socialization of the means of production provides the answer to a new economic order.

But in order to reach this organizational stage the worker must clearly understand both the strength and the limitations of the general strike. He must know that this is a constant testing ground – against the employers first and at a later stage against the entire state machinery.

If the worker is prepared for this struggle and if there is a clear understanding of the nature of the weapons open to us, we shall truly achieve freedom in our lifetime!

**NOTES**

1 The 1914 general strike was catalysed by the government's decision to retrench railway workers in the National Union of Railway and Harbour Servants on Christmas Eve 1913. Martial law was imposed from January to March 1914. The nine strike leaders were abducted from jail by the government and deported to Britain without trial on January 30. They were repatriated later that year.

2 The all-white 1922 Rand Revolt was the first major white mining strike after the entry of unskilled Afrikaners into the mines and, accordingly, the first mining strike led by industrial rather than craft trade unions. Just as craft workers had felt the threat of semi-skilled blacks and unskilled whites fifteen years earlier, newly proletarianised Afrikaners felt vulnerable to replacement by cheaper labour if the colour bar was modified. Consequently, they were the most militant strikers in 1922, and they were given material and moral support by rural Afrikaners. Communists were sympathetic to the vulnerability and poor working conditions of white workers and hoped that their propaganda would push them towards unity with black workers. The strike was brutally smashed, leaving organised white labour in disarray.

3 Colonel Frederic H. P. Creswell was a staunch advocate of white labour. He led the struggle against the importation of Chinese workers and was arrested for his role in the 1914 strike. As leader of the SALP, following his return from a campaign in South-West Africa in June 1915, he promoted the "See It Through" policy, calling for intensified backing for the war. At the SALP conference in August 1915, Creswell's pro-war resolution carried, precipitating the formation of the ISL, first as a faction of the SALP, and later as an independent body. Creswell later became Minister of Labour in the Pact Government and promoted the "civilised labour policies" which protected white labour.

4 The SATUC was generally not sympathetic to the ICU. In 1927 the ICU applied for affiliation on the basis of its claimed 100 000 members to the South African Trades Union Co-ordinating Council, a joint body representing the all-white Johannesburg-based SATUC and the CFLU, whose affiliates included some coloured members. The SATUCC responded with the possibility of affiliation on the basis of 5 000 members, which Clements Kadalie rejected. Kadalie (1970: 178, 221) notes that W. H. Andrews was largely responsible for any co-operation from SATUC and that although the ICU and the SATUC did hold some joint meetings, a split in the SATUC put an end to that.

5 The ICU organised African workers in the Johannesburg General Post Office and Clements Kadalie met with W. B. Madeley, the Minister of Posts and Telegraphs, to seek better working conditions for them. According to Kadalie, this meeting precipitated a government crisis. Kadalie recounts (1970:180-81) that Prime Minister Hertzog had indicated that he did not want Cabinet Ministers to negotiate with the ICU. Madeley, however, agreed to meet with the ICU under the auspices of the SATUC, with W. H. Andrews as intermediary. Although Kadalie contends that Hertzog had the Cabinet reshuffled and left Madeley out as a result of this meeting, Roux (1964:182) argues that this meeting was fortuitous and that the reshuffling reflected disagreements over the accountability of Ministers to the Labour Party rather than to the Cabinet.

6 In the late 1930s Gana Makabeni was leader of a new group of trade unions under African leadership, which in 1938 joined with Max Gordon's Joint Committee of African Trade Unions to form the short-lived Trade Union Co-ordinating Committee. The CNETU was formed in 1942 under Makabeni's leadership after black trade unionists decided not to affiliate to the SATLC, the descendant of the SATUC. It upheld black leadership of the black trade-union movement. In 1945 Communist J. B. Marks became Chair, and CNETU expelled members of the Trotskyist-influenced PTU group.

7 The 1840s Chartist movement in Britain advocated a six-point democratic programme. Their campaign culminated in a mass petition as part of a mobilisation in 1848. Although the campaign was effectively defeated by the British state, its radical democratic legacies were significant for both British Liberalism and the labour and socialist movements.

8 Daniel Tloome, a veteran trade unionist, joined the CPSA in the 1930s, was on the CNETU leadership from 1941 to the mid-1950s and was a leading ANC member. In 1945 he became Chair of the Orlando ANC and in 1949 a member of the National Executive, helping to plan the Defiance Campaign. He was subsequently banned and became printer and publisher of *Liberation*. In 1962 he became a member of the SACP Central Committee, and in 1963 he was house-arrested and went into exile. He later became ANC Deputy-Secretary-General and a member of its National Executive Committee. In 1987 he became SACP National Chair and in 1990 a member of its Politburo and Interim Leadership Group.

9 After the 1950 Suppression of Communism Act, overt political discussion and criticism became increasingly difficult and had to be carried on in non-political organisations. The Johannesburg Discussion Club was formed in 1952, mainly by Communists. Its primary concern was the national question and the relationship of the working-class movement with the national liberation struggle. With the reconstitution of the SACP in 1953 this debate was submerged as the colonialism of a special type thesis became the Party's dominant paradigm, and the Johannesburg Discussion Club faded away. *Viewpoints and Perspectives* was its publication.

10 See Document 9.
11 The M-Plan was formulated by the ANC National Executive, in consultation with its National Action Committee and the SAIC around 1953. It recognised that, because of the repressive laws passed as a result of the Defiance Campaign, the liberation struggle could no longer be based mainly on public meetings and announcements. It aimed to streamline Congress machinery; to facilitate communication between local and national levels without recourse to public meetings; to strengthen local branches and national leadership; and to enhance the relationship between Congress and the people. See Mandela's 1953 Presidential Address to the Transvaal ANC, "No Easy Walk to Freedom" (Karis and Carter 1977a:112).
12 The Socialist League of Africa was a tiny Johannesburg-based group of the late 1950s and early '60s which produced several ephemeral publications: *Analysis* (No. 1, February 1958; No. 2, April 1958; No. 3, May 1958); *Lekhotla La Basabetsi* (No. 1, April 1959); and *The Spark* (No. 2, May 1960; No. 3, June 1960; No. 4, June 1960; Vol. 2, No. 1, December 1960; Vol. 2, No. 3, [c. 1961]). At least one member, Baruch Hirson, worked in COD and tried to provide an internal left critique of what he saw as the moderating influence of Communists. In May 1962 it merged into the NCL. Copies of some of its publications are in the Hirson Papers and in the Mr. P. Duncan Papers (folder 8-71), both at the Borthwick Institute, University of York. This document was originally published as a discussion paper. Hirson (1995:297) states that he authored the document and that it provoked a critical response from Michael Harmel of the SACP. Harmel's critique noted some factual errors which were addressed in a postscript when published in International Socialism. See also A. N. Iphongoma and K. Shanker [Baruch Hirson], "Why did the stay-at-home fail?", *Analysis*, No. 3, May 1958 and "South Africa: Once again on the stay-at-home", *International Socialism*, 6, Autumn 1961, 12-14.
13 Autumn 1956 saw two major international crises. The British, French and Israeli governments conspired to overthrow the Nasser regime in Egypt through military intervention. The action failed faced with international, and particularly American, opposition. It was seen as a major episode in the relinquishing of British and French colonial ambitions. The Suez crisis in Egypt overlapped with the Soviet invasion of Hungary. The objective which was attained was to overthrow a reform government which threatened Soviet hegemony and to replace it with a more compliant administration. This intervention followed closely on the revelations of Stalinist crimes at the Twentieth Congress of the Communist Party of the Soviet Union. Together, they made 1956 a critical year for the international Communist movement.
14 SACTU began organising the £1-a-day campaign in late 1957. See "Unions ready to fight for £1 a day victory" and "'£1 A DAY ... WE WANT £1 A DAY'" in SACTU's bulletin, *Workers' Unity*, 3, 24, August/September 1957.

# Part Two

## The national question

**EDITOR'S NOTE**
*Because of the class composition of South Africa's black population, most socialists in the 1940s and 1950s believed that the national question was inextricably linked to the class struggle. However, Communists elaborated their views of the national question through the theory of "colonialism of a special type". This theory lends itself to a two-stage process of social change in which a multi-class alliance for national liberation is seen as a necessary precondition for the struggle for socialism. Trotskyists analysed the divided polity in terms of the concept of combined and uneven development and believed in the possibility of a permanent revolution. They generally saw the struggle against the colour bar and for democracy as a direct assault on capitalism, believing that socialism was a precondition for democracy. These theoretical approaches were reflected in organisational practice. The moderate wing of the Congress movement, along with Communists, used a multi-racial or multi-national paradigm, while the NEUM saw building a non-racial nation as the road to national liberation and democracy. Africanists, by contrast, saw building an African nation as a precondition for broader black unity and for the overthrow of white supremacy.*

## Document 51
## W. P. van Schoor[1], "The Origin and Development of Segregation in South Africa", A. J. Abrahamse Memorial Lecture, Cathedral Hall, Cape Town, 5 October 1950[2]

A people desiring to emancipate itself must understand the process of its enslavement. In South Africa this process begins far back, but it is in the last 80 years that the history of centuries has been condensed. During this period, the systematic exploitation and oppression of the Non-European people on a deliberate and highly organised basis has been developed to a degree of near-perfection.

In "Rhodes", S. G. Millin says:

If no white man had come to South Africa before 1870, the South Africa of today would have been materially little different....South Africa did not exist for the world, and hardly for itself until its gold and diamonds were discovered.

The real foundations of the modern colour bar system in South Africa began to be laid with the development of the sugar plantations in Natal – where large-scale wage problems confronted the ruling class for the first time – the opening up of the Kimberley diamond mines and, later, of the Rand gold mines. Into this foundation were thrown the methods of exploitation and the traditions which had previously existed. Only in this context is the history of 1652 to 1870 significant for us.

### The Period of Slavery in South Africa

The slaves were brought to the Cape by Dutch commercial capital which tore them away from West Africa, the Malay Archipelago, and Mozambique. During the first five years of European settlement at the Cape, there were hardly any slaves. *[....]* Within 70 years such a change had come about that Baron van Imhoff, Batavian Governor, could castigate the local regime in 1743 by saying: "The majority of the farmers in this colony...consider it a shame to work with their own hands," and, that the European workers at the Cape: "does not do as much as a half-trained artisan in Europe...But having imported slaves, every common or garden ordinary European becomes a gentleman." This slave-owning attitude to labour has persisted, and the Industrial Revolution in South Africa, far from abolishing it, intensified it. The 1925 "Civilized" Labour Policy enshrined this attitude as a law of the land. This transformation within 70 years was brought about by the exploitation of imported slave labour.

The negro slaves, demoralised by their mode of capture, and enslaved with little resistance, developed a fatalistic acceptance of slavery as a permanent institution. Through the years, this attitude has had an extremely bad effect in retarding the Non-European struggle for liberation, and it is beginning to die out only now among the oppressed Non-European people of South Africa.

The imported Malay slaves, many of whom were sent here to serve sentences for resisting the Dutch in the East Indies, did not forget their resistance to enslavement. On the other hand, their relatively privileged position as artisan slaves, with the right to work for wages, developed an attitude of aloofness which likewise has been an obstacle in our struggle for liberation. It is only because of the growing idea of Non-European unity over the past 10 years that this bad heritage is crumbling.

The intermediate position of the "Hottentots" as household servants and farm help also left a bad heritage of subservience and inferiority to the ruling class, together with an isolation from the black worker. These attitudes, arising out of the conditions of the slave system, were intensified and fully exploited by the British in the period which began in 1870. [....]

**The Coming of the British and the Decline of Slavery**
The landing of the British changed practically nothing at the Cape. The 1796 instruction to McCartney ordered the abolition of certain tortures and stressed the need to build fortifications against "the natives of the interior". At the same time, this instruction hinted at a new method of exploitation by ordering the Governor to investigate the possibilities of trade with the "natives". The first British occupation was noteworthy for a merciless war against Ndlambe, with the assistance of the missionaries. The Xhosas, however, still remained undefeated. [....]

The second British Occupation continued from where the Dutch had left off. In 1807 the Slave Trade was abolished (legally, at any rate) in order, among other things, to keep up the price of slaves and to prevent the devaluation of Britain's slave empire in the West Indies, Africa and the East, on the basis of which the wealth of England accumulated. England's Industrial Revolution, which led to the abolition of slavery, would have been utterly impossible had England not practised slavery for two centuries before. [....] The much-boosted Ordinance 50 amounted to nothing other than a labour ordinance to regularise and legalise wage labour for "Hottentots and other free persons of colour at the Cape of Good Hope." It did not abolish apprenticeship, but merely limited it – the slaves remained slaves, and the freed slaves were haltered by Ordinance 50 to a new form of slavery under legal trappings of pseudo-equality. The 1834 Ordinance emancipated the British Government and the slave owners from the burdens of an expensive slave economy. Thus the final period of slavery from 1806 to 1834 may be summed up as [...] the transition from chattel slavery to wage slavery.

**The Period of Cape "Liberalism," 1834-1872**
In order to introduce a system of free wage-labour in the towns and on the farms, the

British followed their age-old policy of first depriving the indigenous people of an independent source of livelihood – above all, of their land and cattle. The land wars of 1799, 1811, 1819, 1834 and in the 'forties against the Xhosas, opened the way for their dispossession by the British. In the middle of this series of brutal aggression, robbery and rapine, the frontier boer took fright and fled from his protector and defender, the British Government, and its hand-maidens, John Philip and Co. This event has gone down into our history books under the official designation of "The Great Trek". The heroes of this period of land robbery known as the "Kaffir Wars", were not the pathetic and small-minded Retiefs, Maritzes and Pretoriuses, but the great defenders of the common property of the Africans, *viz.*, Ndlambe and Makanda, who thwarted for half a century the unholy combination of Briton and Boer. This they did despite treachery from within, and the demoralising conversions to Christianity by the missionaries whose creed was summed up by Dr. Philip in 1828 as follows: "All that is wanted for the Hottentots, more correctly for the natives of South Africa is liberty to bring their labour to the best market." This, be it noted, was the essential contribution of the missionaries to the history of South Africa during the period of expropriation of the African.

The military defeat of the Ama-Xhosa tribes was incomplete after 70 years of merciless warfare by the invaders. The African resisted every effort to enslave him by depriving him of the land. The 1820 Settlers, sent out as "soldiers" to crush the African resistance, were forced to throw away their muskets and become soldiers of fortune in safer fields: "The primary motive in colonising the Eastern Province with settlers of British nationality was to establish a permanent outpost against the aggression of the native tribes." The tragedy of the Nonquase mass-suicide coincided almost miraculously with the interests of Grey's policy: "The self-destruction of the natives helped Grey to carry out his policy...enabled him to fill up the empty and confiscated reserves with European settlers." Tragedy, duplicity and cunning finally succeeded in bringing the Xhosa to his knees within a few years, when the might of arms had failed for three-quarters of a century.

The period 1834-1872 is usually thought of as the period during which, in 1854, the Cape achieved representative government and finally reached the pinnacle of colour-blind democracy with the granting of responsible government in 1872. The meaning of this legal equality has been analysed earlier as the equality of the oppressed with the oppressor. Severe property, income and educational qualifications effectively debarred the mass of the population from the enjoyment of the full franchise. This class and caste political segregation made it easy for the rulers later on to introduce their colour segregation. Actually, this much-vaunted period of early Cape "liberalism" was really a period of the land robbery of the African, carried out by a series of colonial wars which wrought havoc upon the lives and institutions of the African pastoralists. This period was the first serious period of military conquest.

While the Xhosa was being expropriated, the Zulu, under Dingaan, was tragically defeated by the Boers, abetted by British settlers from Natal. The work of Dingiswayo and Chaka was not completely undone by this defeat. After their miserable vassalage under Mpanda, the Zulu people were to rise in defence of their land under Cetewayo and, later, Bambatta. The final military destruction of the Zulu was not achieved by the Boer, but by the British after the discovery of diamonds. The same applies to the Basuto, the Bechuana, Matabele, Swazi and Mashona. *It is a significant fact that the major military conquest of the African, with the exception of the Xhosas, was achieved only after the opening of the sugar plantations and the mines. [....]* During the years 1877 to 1895 the Transkeian territories, Griqualand West, Pondoland, Bechuanaland and Matabele-Mashonaland were annexed. Without these annexations by the British in the "liberal" Cape, the gold mines of the North would never have been able to get their cheap labour. *The military conquest by the Cape cleared the way for the recruitment of cheap labour and for the building up of the whole colour bar system which arose on the foundation of cheap labour on the mines.* The "liberal" Cape made a most substantial military contribution to the colour bar structure of South Africa, which is said by liberal historians to be the work of the Boer Republics. The theory that the complex colour-bar system was forced on the Cape by the Transvaal in 1909 is designed to cover up the contribution which the Cape made to set Colour-Bar South Africa on its feet. Economically, likewise, the Northern Colour-Bar System around the gold mines was based upon the practices of Rhodes in the Kimberley mines of the Cape. The Cape laid the military and economic foundation of the modern Colour-Bar System, and this in the heyday of Cape "liberalism".

**The Voortrekker Republics**
The late Dr. A. Abdurahman, in the course of a speech in Kimberley on September 29th, 1913, said:

> The Northward march of the Voortrekkers was a gigantic plundering raid. They swept like a desolating pestilence through the land, blasting everything in their path, and pitilessly laughing at the ravages from which the native races have not yet recovered.

It is difficult to paint a more graphic and more accurate picture of the Trek in fewer words. It is impossible to remember the Voortrekkers for any contribution they are supposed to have made to the progress of South Africa. But they will always be remembered for their attitude of simple and barbarous brutality towards the African. This attitude has become an integral part of the present-day colour psychology of the South African *Herrenvolk*. The Voortrekker attitude to colour and religion was the central feature of their conception of the universe and life. Their attitude towards the Non-European was that of a master (baas), this attitude being partly a heritage from slavery, arising partly out of the military subjugation of the African and in part from their employment of conquered labour on their farms. In the constitutions of their republics, the Non-European was not considered as a member of the community. In line with the fear-complex of Retief's Manifesto, the Grondwet of 1858 laid down, as one of its basic principles, that "the people desire to permit no equality between coloured people and the white inhabitants of the country, either in church or state". Only a handful of chiefs were granted burger rights. This primitive colour outlook was based more on the military factor than on a system of large-scale labour, as is the case to-day. Labour itself was often a form of tribute, like cattle and ivory. *[....]* Labour was a punishment to intimidate the African. The crude Voortrekker farmer did not from the beginning see the African as a source of cheap labour, but continued for a long time to regard him as an enemy. Gradually, however, the labour requirements of the farmers grew. Labour tax was introduced in return for the use of ground occupied by the Africans in the country which the Voortrekkers had taken from them. The effect was to convert the conquered African into a labour serf. On his own farm the Voortrekker farmer was employer, judge, jury and policeman, as had been the case in the Cape prior to the trek Northward. Based on labour serfdom, this amounted to a crude reproduction of an undeveloped feudal system. In the Transvaal and Free State this narrow feudalism caused large-scale squatting which has continued until recent times despite the 1913 Land Act. Under the Voortrekker land and labour system the African became shackled to the land of which, ironically, he had been dispossessed.

The Transvaal Republic was quite incapable of completely subjugating the unconquered African. [....] Just as the British had saved the frontier farmers in the Cape Colony again and again against the Xhosa, so once more they came to the rescue of the Voortrekkers in the Transvaal. Without British intervention less might have been known of "Voortrekker civilization" than is to-day known about Zimbabwe. Shepstone, the Natal-born Britisher, laid down policy for the Transvaal. This policy was in effect the Grondwet of Kruger's Republic. The "native policy" of the Transvaal Republic after the Pretoria Convention of 1881, was the continuation of the policy of the British in Natal. The so-called Boer policy was in reality a British policy. Under the British in Natal there was at first no legal discrimination. But in 1865, nine years after the granting of Representative Government for Natal, the growth of the sugar plantations made political segregation necessary. A black labourer could not have the same vote as his white overlord. Only exempted Africans could vote. Shepstone introduced in Natal the reserve and location system and began to regard African territories as reserves of cheap labour. This Natal British policy was applied to the Boer Transvaal, and was not repealed when the Boers regained their independence. [....]

We can see that the anti-African legislation of the Boer Republics was not so much the work of the Boer as of the British and that the so-called policy of the North was fundamentally a British policy. The Union of 1910 amounted to a fusion of British policy as developed in the Cape, with British policy as developed in Natal and the Transvaal.

**The Industrial Revolution in South Africa**
In 1870 the diamond pipes of Kimberley began to transform South Africa. In order to obtain and preserve a constant supply of cheap African labour, Cecil John Rhodes introduced into Kimberley, features of the British Native Administration in Natal. Around the De Beers diggings, he erected locations for the African miners. This was the beginning of real residential segregation in South Africa, and of the vast network of labour concentration camps which are to-day to be found in every town, village and farm in South Africa. To crush the spirit of these African labourers, Rhodes introduced rigorous liquor measures. [....] The Kimberley diamond mines gave rise directly to the vast system of migratory labour, flowing between reserves and locations, which is the king-pin of the cheap labour system of South Africa.

[....] In Kimberley, Rhodes and his associates developed a "civilized" labour policy for imported Europeans, and maintained African wages at the lowest level. Out of this arose the high ratio between skilled and unskilled rates of pay in South Africa, unique in the world. Rhodes disarmed the African. [....] To prevent traffic in diamonds from the locations, and to control his supply of cheap labour, Rhodes introduced a stringent curfew and a pass. With Kimberley as its industrial hub, the troops of the British Chartered Company radiated out in all directions to conquer the indigenous people, to rob them of their land and, having rendered them propertyless and impoverished, to recruit them as cheap labour for the mines. In his conquest of Rhodesia Rhodes appointed Native Commissioners as "eyes of the Queen" to guard the newly-won reserves of cheap labour. These were later to become the District Magistrates who today preserve "law and order" in the Territories. Realising that the British Empire required a local European population to manage its affairs in South Africa, Rhodes developed the idea of converting the Boer into the policeman and foreman of Britain, a role which has been assiduously and conscientiously fulfilled by each and every government in South Africa up to the present day. *[....]* From Rhodes' labour needs in Kimberley he realised that the African had to be rendered voteless, rightless and voiceless, and became the father of the policy of trusteeship. This great brigand, brandishing his guns all over Southern Africa, declared of the Africans: "At present they are children only and must be treated patiently and sympathetically". *[....]*

The policy of "baasskap" is as much a British as an Afrikaner policy. *[....]* Kimberley was the birthplace of ideas and practices which were later to become the law and policy of the land. The present-day system of colour bars, segregation and discrimination is basically the product of the Industrial Revolution in South Africa which began in 1870 with the opening of the diamond mines.

With the opening up of the diamond mines the railways began to spread throughout the country *[....]* The fact that Kimberley diamonds were not alluvial made the importation of vast sums of capital necessary. South Africa became a market for the export of capital from Britain. The deep mining operations needed to unearth the gold of the Rand, also required an enormous combine of capital to operate the diggings with heavy equipment. Only monopoly capitalism, concentrated in the hands of the vast concern now known as the Chamber of Mines, could dig out the gold thousands of feet below the surface of the earth and organise its shipment to every corner of the world. "The Spaniards who worked the great mines of the 16th and 17th centuries would have stood helplessly before the gold deposits of the Witwatersrand." The gold mines of the Rand continued the industrial revolution begun by the diamond mines of Kimberley. A network of railways radiated out of Delagoa, Bloemfontein, Port Elizabeth, Natal and the Cape. By 1896, 97 per cent. of Transvaal exports was gold. Rhodes' policy of the Kimberley diamond mines was applied in detail to the Rand. The gold mines consolidated the foundation of the colour system which had been laid in Kimberley. The modern colour bar travelled from the Cape to the North.

The rise of the diamond and gold mines caused a network of recruiting corporations which stretched their tentacles to all parts of the country. The search for cheap African labour was the driving force behind the various measures to drive the African off the land of which he had been robbed by the wars of conquest which I have mentioned. The first important land Act to render the African landless was the Glen Grey Act of 1894 *[....]* This Act was not designed to create a small African peasantry, nor was it designed to give local government to Ciskei Africans. Its aim was the destruction of the African peasant, to deprive him of land and cattle and to smoke him out to the mines to work. *[....]* The labour tax was Rhodes' method of smoking the African out of the reserves.

With the opening of the mines in Kimberley the idea of Union was put forward as practical policy by Lord Carnarvon. The basis of his Confederation Scheme, as of the Act of Union, was the unity of the Europeans of the four provinces in order to subjugate the African completely. *[....]*

The mining revolution, based on cheap African labour, paved the way for a united white South Africa. There are few laws to-day which were not common practice in the running of the sugar plantations, diamond mines and gold mines. The financial magnates of the mines drew up regulations for their black workers which were later consolidated into nation-wide colour laws. The colour-bar system, as I have stated earlier, is essentially a British product. The colour prejudice of the Boer was to become the psychology of the system. The British contribution was material; the Boer contribution emotional.

Union had a secure economic foundation in the diamond and gold mines. The idea of Union was essentially developed by the British statesmen Carnarvon, Shepstone, Selborne and Milner. The Boer statesmen Hofmeyr, Botha and Smuts carried the idea further and put it into effect under the watchful eye of Westminster. Britishers like Patrick Duncan, Phillip Kerr and Lionel Curtis, were organised by Smuts to work out the details of Union. [....] It is often claimed that the Act of Union was a compromise between the "liberal" Cape and the Boer North. Actually it was the union of British-controlled Kimberley with British-controlled Johannesburg. The infamous clause of Union that debars Non-Europeans from sitting in Parliament was discussed as far back as October, 1908, between Lord de Villiers and Selborne. [....] In 1901 Lord Milner wrote:

> A political equality of White and Black is impossible, though I do think that in any South African parliament the interests of the Blacks should be specially represented. Perhaps this can be done by white men.

Notice that here we have the corner-stone of the idea of special Native Representation of the notorious 1936 Bills. [....] The Act of Union, 1910, was the gravestone of Non-European political rights, fashioned by Carnarvon, Selborne and Milner, and put into position by Botha and Smuts. The Afrikaner victims of the British in the Anglo-Boer War became beneficiaries of the British estate handed over to their care, first in the Treaty of Vereeniging, later in the Act of Union, and still later in the Statute of Westminster.

The period 1870 to 1910 saw the construction of the economic and political foundations of the Colour-Bar system and the final destruction of the independence of the indigenous peoples. While segregation had existed in South Africa in various forms before 1870, it was the Industrial Revolution which elaborated it into a system and give it its character as the expression of the Colour-Bar in South Africa. From 1910 onwards the superstructure of the Colour-Bar was built up systematically; weaknesses in the foundation were reinforced and the system of modern exploitation and oppression consolidated by means of a series of colour laws unique and unparalleled in the whole history of mankind.

**The Economic Consolidation of the Colour Bar, 1910-1950**

Apart from the Immigration Act of 1913 and the secondary legislation affecting Coloureds and Indians, the major legislation from 1910 to 1940 was directed against the African. Fundamentally, all Non-Europeans had been enslaved politically by the Act of Union. But having done this, the *Herrenvolk* first concentrated their attention on the African and then, applying the "divide and rule" policy of crushing the oppressed people group by group, found it easy to mop up the remaining rights of the Coloureds and Indians.

In the Botha-Smuts Government of 1910 to the outbreak of the first World War, three major laws were passed. These dealt with mine labour, the migratory labour system and the land question. In 1911 the Mines and Works Act was passed which, amended in 1925, shut the Non-European out of skilled occupations; it applied not only to mines and works, but to railways, roads and buildings. The Chamber of Mines had by this time a sufficient control of a vast supply of African labour. In the mines these Africans did skilled work for unskilled rates of pay. In the mines, particularly, this Act operated as a law to exclude the African from skilled pay rather than to shut him out from skilled work. African wages on the mines have remained practically stationary since the opening of the gold mines. At the same time the skill and productivity of the African miners have grown by leaps and bounds. Technical improvements increased the efficiency of production. *[....]* The greater productivity of African labour and the intensification of his exploitation made it possible for the Chamber of Mines to bribe off the white labour aristocracy without materially affecting its profits. This trend continued after 1911. In 1914 an African miner could unearth 250 tons in six months. After the introduction of the light jack-hammer drill his output rose to 800 tons in six months by 1930. The super-exploitation of the African miner was increased by the very technical development which should lighten labour in any civilized country. Improved technique, more intense sweating of labour, and a freezing of African wages permanently, made the white labour policy possible. *[....]* However, even the greatest technical development and the harshest exploitation of African labour have not sufficed to support the uneconomic burden of this white aristocracy of labour. The Chamber of Mines itself has more and more felt the pressure of this burden and has been able to relieve it of late only through artificial measures such as devaluation, at the expense of other sections of the exploited classes. The 1911 Mines and Works Act created a major economic problem for the rulers of this country, *viz.*, the burden of an expensively paid but comparatively unproductive white labour aristocracy. This system of privileged white labour was later to extend to secondary industry as well.

The second major legislation was the Labour Regulation Act of 1911. Having tied down the African miner as an "unskilled" worker, the Botha-Smuts Government set out to continue building up the labour-recruiting network which Rhodes had established. The African, who had previously been rendered landless, was now prevented from becoming a settled worker in the town. The effect of this Act was to keep the African in a constant state of movement between the reserves and the mine compounds. The migratory labour system received the stamp of law. It serves a threefold purpose. In the first place, it prevents the settling down of a propertied peasantry. Secondly, it prevents the settling down of a permanent urban working class. Thirdly, the migratory labour system is bound up with the system of low wages. In any other country an industry paying high wages would attract a great supply of labour. With the mining industry in South Africa it is the opposite as far as the African is concerned, since an increase in wages would enable him to stay in the reserves for a longer time. In order to preserve a steady supply of labour and to prolong his stay in the mines, low wages are paid. *[....]* If the migratory labour system were to break down it would at once polarise into a landed peasantry in the country and an organised working-class in the town, thereby sounding the death-knell of the cheap labour system whose foundation is the landless worker.

The 1911 Labour Regulation Act gave an impetus to the Chamber of Mines labour recruiting agencies to recruit for labour from the Transkei to the Belgian Congo.

One-third of African mine labour is recruited from outside the Union, and the Rand mines have ramifications throughout Southern Africa. *[....]* It has been estimated that approximately 70 per cent. of the urban African workers are migratory labourers; the corresponding figure for African farm labour is nearly 20 per cent. Of the entire African population, **less than one-quarter is settled permanently in towns, on farms, on privately-owned land or on Crown Lands.**

The Mines and Works Act and the recruiting Act of 1911 were supplemented in 1913 by the infamous Land Act. This Act prohibited Africans from purchasing land, renting land, squatting in return for money rent, or share-cropping. Farmers could evict squatters who refused to become labourers or servants. Farmers were forbidden to draw up new leases with Africans. There was a fine of £100 and £5 for each day that the stock was left on the farm. This Act was clearly designed to keep the African landless, to deprive him of his cattle and to convert him into a labour serf or a labourer. Sol T. Plaatje has recorded the terrible plight of the African who was thus forced off the land. But the plight, immediately after the Act, of thousands who were rendered homeless on lands once their own was but the beginning of a series of miseries which attended the various Land Acts which followed. The Glen Grey Act, the 1913 Land Act, the 1936 Native Land and Trust Act were part of a series of laws to deprive the African of his independent means of subsistence, his cattle and his land, and to strip him of every possession except his labour power. Farm wages after the 1913 Land Act dropped suddenly, and to-day the farm labourer earns from £5 to £18 a year. The rural squalor, aggravated in the Western Cape by the "tot system", is better imagined than described. The presence of a large, cheap farm labour supply has preserved the ignorance and sloth of the white farmer. Technical progress has been slow and methods of production have remained as primitive as in any other backward country in the world. In 1931 the average cost of irrigation in India was £3 an acre compared with a corresponding cost of £20 per acre in South Africa. *[....]* The present position is probably much worse. The rural population has decreased relatively. Almost the whole of farming is subsidised by the labour of the African mine worker. The Segregationist Land Acts have kept South African agriculture in a state of abysmal backwardness. This has thrown almost the whole of South Africa into the clutches of the Chamber of Mines which is not only the largest employer in the world – of workers concentrated together – but completely dominates every other enterprise in the country. *[....]* If in general we can say that the system of segregation has retarded the free development of technical progress by confining 80 per cent. of the population to unskilled work, this is particularly true of farming. This is the real meaning, the real effect of the policy of Milner *[....]*

The first World War, as far as the Non-Europeans were concerned, ended where it had begun, *viz.*, with the consolidation of segregation. In 1918 the Factories Act, subsequently amended in 1941, introduced segregation into the factories, culminating in the maximum "apartheid" inside the factory. Work-benches, rest-rooms, entrances, etc., made the South African factory unique in the world. Of late, separate factories for Europeans and Non-Europeans have been built. Segregation is more rigorous in the factory than in the mines! Secondary industry, the pride and hope of the Liberals, flourishes on the basis of segregation and encourages colour discrimination as much as farming or mining. Like agriculture, secondary industry is heavily subsidised. The development of the mines eventually led to the growth of manufacturing industries. *[....]* Rapid development of secondary industry in South Africa took place when South

Africa left the gold standard in 1933. By 1948 there were two and a quarter times as many factory workers as in 1935. The power used increased two and a half times. The volume of the output doubled from 1934 to 1939 and is to-day three and a half times as much as when South Africa left the gold standard. The heavy sector of industry, steel, iron and engineering, increased its output three and a half times between 1936 and 1948. Heavy engineering, directly connected with the gold and coal mines, is the greatest single section of so-called secondary industry. This section has compounds and even labour recruiting like the gold mines. Although secondary industry to-day employs 150,000 more workers than mining, it is less monopolised, less concentrated and copies the labour policy of the Chamber of Mines.

The factories of South Africa have been built on the basis of segregation, for the 1918 Factories Act coincided with the rapid growth of secondary industry. At the same time, segregation has shut the Non-European factory workers, who form two-thirds of the workers in secondary industry, out of skilled employment. This has retarded the natural progress of technique and modern methods of production in industry. The result of segregation in secondary industry is that the productivity of the average industrial worker in England is three times that of the industrial worker in South Africa. This is due to two factors directly connected with the segregation policy of White South Africa. The first factor I have mentioned, *viz.*, the exclusion of Non-Europeans from skilled work. When 80 per cent. of the population is forbidden to handle modern machinery, technical progress must necessarily be slow. When the bulk of the remaining 20 per cent. is engaged more in the role of overseers, clerks, managers, directors, coupon clippers, etc., technical progress must be slower still. This is the second factor which retards technical progress, *viz.* the fact that **the average white worker in South Africa produces less than he receives**. *[....]*

On the gold mines the average worker produces £106 of new value every year. The white worker receives four times this value in salary! He receives four times as much as he produces! He costs the country at least £300 a year. The average Non-European worker on the mines produces three times as much as he earns. The wealth of South Africa is created by its Non-European labour which has to support on its back the European employers as well as the European workers. In secondary industry the average white wage is equal to the average value added per year by the worker. Economically the European worker in secondary industry is dead weight. According to the figures, it would make no difference if he were there or not. In secondary industry the average Non-European worker earns less than £100 per year and produces £350 per year – three and a half times as much as he earns! Segregation has thrown the entire burden of production on the shoulders of Non-European labour. The Non-European receives for this labour the most oppressive, humiliating and degrading treatment that is possible, and is left to pick up a living while the white worker lives off the luxury of the colour bar. In secondary industry the European worker receives three and a half times as much as the Non-European worker. On the mines the white worker gets 12 times as much as the black worker. Sixty years ago the white worker earned seven times as much as the black miner who then earned exactly as much as he earns to-day, *viz.*, £3 per month plus food. On the farms the ratio has still to be worked out.

There is no evidence that the ratio of white to non-white wages in secondary industry is decreasing. Secondary industry houses its Non-European workers in compounds, locations and townships, working together with municipal authorities. The segregation housing schemes and locations preserve the poverty of the worker and keep wages down. On the mines and in some heavy engineering enterprises, company and concession stores provide a minimum calorie diet as cheaply as possible to depress wages. The migratory labour system further depresses the living standards and wages of the Non-European. These low living standards of Non-European labour are at present the basis for the high standard of living and wages of the European workers. [....]

While in depression the employers will squeeze every ounce they can out of Non-European labour before they attack the living standards and wages of European workers, there is no doubt that this heavy cost structure of the white worker will not be permanently tolerated by the employing classes. In depression the low wages of the Non-European will fall still lower and eventually will act like a magnet on the wages of the whites. Poor whiteism was a product of these low wage levels of the Non-European. All the "apartheid" in the world will not save the white worker in the long run from crashing headlong into the abyss of poverty which is the lot of the Non-Europeans in South Africa. As long as the economic and political structure is stable and can withstand the great stresses and strains which segregation imposes on it, this fate will not overtake the white worker. But nothing is permanent, not even, and least of all, the elaborate segregationist economic structure of white South Africa.

The 1911 Mines and Works Act and the 1918 Factories Act formed the corner-stone of the 1922 Apprenticeship Act, the 1924 Industrial Conciliation Act, the 1925 "Civilised" Labour Policy and the 1925 Wage Act. The Apprenticeship Act further debarred Non-Europeans from becoming skilled workers. The Industrial Conciliation Act prevented the free organisation into recognised unions of African labour. The Wage Act regulated wages and excluded the majority of Non-European workers – those in mining, agriculture and domestic service. The "civilized" labour policy regarded the Non-European labour on which white civilization was built up as uncivilized. [....] The Anglo-Boer war had ruined many transport riders, small farmers, etc., and separated thousands of Europeans from the land. The first World War continued this process. The rural European "bywoner" and labourer could not compete with the African, Coloured and Indian farm worker. They migrated in thousands to the towns where, faced with the only work of which they were capable, unskilled labour, they once again failed against the Non-European industrial worker. This inability to compete with Non-European labour in country and town was not simply due to lack of training; it was due to an attitude of contempt for labour, which was regarded as "Kaffir work". It was due to a long separation from, and an almost lost acquaintance with, the process of labour [...] The Wage Acts and the "civilized" labour policy were designed to drive out enough Non-Europeans from unskilled occupations to make room for the so-called poor whites. Two years before the "civilized" labour policy, these numbered 160 000, according to official figures. The Carnegie Commission Report, published after the "civilized" labour policy, estimated the number at 300 000. Within 15 years of the "civilized" labour policy almost all the poor whites were absorbed on the railways, roads, transport, defence and public works. **The Non-European had to pay the bill for the elimination of poor whiteism from South Africa**, which was achieved by means of the segregationist "civilized" labour policy. Today, the former poor white earns about twice as much as the average Non-European industrial worker. To-day the former rural poor white is mainly an urban dweller who receives compulsory education, first-class housing, and all the other amenities of an urban civilization, whereas less than one generation ago his forebears were living under conditions in many ways as bad as those of the average Non-European of to-day. The offspring of the erstwhile poor white has become a pillar of support for the policy of white supremacy. *[...]* to-day the former poor white has been converted by the "civilized" labour policy into a full-blooded European. The 1935 Workmen's Compensation Act and the amendments to the Factories Act, the 1937 Amended Wage Act – these further consolidated the legislation, binding the economic colour bar dealt with in the Acts described up to now.

**The Social and Political Consolidation of Segregation**
Having laid a secure economic foundation in the legislation of the Mines Act, the Labour Recruiting Act, the Land Act, the Factories Act, the Wage Act and the "civilized" labour policy, the oppressors built up a complicated system of social and political segregation on the legislative foundation of the 1910 Act. The major political segregation laws after 1910 flowed from the Native Affairs Act of 1920. This Act made room for local African councils under European control, formed a Native Affairs Commission and segregated the Africans administratively. The 1920 Act was the forerunner of the 1936 Representation of Natives Act which removed the remaining Cape Africans from the common roll, created the Native Representative Council and segregated the African politically by means of separate European representation in Parliament and Provincial Council. It also extended the local Advisory Boards.

In general it completed the political segregation of the African. This was the logical result of having rendered the African landless and, on the basis of this landlessness, having enslaved him on farm, in factory and on the mines. The *Herrenvolk* could not allow the labour which created its wealth to have a say in the affairs of the country and, thereby, in the distribution of this wealth for the benefit of all. Milner and Selborne had long before indicated the general plan for the Native Affairs Act. The Liberals fully approved of these measures. *[....]* To-day the Liberals work the Slave Acts, continuing in the tradition of John Philip who regarded the African only as cheap labour. Not a single European party disagreed with the policy of political segregation and white supremacy. *[....]* Unfortunately, the Liberals, working through African quislings of the Native Representative Council and the African National Congress, dragged so-called organisations of the people, including the late Communist Party, into collaboration with the 1936 slave bills. The British and their "Liberal" hand-maidens had for long conceived of the political segregation embodied in the 1920 and 1936 Acts. *[....]* With the African emasculated politically, the rulers proceeded to segregate the Coloured and Indian politically.

The first serious step in this direction was the introduction of the Coloured Advisory Council in 1943. After being rendered unworkable by the boycott movement initiated by the anti-C.A.D., the C.A.C. collapsed, but the idea of working through a quisling Coloured Council was continued by the present Nationalist Government. The administrative segregation of the Coloured people is to-day practically complete with the provision, recently, for the establishment of a Coloured Affairs Department. The pre-Union Coloured male franchise was rendered worthless in the 1910 Colour Bar Act of Union. The Coloured vote was further emasculated when European women were given the vote about 20 years ago. It was still further reduced when the Cape African voters were removed on to a separate voters' roll. To-day the pathetic remnants of the Coloured man's vote is on the threshold of removal from the common roll. The administrative and political segregation of the Coloured people is rapidly nearing final perfection.

The Cape Indian vote falls into the same category as the Coloured vote in the Cape. *[....]* In the case of the Indians, two policies can be discerned, one affecting the Indian plantation labourer, the other the Indian merchant class. Useful though this merchant class is to the *Herrenvolk* in preventing the Indian from coming into the Non-European Unity Movement, at the same time the wealth of this class is being coveted by the European businessman. Today the Indian businessman cannot invest freely, cannot acquire property freely, cannot trade freely and is facing expropriation, ruin and repatriation. The dispossession of the Indian merchant class would bring new wealth to the *Herrenvolk* of South Africa and enable them to continue the policy of bribing off the white workers. This is the economic content of the anti-Indian segregation policy. Political enslavement of the African, Coloured and Indian is practically complete. The Suppression of Communism Act of 1950, smashing the few remaining rights of free speech, assembly and organisation which had previously been undermined by the Riotous Assemblies Act, brings the system of dictatorship to a point of completion and makes South Africa the perfect totalitarian state in relation to the Non-European. *[....]*

From 1910 to 1950 the system of segregation in every walk of life was consolidated on the foundation of the industrial revolution in South Africa. This period of the basic reconstruction of South Africa was preceded by the period of the wars of conquest and the dispossession of the African peasant. Into this economic foundation were thrown all the prejudice and oppressive practices of two centuries of slavery at the Cape. This is the history of South Africa.

We have had a long struggle against tyranny. Hundreds of thousands of Non-Europeans perished as the heroes of this struggle. Gonnema, Stuurman, Ndlambe, Makanda, Dingaan, Moshesh, Cetawayo, Bambatta, resisted their military conquest and the expropriation of their land. Hundreds of Non-Europeans perished in the struggle against tyranny at Bulhoek, Bundelswarts, Marabastad and on the Rand. But in all these struggles the Non-European people have been defeated, and the history of South Africa has been the history of blood and tears. Yet this system of unparalleled despotism has unified the Non-European on the basis of a terrible common oppression. Out of the common interests of the oppressed people of South Africa have arisen new cries, new ideas, new methods of struggle. The ideas of Non-European unity, non-collaboration with the oppressor and full democratic rights have become deeply rooted in the minds of thousands of the oppressed. Out of these new ideas the struggle for freedom will grow into a reality. We who have thus far been the victims of South African history, will play the major role in the shaping of a new history. In order to make that history, we must understand history. A people desiring to emancipate itself must understand the process of its enslavement.

Document 52
K. A. Jordaan, "A Critique of Mr. W. P. van Schoor's
'The Origin and Development of Segregation in South Africa'"[3],
*Discussion*, 1, 3, June 1951[4]

**Introduction**

It was during the course of a Memorial Lecture held under the auspices of a Cape Province Coloured teachers' organisation in October, 1950, to honour the memory of one of its members, that Mr. W.P. van Schoor propounded his ideas on a subject which was finally published in booklet form *[....]* Except for the acclamation of the author as a "new historian" by the sponsors of the book, and a brief report on it in the local press, Mr. van Schoor's work passed without comment, discussion or analysis. This cannot surely be the end of a historical work which represents a radical and decisive departure from all the histories hitherto written on South Africa. For here is an author who has boldly undertaken the task of writing a short history from the point of view and in the interest of a general evolution of South African humanity to higher social and political forms. The author himself epitomises the function of historiography in the first and last sentence of his booklet: "A people desiring to emancipate itself must understand the process of its enslavement." *[...]* the author attempts to explain not only how the present South Africa evolved out of the past, but how the genesis of this country has created the complex and intricate problems, the solution of which falls four-square on the people of South Africa themselves. The book is therefore not merely a matter of academic interest, of historical draughtsmanship and accuracy in the presentation of our historical past. No. The author clearly sees in history the key to the understanding of the present which in turn is the indispensable guide to the future. That is why Mr. van Schoor's work is an entirely new approach to South African history. That is why it demands the attention of all those who are interested in the continued evolution of South Africa. It is indeed a reflection on the inspirers of the Memorial Lecture that, for reasons best known to themselves, they have remained silent on a work which they merely dismissed by an unwarrantable and meaningless eulogy.

Mr. van Schoor has entered a field of study which has up to now been completely monopolised by the official historians in the service of the ruling classes and in the interests of the status quo. *[....]*

In the appraisal of Mr. van Schoor's work I will use the author's own dictum *[...]* as the yardstick for the critique. Having read the book one must therefore ask oneself the following questions: Do we now understand the process of our enslavement? Do we understand the evolution of modern South Africa and the present national set-up in the light of this work? Do we have a better understanding and appreciation of the manifold problems which face the peoples of South Africa in their democratic strivings? What theoretical and political lessons can one draw from the author's analysis of the process of our enslavement? Does Mr. van Schoor indicate the course of South Africa's future evolution? *[....]*

## THE BANEFUL EFFECT OF THE AUTHOR'S ANTHROPOLOGICAL APPROACH TO OUR PROBLEMS

**1. The Need for a Social Approach to History**

Political theory influences our political orientation, poses our practical tasks and clarifies our aims. It is the indispensable guide to political struggle. On the correctness of our theory depends the whole future of the liberatory movement. But what determines our political theory? The most painstaking historical and sociological analysis. Every political in the emancipatory movement, engaged in the interpretation of historical evidence and the assessment of the forces at work in society, must realise the cardinal importance of this work.

Documentary evidence is the raw material out of which the historian reconstructs the past to explain the present. But it is impossible to understand the present if one merely regards history as a series of events. [....] it is the fundamental task of the historian to discover the laws and the forces which generate events and which lead to the rise and fall of special institutions. It is on this basis that history becomes a science, and the indispensable aid in the interpretation of the present. And it is on the basis of determining the general laws underlying the social changes that the future becomes predictable. [....]

If politics is therefore the expression of fundamental class interests which have their basis in economy, then it is clear that economics is in the final reckoning the determining factor in social change. The question of race and colour, racialism and colour prejudice, while they often tend to have a logic of their own, are finally merely the superstructure of basic class conflicts.

The temptation every student of South African history should therefore learn to resist is the temptation to conceive of South Africa's evolution and the process of our enslavement in terms of anthropological entities. [....] in South Africa, beset as it is with multi-racial problems, it is a great inducement – incidently the easiest way – to explain the nature of our historical and political problems in terms of race, racialism and colour. For it is precisely in this country that social or class conflicts tend to coincide with the lines of the race and colour.

## 2. The Author's Preoccupation with Racial Categories.

The greatest weakness of Mr. van Schoor's book from which all its other weaknesses naturally flow is the author's inability to resist the temptation. The result is the other side of the coin of Herrenvolkism from which political poison can and must follow. While the official historians have hitherto attempted – and attempted with some degree of success – to paint the white whiter and the blacks blacker, Mr. van Schoor tries to paint the white black and blacks white. The result is the same. Not only does he not find any difference between the Dutch and the British policies in South Africa, not only does he regard the white workers, the white labour aristocrats and the mining magnates as a homogeneous white mass, but he proceeds on the basis of his racial approach to identify slaves with Hottentots, Hottentots with Bushman and the Bantu with the Cape Coloured people. And how does he attempt to effect this? By approaching history in reverse. I am referring to his naive attempt to explain the past in the light of the present national set-up, rather than the present in the light of the past. [....] In his attempt to project preconceived political notions on to the historical past, the author forces historical facts into a political straightjacket and proceeds to write some questionable history. Let me illustrate. As a consistent democrat, the author rightly sees the political need for Non-European unity as the indispensable pre-requisite for the launching of a mass democratic movement. The only honest way of approaching such a question is to dwell on the indivisibility of Non-European oppression which has placed all the racial groups, Coloured, Indians, Malay and African in the camp of the oppressed. But the author seeks to "justify" the idea of Non-European unity by obliterating the lines of distinction between the Non-European racial groups and by transferring this idea into the historical past. Thus he writes that the institution of slavery "has had an extremely bad effect in retarding the Non-European struggle for liberation and is beginning to die out only now among the oppressed Non-European people of South Africa." It would therefore seem that the Non-European as a whole at one time existed in the state of slavery. History, however, has it that neither the Bantu, the Hottentots, the Bushman nor the Cape Coloureds were legally chattel slaves. Only a small percentage of the present black population, namely the Malays and a few Coloureds, has slave antecedents. It was the policy of the Dutch not to enslave the indigenous people of South Africa. How this institution of slavery therefore hampered the struggle for liberation is difficult to understand.

A number of anachronisms creep into the book in the author's attempt to explain the slow development of Non-European unity. Thus we hear that it was because of "their relatively privileged position as artisan slaves that the Malay slaves "developed an attitude of aloofness." As if they had then as slaves to unite with the tribal Bantu groups! As if the need for Non-European unity arose not in recent years but in 1652! Then we are asked to accept the idea that the "bad heritage of subservience and inferiority to the ruling class is due to the "intermediate position of the Hottentots as household servants...together with an isolation from the black workers"! Why the Hottentots should have united with other blacks and who were tribalists, not workers, then is difficult to understand. *[....]*

### 3. The Author's Tribal "Heroes": an Example to Democracy?

The black chauvinist is as determined as the white chauvinist to create his stock of national heroes. *[....]* Thus at a time when the Non-Europeans cannot speak of any national heroes, Mr. van Schoor, in his attempt to give his racial approach to history a sort of moral sanction, turns the wheel of history back to fish out "national heroes" for the Non-Europeans. And from where? From the primitive Bantu and Hottentot tribes! It is difficult to understand why a consistent democrat like Mr. van Schoor should elevate a number of tribal chiefs to the position of "national heroes" and by implication deprecate the dissolution of the primitive tribal societies and the development of industrialism – the indispensable pre-requisite for a democratic society in South Africa. *[....]*

The study of the movements of various Bantu tribes clearly reveals that each tribe was bent on territorial expansion which it tried to realise at the expense of the extermination of another. The Zulu king, Chaka, had during the early nineteenth century extended his domains by a rigorous military system and a terrible discipline. The neighbouring tribes, particulary the Xhosa, were forced to flee in the face of Chaka's expansionist policy and rule of terror. *[....]* Mr. van Schoor *[...]* eulogises the work of Chaka who had terrorised Gaika and Ndlambi. *[....]* One must certainly defend the tribes against the land robbery of the Dutch and the British, but to eulogise and hold up as an example the primitive chiefs is not the work of a modern democratic movement.

To the black chauvinist van Riebeeck occupies the same place in South African history as the doctrine of "Original Sin" in theology. It is to this humble servant of a commercial company that all the ills of society are attributable. *[....]* And what is the upshot of it all? Every evil is laid at the door of the white man. *[....]*

## SOUTH AFRICA HAD NO FEUDAL PHASE IN ITS HISTORY
### 1. The Author Leaves the Door Open for the "Feudal Theory"

*[....]* having developed at a slow tempo under commercial capitalism from a half-way house to a commercial colony, the Africans were rudely torn away from their tribal mode of life and geared to a modern industrial machine as wage earners. The dependence of the mines on cheap labour made the task of expropriating the Africans from their tribal lands the unpostponable demand of the incipient capitalists. The disintegration of African tribal life was accordingly effected by taxation and wars and the subsequent need for European coinage and goods. In the course of a few decades after 1870, the Africans were violently hurled into the streams of capitalism by sword and fire. The Industrial Revolution in South Africa gave them no opportunity, no breathing space to settle down with the dissolution of tribal life as private landholders. Under the tremendous impact of capitalism, they were forced and absorbed into the economic veins of capitalism, bearing heavily the scars of tribalism. The Africans knew of no stage between tribalism and the cash nexus.

It must not, however, be taken to mean that industrial capitalism destroyed every vestige of the pre-1870 institutions. *[....]* In South Africa the industrialists have judiciously preserved the outer forms of chieftainship, tribal categories and combines and integrated these with modern industrial forms. But this preservation of the shells, of the relics of the past are not the fundamental characteristics, the essence of the social order. They are mere incidentals, mere reminders of the past.

The whole argument in Mr. van Schoor's book, as a few good passages indicate, tends to bear out the above argument. This is the author's best contribution. However, in the author's characterisation of the Voortrekker republics, the African labourer and the migratory labour system, he draws certain unwarrantable conclusions which point to the existence of feudalism at a certain stage in South Africa's development as well as the existence of feudal elements today. One therefore gains the impression that he is leaving the door wide open for the theory that South Africa is feudal now seeking shelter from the intellectual storms. This makes it necessary to deal with some of his remarks on this subject. For from the theory South Africa was and is feudal, definite political conclusions must flow.

On the political plane this theory wears the ballroom dress of the "agrarian" slogan. Thus according to the advocates of this theory, the fundamental political task is to rid society of the feudal stalactites and stalagmites and achieve for the people the full and legal ownership of their land, like the August 4th decrees of the French Revolution. The fundamental demand of the people, according to them, is therefore for land. *[....]*

### 2. What is Feudalism?

*[....]* Feudalism is a state of society in which the political, economic and legal status of every individual came to be inextricably bound up with a contractual relationship based on the tenure of land. *[....]*

In the Boer pastoral communities no feudal system could emerge, because the pastoralists lived in a semi-nomadic state. For feudalism, to quote Franck-Brentano, is agriculture without movement. They held land from the Company on a system of rent, not military, clerical or labour services. The Hottentot and Bantu servants rendered labour services in return for food, not for grants of land. In point of fact, until 1828, the Hottentots could not own land or work a plot of land. Under feudalism, personal services to one's master had to be territorialised, that is, they had to be accompanied by a grant of land. The Hottentots were, in short, not medieval serfs.

Politically, feudalism means the decentralisation of political power and its delegation to a number of strong feudal lords by the king. *[....]*

The Voortrekker states were, on the other hand, centralised in the People's Council or Volksraad which made laws for all the Boers. Everyone came under the jurisdiction of the central authority. The local authorities – the landdrosts and field cornets – merely carried out the instructions of the central authorities to whom they were responsible. The tendency was always in the nature of centralisation which is inimical to feudal political theory.

A few liberal historians, notably De Kiewiet and Agar-Hamilton, are quick to draw comparisons between Voortrekker-Bantu relations and feudalism to show that the Boers established a stable system in which their relations with the blacks were based on reciprocity of rights and services. It is a pity that our "new historians" should fall into the same error, which is tantamount to the whitewashing of white-black relations.

The liberal historians have subtly tried to see in the practice of a number of chiefs to place themselves under the protection of white farmers a resemblance to the feudal practice of "commendation". But this is precisely why it is not feudalism. "Commendation" or "recommendation" was merely the means whereby the feudal system was built up in the course of centuries during which the weak and helpless placed themselves under the protection of the strong. It is not a feature of feudal society itself. The practice of "commendation" must, in a word, be discontinued to end chaos and anarchy and stabilise the feudal structure.

The Voortrekkers could not carry the practice of "commendation" to a logical conclusion by integrating the Bantu into their pastoral economy. The very similarity of the Boer and the Bantu economies, based as they were on land and cattle, was hostile to such assimilation. Their interests were indeed so similar that they both constituted themselves into two armed camps. The result was territorial segregation. To be sure, Bantu children and adults were, through their chiefs, recruited as farm hands and domestic servants. But such services were not accompanied by grants of land. They were not feudalised. Some petty chiefs, on the other hand, seeking refuge from other tribal "heroes", were given temporary residence within the borders of the Transvaal Republic. But even the liberal historians have to admit that such protection as was offered them was a very insecure and hazardous one. At any time they could be expelled. Their temporary residence was therefore not part of perpetual feudal contracts, of feudal tenure and territorialisation.

Feudalism offered three main obstacles to the free development of capitalist commodity production. The abrogation of these barriers constituted the historic mission of the capitalist class.

Firstly, the capitalist entrepreneur was faced with the task of creating a proletariat *[....]* The solution of the first problem was the solution of the second: the creation of a home market for the mass-produced goods of the industrialists. *[....]*

The third problem was political: how to absorb the scattered political power that existed under feudalism into the hands of a central authority which could legislate in the interests of the capitalist class. The creation of the centralised political state was finally achieved.

In South Africa the mining magnates were faced with the same problems which were, however, complicated by the presence of a compact tribal system. They could not effectively achieve the expropriation of the Africans by an enclosure system. The indivisibility of primitive tribal communalism called for more bloody measures. Wars and taxation had to accomplish the dissolution of tribal life.

The call for Confederation of the various provinces was not a mere move for white unity to crush the Africans, as Mr. van Schoor alleges it to be. It was a political move by the mining magnates to create a centralised authority which could protect and legislate in the interests of the capitalist economy. The South Africa Act, 1909, created the central state power.

## THE INDUSTRIAL REVOLUTION IN SOUTH AFRICA
### 1. Modern South Africa is Rooted in the Industrialisation of 1870

The foundations of modern South Africa were laid neither by the Dutch East India Company in 1652 nor by the British liberal Cape in 1806. The present-day society of this country has its roots in the Industrial Revolution which began with the opening up of the diamond mines in Kimberley and the gold mines on the Witwatersrand towards the end of the third quarter of the nineteenth century. *[....]*

If twentieth century South Africa is not the product of either early Dutch society or the old liberal Cape, then neither is it the product of the patriarchal Voortrekker pastoral society. Moreover, neither is it a synthesis of the Voortrekker north and the liberal south. It is the creation of an entirely new economic system which, by its new techniques in the process of production, radically altered the old social relationships, evolved new classes rooted in the new process of production and produced a modern political structure to give expression to this change. Up to 1870 South African history is characterised by the slow tempo of her development; after 1870, this country took a tremendous leap which brought her within the course of a few decades into line with modern industrial forms. The introduction of new techniques for the exploitation of the mines is the driving force of this social revolution.

The Cape Colony, the basis of whose subsistence was agriculture, commerce and pastoralism, had no policy of residential, social and political segregation within the orbit of commercial capitalism. Neither did it have a colour bar. It finally and legally recognised the equality of all races. And although social differentiation in practice took the form of colour, this is because class and colour lines coincided. The Hottentots and early Cape Coloureds, in addition to the detribalised Bantu on the eastern frontier, came to be the exploited class within the framework of political and legal equality. When, therefore, one compares the present national set-up with the British Cape, then it is clear that British liberalism was a force before 1870. The Industrial Revolution reversed this trend of political and economic assimilation, and gradually abrogated the time-hallowed liberal policy of political and legal equality.

The Voortrekker pastoral society, on the other hand, was economically and socially incapable of integrating the black into its subsistence economy lest it be consumed in the process. The very similarities of their respective modes of life, based as they were on land and cattle, precluded the possibility of such a development. The Boers therefore pursued a policy of what one can call territorial segregation. This segregation was based on the complete separation, socially and economically, of the Boers and the Bantu. Thus it has not connection with the modern system of social, residential and political segregation which flows from the integration and interdependence of black and white.

*[....]* The essential basis for South Africa's rapid industrialisation since 1870 was the presence of a large permanently settled white population in this country at the inception of mining. British Imperialism had to consider this white element when it embarked upon the intensive exploitation of the country, before as well as after the discovery of gold and diamonds. Without this population in 1870, Great Britain would have occupied this country on military lines and administered it on the same lines as the South American states or West African colonies. There would have been no such constitutional progress of the various colonies to responsible government which formed the basis for Union and complete political autonomy. There would have been no industrial progress in the form of manufacturing industries. For without the whites, South Africa would still perhaps have been a large mining camp. The presence of a large white population is intimately bound up with the rapid industrialisation of modern South Africa.

Let it be understood that Britain never really had it all her own way in South Africa. She was forced to grant the whites certain political and economic rights which would never have come, or at least come very much later, had they not been here in 1870. The Boers fought hard for and forced Britain after the Anglo-Boer War to give them those privileges which they today enjoy in the form of a colour bar, industrial and social, a labour aristocracy and a full democracy. Without them it is difficult to conceive the present-day South Africa with these social institutions.

In an analysis of the modern colour bar, it is necessary to pose and answer the following questions clearly: What is the colour bar? How and where did it originate? How was it consolidated? What are the conditions for its elimination? All these questions are of vital importance to the democratic movement. Yet our author fails to answer any one of these questions. *[....]*

## 2.  The Foundations of the Modern Colour Bar
*[....]* The industrial colour bar and all its concomitants – social and political segregation – are the products of capitalist commodity production which began in Kimberley and on the Witwatersrand. The dependence of modern techniques of capital on labour called for the concentration of labour in the industrial centres. The Bantu had, in short, to be swung into the new industrial system. Skilled labour had to be imported from overseas. In this process of economic integration, economic circumstances, practice, white public opinion which were finally sustained by law, made a strict separation in the two types of labour employed; skilled work at high rates of pay was from the outset the monopoly of the whites; unskilled work at low rates of pay came to be associated with black labour. In the mining industry this practice finally received the sanction of the law by the Mines and Works Act of 1911. It was subsequently extended to other industries. This is the industrial colour bar.

Mr. van Schoor merely sees the hand of Herrenvolkism in this arrangement. "In Kimberley," he says, "Rhodes and his associates developed a 'civilised' labour policy for imported Europeans and maintained African wages at the lowest level. Out of this arose the high ratio between skilled and unskilled rates of pay, unique in the world." We do not know in what respects this high ratio between skilled and unskilled rates of pay is unique in the world. What is unique is the fact that in South Africa a large group of people is excluded from occupying skilled jobs in a modern industry. There is no parallel anywhere else. To see in this arrangement merely race and colour is meaningless. One must take into consideration the class interests of the mining capitalists who are mainly concerned with quick profits. According to our author it seems that the industrialists were bent from the outset on raising the wage rates of the whites and correspondingly lowering the wage rates of the Africans. This then raises the question whether this arrangement was the cause or result of prejudice or whether the two interacted to cement both.

Let us understand that the Africans who appeared on the industrial field had no knowledge and skill in the use of modern instruments of labour. Unskilled work naturally fell to their lot in the formative stages of mining. Moreover, at the time of the opening of the diamond mines, the vast majority of the Africans came of their own accord in search of European goods and guns. The task of destroying African tribal life was not yet under way. Under such circumstances, the Africans worked for low wages.

On the other hand, South Africa had no skilled whites to operate the complex machinery. Skilled artisans had to be imported. To induce them to come high wage rates were offered. This division between white labour and black labour was therefore made more emphatic because skilled labour from Europe had to work alongside black workers who had just appeared on the scene of civilisation. Thus the wages the African workers received in the early days of mining were about ten shillings per week with rations, while the white workers received from £4 to £5 per peek in the case of overseers and from £6 to £8 in the case of mechanics and engine drivers. When African labour was scarce their wage rates rose to even thirty shillings per week. Coloured artisans were also employed in skilled occupations. It is therefore clear that this division between black and white labour is attributable to the objective, economic circumstances of the time, and not to racialism and colour prejudice. "The white workers," writes De Kiewiet, "stood out more sharply because they were for the most part not of South African birth."

With the rapid dissolution of African tribal life after 1870 starving Africans appeared on the mines, eager to work at the lowest rates. This partly and temporarily solved the labour problem and depressed African wages still more. The gulf separating black from white wages consequently widened.

### 3. The Economic Interpretation of Colour Prejudice

*[....]* While Mr. van Schoor finally says that the modern colour bar system "is essentially a British product", he wrongly attributes colour prejudice to the Voortrekkers. *[....]*

The colour prejudice we know today is not the product of the Boers but of the peculiar conditions and circumstances under which the Industrial Revolution developed in this country. The pastoral semi-nomadic Boers had a military hostility and fear of a similar economic group which they could only distinguish from themselves by religion and colour. The two groups could not be integrated into one society because their economic habits were so similar. The colour prejudice we know today flows from the integration of black and white in an industrial society in which the preferential treatment of the whites by the British has revolutionised the whole psychology of the Boers. The Anglo-Boer War was a sharp lesson to the British that without granting concessions, privileges and rights to the Boers, her rule over South Africa with its teeming millions would be unstable. *[....]*

Objective conditions themselves first inculcated the idea of colour prejudice into the white. The particular disposition of black labour, on the one hand, and white labour, on the other hand, produced the idea that the division between skilled and unskilled labour and high and low rates of pay was a natural, permanent and immutable one. They came to regard this division as a legitimate institution imposed from above, and not the product of the peculiar circumstances from below. Shortly after the inception of diamond mining, the whites of this country developed a strong feeling of colour in relation to the productive process. De Kiewiet says that before "the diggers were themselves reduced by the capitalist mining companies to the state of employees, they had decided that no other place was open to the native than that of low-paid and unskilled labour".

This colour prejudice rapidly become more intense when two important social forces arose out of the new techniques of production: a South African born white artisan class and a black proletariat.

The Industrial Revolution in South Africa not only led to the dissolution of tribal life, it also dealt a death blow to the isolation, the particularism of the Boer subsistence economy. For when the demand for agriculture and pastoral products to feed the industrial population became great, the white farmer began to exploit their farms as fully as possible to produce for a large market. The demand for agricultural produce had even led the mining companies to speculate in land and buy large areas which they began to exploit to feed the industrial population. Land prices rose rapidly; many farmers could not adjust themselves to this revolution in agriculture and sold out. The new capitalist farmers, in order to exploit every available stretch of land, were less and less inclined to give the ruined whites refuge on their estates. The white bywoners who had, because of land hunger, taken refuge on the estates of the big farmers, were evicted. Black labour was preferred to white labour on the farms. And so the exodus to the industrial areas began. There they were confronted by a mass of cheap black labour with whom they could not compete in unskilled work. Neither were they trained for skilled work. The Industrial Revolution had produced the "Poor White Problem".

What does Mr. van Schoor say about the "Poor White Problem"? He writes: "...the inability to compete with Non-European labour in country and town was not simply due to the lack of training; it was due to an attitude of contempt for labour which was regarded as Kaffir work." This is a misunderstanding. The white employers of labour preferred the Bantu labourers to white labour. Economics overruled consideration of race and colour prejudice.

With the inability of the impoverished whites to compete with the blacks in industry, with the gradual acquisition of technical skill by the black workers and their utilisation to a small extent as semi-skilled and skilled workers, and with the preference of the mining companies for cheap black workers, there was a loud public outcry against this stage of affairs. The impoverished whites began to place the blame for their economic ruination on the shoulders of the blacks. This fed colour prejudice. Public and political opinion grew for the protection of the whites in industry. The position was aggravated by the cleavage of interests between white employer and white worker whose high wage demands the former would not meet. For the higher the wage rates demanded by the white workers became, the more limited became their opportunities to find employment and the more blacks were conscripted. To be sure, the encroachment of the blacks on skilled occupations was very slight indeed. But so sensitive were the white workers to the idea of associating white labour with skilled jobs and high wages that they began political agitation for the preservation and consolidation of the status quo. *[....]* Their racialism, their colour prejudice, had an economic content – their demand for a place, a protected place, in industry. Their colour prejudice was not the cause for the separation of black and white in industry but the product and consolidator of it. *[....]*

## 4. The Consolidation of the Industrial Colour Bar

Such is the genesis of the modern colour bar. Since its conception almost fifty years have elapsed during which it has shown no obvious signs of collapsing. On the contrary, it has permeated every industry which has developed in South Africa. It is being maintained despite the fact that the rationalisation in production which largely eliminates the need for "skilled" operatives has developed at a rapid rate in South Africa. It is being maintained despite the fact that the African workers are becoming more and more acquainted with the production methods of modern industry and are capable of doing most of the so-called skilled work, or could do so with very little training. It is being maintained despite the fact that it is the chief source of annoyance and financial loss to the Chamber of Mines. Today, political expediency which had forced upon the Chamber of Mines the colour bar, is being mercilessly pounded by the laws of economic necessity which no longer sees the justification of the indefinite continuation of a white labour aristocracy. Profits are dwindling; cuts shall have to be made somewhere. This top-heavy social institution is being strained to the utmost. The economic base is now pounding the superstructure of political expediency, race and colour prejudice.

After the Great War of 1914-18, however, the colour bar has become more rigid. Not only did the extension of the statutory colour bar to other industrial fields consolidate the labour status quo, but the increase in power and co-ordination of the white trade unions and the corresponding lack of organisation, lack of rights and docility of the black workers led to increased rates of pay and better working conditions for the white workers.

"Segregation is more rigorous in the factory than in the mines," writes Mr. van Schoor. Is this really so? In the factory, to be sure, there is not the same rigorous enforcement of the statutory provisions of the colour bar. Non-European factory workers are more intimate with the technical processes of production and receive rates of pay which are superior to those of the Chamber of Mines. The author, however, says that the "ratio of white to non-white wages in secondary industry" is evidently not decreasing. But a careful study of the wage rates of the two groups shows that there has been a definite narrowing of the gap. In 1915 the ratio was 4,85; in 1919 it was 4,84, and in 1924 it was 4,5. Then there was an increase to 4,27 in 1927, but in 1929 it fell to 4,08. In 1938 the ratio was 4,36 and it fell to 3,5 in 1944, rising to 3,47 in 1945. This decrease, slight though it is, proved that the economic demands of the Non-European workers are increasing. It vaguely foreshadows the future of the Industrial Colour Bar.

In the gold mining industry the colour bar is rigidly being maintained. From 1911 to 1915 European wages amounted to an average of £330 annually. In 1920 European wages averaged £501 and then declined to £372 in 1923. In 1938 it was £404, and in 1947 it was £579. As regards Non-European wages, the average cash wages for 1911 was £28 5s.; for 1923 it was £34 1s., and in 1938 £36 6s. "In 1938 both average cash wages of Natives and average European wages were almost 21,3% above the 1911 level." The gap is being maintained. For example, the average increase of European wages in the diamond industry was 23% from 1911 to 1938, and for Non-Europeans for the same period it was 11,7%. In the coal mining industry the average increase of European wages from 1911 to 1938 was 39,4%, and for Non-Europeans 37,3%.

In July, 1918, the Chamber of Mines recognised the Status Quo Agreement which reaffirmed the colour bar system in the mining industry. *[....]*

In an attempt to modify this agreement, the Chamber of Mines precipitated the 1922 strike. *[....]* In 1926 the Mines and Works Act was amended to exclude Africans and Asiatics from acquiring certificates of competency to do skilled work. For already, in 1925, the Mining Regulations Commission had spoken of the competition of the African labourer which would lead to the elimination of the European worker "from the entire range of mining operations".

There can be no doubt that the Chamber of Mines views the white worker with an ambivalence of emotions. For the conditions and circumstances under which the colour bar arose have vanished. Political considerations are, however, still stronger than the need to cut down on the heavy cost structure, either by reducing European wages or by replacing the whites in skilled jobs by black labour. But so great is the strength of the organised white working class, so strong their political voice, and so docile and rightless the unorganised workers that legislative and administrative measures are still the main props for the support of the colour bar in industry.

### 5. The Conditions for the Elimination of the Colour Bar

What then are the conditions necessary for the elimination of the colour bar? For this is the fundamental task of the political movement for democracy: to bring the wage rates of the black worker to the level of Europeans and to eliminate the artificial barriers separating "skilled from unskilled" in industry. Two factors combine to this end: in the automatic process outside human agency and in the political struggle through human agency to bring about its abrogation.

Mr. van Schoor only sees the former *[....]* The problem of raising the standards of life of the black workers does not enter the mind of the writer. Moreover, he ignores the rapid increase in the number of proletarians settled permanently in the towns where, it is clear, they will one day organise into a mighty social force and play the decisive part in the struggle of the abolition of the colour bar. *[....]* The elimination of the industrial colour bar is inextricably bound up with the increase in the number of permanent black workers. For such a development will indubitably lead to the organisation of the black proletariat and their participation as a force in the industrial struggles that lie ahead. Yet Mr. van Schoor only sees the objective factor of economic necessity. Such an automatic abolition of the colour bar is the dream of opportunism and the product of political abstentionism.

The Non-Europeans have up to now been putty in the hands of the employers, not only because they are voiceless and voteless, but because they are not an organised force that can struggle for higher wages and better working conditions. But Mr. van Schoor must not consider that they will remain a permanent, docile mass, incapable of any struggle. Such an attitude of mind is already the beginning of capitulation to the status quo. This striking omission of the role of the liberatory movement to wrench away the props that support the colour bar is the beginning of defeatism, of lack of faith and optimism in the democratic struggle. History is made by people under definite conditions. That history will only be made when the proletariat step into the political arena as an organised industrial force.

### 6. The Economics of Black Chauvinism

Mr. van Schoor's anthropological approach once more reveals its baneful influence on the author's assessment of black and white wages and the productive output of the respective labour groups. [....]

He argues that "the European worker in secondary industry is deadweight." [....]

We are therefore given to understand that the South African capitalists are not really interested whether the white workers produce new social values. It seems that racialism and colour prejudice overrule all economic considerations. According to Mr. van Schoor, the black workers alone contribute towards the productive output. In other words, technical skill, the economic planning commissions, the skilled overseers and engineers play no part in the productive output. All production is dependent – on whom? On the semi- and unskilled black workers who are not allowed to handle modern machinery freely. Thus we finally have the formulae: Skilled workers = unproductive; unskilled work = productive; white = unproductive; black = productive.

That the author is not at all serious about the above statement is proved by two statements on production: "When 80% of the population is forbidden to handle machinery, technical progress must necessarily slow." So? The Non-Europeans are not very productive after all! Technical skill is, after all, necessary to industry! The whites, after all, produce new values! [....]

Even in a democratic society, skilled workers will have to be paid more than workers who are less skilled. For without this technical skill production will be slow, poverty will continue to haunt democracy and elementary needs will not be satisfied. Does the writer imagine that unskilled workers and manual workers can build a democratic society? The reason for the low productivity of this country lies in the fact that the Non-Europeans are not allowed to participate fully in the process of production. The abolition of the colour bar, therefore, also means a tremendous increase in production.

### 7. The Proletariat as the Greatest Force in the Country.

[....] Since the opening of the mines, the establishment of factories and the beginning of capitalist agriculture, the areas allotted to the Africans have continually shrunk. The result is continued proletarianisation. Africans are forced by land hunger, the need for money to buy European goods and pay their taxes to seek work in the urban areas. The reserves were never set aside to sustain the Africans. Thus, before the depression of 1929-36, the income from production of African families in the reserves was £4 0s. 1d. per annum. Today the reserves are a large creche for old woman and children and a short place of rest for the migratory workers.

Since Union the African population has continued to flow from areas of predominantly African population to the urban centres and European farms. They go yearly from the reserves to the towns; from the towns back to the reserves; from the reserves to European farms and back to the reserves and from farms to the towns and back to the farms. This perennial movement is a unique characteristic of the black proletariat. It is our task to understand how conditions, administrative measures and economic forces dictate this complex migratory labour system.

Once again Mr. van Schoor is unable to see the migratory labour system as a process of development. He simply says: "The Kimberley diamond mines gave rise directly to the vast system of migratory labour flowing between reserves and locations..." How and why this came about he is unable to tell us. Later we hear that, having been rendered homeless, the African was prevented from becoming a settled worker in the towns by the migratory labour system. Then he writes that this labour system also "prevents the settling down of a propertied(!) peasantry." The author here confuses cause and effect. The migratory labour system, contrary to the author, is not the cause of the inability of the Africans to become either a peasantry or a settled urban proletariat, but precisely the result of it. By various administrative measures the Africans are forbidden to settle permanently in urban centres. This is the meaning of the pass laws. After the expiration of his labour contract the pass laws forced him to return to the areas specially set aside for Africans. But here he cannot stay for long because the reserves were never meant to be self-sufficient areas. Poverty and land hunger compel him to seek work in the towns or on the white farms. The result is that he oscillates between reserves and urban areas for European farmers. [....]

Yet, in spite of these administrative measures which prevent the emergence of a permanent urban African proletariat, the very poverty of live in the reserve, the increasing economic demands of the Africans, and the consequent desperate need to augment their frugal incomes, are leading to more and more Africans into the ranks of permanent urban dwellers. Their labour contracts and their stay in the industrial centres are becoming larger. The extension of the urban localities themselves bears testimony to this fact. [....]

Mr. van Schoor: "...if the migratory labour system were to break down, it would at once polarise into a landed(!) peasantry in the country and an organised(!) working-class in the town. . ." [....]

The author does not give us the conditions under which the migratory labour system would break down. He cannot see that the labour and economic needs of the industrialists would finally force them to abolish the migratory labour system and allow the migratory African workers to become an integral part of urban life. This is an inescapable development in our social evolution. The wheel of history cannot be turned back either to the revival of tribalism or the settling of the Africans on the land as small producers. Such a development is repugnant not only to the historic process and the development of industry but also to the democratic movement, which can only triumph on the basis of increased industrialisation.

The African worker is not a proletarian in the true sense of the word. Firstly, he is not a permanent urban dweller and therefore does not form an integral part of industrial life, socially and culturally. Secondly, he is debarred by industrial legislation from participating in all the technical processes as a skilled and efficient worker. The development of capitalism will undubitable also lead to the development of a fully-fledged proletariat.

Of the great importance to the liberatory movement is a strict understanding of the forces which are driving more and more Africans irresistibly forward into the capitalist economy as proletarians. The great task of the liberatory movement is to facilitate this development by its struggle for the abrogation of all the administrative measures which prevent the Africans from becoming a settled proletariat; by calling for the abolition of the Industrial Colour Bar to raise the living standards of the African and develop his technical skill; and by demanding political and civil rights to make him a full citizen of this country. [....]

## CONCLUSION

[....] This analysis has attempted to show that the weakness in the book flow from a wrong orientation and approach to our social and political problems, an approach which, taking racial categories as its point of departure, has the tendency, though not always, to go to the other extreme of Herrenvolkism – black racialism. It is a tendency that is all too prevalent in Colonial countries where class oppression and exploitation assume the form of and coincide with race and colour. But it is precisely the task of the democratic movement to strip this Colonial oppression of its racial garb and reveal its class content.

All the differences which this critique has with this book are consequential upon the author's anthropological approach. In many respects they are indeed slight, being a matter of emphasis, of underlying principles, of seeing the wood for the trees and objectivity. And although we have reached an important stage in Mr. van Schoor's work on the road to sociological clarification on our political problems, I still consider that our main task in the field of history at present is to deal with and refute the arguments of the official historians writing South Africa's past. They still reign supreme. We are grateful to Mr. van Schoor for having taken another step in this direction. For the clarification of our past is the condition for the clarification of our present, and the clarification of our present the condition for the clarification of political theory and our future. The leadership of the enslaved masses must first understand the process of enslavement before they can lead them on the road to emancipation.

## Document 53
## M. Harmel[5], "Observations on Certain Aspects of Imperialism in South Africa", *Viewpoints and Perspectives*, 1, 3, February 1954

*[....] TWO NATIONS*
*[....]* On the one hand the most superficial observer can detect all the main features of advanced monopoly capitalism flourishing in South Africa. Cecil Rhodes set a precedent when, having cornered the diamond market and amassed a fortune, he did not go "home" to England but settled in this country to be a "big frog in a little pond" and to enjoy in public life those political plums which other pirates of his stature assign to paid agents. Though massive investments from overseas continue to predominate in the Unions mining and other key industries, the section of the bourgeois monopolist class which has settled more or less permenantly in the Union has become as "native" and fixed a feature of the local picture as this essentially cosmopolitan gang can ever be. Though closely linked with and, in an exceptional way, dependent on foreign – Anglo American – imperialism, this groups corresponds closely in its relationship to the Union's economy and polity to the position enjoyed by monopoly capitalism in other imperialist countries. The white "secondary industry" bourgeoisie, middle and professional classes, and "labour aristocracy" also (with certain significant modifications to be discussed just now) correspond to their counter parts, in, say, England or America.

On the other hand, there is no qualitative difference between the status of the Africans (and, in the main, the other non-white population groups) in the Union and those elsewhere in Africa – or the people of any other colonial territory. "Colonial" living standards, deprivation of political rights and constitutional liberties, the deliberate efforts to prevent their economic and cultural developments – all these are characteristic of colonialism.

Similarly, the relationship between the white rulers of South Africa and the non-white masses is essentially imperialistic. No concessions here, no pretence even at representing the will of the people.

In a word: there are two nations in South Africa occupying the same state, side by side in the same area. White South Africa is a semi-independent imperialist state: Black South Africa is its colony. This almost unique dualism of South Africa has its roots in our history. (I say "almost unique" because obviously Rhodesia and parts North are developing a similar pattern today).

*TWO PATTERNS*

Two main patterns of colonial domination by European over non-European countries may be observed during the eighteenth and nineteenth centuries.
1. In Asia, and Africa, north of the Cape colony, the ruling classes of Britain, France, Belgium, Holland, etc., were concerned predominatly with the seizure and transport back home of natural wealth (including people, as slaves) of these countries. *[....]*
2. In North America and Australia, although colonisation began with the same aim, a second aim developed which was to have the most fatefull consequences. One of the fruits of the development of capitalism (the "industrial revolution") in Britain and other West European countries was the destitution of millions of peasants, driven from the land. No amount of "pass laws" and "influx control" could prevent the steady drift of these masses of starving and desperate people to the towns. Industry, however rapidly developed, could not absorb them. The Governments decided to get rid of thousands of these unwanted surplus proletarians by shipping them abroad to "the colonies" – above all to North America and Australia. *[....]*

Two quite seperate types of colonial countries emerged from these different processes. In colonies of the first type, such as India and Central African territories, the Europeans came not as dispossessing "settlers," but as administrators, civil servants, missionaries, police chiefs, plantation managers and overseers, and the like. They came not to settle and found dynasties, but to get rich quick and go home. They left the native populations, for the most part, in the possession of their lives, and much of their land. In colonies of the second type, such as North America, and Australia, the white colonists organised ruthless warfare against the indigenous peoples. By force and fraud they deprived them of their ancestral land. By massacres and starvation they all but exterminated them.

These two types of colonies followed different types of economic development. In colonies of the first type while force was excerised to ensure a sufficient supply of labour for imperialist owned plantations and mines, the capitalist evolution of the colonial economy was not encouraged. In fact, although imperialism, brought into being the two classes typical of capitalism (a working class, of wage earners, and a commercial and even an industrial bourgeoisie) the imperialist leaned heavily on the pre-capitalist ruling classes (feudal princes and tribal chiefs) as a means of maintaining their hold and preserving stability. This system of so-called "indirect rule" meant that the imperialists deliberately discouraged "normal" capitalist development, deliberately preserve, and perpetuated outworn and reactionary institutions. Similarly, though they built roads, railways and harbours the Imperialists did this solely in order to get the natural wealth out of the country, not to foster internal development and communications. Though at first a "revolutionary force", disrupting traditional economies, imperialism rapidly assumed a completely reactionary role, strangling economic progress.

The white settlers in second-type colonies brought with them fully developed capitalist relationships and techniques. Once the resistance of the original, non-European populations had been overcome, the newly-conquered territories provided ideal conditions for the very rapid development and expansion of capitalism: no feudal relationships, classes and interests stood in the way; no land-owning and serf-owning aristocracy; all goods were commodities, and all payments and wages were in money. [....]

*Union not Wholly of Either Type*
The Cape Colony was never really regarded by Britain as a suitable settlement for the "dumping" of surplus population. There was one attempt to establish a "New England" type of colony – in the Eastern Cape, in 1820 – and a shipload of convicts destined to be landed in Cape Town was prevented by the townsfolk from disembarking its passengers. But the determined resistance of the Africans, particularly the Xhosa people, whom the whole protracted series of horrible "Kaffir Wars" had failed to conquer or subdue, made the whole idea of expansion dangerous and costly; nor, prior to the discovery of gold and diamonds, did the interior appear to offer attractive rewards to imperialist adventures.

For these and other reasons South Africa did not develop along "North American" lines. The white settlers themselves (apart from the Cape coastal towns) were organised on the basis of pre-capitalist relationships – a predominantly pastoral subsistence economy. Armed with rifle and ox-wagon they could and did conquer various tribes and establish areas of settlement; they were not strong enough to completely dispossess, still less to eliminate, the vigorous African tribes.

With the opening up of Kimberley and then the Witwatersrand, South Africa came dramatically and overwhelmingly into the picture of modern capitalist imperialism.

*Problems of the Imperialists*
The overseas investors who exported millions of pounds worth of capital to the Witwatersrand were faced with serious problems. To protect their investment and to reap the rich rewards they hoped to gain in gold, they required a stable and subservient political system. This requirement was not met by Kruger's semi-feudal farmers' republic, constantly at war with the African population, stubbornly refusing to remould itself as a bourgeois society or to accept the hegemony of the gold mining interests.

Secondly, the imperialists required a mass, stable, cheap labour force of the colonial type if they were to derive maximum profits from gold-mining. This requirement was not met either by the Boer farmers, who satisfied their limited needs on the farms, or by the African tribesmen, whose independence had not wholly been broken, and who were able to subsist economically on land held tribally, or as share-croppers and squatters on land which had been seized but not cleared by the Boers.

Victory in the Boer Wars did not, of itself, adequately solve either problem. Events, ever since 1776, had proved the impossibility (and the ruinous expense) of running a colony with a settled population, on traditional lines – i.e. with an imported civil service, army, police, etc. And attempts to staff the mines with imported labour (Cornish, then Chinese) failed.

*The Solution*
The political and economic structure crystallised in the Act of Union provided a

working answer to these problems. The white population of the Union was entrenched as a privileged oligarchy, providing a stable and reliable basis of government. The Africans were dispossessed of most of their remaining land and squatting rights, pauperised and driven by a complex of economic and legal measures, backed up by a massive police and administrative system, to sell their labour-power at sub-economic rates.

Economically, the Union of South Africa is founded on the subjection of the non-European population and the super-profits derived from the colonial-type exploitation of their labour.

The imperialist-monopolist group (closely linked with British and American finance-capital) which exerts a decisive influence in the country's affairs shares the fruits of cheap labour with the agricultural, industrial and commercial capitalists; the white middle-class and professional groups and the upper stratum of the white working class are also permitted to share directly and indirectly in the imperialist robbery of the non-whites (e.g. by being granted "sheltered" employment, by rather higher living standards, cheap domestic labour, exemption from heavy work, etc.).

*A Few Conclusions*
I have attempted to give a brief sketch of the origin and nature of the curious duality of South Africa: at one and the same time an imperialist state and a colonial country; with two populations enjoying entirely different statuses – and determined artificial apartheid measures directed against their natural tendency to integrate.

I make no apology for the tentative and preliminary nature of the treatment of this theme: its full development would of course require a substantial volume.

At the same time, it is interesting to note a few conclusions which I think follow from this approach.

1. In the first place, it is idle to imagine that there are any sort of revolutionary or progressive potentialities among the white bourgeoisie in South Africa. People like E.S. Sachs who chatter about "progressive capitalism,"[6] or those who place their confidence in the new Liberal Party are making entirely false analogies with countries quite different in character, in historical circumstances far removed from ours. The secondary industrialists of this country are basically junior partners of imperialism; the last thing they would advocate would be the abolition of the imperialist system on which they depend.
2. Afrikaner republicanism and "anti-imperialism" (except as a bait to catch the nationalist vote) has ceased to exist as a serious political phenomenon.[7] The pre-capitalist Boer farming economy has disappeared, become absorbed in the capitalist economy of white South Africa. The Afrikaans farming bourgeoisie has merged with the new and rising Afrikaner industrial and financial bourgeoisie. Very much the same remarks apply to them as I have made about the secondary industrialists above. The Malanists today must be classed with Chiang Kai-Shek, Syngman Rhee and Tito as the most ardent and staunch supporters and defenders of imperialism.[8]
3. The continuing development and growth of white capitalism in South Africa leads to an ever-increasing, insatiable demand for cheap labour (note the present grave shortage of labour in the mines) which can only be met at present by intensified repression and pressure against the African population.

4. The whole system is increasingly being challenged and threatened by the growth of the non-white national liberation movement: the advanced progressive anti-imperialist tendency in our country. Here should be noted certain features of the national liberation movement which differentiate it from similar movements in other colonies:
(a) It results from the monopoly of commercial and economic opportunities which has been preserved for the white group that the emergence of a significant capitalist section among the Africans has been deliberately frustrated. The African liberation movement is not dominated by the unstable and potentially treacherous elements which have led similar movements elsewhere. It is a movement of workers and peasants, professional people, middle and commercial classes, in which the progressive, working class tendency plays an increasingly influential part.
(b) The demand for national independence takes a different form in South Africa from that taken in countries dominated by overseas imperialist states. Since the imperialist oppressor lives right here the demand is not for "independence" but for self-government, democracy, that is to say, for equal rights and opportunities for all. (Superficially, this struggle resembles the franchise struggles of the bourgeois democratic revolutions of the Eighteenth and Nineteenth Centuries: this resemblance should not blind us to its real character as a national struggle for self-government and self-determination.)
(c) Since the liberation movement is not a predominantly bourgeois movement it does not subscribe to the reformist and idealist illusions which characterise bourgeois movements (including national movements) in the twentieth century and which spring out of their fear of the awakened masses in their hope of wresting concessions from the ruling class. The Defiance Campaign in this country was quite different in purpose and content from the classical Gandhi-ite "satyagraha" movement: it was seen as a means (a very effective one too) of propaganda and organisation, rather than an attempt at "conquest by submission." Passivity, of the so-called Unity Movement type, consisting of negative boycotts and "non-collaboration", is widely recognized today as a timid intellectual substitute for resistance. (Which is not to say that well-organised boycotts with mass backing cannot be in suitable circumstances useful educating and organising techniques).
(d) The liberation movement has concentrated on formulating political demands. But the economic content of national liberation in South Africa must inevitably centre in redivision of the land and the nationalisation of the principal means of production (for the power of imperialism in this country can only be broken by divorcing the imperialists from the means of production). As the movement grows in strength, confidence and political clarity it is bound to give expression and emphasis to such demands.
5. The enormous burden of the top-heavy administrative and police apparatus which is required to maintain the imperialist system in this country (and which is bound to increase year by year) and the increasing inroads made into their own rights and privileges (in a police state) must sooner or later make their impact upon the white working population of South Africa as well. Whether they will, in the long run, reject the role of a counter-revolutionary army for which they have been cast by the Chamber of Mines millionaires, depends on many factors. Not the least of these factors is the effectiveness and perseverance of that clear-headed and courageous

band of white democrats which has already identified itself with the aims and the struggle of the liberation movement.

*DISCUSSION*

The following points were raised in the discussion:
1. A distinction must be made between the mining industry with a need for cheap labour and secondary industry with a need for expanding markets and stable skilled labour. The political repercussions of such a policy, however, would probably stop the secondary industrialists from demanding these economic reforms. The Chamber of Industries, for example, has never really demanded the abolition of the colour bar for just this reason.
2. The leaders of the Liberatory Movement are not large capitalists. They have no vested interests which might lead them to "sell out." In the circumstances of a poor uneducated community, would one find leaders coming from the educated and professional groups or from the industrial proletariat? Alternatively, can the leadership come from the Non-European trade unions?
3. It is not a national but a class question. For example, amongst Africans we have workers, petit-bourgeoisie and capitalists and each is interested in his own troubles. Congress does not represent anything but itself and certainly is not a workers' movement. Passive resistance is a bourgeois idea. In fact, issues taken up were bourgeois issues.

*A NOTE BY THE SPEAKER ON THE DISCUSSION*
*[....]*
1. *On alleged "progressive capitalism" and the role of secondary industry*
It is true that there are certain contradictions between different sections of the white imperialist class in South Africa. Manufacturers of consumer goods compete for cheap labour at a disadvantage with mining and farming employers, because the complex of "cheap-labour" legislation (passes, taxes, reserves, urban areas, etc.) operates primarily in the interests of the latter employers. Secondary industrialists therefore are obliged to offer slightly higher wage rates, and their spokesmen frequently criticise the pass laws etc. Moreover, they seek a more stable, experienced and better-educated labour force. If higher wage-rates were paid for mine and farm labour they would benefit by an increased demand in the home market.

It would, however, be gravely mistaken to overemphasise these factors, or to make a false analogy with, for example, the American Civil War (with, I suppose, the South African clothing and furniture manufacturers in the role of the Northern capitalists fighting the slave-owning planters of the South).

This analogy completely overlooks the characteristically imperialist structure of South Africa, and the basic position of the industrial and commercial bourgeoisie as junior partners in the super-exploitation of colonial-type non-white labour. Their continued existence as a class is dependent on the continuance of this imperialist structure. The abolition of white domination would inevitably bring with it the destruction of the white monopoly of capital and of commercial opportunities.

Moreover, we cannot lose sight of the fact of the very substantial economic dependence of manufacturing interests on the predominant primary industries. Much of the engineering industry produces mining and farming equipment, or equipment for closely related and subsidiary purposes. In addition to these direct links, the great mining and financial interests own directly or indirectly (through the banks) a big and growing share of industrial capital. This is precisely what is meant by monopoly capitalism, the merging of finance and industrial capitalists into finance capital.

These important factors help to explain why the "secondary industries" have never gone so far in their occasional criticisms as to establish any political party of their own. (The Liberal Party, no doubt, aims to attract their support, but there is not the slightest sign that they have succeeded; the Liberals will only be supported by capitalists in the event of their appearing to have some prospect of diverting the "dangerous" non-White Liberation Movement – and even then their support is as likely to come from the Chamber of Mines as the Chamber of Industries. The Mines, after all, are the mainstay of the Institute of Race Relations).

It is time to discard illusions about "progressive capitalism" as a significant factor among any section of the merciless exploiters who constitute the white imperialist group. We are not living in the period of nineteenth century expanding capitalism, but of shrinking twentieth century imperialism. The decisive conflict in our country is that between white imperialism on the one hand; and on the other, the various classes among the non-white people, headed by the working class, and aiming at national emancipation and full democracy. In this conflict the white manufacturing and commercial bourgeoisie are allied with imperialism, a part of imperialism. Of course, these considerations do not apply to the groups among the white population (workers, professional people, etc.) who do not directly derive profits from colonial exploitation and may, as I have indicated, be regarded as potential allies of democracy, in certain circumstances.

2. *On the Class Character of the Non-White Liberation Movements*

The special feature of imperialism in South Africa is the existence of the large population of the dominant imperialist nationality, side by side in the same state territory as the oppressed colonial people. This has resulted in the virtual exclusion of the non-white peoples, especially the Africans, from the commercial and other opportunities which the development of imperialism afforded to a small minority in other colonies, and the virtual monopolisation of those opportunities by the dominant white group. Despite the exceptional capitalistic development of South Africa, this country has not experienced the growth of a "Native bourgeoisie" to anything like the extent that has occurred in India, Indonesia or even the Gold Coast and other African territories unsuitable for white settlement.

It is true that despite all past restrictions, Indians and Africans have in many instances managed to establish themselves in the most precarious and least-rewarding section of the capitalist class – retail trade, and as urban landlords, on the fringes of the transport industry, etc. But three important factors are worth noting about the small bourgeois group – firstly, nowhere have non-white employers been allowed to enter the field as substantial competitors in the labour market. There are no large-scale non-white employers and direct employers of labour. Secondly, the non-white commercial class is exceptionally small, not only in relation to the white bourgeoisie, but also in relation to the total non-white population, and to the working class. Thirdly, the foothold which this class has established is extremely tenuous and constantly threatened by the ruling group which wants to seize every advantage for itself and reduce the entire non-white group to a proletarian status. (Consider the intention and current use of the Group Areas Act against Indian and other non-white merchants).

In addition to these petty capitalist elements the non-white population comprises a relatively small (for the same obvious reasons) group of professional people, mainly teachers, chiefs and other civil servants and small handicraftsmen. Far the most important sections are the industrial, mining and agricultural working class, and the peasantry which (because of land shortage and the migratory labour system) is increasingly merged with the working class.

The National Liberatory movements comprise an alliance of all these classes and groups for the common aims of equality, self-government and land. This is a familiar characteristic of such movements among oppressed colonial peoples everywhere. The development of many of these movements has been marked by the dominance of the bourgeoisie, and in critical periods a split among the capitalist elements, a section of which has treacherously betrayed the movement in order to reach a compromise with imperialism at the expense of the masses.

While it would be wrong to assert that the movement has been free of such tendencies in our country, or will be free of them in the future, it would be still more wrong to generalise mechanically from overseas experience and to assume that the Congresses are mere "bourgeois affairs" which "pure working class elements" should stand aloof from, or attempt to disrupt. Apartheid South Africa allows little or no room for a compromise with non-white capitalism; the economically and numerically small character of non-white capitalism, and the consequent threat of its complete extinction by white imperialism, has made it both less influential and more revolutionary than, say, the giant Birla and Tata concerns in India or the big bankers behind Chiang-Kai-Shek.

In recent years, particularly, the militant working class tendency has wielded increasing influence in our national movements. In the Indian Congress, the progressive working class policy of men like Dadoo and Naiker has completely displaced the compromising line of the former bourgeois leadership; and a similar development has taken place in the A.N.C., especially in the Transvaal. But the policy of genuine workers' leaders in these movements is not to drive out the allied classes, but rather to broaden out the movements, and to make the alliance of all oppressed people firm and enduring. It is significant that the ultra-"left" sectarian policy of certain Congress members was resoundingly defeated at the October 1953, Transvaal Annual Conference of the A.N.C., which at the same time gave an overwhelming vote of confidence to its working class and progressive leaders.

3. *On the Allegation that "It is not a National but a Class Question"*

Of course, every question is at its roots "a class question" but one can have little patience with the pedantic arm-chair socialist types of "theoreticians" who are apparently unable to see that on practically every main issue of home and foreign policy, the outlook and aims of such a bourgeois element as, for example, Dr. Moroka, are far more progressive in content than such working class elements as the Mineworkers' Union, the S.A.R. Staff Associations or the S.A.T.L.C.[9] In case anyone should mistake these arm-chair socialists with authoritative spokesmen of any sort of progressive opinion, it is time to say that this point of view, like that of a previous lecturer who suggested at the Discussion Club the abolition of the national character of the Congresses (which means, in effect, their liquidation) represents a crude opportunist distortion of, and deviation from, scientific political theory.[10]

## Document 54
### K. A. Jordaan, "What are the National Groups in South Africa? A Contribution to the Symposium", Forum Club, Cape Town, May 1954[11]

In analysing a subject of this nature [...] it is necessary to warn against a definitional approach to the national question and the problem of nationalities and its mechanical application to a given situation without a thorough assessment of the extant social and political arrangements. The truth is always concrete.

1. *The National Question: General Considerations*
According to the classical meaning of the term, the national question presents itself as the problem of altering the relations one nation has with a foreign nation. The one is the oppressor; the other is the oppressed; the one is the hammer; the other is the anvil. The oppressed nation seeks to alter this relationship with the oppressing nation by its struggle for national independence and its demand for self-determination, that is, the right to separate state existence.

The Polish question of the nineteenth century is the classical instance of the nationalities problem.[12] For more than a century the Poles lay under the heel of Russian absolutism as well as of German militarism. Thus, on the one hand, they were subjected to a rigorous policy of Russification, and on the other, to a policy of Germanisation. These policies were a calculated attempt to stamp out these traits and characteristics whereby the Poles justified themselves as a separate national group with their separate interests, and ipso facto, their right to a separate state existence. To this end, therefore, the Polish language was not recognised; the chief posts in the Polish government were filled by members of the foreign overlords; only the languages and customs of the oppressing nations were given official recognition. In this way, the Polish nation was lashed to the war chariot of foreign nations and sucked dry, economically, culturally and politically.

India furnishes us with the second example of the national question. Because of the multi-national set-up in that country, there are two prongs to the national question: firstly, the political liberation of all the Indian national groups from Imperialism: and secondly, the right of every Indian national group to complete cultural and political autonomy within the orbit of an independent India. This movement for autonomy by the Indian national groups is a very strong one because they had since time immemorial existed as distinct cultural groupings. Their desire for a separate existence is theirs as of historical right, like the Poles or Czechs.

Four main conclusions can be drawn from these two examples of the national question. Firstly, a homogeneous national movement develops strong centripetal forces whereas a heterogeneous national movement generates powerful centrifugal forces. Thus, on the one hand, the movement for German unification led to the assimilation of all the *disjecta membra* of the German nation under one central state, while, on the other hand, the dismemberment of the multi-national Austro-Hungarian Empire culminated in the formation of various states.[13] Secondly, national liberation involves the combined movement of all classes and groups composing the oppressed nation. Thirdly, the national struggle is primarily directed at the overthrow of political and legal discrimination between one nation and another. It does not necessarily involve a change in the economic structure of the liberated nation. And finally, a successful national struggle, while it means the liberation of the oppressed nation from the oppressing nation, does not necessarily imply the extension of full democracy to the constituent elements. To be sure, the political oppression and economic exploitation of one class by another or of one group by another can still continue within the liberated nation itself.

2. *The National Question in South Africa*

What, then, are the *differentia specifica* of the national question in South Africa? How are we going to apply the classical slogan of "national independence and the right to self-determination" to our problem of national liberation? There is no doubt that we are not dealing here with the problem of changing South Africa's relations with a foreign nation. The Act of Union, 1909, the Statute of Westminster, 1931, the Status and Seals Act, 1934, all gave South Africa its full political independence as a nation as well as its right to independent state existence.

Our national question revolves around the question rather of the internal arrangements of the South African State. The form of this multi-national state must be distinguished from its content. Within the framework of this independent nation, four-fifths of the people are oppressed by one-fifth. Concretely speaking, certain South African groups are oppressed by other South African groups. The African, Indian and Coloured South Africans are oppressed by British, Afrikaner and Jewish South Africans. Our national problem therefore presents itself as the struggle of four-fifths of the nation to alter their status under the state within that nation and to attain the same status enjoyed by one-fifth of that nation. This involves three things: the equalisation of political and legal rights (the full franchise); the right to sell one's labour power in any field of economic activity (the abolition of the industrial colour bar); and the right to buy and possess property in any area (the abolition of the reserves and so-called native territories, as well as the abolition of laws which restrict on the grounds of colour the right of buying and selling).

The South African national question therefore differs from the national movements in other countries in that it does not aim at establishing new and different relations with an outside nation or people. It aims at establishing new and different relations within the South African nation itself. Secondly, our national question is unique also in this respect, that the solution to the national question is at one and the same time the solution to the question of democracy. More concretely: our movement is national because it aims at the overthrow of the oppression of peoples by other peoples within the same nation; our movement is democratic because the overthrow of such oppression automatically leads to the extension of democratic rights possessed by one-fifth to four-fifths of the nation. Ours is, in short, a truly national democratic movement.

In determining the character and the future of our national democratic struggle, one must beware of using as the point of departure those artificial Herrevolk racial divisions. It is unfortunately an indication of our political primitiveness that certain political groups and individuals can conceive of our struggle, our organisational forms and the future of South African society only in terms of those racial categories foisted on us by Herrenvolkism. Thus there are people who conceive of our struggle as a purely African demand for land, as if the Africans would be satisfied with land alone. Others consider the democratic struggle purely as a Non-European struggle. And there are some who are perpetuating the tradition of racial separation by incorporating into their political organisational forms those racial divisions which Herrenvolkism is preserving in society at large.

Our movement is, on the contrary, a movement which embraces all those people who are opposed to the present system of national oppression and race discrimination. Our movement has a place for every person who subscribes to its programme. It follows therefore that there is a place for every South African in the society of the future. This must necessarily be so, because the movement does not only offer the oppressed peoples but the whole nation a solution to the present-day problems facing the country. And in freeing the oppressed peoples, the movement thereby also frees the whole of South African humanity. For no people oppressing other people can be free.

It must not, however, be taken to mean that the national movement will make the slightest concession to white arrogance or chauvinism. It emphatically asserts that in establishing a democratic republic the majority of the nation, the Africans, will clearly leave their imprint on the form the state is to assume. From the point of view of their number alone, it is indubitable that the Africans will dominate the councils of the new nation.

3. *The Problem of National Groups*

What is a national group? It consists of people who, by virtue of their common racial geographical or linguistic antecedents, consider themselves or are considered to be a distinct or separate racial entity. In the light of this definition, the Africans, the Coloureds, the Indians and the Africaners can be regarded as national groupings. The question now arises: Should we sponsor a movement for the complete separation of these national groups and their separate existence in their separate territories? Is there a demand for such a dismemberment of the South African nation?

There is no evidence that any national grouping is raising any demand for an existence separate and apart from the rest of South Africa. There is, moreover, no demand by any national group for the development of their own special culture. On the contrary, the members of every national group feel and consider themselves to be an inextricable part of one nation, and they resist any attempt to divide them from the rest of South Africa. To be sure, if there is any move at present for cultural differentiation, then it emanates from the ruling classes themselves. The Nationalist-sponsored Bantu educational system is a case in point. This system seeks to revivify and to encourage those obsolete Bantu traits and characteristics which are the relics and the reminders of the tribal past. Contrary to any demand by the Africans, for example, the use of the Bantu vernacular in schools is being made compulsory. And by encouraging a peculiar Bantu culture and mode of life, the ruling classes are trying to justify their special treatment, that is, their inferior status in the South African nation. The move for a Bantustan also comes from the Herrenvolk, though the Africans are implacably opposed to any special treatment or to any special home.

It is reactionary from two points of view to advocate the recrudescence of an obsolete Bantu culture. It is reactionary because it constitutes an attempt to unwind the historical film in reverse when the historic process is tending to knit more closely every section of the South African nation to meet the needs of a modern industrial system – the fundamental pre-requisite for the socialist reconstruction of any society. It is reactionary because it means the aiding and abetting of Herrenvolk schemes to differentiate between sections of the nation in order to safeguard European interests.

There is no doubt that our problem of national groupings differs from the nationalities question in India. The peculiar historical evolution of this sub-continent precluded the development of any distinctive culture by any national group. The industrial revolution in this country which began with the discovery of gold and diamonds gave the Africans no opportunity whatsoever of establishing on the smoking ruins of tribalism any peculiar culture of their own and of becoming a distinct national entity. They had perforce to take a tremendous leap from tribalism to modern wage slavery and assimilate the culture of a progressively higher type of society. Where certain aspects of the tribal past still exist, then those are assiduously preserved by the ruling classes and combined with the most modern forms of exploitation and oppression. This is the law of combined development. The Boers, also, were at no time able to evade the dynamics of capitalist development in this country. When they were able to establish simple peasant republics, these were at all times dependent on British capitalism economically, and subjected to the corrosive and assimilative forces of that system. The Coloureds themselves are not a race or nation aspiring to independent existence. Having been part and parcel of the European people for over two centuries, they had their links with the white severed by the Union. They are Europeans and know of no other culture. Finally, the Indians are of such diverse racial antecedents that one cannot conceive of them as a cohesive and homogeneous group. A national grouping demands a separate national existence on the grounds of historical and cultural rights. In South Africa, no national group is making such a demand because no national group has any distinct cultural or historical traditions.

Despite the attempts of the Herrenvolk to accentuate our differences, the democratic movement, on the contrary, emphasises the similarities of the nationally-oppressed groups. And these similarities are our common and indivisible oppression, our common interests and our common destiny. We emphasise the fact that we are not only one nation economically. We also emphasise the fact that we are one nation psychologically, because we think of ourselves, we act and react like members of one nation.

It is quite possible that after the consummation of the democratic struggle, a section or sections even of the South African nation would ask for autonomy, even if only for cultural autonomy. The thing cannot be anticipated. Certainly we will grant any group this right to cultural autonomy or secession. But to raise this problem now when there is no demand for it, is to confuse the epilogue of the struggle with the prologue. We will give cognisance to these things if and when they do arise.

4. *The National Struggle in Relation to Socialism*

Every national movement has as its objective the triumph of capitalist democracy. This is a fundamental proposition of the materialist conception of history which it is necessary to reiterate in view of the many misconceptions on this score. While it is clearly linked up with the struggle for socialism and while it is true that historical stages can be telescoped, a national liberatory movement must not be confused with the movement for the social ownership of the instruments of labour. The one involves a political revolution, nothing more, nothing less; the other argues a social revolution to change the very economic basis of society.

Let us take two examples to confirm this postulate. The Indian national movement has as its task the complete elimination of British Imperialism as a political factor from the Indian body politic. A bloc of three classes was formed to this end; the capitalists, the peasantry and the proletariat. Each class, let it be noted, temporarily liberated itself from its own peculiar economic interests to join in a united front with other classes for the political liberation of the oppressed Indian nation. The question of the radical alteration in the economic base of India did not and, indeed, could not crop up. For how can it be tackled by a bloc of classes with conflicting economic interests and aspirations? In South Africa, secondly, the national movement is not directed against the present property relations. It is calling for a radical change in the form and application and not the content of capitalist laws. The demand for the full franchise, the demand for the abolition of the colour bar and race discrimination – these all involve political changes, not changes in the basic capitalist system of production.

The question now arises: Can our democratic struggle be consummated within the framework of the existing capitalist system? It is here that we have to distinguish between the formal programmatic demands of the movement and the practical results of their implementation. The theoretically possible must be distinguished from the practically probable.

Our revolution is clearly bourgeois, or more correctly, capitalist democratic, in its formal aspect. But who is going to make this revolution? The white capitalists have consistently displayed their impotence to consummate their own revolution by fighting against those obsolete institutions which are stultifying the free development of capitalism. Does this task therefore devolve on the Non-White bourgeoisie? Once again, South Africa is singular in the respect that, unlike India, Indonesia and China, she has no native bourgeoisie of any numerical significance. For at every turn in its evolution, capitalism has prevented the emergence of any large Non-White bourgeoisie either in the form of industrialists or peasants of trading and commercial classes. Our movement does not consist of a bloc of these classes. The Proletariat constitutes the preponderant majority in our national struggle.

It seems to me that the belated historic task of the capitalist class is now being shouldered off on the proletariat. This, to be sure, is nothing new in the history of revolutions. It is part of the law of the uneven development of capitalism. The oppressed have had no tradition in private ownership under capitalism. I venture to suggest, therefore, that the proletariat will emerge at the head of the national movement and proceed to solve the contradictions of capitalism by proletarian methods of class struggle. More concretely, the national movement will find it impossible to solve the problem of democracy and the aspirations of the dispossessed elements within the framework of capitalism. Two examples will suffice. The abolition under capitalism of the laws regulating land ownership will in fact place all the land in the possession of the moneyed classes and leave the landless more landless. The abolition of the colour bar in the economic sphere will not satisfy the aspirations of the proletarian majority in the national movement to enjoy the fruits of their own labour.

The democratic struggle will therefore be uninterrupted and permanent in character by transforming the political revolution into a social revolution and reconstructing society on socialist principles. The task will greatly be facilitated, not only by the presence of a weak and insignificant local bourgeoisie, but by a tottering capitalist system on a world scale. That is the main conclusion we can draw from this analysis.

## Document 55
## H. J. Simons[14], "Nationalisms in South Africa",
## Forum Club, Cape Town, May 1954

1. Every political question ought to be examined in the light of (a) the theoretical principles relevant to the problem and (b) the specific and historical conditions applying at the time and place under consideration.
2. The "national problem" which we are here discussing is, firstly, what are the "nations" or "national groups" in South Africa and, secondly, and mainly, what is the correct attitude towards them – correct, that is to say, for South Africans who wish to replace the existing system of exploitation by a free and harmonious multi-racial society.
3. Our theory provides us with a definition of "nation" that can be applied anywhere. It is an aggregate or community of persons having a number of specific characteristics in common: language, territory, economy, traditions, and psychology. Some students would include another attribute: the desire, realized or unfulfilled, for self-government.[15]
4. Leaving aside for the moment the question as to which groups in South Africa fall within the scope of our definition, let us examine the standards by which we are to measure the values of nationalism as a political force.
5. We can do no better for this purpose than look at the comparable experience of other countries where the related issues have come under scientific scrutiny by persons looking for a guide to the reconstruction of society on a rational basis.

*MULTI-NATIONAL STATES OF EUROPE*
6. One important source of experience comes from the controversies over the multi-national empires of Austria-Hungary and Tsarist Russia, which had spread outward, absorbing border regions and their inhabitants and subjecting them to alien rule. The policy of the dominant classes in each empire was to hold it together by force, resisting separatist movements and repressing the language and culture of the minority groups.
7. The middle class liberals and working class social democrats who struggled for the liberation of the oppressed nationalities developed two opposing viewpoints: the concepts of "cultural autonomy", and of "national self-determination".
8. The Austrian and Russian social democrats who urged the former policy wanted equal recognition for the Slavs, Magyars, Czechs, Poles and other "national" minorities, which were, however, to remain within the framework of the multi-national society. Each "nation" would have its own representatives in the central legislature (a form of "communal" representation), and its language would be given equal status with any other in schools and official circles. It would manage its own affairs as far as possible.
9. These claims of the "cultural autonomy" school were really implied also in the "right of self-determination"; but the adherents of this policy went much further in that they wished to secure to the nation the legal and political right to secede from the imperial state and establish itself in a separate territory as an independent state.
10. Although the theory emphasised the discretionary nature of this right, and the possibility of the nation preferring to remain within the empire (which it would do as a result of free choice only if the advantages of remaining in the empire clearly

outweighed those of secession,) the struggle for the recognition of the right inevitably carried in itself a threat of dissolution. The ruling class therefore resisted the claim. In the upshot, it was established by means of mass support, insurrection and war, out of which emerged the national states of eastern and central Europe.

## COLONIAL NATIONAL MOVEMENTS

Before considering the lessons to be drawn from the European experience, we might turn our attention to another type of nationalism which developed during the course of this century in Asia and Africa under the domination of European imperialist states.

12. The conditions shaping the national movements in Asia and Africa differed from those operating in Europe in the following respects:
(a) the imperialist state and the colony were situated in different continents; consequently conquest and domination were carried out by relatively small numbers of emigrants from Europe who became the ruling class in the colonies;
(b) the colonial peoples differed from the imperialists not only in culture but also in physical type, and the physical differences rather than the cultural became the basis for discrimination;
(c) cultures in the colonies were tribal and feudal, but in any event pre-industrial, and the effect of imperial conquest was to undermine and reshape the traditional culture in the process of exploiting resources by modern techniques;
(d) contact between the imperialist representatives and the upper social classes of the colonial peoples was slight and formal, in contrast to the intimacy of the relationships between the upper classes of the dominant and minority nationalities in the multi-national states of Europe.

13. Nationalism in the colonies bears the imprint of these characteristics. It attaches less importance to the recognition of language and culture than to the achievement of equal and democratic rights; it works for the elimination of the gap in education, technical skill and living standards between the people of the colony and the inhabitants of more advanced countries; and it demands, not a separate territory for the national group, but self-government and the right to secede from the empire.

14. These features result from the special geographical, cultural and ethnic (i.e. racial) factors involved in the type of exploitation found in overseas colonies.

    We may conclude that the Europeans will not become a permanent community in the colonies as members of multi-national societies, though we should not rule out the possibility of the colonies becoming full and autonomous partners with European states in a socialist commonwealth.

## IN SOUTH AFRICA

15. The special features of South African nationalisms arises from the combination of an imperialism and its dependent colony in a single political and geographical region. The large, permanently established European population attempts to dominate the rest of the population in typical colonial fashion, while the various national groups have interacted and fused in a manner closely resembling the integration that takes place in multi-national societies such as developed in Europe.

16. Because of the colour bar on the one hand and the high degree of interaction between the national groups on the other, the oppressed nationalities do not raise the demands characteristic of national movements in European history or in the colonies.

17. They do not demand "cultural autonomy" or "self-determination" or "secession." In fact, these concepts are regarded with doubt or even hostility, because they resemble outwardly the "ideology" of the racialists who use them to mask and justify race oppression.
18. The African, Indian and Coloured people are not deceived by the Nationalist appeals to "respect and preserve their way of life", to "develop along their own lines", or "build a separate Bantustan" (this last proposal being varied in the case of the Indians with the insolent demand that they return to "their" country.) The oppressed nationalities recognise in these formulae of apartheid a thinly-veiled attempt to perpetuate non-European backwardness and inferiority for the purpose of an exploitative economy.
19. It is the racialist in the European ruling class who stresses the "peculiar" features of "Bantu" culture, urges the African to "respect the ways of his forefathers", forces him through the Bantu Education Act into a separate education system, revives the traditional rule of tribal chiefs under the Bantu Authorities Act, and instructs him that his "national" home is in the reserves, not in the "European town and cities."
20. We all know that similar efforts are now being made to transform the Coloured people into a "nation" by such means as the Group Areas Act, Population Registration Act, Mixed Marriages Act, a Coloured Affairs Department and the rest of the segregation paraphernalia.
21. Our hatred of apartheid and the other varieties of racialism should not blind us to the advantages of a genuine, healthy and dynamic nationalism. It is necessary, however, that we examine carefully and even suspiciously any theory, no matter how well-intentioned, that savours, even if only superficially, of the Nationalist formula: "development along own lines". That, certainly is not what the movement for national liberation wants in any shape or form.

*THE DEMAND FOR EQUALITY*
22. The national liberation movement demands EQUALITY. And that demand is not the same as the programme of "cultural autonomy" or "secession." Equality does not imply a withdrawal from or expulsion of the European population. It contemplates a common society with Europeans on a completely equal basis.
23. Equality means, in the first place, equality in law: the removal of all statutory and public forms of racial discrimination; the abolition, in short, of the colour bar. This kind of equality is implicit in the theory of the "liberal" state based on private ownership of the means of production, free competition and parliamentary democracy.
24. Legal equality does not itself ensure social equality. The latter can come about only through the elimination of the taproot of inequality, namely private property. To achieve actual equality, the people will have to introduce social ownership of the productive section of the economy.
25. The national liberation movements in South Africa limit their demands to the first kind of equality and must therefore be described as a form of inter-class nationalism which embraces both an exploiting and an exploited class.
26. This kind of nationalism is progressive as long as it opposes discrimination and oppressive policies, but the exploiting element is always a source of potential support for class discrimination, that is, inequality caused by private ownership of the instruments of production.

27. A recent case of the emergence of the exploiting element in colonial nationalism comes from the Gold Coast, where the Prime Minister, Dr. Nkrumah, associated his government and party with the attack upon socialism. India and Indonesia provide other similar examples.
28. Prediction is always tempting, if dangerous. Yielding to temptation, I should say that the influence of the exploiting element in the South African national liberation movement is likely to decline because of the effects of the colour bar, which is designed to stifle the growth of social classes above working-class level in the African, Indian and Coloured communities. While the "middle class" grows very slowly or even declines, the number of urban workers grows rapidly because of the rise of industry. We may therefore expect to find that the national movements acquire a definite working class character.

*MORE OR FEWER "NATIONS"?*
29. Workers like other people want to use and develop their language and preserve their customs. They therefore resent and resist restrictions being placed on their "national" culture.
30. I think it is right to say, however, that workers are less involved emotionally in their "national" culture than such persons as teachers, ministers of religion, journalists and writers, traders and professional people. The latter associate almost exclusively with their own people, also in business, and have a strong material, as well as intellectual, interest in cultivating pride in the national language and tradition. Workers, on the other hand, mix at places of employment with members of other national groups, and tend to develop an "international" outlook based on common class interests.
31. For these reasons, a national movement led by workers is less likely than one led by exploiting elements to exaggerate the importance of purely "national" issues.
32. Personal experience leads me to believe that African working men and women of the kind active in the A.N.C. do not want to divide their people into "nations" according to language: Xhosa, Zulu, Tswana, Sotho, Pedi, Venda and so on. They put the emphasis on the common factor: they are all "Africans", victims of the colour bar, and linked in a common struggle. They view with suspicion efforts to encourage a "tribal outlook and condemn them as a "divide and rule" device.
33. I think they are right. Africans are engaged in a gigantic task of nation-building under great difficulties. Their whole attention is concentrated on mastering the new environment of which they have become part, and of adapting their traditional life pattern to these new circumstances. There is much in the old tribal culture that is a handicap and burden. Their only hope lies in forging ahead to build a wider society embracing Africans of all tribal origins.
34. It is the racialist who stresses the differences between people, who wants to "preserve" chieftainship, "Native law", and "Bantu tradition." Does he do it in order to help the African, or to save his own privileges and power?

*OBJECTIVES*
35. To conclude, I should say that the African, Coloured and Indian people are not trying to drive the Europeans out of the country, or to break away from a common society and form a separate, independent state, or to divide the population along racial lines into distinct "cultural communities."

36. On the contrary, their struggle is aimed at the creation of a common South African society guaranteeing equality of rights and opportunities to all sections and races.
37. In this struggle, the working class is likely to become the dominant and leading factor, and its policy will centre around the common interests of all workers, regardless of race.
38. It would be wrong to disturb or deflect this development by stressing tribal, racial or cultural differences. On the contrary, the stress should be placed wherever possible on the values and interests common to all persons in the national liberation movements.
39. This international outlook is quite consistent with the demand for the full and equal recognition of the languages used by the different sections of the people.


## Document 56
## Thomas Ngwenya, "What are the National Groups in South Africa?" Forum Club, Cape Town, May 1954

*[....]*

1. South Africa's population is composed of four racial groups: Africans, Coloureds, Indians and Europeans. Together these four racial groups constitute the South African Nation.
2. The division of the South African population into these racial groups has been artificially perpetuated and natural absorption and assimilation arrested, by the economic, social, political and cultural interests of capitalism.
3. The whites have been elevated to a status of supremacy, and the Non-Europeans reduced to "hewers of wood and drawers of water". A cunning policy of "divide and rule" has furthermore, been applied by the ruling class in order to prevent unity and solidarity of the oppressed.
4. Racial differences manifest themselves in terms of differences of colour, hair-texture, cephalic index, nose shape, etc. According to these the oppressed are grouped into the categories of Coloured, Indian, African and White. They also differ in respect of their historic origins, language, customs and traditions. However, the common oppression the Non-European races of the country endure, over-rides and obliterates nationalistic sentiments which may be expressed occasionally owing to race, possession of a common language, customs and traditions.

    Whilst cultural groups have discussed the future of certain Bantu languages and customs and their preservation, in not a single instance have the people thrown these up as political demands. Which can only mean that experience and intuition are teaching the people that the struggle for national emancipation lies upon the plane of concerted political action against the ruling class. Just as we condemn Bantu, Coloured, Indian or White chauvinism so we have to reject efforts to organise the oppressed upon the basis of cultural demands [rejecting] linguistic autonomy etc., etc.
5. Furthermore, whatever differences of race, language, customs and traditions tend to separate South Africans (fostered as these are by the state), the complex web of

relationships created by a unified economic system into which everyone in our society is drawn, whether as employer or labourer, white, black, Coloured or Indian, whittles away "national" or racial differences that exist. Integration has been taking place on all planes all the time. The official languages of the country; the culture, arts, crafts, industries and ideas of the dominant white group, are being assimilated all the time, precisely because the people have to find a place in the economy of the country, gain entry into the labour market.
6. In the throes of this process, the pursuit of national autonomy for different racial or linguistic groups, simply has no meaning. A national-cultural emersion of the whole population is taking place out of this fluid situation. It will inevitably end up in the birth of a democratic state in South Africa.
7. The task confronting us is the creation of a unified national liberatory movement which will serve as the midwife in that process.

## Document 57
## Lionel Forman[16], "Self-Determination in South Africa: A Contribution to Discussion", *Liberation*, 37, July 1959

In modern times the right of nations to self-determination has become a rallying call of oppressed peoples all over the world.

What does this demand mean? Essentially it means that a nation has the right to determine its own destiny, and this in turn means that, if it forms part of a multi-racial state or empire, it has the right to secede and lead an independent political existence.

That is self-determination. But what is a nation? People use this word in many ways. Everyone has for example heard talk of a South African nation, a Zulu nation, and African nation. In each case something different must be meant, for the Zulus form part of the African people and the Africans part of the South African people. They cannot all be nations unless one gives the word nation a very amorphous meaning like community, or people. Social scientists have therefore analysed the specific characteristics which make a community tightly knit and integrated, and capable of leading a separate existence. The definition they have adopted is that a nation is a historically evolved, stable community of language, territory, economic life and psychological make-up, manifested in a community of culture.

A community possessing all four of these essential features, and lacking none of them, is capable of leading an independent political existence in the world of today; and such a community is therefore entitled, as of right, to receive from all true democrats in the other nations of the multi-national state or empire of which it forms part, the fullest support for its demand for self-determination.

South Africa is not a single nation but a multi-national state. What is the position with regard to the Africans, who constitute the majority of the population of this State?

They too are not a nation. To a very large extent they have become, as the result of their common oppression, and the unifying efforts of the ANC, a single political community – but, like South Africa itself, it is a multi-national political community containing several languages and cultures.

## AN AFRICAN NATION?

Are the Africans developing into a single nation? The answer seems to be "Yes", and a single African nation is likely to develop before a single South African nation does.

The beginnings of a single South African national consciousness can be traced back to the 1880's.

Until the 19th century the economic basis did not exist for the amalgamation of the numerous African tribes into states. They were cattle-grazers and small scale formers, and as they required large areas of pasture and lived at subsistence level the tendency was towards dispersal rather than concentration of population. Even when, with the accumulation of wealth, a ruling class and a state developed, it was capable of exercising its authority only over a limited area, and when conflicts of interest arose it was powerless to prevent dissident groups within the tribe from moving off to pastures new.

As new techniques were acquired, making possible a greater division of labour and the development of a standing army, groups of African tribes would have developed towards a statehood and unification just as people did in Europe, and this is clearly demonstrated early in the 19th century by the Zulus from the time of Tshaka and the Basuto from that of Mosheshoe.

Unification in this form however was smashed in its infancy by British imperialism.

Nevertheless, it is not impossible that British imperialism hastened the development of a single African nation rather than retarded it. The huge inflow of capital which came with the discovery of diamonds in 1870 and of gold sixteen years later transformed South Africa from a collection of primitive pastoral and agricultural communities into a single economic unit and smashed the tribal system and sped up the process of unification of the Africans.

Long before the industrial revolution wrought by the discovery of diamonds and the imperialist intervention in South Africa the voluntary amalgamation of all the black people to make a stand against the white advance had been a dream of the most farsighted African leaders and the nightmare of all the Europeans. But it had remained a dream.

Far from there being unity of the African tribes, a handful of Europeans were able to exploit inter-tribal conflicts so skillfully that in every decisive campaign by far the main burden of fighting, on the European side, was borne by Africans.

At the same time a tiny African petit-bourgeoisie composed of mission assistants, priests, teachers and clerks was coming into existence in the Eastern Cape, and in the early 1880's the first bodies cutting across tribal barriers, the first **African** bodies came into being. Most important of these were Mutual Benefit societies at Kimberley, (embryo trade unions), the African Educational Association (composed of teachers and priests around the mission stations of the Eastern Cape), and the general political organisation, Imbumba Yama Afrika.

The last-named may be described as the first Non-European national organisation – the direct forerunner of the African National Congress. Like the Afrikaner Bond it came into being as the result of the heightened national oppression which followed the decision of the British, in 1874, to establish complete control over Southern Africa.

From the formation of Imbumba onwards, the drive towards the unity of all Africans continued steadily. By the time of Union there were political organisations uniting men not as members of tribes but as Africans (though the word "African" was not yet used) in each of the provinces, and with union their merger into the South African Native National Congress was a natural development.

With Congress came the conscious assertion of a single African nationhood. In fact, however, the Africans do not yet constitute a single nation in the sense in which we are using the word.

Does this mean that the ANC is incorrect to demand self-determination? Of course not, for (quite apart from the fact that there may be circumstances in which even a single "pre-nation" should be supported in the demand for self-determination) the Africans are a political community made up of several national groups on the verge of nationhood, and as we shall see their right to self-determination cannot be disputed.

## *ZULUS, AFRIKANERS, COLOUREDS*

This brings us a stage further. What is the position with regard to the different national communities which make up the African people? Let us consider the Zulus.

With their common language, territory and culture, the Zulus have the main requisites of nationhood.

We have only to settle the question of whether there can be said to be a common Zulu economy, or, in the words of Potehkin in his recent Liberation article, "a single national market."[17] The main prerequisites for the development of such a market are "the geographical division of labour and the existence of developed exchanges on a profit basis within a capitalist mode of production."

If we take this view, the only thing separating the Zulus from true nationhood is the stifling of their economy by the colour bar. Abolish the colour bar and the Zulus will become a nation almost overnight. They are a form of the community known in Russia as a "Narodnost", the closest English translation of which is "nationality," and as that has a different connotation in English, I would suggest that we use the word "pre-nation."

What has been said of the Zulus applies, subject to modification, also to the other African peoples in South Africa.

What of the Afrikaners? No South Africans can vie with Verwoerd's Nationalists in the fervour with which they express the conviction, not only that the Afrikaners are a nation, but that they are the nation.

Here again we are at odds about a definition. The pure lily-white Afrikaner volk about which the Verwoerd Nationalists declaim are not a nation but an hallucination. If there is an Afrikaner nation in South Africa it does not consist of the 1½ million Afrikaners who can claim white identity cards, but of about 2½ million people – for once you break through the racialist smokescreen it becomes clear that the one million Afrikaans-speaking Coloureds are a part of the same national community as the 1½ million Afrikaans-speaking whites, common territory, language, economy culture and all. Except for the political and social discrimination there is nothing at all to distinguish the very substantial proportion of Afrikanerdom which, though technically Coloured, passes for white, from the proportion which is too dark, or too proud, to pass.

And what is so ironical is that the Coloureds are one of Afrikanerdom's greatest national assets. With them Afrikanerdom has a territory where it is in the majority, with a few good-sized towns; and it has a much better balanced class structure.

Although the present leaders of white Afrikanerdom would choke at the idea, it is very possible that under conditions of freedom the single white and Coloured Afrikaner nation will be one of the first to consolidate itself, and that its Afrikaner language and culure will blossom as never before.

At the same time it must be noted that the position is by no means static. The political discrimination against the Coloureds is creating something akin to a Coloured national consciousness, separated from that of the white Afrikaner, and comparable with that of the Negro in the U.S. The South African Coloured People's Organisation is thought of as a national organisation like those of its African and Indian allies in the Congress alliance. But an optimistic estimate of the time required for winning freedom would preclude the development of a separate Coloured nation born of "race" oppression.

There appear, therefore, to be several communities in South Africa which will swiftly become nations when the national oppression which strangles their economic development is ended.

## *SELF-DETERMINATION AND SECESSION*
This brings us to a discussion of the form which the demand for self-determination is likely to take.

When other oppressed nations, particularly those of Africa, have put forward the demand for self-determination, the form of self-determination contemplated has almost always been that of secession (although informal political links with the former oppressor nation may be maintained, as is the case with the independent nations of the Commonwealth.)

In South Africa, however, as far as the Africans are concerned, self-determination has a different significance. For them it is not a question of calling upon an oppressing **majority** to permit them independence in their own territory; nor one of calling upon a **foreign power** to withdraw.

For the **Africans** are the majority. In a democratic South Africa they can have no fear of being subjected to discriminatory laws by another South African nation, and therefore the demand for Africans to secede from anywhere would not make sense.

The form that the demand of the Africans for self-determination takes, therefore, is simply that for full equality. And as the African pre-nations draw their whole strength and hope from their inter-national African unity, the demands of the individual pre-nations, are identical with and inseparable from those of the Africans as a whole.

The mere winning of the full and free franchise would guarantee the Africans self-determination, constituting, as they would, the majority of the electorate; there would, in effect, come into being an independent African state, with (if the Freedom Charter is the basis) full protection for national minorities.

This leads us to a question which is going to be raised more and more frequently as the realisation grows that the Freedom Charter is neither treason nor a dream. What does the Charter mean when it says "All national groups shall have equal rights." And what is meant by the term national group?

One answer we may give is that these are things which must be thrashed out at a national convention to plan the new state form, and that if people want to know the answers they must urge the holding of such a convention.

But such a reply, good as it is, is not altogether satisfactory. The new state may not come about as the result of around-table conference! We should begin to think about answers now; not fixed and inflexible answers – for conditions change – but answers nevertheless.

## *A FEDERATION*
Does the answer lie in some form of multi-national federation comparable say with that of the Soviet Union, India, Switzerland or China?[18]

I would suggest it does. The Freedom Charter guarantees the right of all national groups to develop their own languages and cultures. For the first time the national cultures will be able to blossom, stimulated by (among other things) free, equal and compulsory education, of the highest standard, available in the national languages.

The example of the countries has proved that only by the fullest development of national cultures will it be possible to secure the maximum participation of the backward nationalities in the work of constructing a new South Africa.

It may seem strange that the best way to achieve the **fusion** of national cultures in the future into **one** common culture, is to favour the blossoming of many cultures first.

As Pandit Chandra put it: "Disunion for the sake of union. Just think! – It even smacks of the paradoxical. And yet this 'self-contradictory' formula reflects the living truth of dialectical reasoning."

The national cultures must be permitted to develop and expand and to reveal all their potential qualities in order to create the conditions for their fusion.

National cultures do not blossom in the air. They have to be rooted in the firm soil. And national cultures, plus territory, plus the unshackled economy which freedom will bring, means nations. The perspective is opened of a South Africa which is an economically integrated brotherhood of equal and autonomous nations, united in a single state, in which racial discrimination will be a crime.

This development and expansion is not merely a matter of the happy future "when freedom comes".

It is obvious that to really get to the hearts and minds of the people, particularly the backward rural masses it is necessary to develop to the full a presentation of our message which has its roots deep in the popular culture – and to do this **immediately**.

It is necessary to produce democratic literature in the language of the people – not merely in **translation** but in the original idiom. Because English is the most widely understood language it is natural that it should be so widely used for conferences and country-wide newspapers. But this is no excuse for neglecting the **majority** of the population who have not been fortunate enough to obtain sufficient education to read or to follow an argument in English. In this respect we could learn from Indian democrats who also use English as the international tongue, but at the same time produce extensive literature in the vernacular languages.

If there is any neglect of these people it is still a hang-over from the old days when there was a feeling that the intellectuals were the only important people in Congress and when, in turning their backs on tribalism, the intellectuals tended to turn their backs also on their language and culture.

The need to remedy this situation is already widely recognised. The effect of the deeply moving and inspiring African political songs and music which has been created in recent years is evidence enough of the importance of this type of development. Now what are required are plays and poems and dances of liberation which will inspire and teach people who know no English, and which will give them that added consciousness of dignity which pride in a national culture instils.

## Document 58
## Robert Mangaliso Sobukwe, "The Opening Address at the Africanist Inaugural Convention", 4 April 1959[19]

*[....]*
*INTERNATIONAL SCENE*
We are living today, Sons and Daughters of the Soil, fighters in the cause of African freedom, in an era that is pregnant with untold possibilities for good and evil. In the course of the past two years we have seen man breaking asunder, with dramatic suddenness, the chains that have bound his mind, solving problems which for ages it has been regarded as sacrilege even to attempt to solve. The tremendous epoch-making scientific achievements in the exploration of space, with man-made satellites orbiting the earth, the new and interesting discoveries made in the Geophysical Year, the production of rust-resistant strains of wheat in the field of agriculture, the amazing discoveries in the fields of medicine, chemistry and physics – all these, mean that man is acquiring a better knowledge of his environment and is well on the way to establishing absolute control over that environment.

However, in spite of all these rapid advances in the material and physical world, man appears to be either unwilling or unable to solve the problem of social relations between man and man. Because of this failure on the part of man, we see the world split into two large hostile blocks represented by the U.S.A. and the Soviet Union respectively. These two blocks are engaged in terrible competition, use tough language and tactics, employ brinkmanship stunts which have the whole world heading for a nervous breakdown. They each are armed with terrible weapons of destruction and continue to spend millions of pounds in the production of more and more of these weapons. In spite of all the diplomatic talk of co-existence, these blocks each behave as though they did not believe that co-existence was possible.

*AFRIKA'S POSITION*
The question then arises, where does Afrika fit into this picture and where, particularly, do we African nationalists, we Africanists in South Afrika, fit in?

There is no doubt that with the liquidation of Western imperialism and colonialism in Asia, the Capitalist market has shrunk considerably. As a result, Afrika has become the happy hunting ground of adventuristic capital. There is again a scramble for Africa, and both the Soviet Union and the United States of America are trying to win the loyalty of the African states. Afrika is being wooed with more ardour than she has ever been. There is a lot of flirting going on, of course, some Africans flirting with the Soviet camp, and others with the American camp. In some cases, the courtship has reached a stage where the parties are going out together, and they probably hold hands in the dark, but nowhere has it yet reached a stage where the parties can kiss in public without blushing.

This wooing occurs at a time when the whole continent of Afrika is in labour, suffering the pangs of a new birth, and everybody is looking anxiously and expectantly towards Afrika to see, as our people so aptly put it, *ukuthi iyozala nkomoni* (what creature will come forth). We are being wooed internationally at a time when in South Africa, the naked forces of savage Herrenvolkism are running riot; when a determined effort is being made to annihilate the African people through systematic starvation; at a time when brutal attempts are being made to retard, dwarf and stunt the mental development of a whole people through organised "miseducation"; at a time when thousands of our people roam the streets in search of work and are being told by the foreign ruler to go back to a "home" which he has assigned them, whether that means the break-up of their families or not; at a time when the distinctive badge of slavery and humiliation, the "dom pass" is being extended from the African male dog to the African female bitch. It is at this time, when fascist tyranny has reached its zenith in South Africa, that Africa's loyalty is being competed for. And the question is, what is our answer?

Our answer, Mr Speaker and children of the Soil, has been given by the African leaders of the continent. Dr Kwame Nkrumah has repeatedly stated that in international affairs, Afrika wishes to pursue a policy of positive neutrality, allying herself to neither of the existing blocks but, in the words of Dr Nnandi Azikiwe of Nigeria, remaining "independent in all things but neutral in none that affect the destiny of Africa".[20] Mr Tom Mboya of Kenya has expressed himself more forthrightly, declaring that it is not the intention of African states to change one master (western imperialism) for another (Soviet hegemony).[21]

We endorse the views of African leaders on this point. But we must point out that we are not blind to the fact that the countries – which pursue a policy of planned state economy – have outstripped, in industrial development, those that follow the path of private enterprise. Today, China is industrially far ahead of India. Unfortunately, however, this rapid industrial development has been accompanied in all cases by a rigid totalitarianism notwithstanding Mao Tse Tung's "Hundred Flowers" announcement.[22] Africanists reject totalitarianism in any form and accept political democracy as understood in the west. We also reject the economic exploitation of the many for the benefit of the few. We accept as policy the equitable distribution of wealth aiming, as far as I am concerned, to equality of income which to me is the only basis on which the slogan of "equal opportunities" can be founded.

Borrowing then the best from the East and the best from the West, we nonetheless retain and maintain our distinctive personality and refuse to be the satraps or stooges of either power block.

*RELATION TO STATES IN AFRIKA*
Our relation to the States of Afrika may be stated precisely and briefly by quoting George Padmore's book, "Pan Africanism or Communism".[23] Discussing the future of Africa, Padmore observes that "there is a growing feeling among politically conscious Africans throughout the continent that their destiny is one, that what happens in one part of Afrika to Africans must affect Africans living in other parts".

We honour Ghana as the first independent state in modern Afrika which, under the courageous nationalist leadership of Dr. Nkrumah and the Convention People's Party, has actively interested itself in the liberation of the whole continent from White domination, and has held out the vision of a democratic United States of Afrika. We regard it as the sacred duty of every African state to strive ceaselessly and energetically for the creation of a United States of Afrika, stretching from Cape to Cairo, Morocco to Madagascar.

The days of small, independent countries are gone. Today we have, on the one hand, great powerful countries of the world; America and Russia cover huge tracts of land territorially and number hundreds of millions in population. On the other hand, the small weak independent countries of Europe are beginning to realise that for their own survival, they have to form military and economic federations, hence NATO and the European market.

Besides the sense of a common historical fate that we share with the other countries of Afrika, it is imperative, for purely practical reasons, that the whole of Afrika be united into a single unit, centrally controlled. Only in that way can we solve the immense problems that face the continent.

## NATIONAL MOVEMENTS IN AFRIKA

It is for the reasons stated above that we admire, bless and identify ourselves with the entire nationalist movements in Africa. They are the core, the basic units, the individual cells of that large organism envisaged, namely, the United States of Africa; a union of free, sovereign independent democratic states of Africa.

For the lasting peace of Afrika and the solution of the economic, social and political problems of the continent, there needs must be a democratic principle. This means that White supremacy, under whatever guise it manifests itself, must be destroyed. And that is what the nationalists on the continent are setting out to do. They all are agreed that the African majority must rule. In the African context, it is overwhelming African majority that will mould and shape the content of democracy. Allow me to quote Dr. Dubois, the father of Pan Africanism[24]: "Most men in the world", writes Dubois, "are coloured. A belief in humanity means a belief in coloured men. The future of the world will, in all reasonable possibility, be what coloured men make it." As for the world, so for Afrika. The future of Africa will be what Africans make it.

## THE RACE QUESTION

And now for the thorny question of race. I do not wish to give a lengthy and learned dissertation on race. Suffice it to say that even those scientists who do recognise the existence of separate races, have to admit that there are border-line cases which will not fit into any of the three races of mankind.

All scientists agree that all men can trace their ancestry back to the first Homo Sapiens, that man is distinguished from other mammals and also from earlier types of man by the nature of his intelligence. The structure of the body of man provides evidence to prove the biological unity of the human species. All scientists agree that there is no "race" that is superior to another, and there is no "race" that is inferior to others.

The Africanists take the view that there is only one race to which we all belong, and that is the human race. In our vocabulary, therefore, the word "race" is applied to man, has no plural form. We do, however, admit the existence of observable physical differences between various groups of people, but these differences are the result of a number of factors, chief among which has been geographical isolation.

In Africa, the myth of race has been propounded and propagated by the imperialists and colonialists of Europe, in order to facilitate and justify their inhuman exploitation of the indigenous people of the land. It is from this myth of race with its attendant claims of cultural superiority that the doctrine of white supremacy stems. Thus it is that an ex-engine driver can think of himself as fully qualified to be the head of the government of an African state, but refuse to believe that a highly educated black doctor, more familiar with Western culture than the White premier is, cannot even run a municipal council.[25] I do not wish to belabour this point. Time is precious. Let me close the discussion of this topic by declaring, on behalf of the Africanists, that with UNESCO we hold that "every man is his brother's keeper. For every man is a piece of the continent, a part of the main, because he is involved in mankind".

## IN SOUTH AFRIKA

In South Africa we recognise the existence of national groups which are the result of geographical origin within a certain area as well as a shared historical experience of these groups. The Europeans are a foreign minority group which has exclusive control of political, economic, social and military power. It is the dominant group. It is the exploiting group, responsible for the pernicious doctrine of White Supremacy which has resulted in the humiliation and degradation of the indigenous African people. It is this group which has dispossessed the African people of their land and with arrogant conceit, has set itself up as the "guardians", the "trustees" of the Africans. It is this group which conceives the African as a child nation composed of Boys and Girls, ranging in age from 120 years to one day. It is this group which, after 300 years, can still state with brazen effrontery that the Native, the Bantu, the Kaffir is still backward and savage. But they still want to remain "guardians", "trustees" and what have you, of the African people. In short, it this group which has mismanaged affairs in South Africa just as their kith and kin are mismanaging affairs in Europe. It is from this group that the most rabid race baiters and agitators come. It is members of this group who, whenever they meet in their Parliament, say things which agitate the hearts of millions of peace-loving Africans. This is the group which turns out thousands of experts in the new South African Science – the Native mind.

Then there is the Indian foreign minority group. This group came to this country not as imperialists or colonialist, but as indentured labourers. In the South African set-up of today, this group is an oppressed minority. But there are some members of this group, the merchant class in particular, who have become tainted with the virus of cultural supremacy and national arrogance. This class identifies itself by and large with the oppressor but, significantly, this is the group which provides the political leadership of the Indian people in South Africa. And all that the politics of this class has meant up to now is the preservation and defence of the sectional interests of the Indian merchant class. The down-trodden, poor "stinking coolies" of Natal who, alone, as a result of the pressure of material conditions, can identify themselves with the indigenous African majority in the struggle to overthrow White supremacy, have not yet produced their leadership. We hope they will do so soon.

The Africans constitute the indigenous group and form the majority of the population. They are the most ruthlessly exploited and are subjected to humiliation, degradation and insult.

Now it is our contention that true democracy can be established in South Africa and on the continent as a whole, only when White supremacy has been destroyed. And the illiterate and semi-literate African masses constitute the key and centre and content of any struggle for true democracy in South Africa. And the African people can be organised only under the banner of African nationalism in an All-African Organisation, where they will by themselves formulate policies and programmes and decide on the methods of struggle without interference from either so-called left-wing or right-wing groups, of the minorities who arrogantly appropriate to themselves the right to plan and think for Africans.

We wish to emphasize here that the freedom of the African means the freedom of all in South Africa, the European included, because only the African can guarantee the establishment of a genuine democracy in which all men will be citizens of a common state and will live and be governed as individuals and not as distinctive sectional groups.

*OUR ULTIMATE GOALS*

In conclusion, I wish to state that the Africanists do not subscribe to the fashionable doctrine of South African exceptionalism. Our contention is that South Africa is an integral part of the indivisible whole that is Africa. She cannot solve her problems in isolation from and with utter disregard of the rest of the continent.

It is precisely for that reason that we reject both apartheid and so-called multi-racialism as solutions of our socio-economic problems. Apart from the number of reasons and arguments that can be advanced against apartheid, we take our stand on the principle that Afrika is one and desires to be one and nobody, I repeat, nobody has the right to balkanise our land.

Against multi-racialism we have this objection, that the history of South Africa has fostered group prejudices and antagonisms, and if we have to maintain the same group exclusiveness, parading under the term of multi-racialism, we shall be transporting to the new Afrika these very antagonisms and conflicts. Further, multi-racialism is in fact a pandering to European bigotry and arrogance. It is a method of safeguarding white interests irrespective of population figures. In that sense it is a complete negation of democracy. To us the term "multi-racialism" implies that there are such basic insuperable differences between the various national groups here that the best course is to keep them permanently distinctive in a kind of democratic apartheid. That to us is racialism multiplied, which probably is what the term truly connotes.

We aim, politically, at a government of the Africans by the Africans for Africans, with everybody who owes his only loyalty to Afrika and who is prepared to accept the democratic rule of an African majority being regarded as an African. We guarantee no minority rights, because we think in terms of individuals, not groups.

Economically we aim at the rapid extension of industrial development in order to alleviate pressure on the land, which is what progress means in terms of modern society. We stand committed to a policy guaranteeing the most equitable distribution of wealth.

Socially, we aim at the full development of the human personality and a ruthless uprooting and outlawing of all forms of manifestations of the racial myth. To sum it up, we stand for an Africanist Socialist Democracy.

Here is a tree rooted in African soil, nourished with waters from the rivers of Afrika. Come and sit under its shade and become, with us, the leaves of the same branch and the branches of the same tree.

Sons and Daughters of Afrika, I declare this inaugural Convention of the Africanists open. IZWE LETHU!

## NOTES

1. W. P. "Willem" van Schoor (1913-71) trained as a teacher and lectured at Söhnge Training College in Worcester, where A. J. Abrahamse was a colleague. In 1937 he co-founded the New Era Fellowship in Cape Town and presented its first lecture, on "Imperialism". In the 1940s he worked in the FIOSA. In 1951 he was elected President of the TLSA, and he campaigned against the introduction of tribal divisions in education, coining the term "bush college" to describe the segregated black colleges set up by the government in the early 1960s. In 1951 van Schoor and Leo Sihlali of CATA set up the Cape Teachers' Federal Council, with the TLSA and CATA as affiliates. His criticism of the Eiselen-de Vos Malan policies for inferior education in his 1955 TLSA presidential address led to his dismissal as a teacher, part of a government crackdown on teachers who were challenging "gutter education". He was on the National Anti-CAD Committee and a leading figure in the NEUM. In the late 1960s he moved to England.

2. For considerations of space, the footnote references within the original document have been omitted. The sources cited in the original text include: H. C. Armstrong, *Grey Steel*; Economic and Wage Commission: U.G., 1926; Eybers, *Select Documents*; Haily, *An African Survey*; C. Headlam (ed.), *Milner Papers, Vol. II*; J. H. Hofmeyr, *South Africa*; C. W. de Kiewiet, *Social and Economic History of South Africa*; *Mixed Marriages Commission Report*, 1937; *A Monthly Bulletin of Statistics: U.G.*, May 1948; Nxele [Hosea Jaffe], "History of Despotism" Series, *The Torch*, 30 January 1950; Ordinance 50, 1828; *Selborne Memorandum on the Union of South Africa*, 1908; Sir J. G. MacDonald, *Rhodes: A heritage*; J. S. Marais in I. Schapera (ed.), *The Bantu-speaking Tribes of South Africa*; S. G. Millin, *Rhodes*; Sol T. Plaatje, *Native Life in South Africa*; Rose Innes, *The Glen Grey Act and the Native Question*; E. Roux, *Time Longer than Rope*; J. C. Smuts, Speech, House of Assembly, 13 March 1945; *The Torch*, 18 August 1950; S. van der Horst, *Native Labour in South Africa*; E. Walker, *Lord de Villiers and His Times*; and *Year Book of the Union of South Africa*, 1926.

3. See also Dr Z. Sanders (Zena Susser), "Some comments on K. A. Jordaan's 'Critique of W. P. van Schoor's *The Origin and Development of Segregation in South Africa*'" and K. A. Jordaan, "A reply to Dr Sander's Historical Criticisms" both in *Discussion*, 1, 4, December 1951, 40-9.

4. For considerations of space, the footnote references within the original document have been omitted. The sources cited in the original text include: J. A. J. Agar-Hamilton, *The Native Policy of the Voortrekkers*; C. de Kiewiet, *A History of South Africa, Social and Economic*; *The Economist*, 10 March and 17 March 1951; J. H. Hofmeyer, *South Africa*; W. M. Macmillan, *Bantu, Boer and Briton*; J. M. Tinley, *The Native Labour Problem of South Africa*; *Union Year Book*, 1948; and S. T. van der Horst, *Native Labour in South Africa*.

5. Michael Harmel (1915-74) was one of the major CPSA ideologues from the 1940s, a strong proponent of the Party's closer ties with the national struggle and the Congress movement in the post-war period. He joined the CPSA in 1939, was secretary of the Johannesburg district committee from 1940 to '46 and a member of the CPSA central committee from 1941 to 1950. Out of the seventeen members on the central committee, only he and Bill Andrews opposed the Party's decision to dissolve in 1950. In the 1950s he played a leading role in the COD. He was on the editorial board of *Liberation*, the Johannesburg representative of *New Age* and a founder of *African Communist* in 1949. Subjected to repeated state harassment, he left South Africa in 1963. In London he edited *African Communist* and published *Fifty Fighting Years* (1971) under the pseudonym A. Lerumo. This document represents an early elaboration of the colonialism of a special type thesis. Harmel was married to Ray Adler (b. 1907), a Lithuanian Jewish immigrant who worked as a seamstress. She was a member of the CPSA and the GWU and was highly critical of the GWU's decision to set up a separate branch for coloured workers in 1940.

6. In *The Choice before South Africa*, E. S. Sachs (1952:8) wrote: "Capitalism can still play a progressive role in South Africa, provided backwardness, reaction and foreign domination are eliminated from our national life." Essentially, he argued that South Africa's extreme racism and exploitation were due to the mining and agricultural sectors, which had developed on the basis of cheap labour. The growth of manufacturing capitalism was premised on a free and mobile labour market, raising the possibility of breaking from an outmoded political system and achieving real democracy. He called for a united front to defeat the NP, for building a strong Labour Party and adopting a "New Deal" to win over progressive whites, especially Afrikaner workers.

7. In the late 1930s, some socialists had argued that Afrikaner nationalism could play a progressive role in the struggle against British imperialism, a claim that was a legacy of the Anglo-Boer War. Sachs (1952:209-16), who had organised Afrikaner women garment workers, makes a similar argument, believing that most Afrikaner workers were becoming disillusioned with the NP but would not readily vote for the UP.

8. Chiang Kai-Shek was leader of Nationalist China prior to the Communist victory in 1949. He then retreated to Taiwan where he was supported by the United States. Syngman Rhee was leader of South

Korea during and after the Korean War. He was supported by the United States and its allies. For the Left he symbolised the corrupt dictatorships aligned with the West during the Cold War. Tito was a Yugoslav Communist and leader of the Partisans during the German occupation. He was supported by the Allies in preference to the alternative resistance led by Mihailovitch. Subsequently, Tito became leader of post-war Yugoslavia but quarreled with Stalin and became the target of Communist vilification. Yugoslavia became for some on the Left a model for socialist construction, independent of both Communist and Social Democratic politics.

9   Dr James S. Moroka (1891-1985), a physician trained at the University of Edinburgh, was an early leader of the AAC. He then served on the NRC from 1942 to '50, arguing the need to expose the institution's bankruptcy from within. Paradoxically, in 1949 he was elected as ANC President-General on the pro-boycott platform of the ANC Youth League, even though he was still in the NRC and not at the time an ANC member. In 1952 he lost his bid for reelection to Albert Luthuli. The Mine Workers' Union and the South African Railways Staff Associations were organisations of white labour. Until 1953 the SATLC did not have a colour bar but that year it began excluding Africans.

10  Both the NEUM and the Congress movement were subject to criticism, mainly from the Left and from liberals, for their sectionally-based federal structures. The COD was subjected to such criticisms from its formation in October 1953. In theory, its membership was open to all South Africans; in practice, it was a white organisation. Some white Communists refrained from joining for that reason, and the Liberal Party proudly contrasted its non-racial organisation with that of the COD. Discussion of the "One Congress" question escalated through the 1950s. See, inter alia, "Fusing the Congresses", *Liberation*, 37, July 1959; Lazerson (1994:211-18); and Hirson (1995:275, 278).

11  The joint symposium convened by the Forum Club and the South Africa Club in May 1954 marked a rare co-operative effort by Communists and Trotskyists. In their foreword to the proceedings, the organisers, Enver Marney of the Forum Club and I. O. Horvitch of the CPSA, noted the effects of political sectarianism on the liberation movement: "Our movement suffers not only from sectionalism (racialism), but is also ridden by a crippling sectarianism which puts the interests of sects above the interests of the movement, and is the main obstacle in the way of vigorous discussion and the achievement of theoretical clarity. In the absence of discussion sectarianism thrives and the best interests of the whole movement are sacrificed."

12  Polish nationalism continued as a significant force during the nineteenth century despite the dismemberment of the Polish state. Its principal manifestations were through language and Catholicism. Following the end of World War One, a separate Polish state was reconstituted as part of the Versailles settlement. Its boundaries proved a significant focus for the German agitation for revision of the Versailles Treaty and in 1939 Poland disappeared again as a consequence of both German and Soviet invasion. After the end of World War Two, a Polish state was again born but with significantly different boundaries to those of its inter-war predecessor.

13  German unification was effectively achieved at the end of the Franco-Prussian War in 1871. The method produced a strong state, the heir to its Prussian predecessor. The King of Prussia became Emperor of the new Germany and Berlin, the Prussian capital, became the Imperial capital. This outcome met with some opposition in other parts of the new Reich. One crucial step in the process had been the Prussian-Austrian War of 1866 where military victory for Prussia ensured that Austria, although German-speaking, would not become part of a unified Germany. Instead, Austria remained until 1918 the administrative centre of the multi-national Austro-Hungarian Empire. This included not only the Magyars of Hungary but also large numbers of Slavs.

14  Harold Jack Simons (1907-95) – a Communist intellectual, author and renowned teacher who received a Ph.D. at the London School of Economics and lectured in African law and administration at UCT. He became a Communist c. 1934, while in London. He was tried for sedition following the 1946 African Mineworkers' strike, a member of the CPSA Central Committee at its dissolution in 1950 and repeatedly banned in the 1950s. In 1965, banned from teaching, he and his wife, Ray Alexander Simons, went into exile for many years where they completed *Class and Colour in South Africa*. He taught at the University of Zambia and, after his retirement, at MK camps in Angola. A member of the ANC, he helped prepare a draft constitution for South Africa's democratic transition.

15  Both Simons and Forman based their work on Stalin's definition of a nation. Stalin's principal work on the subject is "Marxism and the National Question", first published in 1913. In this work he defines the characteristic features of a nation as "... a historically evolved, stable community of language, territory, economic life and psychological make-up manifested in a community of culture. ... It is only when all these characteristics are present that we have a nation. ..." Despite their common starting point, Simons and Forman reflected two poles of thought within the SACP on the national question.

16  Lionel Forman (1927-59) was from a white working-class background and became politicised at a young

age. He joined the Jewish youth group Hashomer Hatzair but switched to the YCL when he was 15. He was a student activist at UCT and worked for *The Guardian*. In 1949 he began studying law at the University of the Witwatersrand. In the early 1950s he spent two years in Prague as a representative of Nusas, which he had convinced to retain its affiliation to the Prague-based International Union of Students. On his return to South Africa in 1954 Forman temporarily took over the editorship of *Advance*, whose pages he used to promote a discussion of the national question. He later edited *New Age*, and he wrote a number of short people's histories of the socialist and national liberation movements. Forman was very much an iconoclast within the SACP and a strong critic of its internal efforts to suppress critical thinking. This article was written around 1954. However, the dominant Party view considered it too controversial to publish at that time, and it was published in 1959 with the support of Ruth First. See Forman and Odendaal (1992).

17  I. I. Potekhin was a Soviet Africanist and the first Director of Moscow's Africa Institute. His mimeo, "Extract from 'The Formation of the South African Bantu into a National Community'" (c. 1953), circulated widely on the South African Left, and his ideas were very influential in the SACP. Potekhin and Forman corresponded on the national question. Potekhin argued against the "two camp" approach which dominated Soviet thinking from 1947 to the 1950s and which saw world politics polarised between anti-democratic imperialist forces and democratic, anti-imperialist forces. Initially, the two-camp approach ruptured the earlier alliances between Communists and the national bourgeoisies or aspirant bourgeoisies of oppressed or colonial countries. Potekhin maintained that anti-imperialist struggles in oppressed nations entailed a revolutionary alliance of all classes and that in sub-Saharan Africa such alliances were led by the national bourgeoisie and intelligentsia. He believed that national consciousness reflected the aspirations of the social classes to which it was tied. In South Africa, he argued, African nationalism was developing along contradictory lines. In his view, Africans comprised a proletariat and a bourgeoisie which was permeated by anti-white race consciousness rather than the national consciousness necessary for self-government. But working class and Communist influence in liberation politics was growing in the post-war period, while the influence of the African bourgeoisie waned. As a result, two tendencies were developing within the African national liberation movement: one, a movement towards a united anti-imperialist front and two, a movement towards a united African national consciousness. However, Anglo-Afrikaner imperialism artificially preserved feudal remnants in tribal form, which impeded the development of a single African nation; moreover, the linguistic basis for such unity did not yet exist. Despite the post-war efforts at joint activity by Africans, Indians and coloureds, South Africa was developing into two separate nations, with additional national groupings. Potekhin advised Africans to form one national front and organise against national oppression with other sectional groups.

18  The characterisation of the Soviet Union, India, Switzerland and China as multi-national federations is insufficient. The United States and Switzerland are often taken as classical examples of federalism. Wheare (1963:1) defines a federal government in the broadest sense as "... an association of states, which has been formed for certain common purposes, but in which the member states retain a large measure of their original independence". But he notes additional criteria (1963:46): firstly, a similarity of institutions in the federated states; secondly, the absence of autocracy or dictatorship, as that would "... destroy that equality of status and that independence which these states must enjoy, each in its own sphere, if federal government is to exist at all". Although in a constitutional sense, the four states all share traits of a federal as opposed to a unitary system, they vary greatly in the degree to which the federated republics are subordinated to a central power and to which power is devolved or decentralised.

19  For other documents of the Africanist Inaugural Convention which launched the PAC see Karis and Carter (1977a:510-37).

20  Dr Nnamdi Azikiwe (1904-96) was an American-educated leader of Nigeria's anti-colonial movement. In the 1930s he was involved with the Nigerian Youth Movement and the more radical West African Youth League, and he edited the influential West African Pilot. After World War Two he became Secretary and President of the National Council of Nigeria and the Cameroons, preeminent nationalist organisation of southern Nigeria. In 1960 he became the first Nigerian Governor-General of the Federation of Nigeria and from 1963 to '66 was President of the First Republic, until deposed by a coup d'état. He helped negotiate an end to the Biafran civil war and later returned to party politics.

21  Tom Mboya (1930-69) was a Kenyan nationalist who began his career as a trade union leader. He was educated at Catholic mission schools and at Ruskin College, Oxford. In 1955 he became Secretary-General of the Kenyan Federation of Labour. He was a founder and Secretary-General of the Kenyan African National Union from 1960 until his assassination in 1969. He aligned himself with Jomo Kenyatta, and as Minister of Labour (1962-3), Minister of Justice and Constitutional Affairs (1963-4) and Minister for Economic Planning and Development (1964-9) promoted his belief in free enterprise with state regulation.

22  Karis and Carter (1977:512) point out that the PAC began receiving financial assistance from China in

1961 and that, when Sobukwe's address was reprinted in *The Basic Documents of the Pan-Africanist Congress of South Africa* in March 1965, the PAC deleted this sentence. In the late 1950s Mao Zedong put forward the slogans "Let a hundred flowers bloom" and "Let a hundred schools of thought contend". Their intention, he argued, was to promote the flourishing of the arts and sciences in conditions where, despite the ongoing building of socialism, the country retained social contradictions from the remnants of the bourgeoisie, landlord and comprador classes and urgently needed to speed up social and economic development.

23 George Padmore (1902-59) was a Trinidadian radical and Pan-Africanist who campaigned for African independence, unity and socialism. With C. L. R. James, he organised the International African Service Bureau. His book, *Pan-Africanism or Communism? The coming struggle for Africa*, reflected his disillusionment with orthodox Soviet Communism.

24 W. E. B. Dubois (1868-1963) was an African-American pan-Africanist, civil-rights advocate, historian and sociologist who studied at Fisk, Harvard and Berlin. A critic of Booker T. Washington's moderation in the U.S. civil-rights struggle, he helped found the National Association for the Advancement of Colored People. He became a citizen of Ghana, where he spent his last years.

25 The "ex-engine driver" refers to Roland Welensky (1902-92), a Rhodesian politician born in Bulawayo who began working on the railways when he was 14 and was heavyweight boxing champion from 1926 to '28. In 1933 he became leader of the Railway Workers' Union in Northern Rhodesia, founded the Northern Rhodesia Labour Party in 1941, and was appointed Director of Manpower. He held several ministerial appointments and was Prime Minister of the Federation of Rhodesia and Nyasaland from 1956 until its collapse in 1963. He opposed Rhodesia's UDI and unsuccessfully opposed Ian Smith before retiring.

# Part Three

## The agrarian question

**EDITOR'S NOTE**
*Although the principal efforts to address South Africa's agrarian question and to organise in the reserves have come from socialists concerned with the revolutionary potential of the rural population, the socialist movement's theoretical and practical attention to the agrarian question has been sporadic. The South African Left has been divided between a majority which prioritised the urban working-class movement and a minority which saw the agrarian question as the backbone of any social revolution. This dichotomy resulted in an oscillating practice between town and country. For the NEUM, the agrarian question was the alpha and omega of the South African revolution, in that the national and political aspirations of the African majority flowed from land hunger. Within the NEUM, the agrarian question became a subject of acute debate during the late 1950s. Although the SACP and the Congress Alliance were more urban-orientated, Communists likewise did important organising work in rural areas. The similar observations and analyses of rural protests made by socialists of different traditions is striking.*

## Document 59
## Letter from Ruth First to The Secretary, South African Institute of Race Relations[1], 17 August 1944

*Young Communist League of South Africa*[2]

Box 5498

128 Main Street,
JOHANNESBURG.

August 17, 1944.

The Secretary,
The South African Institute of Race Relations,
University of the Witwatersrand,
Johannesburg.

Dear Sir,

We wish to draw your attention to the dangerous implications in the resolutions on African farm labour which will be moved at a special congress of the Transvaal Agricultural Union in Pretoria on August 17.

The main points contained in the proposals as reported in the "Daily Mail" of July 28, 1944 are as follows:

1. The apprenticeship (presumably compulsory) of Africans from the age of 14 for a period of 3 years.
2. The compulsory registration of labourers providing for identity cards.
3. The establishment of a Committee by the Minister of Native Affairs in consultation with agricultural unions to control African farm labour.
4. The objection to interference by the Native Affairs Department in disputes over labour contracts between farmers and labourers.
5. The prohibition of young Africans not liable for poll tax, from working in urban areas unless their parents live there.

The proposals are Fascist in character and reminiscent of Nazi forced labour. Should they be adopted they will virtually reduce Africans to conditions of serfdom by restricting their freedom to seek more remunerative employment.

We hope that your Institute will take up this issue and strongly protest against the resolutions outlined above.

Yours sincerely,

Ruth First
Hon. Secretary

## Document 60
Letter from J. D. Rheinallt Jones[3] to Ruth First, 31 August 1944

31st August, 1944.

Miss Ruth First,
Hon. Secretary,
Young Communist League of South Africa,
P. O. Box 5498
JOHANNESBURG.

Dear Madam,

Your letter of 17th August was placed before the General Purposes Committee of this Institute. While being fully alive to the objectionable features of many of the proposals put forward before the Transvaal Agricultural Congress, the Committee feels that other measures than a mere protest would be more fruitful. We have learned from several sources that the rebuke of the Minister of Native Affairs had a salutary effect upon the Agricultural Conference. The Institute has for some time been active in pressing constructive proposals upon the Government, and the General Purposes Committee feels that these are likely to be more fruitful than sporadic protests.

Yours faithfully,

J. D. Rheinallt Jones
DIRECTOR

## Document 61
A. Mon [M. N. Averbach][4], "A Comment on Trotsky's Letter to S.A.", *Worker's Voice*, 1, 3, July 1945

*[....]*
**HOW THE LAND QUESTION WAS CREATED**
In order to understand the present land problem in South Africa, it is necessary to see

how it was created. It is necessary to grasp that the landlessness of the Africans in particular has flowed from the imperialist policy of creating a migratory African proletariat kept in readiness in vast reservoirs of labour – the Reserves – driven out of these reserves by landlessness, starvation and the poll tax, and controlled in the cities by means of compounds, pass laws, etc. In short, the land question cannot be separated from the question of the way in which imperialism built up a supply of cheap African labour. Here the land question is not only the problem of fighting against landlordism, but furthermore a problem of fighting imperialism with its strongholds in the cities. Just as the rural African, in most cases, is also a city worker for part of his life, so the land problem is tied up with the problem of the anti-imperialist fight which has its bastions in the big cities of South Africa. Imperialism has gone about its task of subjugating the toilers here by building up an intricate network of colour bars, segregation, race-oppressive legislation and institutions, all of which it has created, built upon and maintained with increasing brutality and intensity in order to preserve, tap and control a supply of cheap labour. In order to have at hand a ready source of controllable cheap labour imperialism has deliberately prevented the development of an African peasantry, for such a peasantry would live off the land, would reduce the number of human beasts of burden to be exploited in the mines, factories and on the farms, and slow down or threaten to stop the migration of cheap labour from town and farm to reserves and back again. Imperialism has uprooted the African tribalist, expropriated the African small farmer, prevented their growth into peasants, extended their landlessness and kept them in a state of permanent flux between the slave conditions in the cities and the starvation conditions on the reserves – in short, imperialism has created the land question as part and parcel of its mechanism of depriving the Non-Europeans of their rights, of their land, of opportunities – part of its mechanism of the colour bar and segregation and race-persecution. The landless Non-European is landless not merely because he has not got the money to purchase land, but, above all, because the machinery of state mercilessly carries out the policy of the economic bosses – to oppress the Non-European nationally in order to exploit him economically. His colour prevents him from becoming a peasant. Under such conditions it is clear that the struggle for land is an integral part of, and not distinct from or raised above, the struggle for full democratic rights. In the sense that this struggle for democratic rights means the abolition of race-discrimination, the struggle for land means the struggle for the rights of Non-Europeans to own land and become farmers. But in the scientific sense of the term "realising the task of the bourgeoise democratic revolution", the struggle for "democracy" embraces the struggle, furthermore, not merely for the right to the land, but for the actual division of the land (as was the case with the 1789 French Revolution). Finally, since this land cannot be won except through a struggle against imperialism and the South African capitalists, and since the land can be divided only after it has been expropriated from the big landowners, farmers and land-companies, the struggle for land, as part of the struggle for the realisation of the tasks of bourgeois democracy in South Africa can be won only through the socialist revolution, i.e., only, in Trotsky's words: "Through methods of proletarian class struggle". This is the the road leading to the solution of the problem of landlessness. This, the road of the toilers of South Africa, can be trod only if we see the road from the past which has brought us to the present position from where we are to set out along the path of national and agrarian emancipation, through the social revolution. *[....]* Here we are concerned with this path inasmuch as it led to the land problem as it confronts us to-day.

While the Whites robbed the Africans of the land they forced the African into smaller and smaller areas of land which became "reserves", into which the African was driven or whither he escaped from the attacks of the British and Voortrekkers. By means of brutal wars against the Africans in the Cape, Free State, Natal and the Transvaal, the Africans were savagely driven off their land and herded into small areas (or, in some cases, driven farther north out of the Union). The African was EXPROPRIATED by sword and fire.

Near the end of this process the imperialists began to industrialise the country and to employ masses of cheap labour on the Natal plantations, on the diamond mines, the gold mines, on the industries connected with these mines, and at the big ports. They used the "reserves" where the expropriated Africans had been driven as real reserves – as reservoirs of cheap labour. To force the Africans off the reserve lands the ruling class tore more and more land out of African ownership and occupation, starved the reserve-population, concentrated them into villages inside the reserves, imposed money-taxes on the male Africans (and are now, in the Transvaal Provincial Council, considering a poll tax for African women as well), entangled the tribalists in debt to traders, and recruited Africans through Chamber of Mines recruiting agents. In the cities the bourgeoisie built up an elaborate system of compounds, passes and regulations to control the migratory labour from the reserves. To prevent the formation of a stable, hereditary urban proletariat which would become used to the traditional methods of organisation and struggle – trade union and political – of the city working classes all over the world – the imperialist bourgeoisie segregated the Africans from each other tribally or otherwise, and from city political life by means of compounds, and allowed a drift back to the reserves after some time of slavery in the towns. At the same time, while preventing the formation of a stable urban African proletariat (which has nevertheless developed as a result of the process of urbanisation and industrialisation characteristic of all capitalist countries and countcracting the segregation policy of the imperialists here), the imperialists simultaneously and even more energetically prevented the formation of a settled African peasant in this country, either on the farms or in the the reserves. In this way the economic purposes of the imperialists – namely, the exploitation of cheap labour – were served through the policy of segregation, and the prevention of both a settled proletariat and peasantry among the Africans. Combined inevitably with the policy of segregation and the colour bar went the whittling away of the few rights possessed by the Africans in the form of the vote. The fate befalling the Africans steadily extended itself to the Coloureds and Indians, and segregation, the colour bar and race-discrimination became the modus operandi of the imperialist masters of South Africa, and their central instrument in maintaining and widening their economic exploitation of the peoples and resources of South Africa.

From this outline it is clear that the land question was historically created by the labour-demands of the imperialist bourgeoisie and the big farmers. Furthermore, that the land question is inseparably bound up with the whole race-oppression of the Non-Europeans, and that the land struggle cannot be divorced from the fight for full democratic rights. The land problem, created by imperialism, forms part and parcel of the entire problem of national oppression. The land struggle is part of the struggle against imperialism and national oppression. It is from this standpoint that we have to look upon the rural struggle; and it was from this angle that Trotsky approached the question as is shown by the opening sentence of his critical remarks: a sentence which contains the essence of the correct approach to the national question here:

> The South African possessions of Great Britain form a Dominion only from the point of view of the White minority. From the point of view of the black majority, South Africa is a slave colony.

Although this is only a mere sentence, and although Trotsky did not elaborate this, his own description of South Africa, it sums up the entire position, by stating the general fact which stands out when one views the South African scene – namely, the peculiar, unique relations between the national groups which exist in South Africa, and the manner in which these relations are geared to the economic machinery of wage-exploitation and profit-making. From this correct stating of the main fact of South African conditions – its chief peculiarity – flowed Trotsky's emphasis of the national question in general with regard to South Africa and especially in relation to the land question. The factual description of South Africa given briefly by Trotsky is made the more important as a base for a correct approach by the addition of a correct history of the colour-bar and land mechanism employed by imperialism in its industrialisation of the country.

## THE COMPOSITION OF RURAL AFRICANS

Having used this mechanism to create and preserve a reservoir of cheap migratory African labour, thereby holding back the formation of a settled African city worker, and still more the growth of an African peasantry, imperialism and the rich farmers fashioned a rural African population consisting of the Reserve dwellers and the farm workers, leaving practically no room for an African peasantry. The theses to which Trotsky replied informed him of the undeniable demand for land which exists among the rural Africans, but erroneously gave him the impression that there was in existence, economically, materially, in actual fact, a peasantry among the Africans who lived mostly off the land and only wanted more land. Consequently Trotsky speaks in his letter of the African "peasants". While it is true that millions of Africans cry out for land, and wish to become peasants, they are, in this sense, peasants by aspiration only. They aspire towards becoming a peasantry, but are not a peasantry in actual fact, with the exception of a small layer of small African farmers in the Transkei and, on a very small scale, in other reserve and rural areas. The fact that an African peasantry, speaking generally, does not exist, does not diminish the weight of the slogan for land, but lends added strength to this demand, in view of the pressure which the landlessness exerts on all those Africans driven to work in the towns, against their feeling to till and live off the land.

About one-half the total African population of South Africa is directly dependent for its income upon the labour of the three-quarters to one million city African workers. The figures in the Mine Wages Commission Report of 1943-44 showed that the families of the mine workers and the V.F.P. workers were almost entirely dependent upon the wages earned by these workers during their stay in the towns, and that their income from their scanty rural occupations and possessions amounts to a negligible quantity. It is no exaggeration to state that practically the entire Reserve population of about half the total Africans in the Union are not dependent on the land, but on the wages of their relatives in the cities. The Reserve dwellers are, in fact, tribal-proletarians, and the centre of their livelihood lies in the towns and cities. These tribal-proletarians are gradually forced to lengthen their stay in the cities and thus the proletarian side of their social character is steadily becoming the predominant factor, not only in the way of living, but also in their outlook. In spite of the compound system and the pass laws and the various laws and regulations tending to keep them away from becoming proletarians in their outlook and forms of struggle against the employers, the deep process of industrialisation in South Africa, particularly in those industries connected with the mines and in the big "secondary" factories, is increasingly transforming the tribal-proletarian into a city proletarian. Hundreds of thousands of Africans live more or less permanently in the cities, and the remainder spend more and more time, in spite of their continual migration, in the cities. Not only are the overwhelming majority of reserve dwellers not peasants in material fact, but even their peasant outlook is steadily being changed into a proletarian one by the development of industry. Nevertheless, while this change goes on in the outlook of the reservists, the fact that landlessness, land-hunger and intolerable conditions on the infertile reserve lands are used, together with taxes, to hound them into the towns, causes the migratory Africans, even those spending some time in the cities, to see in his landlessness the cause of his travelling to the towns, and consequently to long for and demand land. The horrible conditions under which he becomes a proletarian encourages him to strive to become a peasant, even while his living is made as a proletarian. The processes connected with migratory workers develops both the proletarian and the peasant sides of his outlook.

The other half of the total Africans in the Union live chiefly on the farms of the rich Afrikaner farmers and the big imperialist land-companies, including those farms controlled by the Chamber of Mines. The farm Africans are predominantly agricultural proletarians, and not peasants. Gradually, by means of the application of all sorts of laws and amendments, especially since the 1913 Land Act, the Government has discouraged "squatting", tenancy, and share cropping, and to-day the bulk of African farm workers live off wages paid by the farm-owners. According to a statement made in 1944 by the Minister for Native Affairs, about one million Africans on farms are wage-earners. This means that virtually the total farm population (African) are agricultural proletarians and their dependents. The tendency towards wage-labour on the farms, the destruction of those "peasants" who, in one way or another, were dependent not only on wages, but also on their own plots, crops, cattle, etc., has made it necessary for the African farm worker to struggle for higher wages, shorter hours, etc., as is the case with his urban brother. While being forced to wage this proletarian struggle, the struggle of rural wage-labour against capital, the African farm-worker also strives for land, especially those who are not living permanently on the farms, but are migratory between the farms and the reserves. On the other hand, those Africans who flow between the cities and the farms more and more look towards higher wages than towards land. Again, the process produces two directions – a tendency towards a proletarian outlook, and also towards a peasant's aspirations. On the farms the struggle for wages has to be coupled with the struggle for land, and both in general cannot be separated from the struggle against the colour bar.

This then is the present-day composition of the rural Africans. There is no African peasantry of any significance in fact – there is a demand to become a peasantry – and there is a profound and overwhelming tendency towards proletarianisation and a proletarian outlook. Under these conditions it is impossible to make political headway if one isolates the so-called peasant struggle – for land – from the fight which confronts the proletarian, especially the Non-White proletarian, in the cities and on the farms.

## LINKING THE LAND TO THE NATIONAL SLOGAN

Although Trotsky himself was not furnished with theses which clearly described the rural African in these terms, he nevertheless perceived that the land struggle was factually related to the national problem and he held that the task of revolutionary socialists was to link the slogan for land to the slogan for national liberation. He went much further than this and said that the land struggle is important only inasmuch as it is regarded as a stepping stone towards the national struggle, and that the revolutionary's duty was to lead the African ruralist, step by step, from the land struggle to national and political consciousness. [....]

Trotsky [...] clearly subordinates the land to the national struggle. And he does this EVEN working on the assumption that there was a large African peasantry in existence, i.e., a mass of people whose mode of living is based on the possession and occupation of land. But Trotsky's conclusion that the task is to RAISE THE RURALIST TO NATIONAL AND POLITICAL CONSCIOUSNESS is made all the more weighty when we take into consideration the fact that, as things are, the national problem bears down upon the "rural" African with tremendous force. It is doubtful whether the majority of Africans feel the shortage of land (the "agrarian oppression") more than they feel the poll tax, The Reserve and compound segregation, the anti-African labour laws, the discrimination in social life, the industrial colour bar, the lack of political rights, the pass laws, the non-recognition of African trade unions, AND the anti-African LAND ACTS (in short, the "national oppression"). Under such conditions Trotsky's emphasis on the need to subordinate the land struggle to the national struggle becomes still heavier. In the practical struggle the task of translating this emphasis into action, is also facilitated by the fact that the colour bar, segregation and all sorts of anti-African laws burden the African terribly, possibly even more than the land-hunger itself. At the distance from which he wrote, without even knowing South Africa, Trotsky could yet question the theses' claim that the land-question was more important than the national one, EVEN for the "peasants". Hence Trotsky's questioning remarks: "....It is quite possible ..."

In thus establishing the connection between the land and the national slogans Trotsky rendered great assistance to our organisation when it was busy shaping the programme during its first years. As far as the programmatic side of our development was concerned this was the chief value of the letter. And, with regard to our practical organisation work in handling the land-problem and the rural toilers Trotsky pointed out what our comrades have long maintained: that our first duty is to organise the CITY workers, and ONLY THROUGH THE ADVANCED URBAN WORKERS could we organise and properly approach the rural masses. This is the more important for a party which has not reached the status of a party, has insufficient members and sorely lacks personnel, everyone being urgently required for the growing volume of work in the cities. [....]

## THE ALLIANCE BETWEEN THE CITY AND THE RURAL WORKERS

From theoretical and organisational considerations Trotsky drew the conclusion that the ruralists can be organised chiefly, if not only, through the medium of the advanced city workers. This task is actually facilitated by the peculiar conditions which exist in

South Africa. The fact that the majority of Africans come to the cities and spend a growing period in the mines, or factories, etc., actually brings the "ruralists" into touch economically and politically with the urban workers. The alliance is born in the towns. To this extent the political gulf between town and country is half bridged by the migratory labour situation in this country. The fact that the majority of African reservists are either city proletarians or agricultural proletarians for the major portion of their working, if not their whole, lives, enormously simplifies the task of establishing contact between the permanent city and city-reserve workers. This does not mean that the task is itself simple. By no means! Not a few have sacrificed their lives in attempting to work inside a compound; who are segregated rigorously from the city influence, from other compounds, and in which tribal feuds are stirred up to divide and rule the Africans. But the work is simpler than doing organisational work among the ruralists in the country itself, and this latter work is rendered a task mainly of the migrant workers themselves upon their temporary return to their territories.

The organisational alliance of the workers of town and country, however, has to be based and can be based on far more than the possibility of contact in the towns. It is made possible and necessary by the fact that both the urban and the rural Africans, and all Non-Europeans, are commonly oppressed by their lack of democratic rights. On the basis of the struggle against the colour bar, against segregation and race-discrimination – by means of a struggle against the Imperialist-National policy of divide and rule and for the unity of all the Non-Europeans as a major step in the struggle to build up the unity of all the oppressed in the country – both Non-White and White – on this basis the alliance between the workers of town and country can and must be built. Here in this country, it is not so much, in fact hardly, a question of the "alliance between the proletariat and peasantry", but rather a case of building up the alliance of the city workers and the farm workers, the vast majority of whom are wage-slaves and commonly oppressed by the colour bar, segregation and lack of rights (including the right to land), and all of whom are held in bondage by imperialism, which is chiefly responsible for their misery. By means of the national struggle and by means of building up a powerful mass national organisation of all the Non-Europeans and their White supporters in order to wage a determined struggle against imperialist oppression, the toilers of all nationalities and from town and country will be united against a common foe.

This national organisation is essential to effect this unity. But the national struggle and the national organisation cannot triumph unless the whole course of this struggle for liberation and democratic rights opens up the way to the socialist revolution, to the setting up of a Worker's Government for South Africa and the expropriation of the imperialist and nationalist bourgeoisie – the only revolution and the only government which can introduce democracy for all and divide out land among the landless in South Africa.

But this organisation and this struggle cannot travel a correct path unless guided by a revolutionary Leninist party of the workers.

Unless this party is built speedily and yet soundly, so that it can organise the city workers politically and shape the policy and orientation of the national organisation by means of this proletarian support exercised inside the national organisation and upon it from outside, unless our party is built, there is no hope for the national movement, nor for the landless toilers. When this party will have been built on such a scale that it can lead the fight for the conquest of power in this country, then the toilers of this land and of all Africa will fully realise the great role which Trotsky's few lines have played in developing the programme and action of our organisation.

## Document 62
## I. B. Tabata, The Rehabilitation Scheme: A New Fraud, December 1945

To understand this Rehabilitation Scheme we must see it as something which will complete the exploitation of the Black man. We must see it fitting into and following upon all the laws already passed against the African peasant. At the same time we must see it as a link in the long chain of oppression affecting the whole African population. It flows directly from the basic policy of the country, known as the "Native Policy". And if we understand this "Native Policy" then we shall be in a position to understand not only the meaning of the Rehabilitation Scheme, but also all other measures passed against the Black man.

The whole ruling class without exception – whether it is the United Party, the Labour Party or the Malanite Party – are agreed on this Native Policy. That is, they are unanimous on the policy of keeping the Black man as a slave to minister to the needs of the White man and as a beast of burden to create wealth for him. The only difference that exists among the ruling class on this question, is a difference as to the METHOD. There is the old Boer method, that of the feudal landlord – the method of the sjambok. Then there is the much more cunning method used by the British Imperialists – the method of creating a set of circumstances which will force the African to toil for the White man. It is the second method, of British Imperialism, that has proved to be by far the more efficient. All the laws passed and the regulations made for the Black man are connected with this policy. To understand this is to have a key to the understanding of a mass of apparently contradictory laws. With this key, every law, every enactment is seen to fall into its proper place as a step in the steady progression towards the further exploitation of the oppressed people.

*THE CREATION OF A SET OF CIRCUMSTANCES*
After the African people had been conquered and their land taken away from them, they were herded together into small strips of land known as the "Native Reserves". These were deliberately made small so that hunger would drive the African out of the Reserves to labour for the White man. With the discovery of the gold mines and the resulting expansion of trade and industry, the building of railways and the growth of agriculture, the demand for African labour reached such huge proportions that the Government had to devise means to squeeze them out of the reserves at a still faster rate. So they imposed a hut tax payable in cash which could only be earned by working for the Europeans. But this was not enough, so they applied a drastic measure known as the Land Act of 1913. This act prohibited Africans from buying land except in the overcrowded reserves and made it illegal for them to occupy land on White farms on a rental or squatter system. Without warning, thousands of people were forced to sell their possessions and hire themselves out as labourers to the farmers or on the mines.

But the insatiable greed of the rapacious mine-owners and farmers demanded a still more violent expulsion of the African from the land. They therefore introduced the Poll Tax, hypocritically named the Natives Development Act. Under the pretence of bestowing a benefit upon the African they devised a more vicious method of forcing him out of the lean Reserves, and significantly made non-payment of the tax a criminal offence. But still the demand for labour was greater than the supply, so that still more efficient schemes had to be evolved by the rulers. In 1936-1937 they passed the notorious "Native Acts", the Native Representation Act and the Native Trust and Land Act, the very names of which were an outrageous lie. The form of representation provided under the Native Representation Act was a monstrous deception and a mockery. Three people were to represent 8 million as against 150 representing 2½ million. And who were these three people? Members of the exploiting groups representing the exploited! The whole idea is ludicrous. The jackals sit in council to discuss the fate of the sheep and ask the sheep to elect a few jackals to represent them! The Native Trust and Land Act is no less fraudulent, for the last thing it does is to give more land to the Africans, as they have learned through bitter experience since the Act was passed. [....]

The process of creating a set of circumstances to force the Black man to labour had been going on for decades and therefore when Hertzog introduced his Native Bills in 1936-37, the whole ruling class thought that this time the job was being completed. They were delivering the last blow and, as they said, with smug self-satisfaction, the "Native Question" was being finally "settled". But no sooner had they made their plans for hounding Africans out of the Reserves than they realised that the expected rush of labour was not flowing out in sufficient number to meet their ever-increasing requirements, nor was it going exactly where they wanted it to go – i.e. to the mines and farms. Loud complaints of labour shortage were heard form all over the country. The representatives of the farmers were screeching in Parliament that their wheat was collecting rust and their mealies were rotting in the fields for lack of Black hands to gather them in. They complained that "hordes" of Africans in the Reserves were basking in the sunshine and drinking beer or flocking into the towns, attracted by bioscopes and a life of indolence. The Government wasn't doing its job properly and ought to be kicked out. Then Smuts calmly pointed out that his critics didn't know what they were talking about; he and his Government had the situation well in hand. He had sent his Minister of Native Affairs to discuss the labour shortage with the Agricultural Union.[5] (The Minister of NATIVE Affairs, if you please, goes NOT to the "Natives" but to the farmers to discuss the fate of the "Natives." He (Smuts) regretted that the farmers had not co-operated and followed the example of the mines in the handling of their labour problem. He went on to assure them that: "The Government would have to take steps to come to the assistance of the farmers.....to create an organisation for the recruitment of farm labour.....These were the matters that were being discussed with the Agricultural Union." (Hansard, 14th March, 1945.) The Government was not asleep. It had plans, comprehensive plans covering the whole African population; it has schemes for those in the Reserves and for those in the towns.

By day and by night, during peace and during war, the rulers never cease laying their plans. [....] But it was only after the war that the Africans began to realise what had been happening. Even before the war was over, when the rulers were already feeling more confident after the threat from the Germans and the Japanese was removed, the

Africans had a foretaste of what was in store for them. These plans are on a national scale, covering the whole front, not only of the African population but of all Non-European people. On the African front, they take one form in the Reserves to meet conditions there; in the towns they take another form and are called by different names. But their purpose is one and the same, namely, the complete regimentation of African labour. Africans have to be hounded out of the Reserves and the so-called "redundant Natives" have to be hounded out of the towns and all driven, from whatever direction, into one inescapable channel leading to the White farms and to the mines, which are regarded as "the economic fly-wheel of the country" and therefore indispensable to its whole economy.

*THE REHABILITATION SCHEME*

The latest plan for those Africans in the Reserves goes by the grand name of the Rehabilitation Scheme. As always in the past, the rulers would like to make out that it is something which will greatly benefit the Africans. They argue that soil erosion is rampant; that it is increasing every day and is rapidly turning the Reserves into a desert. Yes, we agree. This is all terribly true. Then they say that the soil *[- - -]*. Very good. We also agree. But how? That is the crux of the matter. Before you can treat a disease, you must find out the cause of it, and it is here that we take our point of departure. The rulers argue that soil erosion is due to overstocking and that therefore the African people should drastically reduce the number of their cattle. This is a preposterous argument. Today our people are disease-ridden because of malnutrition; they haven't the oxen to plough; the majority of the babies to do not survive the first year because mothers are too starved to be able to feed them. Children are dying like flies from all sorts of disease because there isn't enough cow's milk to build up their resistance to disease. These well-known facts give the lie direct to the statement that the Africans keep too many cattle. On the contrary, they have far too few cattle for their requirements. It is not that the cattle are too many, but that the *land is too small*. There is an appalling shortage of land. *[....]*

Once these bare facts on the real position of the division of land between European and African are revealed, *[...]* the arguments of the rulers become exposed in all their enormity as a fraudulent hoax. One is amazed that with so little land for the Africans there is even a blade of grass left in the Reserves. That there is still some grass at all is proof that, compared with their former state, the people have no cattle left. In fact, looking at the tiny strip of land into which so many people are concentrated and herded together, one would expect that the people alone, without any stock, would have trampled the soil bare with their feet. It is quite obvious that THERE CAN BE NO TALK OF REHABILITATION IN THE RESERVES WHILE THE LAND POSITION REMAINS AS IT IS. No amount of juggling with words will alter the plain fact that the rest of the problem is LAND HUNGER. It is not that the Government does not realise this. Their ignoring of this stark fact, and their stressing instead of overstocking reveals the real issue. (Those cattle again – they have always been a sore spot with the rulers!) They are not concerned with the welfare or prosperity of the African people in the Reserves. If they were really concerned about it, before talking about anything else, they would go straight to the root of the problem and give the Africans MORE LAND commensurate with their numbers. But this would be the negation of their whole policy. For the shortage of land is not an accident; it is the basis of cheap labour.

As we watch the Rehabilitation Scheme unfold we see clearly what its effect will be. It proposes to shift the population and reshuffle it in such a way that the "residential sites" are together on one side so as to leave an open space where there will be arable land on the one side and grazing fields on the other. This may sound plausible to some people. But what follows? It will establish three types of new village settlements. Type (a) will be built near forests for those people who will be employed to work there. Type (b) will be placed near factories, presumably to be established by the Government for those people who will be employed. In both these types of villages the workers will be able to return to their families every night. Type (c) will be reserved for those workers who will be employed far away in places like the mines and the towns and can only return to their family at intervals of many months.

All these village-settlements will be subject to rigorous supervision and the only people who will be allowed there will be those employed in the respective concerns. In those villages nobody will be able to live by ploughing because there will be no arable land attached. They will not be able to keep cattle or any other stock because there will be no grazing land attached. Of course there is a suggestion that milk will be sold cheaply to the people. Those Africans occupying the village-settlements must be servants and live only on their wages. (Let us not ask what wages!) But this is not quite the whole point. The important thing is that the people will be permanently divorced from the land. They will be entirely deprived of any means of independent existence and rendered destitute, without land and without cattle. "Abandon hope all ye who enter here."

All this talk about special villages around forests, factories and so on, is spurious talk. What forests are there in the Reserves to warrant special villages? How many people could these forests absorb all told? As for these nebulous factories, precisely where and when are they going to be built and for what purpose? Are they charitable institutions? How many people will they absorb and what wages will they pay! Has the Transkei suddenly revealed itself as a fertile field for business speculation with attractive factory sites all over the place and raw materials galore? No. These village-settlements are traps. They will actually be labour depots to feed the mines and the farms.

In this light, the proposed reshuffling of the population reveals itself as a device which will comb out all those Africans who have no arable land registered in their name. Only those who already possess arable land will get sites in the "residential area". The rest will be pushed on to the village-settlements (a), (b) or (c), according to the nature of their previous employment or the whim of an official in charge of the reshuffling operations. It is a well-known fact that the majority of the people in the Reserves have no land. It is only the old people who have plots registered in their names. An old man may have four of five sons all married and living with him because they have no allotments, despite the fact that for years they have been paying the extra tax for those allotments. All those will be driven out into the village-settlements. Only the old man will be left in the Reserves. The mines and the farms have no more need for them; they have already been sucked dry and now they may go and die in the Reserves. It is young blood that is wanted. The young men must be driven from their homes into the village-settlements, the labour depots, and from there they must enter the inescapable channel that leads to the mines and the farms. This will be the real effect of the Rehabilitation Scheme. Thus Smuts' promise to the farmers of an increased labour supply will be fulfilled.

*CONTROL OF AFRICANS IN URBAN AREAS*
The Africans living in and entering the towns do not escape. The machinery for dealing

with them is different from that employed in the Reserves, but it has the same effect. They come under the Urban Areas Act of 1923 with its many Amendments for the control of Africans in towns, so that now it is only necessary to create a set of regulations under the existing laws. The latest scheme for urban Africans, then, goes by the grand name of a "Housing Scheme", accompanied by the new Pass System grandiloquently called "Regulations for the PROTECTION and control of Natives in town." By this time their language has become familiar to us – a vicious attack is always cloaked in fine words and the appearance of bestowing a benefit upon its victims. The more vicious the attack, the more pretentious is the language. Their grand "Housing Scheme" means nothing else but locations and their "Regulations for the protection of Natives" are nothing less than the old Transvaal Pass System extended to the Cape.

Let us now examine both these schemes which are in fact two complementary parts of one and the same plan of urban control. The people, especially those in the Cape, do not always realise the full significance of locations. Many Africans think that locations are built because of two reasons (a) that Europeans do not like to live side by side with Black people, and (b) that municipalities want to provide cheaper and better houses for the poor Non-Europeans. The former reason is used by the Malanites with their usual brutal frankness because for them residential segregation (i.e. locations) is the logical completion of the accepted policy of segregation in the political as well as the economic sphere. On the other hand the second argument is typical of the more subtle methods employed by British Imperialism and its agents, the Government supporters and the liberals, and so-called "friends" of the African. Even the Minister of Native Affairs, while steering the Native Laws Amendments Bill through Parliament (1944) and in the very act of launching a new attack upon the people, beat his breast and shed crocodile tears over "these unfortunate Natives who come to the Peninsula to look for a better job and a better living, but who are living under the most appalling conditions". As usual they give any and every reason for their schemes except the correct one.

The real reason for creating locations is to isolate the Africans and concentrate them in one spot for the purpose of bringing them under complete control. An independent African living in town may, by virtue of occupying or owning a house, become a voter and possess certain human rights (limited though they may be) which safeguard him from being treated as a sub-human chattel. But in a location he is deprived of these rights. He many not become a voter by virtue of occupying a house, no matter what its valuation is or what monthly rent he pays. The location is no place for an independent African. A location is a glorified compound which only those may occupy who are required for the needs of the urban employer or who are actually employed. Just as on the mines no man may occupy a compound unless he is actually employed on that mine, so no man may live in a location unless he is employed in that town to which the location is attached. The only difference is that in the town compound (i.e. the location) a man may be allowed to live with his wife and family.

But their plan for complete urban control required something further, namely, the pass system. The latest scheme, the introduction of the Pass System to the Cape, is designed as the completion of this process of the control of Africans in the town. Every Black man in town is to be docketed, so that there is a complete check-up on how many there are, what their employment is, and where they stay. Every Black person must carry a pass to show that he is looking for work, a pass to show that he has got work, a pass to show that he is allowed to be in the urban area, or a pass to show that he has to clear out, or a pass to show that he does not need to carry a pass. These apply to every man, woman and child. As we know, in a concentration camp all the inmates are tagged and docketed; and in a prison each man had a number written in large letters on the shirt he wears. Here, African casual labourers and independent contractors must wear a badge placed in a prominent place on their person. A dog, too, wears a badge around its neck to show that its licence has been paid. But that is not all. The rulers have made preparations also for those who will be driven by hunger out of the Reserves and other parts of the country to come and seek work in the towns. They have made provision for a recruiting system like the Native Recruiting Corporation for the mines, so that all Africans coming into town must pass through this recruiting channel that leads to the labour-depôts in town. But in case some should escape the recruiting channel and get into the urban area on their own – they have made plans for them, too.

As Smuts pointed out during the debate on the control of the "influx of Natives" into town, it is extremely difficult to prevent them from coming in. The country is wide and they come from all over. [....] So what should be done? Smuts proceeds to suggest a way out. "It is very much better," he said, "to create THE BOTTLENECK HERE. The Native comes here to look for employment in a big centre and here we can get hold of him. Here he comes under the CONTROL of the administration. The Pass Regulations, then, make provision for those people who enter town in this way. On their arrival they would have to go, within 24 hours, to report to the urban authorities and get one or more of the many passes. The whole scheme is such that there is no loophole of escape. Every Black man, woman or child who puts foot into town is docketed and comes under rigid control. He is here, stripped of all rights and completely at the mercy of the urban authorities.

Thus this grand "Housing Scheme" reinforced by the Pass System, this drive to herd Africans into locations, reveals itself as part of the whole comprehensive Plan to force the African population into urban labour-depôts, from which they must enter the inescapable channel leading to the White farms and the mines. For with the rigid system of urban control, the concentration and regimentation of labour, it will be an easy matter to distribute it and apportion it according to the precise requirements of the ruling-class concerns. And of course the most powerful groups in the Government, namely, the mine-owners and the farmers, will receive first consideration. The rulers have indeed laid their plans on a nation-wide scale. In the towns they propose creating bottle-necks at the labour-depôts; in the Reserves the bottle-necks are to be the so-called village settlements. Here we have a picture of the whole population forced through bottle-necks and dammed up in labour reservoirs. From these reservoirs channels are created, leading to the White farms and the mines. This will result from their Rehabilitation Scheme in the Reserves. This will result from their Housing Scheme and their Pass Regulations in the town.

*UTILITY CORPORATION*
Even this is not all. The Fascist mind which conceived these plans knows no limit. Not content with preparing for the complete enslavement of the adult Black population, they now propose to deal with our children, too. A Government body known as the Social and Economic Planning Council has worked out a scheme whereby the Government is asked to form what they call a Utility Corporation, "to train Natives aged 14 to 19 and form them into service units to undertake farming and industrial work".

As usual they declare the scheme to be "for the welfare" of the Africans. Let us see what this amount to. The Utility Corporation is to recruit young boys of 14 to 19. The parents have to sign a contract handing their children over to the Corporation for the period of five years. The boys will be housed in tents in various camps throughout the country. They are supposed to receive "scholastic and vocational training" and will be called "students". But the very purpose of creating this Utility Corporation, as declared by the Government body itself, namely, "to form service units to undertake farming and industrial work" – explodes the myth of "scholastic and vocational training" and exposes the hoax. In fact, the boys will be hired out to farms and industrialists in the respective districts, and these will pay, not the boys for their services, but the Corporation.

The enormity of the fraud of doing something for the "benefit" of the young Africans, comes out in the payment which the Corporation in turn proposes to give the boys for their labour. For the first year they are to get 3d. a day; in the second year, 9d. a day, with deferred pay of 3d. In the third year they will get 1s. a day, with deferred pay of 6d.; in the fourth year, 1s. 3d. a day, with deferred pay of 9d.; in the fifth year, 1s. 6d. a day, with deferred pay of 1s. At no time in the five years, therefore, will the boys get more than 6d. a day! Then the deferred pay will be invested and the interest will go to the Corporation, which will thus make its profits by hiring the boys out to the farmers and industrialists and proceed to make further profits by collecting the interest from the deferred pay. When we consider that they propose to recruit 60,000 boys for a start, then we have some idea of the amount of money they will make out of our children.

But again and yet again. That is not the end of the matter. Just as the other schemes of the rulers will wrench the people from the soil, strip them of all rights, herd them together in labour-depôts and hold them under complete regimentation, so this proposed Utility Corporation Scheme for our children will create child-labour battalions at strategic points all over the country. There is a completeness and thoroughness about their plans that is truly diabolical. In case the schemes for the adult population do not work out with clock-like perfection (for they have found this to be so in the past) they will have in readiness a supplementary army of boys. And these child-battalions can also be used for another purpose. They can be used to scab on their parents if they should go on strike for higher wages.

*INTER-CONNECTION OF INTERESTS*
These sinister moves which will turn the whole African population, adult and child, into a regimented labour-force, are a grave threat to the whole working class of South Africa.

*[....]* The primary purpose of the exploiters is to maintain their rate of profits at a high level. During a depression this is effected by reducing the wages of the workers. Now organised labour resists this through its trade unions, so it is necessary for the rulers to devise means of smashing them. There are two ways of doing this. The one is by collaring the existing unions and turning them into company unions under the control of the bosses. The other is by smashing them outright. Already attempts are being made to do the former and they are starting with what they regard as the weaker unions, i.e the Coloured and Indian Unions. It is certain that if the European trade Unions do not come decisively to the aid of the Coloured and Indian Unions, they, too will be attacked in the same way. African trade unions are in any case not recognised by the law, and sad to say, the powerful European unions are in agreement with this. In spite of

non-recognition, however, the African trade unions have been growing from strength to strength and fighting for and getting improvements in their conditions of work. The Government now seeks to curb and undermine this development by giving them a form of "recognition" – which actually hands them over holus-bolus to the control of the Native Affairs Department.

As to the other alternative open to the Government, namely, of smashing the trade unions outright, preparations have already been made. The rulers know no other than the old and well tried-method of "divide and rule", of setting one section of the oppressed against the other. This is what they want to do now on a wide scale. The white worker has been so well bribed at the expense of the Non-European worker and so long fed on colour prejudice, that he has been completely blinded to his real position as a worker and has aligned himself with the exploiter against the Non-European. Up to now he has not only connived at the oppressive measures directed against his fellow workers, the Non-Europeans, but he has actively assisted the Government in enslaving them. So blind is he that he does not even realise their depressed and helpless condition constitutes a threat to his own position, and that in fact the Black man is eventually going to be used against him.

The system of recruiting Black labour is designed to lower the wage level of the African people. But this is in itself a threat to the wage level of the Coloured and Indian worker and, in the long run, of the White worker, too. The recruiting system accompanied by the damming up and regimentation of African labour constitutes more than a threat to the whole working class.

In the final analysis organised labour has only one weapon of defense against an attack on its wage level and that is a strike. At the present moment recognised trade unions (i.e. European, Coloured and Indian trade unions) can boast of and rely on their Industrial Conciliation Boards and other channels of negotiating with the employers. But when a crisis arises and the employers brush aside the Industrial Councils, etc., then the trade unions have to resort to strikes. But this is precisely the contingency which the ruling-class has prepared against. They will have in readiness the mass of controlled Black labour to be used as the strike-breakers against them. The White, Coloured and Indian trade unionists will have their trade union cards in their hands, but they will be without work unless they knock the bottom out of the trade union movement. In other words, one section of the workers will be used against another section. This then clearly indicates the inter-connection between the struggles of the different sections of the workers and oppressed peoples. It is a vital necessity for the workers to view their struggles against the exploiters, NOT as sectional, isolated and unconnected problems, but as forming one individual whole. Thus what might have appeared on the face of it as simply an attack on one section, the African, reveals itself as in fact an attack on all sections of the workers and oppressed people.

In this light the various schemes of the rulers constituting their whole comprehensive plan on a nation-wide scale can be seen in a chain – the long chain of oppression, the Rehabilitation Scheme in the Reserves with its bottle-necks in the so-called village settlements, the Housing Schemes in the towns together with the Pass Regulations, leading to the bottle-necks of the urban labour-depôts – those might appear as two distinct schemes effecting respectively and separately the Africans in the reserves and those in the towns. On closer examination, however, it becomes evident that these two streams of dispossessed people would be disgorged into one common channel leading primarily to farms and the mines. In this the African population throughout the Union is involved. Likewise the creation of child-labour battalions under the "Utility Corporation" Scheme assumes a sinister significance. It concerns not only the enslavement of the African children, but is inseparably bound up with and merges into the plan of enslaving the whole African people. These child-battalions living under a military-like discipline can be used (as already pointed out above) to depress still further the wage level of the adult African. In the event of strikes for higher wages they can even be used as scabs against their parents. But finally, the damming up and the complete regimentation of African labour, both adult and child, does not concern the African alone. It has still further sinister implications. For this Black labour forces constitutes a threat to the wage level of the other sections of the working class. In the event of economic crisis they can be used a strike-breakers to smash any attempt of the other sections to defend their positions. It is the whole working class that is involved.

*INTER-CONNECTION OF STRUGGLES*
As already stated, to understand the Rehabilitation Scheme, it was necessary to see it as part of the whole comprehensive plan for the exploitation of the Black man. It was necessary to see it as flowing from the basic Native Policy of the country. And with this key we could understand the effects not only of the Rehabilitation Scheme, but of all the other apparently unconnected schemes of the government concerning the Black man. More than this, we were able to see the vital inter-connection between their various plans for the Africans and the other sections of the Non-Europeans, and for the workers as a whole. In other words, we begin to understand the inescapable unity of oppression.

But it is not enough merely to understand. Understanding as an end in itself is worthless. It would be ludicrous for a prospective victim, when confronted with a huge octopus about to devour him, to sit and comfort himself with the thought that he understands the intricate workings of the monster's anatomy. Understanding, however, is essential. It is essential precisely because it provides a basis for the correct line of action. A clear idea of the inter-connection between the various schemes of the government for all sections of the Africans and indeed all sections of the Non-Europeans, leads the way to a clear understanding of the nature of our resistance to those oppressive measures. THE FORCES OF OBJECTIVE CONDITIONS DICTATE THE FORM WHICH OUR STRUGGLES MUST TAKE. The more clearly we grasp their real nature and their full implications, the better prepared we are to evolve just those weapons essential to a determined and successful resistance. It is imperative for us to evolve just that form of struggle which can measure up to and meet the situation.

Failure to do this must lead to disaster. We must be prepared to discard the old out-look and the old methods which were based on ignorance of the forces at work. Tribalism is a thing of the past. We must throw off the isolationist attitude, the pre-occupation with merely local problems and the narrow parochial outlook. No single tribe, however important, or lowly, is signed out for special oppression. No village, big or small, suffers from a special set of laws. Neither is the rural African exploited as distinct from the African living in the towns. One and all are subject to the same oppressive measures. OPPRESSION IS INDIVISIBLE.

The government plans for the whole and each scheme is part of a single comprehensive plan. Each scheme or attack is in the nature of a sortie in a long, nation-wide front. It is precisely this circumstance which imposes on us the duty and necessity to view

OUR STRUGGLE ON A NATIONAL SCALE. It is this circumstance which imposes upon us the necessity to evolve the political machinery which will draw together every section of the African people; the peasant and the townsman, the farm-labourer and the mine-worker, the professional and the worker throughout the length and the breadth of the Union. This unifying body will be the focal point of our struggle. It will draw together all sections and at the same time be the source from which ideas will be disseminated and from which will emanate our strength and all our plan of action.

Already these different sections have their organisations. The peasants have their farmers' associations, the teachers have their teachers' associations, the workers have their trade unions, the ministers their ministers' associations, etc. But each one of these struggles in isolation independently of the others, as if they alone existed and suffered from oppression. Up to the present moment they fail to realise that the problem which faces each sectional organisation is a particular aspect of one common oppression. Up to now a great deal of time and energy have been uselessly dissipated by each organisation going into battle single-handed. The whole race is scarred because single warriors have indulged in isolated skirmishes and have been worsted in the attempt. It is a spectacle that must seem futile and stupid to anyone who understands the full extent of the forces ranged against us. The very nature of these forces demands that all our struggles must be co-ordinated and unified in that each organisation becomes part of a whole and works in connection with all the others. In such a case – to put it in military parlance – the struggles of each are in the nature of a defensive sortie directly related to the others along a nation-wide front. Thus the single organisations throughout the country constitute battalions operating as part of one division in a whole mighty army.

Each struggle must be seen as a particular aspect of resistance to one common oppression. And this common oppression flows from one source – THE LACK OF POLITICAL RIGHTS.

Now the body which co-ordinates, concentrates and unifies this political struggle is the ALL AFRICAN CONVENTION. Its organisational form is best suited to meet the needs of the objective conditions of to-day. Its policy and programme as expressed in "The New Road" and the Ten Point Programme clearly voices the aspirations of the oppressed. Already the people are beginning to realise the vital rôle of the All African Convention in leading them along this New Road in the struggle for liberation. And it is the duty of all Africans to build up and strengthen this organisation.

We have, however, to extend our vision to a still wider Unity. As was pointed out above under the heading "Inter-connection of Interest", the various schemes of the Government for the different sections of the African people actually involve the regimentation of the whole African population. Moreover, this regimentation has sinister implications for the other sections of the oppressed people, the Coloured and the Indians, and finally for the working class as a whole. This reveals the identity of interests of all sections. In other words, the oppression of the African, the Coloured and the Indian is indivisible, so that an attack on one section has repercussions on the others and is in fact an attack upon all. This fact points directly to the necessity of placing our struggle on a wide basis.

It us not enough therefore to co-ordinate and unify the struggle of the different organisations among the Africans under the All African Convention. Neither is it enough for the Coloured people to co-ordinate their struggles under the Anti-C.A.D. and the Indians likewise under their organisation. To speak again in military parlance, the various battalions of the Africans together constitute a division; those of the Coloured and the Indians form the other divisions, and the three together constitute one mighty army of the oppressed Non-Europeans in the struggle for political rights. We have learned from bitter experience that all our failures in the past have flowed from the main weakness, LACK OF UNITED ACTION. Too long have we suffered from that terrible disease of racial prejudice. Too long have we been blinded by the segregationist mentality inoculated into our veins and fostered by the rulers in order to keep our ranks divided and ensure a policy of isolationism. Too long have we indulged in petty squabbles among ourselves, in faction fights between tribes, antagonism between town and country, distrust and bitterness between African, Coloured and Indian. And all the time the juggernaut of oppression has been ceaselessly and steadily crushing the body of the Non-Europeans.

Those leaders who do not realise this and still follow the old road of isolationism are either fools or traitors. Those leaders who still continue to keep the sections of the Non-Europeans separate, who still find some excuse, some spurious argument for keeping us divided, are consciously or unconsciously repeating the old arguments of the ruling-class, and merely echoing their masters' voice like a cracked gramophone record. They do this either deliberately or because the poison of the segregationist mentality has so seeped into their system that they cannot help themselves. In either case, they are serving NOT the interests of the oppressed people, but the interests of the ruling-class, because by such tactics they are paralysing the struggle for liberation.

The struggles of the Africans, the struggles of the Coloured and of the Indians are inseparably connected. It is not a question of the disabilities of the Africans or the disabilities of the Coloured or of the Indians. It is not a question of this particular law or that particular law. IT IS A QUESTION OF A WHOLE OUTRAGEOUS SYSTEM OF OPPRESSION. You cannot lift that oppression from one section and leave the other straining under its yoke. You cannot hope to liberate one section without at the same time liberating all.

In full realisation of this fact, the different sections of Non-Europeans have come together to form the Non-European Unity Movement. Upon it falls the gigantic task of bringing together and unifying all the struggles of all sections of the Non-Europeans. Its policy is firmly based on the demands formulated in the Ten Point Programme. All our energies must be directed to the building up of this Unity, for it is the essential prerequisite for a serious and determined struggle. The road of the Unity Movement is the only road that leads to the liberation of all the oppressed Non-Europeans of South Africa.

## Document 63
## Letter from the Chairman of the Planning Committee, Libode, to the Chief Magistrate, Umtata, 8 February 1947

Planning Committee
c/o The Magistrate,
Libode,
8th February, 1947

The Chief Magistrate,
UMTATA.

*The Rehabilitation Scheme: "The New Fraud"*
*by I. B. Tabata.*

With reference to my telephone request of the 6th instant to be supplied with the above publication, which is returned herewith, I have to inform you that the subject matter is not, as I was led to understand, an attack against the Planning Committee's action and proposals in these Territories, but rather against the whole Government's Native Policy in the Union, with which it is argued the Rehabilitation scheme is designed to fit in, so as to hound the people out of the Reserves and force them to work on the Mines and Farms, and by doing so, perpetuate the suppression of the Black man and keep him, as is claimed by the author, "as a slave to minister to the needs of the White man and as a beast of burden to create wealth for him." It is a call to all Non-Europeans to come together to form a Non-European Unity movement to fight for the Ten Point Programme advocated by the All African Convention.

The well known arguments regarding "Land hunger", "More Land" "More stock" etc., are cleverly treated and while it is submitted soil erosion is rampant, no constructive criticism is advanced to improve the position. The true aims of rehabilitation which have been clearly demonstrated in plans so far approved are sidetracked and much play is made of the so called Village Settlements, both rural and urban, which are envisaged as centres where individuals have no rights and from where they will be compelled to go forth and work for their rulers the White Men. The article abounds with cleverly distorted facts and half-truths which are made with the sole object of disproving and casting suspicion on the motives of the Government regarding the native people. Credit is not given for any benefits introduced while all action not favoured by the people is taken and argued to prove and establish a case of the Government's lack of sincerity which is regarded as a blind to its true motive of suppression.

Circulation of a publication of this nature especially in view of the attitude adopted by the United Nations towards the Union can and will do much to create dissension among the native people, and as it possibly would not be good policy for the Government to suppress it at this stage, intensified propaganda should be embarked upon by officials and others to counteract its subversive results and pass on to the people the Government's true aims in regard to rehabilitation. The carrying out of rehabilitation planned at Buttersworth, Mount Ayliff and Libode will in itself be a demonstration of the Government's bona fides and should allay suspicions of any ulterior motive in the matter.

CHAIRMAN OF THE PLANNING COMMITTEE.

## Document 64
## Progressive Forum⁶, Johannesburg [June 1950]

We would like to bring to your attention an important problem. In the rural areas of South Africa the government is applying what is known as the Rehabilitation or Land Betterment scheme. They claim that this is an attempt to save the soil and improve the economic condition of the peasants in the reserve. The government officials blame the bad state of affairs on the farming methods and laziness of the Africans. They "forget" to mention that the people in the reserves are starved for land, are given no education and are forced to spend a large part of their time working on the Rand Mines. In fact the government's main interest in the reserves seems to be to keep up the supply of cheap labour.

Knowing all this the people have resisted the scheme. They regard it as fraudulent and pernicious. They refuse to sell off their cattle, they say that if the land is overstocked, they should be given more land. They are struggling desperately, putting forward the slogan of NON-Collaboration with the oppressor. This is the same idea of Non-collaboration which has become the most important issue in our political world.

On Wednesday, June 7th, Dr. E. Roux (author of "Time Longer than Rope") will lecture to the Progressive Forum on THE REHABILITATION SCHEME. Dr. Roux will try to prove that that scheme is for the good of the people. He will try to prove that Non-Collaboration means cutting our own throats.

As the government tightens up the laws which prevent us from getting our Freedom it becomes more and more important to understand clearly the problems of the organisation of National Movements. And to do that we must be sure that we understand the idea behind Non-Collaborationism, a slogan that has been gaining more and more support from the major Non-European political organisations.

The Progressive Forum holds meetings regularly at the Bantu Mens' Social Centre to discuss issues which interest and affect you. Come along and give YOUR opinion. Everyone is welcome.

*Date:* 7th June, 1950
*Time:* 8-15 p.m.
*Place:* Bantu Mens' Social Centre, Eloff St. Ext.
*Speaker:* Dr. Edward Roux
*Subject:* The Rehabilitation Scheme

## Document 65
## Z. Sanders (Zena Susser), "Aspects of the Rural Problem in South Africa", lecture delivered to the Johannesburg Discussion Club on 1 December 1952,
*Viewpoints and Perspectives*, 1, 1, 21 February 1953

*[....] Discussion of Policy*
Our analysis has shown a growing pauperization and proletarianisation of the rural

Africans, but also a growing contact with the towns and with the concepts of the industrial worker and miner. On the one hand the needs of the people for food, clothes, money, health, freedom are gradually becoming felt and conscious; on the other hand new ideas of policy and action are finding their way to the rural areas. We have shown that the most powerful factors which maintain the depressed condition are lack of mobility and lack of land. This situation arises out of the present economic system of the country – on the one hand, the system of migratory labour demands such conditions, on the other the rapid development of capitalism is tending to dispossess the rural people still further. The contradictions of capitalist economy emphasise the disabilities of our rural people, because while they are being dispossessed they are yet prevented from selling their labour in the best market. This the people begin to understand. Their need for mobility is underlined by the difficulties which face them when they are driven to migrate illegaly, and the need to move is a direct outcome of their lack of land.

Because the immigrant to the city is often forced to move from town to country and back, he is able to identify himself with, or at any rate, to recognise the needs of the industrial proletariat. These are obviously closely linked with his own. The industrial worker also needs mobility; he needs in addition the abolition of the industrial colour bar, which is the technique that operates most powerfully to keep him in desperate poverty, unable to advance and unable to attain class cohesion. The contradictions between the methods of farming and mining on the one hand and industry on the other must lead to the breakdown of the industrial colour bar by a process of slow attrition; in the meantime it serves to emphasise and sharpen the recognition of this need by the worker.

*Development of Capitalism*
While the economic forces of our capitalist economy are gradually driving towards the breakdown of restricted mobility and restricted skill, the most effective bulwark of this system is an uneducated European electorate on which the mining and farming interests can rely. Thus an immediate and obvious demand both for city and rural dwellers is extension of the franchise.

Who will make these demands and how can they be made effective?

It is not difficult to show that since 1910, when South Africa obtained the forms of political independence, the Union, after the stimulus of industrialisation that followed the discovery of golds and diamonds, has rapidly taken on the shape of a capitalist economy. Pervading this economy are the remnants of colonialism, namely the colour bar in all its manifestations (we do not deny that it is an integral part of the present system, but it is in direct contradiction to the direction of capitalist development), the tribal system, segregation, the limited franchise and the systems of migrating labour. Similarly in some European countries before 1917 there existed a capitalist economy heavily loaded with the remnants of feudalism. Before advance could take place it was necessary to destroy and abolish the institutions of feudalism – this was described as the completion of the bourgeois democratic revolution, and it was achieved by the workers with the peasants, and the petit bourgeoisie and bourgeois up to a point, as their allies.

*Criteria for Advance*
In light of this, we can proceed to answer questions. Certainly in the Union, before advance can take place, the institutions of colonialism must be abolished. The people who make the demand are the people who suffer from them, namely the Non-Europeans,

and up to a very limited point, those "liberal" Europeans who represent the needs of industry. Because we have here capitalism developing amongst people who were never highly organised enough to produce a rich and powerful class, e.g. landowners, and because the rigid colonial institutions have prevented the emergence of any economically powerful group from amongst them, even under capitalism, their liberating movement is particularly lacking in complexity. It has no bourgeoisie worth speaking of to reckon with. Those who seek liberation are industrial workers, rural workers and migrant labourers, with a smattering of petit bourgeoisie. And here their needs are largely in accord. It is not a "national" liberating movement in the tru sense of the word. The Europeans, the Indians, the Coloureds, the Malays and the Africans do not each form a separate nation. None of them have any of the attributes of a nation, but only some racial distinction, and to call them nations would be absurd. There is but one economy in South Africa, several cultures which are tending to assimilate into one culture, several languages which must at some time assimilate, and one geographical and political unit. Thus the problems are these of a capitalist country with remnants of colonialism still existing, and the chief opposing forces are the capitalists and the industrial workers. The first handicap of the workers is the colonial forms that hold them in chains, without destroying these they cannot advance. Their allies in this struggle are natural and to hand; the rural workers and the migrant labourers. Their contact and distribution is so intimate that of necessity the migrants will carry home with them the same objectives and the same struggle. To make the struggle effective the major protagonist, the industrial proletariat, must first achieve cohesive organisation. This is difficult precisely because they are so invaded with temporary rural migrants, but once achieved, the wide spectrum of such an organisation will make it all the more powerful. The policy based on the needs of these workers and migrant labourers must be towards mobility and breakdown of the industrial colour bar (and consequently of the migratory labour system) and unqualified franchise.

We need not speculate at this stage on what is likely to follow the achievement of these aims; they are far reaching in themselves.

*CONCLUSION*

The attentive reader will have noted that the need for land had not been dealt with. We believe that no advance in this respect is possible without the accompanying abolition of colonial institutions. It is a just demand and should be made, but its achievement will surely be a later event than the abolition of the pass laws and the industrial colour bar, and perhaps even the full franchise. The immediate limiting factor is, of course, the orientation of the ruling groups in the country and its electorate base. On such a basis no demand for land has substance. Land reform could only be an expansion of Native Trust policy, and obviously no South African government based on the present electoral could or would wish to undertake the purchase of four-fifths of South Africa for Africans. Equitable distribution by this means is obviously a ludicrous pipedream. The freedom to buy and sell land may appear not a very radical demand. But it would mean scrapping the reserves and thus the breakdown of the system of migratory labour, which is a fundamental feature of our present economy. Again, no government based on the present electorate would consider such a change. In any case, without the abolition of other colonial restrictions, this freedom must lead quickly to complete dispossession of the African, and to no fundamental change in his condition save to intensify his economic problems.

The abolition of colonial institutions would lead to a revolutionary change, i.e. the achievement of a new and more advanced political form. It might then be possible to establish freedom to buy and sell land. But the fundamental need of rural dwellers is simply for more land, which necessarily entails some form of redistribution. Precisely how this should best be done would depend on the conditions obtaining at the time, on the rate of development of the economy as contracted with the rate of political development of the people, on how and when the necessary political changes come about. So that a sound policy would not take into account the detail and minutia of a redistribution of land, but would simply note the need and make the demand for more land.

## DISCUSSION

*Mr. Holt.* I should like to know at what rate this trend towards wage labour is developing? In trying to assess this development rate, certain factors should be taken into consideration. Firstly, the backward farmer is subsidised, therefore economic pressure doesn't necessarily force him to use wage labour. Secondly, he has convict labour on which to draw. Thirdly, the situation one finds on South African farms of wage labourers living in prison-like compounds doesn't seem to be a development towards capitalist production. These wage labourers are not always free to sell their labour as and how they wish.

Another point I should like to make is that most Africans want private ownership of the land and one must take this into account if one is trying to draw them into the Liberatory movement. The slogan "the land to those who till it" is a very good one. By implementing this slogan the African peasant would be able to own his land as it would mean the expropriation of white farms.

*Lecturer.* The compound system does involve a capitalist relationship between labourer and employer. The labourer has only his labour to sell. The overlay of restrictions which prevent his movement from market to market and even locally from farm to farm, does not affect qualitatively this economic relationship with his employer. The amount of wages he can command is affected but the way he works is a capitalist way. The restrictions on movement are a colonial hangover.

While subsidisation obviously encourages poor and outdated farming methods and labour relations, the rewards of capitalist techniques are great enough to be promoting a fairly rapid development in the use of these methods.

*Mr. Sisulu.* The people in the Reserves are not so interested in "buying" land. They want more land more stock. It is important that something be done to prevent these people from being so easily recruited to the mines.

How does one organise forced farm labour who are working in many cases against their own will. The Liberatory movement has not made a thorough study of this group.

*Mrs. Altman.* There is no stable group in the Reserves to form the basis of the Liberatory movement. Assuming the conservation and culling boycott is successful, what happens after the boycott?

*Mr. Rabinowitz.* Despite Mr. Holt's arguments, the trend is definitely towards rural wage labour. Irrigation farming is assuming ever greater importance, and irrigation land is too valuable to use in lieu of wages. Squatters are becoming wage labourers. The trend is towards intensive rather than extensive farming – a trend incompatible with the old systems. The fact adduced by Mr. Holt, that South African farm labour is not free to sell in the highest market is irrelevant. Traditionally agricultural labour is less mobile than industrial labour. Furthermore, in Britain where agriculture is highly developed, the bulk of agricultural labourers are in fact tied to individual employers by reason of their occupancy of housing supplied by that employer or landlord. No one would suggest that this is incompatible with a wage-labour system.

From the tone of the discussion it would appear that it is generally accepted that, given the opportunity, all Africans would want to be farmers. This misconception could lead to serious errors. A growing number of Africans are (as are people in all countries) drawn to the cities by greater opportunities, better amenities, education for their children, etc. The city-born know nothing of farming. From the point of view of the economy, it is incorrect to assume that 80% of the population will be permanently required as food producers. In America, 13% fulfil this function.

A correct assessment of the position is necessary in order to determine what are the legitimate aspirations of the African peasantry. From this would be determined his political role and also the best methods of expressing and canalising his political potential.

*Dr. Roux.* I should like to raise the following points for discussion:
1. The present campaign has found its support predominantly in urban areas, except for certain cases in the Eastern Province, where the most striking example was seen in Peddie.
2. The Unity Movement recommended the boycott of Government conservation measures, these reaching their highest point at Witzieshoek and in Natal where people were prevented from building fences.

This policy was based on the feeling that conservation measures are a form of oppression. I disagree with them as I regard conservation as being in the same category as other preventative measures such as vaccination. In Port Elizabeth, for example, the rioters burnt down schools, cinemas, etc. Although the African National Congress later admitted that it was not good politics to burn down schools, I consider this similar in nature to conservation sabotage.

The Liberatory movement has never tried to use the Reserves as an economic basis of struggle. I maintain that the Transkei, if properly organised on a collective basis, could be the granary of South Africa. The people in the Reserves could build up their economic strength to use as bargaining power to increase mine wages. The existing tribal organisation in the Reserves could do this if the desire and knowledge were not lacking, and they would then use the conservation methods to help to achieve this aim.

*Mr. Papert.* Because they are the most permanent source of labour on the mines, the peasants are the backbone of South African economy. The function of the Reserves as a whole and of the rehabilitation scheme is merely to provide additional labour for the mines. If betterment schemes were to be resisted a serious blow would be dealt to the Chamber of Mines who would then find its supply of cheap labour considerably curtailed. Similarly, Dr. Roux's suggestions in regard to the Transkei is wholly unfeasible as the Chamber of Mines and the Government would never permit the re-organisation of the Transkei on a collective basis – again because it would endanger their potential source of labour.

It is not so much a question of Africans overstocking the land, as of their having insufficient land. The policy of "resting" certain areas of land by having people move from one area to another merely decreases the amount of land available for production. At the same time it adds to the congestion already present in those areas which have to carry a larger number of people. Contour farming, too, is no answer to the land problem. Again, if there is an insufficiency of land available for the farming, culling will provide no solution, especially in terms of the value set on cattle by all African peasants.

Consequently, all rehabilitation schemes, even if they are honest, still serve the function of the Chamber of Mines. The Native Affairs Department which administers these schemes will has the primary function of looking after the requirements of the Mines in regard to labour. In other words, since it is the Native Affairs Department which is responsible for the administration of rehabilitation schemes, the form of administration practised is similar to that found in the educational sphere – Africans are given some measure of educational facilities, but of a far inferior nature to those available for Europeans.

Because of the importance of land to the people, they can be rallied in terms of land.

*Mr. Slovo.*[7] The major problem as the African peasant sees it, is lack of land. When he sees a government conservation official, that official is a symbol of frustration. For that reason I don't think one can compare, as Dr. Roux has done, conservation sabotage with the burning of schools. The farmer might not be in every case an expression of political consciousness but it is an expression of their desire for more land. As such one cannot condemn conservation sabotage but one must try to direct it into positive channels.

I find the formulation of policy in the paper inadequate. The perspective suggests that the proletarian is going to lead the struggle. Appealing to peasants in their capacity as migrant industrial workers is completely impractical. As peasants they demand more land one can't ignore this unless one ignores five million potential supporters. Once can compare the position here with that in China where it was originally said that the proletariat must lead the struggle. However, when it came to making an appeal to the soldiers, for example, they appealed to them not only in terms of the proletariat struggle but in terms of the problems of the land shortage. One must take into account the aspirations of the people. *[....]*

Document 66
Hosea Jaffe[8], "The First Ten Years of the Non-European Unity Movement", Excerpts from a lecture delivered to the Cape Flats Educational Fellowship, December 1953

*[....]* The 10-point programme is not a mere rallying call, but a programme, every point of which we shall put into practice. Ours is not one of these programmes which are buried when they should be practised, but the practical basis on which to begin to build a new South Africa, i.e. it is a minimum programme which we seriously propose should be put into practice and which we intend to see put into practice. Thus, the redivision of the land is an open immediate demand of the 10-point programme (all its points are minimum, immediate demands). The 7th points says a *new division of the land in conformity with the existing rural population living on and working the land, is the first task of a Democratic Parliament.* Point 7 calls for (a) the repeal of all discriminatory land-laws (b) the abolition of serfdom and semi-feudal relations and (c) for the redivision of the land to the tillers of the land.

The 7th point is a good illustration of the fact that, throughout the 10-Point Programme views democratic rights in the *broad historical sense* and not merely as legal equality. By full democratic rights we mean (a) all these questions which capitalism has to, did, or tried to solve in the classic "bourgeois revolutions" when it was being born (England in the 17th century, France in 1789 and 1848, America in the War of Independence and the Civil War, Germany in the Reformation and 1848, Italy in the Renaissance and later Russia in 1861, 1905 and February 1917, etc.,) and (b) the unsolved "bourgeois democratic" questions of the modern 20th century anti-imperialist colonial movements, which are taking place when capitalism is dying (China 1949, N. Korea 1946 and later Indo-China 1947 and later, the struggles in Malaya, Kenya etc., and the struggles yet to come in India and elsewhere.) In these struggles the workers backed by the peasants, have to solve the problem which the colonial capitalists can no longer solve and which, indeed, they oppose, because they are tied up both with foreign imperialism and "native" landlordism. Because capitalism has failed to satisfy the peasant's demand for land in semi-colonial and colonial countries, the workers lead the peasants in this struggle, they divided the land in China and North Korea, are dividing the land in Indo-China and still have to and most certainly will divide the land in India and other non-liberated countries, whether these be colonies, protectorates, semi-dominions, dominions or republics. Under these conditions the redivision of the land is a *liberatory* and *progressive* demand for backward countries – the FIRST STEP towards modern farming techniques, farms and relations, which do NOT obtain to-day in the colonial world despite the capitalist invasion and even conquest of the countryside (e.g. in South Africa capitalist farming is subsidised, backward, rests on cheap labour, ruins the top soil, retains semi-feudal forms and practices and at the same time holds the farm toilers down in Bethal-like fascist vice. Redivision is a progressive step compared with this *reactionary* system of cheap forced labour, rural compounds, the tot-system, squatting, Masters and Servants Acts, farm-schools and the rest of rural backwardness and tyranny in South Africa). What is historically necessary is progressive. Mechanical economism will condemn redivision as reactionary, wherever it takes place, and make no distinction between countries like England and America and retarded colonial countries like South Africa and India. Because they are *against* redivision as a necessary step towards further progress, they will be found to attack redivision (and with it the 10-Point Programme) from the Right and also from the "Left". Arguing against redivision from the Right, they say it is "socialistic" (which of course is complete nonsense, because socialism means collectivisation, state farms etc.). Arguing against redivision from the "Left" they say it is "reactionary". This argument forgets that history is a process, forgets that Herrenvolk farming is reactionary and that redivision is a progressive and necessary step even in India and Egypt where redivision will mean average holdings of about *5 morgen*, whereas in South Africa redivision will mean average holdings of about 100 morgen per rural family, which is an area large enough to demand mechanisation, modern practices and co-operation, steps that will be taken voluntarily and the more easily because the new peasant owners will have come from the workers in the mines, heavy industry and transport where they run the modern basic key industries, albeit on a segregated and migrant basis. We must view redivision historically and neither idealistically nor mechanically and then we will know how to answer those who want to revise the 7th Point of the 10 Point Programme whether they regard redivision as "too much" or as "too little" for them. The "too much" revisionists reject the small semi-landed would-be speculator group, and the aspirant middle class among the Non-Europeans. The "too little" critics reject the labour aristocracy ostriches and oblomovs in society.

For us as colonial oppressed the land question is the major democratic problem to be solved by means of liberty, by means of the full franchise and full citizenship. We have to solve the national (political) question in order to begin to solve the land (economic) question. At the same time the demand for and the actual redivision of the land will make the struggle for liberty advance with seven-league boots. And so we say "Land and Liberty".

And when we say "Land" we do not mean the right to buy land, we mean the *"new division of the land"* as our Programme explicitly says and which is a classic and *modern democratic* demand of and for the peasants. Inasmuch as we demand the right to buy land, we do not raise this demand in isolation from the operative phrase: "on the same basis as the Europeans" i.e. we raise this limited demand as a *demand for the abolition of discrimination in property rights* and as nothing more. It is by way of opposition to Group Areas servitudes and the Land Acts. It is not a slogan it itself, but a demand for the repeal of discrimination. We do not raise this demand to satisfy speculators and investors at the expense of the people. We raise it as part of our struggle for equal rights and never pretend that it is a solution to the question of land hunger. The right to buy land favours the Herrenvolk and its hangers-on and cannot even initiate agrarian reform. In relation to the redivision of the land among the landless peasants the isolated right to buy land is a reactionary demand. Indeed, a democratic land law in S. Africa would either abolish this right for everybody white or Non-white (e.g. N. Korea Land Law) or grant it after the free statutory redivision of the land (e.g. Chinese Land Law). We do not demand the right to buy land as such (e.g. freehold in the new western areas location or Servitas freehold in Coloured Locations, or "Economic" housing schemes), because *we subordinate the right to buy land to the question of equality*, (e.g. we oppose freehold in location schemes or freehold in the Reserves because this is Group Areas, discrimination and inferiority). We do not say the right to buy land, we say, equal rights to property (land, houses, shops etc.) with the Europeans, the right to live, work or farm anywhere we please and not in segregated areas. (confusion on this question made some civics accept "Economic" Housing, until we put them on the right road again.) And, secondly, we subordinate even the equal right of everyone e.g. speculators, landlords) to buying land anywhere to the right of every *peasant* to the land i.e. 1. we subordinate the right to buy land to legal equality and 2. we subordinate the legal equal right of everybody to buy land to the redivision of the land amongst "these who live on and work the land" – i.e. amongst the toiling peasantry. The right to buy land is *relative* in this double sense and only in this *relative* sense do we raise it as a demand. The furthest a democratic parliament can go in S. Africa on this right is to everybody insofar as residence (consumption) is concerned, but, so far as farming (production) is concerned, it must necessarily and justly re-divide the land among the landless (and penniless) peasantry and abolish for white and Non-White alike (even though in practice it will apply mainly to the former) the right to land speculation, landlordism, absolute (feudal-like) rent, mortgage and rural parasitism. There will be a new Land Law a democratic land law, abolishing the anti-Non-European Land Acts of the Herrenvolk (1894, 1913, 1936) as well as the Europeans Only Land Acts which give every European the right to buy farms, European Land Settlement

Acts, subsidise farming etc. Both sets of Land Acts (Anti-Non-European and pro-European, so to speak) will be replaced to a New Land Act, along the lines described above. And this we demand right now, as a minimum demand of our Programme.

Maybe it will be argued that we are demanding in this respect, more than the Europeans have in this case. Yes, but there is a land-problem also for a section of the Europeans (as land statistics for European owned farms show clearly) and where "European democracy" is not democratic we cannot accept it as democratic. *We do not fight for democracy as the Herrenvolk sees it, but as we, the oppressed, see it.* "European democracy" has a Suppression of Communism Act which applies in law equally to white and Non-white and we oppose it because it is *undemocratic*, even though it is not colour-discriminatory. The European democrats discriminate against "their" women, but we demand equality irrespective of sex, which goes further than what the Europeans have. The European democrats have indirect taxation which in law applies equally to white and Non-white, but we demand the *abolition of indirect taxation. [....]* So, too, it is consistent for us to demand a NEW division of the land, i.e. a New Land Act replacing all the old anti-Non-European, speculators, landlords' Land Acts. We do so because we interpret democracy in the broad historical sense which includes the agrarian question and not in the narrow legal sense, which excludes the agrarian question. And by the broad historical sense we mean as part of a minimum programme. A maximum programme means collectivisation, state farming, socialisation etc. and this is not part of the 10 Point Programme (even though socialists have been known to redivide the land in backward countries. As to the means whereby the land will be equitably redistributed, this is not yet a question of practical politics. Redivision to those who work and live on the land by means of nationalising the land and giving occupation to individual peasants (as in Russia in 1917). Redivision might take place through private ownerships of the land by toiling peasants, without the right to mortgage, buy or sell (as in North Korea) or with buying and selling rights (as in China under Mao Tse Tung).

But in all these cases the peasants got the land free and did not have to buy it. And each of these methods and forms of redivision has many variants. The method of redivision is a matter for a democratic parliament and the above methods, including nationalisation are each and all both classically and theoretically "bourgeois-democratic" methods and not socialistic methods. *[....]* Whatever the method of redivision (and I think that under S. African conditions the peasants do and will at first want individual titles to non-marketable land) the fact is that redivision is one of our clearly expressed minimum demands, that our programme says clearly that this redivision must be done by a democratic state and hence, by implication, not by private buying or selling (which cannot give land to the toiling peasants) and finally that also by clear implication, that the land will be given free to the toiling peasants from whose ancestors it was stolen by force and whose labour has in any event paid for it a hundred times over. By suitable constitutional means of its own, the state will take the land out of the hands of the Herrenvolk land-barons and distribute it free and equitably among all toiling peasants whether they be Non-European or European. This will translate Point 7 into practice. What concerns us immediately is the need of the landless peasants for land, the cry of the overwhelming majority of the population for land and the necessity to call for and to demand and to struggle for the redivision of the land by means of the struggle for liberty, to show that Point One (franchise) on the Programme is the key to

Point 7 (land). But if we reduce the 7th Point to the right to buying and selling land, then we are substituting the national question for the land question, instead of making the national question the key to the solution to the land question on which it rests. Then in fact and theory, we are abandoning the agrarian question and sacrificing the landless peasants on the altar of legal equality. This is not our policy and those who disagree with us on this question are outside our movement. *[....]*

## Document 67
### K. A. Jordaan, "The Land Question in South Africa", *Points of View*, 1, 1, October 1959[9]

*[....]*

THE HISTORICAL DEVELOPMENT OF THE LAND QUESTION IN SOUTH AFRICA
*[....]* The land question in South Africa is not an agrarian problem in the classical connotation of the term. Indeed, this essay sets out to establish the thesis that the problem of land, as the exclusive and predominant source of livelihood of independent farmers, is one that affects only a small stratum of the people. In this sense there is no land problem for the vast majority of the people. This statement, sweeping as it is at first sight, bases itself on the unique social relations in our countryside as a result of a singular historical development.

Firstly, the preponderant majority had been systematically uprooted from the land and swung into the orbit of an exploitative society as wage earners. This root and branch expropriation was undertaken and is at present being intensified to meet the insatiable labour requirements of agriculture, mining and manufacturing industry. The Africans were given no opportunity to settle down as smallholders on the smouldering ruins of tribalism and gain a livelihood as independent farmers. Nor were they allowed to develop the traditions of private property in land. Since, however, a peasantry can arise and eke out some sort of existence under the most adverse conditions, it has always been ruling class policy, sanctified by custom and hallowed by tradition, to subject the oppressed to mass evictions from areas where they might take root and then to remove them to districts where they may become more dependent on and accessible to the employers of labour. Our agrarian problem is certainly not a peasant problem. It is the problem of an agricultural proletariat on European farms, of ruined cultivators in the Reserves, the worker aspect of whose economic habits is being emphasised at the expense of their peasant character.

Secondly, under the impact of industrialisation and the irrevocable capitalist process of transforming ever larger layers into wage workers, the landless Africans today, like the landless Afrikaners of yesterday, are seeking to escape from rural poverty by migrating to the cities where industry offers them better scope for employment. Whereas in India a peasantry was deliberately created to supply Britain with raw material, South Africa was, by contrast, never regarded as an agricultural colony. Very early in her career, South Africa came to be regarded, not as a supplier of goods, but as a supplier of labour, first to feed a predatory pre-capitalist subsistence economy, and then the mines, capitalist agriculture and industry. Whereas in India the masses saw no outlet for their land problems, the people of South Africa saw in industry an escape from rural unemployment; or otherwise they perforce became agricultural labourers; thereby developing down the years a psychology different to that of a landholder.

And thirdly, in as much as industrialisation and its concomitant – urbanisation – is an irreversible trend, the problem of developing the rural productive forces, in a period of large-scale production, cannot be solved by a return of the dispossessed to the land and their reversion to small-scale farming. The peasant, as the pack animal of mankind, is clearly an anachronism in such a dynamic set-up and it would therefore be anti-historical to call him to life again.

In every Colonial country, nascent capitalism must create a social buttress for its rule by creating a middle class and, more particularly, a landlord class. Up till 1870 this country was regarded neither by the Dutch nor by the British as a source of raw material which would have necessitated the creation of a peasantry to sweat and toil for an overseas market. She fulfilled the role of a military outpost to guard the approaches to the East, both for the Dutch Company and Britain. During this period the problem of colonising the interior did not fall within the purview of both Dutch and British policies. Indeed, to save the British purse from administering territory which was unprofitable, the Sand River and Bloemfontein Conventions of 1852 and 1854, respectively, repudiated English authority over the area north of the Orange River.

Of cardinal importance, however, is the fact that a large and growing number of white settlers had come to regard this country as their very own and consequently severed all connections with their country of origin. [....] That white colonisation began from the south at a time when the African tribes were moving in from the north and expanding along the eastern seaboard is of crucial importance. That both groups were semi-nomadic pastoralists, bent on occupying new grazing areas, is a circumstance that precipitated the land wars. [....]

All the communities comprising the South African nation are the descendants of immigrants from across the seas and of those who migrated to this country from North and Central Africa. No group can therefore lay claim to South Africa or any portion thereof on the grounds of original occupation. If the Hottentots had any right at all to dislodge the Bushmen[10] – the first wave of migration from the North – then the Africans, as the last arrival from across the Zambesi, had the same right to dislodge both. And by the same token the Europeans had the right to expropriate all. The approach to the land problem must transcend the claims of "races."

The contact of Boer and African pastoralists in the Fish River basin during the early 1770's set the stage for a conflict which was to rage for a century. [....]

With the expansion of Boer territory, his labour needs increased. After every war, indeed, the Boers willingly took the impoverished tribesmen as farm hands. The land wars were also labour wars.

The introduction to the Africans of European goods by the system of bartering created new needs among them, undermined tribal crafts and destroyed the unity between tribal agriculture and industry. In this way the self-sufficiency of tribal life was destroyed. [....]

If the first step in the process of Colonial conquest is the expropriation of the people's land then the next step is the appropriation of their labour. This stage was ushered in by the discovery of diamonds and gold. Mining made necessary the introduction of machines which in turn called for the concentration of hired labour in and around the productive units. Such labour meant detribalised labour. The Africans had thus to be released from the protective system of tribalism and attached to the industrial machine. It is understandable therefore that in the decade following the opening of the mines, the most serious wars were waged against the Africans and the most obnoxious taxes imposed.

Not only did mining lead to the dissolution of tribal life. It also dealt a death blow to the particularism of the Boer subsistence economy. For when the demand for agricultural and pastoral products to feed the industrial areas became acute, the patriarchal farmer now began to rationalize his farming to produce for a market. Land itself became a machine, requiring a working class and a market. Land prices rocketed. The capitalists themselves began to speculate and invest in land. Those farmers who could not adjust themselves to the new conditions of production sold out and swelled the ranks of the new proletariat. The modern farmer took his place. The capitalist became territorialised. The land question began to assume the form we know it today. [....]

## II
## THE CLASS STRATIFICATION OF RURAL SOCIETY

1. How do we analyze the rural classes? [....]

The purpose of this section is to show (a) that the vast majority of the rural oppressed are relentlessly being transferred, by the logic of objective conditions, into the working class ranks; and (b) that as a result of the rationalization of agriculture, the landlord system of agriculture is on the way out and is being replaced by the capitalist farmer.

These conclusions are of seminal political importance. They argue that the driving forces of the agrarian struggle are fundamentally the proletarians and semi-proletarians who are perforce shedding all illusions of solving their problems under a regime of small private ownership. Their problems have become or are becoming those of earning better wages, of obtaining better conditions of service, of disposing of their labour freely, unshackled by the colour bar. Furthermore, these conclusions argue that, under conditions of increasing mechanization, a division of the land is a retrograde step when large scale production has come to dominate our system of agriculture. [....]

There are, to be sure, bondage conditions in the countryside. The nature of these must, however, be determined by a study of the concrete situation. This will show that outside the Reserves, firstly, the people, having been uprooted from the land, and seeking freedom of movement to sell their labour power in the best market, are prevented by a spate of legislative and administrative measures from leaving the rural areas. They are, in fact, directly or indirectly forced to take employment as farm labourers on terms dictated by the farmers. Their bondage conditions do not however, flow from a forcible connection with plots of land which are used by the landowners as a means of exploiting them.

The Reserves, on the other hand, are simply a labour reservoir to feed the large farms and mines with migrant workers. Their bondage conditions reside in the fact that they are of set purpose given allotments so small as to force them out periodically to the mines or to the large farms to gain a livelihood, and then to return to the Reserves. Under the impact of capitalism, however, this ruling class arrangement is breaking down everywhere. It is, above all, not a part of the agricultural system proper, but a special concession to the gold mining industry which, by paying them the low wage of about £4 a month, cannot allow them and their families to be permanent residents on the Rand.

If, then, it as essential to secure the break-up of feudalism by freeing the peasantry from unpaid labour services and giving them unfettered ownership rights over their allotments and the parcels of land into which the landlord's estate is divided, then in

South Africa the predominance of capitalist farming, hiring essentially wage workers, does not permit of such a division when large farming units, under increasing mechanization, each form an inextricable whole.

## 2. *The Reserves*

In the democratic phase of the liberatory struggle, the majority of the people are on the land. Under feudalism this rural bias of the demographic arrangement obtains because the majority of the people, being peasants, are tied to the estates of the landlord class. Their status is rigidly prescribed by the fundamental feudal law that land cannot be bought or sold. This freezes their status and arrests the crystallization of classes.

12.1 per cent of the Union's land area, covered by the Reserves, and regarded by officialdom as the abode of 42.6 per cent of the African population, cannot be bought or sold. The enforced sojourn of a large section of the people in these congested areas putrefies rural productive relations, aggravates the problem of earning a livelihood on the land and, by depriving the urban areas of labour, acts as a break on the escalator of industrial advance.

Despite the incrustation of rural social relations by a set of obsolete laws, capitalism none the less bids fair to undermine those institutional elements inimical to its continued development. This is demonstrated by the rapid rate of urbanisation and the marked tendency of the reservists to stay in the cities for longer periods, to call for their families and then sever all connections with the "Native Areas." *[....]*

As such a small area has to contain such a large population, the proceeds from farming are dwindling. The African has consequently to depend in increasing measure on the sale of his labour power outside the Reserves. *[....]*

As a result of population increase, the sub-division of communal holdings has been proceeding apace. But men now prefer to leave the Reserves rather than take over a fraction on which they cannot subsist. In 1950 in the village of Rabula of Keiskammahoek one-third of the arable plots were lying fallow. The men, even those who held freehold allotments, preferred to work in the cities rather than be part-time peasant farmers. *[....]*

It is not surprising that men endowed with freehold rights in land become absentee landlords. In the Rabula district nearly a quarter of the owners of freehold land did not live in the village but were in the cities. Many had their wives with them. The people who occupy freehold and quitrent villages may of course stay away for long periods, but the migrants from communal and Trust holdings cannot do so if they wish to retain a plot of their own. The colour bar of the cities, from which they can be removed on any pretext, forces many to retain a connection with the land.

In 1951 85 per cent. of the income of the people of Keiskammahoek came from cash earnings, mainly in the towns and none of the families made a living out of farming even if they were to improve their techniques.

The limited land resources cannot accommodate the large population. They place severe restrictions on the number of livestock, as well. The result is a severe decline in production. *[....]*

There appears to be certain reservists who in certain areas and under certain conditions are able to eke out an existence in farming. Thus in the pastoral farming regions the Africans generally are able to sell 50 per cent of all their produce. And on the irrigation schemes under European supervision 45 per cent. of the produce are sold. The overall picture is that not more than 25 per cent of the agricultural produce of the

Reserves are sold and about 40 per cent of the livestock.

To assert therefore that there is no peasantry will be as sweeping and misleading as to aver that there is one. The trends of development are all-important, and these present us with the inescapable conclusion that the Africans in the Reserves are perforce emphasising the working class aspect at the expense of the peasant aspect of their economic activities. They may be regarded as semi-proletarians who are prevented from becoming full-blown city dwellers by the pass law system and the forcible connection they have to retain with the Reserves.

Under the Nationalist regime the disintegration of the reservists as part-time peasants has been intensified. Any distinction between freehold, quitrent, communal and Trust tenure is a distinction without a difference. For no person, even with freehold property, may sell, lease or transfer his land without the consent of the Minister of Native Affairs. The principle of "one man, one lot" is rigorously being enforced to drive the members of the family on to the labour market. The fragmentation of plots is being stopped, ostensibly in the interests of furthering the Rehabilitation Scheme, but in reality to eliminate every vestige of economic independence. Squatting on Crown land is no longer permitted. Nor may such land be used for the grazing of their cattle, whose numbers are steadily dwindling as the small allotments cannot support them.

Forests are also being enclosed. Even scrubland and grassland, which served as communal grazing, are being fenced off. People are being cleared off their allotments and accommodated in rural villages. The land is being divided among a few. And yet influx control is being tightened up so that the Bantustan dream may be realised.

The gold mines, however, are a big factor contributing to the perpetuation of the migrant labour system. They cannot afford to pay an African a wage which can support his family in the cities. The Report of the Witwatersrand Mine Native Wages Commission said: "The ability of the Mines to maintain their native labour force by means of tribal natives from the reserves at rates of pay which are adequate for this migratory class of native but inadequate in practice for the detribalised urban native is a fundamental factor in the economy of the Gold Mining Industry."

It is clear, then, that the migrant labour system is to a large extent responsible for preventing the development of the semi-proletarian reservists into a settled urban working class.

### 3. *The development of Capitalist Agriculture*

According to the 1952-3 Agricultural Census, 87 per cent of the total farming area was taken up by farms over 1 000 morgen each and 13 per cent by 876 farms with an area of 10 000 morgen each. These facts reveal the importance of large scale farming. Of all the European-owned or -occupied farms, 69.27 per cent. were owned by the occupier in 1953; 11.7 per cent were rented for cash; 7.64 per cent were managed for other persons and 2.61 per cent were worked on a shares basis. The "engrossing" of farms had encouraged absentee landlordism which in some areas has risen to 30 and 40 per cent.

The increase in the number of tractors is indicative of the extent of mechanization. [....]

Owing to climatic conditions in this country, and the barrenness of much of the land, extensive farming is the general rule, more especially as stock farming plays such a dominant role. For example, of the approximate 101 million morgen owned by the whites, only 6.04 million morgen was under cultivation as far as the chief cereals are concerned.

In 1953 with less than 6 per cent of the country's area under cultivation, it has been reckoned that only 9 per cent can be brought under cultivation. Let the "divisionalists" take cognizance of this.

The Department of Native Affairs distinguishes between three classes of African workers in the rural areas: the wage workers (huurvolk); labour tenants (woonvolk), and squatters (sitvolk).

The term "labour tenancy" is used to describe "the system the main features of which, subject to innumerable differences in detail from district to district and even in the same district, is the giving of services for a certain period in the year to the farmer by the native and/or his family in return for residence on the farmer's land, to cultivate a portion of land and to graze his stock on the farm."

Squatters are of two kinds: those who live on Crown land and those who are given land by the farmer in return for a share of their produce or for a money rental. The former are now being accomodated in rural villages.

It is difficult to distinguish between the three classes as listed by the government, especially as the economic standards of all are so low. Moreover, like the labour tenants, the wage workers are also often allowed to graze a limited number of stock and cultivate a patch on the farm of his employer.

Labour tenancy is clearly an anachronism. It has disappeared in the Cape Province where mechanization has developed furthest. This must necessarily be so because the scientific farmer, with his eye on the market, will bring under intensive exploitation all his available land. The farmer is calling upon the labour tenant to do more work and it is usual these days to give him a wage as well. The system still flourishes in the more backward farming regions.

The system of squatting on European farms is being abolished. Not only are the scientific farmers taking the steps to do so, but the State is actively intervening to eliminate this class. [....]

There are certainly elements of bondage conditions under which the workers have to labour. Firstly, influx control immobilises labour and, by creating a surplus labour supply in the countryside, places the farmer in a commanding position to dictate the terms of the contract. In this way the wage standards are severely depressed. Secondly, because of the Land Acts and the extremely limited opportunities for Africans in the rural areas with regard to choice of work, they, their children and their grandchildren have perforce to be farm workers all their lives. Thirdly, in terms of his private contract with the farmer, a contract that cannot be legally enforced – at least as far as the rights of the workers are concerned – the African is exposed to the risk of expulsion and finding himself without a home if he does not bend completely to the will of his master. Finally, by contracting the worker together with the members of his family, who can be called upon at any time to render services as well, no one is permitted to leave the farm without the express consent of the farmer. This relationship smacks of the feudal patriarchal system, if not in law, then at any rate in social and economic fact.

Agriculture in South Africa thus presents a picture of contrasts. On the one hand, a high development in techniques and methods of exploitation for the market; on the other hand, the retention of a system of immobilised landless labourers tied to land, lacking freedom of movement and living in abject poverty and ignorance. The combination of different stages of the historical journey within one and the same sector of the economy invests it with the elements of inevitable and ineluctable radical change, to bring it into line with the demands of modern society.

It is worthy of note that farms remote from the industrial areas pay extremely poor wages, but those near the cities, like the diary farms, have necessarily to pay more because of the relatively higher rates of industrial enterprises.

The recent tightening up of influx control has eased the position considerably for the farmers and temporarily, at any rate, dispelled their fear of having to raise their wage rates in order to keep the services of their workers. As a matter of fact, the determination of the Nationalist government to reverse the process of urbanisation is leading to the creation of a surplus rural labour force. And under such conditions the Africans are in for another period of wage cuts and a further depression of their already low living standards.

Farmers are complaining that their workers are becoming "defiant" and "insolent." They are observing that they are becoming dissatisfied with their lot which they had hitherto borne with monumental patience. Most of the farmers ascribe these changes in their attitude to "communist propaganda" and the dissemination of African National Congress ideas. There is no proof for this averment. Investigations have revealed that their dissatisfaction may rather be attributed to changes in the objective situation, not so much in the rural areas, but in the industrial centres.

The flooding of the countryside with mass produced cheap industrial goods is creating new wants among them. It is their inability to gratify these wants that is causing them to display their dissatisfaction in an overt manner. They are beginning to compare their own abject poverty with the luxury of the cities and the higher wage standards of the urban Africans. Their own position consequently grows more intolerable. Some are beginning to demand higher wages. Many, move freely to the cities. The recent demonstrations against influx control is a case in point. *[....]*

Whether capitalist agriculture in South Africa will be able to survive on the basis of civilised wage standard is a vital question. Up till now it could give itself an extended lease of life only by relying on generous State subsidies and a lowly-paid labour force. What De Kiewiet calls the "subsidization of inefficiency" in respect of farming is an organised drain on our resources.

The lines on which the productive forces in the countryside can be developed to ensure economic well-being for all is thus a question of the first-rate importance.

### III
### *PROGRAMMATIC ASPECTS OF THE LAND QUESTION*
1. *The Character and Driving Forces of our Struggle*

Intimately connected with the land question and a solution to it are the character and driving forces of the struggle that is now inscribed on the historical agenda of South Africa. What are the demands of the oppressed and exploited sections in South Africa? Which are the viable classes in this struggle? What part does the struggle for land play in it?

The immediate demand of the movement is for equality, before the law. Such a demand, confined as it is to the legal and political fields, does not call into question the existing capitalist property relations. In point of fact, it seeks to abolish a political superstructure which, by discriminating between different sections of society on the grounds of status, stifles the development of the productive forces and prevents the fullest utilisation of the human resources in the interests of further social development. In this sense our struggle is bourgeois democratic or, more correctly, capitalist democratic.

Every capitalist democratic struggle sets itself the three following tasks: (1) the equalisation of political and legal rights (or the franchise); (2) the right to sell one's labour freely in any field of the social economy (the right, that is, to be free from feudal dues and to move about freely; and (3) the right to buy and sell land (or the right of the peasants to full ownership rights).

As the peasantry forms the vast majority in a classical democratic struggle, the foundation of a successful bourgeois struggle is the creation of a class of free peasants; free, that is, to dispose of their labour; and free to dispose of their allotments. The bourgeois shibboleth of "free contracts" must replace the medieval concept which freezes the status of an individual and stifles the free play of economic forces, thereby arresting class differentiation.

In South Africa the consummation of the democratic struggle will involve, under (2) above, the abolition of the industrial colour bar and the pass law system which ties an already uprooted mass of people to the rural areas; and under (3) the abolition of the so-called Native Reserves and the Land Acts which restrict the ownership and free exchange of landed property. [....]

If our struggle is broadly characterised as bourgeois democratic, then we must seriously ask ourselves whether the bourgeoisie can initiate it.

It is to be noted that the bourgeoisie in this country has already been territorialised as a result of the expropriation, by sword and fire, of the tribal system. There is, secondly, no significant peasantry attached to the soil whom they must liberate to create a labour force and a national market for their goods. The land wars had taken care of this problem for them: and so also did the creation of labour reservoirs.

What is the attitude of our bourgeoisie to this propertyless mass if we consider for a moment that they wish to struggle for a colour barless capitalist society? If the bourgeoisie deserted their own struggle in the face of a plebeian minority in the classical democratic social movements, is there any reason to believe that they will forge an alliance with a plebeian majority in South Africa?

Capitalism has, indeed, made great strides under the colour bar system. We must therefore seriously ask ourselves the question whether the colour bar is not the signal modus operandi of capitalism in South Africa; whether the advantages which the colour bar gives the capitalist do not overrule the disadvantages of the system. For, example, mining can thrive only with the aid of a poorly-paid labour force. And the same applies to agriculture.

What about the so-called progressive capitalist class – the secondary industrialists? They certainly do feel that the abolition of the industrial colour bar and the restrictions on the flow of labour will give a tremendous impetus to capitalist development. But they are afraid to struggle for their removal: the repercussions are fraught with dynamics. They sensibly feel that, in the absence of a peasantry which as an owning class acts as a social buffer and security against "popular tumult," an organised, settled working class constitutes a threat, not only to the system of super-exploitation, but also to property itself.

It seems to us that, despite the great inconvenience which the colour bar causes, the industrialists see in it a weapon for their own preservation, just as the classical bourgeoisie saw in the retention of certain feudal elements and a bonapartist regime the means whereby the workers could be kept enslaved to the capitalist system. The colour bar, indeed, ensures their super-profits, prevents the workers from organising for increases, decimates their ranks and stifles the development of a working class consciousness. Hence the industrialists will continue to avoid the struggle like the plague. To be sure, there is, in the ultimate reckoning, a community of interests between mining, agricultural and industrial capital when it comes to the question of protecting property and keeping the workers chained to it.

Our democratic struggle cannot be brought under the classification of bourgeois democratic struggles. It is being waged without the bourgeoisie and against the bourgeoisie. This is the first distinctive feature of our movement.

The second feature of our movement is that the land question is not the sub-soil of our struggle. The fundamental task of our struggle is not the creation of a class of free peasants when the mass of the people had already been uprooted from the land and drawn into the orbit of capitalist society as wage earners.

Every peasant movement is a bourgeois democratic movement since it aims at establishing capitalist laissez-faire conditions in agriculture. But every democratic movement is not necessarily a peasant movement. This distinction is of paramount importance. For if agriculture is already organised on capitalist lines, as in South Africa, if, that is to say, there are large farms employing wage labour and producing for a market, then any rural movement that develops under such conditions may be a democratic struggle but certainly not a peasant struggle. Under such conditions, to be sure, the agricultural system is inextricably bound up with the capitalist system generally. This means that a renovation of agrarian conditions is possible only by abolishing capitalism or by nationalising the land and placing it under the control of workers' associations.

It is not therefore necessary that a capitalist country should have a peasantry.

South Africa finds herself in this singular position of not having to retrace the necessary steps of the classical democratic struggles in the agrarian sphere.

## 2. The 10-Point Programme of the N.E.U.M.

We may take the N.E.U.M. land programme as a convenient starting-point for a discussion on the solution of the agrarian question in South Africa. This political organisation has, indeed, given more attention than any other to a problem whose solution they regard as the alpha and omega of the struggle in this country.

The much-vaunted Point 7 of their 10-Point Programme, over the interpretation of which the affiliated bodies – namely, the Anti-CAD and All African Convention – have fallen foul of each other, thereby renting their movement in twain, reads thus: "Revision of the land question in accordance with the above," where the above is the demand for equality in general and the unfettered franchise in particular. A faulty formulation, to be sure, in as much as it is a manifest absurdity to revise a social question: it has to be solved. What the authors had in mind was the revision of the Land Acts; and this is explicitly stated in the explanatory remarks on and appended to the Programme. The section germane to Point 7 reads: "The relations of serfdom existing on the land must go, together with the land acts, together with the restrictions upon acquiring land. A new division of the land in conformity with the existing rural population, living on the land and working the land, is the first task of a democratic Parliament."

Point 7 therefore regards the equalisation of political and legal rights as the first step towards and the key to the solution of the land question. For such equality must willy-nilly abrogate the Land Acts which place restrictions upon the acquisition and disposal of land. But does the Programme espouse a laissez-faire policy in respect of buying and selling? Not at the inception of the democratic rule, at any rate, because the first task of the democratic Parliament is to undertake the re-allocation of the land on an egalitarian basis among the farm workers, labour tenants, squatters and independent peasant farmers – in short, amongst those who are "living on the land and working the land...." Such a dotation argues the expropriation of the land barons ("by constitutional means", as a NEUM spokesman has it.).

On an important question the Programme maintains a pregnant silence: whether the land thus parcelled out is to be a negotiable asset or pass permanently into the full dominion of the democratic State charged with the function of following up this "new division" with periodic redivisions in the interests of equity. Is the term "acquiring land" the same as "buying land" from private holders or is land to be acquired only from the democratic State as the sole owner? In short, should the NEUM hitch its destiny to the star of private property as a plenary power or should it seek to abolish private ownership in land? It is precisely on these mutually exclusive conceptions of agrarian property relations that the AAC and Anti-CAD have reached the parting of the ways.

So we have before us a Programme that, in the interests of economic equality, is seeking the fragmentation of all arable land, including the large mechanised farms. It is common cause that such drastic surgical treatment of the ills of rural society must spell the doom of agriculture in this country. A mechanised farm cannot be broken up into peasant holdings any more than a factory can be dissolved into its constituents and divided among the workers. Moreover, tractors are quite uneconomical for the small holdings which the Programme contemplates.

Indeed, with the development of mechanised farming, the productive forces tend to become more and more collective, bringing them into open collision with the system of private property in land. To solve this dichotomy between the productive forces and the property relations, social democracy has always advocated the transformation of property in land into common national property and the introduction of co-operation among those who till the soil. This solution is essential for those countries where there is large land ownership, with large mechanised enterprises, each with one owner employing many wage earners. Under conditions of increasing industrialisation, large-scale farming cannot be mutilated to fit into the Procrustean bed of the small holder.

The mystique of Point 7 lies precisely in this dichotomy immanent in its determination of the land question, that it embraces both progressive and reactionary admixtures. On the one side, there is the progressive move to purge the countryside of bondage and obsolete conditions and place the land at the disposal of the landless. It is this aspect of their Programme that accords with the demands of social evolution. On the other side, however, there is the reactionary dream to universalise small-scale farming under an industrial regime and endow everyone with economic equality under capitalism after the manner of the Russian Narodniki. This is a chimera.

If Point 7 is a nursery for the growth of small proprietors, then a comparison of this with Point 10 of the Programme raises doubts whether the NEUM are such impractical dreamers. Says Point 10: "Revision of the labour legislation and its application to the mines and agriculture." The relevant explanatory remarks call for "the elimination of all restrictions and distinctions between a European and Non-European, equal pay for equal work....the liquidation of indentured labour and forcible recruitment, the full application of Factory Legislation to the mines and on the land....the abolition of payment in kind, and the fixing of a minimum wage for all labourers without distinction of race and colour." The Programme is certainly on firmer ground when it treats of the status of a free agricultural wage earning class. Yet it cannot determine the status of the peasant owning class. Moreover, it is a contradiction in terms to advocate a nation of property owners and at the same time make provision for the treatment of agricultural labourers. If Point 7 falls within the scope of the mischief created by Point 10, how is this contradiction to be reconciled? It may be contended that the Programme envisages only one division of marketable land after which class differentiation under capitalist production will assert itself and lead to the crystallisation of a new rural bourgeoisie and free proletariat.

Thus it is fair to conclude that Point 10 is simply a confession of the impracticability of all schemes such as the equitable division of the land. It is fair to see Point 10 as a substitute for the land reform contemplated in Point 7, as a sop of liberty to those who will not be given any land. The land question remains unsolved. The mountain has brought forth a mouse.

3. *The Land Policy of the A.A.C.*
Having said thus much, there remains the posse of conflicting opinions of the AAC and Anti-CAD on the purport of Point 7. At first sight, the crucial issue between these bodies is whether the democratic State should, in the interests of equity, exercise control over landed property after the initial division by Parliament.

AAC policy is wedded to the idea of unshackled ownership. *[....]*

In the Presidential Address to the 1958 AAC Conference this laissez-faire attitude to landed property was underlined.[11] It was clearly pointed out to the Anti-CAD "divisionists" that "redivision is not part of the 10-Point Programme. When we talk of 'acquiring' land in Point 7 we mean and have always meant lawful acquisition within the framework of the capitalist society of which we are part." By repudiating "a new division" by the first democratic Parliament, the AAC came forward with the slogan of "the right to buy and sell land."

We observe therefore that the AAC take their stand on the question of agrarian relations strictly within the ambit of bourgeois propriety rights. This is the classical juridical approach, no more, no less. Every rural toiler must have the right to buy and sell land freely. This is the basis of the "free economy" the AAC wish to usher in. This approach means the advocacy of rugged individualism which would furnish opportunities for all with the wherewithal and capitalist spirit to embark upon conspicuous expenditure on the conspicuous accumulation of property. And in the manner of the classical bourgeois solution to the land question, it is quite irrelevant to argue, the AAC contend, that those without the necessary financial backing will continue to be landless. Laissez-faire must have its way, even to the extent of the "kulakization" of the more prosperous rural layers.

The practical policy of the AAC consists in helping the cultivator in the Reserves to preserve and enlarge his allotment and gain complete ownership over it. The communal, quitrent and leasehold systems of land tenure must therefore go by the board. So also must those farming strips reminiscent of the manorial system. Full ownership argues the enclosure of holdings and the abolition of communal grazing grounds. Freedom for all to buy and sell must throw the Reserves open to land monopoly and reduce the majority to landlessness.

It is significant that the agrarian policy of the AAC is exclusively directed at solving the land hunger of the small holder in the Reserves. It excludes from its reckoning the 2.5 million labourers on European farms where they eke out an existence, not as peasants interested in land, but as wage workers interested in improving their living standards and gaining personal liberty. Which lends weight to the conclusion that the AAC is a peasant organisation. They regard the peasant as the man of the future and, indeed, reduce all to the bourgeois level of this class. Writes the AAC mouthpiece, Ikhwezi Lomso: "The demand for an equitable distribution of land among the peasant population is and will continue to be for a long time the most powerful driving force of our struggle for it touches the heart-strings of the majority of the oppressed, the African peasant." Here the AAC turn their backs on the rapid assimilation of the oppressed into an industrial economy as workers who will, in ever-increasing numbers, put forward demands similar to those of the European working class, demands which have no connection with agrarian conditions. Moreover, under a free economy the peasantry must rapidly disintegrate and join the ranks of the proletariat. These are the lessons of the West European experience.

If we regard the AAC as a peasant organisation and the 10-Point Programme as an inter-class democratic one aiming to achieve bourgeois democracy, then the laissez-faire policy of that body is more realistic than the Anti-CAD programme to perpetuate the division of the land. Indeed, the AAC may legitimately invoke Point 10 to demonstrate that it is not the intention to perpetuate small-scale farming. Class differentiation under a free economy must then proceed apace. Indeed, irrespective of the Anti-CAD's and AAC's volition, such a development is as inevitable as it is desirable. A plethora of laws cannot overrule such class stratification. It is in conformity with the bourgeois democratic desideratum to widen the foundations of capitalism and wrought clear-cut class differences. Such conditions are the ideal milieu for the struggle against economic exploitation.

4. *An Instructive Historical Episode*

We may then view the AAC land policy from two angles. It contains this progressive element, that it seeks to widen the framework of capitalism and promote its untrammelled development by subjecting all landed property to the laws of commodity exchange. This must lead to the crystallization of a new bourgeoisie, at the one pole, and an agricultural proletariat, at the other. The disintegration of the peasantry is all but complete. The state is now set for a direct struggle between Capital and Labour groups.

If the AAC do not hold these perspectives – and it can honestly be said that this grand strategy does not form part of their programme – then they subscribe to purely capitalist interests in their land programme. It has many parallels in the history of agrarian politics. The most striking one is the famous land reforms of the Russian Prime Minister, Stolypin, during the years 1906-11.[12] *[....]*

Whilst mindful of the motives which actuated the Stolypin Reforms, social democracy welcomed these changes as they were in consonance with the need for capitalist development and conductive to the higher ideal of clearing the ground for the intensification of the class struggle. The social democratic leadership was clearly not interested in a peasantry as an end in itself. In capitalist society the motor force of social change is the working class.

The modus dominandi of capitalism in South Africa rules out the possibility that the rulers may one day contemplate the creation of a free peasantry with the right to buy and sell land freely. For South African history teaches us that capitalism relies heavily on the super-exploitation of a propertyless mass of people who, in the interests of insatiable labour requirements, cannot be allowed to withdraw their services as workers by settling down as independent farmers.

5. *The Anti-CAD Land Policy*

The Anti-CAD first enunciated its interpretation of the NEUM land program in an article, "The First Ten Years of the NEUM."[13] In it the author states that the right to buy land is subordinate to the re-division of the land on an equitable basis by the democratic Parliament. "As to the means whereby the land will be equitably distributed," he continues, "this is not yet a question of practical politics." He leaves this matter to the democratic Parliament which may decide to nationalise the land and give occupation to individual peasants, with or without the right to buy, sell or mortgage. It is, however, his personal opinion that "under South African conditions peasants do and will first want individual titles to non-marketable land." And arguing against the laissez-faire policy of the AAC and for re-division, he considers that "in South Africa re-division will mean average holdings of about 100 morgen per average family, which is an area large enough to demand mechanisation, modern practices and co-operation, steps that will be taken voluntarily and more easily because the new peasant owners will have come from the workers in the mines, heavy industry and transport....".

Seldom has a socialist gone to such a great length to certify to the grave defects in his organs of historical perception.

Let us examine his generous present. Every rural family will be given 100 morgen. As the two million will "voluntarily" (sic!) withdraw from urban industry to become land holders, this gives us seven million rural Africans on the basis of present population figures. The author obviously wants to cause a "demographic explosion." And if one has to make provision for the population increase, one can imagine the terrible congestion on the land and wonder whether the author regards a farm of 100 morgen as a fixed and immutable amount.

More disastrous is his anticipation that the Africans will abandon industry and return to the land. This is nothing less than a conspiracy to unscramble our historical omelette, escape the purgatory of capitalism after the manner of the Russian Narodniki and condemn the country to a vegetable civilisation. And under such a system where equality of poverty will be the rule of life in the absence of a dynamic economy, the peasants will vegetate at different rates to the stage of the petrification of inequalities. *[....]*

It is of course pedantic to calculate the size of an allotment without taking into account such matters as the configuration of the land, climatic factors, irrigation facilities, tools and the touchstone of market control. Here is an agrarian whose comprehension of the land question is limited to the two questions of "land" and "citizens," categories which they abstract from the social order. The result is a superstructure of cobwebs.

The Anti-CAD approach the land question from the point of view that certain historical wrongs must be made right so that a certain unhistorical justice may be done. To assert this claim they are prepared to kick against the historical pricks. Thus in a recent statement there is a vehement condemnation of the brutal way in which the

Africans had been deprived of "their" land. And for this reason there must be a return to the land by all classes whose ancestors had been so ignominiously uprooted. To deny them this right to reverse the process of urbanisation or to give them the right merely to buy back their "ancestral land" is a great betrayal of "landless peasants who slave as agricultural labourers on the farms grabbed by Herrenvolk, or in the mines and factories...". Negrophilism and racialism are the implacable enemies of scientific development.

The claim to abstract rights expresses itself also in the defiant indifference to the utility value of land when the question of a solution to the agrarian problem is approached. There is a divorce between property and usufruct. *[....]*

### 6. The Rationalization of Agriculture

It is a commonplace that the transfer of the working population from the land to the cities has been proceeding ever since the advent of capitalism. This process is, first of all, caused by rural poverty as a consequence of landlessness, and secondly, to the magnetic attraction of expanding industries with their offer of higher rates of renumeration and, generally speaking, to improved social amenities. *[....]*

What is not generally known is that with the mechanization of agriculture fewer hands are needed to produce a certain output; and since moreover, the land area and agricultural resources are limited, it is in the interests of the economy generally, and of agriculture, more particularly, that this exodus of the rustic population should continue. There are, generally speaking, still too many people on the land for all to procure productive employment in agriculture. Accordingly, the supply of labour outstrips the demand; wages are consequently depressed; too many eke out an existence at a bare subsistence level on fragmented plots where their productivity, despite the colossal expenditure of human energy, is next to nothing. Such fruitless labour is called disguised employment which aggravates the imiseration of the people. *[....]*

In the light of the above, how should we then view the call by the 10-Point Programme for the distribution of the land "in conformity with the existing rural population?"

The present distribution of our rural population does not suit the requirements of agriculture and market control. This demographic arrangement is intimately connected with the ruling class policy to confine the oppressed masses in congested rural areas which are unproductive and remote from the market in order that they may continue to fulfil the function of furnishing labour for the pinchpenny agricultural industry and the parsimonious mines. It is a policy that is inimical to industrial development which demands freedom of movement so that the population may distribute itself in accordance with the labour requirements of all the sectors of the economy in general and industry in particular.

To divide "the land in conformity with the existing rural population," therefore, is to bow to the existing outmoded social and political arrangements. It takes the present distribution of the population as given once and for all and, in medieval fashion, regards landed property as so many rural centres around which the population should cluster, without reference to the development of the productive forces and quite in conformity with the patriarchal, sentimental attachment to the soil. *[....]*

It is the task of a democratic government to syphon off more people from the land by abolishing the pass law system and stimulating industrial development on the basis of equal opportunities for all. Then, instead of distributing the land among those who wish to till the soil, it must allow them to distribute themselves freely in relation to the productive areas and the requirements of the market. This means placing the land at the disposal of those who wish to till it, unfettered by the barriers of fences which are the badge of private property. The full development of agriculture calls, in a word, for the nationalisation of the land as the first step in the struggle for liberation. *[....]*

Nationalisation is the most thoroughgoing democratic measure and the last barrier to the struggle for a non-exploitative society. Indeed, in as much as it constitutes a vital encroachment on an important sector of private property, it may be called an important step in the struggle for social equality.

Historical experience has taught us that, with the consummation of the democratic struggle, the progress by the working class government towards an all-embracing rational society must necessarily pass through a number of transitional phases. This historical gradualism, to which the working class must adhere, even if, at times, with ill-concealed impatience, is necessitated by the presence of a peasant majority who must be shown by actual experience the superiority of collectivization before they are prepared to relegate all their illusions about private property and small-scale production to the limbo of forgotten things.

It has been said that the peasants will judge an issue on the basis of actual experience and pre-judge another on the basis of their accumulated prejudices. This points to a dualism in their class psychology of which the working class leadership must take cognizance. They have reason besides their time-hallowed prejudices, a future as well as a historical past. Social democracy must bring out the forward-moving traits in their class make-up without pandering to the backward traits in their character.

How does this historical lesson apply to our struggle? From the point of view of consistent democracy, our struggle is not complicated by a peasant majority. More fortunately, there is not within our movement an organised bourgeois party with a political apparat. In short, our movement does not consist of the classical bloc of four classes which by virtue of the specific weight of the middle and small middle class elements can circumscribe the scope of the struggle and even oust the working class as a minority group. This favourable historical circumstance leads one to suggest that, given the proper social democratic leadership, the workers can be placed in sole control with the consummation of the democratic phase by forming a majority government. They can then make their ascent to human history without having to pass through a number of transitional phases. The political line separating the minimal and maximal programmes is thereby removed and becomes of academic interest only. *[....]*

## NOTES

1. The SAIRR is a research institute which produces an annual *Survey of Race Relations*, conducts research projects and analyses legislation placed before Parliament. Like the Joint Council movement, it was inspired by the visit of Ghanaian-born educator Dr James Aggrey to South Africa in the early 1920s, and it was founded in 1929 under the leadership of J. D. Rheinallt Jones. Until 1948 it acted as a pressure group on the government but the apartheid regime saw it as a dangerous "liberal" body. From an opposing viewpoint, those in the NEUM saw it as "... the home of the Liberals of the Cape, Johannesburg, Natal and particular places like Fort Hare, Lovedale and St. Matthew's" (Ntantala 1992:169).

2. The YCL was formed in 1921 by E. R. Roux and other young people to address the "working youth" – at that time, white youth. Supported by the Young Communist International, in 1924 a small minority of individuals, including Roux and Willie Kalk, successfully pushed a "pro-Native" policy in the YCL and began recruiting Africans. S. P. Bunting, Roux and a few others were then able to push this policy through the CPSA in December 1924, when the majority voted not to reapply for affiliation to the SALP. Apparently dormant in the late 1920s and '30s, the YCL was revived in the early 1940s. In 1940 a group of white students in their teens launched a Junior Left Club. This collapsed and the nucleus attempted, again unsuccessfully, to build up a Youth League. This nucleus subsequently launched the YCL, which ran a Debating Club and Speakers' Training Course. Lionel Forman and Ruth First were active members. From 28 December 1944 to 1 January 1945 the YCL held a National Conference chaired by Hilda Watts and Ruth First. The delegates included: J. Shedrin, B. Uranovsky, R. First, L. Forman, A. Coe, B. du Plessis, S. Reddy, T. Gwala and T. van Huzer. Much of the discussion concerned the relationship between the CPSA and the YCL, with the Party wanting the YCL to include a statement that "the Y.C.L. follows a Communist Party policy" in its constitution. All the YCL delegates agreed that the YCL should maintain its independence while the Party members at the conference, such as Dr Dadoo, argued that complete independence was not necessary. However, Ruth First successfully carried the YCL position. The YCL's request that a representative be allowed to voice its views at the Party Conference was denied. A resolution that the Party appoint a National YCL organiser was defeated on the grounds that the YCL needed its complete independence, a case in point being the rapid growth of an independent YCL in Britain. See *Young Communist League Newsletter*, no. 5, April-May 1945 (editor's possession).

3. John David Rheinallt Jones (1884-1953), born in Wales, was a leading figure in the Joint Council movement and, from 1929, first Secretary, Director and guiding spirit of the SAIRR. He gave evidence before almost all government commissions on African affairs from 1920 to 1950. He was Natives' Senator for the Orange Free State and Transvaal from 1937 to '42, when he lost his bid for re-election to Hyman Basner.

4. Moshe Noah Averbach, who used the pseudonym A. Mon, emigrated from Europe to Palestine and then to South Africa, where he owned a grocery shop in District Six, Cape Town. He joined the CPSA and the Gezerd (*Gezelshaft far Erd*), a Jewish, Yiddish-speaking CPSA-aligned organisation meaning "Go Back to the Land", which supported the settlement of Russian Jews in Birobidjan, in eastern Soviet Union. He and the core of the Lenin Club were expelled from the Gezerd, following the 1932 visit of Comintern representative Gina Medem. He returned to Palestine after World War Two. This document is extracted from Averbach's commentary on Trotsky's 1935 letter to the South African comrades. See *South Africa's Radical Tradition*, Volume One, Document 51.

5. See the discussion of the proposals made by the Transvaal Agricultural Union in Documents 59 and 60. Jan Christian Smuts (1870-1950) – a scholar, a soldier in the Anglo-Boer war, an architect of the Union of South Africa in 1910, Prime Minister from 1919 to 1924 and 1939 to 1948, and a founder of the UN. When Smuts became Prime Minister in 1939 he pushed South Africa to join World War Two, and he and his Minister of Native Affairs, Deneys Reitz, temporarily relaxed influx controls to allow blacks to come to towns, thereby facilitating war-fuelled industrial growth. This temporary liberalisation caused concerns about labour shortages in the agricultural sector and fears amongst whites that segregation would be reversed. But only a few months after the relaxation of pass laws, the government tightened them.

6. The Progressive Forum, an affiliate of the NEUM, was a Johannesburg-based study forum which examined international events and engaged in some discussion of Marxist theory. The PF began as a circle of intellectuals, most based at the University of the Witwatersrand; in the early 1950s it was attended by Jennifer Davis, Baruch Hirson, Andrew Lukele, Dan Mokonyane, Seymour Papert and Roseinnes Phahle amongst others. The PF contained a wide range of political positions, and as a whole it was more overtly socialist than the NEUM; probably a third of its members thought themselves Marxists or Trotskyists. Two conflicting theoretical conceptions predominated in the PF, as in the NEUM. Some thought that South Africa was still backwards, and that revolutionary potential lay in a national struggle; hence organising on a socialist programme was premature. Two reasons were commonly given to support this position: first, the white working class would not support black workers at that stage; second, the

weakness of the black proletariat demanded its alliance with non-working-class sections of blacks like peasants and intellectuals. Such an alliance raised the problem of how to keep the movement from being co-opted. On the other side were those who believed in a single stage revolution, a view which was strongly held by Western Cape Trotskyists, although few dared to espouse this position openly either in or out of the NEUM. The PF's influence went beyond its tiny size – in the early 1950s it numbered about 25, mostly blacks – and it began attracting youth from the township to its weekly discussions. Its influence went as far as Natal, where it had a branch in Dundee and where it played a role in the formation of a pro-NEUM grouping in the NIC around 1951-52. By the late 1950s differences had emerged over the needs for grassroots work and for organisation of factory workers, which paralleled divisions within other NEUM affiliates. The NEUM's lack of participation in township struggles came to the fore as the PF slowly drew township youths from Soweto and Alexandra into its ranks. Pushed by the observation that the ANC was involved in urban campaigns while the NEUM remained aloof, some people suggested working on joint campaigns with the ANC. The majority in the PF remained very much influenced by Tabata's argument that most black workers were migrant labourers, essentially a landless peasantry, to be organised first in the reserves. Hirson, for one, felt that efforts to critically evaluate I. B. Tabata's book, *The All-African Convention*, were stifled. Nonetheless, there was a growing feeling that the NEUM was underestimating the significance of the urban working class. For a number, the NEUM's refusal to actively assist the 1957 Alexandra Bus Boycott was a catalyst to quit the PF. Several PF regulars from Alexandra pulled out with Vincent Swart and Dan Mokanyane, assistant secretary of the Alexandra People's Transport Committee, and formed a South African section of the Movement for Democracy of Content. By the end of the decade the PF was in fragments. See also Hirson (1995:256-64).

7   Joe Slovo (1926-95) immigrated from Lithuania, joined the CPSA as a teenager, trained as a lawyer, became a leading figure in the SACP and Chief of Staff of MK. In the 1950s he was a founder of the COD and on the consultative committee of the Congress Alliance. He was repeatedly banned and was a Treason Trial defendant between 1956 and 1958. In 1963 he went into exile for several decades. In 1985, he became the first white person to serve on the ANC National Executive Committee. As SACP Chair and General Secretary in the 1980s and '90s, he helped move the Party towards negotiations. His 1990 pamphlet, *Has Socialism Failed?* was a critique of Stalinism and committed the Party to multi-party democracy. As a leading negotiator at Codesa, he introduced the controversial "Sunset Clauses" protecting the composition of the civil service, thereby facilitating compromise between the NP and ANC. He was Minister of Housing in the GNU until his death. For his autobiography see Slovo (1995).

8   Hosea Jaffe – a socialist who worked in the FIOSA and subsequently joined the NEUM, helping to build up its network of educational fellowships in the Cape Peninsula. Under the pseudonym Nxele, he wrote a series on "The History of Despotism" in *The Torch*. In 1952, under the pseudonym Mnguni, he wrote the seminal *Three Hundred Years*, an early radical revisionist history of South Africa, which was widely read in Left circles. At the time of the NEUM split in 1958, he sided with Benjamin Kies, arguing that AAC leadership was conceding to African nationalism. Shortly thereafter he left South Africa and lived in Kenya, Ethiopia and Europe. He has written several books and articles on uneven development and on African history and politics.

9   For considerations of space, the footnote references within the original document have been omitted. The sources cited in the original text include: Patterson, *The Last Trek*; *Union Year Book, 1941*; *Viljoen Commission Report*; Roberts, *Labour in the Farm Economy*; *The Student*, July 1957; *Ikhwezi Lomso*, September 1958; Owen, *The Russian Peasant Movement, 1906-1917*; Mandelbaum, *The Industrialisation of Backward Areas*; Gluckstein, *Mao's China*; *Peking Review*, July 15, 1958; Frankel, *Capital Investment in Africa*; Simpson, *The Ejido: Mexico's Way Out*; Brooks, *History of South Africa's Native Policy*; De Kiewiet, *The Imperial Factor in South Africa*; Desai, *Social Background to Indian Nationalism*; Dutt, *India Today*; Agar-Hamilton, *The Road to the North* and *The Native Policy of the Voortrekkers*; Luxemburg, *The Accumulation of Capital*; Plaatje, *Native Life in South Africa* and Van der Horst, *Native Labour in South Africa*.

10  In the original document the first footnote states: "The terms 'Hottentots' and 'Bushmen' are regarded as terms of abuse. It is preferable nowadays to call them respectively, the Khoi-Khoin and the Batwa."

11  See Document 30.

12  As Premier of Russia from 1906 to 1911, Peter Arkadevich Stolypin (1862-1911) enacted a series of agrarian reforms which aimed to prevent a peasant revolution and stabilise the czarist regime by promoting the class differentiation of the peasantry and fostering a small yeoman class to act as a social bulwark against rural uprisings.

13  See Document 66.

# Part Four

## The turn to armed struggle

**EDITOR'S NOTE**

*The turn to armed struggle in South Africa began in the countryside as rural people sought to resist state intervention and repression. Initially, urban-based intellectuals and political activists were reticent about supplying arms to rural areas. However, for most South Africans involved in the liberation struggle, the 1960 Sharpeville massacre marked a turning point, a recognition that the methods of passive resistance and defiance were inadequate means to achieve social reforms. The refusal of the South African state to consider any form of negotiations or reform led perforce to armed struggle. In the early 1960s, the various political organisations within the liberation movement adopted diverse approaches to armed struggle. MK, the armed wing of the ANC and SACP, advocated sabotage as an intermediate step towards guerrilla warfare. Poqo, linked to the PAC, was a loosely-organised network with a populist orientation that lacked a clear-cut strategic view. The NEUM delayed considering armed struggle until 1963. The YCCC and NLF, most of whose members had broken from the NEUM in frustration over its reticence to adopt an activist stance, tried to develop a strategic conception of the relationship of guerrilla struggle to national liberation in a racially-divided society. The tiny NCL/ARM, like MK, also engaged in sabotage but was isolated and lacked a mass base.*

Document 68
Ben Turok[1], *The Pondo Revolt* [c. 1960]

*[....]* AFTER many months of pretence that nothing untoward was happening in Pondoland, the Government has now admitted that 4 769 people have been arrested during the present Emergency.

Reports filtering through the official ban on news indicate that a minor war is in progress in East Pondoland and that hundreds of homes have been razed to the ground, thousands of families broken up and made homeless, and that famine threatens the whole area.

Furthermore, the troubles are no longer confined to East Pondoland but have spread throughout the whole Transkei. The whole of the Xosa people have been inspired by the Pondo resistance and the struggle against Bantu Authorities has been mounted throughout the area. There is now every reason to believe that the situation will continue to deteriorate and is likely to spread to all the reserves of the Union.

Because of the unique character of the struggle in East Pondoland and the example it has set to the other rural peoples, the Pondo Revolt merits special study.

THE PEOPLE OF PONDOLAND
THE Pondo people form part of the Xosa national group. They are renown for their strong tribal ties and the firm unity that has deep roots in their past.

Unlike most of the other African peoples of South Africa, the Pondos were not involved in the numerous wars between white and black – they were never defeated in battle. Pondoland was annexed by the Cape Colony in 1894 but has always been an African territory with European influence limited to a few thousand missionaries, traders and civil servants.

The pride of the Pondo people in their customs and traditions is legend.

East Pondoland, the centre of the present Pondo revolt, consists of the districts of Bizana, Flagstaff, Lusikisiki, Tabankulu and Mt. Ayliff with a population of over 250 000 people. It was intended by the Government to be one of the nine Regional Authorities for the Transkei. But little progress had been made in this respect.

In travelling through Pondoland one is struck by the startling difference between East Pondoland and West Pondoland, where Bantu Authorities have been in force for some time. Here large tracts of land have been fenced off, huts are clustered together in controlled villages, few cattle are to be seen and very little land is now under plough. By contrast East Pondoland presents a picture of vast stretches of lush vegetation where the cattle are fat and much land is under cultivation. There is a general air of greater activity and prosperity.

It was the Government's efforts to enforce its Great Design, in this East Pondoland area of peace and tranquility, that led to the most violent and determined resistance it has yet encountered in the Reserves of South Africa.

## BANTUSTAN – POLICY OF DESPERATION

THE Government's attempts to interfere with the traditional tribal institutions in Pondoland was no chance event, it was the result of a conscious effort on their part to find a new policy for the people of South Africa.

This arose directly from the need of the governing Nationalist Party for some political solution to the critical problems facing them. With events elsewhere in Africa highlighting the rapid awakening of the African giant, and with the increasing political consciousness of the Non-Whites in South Africa, the situation seemed desperate.

In this climate of alarm and uncertainty the evil genius of Afrikaner Nationalism, Dr. Verwoerd, pulled the theory of Bantustans out of the hat to save his party from political bankruptcy. Having taken the plunge with the new policy, the Nationalists were forced, when challenged by opposition forces, into making reckless statements that they knew to be sheer bluff.

"The Nationalist Party is prepared to divide South Africa," said Mr. J. J. Fouche, Minister of Defence.

"If they want it (independence) they will be free to have it," Mr. De Wet Nel said in Parliament.

Nationalists who had been reared on the old fashioned 'baasskap' of Mr. Strydom must have been startled by the finality of Mr. Louw's statement at the United Nations to the effect that the Government believed in "separate Bantu communities which can eventually attain full self-government." And their confusion was even more confounded when this statement received the blessing of Dr. Verwoerd at a public meeting.

The breathtaking boldness of the Nationalist leaders misled many whites. Here was the straw they could grasp in the hope that European privilege and domination could be maintained in the developed areas of the Union at the cost of ceding the poverty stricken reserves, which were valueless to them in any case.

Some even accepted Nationalist arguments that this policy fully justified the Government's attitude of no concessions to the strident demands for political rights by the urban Africans. The poverty-stricken reserves were to be their homelands and they would be expected to find their political emancipation in these overcrowded backwaters of civilization.

However, while the Government was putting up a pretence of preparing the reserves for autonomy, it had to ensure that real power would remain in the hands of its officials. The technique employed was that of seizing hold of the tribal machinery and subverting it from within. Bantu authorities came to mean the conversion of the tribal system which had been evolved by the African people over the centuries and which was basically democratic, into a Government-run institution. The chiefs who were previously the respected spokesmen of the people were turned into puppets of officialdom. Many chiefs showed reluctance to accept the new set-up, but these were either coaxed with promises of greater authority or intimidated into conformity with threats of deposition or even banishment.

OTHER ADVANTAGES
THE Government saw many other advantages to be gained from their scheme. The Bantu Self-Government Act provides for the stratification of African society into a complex system of tribal, regional and territorial authorities. With this machinery the Government hoped to so enmesh the Africans in the various levels of "authorities" that they would lose their perspectives. By giving these councils very limited local powers it was hoped that they would concentrate all their attention on tribal matters and turn away from larger political issues.

Mr. Govan Mbeki maintains that in this the Government was following the traditional policy of the Native Affairs Department.[3] "They had hoped that the Africans would be so absorbed in the discussion of petty matters of local and tribal interest (in the Bunga) that they would cease to aspire to have a place in the political sun."

The Government expected to have more success in this regard with Bantu Authorities because democratic elections had been done away with and they now had almost complete control of the new councils.

THE CREATION OF CLASSES
REALISING its failure to win supporters amongst the African people in the towns, the Government is making concerted efforts not to suffer the same handicap in the reserves. Their first step to gain supporters was the winning over of the chiefs and their installation as puppets within the Bantu Authorities hierarchy. The second step was to foster the growth of a middle-class consisting of professional men and traders. The third was to encourage the emergence of a new class of comparatively well-to-do peasants, farming on large pieces of land. These three categories were to be privileged, but dependent on Government favour. They were to perform a dual function, – to act as the authority over the mass of the Africans, and serve as a constant reminder that collaboration with the Government pays off. In addition the Nationalists would use this upper-crust to disarm their critics. Here, in the Bantu "homelands", they could say, "the Bantu can develop to the highest levels."

SQUEEZED OFF THE LAND
DRASTIC interference with the traditional system of land allocation is involved in the creation of a class of better-off peasant. Land in the reserves was previously controlled communally and farmed in strips allocated to individual peasants by the chief. It is of course true that these strips were too small to enable families to make a living off them and the acute shortage of land left many peasants without strips, forcing them to rely solely on their cattle grazed on the commonage.

Government policy now is to "remove from the land all those who have no arable allotments and place them in special settlements consisting of the landless and the dispossessed." The intention is to drive "the landless sections of the community to be rehoused in rural villages." Of all the drastic and foolish steps that the Nationalist Government has taken in the pursuance of its ideology, this is the most explosive.

This threat of dispossession of their land the African people regard as the removal of their last shred of security. In spite of all their limitations, the reserves have nevertheless been a hedge against the perils of unemployment and the constant hazards of influx control.

What is more, it seems highly likely that the removal of these people from the land is connected with the establishment of the "border industries" to which the Government is constantly referring. Thus, in addition to supplying the present industrial areas and farms with labour, the reserves are to be still further denuded of their manpower in order to staff the White-owned factories to be established on their boundaries.

## THE IMPOSITION OF BANTU AUTHORITIES

MANY of the above facets of Government policy remained hidden for a long time. The chiefs in some areas did not recognise the trap that lay beneath the sugary promises of the Department of Bantu "Development," accepting Bantu Authorities at their face value as a genuine step towards autonomy.

But the Verwoerd tactics never deceived the vast majority of ordinary people – the very people without whom its achievement was impossible. From the start, popular African leaders stated categorically that they had no confidence in the new "Bantu Authorities," and that their aspirations could never be realised within the narrow confines of the reserves. South Africa must be regarded as a single whole, they stressed, and demanded representation in the central authority, Parliament.

African representatives in Parliament launched a determined attack on the Bantu Self-Government Bill. They objected to the political division of South Africa and to the exclusion of any representatives of the African people from the legislative body which made the laws governing them.

More important still, the new policy was rejected by the people in the areas in which it was being applied. While the Bantustan Debate was raging in the political arena, the African people in the reserves were fighting a bitter battle against the imposition of this system.

In some areas the people would have nothing to do with the Government sponsored "celebrations" inaugurating the new Authorities.

"At the first official ceremony to mark the establishment of a Regional Authority in the Transvaal on the 7th August, 1959, near Zeerust, about 250 people attended of the 28 000 people covered by the Authority," states the 1958/9 Race Relations Survey.

During 1958 large sections of the Ba Pedi tribe of Sekhukuniland had resisted the Bantu Authorities system. The acting chief Moroamoche and leading Councillors were banished, 338 Africans arrested, and the area was patrolled by police for the whole of 1959. The whole country was shocked when many tribesmen received life sentences in the drawn out proceedings that followed the disturbances.

Opposition to the "betterment-schemes" which are closely linked with Bantu Authorities was a contributory cause of the widespread demonstrations in Natal in August 1959.

In the Transkei and Ciskei opposition to Bantu Authorities was shown in sudden eruptions of violence in many areas.

## EAST PONDOLAND RESISTS

THE revolt in East Pondoland was destined to be even more widespread than elsewhere. From the start, the Government made the serious error of choosing as their arch-champion of Bantu Authorities, Chief Botha Sigcau, a man already discredited in the eyes of his people. As far back as 1939, when the choice had to be made of a successor to the Paramount Chieftainship of East Pondoland, the Government of the day choose Chief Botha in preference to his half brother, Nelson who was the rightful heir. The Pondo's did not accept this appointment, and resented Chief Botha for having taken office. Thus, when the Nationalists used Chief Botha to introduce Bantu Authorities into the area in 1957, they had lost before they started.

Many efforts were made by the authorities to persuade the Pondos to accept the system voluntarily, but they met with little success. In 1958, all the Pondoland districts were invited to send representatives to a large gathering called by the Minister of Bantu Administration and Development, Mr. De Wet Nel, and Botha Sigcau. The people were led to believe that the gathering was some sort of celebration, but found on arrival that it was an attempt to get Bantu Authorities under way. "Chief Botha announced that he had been promoted to take over the chair of the Chief Magistrate of Umtata, and that in turn some of the Chiefs would be promoted in the various districts. The Pondo court would be enhanced in status, and great changes would be brought about – in short, the people were told that they were getting self-Government."

In practice, however, it worked out that Chief Botha alone made promotions, and it was he who selected councillors for the courts from his own supporters. The people steadily lost confidence in the courts and corruption set in among the councillors who knew that their position depended not on the goodwill of the people, but only on their maintaining their friendship with Chief Botha. It was this cancer in the heart of tribal justice that was one of the main reasons for the breakdown of the tribal structure, and for the subsequent development of a new system during the Pondo revolt.

The rot ate ever deeper into the once healthy organism of tribal life. Government appointees to positions of authority were increasingly spurned by the people, and they had to rely on the might of the law and the strong arm of the magistrates to impose their authority. Many chiefs and headmen found that once they had committed themselves to supporting Bantu Authorities, an immense chasm developed between them and the people. Gone was the old give-and-take of tribal discussion and consultation. In its place there was now the autocratic power bestowed on the more ambitious chiefs who became arrogant in the knowledge that the Government's might was behind them. On one occasion, the Chief Magistrate of the Transkei said, "Don't forget you are the authority and power, and whosoever is against authority and power is against you...be your own police in your own interests....use moderate violence just like a good policeman."

By flattery, coercion, and blatant incitement the Government drove the chiefs into open conflict with their people.

## THE REVOLT DEVELOPS

THE Pondo people are more amenable to rule by hereditary chiefs than other less unified tribes, and less likely therefore to refuse to accept their dictates without good reason, provided – and here lies the crux of the matter – such chiefs or leaders are genuinely representative of the people...it is to be regretted that the Government has continued to insist on upholding the appointment of chiefs and headmen arbitrarily chosen by themselves rather than elected by the people concerned in a democratic fashion." In this outspoken manner the Institute of Race Relations put its finger neatly on the mainspring of the tremendous revolt against tradition and authority in East Pondoland.

The Government was well aware that the people of East Pondoland were opposed to Bantu Authorities from the very first. In 1957, the people voiced their objections at meetings which were held with their chiefs. But the chiefs refused to take up their peoples' grievances with the magistrates, either because they realised that the Government was determined to carry its policy through and would not tolerate opposition, or because they were Chief Botha's men.

Dissatisfied with their chiefs' attitude the people sent deputations to the magistrates directly. In 1957, in the district of Bizana for example, a deputation was informed that their grievances would be referred to Pretoria. Nothing was heard for some time, and a year later, another deputation interviewed the new magistrate at Bizana who told them that he had no record of their earlier representations. The complaints were repeated but once again no reply was received from official quarters.

Frustration and dissatisfaction were building up, until matters boiled over in an outburst of anger at a meeting in the Isikelo location in East Pondoland. Two of the chief's councillors were asked to explain at an Inkundla what benefits the people would get from Bantu Authorities which they had been trying to popularise. When they failed to do so, the meeting decided that they should receive corporal punishment.

Dissatisfied with their own tribal leaders and with the local magistrate, the people sent word to the Chief magistrate of the Transkei asking him to come to the area. Instead of his visiting the troubled area, a detachment of police was sent in to arrest the leading spokesmen at the meeting.

Pondos in the Bizana district were incensed at the arrests and tension mounted. Hut burnings and demonstrations against chiefs, headmen and police interference took place in a growing number of locations during 1959. What was once a closely knit tribe was becoming a seething, intriguing, unhappy people. Tremendous pressure was put on tribal leaders by both the Pondos and the Government and they had to make their choice. Many of them chose to ignore the people's wishes and uphold those of the Government thus alienating themselves from their people completely.

A popular movement arose amongst the people in March 1960, and the Hill Committee, composed of commoners, was established. It was this committee which rallied the majority of the tribesmen in the Bizana district into open struggle against the authorities and their henchmen. The committee summoned a series of huge meetings, attended by thousands of Pondos, to discuss their plight and make plans to carry on the struggle. Inspired by these meetings neighbouring tribesmen from other districts in East Pondoland carried back the news to their areas.

Repeated requests by the Hill Committee for the magistrate to come and hear the peoples grievances were ignored, and instead they were informed that the meetings were illegal and should cease forthwith. At this stage the Government officials made it clear that they would have no dealings with the leaders of the popular movement and would continue to carry out Government policies through the channel of Bantu Authorities.

The Pondos then found that news of their meetings was reaching the magistrate's ears and that their new-found unity was being undermined from within by Government agents. Drastic action was taken against these informers, huts were burnt down, and many of them were forced to flee from the area.

In retaliation, a meeting of thousands of Pondos at Ngquza Hill was attacked by heavily armed police. Eleven Pondos were shot dead and 15 seriously wounded (Some reports put the number at 30 dead and 60 seriously wounded). The meeting had been summoned for mid-day but while the people were still gathering, helicopters followed by spotter-planes appeared over the hill, flying very low. A white flag was raised by one of the leaders as a sign that a peaceful meeting was being held, but soon afterwards vans of armed police arrived.

Tear-gas bombs were dropped, starting a veld fire, and as the gathering scattered in confusion the police opened fire with the same callous abandon as had been witnessed at Sharpeville and Langa.

Twenty-three Pondos were arrested after the meeting on a charge of "fighting". Nineteen were convicted and sentenced to terms ranging from 18 months and 6 strokes, to 21 months.

Subsequently, at an inquest on the shootings, the magistrate found that the firing of Sten gun bullets was "unjustified and excessive, even reckless."

Policing of the area increased after this incident. Saracens and radio cars were brought in. The breakdown between the authorities and the Pondos was complete.

## A COMMISSION IS APPOINTED

RECOGNISING that police massacres could not break the people's resistance, the Government announced that a Commission of Inquiry, composed of Bantu Administration officials, would be appointed to hear their grievances. Grievances there were many, the main one being that Bantu Authorities had never been accepted by the people, only by some chiefs, and that the system must be abandoned. The complaint was made that inferior education was being given to the children under Bantu Education and that the people had lost control of the schools.

Increased taxation was a serious source of dissatisfaction.

Livestock tax had increased from 6d. per head per annum in 1944 to 1/9d. Poll tax had increased by 15/- to £2.5.0 a year, and the original health levy of 1/- a year had become a 10/- general levy.

Other complaints related to the graft in the courts, and the general corruption that had set in among councillors and chiefs. The findings of the Commission were announced at a public meeting near Bizana on October 11th. It is significant that on this occasion the Government was forced to bypass their much-vaunted Bantu Authorities machinery in order to convey their findings to the people, and negotiate with the Hill Committee which had become the generally accepted tribal representative.

The Report contained a number of admissions of errors made in the creation of Bantu Authorities but few concessions on other important complaints. The Commissioners admitted that when Bantu Authorities were formed, the old customs of the tribes around Bizana were not observed... "and the people of Bizana had every right to complain....The laws and customs of the tribes should have been observed and they should have been given an opportunity to say who they wanted (in the nomination of tribal authorities)."

The Commission also found that £20 000 damages had been caused in the hut burnings.

The Pondos were far from satisfied with the Commissions findings. At a meeting on the 25th October, they finally announced their rejection of the Report, and expressed their determination to continue the struggle against Bantu Authorities.

They decided to stop paying taxes.

This momentous decision taken by thousands of Pondos, many of them delegates from distant locations, was a sharp reminder that the Pondos were in a desperate frame of mind. At the same time, five top leaders of the *Pondoland National Committee* surrendered themselves to the police as they had lost their appeal to the Supreme Court and had been refused bail. They had been sentenced to over a year for attending an illegal meeting!

Furthermore, as a mark of their anger at the jailing of their leaders, and in protest at the attitude adopted by most of the White people in Bizana, the people decided to boycott this town. The Pondos felt that the traders in Bizana had shown partiality towards the Government, instead of sympathising with the people from whom they made a living. One Pondo put it this way, "We boycott the traders because they helped the Government in trying to break us. When we boycott them we are boycotting the Government."

The Pondos also protested at the banning from Pondoland of Mr. R. Arenstein, their attorney, who had fought a valiant battle in the Bizana court for the Pondos. As a result the ban was partially lifted, allowing Mr. Arenstein to complete the defence of the cases then pending.[4]

## THE WHITE TRADERS

IT is useful to interrupt the story of the Revolt, at this stage, to take a look at the small islands of Whites in the heart of this African reserve. Recent events have caught the White traders and professional men in Pondoland completely unawares. While some of them did anticipate that the Government's interference with the tribal set up would bring trouble, they, who pride themselves on "knowing the Native," did not anticipate that the Pondo Revolt could take on its present dimensions. Even now, when they have themselves seen the resistance movement unfolding before their very eyes, they are still unable to credit the Pondos they "have grown up with," with the ability to organise so effectively.

And so they spread the story (in whispers), "The Communists are behind it." Or. even more bizarre, in the words of a senior magistrate of Umtata, "Chief Lutuli is organising it all from just over the river in Harding." (One would expect an official of the BAD to know that Chief Lutuli has been either in gaol or in confinement in Groutville, in Northern Natal, during the past year.)

The traders are in an invidious position. On the one hand the Government resents the existence of these pockets of predominantly English speaking people and can withdraw their trading licences at any time, while, on the other hand, the traders are aware that their connivance in the policing of Pondoland could bring even greater Pondo wrath upon them.

The fact remains that the military forces of occupation in Pondoland are using these white settlements as bases, and therefore, in the eyes of the Pondos these people are regarded as collaborators of the Government.

How much different is the position of the majority of white South Africans from that of the white traders in Pondoland?

## THE EMERGENCY IS DECLARED

THE first signal that the Government had decided to suppress the popular Pondo movement and was going onto the offensive, came with the arrest and banishment of Anderson Ganyile, a Pondo leader.[5] The movement of troops towards Pondoland followed, as if war had been declared. The Government even went as far as taking the ridiculous precaution of putting the navy on to guarding he coast of Pondoland against "Russian submarines!"

A State of Emergency was declared, and the previous curtain of silence that had been drawn around Pondoland was drawn still tighter. Recent reports filtering through to the press indicate that hundreds of Pondos have been arrested, screened and treated with extreme brutality.

A New Age eye-witness writes, "A large contingent of armed police and soldiers seal off an area, usually soon after midnight. Each hut is raided by two armed men who take away everything that remotely resembles a weapon. In some areas, even hoes are confiscated."

More recent reports indicate that the declaration of the State of Emergency has added fuel to the long smouldering fires of revolt in Pondoland and the Transkei as a whole. Violence and hut burnings are taking place over the whole area.

Above all, the declaration of the Emergency constitutes an outright admission of failure to suppress the resistance of the people, and the Government has yet to explain why it was necessary to introduce the army to stop the work of "outside agitators." It would be more correct to say that the Nationalist army of occupation is now trying to achieve what their forefathers could not manage – the complete subjugation of the Pondo people.

The story of Pondoland is a repetition of those of Zeerust, Sekhukuniland and Zululand. In each of these areas, widespread disturbances took place because of the imposition of Bantu Authorities. In each area the pattern of events leading up to the disturbances was similar. Only, in Pondoland, where the tribe was more unified than in other areas, the resistance has been more determined and more sustained.

## THE LESSONS OF THE PONDO STRUGGLE

EVERY struggle develops a momentum of its own; and as the struggle progresses new concepts arise, new demands are made, and the participants are locked in battle on a higher level. The Pondo Revolt is no exception, as can be seen from the changes that have taken place in the demands and approach of the Pondos during the course of the struggle.

In the first protests against Government dictatorship, the Pondos limited their demands to the issues that were of immediate concern. Even though the Government likes to pretend that the Pondos were stirred up by "outside agitators," the truth is that the Government pressed the people so hard that they had to fight back. Furthermore, initially, their methods of struggle were the traditional ones – the holding of meetings, deputations to the magistrate, and, as the crisis deepened, the burning of huts and expulsion of undesirables from their midst.

But their experience of the Government taught the people that these methods did not suffice. Peaceful meetings were broken up by aircraft, spokesmen at deputations were arrested by armed police, and representations about simple things like dipping were written down to "Communist agitation." The people realised that a Government which based its policies on pure force, and completely ignored peaceful representations, had to be opposed, and that the fraudulent Bantu Authorities had to be rejected in toto.

Thus the Pondos turned their attention to the bigger political issues responsible for their plight, and declared the demand for direct representation in Parliament. "Pondoland will be satisfied with nothing short of sending representatives to Parliament."

The tactics of the Pondos also underwent a change. The boycott of the traders – a new weapon in the reserves – was completely effective.[6] It highlighted the unity of the people, and gained much publicity for their struggle. More drastic still was the decision not to pay taxes, and the adoption of the slogan "no co-operation with the authorities." This step was supported by the decision to call for a withdrawal of labour from the mines and sugar estates which would thus force their employers to intervene.

These methods adopted by the Pondos show a maturity that is extraordinary for a people who were not particularly active in political movements in the past. It shows that the Africans in the reserves are perfectly capable of using their initiative in forging new weapons of struggle when the issues are sharp enough.

New conditions, have also created new forms of organisation. The recent developments have brought great changes in the tribal structure. The system of chieftainship is gone, probably never to return in the old form. The people of East Pondoland have elected the Hill Committee democratically, and it would seem likely that this system will remain whatever the outcome of the present struggle may be. One thing is certain, indirect rule through Chiefs accepted by the people, will never work again. The Government will either have to recognise the newly constituted authority of the Pondos – the Hill Committee – or it will have to rule by outright force alone.

THE BANTUSTAN BLUFF EXPOSED

THE revolt against authority and tradition in East Pondoland has great significance for South Africa. National issues which were still subject to debate and dispute before these events, have now been tested in practice, and shown to be completely unworkable.

Whereas it was previously the opposition parties and organisations which criticised and condemned the theory of Bantustans, it has now been rent asunder by the Africans themselves. "Autonomy," "Self-Government" and "Develop on your own lines" – all the deception of a politically bankrupt Government stand exposed as a hollow fraud, by the heroic resistance of the Pondo people.

Dr. Verwoerd's wondrous vision, elaborated at great length in Parliament, of a dynamic new policy that would solve the critical problems of South Africa, is a vision no more. Instead, there stands the stark reality of the South African police state – shed of all pretence of ruling by consent – ruling by force alone.

This is all the Nationalists have left to offer South Africa. As long as they remain in office there will be more and more Pondolands, with ever increasing strife, bloodshed and misery. This appalling prospect represents a challenge to us all.

## Document 69
### "We Must Learn New Methods of Work", *Congress Voice*, issued by the Emergency Committee of the A.N.C., 2, 2, May 1960

Now that Congress is banned, we have to learn new methods of work. We cannot just go on in the same way as before. If an organisation is illegal it has to observe the *rules of secrecy*, otherwise it will easily be destroyed by the Government.

This article tells you something about these new rules of Congress. They are:
1. Organise in small groups, instead of large branches.
2. Don't ask questions and don't answer questions,
3. Use leaflets instead of public meetings.
4. Centralised leadership instead of general meetings and Conferences.

One of the main rules of a secret organisation are that each member knows as little about the membership and leadership as possible. You know what you want to know, what is necessary for your work. More than that you do not know, and you should not want to know. The police have long ears. They have also nasty methods of torturing people to force them to give information. We know that most of our people are brave and loyal, that they will refuse to become informers on their fellow Congressmen – the worst crime a Congressmen can commit. But some people are too fond of talking. They may give away a secret to a friend, not meaning any harm...and then it is passed on from one mouth to another, until the Special Branch picks it up. Or some few people may even give way under pressure. If people do not know something, then they can not tell it to anyone. So here are two good rules for anyone who wants to help Congress in its freedom struggle:

1. DON'T ASK QUESTIONS. Do not try to find out who is in the Congress, or who is leading, or who is on a Committee. One who asks questions – whether he realises it or not – is not helping, but harming our Congress.
2. DON'T ANSWER QUESTIONS. If anyone asks you questions about people in Congress – ask him if he doesn't know that Congress is underground. "I don't know the answer, and if I did I wouldn't tell you." That may seem rude – but it is the right answer.

### IT JUST CAN NOT BE DONE THAT WAY

When our Congress was legal we always had general meetings and conferences to elect our leaders. That is the right way, and the democratic way. But we can't do it that way now that Congress is underground. Just think what it would mean. You have a general meeting, and if there is one spy there every member is gone. You have a conference, and one person can give away every delegate and every committee member. It just can't work. In fact if we try it will be the surest way to a smash the A.N.C. People will just have to have confidence and to be disciplined until we have fought and won our struggle for Congress to be open and legal again.

Another matter. There must not be any big meetings, If a branch has many members, they must not all meet together. They must divide up into little groups of three and four, to meet carefully and carry on the work. Their work must be organised and co-ordinated by a small executive appointed by and responsible to the Emergency Committee. That may sound very harsh and dictatorial. But it is the only way we can carry on Congress at this difficult period. There used to be some people in Congress who were forever arguing and quarreling about leadership. These people must change their ways, or else they are of no use to the movement at this stage. Serious and devoted fighters for freedom will not question these new rules. They will carry them out without hesitation.

### *NO PUBLIC MEETINGS*

Just suppose we had to call a public meeting in the name of the African National Congress, fly the green, gold and black banner and address the masses as we have always done in the past. That seems very inspiring and courageous. But, just think what would happen. In no time the police would arrive, put all the speakers and the audience in jail to join the thousands of others already inside. Soon every Congressman would be in jail, without anyone outsid to give leadership to our people. Thinking we are brave we would in fact be running away from the struggle. It is true we must be ready to go to prison if that is necessary in the interest of freedom. We Congress people are not afraid of prison. To prove that, look at all our brave leaders, now and for many years past, who are experienced prison graduates. But we must know that there are times when the right thing to do is not to go to jail, when it can be avoided, but to carry on the political work outside, and to keep the Congress going.

So we have to work underground. Now, just what does it mean, this *"underground"*? Does it mean that we just meet in little groups and make no attempts to lead the people? No, because the purpose of our Congress is to give leadership, and if we do not do that we might as well do nothing at all. Being underground means that we have to give leadership in a different way from before. We must rely on leaflets rather than meetings. In giving out leaflets we have to be careful not to be caught. Being underground means that we are a *secret society*. And the first rule of a secret society is that the members have to know how to keep secrets. That means – to put it crudely – to keep our mouths shut.

There are two ways we can learn these rules. The one way is to carry them out, and learn the new methods of work quickly so that we can make Congress a mighty organisation in the near future. The second way is to ignore the new rules, to behave recklessly and irresposibly, and see hundreds of our best people put out of action before we learn the same lesson the hard way. Let's hope we shall learn the rules the *first* way.

We do not like secrets. We have always been proud to be in Congress to do everything openly and publicly, to know we have nothing to hide and nothing to be ashamed of. It is this vicious White Supremacy Government, headed by Hitler-lovers like Verwoerd, Louw and Erasmus, that forces us to go underground and to work secretly.[7] All the same, once we are forced to work secretly we must do it properly, skilfully and effectively, so that the time will be brought nearer when this Government and its Fascists laws are got rid of, and we can live free lives, and organise and speak with freedom.

---

Document 70
*South Africa: An Analysis of the Political Situation in South Africa and the Nature of the Struggle for Liberation*[8] [late 1961]

*[....] THE STRUGGLE INTENSIFIES*
*[...]* the true struggle today has reached a new level. It has acquired depth and breadth

and is moving forward with a new momentum. The All-African Convention has once more issued a call for UNITY. It has called upon the oppressed in all walks of life to organise themselves into a Nation. For it is only as a Nation acting under a single unified command that they can prove themselves equal to the demands of the crucial situation.

The All-African Convention could now speak with greater authority, which it had earned over a long period during all the struggles of the peasants. It has earned the respect of the people, not only because its leaders has been instructed to remain in the country and face persecution together with the masses, but also because it has not hesitated to criticise the masses when it had considered them to be making mistakes.

To give one example: before the ill-prepared revolt in Pondoland in 1960, the peasant leaders had come all the way to the Eastern Cape to consult the Executive of the All-African Convention. They were advised against the revolt. However the masses ignored the advice, with disastrous results.

Now the fearlessness of the Convention leaders in going against the stream has borne good fruit. To-day most of those villages committees that participated in the Pondoland revolt belong to the All-African Convention. In addition to this, the leaders have come as individuals into the African Peoples' Democratic Union of Southern Africa (APDUSA), a national political organisation which is itself affiliated to the All-African Convention and the Unity Movement.

The last six months have seen the All-African Convention grow by leaps and bounds. In addition to the village committees all over the Transkei, it has now won over the *[MAKULUSPAN?]*, numerically the biggest organisation in all South Africa.[9] We have been penetrating also into the towns, where the firtst time African, Coloured and Indian workers and intellectuals are joining as individuals the new organisation, the APDUSA, which has captured the imagination of the oppressed.

As we write this document, news is coming in that the Verwoerd Government is letting loose its terrors on members of the African Peoples' Democratic Union of Southern Africa. And still the press maintains its silence.

*UNITY ESSENTIAL TO A PROTRACTED STRUGGLE*

If the history of the last twenty years has taught us anything at all, it is that the Movement will continue to suffer the unnecessary losses of our brave men and women, UNLESS UNITY IS ACHIEVED.

It has taught us:
(a) That unity is a prime necessity for the successful conduct of a protracted struggle.
(b) That a pre-condition for a united struggle is a complete break with the agents of Imperialism in South Africa.
(c) That the maximum unity can only be achieved in the actual conduct of the struggle, provided that the struggle is an independent one, free from the influence of the ideas of an enemy class, and has a principled base and a correct policy.
(d) That a nation-wide organisation under a central command is essential for the waging of a protracted struggle for liberation.

This means that the numerous organisations must be brought under one leadership. A national political organisation, like an army, has its strategy and its tactics, which must be synchronised and put into operation under a single unified command. If this is not done, anarchy will reign, with frustration disillusionment and wastage of human life following in its trail.

It should be added here that within the country itself, contrary to the beliefs abroad, there exists to-day far greater unity amongst the oppressed people of South Africa than there has been since the crisis of 1935, when all the African organisations of that time together decided to created the federal organisation, the All-African Convention, as the mouthpiece of the African people.

*NEO-COLONIALISM THE DANGER*
In conclusion, we feel that it is a matter of great urgency to point out that the struggle in South Africa has reached a critical stage which might decide the course of events and the fate of our people for a long time to come.

We ask the independent States in the continent of Africa who are committed to the assistance of their brothers in the South, to make a careful study of the complex situation in our country and to give us such assistance as will save us from the fate of NEO-COLONIALISM.

The decisions taken by them at the Addis Ababa Conference have far reaching implications. It is for this very reason that we would urge that a full understanding of our complex political problems is of paramount importance.

It is within the power of the independant States of Africa to give such assistance as might be used to land us in the quagmire of neo-colonialism.

It is equally within their power to assist in putting the struggle of the oppressed people of South Africa on the road leading to true independence, a road that leads to the achievement of that society where there will be no exploitation of man by man, a society in which every man and woman shall have the opportunity to develop his or her potentialities to the utmost. *[....]*

## Document 71
## National Committee for Liberation, Announcement [20 December 1961]

The National Committee announces that on 20 December 1961 it destroyed power lines in Johannesburg.

The National Committee for Liberation has been responsible for:
1. The removal of banished people to places of safety
2. The transportation of people overseas.
3. The taking of 20 nurses to a point of embarkation to Tanganyika.
4. The burning of the records at the Bantu Administration Tax Office in Delvers St, on 24/9/61
5. The destruction of a power line on the 9/10/61.

The NCL has taken this action as there is no longer any legal democratic way to oppose the Nationalist Government.

The NCL welcomes the appearance of the "Assegai of the Nation". Both the "Assegai of the Nation" and the NCL support the Liberatory Movement. However, no one group has the responsibility for fighting for the freedom of its country.

The NCL is a non-racial organisation whose members hold varying political opinions, our attack is against the Nationalist Government and not individuals, and our members are trained to protect the lives of people in all circumstances.

We warn the Government that we will fight until the last vestige of white domination has been eradicated. We stand for a non-racial state based on equality for all and we will cary on the fight until this has been achieved.

## Document 72
"A Landmark in South Africa's History: The Sixth National Conference of the South African Communist Party", *International Bulletin*, no. 4, December 1962

*A SUCCESSFUL CONFERENCE*
The Sixth National Conference of the Party was recently held. Like all previous conferences of the Party, it took place underground inside South Africa. Conditions were exceptionally difficult, the Verwoerd Government having intensified greatly its fascist repressive measures. Despite this, all districts of the Party were represented at the Conference. The delegates, most of whom were African workers, came from all parts of the country. The main tasks of the Conference were:
* To consider and adopt the new PROGRAMME of the Party.
* To discuss the REPORT of the Central Committee and consider the main tasks of the Party in the light of the present international and South African situation.
* To elect a new Central Committee.

These tasks were completed in an atmosphere of the greatest confidence, unity and determination. The Conference is an important milestone in the development of the Party.

In its report to the Conference the Central Committee pointed out that as the main task before the delegates was the adoption of the new Party Programme, it did not propose to submit an exhaustive review of world and local affairs. "During the past few months several documents dealing with important problems of the movement here and internationally have been circulated, and all units of the Party have sent in their views and comments on them. These documents and the policies contained in them, form part of the political policies of the Central Committee which you are asked to consider, asked to confirm or alter as you think fit."

### THE SOUTH AFRICAN SCENE
Turning to South African affairs, the Report pointed out that events since 1960 had fully borne out the view of the 5th National Conference that the government was increasingly turning to the use of violence and military force against the people and relying on rule by decree to replace the rule of law and that the people could no longer rely on traditional non-violent methods of struggle and protest, but would have to find new answers if their cause was to be victorious. *[....]*

It was true that the methods of terror had led to a temporary decline in the mass struggle. But the conditions causing the crisis and the inherent instability of the regime had not been removed: they had been intensified.

"The cause of the crisis, leading directly to the policy of police and military dictatorship is the internal political opposition of the people in this country. Internal political opposition has not been stopped by the new methods. But it has to a large measure been forced into silence; it has been weakened and brought to some extent under government control. In the past period we have not managed to overcome this effect of the new methods of dictatorship. Hence the absence of large-scale mass political activity."

The lull in political activity did not mean that the people had resigned themselves to apartheid. The government had made no concessions; indeed oppression was steadily worsening. Nor had the government inflicted any real defeat on the forces of resistance. There were bound to be new upsurges of the people's struggle, more determined and realistic than ever.

"The swing to dictatorship has led to the rapid development of new understanding amongst the people, to a rapid re-appraisal of the policy of non-violence which we had already criticised as wrong and harmful at the time of our last conference. It has led to new preparations for new forms of struggle, to the opening blows in a campaign of force against the government. It has led the whole people's movement into improving its illegal apparatus, into preparing itself for illegal action. The swing to dictatorial methods of rule has thus paved the way for a new, people's offensive against the government, based now on a combination of violent and non-violent methods. Already in the mass response to the demonstrations of the past few weeks we can see signs that the new methods of popular resistance have revived the spirit and morale of the masses; and thus have brought us once again within striking distance of a new round of mass struggles.

"The strengthening of the government by means of the open rule of force has thus been shown to be a temporary process. The balance is swinging once again in favour of the people; new opportunities for mass struggle, mass action are arising. It is necessary for us to understand not just the negative side of government oppression but also the positive aspect, the new mood, the new possibilities, the new fighting spirit it is producing. Without such understanding and appreciation we will be unable to lead the people forward.

"The most urgent need of the whole movement is now to devise new methods of mass work and mass agitation to meet the new situation. If we can do so, then we will be able to exploit fully the weakness of the government. We will be able to reveal the reality of the situation – which is that the government is inherently weak and unstable *when the masses are in action*; that it can only show a convincing façade of strength when the people are passive. A start has been made by certain sections of the people to develop violent forms of anti-government action on a small, widely separated and sporadic basis. But this form of action is not and cannot be the whole answer for the peoples movement. In the long run the peoples' movement must find *mass methods* of struggle, both violent and non-violent, into which the whole democratic movement and all its supporters can be drawn, Without this approach, we will be unable to break the stalemate that appears to exist in South African politics; we will be unable to break out of the period of comparative inaction which has characterised the peoples' movement for over a year."

*The Future of the United Front*
The Report went on to discuss the future of the united front of national liberation, the

building of which remains the central task of the Party. Reference was made to a recent statement circulated by the Central Committee for discussion, dealing with developments within the Congress alliance; a statement which had been overwhelmingly endorsed by units in written statements of their viewpoint.[10]

"The character of the Congress Alliance has been changing during the past few years. The African National Congress was declared illegal followed by the Congress of Democrats. Continued stress in public work on the "Alliance" would give the impression that the "Congress movement" now consisting only of the South African Indian Congress, South African Congress of Trade Unions and South African Coloured People's Congress – had inherited the leadership of the national liberation movement. But in fact the leader of this movement is and always has been the African National Congress. The united front must remain. The reality of the alliance has never been its formal organisational set-up, its joint committees and joint utterances, but rather the fact that, at all times, there has been consultation and unity between the various congresses. This is the essence of the alliance which we must struggle to preserve, not the organisational apparatus which is no longer feasible with so much of the alliance already illegal."

"New forms of united front are also being developed. The main underground resistance movements – the African National Congress and the Communist Party – share a common immediate objective, the overthrow of White Supremacy, and the winning of the Freedom Charter. Although there is no formal relationship between these two bodies the masses of the people increasingly recognise that together they form the main leading forces in the freedom struggle. A new unity is growing in practice between the illegal peoples' organisations, on which the people's hopes of liberation now centre. We must take care therefore, not to present the legal Congress alliance as the sole symbol of leadership of the people's struggles. For it is not, and under present conditions cannot be. Attempts to portray it as such will only result in discouraging the people, leading them to a loss of confidence in the movement, and ultimately alienating them from the movement.

"In the same way a distorted presentation of our image abroad has alienated some people outside this country from us. Members returning from both official and unofficial visits abroad – and especially in Africa – have reported that generally, amongst African peoples and leaders, our policy of a multi-racial democratic alliance in the struggle for national freedom is not understood or supported. Undifferentiated hostility towards Whites and Asians leads them to suspect or despise the policy of the national liberation movements in this country. They regard that policy as some form of partnership of the Welensky type[11]; they consider it to be a concealed form of White leadership of the African national movement; they deduce from this that the Congress movement here is liberalistic, moderate, timid and compromising."

Unlike South Africa, with its long tradition of Communist and working class organisation, there have been no significant elements in the White and Asian minority communities uncompromisingly joining the Africans' freedom struggle. The Whites themselves, in most cases, are not a permanent and substantial part of the native population as they are in this country. Most of the leaders of the liberation movements are bourgeois nationalists.

"Influenced by the chauvinistic attitudes peculiar to bourgeois nationalism, they are generally not well informed about South African conditions, and tend to judge our actions not in the light of our real circumstances, but in the light of their own political experiences and their own conditions. From this rather narrow, parochial basis, they are attempting to develop a policy of universal application to Africa – and they find that the policy of the Congress movement here does not fall precisely into line. National chauvinism is strong wherever the working-class movement is weak, as it is in most of Africa. In Algeria the racial situation is closest to our own. Political struggle has been the sharpest and longest in Africa. The working class movement is highly developed with strong unions and its own political party. Significantly it is in Algeria that there is the greatest measure of agreement with Congress policies and acceptance of them as correct and militant in our special conditions. But elsewhere pressure is exercised indirectly by many leaders of African opinion to bring about a reappraisal of the non-racial Congress policy.

"To some extent, also, the reasons for misunderstanding and failure to appreciate our policies arise from certain errors in the work of the Congress movement itself. A tendency has grown up to allow the Alliance as such to overshadow the reality of the movement – which is that the A.N.C. is the leading core of the Congress movement, representing the African majority whose liberation is the main content of the liberation struggle. It is the alliance which has been seen abroad, increasingly as the Congress movement, and not the real national organisations, vastly unequal in size and in importance which make it up. The effect has been, in propaganda abroad, to eclipse the leading role and nature of the A.N.C.; and to mute the leading aim which is the liberation of the African majority. This tendency has become increasingly evident since the illegalising of the A.N.C., for since then the alliance has apparently been not one headed by the national movement of the African people, but instead to be manned by non-Africans seeking to speak for – and thus perhaps to lead? – the African majority.

"In correcting this false image projected abroad, there is a danger of going too far. We must not, under any circumstances, allow the fine spirit of internationalism which has characterised the Congress movement to give way to a narrow chauvinism, to racialism. We are under heavy pressure from elsewhere in Africa to adapt ourselves to the outlooks of bourgeois nationalism; we live surrounded by a society steeped in racialism and chauvinism; we operate in difficult conditions where the main aim of the Congress movement is illegal and thus restricted while its other members are not; and we suffer, as is said earlier in this report, from a tendency to concentrate too heavily on our own and African affairs to the exclusion of world affairs. All these factors make it imperative that our Party be constantly vigilant and on its guard not to fall into nationalist errors. We must wage a struggle against national chauvinism, no matter what our critics may say. We must not, under any circumstances, alter any aspect of our policy in any way to make it acceptable to our critics. We must judge our own conditions for ourselves, and formulate our own policies as we see fit in the best interests of the South African people. We must not allow our policies to be adapted opportunistically, to suit the views of others in order to gain their support, no matter how valuable or important that support may appear to be in the immediate problems we face. But at the same time, we must find a way to correct the erroneous image of the liberation movement which has been presented to people outside.

"We have no reason to change or to apologise for the character of the South African freedom movement as it really is: primarily a movement of the African people, the African National Congress, which has sought and has found loyal allies in organisations of the Indian and Coloured people, of militant non-racial trade unions, of democratic Whites. But we must not allow or give any pretext for a false and distorted picture of that movement to be projected abroad or at home by P.A.C. and other unscrupulous twisters of facts."

*The Fight against "Bantustans"*

Much of the attention of Conference was devoted to developing the struggle against the fraudulent and vicious scheme of the Verwoerd Government to partition South Africa: granting "independence and self-rule" to the Transkei and other so-called Bantu Homelands, while treating Africans as "aliens" in the remaining 87 per cent of South Africa. *[....]*

## PROBLEMS OF PARTY ORGANISATION

After dealing, with a number of other question of policy, ranging from methods of struggle, to South-West Africa and the Protectorates, Conference considered problems of improving the work of the Communist Party in the exceptionally difficult conditions prevailing in the country.

The Central Committee report drew attention to certain recent weaknesses in the sphere of discipline and party conduct. Cases had even arisen where members had opposed Party policy in meetings of mass organisations. Inner-Party documents had, through carelessness, been allowed to fall into the hands of the police; gossiping and loose talk about Party and other confidential matters had occurred. There was a chronic tendency to deal with Party directives in a tardy and cumbersome manner. The Report said that without discipline of a high level–

"Our Party, as a unified and united body of people with a single political line will disappear. We must now insist that our Party discipline be maintained on the highest level, that no members be permitted under any circumstances to oppose the Party policy except in inner Party discussions organised for that purpose. Especially in our conditions, breaches of Party discipline are a menace to the safety and continued existence of the Party and all its members, and must be treated sternly as such.

"The main weakness in our discipline, however, is not in the matter of supporting the Party line – in which our standards have been generally high. The main weakness has been in the matter of carrying out the Party rules and regulations scrupulously. Discipline requires every member to accept and carry out the decisions of the party; and amongst the important decisions of our Party are the ones covered by our rules – decisions affecting our security system, decisions regarding the handling of Party confidences and documents, decisions regarding prompt carrying out of Party tasks. It is in these respects that discipline has declined noticeably and dangerously in the recent period. This situation we cannot tolerate. Let this Conference be a turning point.

"Henceforward we must tighten up everywhere; we must put an end to loose talk and gossip, and treat with the utmost severity every breach of security, for without this we will not be able to survive the growing fierceness with which the government is attempting to destroy us.

"While laxness has developed on the one hand, an equally dangerous attitude of *recklessness* has also grown up on the other – an aspect of our laxness in observing our own security rules. We have suffered heavy casualties during the past year as a result of this spirit of recklessness, which has led in many cases to the overriding of security rules. *[....]*

"How do these breaches in our security and discipline arise? Largely they are the result of getting into a rut. We have been carrying on for so long that we begin to grow contemptuous of the enemy; we develop a type of fatalistic belief in our ability to outwit and outlive them; we no longer think deeply over every step we take, everything we do, but tend just to carry on in the way we have found satisfactory before, or to 'take a chance'. [....]

"Routinism has particularly handicapped our whole communications and contact system. We have recently had examples like these; one district complains that three weeks' notice of a leaflet distribution is too short a time for them to inform their members; another district forwards in September replies from a unit to a document titled 'Tasks of the New Year'. Repeatedly requests from the centre for the views of members go unanswered; repeatedly communications from units to the centre seem to vanish into space, with no echo or reply returning. [....]

"Especially on the side of personnel, there is a tendency always in an organisation such as ours to 'routinisms' – to keeping the man in the job because he has always been in the job. Normal democratic procedures – election of officials, criticism at general meetings etc. are not always possible in our conditions. We must find other ways to carry out the process of democratic renewal. When last did any district or the centre itself review its personnel, and ask whether they are doing the job properly, whether they are still the best people for the job or only hold the job because they have always held it, have not new cadres developed? In this matter, the sweeping democratic spirit of the new rules of the C.P.S.U. should be an inspiration to us.[12] [....]

After a full discussion on this aspect of the Report, Conference adopted the following Resolution on Organisation:

> During the past period, attitudes of 'routinism' have developed in our approach to matters of organisation, discipline, security and selection of personnel. Conference regards 'routinism' as the main weakness in our internal work, and resolves therefore to conduct a campaign throughout all sections of the organisation to review, and where necessary renew organisational methods and personnel, in order to equip our organisation for effective and quick action in present circumstances.

In particular, it calls for the following steps to be taken:

i. For all security regulations to be strictly applied, and for appropriate disciplinary action to be taken wherever breaches of these regulations occur.
ii. For constant vigilance against recklessness in the making and carrying out of decisions.
iii. For a complete review and shortening of our whole contact and communication system at district and centre levels, with a view to increasing the speed of communication.
iv. For a review and, where necessary, a replacement of personnel in positions of responsibility, in order to ensure that the best possible people fill all such positions.
v. For a review of the work and functioning of all units, and a re-allocation of detailed tasks on the basis of specialisation of as many units as possible in particular fields of work.

The Report of the Central Committee concluded by stating that favourable conditions existed for a big advance in the influence and standing of the Party. The severe anti-Communist repressions of the Nationalist government had the effect of fortifying the people's confidence in and respect for our Party. "In our ranks, in the Central Committee and at this Conference there is tremendous confidence that we can overcome our difficulties and make a great leap ahead. We can make that leap ahead if we see to it that all sides of our work go forward together – our political line, our organisation, our discipline and our understanding. Our new Programme gives us the basis for a vast educational drive among the politically conscious people of our country. It will enable us to explain more precisely and adequately than ever before what we stand for, what we believe, who we are. If we make use of this weapon we can make the coming year a year of great advance for our Party. We can see that the Party grows greatly in numbers and in the understanding of each member; that its influence extends to still wider sections of the population; that we play a more vital part in uniting and leading the people of our country for the downfall of White domination, for national democracy, peace and socialism."

### THE NEW PARTY PROGRAMME

Much of the time of the Conference was taken up in discussion of the Draft Programme which had been submitted well in advance by the Central Committee and circulated to all units for thorough discussion. [....]

"The Programme as a whole was adopted with only minor amendments to the Revised Text. Delegates, voicing the views of the rank and file of the Party in all districts, expressed the warmest enthusiasm about the new Party Programme as a great and inspiring document, a major achievement of our Party, summing up its experiences, throwing light on all our problems, the key to freedom.[13] The Conference also amended the Rules of the Party, strengthening the sections dealing with collective leadership, democratic centralism and discipline." [....]


Document 73
"Why Revolution?", *Assegai*, no. 2, March 1963

From March 21st till April 10th 1960, and for periods ranging from 1 day to the full 3 weeks, more than 500 000 workers brought industry to a standstill in the urban areas of South Africa. Without any sort of organised strength (not more than 10 per cent could have been organised into trade unions), and, more importantly, without their own political organisations to guide them, South Africa's young and virile workers, nevertheless, shook the capitalist state to its foundations. Only the most ruthless measures – the banning of the national organisations, the A.N.C. and the P.A.C.; the declaration of the State of Emergency the detention of 2 000 political activists, the arrest of 18 000 of our youth for shipment to the farms, the «legalised» brutality and hooliganism of the armed forces – restored «law and order» in the workers' residential suburbs.

The revolt of the masses which, in the immediate past had sped through the countryside – from Witzieshoek to Zeerust, from Sekhukhuniland to Zululand – and touched the urban-areas (Alexandra Bus Boycott, June 26th Stay-at-Home 1957), now erupted with full force in the towns. In the short period of three weeks, the quickening pulsebeat of the peoples anger with, and resistance to, their continued exploitation and oppression, drummed out its warning of impending doom to, and for, our monopoly capitalist, racist rulers.

*Though we did not win the battle that was triggered off by the Sharpeville massacre, there can be no doubt that the days of capitalist exploitation, national oppression and colour discrimination are rapidly drawing to a close.*

No longer is it a question of – WILL we be free?

Today it is a question of HOW?

For, though the peoples' upsurge was beaten back and battered down, the struggle continues and today has entered a new phase.

In Pondoland, in the very centre of the government's alleged stronghold amongst the African people, the Tribal Authority, with Matanzima at its head, exists in name only. Because of the uprising of the Pondoland peasants and their revolt against the Bantustan Bluff, the white rulers have been forced to declare a State of Emergency which has been in operation for the last three years. Matanzima, the government stooge, can only move around with a heavily armed bodyguard. Tribesmen have rightly sought to end his evil career. It is only a matter of time. The peasants quite rightly have shown that there is no place in our death and life struggle for sell-outs and quislings. Either you are with the people or with the government. There can be no two ways. Hundreds of Pondos have been ruthlessly killed, but still the struggle continues, in spite of all the modern arms of the white rulers.

For over 2 years "Mountain Committees" have voiced the demands of the reserve peasants: «DEMOCRACY, *not* tribal authorities; land, *not* fraudulent betterment schemes; no taxation *without* representation; proper, scientific education, *not* Bantu Education; seeds, tractors, ploughs, *not* dipping tanks, etc.»

The "Mountain Committees" are the real tribal authority. And, the example of Pondoland (about which we have more to say in another article) must soon spread to other reserve areas as well.

STATE VS PEOPLE

In the towns, because the State of Emergency solved none of our problems, (poverty wages; no political rights; high rents; passes, and the extension of the pass laws to African women; inefficient, not enough, and, far too expensive, transport services; long hours of work and so on, are still the reality of our everyday lives,) our anger and resentment has not disappeared, our determination to end domination and oppression has increased.

On the other hand more vicious laws have been bulldozered through the White Parliament. Following the 3 day strike in Easter, 1961, hundreds of our people were arrested, and many forced to go underground. The Sabotage Act, making it a hanging offence to effectively oppose White Supremacy, house arrests, an increase in banning, banishment and imprisonment, together with a better equipped all white army, with British, French and Belgian arms and aircraft, the training of white civilians in rifle shooting – this is the answer of the ruling class to our demands for higher wages and a full and equal share in the government of our country.

Driven below the surface our revolt has re-appeared in better organised and more prepared forms of class and national warfare against capitalist class rule and the political system of white domination. The emergence of Umwonto We Sizwe, its allegiance to the National Liberation Movement and its non-racial character, shows that with correct political organisation, leadership, strategy and tactics, we shall triumph, although many of us will die our struggle to be free men. Every new assault by us drives the White supremacists further into frenzy and desperation.

By correctly applying the theory and practice of scientific socialism to the experiences of our people and to the objective conditions that exist in South Africa, and, by participating fully in the struggles of the masses, South African Marxists can provide the Workers in town and country, and all the oppressed and exploited millions, with the leadership, guidance and organisational strength needed in the struggle for democracy and socialism.

*Why do we stress the role of the working class, working class ideas and the emergence of Sabotage in the present period of South African history ? Because more than any other events in the past history of our people, the explosions which shook South Africa, first during March/April 1960, and then in December 1961, plunged our country into the very heart of the anti-colonialist and World Workers Revolution.*

## THE WORLD WORKERS REVOLUTION

Socialism is that stage in the development of human society that leads mankind into Communnist society. The motive power of the world socialist revolution is the world workers revolution. Historians of the future will describe the period of social development which mankind is now passing through, as the epoch of socialist or, world revolutions. It is the period of change from capitalism to socialism.

Unleashed against the background of the first (1914-1918) imperialist world war, the world workers revolution recorded its first victory in the 1917 October Russian Revolution. The past 40 odd years have seen socialism grow tremendously in strength, whilst capitalism has, with ever-increasing speed, grown weaker. Despite reverses and setbacks that have been suffered during this period, socialism is today incomparably stronger than it was in 1917 when, the Russian working class under the brilliant leadership of the Russian Bolshevik (Communist) Party, seized power.

In the U.S.S.R., the Eastern European Peoples' Democracies, in China, North Korea, North Viet-Nam and Cuba, the material and cultural base for the transition to Communism has been, or is being laid; and swift gains in the living standards and general well-being of the people are recorded annually. Socialist construction is leading the people to a fuller, happier and freer life.

In France and Italy mass Communist Parties stand in the forefront of the peoples' struggles for peace, democracy and socialism; in the remaining west European countries, in the United Kingdom, in Japan and in the U.S.A. itself, the active resistance of the masses to the devilish schemes of the imperialists, combined with the strength of the socialist world, frustrates the plans of the monopoly capitalists to plunge mankind into a third world war in order to re-impose imperialist rule throughout the world.

With the ending of World War II (1945), movements of national liberation in the Middle East and Asia, Latin America and Africa have, with increasing speed, freed one colonial and semi-colonial country after another from the shackles of imperialist rule. Each declaration of independence strikes another mighty blow against the 20th Century colonialists.

## ANTI-COLONIALIST STRUGGLE

In Africa today there are 32 Independent States; all freed from the political domination of British, French and Belgian imperialists and colonialists. The fight to free themselves from the economic domination of the colonialists is gaining great momentum, although the wily Imperialists are using, all their tricks to make a comeback through the back door. America's role in the Congo; Britain's stand in Katanga; the offering of associate E.E.C. (Common Market) membership to the newly independent countries (which has been rightly recognised for what it is – neo-colonialism) are all apt examples.

Though in some of the independent states a capitalist, not a socialist path of development, has been chosen by the leaders of the liberation movements, even this development weakens imperialism, intensifying the contradictions within the capitalist sector of the world. Desperately though they struggle to retain their positions, using the age-old methods of brutality, violence, cunning and bribery (until recently in Algeria, in Kenya, the Congo, Angola, Mocambique, and the attempts to split the young African Trade Union Movement through funds issued by the International Confederation of Free Trade Unions, are some obvious examples in-Africa alone), defeat stares the imperialists in the face.

Until a short while ago, Marxists throughout the world, were concerned whether socialism in the U.S.S.R. could survive in a hostile world. Could an isolated and surrounded socialist state survive in a hostile, aggressive, capitalist world? Today we no longer ask this question; today we ask: how long can capitalism survive in the face of socialist advance?

Following upon World War I, one-sixth of the world Withdrew from the capitalist camp; following on the defeat of the Nazi-Fascist Alliance (World War II), the scale dipped even further in favour of socialism. *While recently, Cuba, a little island on the doorstep of the U.S.A., has successfully fought against gigantic odds for her right to build socialism, and her achievements are a source of encouragement and an outstanding example for us all.*

Today over one-third of humanity, one thousand million people, have embraced socialism.

## THE SOUTH AFRICAN REVOLUTION

The world-wide transition to socialism and South Africa's place in the world workers revolution has too often been lost sight of by many South Africans in the past. In the present state of the world the revolution should not be divised into two separate stages: first the national or democratic revolution and then the socialist revolution. Instead we must recognise now that socialism is the aim, with the achievement of national liberation, or the ending of the apartheid system, as only the first phase of the whole struggle. By recognising this the South African working class is given its correct place as leader throughout the South African Revolution. Because South Africa is a capitalist country, the most revolutionary class in our country is the working class. It has literally nothing to lose but its chains against the rule is important and if the revolutionary potential of the of capital. But the first phase of national liberation other classes and strata amongst the oppressed are ignored, this can lead only to the isolation of the working class movement from the masses – this must be avoided.

Of course, this does not mean that the peasants are to be ignored. The armed uprisings in the reserves (Sekhukhuniland, Zeerust, Pondoland) show that the peasants in South Africa will and can resist the authorities very effectively. But their ultimate success depends on the resistance of the workers in the towns. *The close alliance of the workers and the peasants is therefore an absolute necessity.*

Superimposed on the basic class divisions in South African society is the political system of white domination. Non-white South Africans are oppressed as migratory and/or rigidly-controlled, settled wage labourers. Despite the fact that some Africans have emerged from the ranks of the working class, all Africans are subjected to the same oppressive laws. Though non-white merchants, intellectuals, small farmers, professional men and so on, are also oppressed, it is first and foremost, as *workers*, that we oppressed. It is our *labour power* that the South African ruling class must be able to purchase if its neevr ending search for profits is to continue. The ruling class are small in number, whilst we are many. Even though it has the guns and the tanks, the army and the police, on its side, the South African ruling class knows that we are many; to strengthen its forces it bribes the white workers and dares not allow any African, Indian or Coloured attain «equal status» and thus expose the myth of «white supremacy».

UNITY OF VARIED INTERESTS

Because of the contradictions which exist in the Government's system of white domination, the few non-white South Africans who are no longer workers must also be kept in chains, suffering the same oppression as the millions who are exploited down the mines, in the factories and on the land. *Therefore the tendency is for all to join together to fight the Apartheid laws.*

Therefore national movements are formed to wage a joint struggle for a common programme, such as the Freedom Charter. These national movements are alliances of different classes and strata formed to resist the racial policies, which, though aimed directly at the workers to secure for the capitalists the maximum profits at the expense of the increasing poverty and ruination of the working people, deprives other sections of the non-white people of their land (Group Areas and Native Resettlement Acts, etc.), of their vote (Representation of Voters Act, etc.) and other rights.

Therefore the revolt of the non-white South African masses is a direct attack on the system which oppresses and exploits them.

CAPITALIST FRONT

South Africa, as we have already said, is a capitalist country. This means that, not only do the means of production, distribution and exchange belong to the capitalists, but that state power (making the laws, governing the country, control of the police and army, etc.) also belongs to the capitalist class as a whole. Different sections of this class contend with one another to manage the affairs of all the capitalists. At present the Nationalist Party is the chief executive of the capitalist class, but whether the Nationalist Party or the United Party or the Progressive or Liberal Parties contend with one another for this position, all these parties agree that state power must belong to the capitalist class at the expense of the workers and oppressed. By holding the state power they seek not only to further the aims of the whole capitalist class (with particular reference to that section of it that they personally come from and represent) but also to keep to manageable proportions, by terror, by "concessions", by reforms, or, in some way, the struggle of the workers and toilers.

As the revolutionary stirings of the oppressed and exploited grow in intensity the capitalists seek to present a "united front" to the world. A South African Foundation is formed (including Nationalist, United Party and Progressive Party supporters) to sell South Africa to their fellow capitalists and imperialists overseas, and a «Declaration of 69» is published. There are boasts of cheap labour costs and large advertisements appear in British newspapers, whitewashing apartheid, urging large scale capital investment, and encouraging a «European immigration» to «Sunny South Africa». Fine sounding phrases are dished out to cover up the naked brutality, bullying and bluff. In the present period of the South African revolution they strive, desperately, to maintain the system of production for private profit – increased manufacture of armaments (the extreme logic of monopoly capitalism, production for death so that capital might live). Some examples of the arms build up are: the record 1962 Defence Budget of R120 million (£60 million); the three new armaments factories to be set up in the Republic at a cost of £10 million; and the strengthening of the links between African Explosives and the British firm of I.C.I. for munitions manufacture. But the contradictions inherent to capitalism cannot be hidden; the competition between different sections of capital cannot be glossed over, the conflict between the exploiters and the exploited cannot be hidden, the conflicts between production for profit and the wants of the toilers, all keep bursting to the surface. With foreign investment in South Africa at over £1 600 million, and the economy closely linked to the overseas imperialists (the United Party representing the tie-up between Anglo-American and South African capital even more than the Nationalists) it is not surprising to find a MacMillan and a Lord Home echoing the sentiments of an Oppenheimer, or Mosenthal, or Sir Francis De Guigaud.

WAY FORWARD
Today, however, in the period of the world-wide advancee to socialism and the increased importance of the Afro-Asian states, the imperialist efforts to keep going at all costs does not make it easy to pass off the failings of the system on wicked, cruel or evil men who are mad, or on sunspots and the like.

*There is nothing wrong with South Africa today which Socialism cannot put right; but everything that is wrong with our country – national oppression, colour discrimination, poverty wages, no land, sickness, illiteracy, convict labour, passes, the anarchy of production for markets... – cannot be set right by capitalism.* They are the logic of capitalist class rule as it has developed in South Africa; they all spring directly from the system itself. It is nonsense, therefore, to say that «socialism is not the immediate problem». Socialism, now, is a burning necessity for our peoples.

The immediate task in the South African Revolution is the breaking down and the abolition of colonial and national oppression, the freeing of our economy from monopoly (foreign) control and, the economic and social reconstruction of our land. This means the violent overthrow of the present rulers and all they stand for, and the building of a people's democratic republic headed by, the industrial workers, in the friendliest alliance with the peasants, all toilers and progressive forces.

# Document 74
## "The Peasants' Struggle", *Assegai*, no. 2, March 1963

It was reported recently in the Johannesburg Star that the centre of underground political activity had shifted from the towns to the countryside. If this is intended to mean that the African workers in the towns have abandoned their struggle against the evil apartheid system and oppression, the present rulers of South Africa and the exploiters of African labour are deceveing themselves. The continuing sabotage in the main cities gives the lie to this wishful thinking. On the contrary, the struggle has become sharper, the use of force by the state being answered in its own coin. It is likewise an illusion to imply that a militant struggle is something quite new in the countryside. Is the Star (the mouthpiece of the Oppenheimer Chamber of Mines) unaware of what has happened in the past few years in Pondoland, Zeerust, Sekhukhuniland and Zululand, while the Government has been trying to impose its Bantustan fraud on the people in the so-called «reserves»?

The various attacks of the Government and its stooges against the people, like the enforcement of passes for women, cattle-culling, Bantu slave education, heavy taxation, etc., have met with a spontaneous response, in the form of demonstrations and actions, which have led to vicious reprisals from the Government. These reprisals in turn have caused the people to organise themselves to resist, with force, the violence of the police and army. They have gone over to the offensive in a number of places and several chiefs, who had sold out to the oppressors and become stooges in return for government bribes, have been killed. Their huts have been burnt. Fences which barred the peasants from their own land have been torn down.

## PONDOLAND'S EXAMPLE

The most successful campaign has been waged in Pondoland. In 1957, the Government introduced legislation making it an offence for any African to refuse forced labour or leave Pondoland without a valid document. It also enforced the Stock Limitation Act, thus making it compulsory for the people to dispose of their stock without compensation. Cattle are used to till the land and without them the peasants starve.

The following year, in 1958, the Government passed the so-called Bantustan Act which aimed at the same time to quieten its external critics and to strengthen its hold on the Transkei as a whole and Pondoland in particular. In appearing to grand «self-government» the Government actually made these territories into gigantic slave camps. The Transkei Territorial Authority was set up, with 123 stooge chiefs and Government appointed members. The legal chief of Pondoland, Nelson Sigcau, was banished and Botha Sigcau a willing tool of the oppressor, was put in his place. Those who opposed the regime's oppressive laws were flogged or imprisoned and tortured.

## THE PEOPLE'S RESISTANCE

The anger of the people began to grow. On June 6th, 1960, thousands from Eastern Pondoland marched to present their demands to a Government Agent at Lusikisiki town. At Ngguza Hill the police intercepted the crowd and, using helicopters, fired on the demonstrators. 31 people were killed. This event sparked off resistance all over Pondoland. The people organised themselves to fight back. Houses of stooges and collaborators were burnt and some of them were killed. Botha Sigcau sought refuge in Natal. Government offices were razed to the ground and the authorities lost control of the situation. *The people took to the hills and ruled themselves for the first time, by «Mountain Committees,» a real example of people's democracy in action.* The Government declared a State of Emergency in Pondoland in November, 1960 and this is still in force today. Over 5 000 peasant leaders were arrested, and 32 were sentenced to death, 11 of whom have already been hanged. Though the iron first of the government and its agents regained control, the fight still continues. The arch-stooge Kaiser Matanzima lives in fear of his life and has, so far, only avoided assassination by white police and army protection.

## PARLIAMENT FOR SLAVES

In December 1962, an armed clash with the police took place when a band of Africans marched on his home at Aamata while this self-styled Paramount Chief was forcing the new constitution of the Transkei through the Territorial Authority. A special session of this body was held on the 13th December, to push through the Government's plan to rule the Transkei through a supposedly «independent Parliament.» Despite increasing opposition from Chiefs like Sabata Dalindyebo, head of the most powerful tribe in the Transkei, the (emigrant) Abatembu, and the Pondo Chief, Tutor Ndamase, this puppet body adopted all the Government proposals. Chief Dalindyebo was unable to put forward the proposals which the people had urged on him but he clearly stated that under the new proposals the Transkei would be cut of from the rest of South Africa and turned into a pigsty; and that the Tembu demand freedom for all the Africans of the Republic.

## LEARNING FROM EXPERIENCE

It appears that all legal opposition to the oppressors will soon be at an end and the people of the Transkei and all the other «reserves» and «Homelands» will have to use the methods of armed struggle to an ever-increasing extent, using their experience and organising themselves under sound leadership to destroy the whole evil Bantustan machine.

From this struggle two points are clearly illustrated. By organised resistance and fighting on their own ground the Pondo people more than held their own against the local oppressors, thus showing that victory is possible. It needed extensive forces of the state and its army to subdue them, and this is only partial and temporary. *At the same time the peasants realised that their fight was not a local one, the authorities had the entire state machine behind them and to bring them down the struggle becomes part of the mass movement of all the South African people.* Thus Bantu Authorities was seen more clearly in a wider perspective – to defeat it the whole system of Apartheid itself must be brought to an end. If the fight of the Pondo people, with their very limited resources can cause such an emergency it is clear that the combined forces of the mass of the South African people can defeat the armed forces of the State.

## UNITY OF WORKERS AND PEASANTS

Brutal tyrants like Matanzima show that not only White men can act as oppressors and do the dirty work of the ruling class. Like the notorious Tshombe they act in the interests of the white exploiters because they belong to the exploiting class themselves and support that class. They know that if it is over-thrown they will lose the wealth and privileges which come from their ownership of the means of production – in this case, the land, which rightfully belongs to the landless peasants. *Here we see how the interests of the peasants in the «reserves» or «Bantustans» and the interests of the workers in the towns are the same – the overthrow of the ruling class and the seizure of the means by which wealth is produced; in the towns, the factories and mines, in the countryside, the land.*

We see also that the struggle of each helps the struggle of the other – sabotage in the towns destroys the property of the rulers, disturbs their communications and forces them to employ large numbers of men in trying to track down the attcakers. Like-wise guerilla activities in the country harasses their army and breaks down the machinery of administration. In both cases the people are rallied to the cause. The strength of the people grows and the stage is set for the final overthrow of the oppressor class. This two-pronged strategy formed the basis of the successful Algerian Revolution. A similar unity of workers and peasants in a common struggle was the way in which the Chinese people defeated the forces of imperialism and set up their People's Republic.

The key to the struggle is organisation and clear objectives. Wherever the masses have organised themselves into militant, well-disciplined forces, there they have achieved the best results. This is where the need for clearsighted and well-trained leadership is most urgently felt. The people must be made aware of who their enemies are and how best they can be defeated. We must study the actual conditions and learn from our own successes and mistakes as well as those of others. No opportunity must be lost to weaken the enemy, whether the Nationalist Government, the bosses of mining and industry, the bourgeoisie, whether white or black, the big landowners or the stooge chiefs. With courage, planning and clear thinking, victory will be ours.

## Document 75
*APDUSA and the nation,* June 11, 1963

[....]
WHY A.P.D.U.S.A.?
The growing process, the maturing process of the Nation has [...] been slow and a painful one. It is not enough merely to talk of unity, it is not enough to pay lip-service to the ideals of a unified nation. The Nation had to be built. It had to be built out of and with the living substance of the oppressed peoples of South Africa. And this nation had to learn the discipline of a Nation. The oppressed have to learn all the implications of Nationhood.

Ideals have to be turned into a living reality.

For the work of building the unity of the Nation has been slow and difficult. Remnants of the past remained with the oppressed. They is why even today young people all over the country are selling their lives. And selling it cheaply. This is why all over there is wild talk about getting arms, about planting bombs on pylons and buildings. All this sounds very brave, very heroic. But all the sacrifice is in vain, because the unity of the Nation is still lacking. The oppressed are still like an army that sets out to do battle before it has even learnt to march. This is happening because people have become desperate.

All this terrorism can only lead the Nation further into the morass, This must happen because wild action, stunts and adventurism, without any political content and devoid of discipline and direction, is purposeless and wasteful. It is self destructive. The Nation is wasting its energies, wasting its strength.

The Herrenvolk have shown that they are acutely conscious of the growth taking place amongst the oppressed people. The oppressed have yet to develop that same consciousness. Because the work of building the unity of the Nation has been so slow and so difficult the N.E.U.M. in 1961 created the *AFRICAN PEOPLES DEMOCRATIC UNION OF SOUTHERN AFRICA.* (APDUSA). It is the task of APDUSA to mould the unity of the Nation, to bring the oppressed into the N.E.U.M. To forge the links that will bind all the oppressed together in the struggle against oppression.

APDUSA is the instrument through which the Nation will find its freedom. APDUSA is the instrument whereby the Nation will rid itself of all the poverty, the misery, the ignorance and the squalor that blights all of life in this country. APDUSA is the instrument through which the unity of the Nation will be forged so that the Nation of South Africa will become a free and proud people.

Throughout its history the N.E.U.M. has set the pace for South Africa. It taught the oppressed the need for unity. It armed the oppressed by giving to the people those weapons which were essential to the throwing off of the slave-mentality. Long ago it fought against the forerunners to the system of Bantustans when it taught the oppressed to reject the Institutions of slavery, like the old Bunga, the Natives Representative Council, the Coloured Advisory Council and the Coloured Affairs Department. It led the people of South Africa in the struggle against the Rehabilitation Scheme, which was designed to destroy any means of independence and subsistence of the toiling masses in the reserves and force them out as cheap labourers into the Mines and onto the farms. It led the struggle against the destruction of Education when it fought the Bantu Education Act. In its short history already there have been many who have had to pay the price for this vigilance. The scores of teachers who were dismissed because they opposed Bantu Education. The persecution and the hounding of the CAPE AFRICAN TEACHERS ASSOCIATION (which is affiliated to the N.E.U.M.). The Bannings of individuals, the attacks on the leadership of the N.E.U.M.

The Nation cannot afford this any longer. Just as it cannot afford the senseless waste that is taking place each day. The Nation must draw itself together. The toiling masses must draw themselves together. The individual must make himself a part of the Nation. The unity and discipline of all the oppressed must come under the central command of the Non-European Unity Movement and every single individual who tries to stand aside, who uses the argument that he is afraid of losing his job, that he is afraid of being cast into prison, that he is afraid – every single individual must take his place in the ranks of the oppressed Nation. Because he who stands aside, and he shouts loudest about "Action, Action", he is holding back the Nation. He is guilty as the worst enemy of the oppressed is, of the crime of subverting the aspirations of the Nation.

APDUSA was formed to hasten this growing process. APDUSA was formed precisely in order that the Nation shall be able to say enough, we shall not tolerate this any longer. APDUSA is the instrument through which the vast mass of the people must find themselves inside the N.E.U.M., inside the ranks of the oppressed Nation. And the task of each APDUSAN is that of organising for the Nation; of drawing in his fellow-workers, his friends and his relatives. In this manner the oppressed Nation of South Africa shall cease to be a nightmare in the dreams of the tyrants, but shall become a living reality.

And so the darkness that lies over the whole of our country shall be lifted. It can only be lifted through APDUSA and the N.E.U.M. By building the unity of the Nation, by strengthening the political head of the Nation, by giving political direction to the Nation – we shall destroy the darkness and flood the country with the light of democracy. *[....]*

## Document 76
## The Speakers' Notes – A Brief Course on the Training of Organisers [Document found by the police during the Rivonia raid of 11 July 1963][14]

*Introduction*

A. You have been appointed to perform the important task of organising the units of Umkonto Wesizwe. You will realise at once how tremendous your task is, and that a great trust has been placed in you by the high command.

B. The purpose of your appointment is to see to it that you recruit the best elements among the African youth into the ranks or even the vanguard of our liberation army – the cream – the defenders and the liberators of our country. Thousands of young men in each region are urgently required.

(For this reason you will be required to work according to a programme to achieve your target).

C. The salient features of your work will embrace the following:–

1. You must *inspire confidence* among the population in the area of your jurisdiction, and you must be well-informed about your subject. You will be required to study the local conditions and the requirements of the population in the area.

2. The organiser must be able to *give information* about the causes which led to the formation of Umkonto Wesizwe. This means that one should be able to apply the brief history of the struggle, culminating in the formation of Umkonto.

3. One must *know the character of Unkonto* as an organisation. One must *know about sabotage*, its purpose and one must *know about guerilla warfare* as a distinct form of warfare from regular warfare. In other words, one must study the character and tactics of guerilla warfare.

4. The organiser must be able to satisfy the people on the following questions:

(a) Why is that we do not immediately prepare the people for open warfare, instead of wasting time with guerilla warefare and sabotage?
(This question has already been raised by Leballo and others).

(b) Why do we not do what the P.A.C. is doing? That is why do we not prepare the people for a sudden simultaneous attack in the big cities?

(c) Will the guerilla warfare develop ultimately into full-scale war, and under what conditions would this be done?

(d) Whom are we fighting and what forces has the enemy at his disposal? Can they be defeated?

5. *The aims for which the war is being waged* must be explained with absolute clarity, as it is imperative and vital that the people should understand and be convinced of the need to risk their lives for their ultimate freedom. This, in fact, is the key to the success of your recruiting campaign. Without this explanation you will never be able to get

your volunteers.

6. Particular attention must be paid to the question of *relationship* between *Umkonto and the masses* of the people, as well as to the role of the masses since our success depends on the support of the masses in the struggle.

7. Having posed these problems, it is necessary for us to deal with them in a lecture form to enable the organiser not only to understand policies but to equip him sufficiently so as to enable him to analyse policies of forces lining up against each other. *[....]*

SECTION A.
### HISTORICAL BACKGROUND 1880-1910 TO THE CAUSES WHICH LED TO THE FORMATION OF UMKONTO WE SIZWE

The period between 1880 and 1910 will show that it was the end of what we may call purely and simply a military struggle, and the beginning of a political struggle. Prior to this period, our country was characterised by bloody wars between the White from Europe and indigenous people of South Africa. The first of these wars on record was in 1659 in Cape Town, between the Dutch settlers and the Hottentots, under the leadership of Autshumayo, and continued thereafter for a period of 200 years at regular intervals. *[....]*

We have chosen the latter period because our main concern today is a political struggle and that period was the beginning of a political struggle.

The end of the 19th century saw the complete subjugation of the African people and the end of the military struggle over the land question. But it also saw the beginning of a political struggle based on political rights – franchise, land and freedom of movement. By this time Europeans had become firm rulers and masters over the African lands. The wars of conquest had ended in their favour. *[....]*

SECTION B.     **THE CONSTITUTIONAL STRUGGLE 1910-1960**
*[....]*

SECTION C.     **THE CHARACTER, THE NATURE AND POLICY OF THE NATIONAL LIBERATION MOVEMENT**

The national liberation movement in South Africa has its roots in the struggle against White domination, oppression and exploitation. In particular against the three main pillars of the suppression and domination – the denial of franchise as enjoyed by Whites, restriction of movement under the pass laws and the confiscation of the African land. The national liberation movement came into existence at the close of the 19th century. Its spearhead was the African National Congress, which was established in 1912. Other organisations which constituted the United Front, were the African Peoples Organisation for Coloureds, which existed up to 1950, the South African Indian Congress, the Communist Party founded in 1921 and which was banned in 1950, and other workers' organisations which arose from time to time, such as our present South African Trade Union Congress.

Although the African National Congress is nationalist in character, it was never racialistic. From its inception it accepted the realities of the situation in our country and worked with men of all colours. There was a close alliance between the African National

Congress and the African Peoples Organisation. The last joint struggle waged by the above mentioned organisations was in 1950 – the May Day and June strikes which were called in protest against the Nationalist suppressive measures and the killing of the non-Europeans.

*Policy*

The policy of our national liberation movement is the Freedom Charter. The Freedom Charter came into being when the African National Congress, after the Defiance Campaign of 1952 called on its partners in the Alliance to come together and discuss the possibilites of summoning a People's Congress to draw up a Freedom Charter. This was done in 1954 at Kliptown, when 3 000 delegates met, coming from all parts of South Africa, representing all groups in the country – black and white. *[....]*

## SECTION D.     THE BIRTH OF M.K.

For more than 80 years the people sought to bring about reforms by constitutional means. But policies committed to white domination of the blacks have been intensified. The Government and Nationalist Party are arming and mobilising the entire white population because they fear the ultimate consequences. They arm themselves, not because of their strength or confidence, but because they are weak. Verwoerd and his gang are a government of frightened men. They show it through their policies of segregation, white trusteeship, apartheid, race federation, Bantu authorities, self-rule, self-government, independence in their own homelands.

A careful study of the Transkei plan, for example, will show clearly that the whole thing is a fraud. These measures are born of fear and panic. They are afraid; afraid of the people whom they misgovern. The Nats do not have the slightest intention of letting up on a single one of the fundamental pillars of apartheid, of giving the people land, votes, freedom, education, higher wages, skilled jobs or any other necessity for which the people are crying out.

The government has driven the peoples' leaders and their movements underground. Jailed them, placed them under house-arrest, forbidden their activities under the most extreme penalities even up to death. By doing this, they are forging the means of their own destruction. The people can take no more. When all attempts at legal, constitutional and non-violent forms of political struggle are denied, and the government declares war on the people, the people are left with but one choice. They too, must arm themselves and fight for freedom and the overthrow of white supremacy. And so the organisation M.K. is born to wage a revolutionary armed struggle to overthrow white supremacy. Its immediate aim is to speedily bring about the achievements of the objects for which the A.N.C. and the national liberation movement are struggling.

*Why did it start with Sabotage?*

Sabotage is an invaluable arm of people who fight a guerilla war. In the initial stages it fulfills the strategic task of creating the conditions necessary for the formation of guerilla units from among the people. But sabotage must be distinguished from terrorism.

*There are two types of sabotage.*
1. Sabotage on a national scale against determined objectives.
2. Local sabotage against lines of combat.

In regard to the first, sabotage on a national scale should be used principally in disrupting communications, transport, railroads, railroad installations etc. It is the civil branch and should be carried out only outside the areas dominated by the guerillas.

Its organisation is commanded by the centralised high-command of the revolutionary army who are responsible for deciding the targets to be attacked. Vital industries, arms factories, will at certain times be destroyed but this may bring about vast unemployment of workers and consequently must be carefully considered. The importance of sabotage against communications must be stressed. The great strength of the enemy is his network of communications. His ability to move freely across the country. We must constantly undermine that strength by knocking out railroads, bridges, electric lights, telephones and in general, everything that is necessary for his normal modern way of life.

Although sabotage is aimed principally against communications, we must, through various means, render useless all factories, all centres of production, that are capable of giving the enemy something needed to maintain his offensive against the peoples' forces. Emphasis should be placed on cutting supplies and blocking the roads.

*In every action of sabotage the system of hit-and-run is employed.* It is not necessary to put up serious resistance but simply show the enemy that in the area where the sabotage has occurred there are guerila forces disposed to fight.

In regard to the second type of sabotage, we must little by little paralyse the cities and towns in the zones surrounding the guerilla operations. The two main types of operations are physical acts of expediency and general political acts. These two types should not be entrusted to the same people or leadership.

When the aim is to achieve the maximum effects – to affect the breakdown of a total factory, specialists are used to do everything themselves. These are people who are placed under the strictest security. They conduct no other political work. Acts which are part of mass action require no great skills.

## Document 77
## Yu Chi Chan Club[15], *Pamphlet No. II: The Conquest of Power in South Africa* [1963]

In South Africa a class struggle is being waged, a struggle which is blurred by the historical accident of race, i.e. by the utilization of the existence of colour groupings by the ruling class. Precisely as a result of this policy of the ruling class it is an historical fact that the most revolutionary sections of South African society are to be found among those who are commonly callrd the Non-Whites. The most exploited classes of South African society are at the same time racially or nationally oppressed. These classes constitute the majority of the Non-Whites. The petty bourgeoisie, the intelligentsia and the merchant class among the Non-Whites form a small but powerful and potentially dangerous section of the oppressed and exploited masses. By virtue of their position in society they have constituted the leadership of the masses up to now – whether this leadership has been revolutionary or reactionary is for the moment not at issue.

A very important social class in South African society is the white working class.

They have been bribed off by Imperialism and the national bourgeoisie for decades. So much so that today they form the main pillar of the colour-caste, capitalist system. While it is obvious that the class interests of these workers lie with the majority of the Non-White population, and while it is clear that they will eventually have to join hands with their class brothers as a result of the developing historical process, it must be equally clear that at the moment and for the foreseeable future their immediate interests coincide with that of emergent Fascism in this country in every respect. This is especially so in view of the treacherous role played by the official working-class organisations in this country and by the grandiloquent isolationism and rabid racialism of large sections of the national liberatory movement. It is from this white working class that the main supports of the ruling class have been and are taken in the form of police, army, navy etc.

*[...]* we turn directly to the question of the conquest of power, which has been put on the order of the day by the tremendous rate of political development in this country in recent years as also by the spectacular events on the continent of Africa, in Asia and in Latin America. Although it would have been simpler to tackle this question directly, it becomes necessary to deal briefly with the question of force or violence i.e. to put it in its proper perspective in this country.

*[....]* In Europe the propaganda of all parties (including the workers' parties) was (and is) concentrated on the national army in times of crisis. In other words, any revolution in Europe had one, almost fatalistically constant factor, i.e. the position of the army in regard to the contending classes. For this reason the main purpose of European political organizations (as indeed in all classical, class-society) was to ensure its political leadership. The army would normally tend to side with the forces which promised internal stability. Naturally when the revolution was a radical social revolution there was less readiness on the part of officers (who as a rule came and come from the ruling classes) to join the revolutionaries. Then the scene of revolution would shift to the army itself for a time. *[....]*

From the introductory remarks in this pamphlet it will have become clear that such a position does not obtain in South Africa at all. Of course it is hardly necessary to answer those elements which think of the revolution in terms of an isolated general strike. These people are as trapped in European conceptions as those who see the white army and state machine intervening (or not intervening) on behalf of the oppressed and exploited masses. We state categorically that no matter what the state of political organization and consciousness of the masses, if they do not have an answer to the diabolical role of the army and other arms of the state in time of crisis, their activities must end in a bloodbath and victory for the state they wish to bring to its knees. In other words, the political movement of the workers and rural poor must be prepared to deal with the state machine on the level of force. Non-Violence, Passive Resistance etc. have been exposed sufficiently in practice. These are the methods of the liberal bourgeoisie (cf. India), which is not so liberal when it comes to workers' rights (cf. India).

In South Africa, the inevitably violent reply of the state to passive resistance campaigns in times of economic crisis can end only in one thing viz. Imperialist intervention in the form of U.N.O. or Afro-Asian embraces which will certainly be deathly in the struggle of the workers of this country. Let there be no doubt about it: Non-Violence means in the final analysis Imperialism under a (temporarily) liberal mask. In effect the same fate awaits those "red-hot", economist protagonists of the isolated general strike, or the isolated sabotage. For, in essence these unfortunate people depend on the kindness, disunity and lack of decision of the state on the one hand, or on the recuperative potential of the masses on the other hand. It is an historical fact, however, that the same masses who can "spontaneously" create miracles, can as "spontaneously" be shocked into semi-permanent inertia by the incredible viciousness and brutality of state repression.

None of these possibilities, therefore, neither Non-Violence, nor the isolated general strike, nor the isolated sabotage attempts and certainly not the dependance on the vacillation of the white army holds out any realistic basis for a concrete conception of the method of conquest of power. Yet we maintain that it is highly essential for an effective mass struggle against the prevailing system to give the political cadre a concrete conception of the forms in which the struggle for power must culminate. As there can be no imitation of European (classical) forms in this country it must be obvious that in this important and even decisive respect we have to look for "models" elsewhere. We have to do so consciously because in the very nature of our struggle will not allow of what is called spontaneity in regard to the form of struggle. Spontaneity in this question = suicide. To put it differently: in the same way as only a class conscious organization of the workers and the rural poor can lead the political struggle, so too only a class conscious, trained organization of soldiers can meet the threat of the highly-trained, albeit frightened army of the South African state. This is the logical conclusion of the policy of non-collaboration which is the policy of class independence.

Having said the above it now remains for us to turn to the kind of warfare in which our struggle will involve us. Which are the forms in which the class warfare in South Africa will terminate? History itself has given us the answer in the form of Guerrilla Warfare. It is a term which has been distorted and coloured with all kinds of heroism, wrong conceptions and plain agent-provocateurism. In the following we treat this subject as an integral part of the class struggle for power.

## GUERRILLA WARFARE
## WHAT IT IS AND WHERE IT FITS INTO THE STRUGGLE

Guerrilla warfare is a specific aspect of warfare as such. It is, therefore, necessary to pose the question: What is War? This question was answered in the classical way by von Clausewitz: War is the continuation of policy by other means. *[....]*

Since guerrilla warfare is an aspect of warfare as such, it will be clear that it too is subject to the political strategy and principles of the class or group which uses it. However, its applicability in a given situation is determined not by political considerations, but rather by considerations of a military nature. In other words, we can be justifiably accused of discussing questions of a military-technical nature. That is true, but it is equally true that these technical questions have become decisive at the present stage of the class struggle. Hence our pre-occupation with them. Guerrilla warfare has been defined as follows: "It is a weapon that a nation inferior in arms and military equipment may employ against a more powerful aggressor nation". On the basis of this definition it might appear as if guerrilla warfare is not applicable to civil war and that it only applies to countries invaded by militaristic, foreign Imperialism. *[....]* It is necessary, therefore, to prove the applicability of guerrilla warfare and its methods in classical civil war, for we are far removed from those chauvinistic groupings, who would insist in the teeth of all history that the white man in this country is a foreigner who has to be driven into the sea.

Firstly, it is true that in almost all historical examples of the application of guerrilla methods, these have played only a subsidiary and complementary role to that of the regular army. They were employed mainly to introduce (from the military point of view) mobility into the army of the defending nation (as opposed to the dependance on positional warfare of the militarily superior aggressor nation). Guerrillas were used, apart from their political, patriotic role in rousing the people and involving the civilian masses in the war, to turn defence into attack. [....] while the guerrillas might have been a more or less decisve factor in victory, they were subject to the general strategy of the regular forces, i.e. did not themselves dictate general strategy. [....]

In a country such as South Africa where the regular army is bound hand and foot, like the classes from which it is conscripted, to the policies of the ruling class, where the revolutionary classes have no army of their own and can only depend on foreign intervention at their peril, the question obviously poses itself in the following manner: Can guerrilla bands be turned into a regular army systematically? [....]

Algeria, Cuba and to a lesser extent Angola are the examples which bear out our answer. In all these countries, more especially in the first two, guerrilla bands of vanishing magnitude were turned into regular armies in the course of the struggle through desertions, political propaganda and state repression of the civilian population. In the final stages of the struggle, before the actual conquest of power guerrilla bands from all over the country swelled together and turned to classical positional warfare, assisted by sabotage, strikes etc. in the cities to gain victory. In Algeria a petty bourgeois-Imperialist compromise prevented the struggle from being carried through to its logical conclusion. Be that as it may, it will become clear later on that South Africa's movment is in the fortunate position of being able to avoid the opportunism which characterised the Algerian leadership as well as the empiricism that characterises the Cuban leadership. These two countries then, show quite conclusively that the question posed above: Can guerrilla bands be turned into a regular army systematically? must be answered in the affirmative.

Before turning to the political and social implications of guerrilla warfare, it is necessary to conclude this section with a few general remarks about the historical significance of guerrilla warfare i.e. its position from the point of view of world revolution. Guerrilla warfare is the classical form of colonial and semi-colonial revolutions against Imperialism. As such it involves all the problems of the colonial and semi-colonial world, and more especially the problem of the land. This point will become clearer in the next section. Suffice it to say that the guerrilla fighter is essentially an agrarian revolutionary without necessarily being from the political point of view tied to the agrarian classes. Those who make the scholastic distinction between the "proletarian revolution" (when they really mean urban revolt) and the "agrarian revolution" (when they really mean jacquerie) will not be able to understand this question from the point of view of world revolution. The latter will be sympathetic towards it and will also be a very dangerous element politically; the former will sneer at it and condemn it as a primitive substitute for the political class struggle. We attempt to answer both these points of view in the next section. At this stage it is only necessary to point out that in those colonial or semi-colonial countries where there was or is no rational bourgeoisie strong enough to act as the managers of Imperialism, or alternatively, where there is no strong petty bourgeois, collaborationist political organizations of the masses, the struggle has invariably tended or will tend to revolve around guerrilla warfare.

Contrasting examples of the first group would be Tunisia as opposed to Algeria and of the second group Ghana as opposed to Angola, In a period of nuclear development as we are experiencing the guerrilla fighter has, for military and political reasons, come to occupy the same central position in the colonial and semi-colonial anti-imperialist revolutions as the uniformed soldier in the classical metropolitan revolutions.

## THE POLITICAL AND SOCIAL IMPLICATIONS OF GUERRILLA WARFARE
We will deal with this aspect under three headings:
(a) Guerrilla Warfare and the political movement
(b) Guerrilla Warfare and the geographical terrain
(c) The initiation of guerrilla armies

(a) Guerrilla Warfare and the political movement
Guerrilla warfare in South Africa is the logical extension of the national democratic movement in this country i.e. it is the continuation of the policy of Non-Collaboration in a specific form towards the achievement of the same democratic aims. The aims and the general strategy of the political movement and its vanguard organization in this country have been fully discussed in pamphlet no. I of this series. We will therefore only treat this subject coincidentally in as far as it has a direct organizational bearing on the question under discussion.

The guerrilla armies must have the same political goals and political discipline as the political organizations of which it is the military, the strong arm. On this fundamental question there can be no compromise. It is, therefore, essential that every guerrilla unit should have its political officers as well as the normal military officers. Since guerrilla units by their very nature will originally be composed of the most conscious political elements, they will in this sense also form an important part of the political vanguard. They will live among the people in a very concrete sense as we shall see later. Therefore, every guerrilla unit is at the same time a propaganda unit. Guerrillas must therefore be completely conversant with the practical aspects of political education. This will also become clearer when we discuss the equipment of guerrilla units.

We have said that the guerrilla is primarily an agrarian revolutionary. This does not mean that the guerrilla has nothing to do with the cities. On the contrary, a well-organized guerrilla army assigns important functions (sabotage, espionage, diversion, supply etc.) to its suburban units. This is precisely the way in which we have tackled the question, having at our disposal the invaluable experience of the Cuban and the Algerian revolutions. But it must be clear that the tasks of the suburban guerrilla are, at least initially, hazardous ones, as the possibility of being discovered is so much greater. Clearly then, the suburban units will for a long time be involved in purely political and trade union activity, seeking to support the struggle on the land by sapping the vitality of the capitalist state.

On the land, however, the picture is very different. Only one alternative presents itself to the rural poor who have reached the end of their tether viz. either brutal suppression (witness Sekhukhuniland, Pondoland etc.) or underground politico-military struggle, which on the land means nothing more and nothing less than guerrilla war against the state. It should be clear, [—] and political leaders of guerrilla units must know the agrarian programme of our political movement as they know their A.B.C. They must be able to inculcate the attitudes and political ideology implicit in our programme, into their men. This is of fundamental importance, because it will be the rural masses who will initially and for a long time in the future constitute the basis of the guerrilla army. It should be emphasized that we are not advocating any concentration on the agrarian question to the exclusion of the rest of our programme. But it should be equally clear that guerrillas who are forced by circumstances to operate mainly among the rural masses must be able to convey that point on our programme which will rally these masses to our political organization and gain soldiers for the army of liberation. It should also be noted by guerrilla leaders that in the beginning they might find open opposition to our agrarian programme because even this transitional programme is often too radical for the petty bourgeois mentality of the rural masses.

However, these masses become ingratiated to the guerrilla army because of its leadership and clarity. Every success scored against the enemy will gain hundreds of new soldiers and thousands of new sympathizers. Hence, there can be no question of concessions in regard to our programme even though tactical retreat might be a temporary necessity. The stronger the guerrilla army gets, the firmer the hold of the political leadership on the minds of the rural masses, the more progressive ideas and attitudes replace that which has been called the "idiocy of village life", the deeper the revolution becomes, the more boldly the leadership can introduce the theory and practice of radical agrarian reform. Amongst other things one of the main social tasks of guerrillas is the education of the masses amongst whom they work. The fight against rural illiteracy starts during the revolution, not afterwards. The raising of the cultural level, apart from bringing our ideas to the masses on a higher level will also instil discipline into the soldiers and into the masses as a whole. Guerrilla "teachers" will prove to be among the most powerful agents of the political, social and cultural revolution. If we remember the axiom that guerrillas are the fishes in the water of the masses, it will be seen that a [special?] type of treatment of the masses is essential. More of this later!

Having clarified these basic issues it remains now to discuss the political organizations under this heading. Which political organization specifically will lead the guerrilla army? On this question there can be no doubt in our minds. We know that all kinds of petty bourgeois, reformist, adventurist and opportunist organizations are preparing for what they call "guerrilla warfare". In so far as they are creating a technical machine, we need not fear them. Indeed it should be our tactic to unite with them, with a view to taking over their units. In so far as they are propagating their reactionary programmes we have to oppose them on the political level. Indeed it should be one of our first aims to outorganize them by means of better propaganda techniques to spread our historically correct programme. It should be quite clear to all of us, however, that the organization which controls the greatest concentration of popular force in the form of armed guerrillas (N.B. Algeria and Cuba) will in effect lead the struggle. Although its programme might be influenced by the revolutionary masses (in sofar as it is a reactionary organization) it will in the final analysis be able to put back the political struggle and in effect betray it. What must be prevented at all costs is the unnecessary and costly fratricide which threatens to destroy the struggle in Angola. Not only because this kind of activity saps the military potential of the people and weakens their morale, but also because in the African soil it invariably leads to "tribal" warfare and racial pogroms, which are suicidal in the liberatory movement as we see very clearly in the Congo.

Guerrilla warfare cannot succeed without the masses. Hence all counter-guerrilla pipe dreams are doomed to miserable failure in the final analysis. This must be remembered by the organizers of guerrilla units. The guerrilla army is a vital aspect, but only an aspect of the national liberatory movement. Any guerrilla army divorced from the masses and the movement of the masses is doomed to failure. In the period of preparation, therefore, the organizers of the guerrilla army must play a prominent part (even if it is not necessarily a public one) inside the political organizations of the mass movement. When it has been established, no guerrilla unit should ever forget its fundamental political character, especially in its dealings with the people. To forget this would mean to fall back into primitive militarism, which during, and especially after the revolution, could play a treacherous role. Although many decisions which leaders of guerrilla units will face, will be of a purely military-technical nature, no guerrilla unit may ever forget that its decisions must be synchronized with the general strategy of the political movement. It might eg. be militarily expedient to destroy traitors in certain villages, whereas it might be politically premature. In such a case, unless the very existence of the guerrilla unit is at stake, the political considerations must take precedence.

(b) Guerrilla Warfare and the Geographical Terrain

The geographical question is also a political question. It is clear that guerrilla warfare can only be waged in a certain type of country. Fortunately South Africa has all the necessary requirements for this kind of warfare. As the experience of the Boers shows, guerrilla warfare can be waged successfully. In fact this experience must be remembered for another reason. The present regime is acquainted in a concrete sense with guerrilla methods.

Mountainous country, bushy, forested areas or swampy, marshy country are most suited to guerrilla warfare. As expreience in Cuba and in China shows, it is possible, although much more difficult, to wage this kind of war in the plains. In our choice of terrain we are guided not only by geographical considerations, but, in view of the fact that all geographical requirements are present, more especially by the political considerations.

Wherever guerrilla activity will be initiated the people must be politically prepared and at least in principle prepared to support the guerrillas. In South Africa, especially in view of the agrarian nature of initial guerrilla activity the areas which must be prepared systematically are obviously the reserves and to a lesser extent, the white farms. The present Bantustan Rehabilitation Schemes form the best basis on which such activity can be unfolded.

The people have a tradition of struggle, to some extent even of quasi-guerrilla struggle (cf. Pondoland Hills, Ovamboland). They have clear political goals which can serve as a point of departure for our programmatic conceptions. They are armed to some extent. A natural, disciplined politico-military leadership is already in existence. All that remains to be done then is to synchronize the illegal activity in the various areas. Let us caste a brief glance at some of the more important areas.

A. *The Transkei*

This area of course will be the primary field of operations with a view to forming a strong base area. It has all the geographical requirements: mountainous area, adjacent to Basutoland, even a coastline which might prove to be an invaluable assert later on. It is the most densely populated reserve in the country, a constant struggle has been waged there against Rehabilitation and Bantustan for the past 10 years. There is a very long political tradition and many people are already hiding in the mountains. Like all other reserves it has the advantage of being "foreign territory" as far as the state machine in concerned. As such then it will form a natural base area which could easily become a liberated area. The main fight will originally have to be waged against collaborationist impis and leaders. But a note of warning has to be sounded here. Under no circumstances must this fight be allowed to degenerate into a tribal war. It is the one thing which could disastrous to a "speedy" victory.

A special word about Basutoland. The people of this High Commission territory are the natural allies of the South African workers and peasants. Our struggle is theirs. Their support will be essential for reinforcement of the struggle in the Transkei.

B. *Zululand* is in the same position as the Transkei. There the opposition to the government is if anything even more intransigent. However, the actual struggle in the political field is still very backward and unfortunately hindered by rabid racialism. However, this problem can be surmounted if the political organizations are rejuvenated [....] We should remember, however, that Mozambique will not be such a natural ally as Basutoland. Hence concentration should be on the potential assistance which could come from Swaziland.

C. *Sekhukhuniland*

Here too there is a long tradition and strong political agitation. Escape routes, retreat and withdrawal possibilities exist towards the badly-guarded Bechuanaland border. It is essential that direct contact be established with the people's movement in Sekhukhuniland. Geographically the terrain is not too suitable but this is compensated for by the politically favourable climate.

D. *The Great Karroo and the Steppe*

There is only one effective way of reaching the agricultural workers on the white farms viz. via the villages and the dorps dotted all over the barren, hilly interior of South Africa. The importance of these areas will lie initially in their diversionist possibilities. There are from 5 to 10 workers' families as opposed to one or two white farmer families on these farms. Large tracts of land could temporarily and periodically fall into the hands of guerrillas, helping to divert the attention and disperse the strength of the enemy. It is from the point of view of "making noise in the East and attacking from the west" that we have to view the role of these areas. Apart from that, the main supply routes of the enemy (roads and railways) run through this isolated, empty country. The importance of this fact need not be stressed any further.

The main point which has to be realized is that we must approach the agricultural workers through the village groups (see next chapter).

E. *Special Position of South West Africa*

Apart from all geographical considerations (Ovamboland is one of the most natural guerrilla areas in Southern Africa) S.W.A. occupies a very special position in our general strategy.[16]

As far as we know the Ovambos are well-armed. There is a popular political movement, the political programme of which needs some tightening up. The people are prepared to act in the direction of independence. This demand is supported by the world at large and South Africa has often shown its sensitivity on the question. Most probably guerrilla action on an extensive scale will bring about some kind of "Algerian" Independence. This will certainly not be satisfactory in the long run, but from the point of view of providing a strong liberated area, dedicated to the struggle of the South African oppressed it will be an invaluable gain for the struggle as a whole. It is South

Africa's Achilles Heel and we have to concentrate as much activity on it as possible.

To sum up: it must be clear that the areas mentioned are only those we consider to be the best for the initiation and maintenance of guerrilla activity. This does not mean that groups should not be formed when and where possible. However, in our general strategy the areas mentioned will obviously play a more important role. Hence all efforts must be made to establish more and more cells in them. Only once there are units of the army in every single one of these areas can we begin to hope for success in our campaign.

### C. THE INITIATION OF GUERRILLA ARMIES

Guerrilla armies are initiated in various ways. It is only necessary for us to deal with a few important possibilities. Before doing so, it is necessary, however, to discuss the role of the paramilitary cells.

These must be formed in every strategic area. It is not necessary to form more than one or two in every demarcated area, more especially as large numbers increase the danger of espionage and betrayal. The basic principles of formation of these groups should be the same as those guiding the Yu Chi Chan Club. The importance of these groups lies in the intensity of their political engagement, their study of military tactics and strategy, knowledge of the enemy strength and their training for leadership of guerrilla regiments and battalions. Every person in a cell of this nature must be prepared consciously and systematically for guerrilla leadership.

I. *Guerrilla groups formed by cells*

The cell or cells in any particular area must look upon itself as the nucleus of a guerrilla unit. As soon as the time is ripe, politically speaking, the members of the cell go out consciously and deliberately to form squads, drawing upon the population of the area. One cardinal principle must be observed viz. that as far as possible the members of the squad must come from or know the area well in which they will operate. The makes communication easy, the members know the terrain, and the local population will harbour and feed the guerrillas when necessary. All guerrilla units must be linked up regionally and of course nationally. (The technical quesitons of equipment, function and study of the cells etc. must be discussed in Pamphlet no. III).

II. *Guerrilla Groups formed by [other?] organisations*

These must be unearthed. If possible and necessary one or two members of the cells should join them. In any case it is necessary to find out whether or not these groups are conscious politically. If they are, members of the cells must try to take over the leadership of the groups. If this is not possible, some kind of liaison must be established. The struggle itself will weld the groups together later on. Under no circumstances must there be competition for the "ear of the masses". Rather it would be adviseable to organise our strategy in such a way as to synchronize the activity of these groups with our own. If there is any well-founded reason to believe that these groups are following counter-revolutionary policies or that they *[may?]* compromise our position, they must be liquidated without any *[–]*. At no time, however, must the police or any other part of *[the state]* machine be used against groups which are not actively engaged in collaborationist activities. It is recommended that the F.L.N. *[tactics?]* employed against the treacherous M. N. A. groups be studied.[17] It should also be remembered that the very nature of political propaganda of the majority of organizations in this country will result in groups of this nature arising more especially in the cities. They will concentrate on sabotage campaigns, which could be utilized in our interests at certain times.

III. *Guerrilla groups arising from the masses*
This is the main kind of group that we will be concerned with., whether they arise in town or country. As examples of this kind of group we can take the existing ones in Pondoland and Ovamboland. Our approach to such groups must be that of the people. Which means that members coming from the area must join the groups. Their training, clarity in regard to military matters and political goals and strategy as well as their ability to link up the local unit with others in the region and even nationally, will soon lead to them becoming the natural leaders of the groups. At no time must there be attempts to usurp positions of leadership in such groups, even if the policy followed by their local leadership is at variance with our national strategy. In such cases the thing to do is to let the cells and other committed groups know through the national organization of this policy, so that it can orientate itself and endeavour to change the policy of the group in question.

Groups of this kind are to be found in all reserves, where the tradition of military struggle is deeply rooted. The cells or members of the cells should, after having surveyed the area carefully, waste no time in linking up with the most promising and best organized groups. The people are born organizers! Secret organizations are very secret indeed. They have to be, for obvious reasons. "Dead" areas are not so dead at all. Members must be trained to find the best methods of gaining access to groups which are in existence.

CONCLUSION
In conclusion, a few words about our immediate tasks and *[-]ion* of launching the struggle. We have to draw practical conclusions from our our analysis of situation and strategy. The main emphasis apart from general political *[activity]* must be laid on formation of cells in all strategically important areas. These must be *[-]* our general strategy as soon as possible so that they can be *[utilized]* immediately. At the same time information about other existing groups must be gathered systematically. This *[must be]* sifted and treated according to the principles laid down in the *[-]* series. At this stage any decision to form liaison with any other camps must be centrally and *[democratically]* decided upon. This *[saf—]* will not be so *[-]* later on.

Finally, we cannot commit ourselves at this stage to any particular date or method of launching the struggle. Everything is possible. Our only guide will be the political situation itself and the state of preparedness of the masses and our own machinery. When the decision has been taken, however, it must take precedence over all else. Dedication to the tasks decided upon must be *[systematic?]* and unquestioning. Otherwise we will only be assisting in our own destruction.

## Document 78
## Memorandum from the
## Pan-Africanist Congress of South Africa [c. July/August 1963][18]

You will remember that in 1962 Mr. Potlako Leballo[19] and I approached the AFL-CIO for financial aid, this aid to be specifically channelled towards ameliorating the refugee problem that PAC was faced with in South Africa.[20]

The problem remains and indeed things are worse, not better, in this respect than they were. I shall revert to the additional needs later.

In the meantime, since our visit, great things have happened in South Africa. On his return Mr. Leballo set up an efficient organization in Maseru, Basutoland, and energetically and successfully drew together again the links with the rest of South Africa. Within a few months he had reestablished contact with the organization's 150-odd cells all over South Africa.

At this same time the South African authorities were thrown off their balance by what they called the "PAC-Pogo" menace. The whites of one town, Rustenburg, panicked. A general alert of the police and mobilization of the Army was ordered on about 17 March, and went on until 15 April. The South African Government rushed through Parliament panic legislation aimed at keeping Sobukwe in detention indefinitely.

Early April saw Leballo's offices raided by the Basutoland police. Leballo himself after an encounter with what has been alleged to have been the Basutoland police, has never been seen since then.

The South African authorities, however, claimed that by arresting some 2800 members of the PAC they had crushed the organization. This is not true: coded messages received in London inform us that contact has been re-established with all areas, that the spirit of the people is still high, and that the Presidential Council, in the absence of both Sobukwe and Leballo, is maintaining effective control over the underground resistance movement in Basutoland.

(A) Funds are now needed urgently for transport, to enable officials to travel from Basutoland round South Africa, to reorganize.
(B) It is essential that the office in Basutoland be maintained.

The events of 1963 have demonstrated that real and effective opposition to apartheid has to begin from Basutoland which is in a unique strategic position.

It is gratifying to note that over the last two years the Basutoland Democratic Movement (Basutoland Congress Party, B.C.P., leader Ntsu Mokhehle) has been resolutely hostile to Communist and near-Communist elements in South Africa, reinforcing the tough anti-Communism of the young Paramount Chief Bereng.[21] The PAC has enjoyed warm and cordial relations with B.C.P. and the Paramount Chief was showing remarkable evidences of sympathy. He, like Mokhehle, see clearly that the Basuto people cannot stand aside from the South African struggle to end apartheid. Funds spent now on (A) and (B) could make PAC in Basutoland a bastion of democracy against Communism and apartheid.

Recently I have myself attended the Addis Conference, which you know about. Funds may be expected from the permanent secretariat, but past experience has taught us to expect delay here. The urgency of the situation in South Africa demands immediate action.

After the Addis Conference I was deputed to have talks with Mr. Cyrille Adoula,

Premier of the Congo, and the Algerian Government.

Mr. Adoula is most helpful and has offered us places for offices and training camps at both Léopoldville and Elisabethville. The Algerians have offered us various forms of equipment and material. We already have a small ship, capable of traveling from Algeria to the Congo. We are now looking for volunteers to man the ship and to run the office in the Congo. Funds will be necessary for this.

(C) Lastly, if the Basutoland office is necessary as a forward position, its exposed and landlocked position necessitates a main South African headquarters. For reasons of geography this base must be in Southern Bechuanaland, probably in the territory of Chief Linchwe at Gaberones. Chief Linchwe pledged himself at his recent "coronation" to sacrifice for the welfare of refugees from apartheid.

(D) A refugee camp ought therefore to be set up near Gaberones, with funds not only to care for the refugees, but to organize the transport, throughout Southern Africa, of PAC leaders, to feed people and material in and out of Basutoland by the Bechuanaland Air Charter Service (which has signified its willingness to go very far indeed along this road).

(E) Two vehicles have been donated by the Swedish Metal Workers Union. These are at Dar-es-Salaam and need crews to drive them to Gaberones, funds to keep them moving between Congo and Gaberones.

(F) The road from Francistown to Kasane (to connect with Kaunda's Northern Rhodesia through the Chobe-Kasane-Kazungula Gap) must be improved and moved away from the S.R. Frontier. This will, as soon as the Federation is dismembered, open a land route to south Bechuanaland.

(G) It is essential that headquarters staff be able to travel in Africa and the world without the handicap of lack of funds.

We request that the AFL-CIO consider making available immediately the following funds to tide PAC over until African freedom funds are available in sufficiency.

With such funds a powerful strengthening of the democratic movement may be expected. If the democratic movement is not able to mount effective opposition to apartheid, no schemes for social, educational or trade union development will be worth anything.

### PARTIAL COST OF THE ABOVE FOR 12 MONTHS

| | | |
|---|---|---|
| (A) | £700 per month | £8,400 |
| (B) | £150 per month | £1,800 |
| (C) | £300 per month for 2 offices in Congo; Mr. Adoula to pay the bulk of these expenses | £3,600 |
| (D) | £500 per month (approximately) for Refugee and transit camp at Gaberones, BP | £6,000 |
| (E) | Vehicle transport costs, approximately | £10,000 |
| (F) | Road improvement, approximately | £10,000 |
| (G) | International travel £500 per member | £6,000 |
| TOTAL: | | £45,800 |

(or approximately $125,000 US)

# Document 79
## African Resistance Movement, Announcement[22] [1964]

The African Resistance movement (ARM) announces its formation in the cause of South African Freedom. ARM states its dedication and commitment to achieving the overthrow of the whole system of apartheid and exploitation in South Africa. ARM aims to assist in establishing a democratic society in terms of the basic principles of socialism.

We salute other Revolutionary Freedom Movements in South Africa. In our activities this week we particularly salute the men of Rivonia and state our deepest respect for their courage and efforts. While ARM may differ from them and other groups in the freedom struggle, we believe in the unification of all forces fighting for the new order in our country. We have enough in common.

The time for talking is past. The present regime and its supporters, internal and foreign, have shown that they are not prepared to respond in any way to the peaceful demands of the people of South Africa for full participation in all aspects of the political, economic and social life of the country. Instead, opression has increased.

ARM does not only talk. ARM acts. ARM has acted. ARM has declared and will declare itself through action. This is the only language our rulers understand. And ARM, with other freedom forces will harry and resist the opressors until they are brought to their knees.

White South Africa has often been given the opportunity to align itself with progress. It has constantly refused to do so. It has sought only to build for itself on the backs of the people a comfortable bastion of profit power and privilege.

ARM declares its fight not against the whites as such, but against the system they so jealously defend. ARM will avoid taking life for as long as possible. ARM would prefer to avoid bloodshed and terrorism. But let it be known that if we are forced to respond to personal violence – and we cannot forget decades of violence, torture, starvation and brutality against us – we shall do so.

For the present ARM will inconvenience and confuse. ARM will disrupt and destroy. ARM will strike where it hurts most. We will not cease until the present vicious system and rule by force is crushed. ARM does not wish to see one form of domination replaced by another. It works for a full political and social revolution.

To Verwoerd, Vorster and their men we say; you will NEVER stop the pulse of the new society which even now, beats in our factories and cities, our mines and farms – and YOU KNOW IT.

To the people of South Africa, we say;
ARM NOW FOR FREEDOM

## NOTES

1 Ben Turok (b. 1927) immigrated to South Africa from Latvia in 1934. In the 1950s he was a leading member of the COD and organiser for the Congress of the People. He was a Treason Trial defendant from 1956 to 1958, and in 1957 was elected to represent Africans in the Western Cape on the Cape Provincial Council. In 1962 he was sentenced to three years imprisonment under the Explosives Act and, upon release, went into exile. His critical discussion of SACP/ANC/MK strategy (1974) led to his marginalisation in Left Congress circles.

2 For space considerations the footnotes in the original pamphlet have been omitted. The sources cited in the pamphlet include: Govan Mbeki, *The Bantustans: A death trap*; Official Summary of Tomlinson Commission Report; Race Relations Survey 1959/60; SAIRR statement on the Pondo situation; Memorandum sent to U.N. by the Hill Committee; *The Star*; *The Sunday Times* and *New Age*.

3 Govan Mbeki (b. 1910) – a leading figure in the ANC and SACP. Born in Transkei, he obtained a B.A. from Fort Hare in 1937 and a B.Econ. from Unisa in 1940. He joined the ANC in 1935 and was introduced to socialist thought by E. R. Roux and African-American Max Yergan, then a socialist. He was particularly concerned with organising in rural areas and was a leading activist in Transkei and author of *South Africa: The peasants' revolt* (1964). In the 1950s he was fired from his teaching post and became a journalist and editor of *New Age* and organised for the ANC in Port Elizabeth. He was arrested during the Rivonia raid of July 1963 and was imprisoned on Robben Island until 1987. In 1990 he was a member of the ANC's Interim Leadership Committee and of the SACP's Interim Leadership Group.

4 Rowley Arenstein (b. 1918), a prominent, Durban-based lawyer, joined the CPSA in 1938 and later became its Organiser and Secretary in Durban. He was a leading figure in the COD. In 1961 he defended Anderson Ganyile and other leaders of the Pondoland uprising and later assisted in the Rivonia Trial and in the Unity Movement trial of 1971-72. In 1966 he was convicted under the Suppression of Communism Act and served four years in prison. He was under house arrest for 18 years and banned for 26 years, the longest banning order in South Africa. He criticised the SACP's turn to sabotage in the early 1960s, believing that a non-violent transition was possible. In 1983 he became legal advisor to Chief Buthelezi and in the late 1980s was a member of the KwaZulu negotiating team. Unable to practice law since 1967, he was readmitted as an attorney in 1994.

5 Anderson Khumani Ganyile was born in Bizana, Transkei, and educated at Lovedale and Fort Hare, where he was expelled for political activities on behalf of the ANC Youth League. He became a leader of the 1960 Pondoland uprising, was banished to a remote area and, after legal battles, moved to Basutoland.

6 Hooper (1989:156) notes the boycott of white-owned shops in Zeerust, Western Transvaal in 1957.

7 Hendrik Frensch Verwoerd (1901-66) became Minister of Native Affairs in 1950 under Prime Minister Malan and was responsible for much apartheid legislation. As Prime Minister from 1958 to 1966 he ruthlessly implemented those policies. He was assassinated in 1966. Eric Louw was Verwoerd's Minister of Foreign Affairs.

8 This document was a request for funding on behalf of the AAC, NEUM and APDUSA – probably written by I. B. Tabata – for presentation to the PAFMECSA at its February 1962 meeting in Addis Ababa. PAFMECSA included representatives from governments of independent African states and from the southern African liberation movements. The OAU was established in May 1963, and it created the ALC to provide funds and co-ordinate assistance to those liberation movements still fighting white and colonial domination. PAFMECSA, which dissolved in September 1963, was effectively the predecessor of the ALC. Although initially non-partisan towards the ANC and PAC, a combination of factors – evidence of MK's activity in South Africa and the PAC's increasingly apparent disarray – pushed the ALC to favour the ANC. Both the ANC and PAC successfully precluded the ALC from aiding the AAC or APDUSA. See Wallerstein (1968:168); also *Statement by the AAC and NEUM Justifying their Rights to the Funds Voted by the Liberation Committee of Nine* [c. December 1963] and the letter from Dorothy Padmore to I. B. Tabata, 18 June 1964 and Tabata's reply, 30 June 1964 in Unity Movement of South Africa Collection, 1963 and 1964, BC925, Manuscripts and Archives Department, University of Cape Town Libraries. The correspondence discusses Tabata's appeals to the OAU's Committee of Nine for funding and indicates his continued reticence regarding support for armed resistance in Pondoland.

9 The document has a blank space but this may allude to the *Makhuluspani* (Big Team), an organisation based in the Qumbu and Tsolo districts of Transkei which the AAC claimed as an affiliate through the TOB. Its original function was to punish livestock thieves and to raise funds for legal cases against thieves, but in the late 1950s it began to threaten chiefs and others who were seen to be collaborating with the Bantu Authorities. This led to a government crackdown, and in 1960 three alleged *Makhuluspani* leaders were deported from the area.

10 This probably refers to "New Problems of the Democratic Movement", Reel 9B, 2.EY1.45/4, Carter-

Karis collection, 1920-65.
11 The Welensky partnership refers to the Federation of Rhodesia and Nyasaland, which existed from 1956 until its collapse in 1963, and of which the Rhodesian politician Roland Welensky was Prime Minister.
12 In October 1961 the CPSU adopted a much-lauded new programme. This discussed the transition from a proletarian dictatorship to a communist society in the context of the collapse of colonialism and the emergence of socialism as a world system. It emphasised industrial development and the well-being of Soviet citizens, setting 1980 as the target date for achieving the material and technical basis for communism. The Party's new rules increased the emphasis on member' rights and responsibilities rather than on institutional change.
13 This presumably refers to *The Road to South African Freedom*. See Bunting (1981:284-319). Bunting identifies that programme as being adopted at the Fifth National Conference. However, Document 72, above, dates the Fifth National Conference in 1960.
14 For other documentary sources on MK see Bunting (1981: 274-6, 385-96) and Karis and Carter (1977a:716-17, 760-68).
15 The YCCC/NLF produced several pamphlets. Pamphlet No. I, meant to be a political analysis of South Africa, was never written. Pamphlet No. III concerned technical and organisational issues. Despite the Unity Movement background of most of the YCCC/NLF members, the focus here is on a guerrilla struggle in which a rural proletariat, including migrant workers and semi-proletarians, rather than a peasantry, is the main social base. This pamphlet reflects Neville Alexander's influence, amongst others. Alexander, an educationist and political activist, studied at Tübingen University in Germany and received a D.Phil. in German literature in 1961. There, he made contact with members of the exiled Algerian Students' Movement and Algerian Trade Union Movement and with Michel Pablo's tendency within the Fourth International, which gave primacy to the revolutionary potential of the colonial world. On his return to South Africa, he argued that the NEUM should consider armed struggle. But in 1961 he and Kenneth Abrahams of Namibia, a medical doctor, were suspended from the NEUM for their agitation on that issue, and they formed the YCCC to study strategies of guerrilla warfare. Alexander and other members of the YCCC were detained in 1963. Alexander spent ten years on Robben Island and was banned and house arrested on release. In the 1980s he helped to form the Cape Action League and the National Forum Committee. He is a leading member of the Workers' Organisation for Socialist Action and the Workers' List Party.
16 The YCCC took a keen interest in the Namibian anti-colonial struggle. See "Short Report on Activity in S. W. Africa (Ovamboland)", *Liberation*, 1, 3, May 1963 and "A Brief Survey of the Revolutionary Movement in S.W.A." *Liberation*, 1, 2, April 1963 (editor's possession). Namibian workers who came to Cape Town to escape their contracts frequently adopted Afrikaans names, lived in coloured areas and married coloured women in order to avoid carrying passes. In the 1950s, some of these people and Namibian students at UCT were in contact with the NEUM. But subsequently, those Namibian students who joined the NEUM became concerned at the seemingly ambivalent views expressed by NEUM leaders, particularly Tabata, on the issue of Namibian independence. According to Dr Kenneth Abrahams, a member of SWAPO who also joined the YCCC and NLF, SWAPO's turn to armed struggle followed that of the South African liberation movement; influenced by those executive members with NLF links, the SWAPO central executive discussed various approaches to armed struggle. SWAPO initially saw armed struggle as a means to pressure the South African government, to be used along with political mobilisation within Namibia and international pressure through the UN. Once the OAU began financing the training of SWAPO guerrillas in mid-1963, divisions emerged within SWAPO's central executive between a radical minority arguing for a Vietnam-style people's war as a means to democratise the struggle, and the majority, led by Sam Nujoma, who continued to see armed struggle as a pressure tactic. Over the decades, the majority of SWAPO guerrillas were Ovambo and operated as an elite group entering the country on specified missions without merging with the population. This, Abrahams has argued, actually reinforced the colonial government's divide-and-rule policy. (Interview with Kenneth Abrahams, Windhoek, February 1988.) See also *SWAPO Cape Town Branch Report* [c. 1962], *The South-West Commentator*, 2, 3, 28 February 1962; 2, 4, 28 March 1962; and 2, 5, 16 May 1962 (editor's possession).
17 The FLN (Front de Libération Nationale) was the liberation movement in the Algerian War of Independence against French colonialism (1954-62). Led by Ahmed Ben Bella, the FLN gained mass support and guerrilla warfare became widespread in rural areas. The French army responded with a massive attack but its brutality generated much criticism, and in 1958 the conflict led to the collapse of the Fourth Republic. The consequences were a new constitution in France – the Fifth Republic, the political dominance of De Gaulle and the negotiation of Algerian independence in 1962. The MNA (Mouvement National Algérien) was a bitter rival of the FLN.
18 This document was probably written by Nana Mahomo around July/August 1963. Mahomo was a UCT

student in the late 1950s, an organiser for the PAC in the Cape Peninsula and a member of the PAC National Executive. In March 1960 Mahomo and Peter Molotski were appointed as PAC external representatives. In August 1962 a formal exile leadership was formed under Potlake Leballo's leadership. In June 1963 Mahomo and Patrick Duncan began a two-month tour of the United States to raise funds and campaign for an arms and oil embargo of South Africa. Mahomo contacted the AFL-CIO, which made a $5 000 donation. Following an abortive attempt in late 1963 to get military training for PAC members at the FNLA's Kinkuzu camp near Leopoldville, Congo, in January 1964 Mahomo was in London. He became estranged from other PAC leaders and was suspended in August 1964 on charges of financial misdealings and "attempts to create personal loyalties", although Tom Lodge (1983:309) found no evidence of financial corruption. The AFL-CIO continued to fund Mahomo's projects.

19 Potlako Leballo was a highly controversial leader of the PAC. Educated at Lovedale and Wilberforce Institute, he became a teacher. Influenced by Anton Lembede and A. P. Mda, he took over leadership of the ANC Youth League Orlando East Branch and used *The Africanist* to criticise ANC leadership, and he was repeatedly expelled and reinstated by the ANC. At the founding of the PAC, he became its National Secretary. Following Sharpeville, he was imprisoned for two years and in 1962 went to Maseru, Basutoland. There, in March 1963, he called a press conference and announced that the PAC and Poqo were about to launch a nationwide insurrection to overthrow the South African government. This precipitated mass arrests of PAC and Poqo members in South Africa, debilitating the PAC. His later claims to lead the PAC were repeatedly challenged by other PAC officials.

20 The AFL-CIO (American Federation of Labor-Congress of Industrial Organizations) – a federation of labour unions in the U.S., Canada, Mexico, Panama and U.S. dependencies formed in 1955 from the merger of the mainly craft-based AFL, founded in 1886, and the mainly industrial-based CIO, founded in 1935.

21 The Basutoland Congress Party was founded in 1952 as the Basutoland African Congress. Some of its leadership had been involved with and influenced by the ANC Youth League. Ntsu Mokhehle, a founding member, studied at Fort Hare but was expelled following student protests.

22 This document was written by Adrian Leftwich and others. See *State v Daniels*, p. 161, Manuscripts and Archives Department, University of Cape Town Libraries.

## List of documents

**Part One: Building the national movement**
**1.1 Political alliances and unity**
1  Harry Snitcher, *Unite Against Segregation! Communists Condemn the C.A.C.* [1943]
2  Against the C.A.D. *for* Full Democratic Rights [1943]
3  National Anti-C.A.D. Conference Agenda, Oddfellows Hall, Hope Street, Cape Town, Saturday, 29 May [1943]
4  B. M. Kies, "The Background of Segregation". Address delivered to the National Anti-C.A.D. Conference, 29 May 1943
5  Johannesburg Anti-C.A.D. Committee, *Bulletin Number One* [1943]
6  Report of Delegation to All-African Convention and Unity Conference 16-17 December 1943. Presented to 2nd National Anti-C.A.D. Conference, 4-5 January 1944
7  Draft Declaration on unity provisionally adopted at Unity Conference, Bloemfontein, 17 December 1943
8  *The Ten-Point Programme* [1943]
9  Report of the proceedings of the Second National Anti-C.A.D. Conference held at Banqueting Hall, City Hall, Cape Town, 4-5 January 1944
10  Y. M. Dadoo, "The Non-European Unity", *Freedom*, 4, 1, February 1945
11  Peter Meissenheimer, "Smuts' Anti-Indian Bill: Economic Sanctions or Non-European Unity?" *Workers' Voice*, April 1946
12  Non-European Unity Movement. Resolutions passed at 6th National Unity Conference, Cape Town, 29, 30 and 31 March 1948
13  Sarah Mokone [Victor Wessels] "The T.A.R.C.", *Majority Rule: Some notes*, Chapter XIX
14  "Short History of Betrayal", *Freedom*, New Series, 1, 5, 1 November 1948
15  Ruth First, "Progress in Unity Talks: African organisations agree in principle", *The Guardian*, 23 December 1948
16  Joint Sitting of the Executive Committees of the All-African Convention and the African National Congress, 17 April 1949
17  Letter from I. B. Tabata to Robert Mangaliso Sobukwe, 13 August 1949
18  Letter from C. I. R. Fortein to John Gomas, 29 April 1950
19  K. A. Jordaan, "The T.A.R.C. Debacle", *Discussion*, 1, 1, [June 1950]
20  F. Carneson, "The Franchise Action Committee", *Discussion*, 1, 3, June 1951
21  E. L. Maurice, "The Rôle of the Non-European Teacher in the Liberatory Movement", *Discussion*, 1, 5, June 1952
22  Report of the first National Conference of Women held in the Trades Hall, Johannesburg, South Africa, 17 April 1954
23  The Freedom Charter adopted at the Congress of the People at Kliptown, Johannesburg on 25 and 26 June 1955
24  "Wreckers at Work" (Editorial), *Liberation*, 18, April 1956
25  Letter from E. R. Roux to John Gomas, 23 July 1956
26  Letter from Patrick Duncan to John Gomas, 3 October 1956
27  Letter from John Gomas to The Editor, *New Age*, 15 October 1956
28  Brian Bunting, "Problems of the Multi-Racial Conference", *Liberation*, 28, November 1957
29  Kenneth Hendrickse, "The Opposition in Congress", *The Citizen*, 3, 3, 4 March 1958
30  W. M. Tsotsi, "Presidential Address to the All-African Convention Conference", Edendale, 14-16 December 1958
31  S.O.Y.A. National Executive Committee, The Maritzburg Conferences and the Tasks of the Immediate Future, 31 May 1959

**1.2 Uses of the boycott**
32  Babeuf [K. A. Jordaan], "A History of the Franchise in S. Africa", *Workers' Voice*, 5, 5, September 1946
33  "Views on Boycott: Majority support at emergency conference", *The Guardian*, 12 June 1947
34  Moses M. Kotane, "Boycott of Elections under the 'Representation of Native Act'", *Freedom*, 6, 5, September-October 1947
35  "New Tactics Proposed for N.R.C. Boycott: Xuma's Address to African Congress", *The Guardian*, 18 December 1947
36  "N.R.C. Boycott Campaign to be Intensified", *The Guardian*, 18 December 1947
37  "Communist Election Policy Defined: National Conference Decision", *The Guardian*, 8 January 1948

38　I. B. Tabata, *The Boycott as Weapon of Struggle*, June 1952
39　Walter Sisulu, "Boycott as a Political Weapon", *Liberation*, 23, February 1957
40　Anti-CAD, *Why You Should Not Vote!* [1958]
41　John Gomas, *Seperate Representation — Our Damnation* [1958]
42　"Boycott the Dummy Election: 2 000 Demonstrate At Mass Rally", *The Torch*, National Edition, 1 April 1958
43　"Oppositionists in Congress Attack C.O.D. Against Participation in Racial Elections", *The Citizen*, 3, 3, 4 March 1958
44　"The Revolt of the Women", *The Soyan*, December 1959

**1.3　National liberation and trade union organisation**
45　Ray Alexander, "Trade Unionism in South Africa", *Discussion*, 1, 6, 1952
46　D. Tloome, "The Origin and Development of Non-european Trade Unions", lecture delivered to the Johannesburg Discussion Club on 27 February 1953, *Viewpoints and Perspectives*, 1, 1, 21 February 1953
47　"Answer to Government's Apartheid Unions", *The Citizen*, 1, 3, 30 April 1956
48　"The Anti-C.A.D. and the Trade Unions", *The Torch*, 1 April 1958
49　"The Stay-Home Call: Why did it fail?", *Congress Voice*, issued by the Emergency Committee of the A.N.C., 2, 2, May 1960
50　Socialist League of Africa, "South Africa: Ten Years of the Stay-at-Home", *International Socialism*, 5, Summer 1961

**Part Two:　The national question**
51　W. P. van Schoor, "The Origin and Development of Segregation in South Africa", A. J. Abrahamse Memorial Lecture, Cathedral Hall, Cape Town, 5 October 1950
52　K. A. Jordaan, "A Critique of Mr. W. P. van Schoor's 'The Origin and Development of Segregation in South Africa'", *Discussion*, 1,3, June 1951
53　M. Harmel, "Observations on Certain Aspects of Imperialism in South Africa", *Viewpoints and Perspectives*, 1, 3, February 1954
54　K. A. Jordaan, "What are the National Groups in South Africa? A Contribution to the Symposium", Forum Club, Cape Town, May 1954
55　H. J. Simons, "Nationalisms in South Africa", Forum Club, Cape Town, May 1954
56　Thomas Ngwenya, "What Are the National Groups In South Africa?" Forum Club, Cape Town, May 1954
57　Lionel Forman, "Self-Determination in South Africa: A Contribution to Discussion", *Liberation*, 37, July 1959
58　Robert Mangaliso Sobukwe, "The Opening Address at the Africanist Inaugural Convention", 4 April 1959

**Part Three:　The agrarian question**
59　Letter from Ruth First to The Secretary, South African Institute of Race Relations, 17 August 1944
60　Letter from J. D. Rheinallt Jones to Ruth First, 31 August 1944
61　A. Mon [M. N. Averbach] "A Comment on Trotsky's Letter to S.A.", *Worker's Voice*, 1, 3, July 1945
62　I. B. Tabata, The Rehabilitation Scheme: A New Fraud, December 1945
63　Letter from Chairman of the Planning Committee, Libode, to the Chief Magistrate, Umtata, 8 February 1947
64　Progressive Forum, Johannesburg [June 1950]
65　Z. Sanders (Zena Susser), "Aspects of the Rural Problem in South Africa"; lecture delivered to the Johannesburg Discussion Club on 1 December 1952, *Viewpoints and Perspectives*, 1, 1, 21 February 1953
66　Hosea Jaffe, "The First Ten Years of the Non-European Unity Movement". Excerpts from a lecture delivered to the Cape Flats Educational Fellowship, December 1953
67　K. A. Jordaan, "The Land Question in South Africa", *Points of View*, 1,1, October 1959

**Part Four:　The turn to armed struggle**
68　Ben Turok, *The Pondo Revolt* [c. 1960]
69　"We Must Learn New Methods of Work", *Congress Voice*, issued by the Emergency Committee of the A.N.C., 2, 2, May 1960
70　*South Africa: An Analysis of the Political Situation in South Africa and the Nature of the Struggle for Liberation* [late 1961]

71 National Committee for Liberation, Announcement [20 December 1961]
72 "A Landmark in South Africa's History: The Sixth National Conference of the South African Communist Party", *International Bulletin*, no. 4, December 1962
73 "Why Revolution?", *Assegai*, no. 2, March 1963
74 "The Peasants' Struggle", *Assegai*, no. 2, March 1963
75 *APDUSA and the Nation*, 11 June 1963
76 The Speakers' Notes – A Brief Course on the Training of Organisers [Document found by the police during the Rivonia raid of 11 July 1963]
77 Yu Chi Chan Club, *Pamphlet No. II: The Conquest of Power in South Africa* [1963]
78 Memorandum from the Pan-Africanist Congress of South Africa [c. July/August 1963]
79 African Resistance Movement, Announcement [1964]

## Sources

Document 1, Hoover Institution Archives, Stanford University.
Documents 3, 6–9, Abdurahman Papers, BC 506, Manuscripts and Archives Department, University of Cape Town Libraries.
Document 5, Bunting Papers, A949, Historical Papers Library, University of the Witwatersrand.
Documents 11, 22, 32, 61, South African Reference Library, Cape Town.
Documents 13, 49, 54–56, 62–63, 66, 77, courtesy of Neville Alexander.
Documents 16–17, African Collection, Manuscripts and Archives, Yale University Library.
Documents 18, 25–27, 41, courtesy of Doreen Musson.
Documents 19–21, 45, 52, State Library, Pretoria.
Documents 23, 49, 69–70, 78, Patrick Duncan Papers, Southern African Archives, Borthwick Institute of Historical Research, University of York.
Documents 59–60, SOU File, Southern African Archives, Borthwick Institute of Historical Research, University of York.
Documents 29, 43, 47, courtesy of Solly Horwitz.
Documents 34, 68, 72–74, Communist Party of Great Britain Library and Archives.
Documents 46, 53, 65, Historical Papers Library, University of the Witwatersrand.
Documents 64, 76, Southern African Political Materials: The Carter-Karis collection, 1920-1965.
Document 67, Johannesburg Public Library.
Documents 71, 79, courtesy of Andries du Toit.
Document 75, Coloured Radical Political Organisations, Southern African Archives, Borthwick Institute of Historical Research, University of York.

## Select bibliography

African National Congress (1977), *ANC Speaks: Documents and statements of the African National Congress 1955-1976*.
Alexander, Neville (1986), "Aspects of Non-Collaboration in the Western Cape 1943-1963", *Social Dynamics*, 12, 1, 1-14.
Barrell, Howard (1990), *The ANC's Armed Struggle*, London: Penguin.
Basner, Miriam (1993), *Am I an African? The political memoirs of H. M. Basner*, Johannesburg: Witwatersrand University.
Beinart, William and Colin Bundy (1980), "State Intervention and Rural Resistance: The Transkei, 1900-1965", in Martin A. Klein, ed., *Peasants in Africa: Historical and contemporary perspectives*, Beverly Hills and London: Sage, 270-315.
Berger, Iris (1992), *Threads of Solidarity: Women in South African industry, 1900-1980*, Bloomington and Indianapolis: Indiana University and London: James Currey.
Bhana, Surenda and Bridglal Pachai, eds. (1984), *A Documentary History of Indian South Africans*, Cape Town and Johannesburg: David Philip and Stanford: Hoover.
Bohmer, Elizabeth W., comp. (1986-87), *Left-Radical Movements in South Africa and Namibia 1900-1981: A bibliographical and historical study*, Cape Town: South African Library.
Bunting, Brian (1975), *Moses Kotane: South African revolutionary*, London: Inkululeko.

Bunting, Brian, ed. (1981), *South African Communists Speak: Documents from the history of the South African Communist Party, 1915-1980*, London: Inkululeko.

Callinicos, Luli (1993), *A Place in the City: The Rand on the eve of apartheid*, Braamfontein: Ravan and Cape Town: Maskew Miller Longman.

Carr, E. H. (1987), *What is History?* 2nd edition, London: Penguin.

Chaskalson, Matthew (1987), "Rural Resistance in the 1940s and 1950s", *Africa Perspective*, New Series, 1, 5-6, December, 47-59.

Cope, R. K. (1944), *Comrade Bill: The life and times of W. H. Andrews, workers' leader*, Cape Town: Stewart.

Cronin, Jeremy (1990), "Rediscovering our socialist history", *South African Labour Bulletin*, 15, 3, September, 97-99.

Dadoo, Yusuf Mohamed (1990), *South Africa's Freedom Struggle: Statements, speeches and articles, including correspondence with Mahatma Gandhi*, edited by E. S. Reddy, New Delhi: Namedia Foundation and Sterling Publishers and London: Kliptown Books.

Davids, Arthur (1950), "A Critical Analysis of I. B. Tabata's Book – The All-African Convention, Cape Town: Forum Club, reprint, *Discussion*, 1, 2, [c. December 1950].

Delius, Peter (1993), "Sebatakgomo and the Zoutpansberg Balemi Association: The ANC, the Communist Party and Rural Organization, 1939-1955", *Journal of African History*, 34, 293-313.

Drew, Allison (1991), "Social Mobilization and Racial Capitalism in South Africa, 1928-1960", Ph.D., University of California, Los Angeles.

Drew, Allison (1996), "The Theory and Practice of the Agrarian Question in South African Socialism", *Journal of Peasant Studies*, 23, 2/3, January-April, 53-92.

Du Toit, Andries (1991), "The National Committee for Liberation ('ARM'), 1960-1964: Sabotage and the question of the ideological self", M.A., University of Cape Town.

Du Toit, Andries (1994), "Fragile Defiance: The African Resistance Movement", in Ian Liebenberg, Fiona Lortan, Bobby Nel and Gert van der Westhuizen, eds., *The Long March: The story of the struggle for liberation in South Africa*, Pretoria: HAUM, 96-103.

Ellis, Stephen and Tsepo Sechaba (1992), *Comrades against Apartheid: The ANC and the South African Communist Party in exile*, London: James Currey and Bloomington & Indianapolis: Indiana University Press.

Ernstzen, Eric (1950), "The Last Ten Years of the Liberatory Movement", *Discussion*, 1, 2, December, 5a-13.

Everatt, David (1991), "Alliance Politics of a Special Type: The roots of the ANC/SACP alliance, 1950-1954", *Journal of Southern African Studies*, 18, 1, March, 19-39.

Everett, Elizabeth (1978), "Zainunnissa (Cissie) Gool 1897-1963: A biography", B.A. Honours, University of Cape Town.

Fine, Robert with Dennis Davis (1991), *Beyond Apartheid: Labour and liberation in South Africa*, London and Concord: MA: Pluto.

Forman, Sadie and André Odendaal, eds. (1992), *A Trumpet from the Housetops: The selected writings of Lionel Forman*, London: Zed, Athens, OH: Ohio University, and Cape Town: David Philip and Bellville: Mayibuye.

Forum Club (1952), "The National Question and its Relation to South Africa", *Discussion*, 1, 6, December, 1-8.

Gerhart, Gail (1978), *Black Power in South Africa*, Berkeley: University of California.

Hassim, Shireen (1991), "Gender, Social Location and Feminist Politics in South Africa", *Transformation*, 15, 65-81.

Hirson, Baruch (1977), "Rural Revolt in South Africa: 1937-1951", paper presented at the Institute of Commonwealth Studies Postgraduate Seminar, *The Societies of Southern African in the 19th and 20th Centuries*.

Hirson, Baruch (1995), *Revolutions in My Life*, Johannesburg: Witwatersrand University.

Hofmeyr, Willie (1985), "Agricultural Crisis and Rural Organisation in the Cape: 1929-1933", M. A., University of Cape Town.

Hommel, Maurice (1981), *Capricorn Blues: The struggle for human rights in South Africa*, Toronto: Culturama.

Hooper, Charles (1989) [1960], *Brief Authority*, Cape Town and Johannesburg: David Philip.

Hudson, Peter (1986), "The Freedom Charter and the Theory of National Democratic Revolution", *Transformation*, 1, 6-38.

Johns, Sheridan (1973), "Obstacles to Guerrilla Warfare – A South African Case Study", *Journal of Modern African Studies*, 11, 2, 267-303.

Jordaan, K. A. (1952), "Jan van Riebeeck: His place in South African history", *Discussion*, 1, 5, June, 21-36.

Kadalie, Clements (1970), *My Life and the ICU: The Autobiography of a black trade unionist in South Africa*, edited and introduced by Stanley Trapido, London: Frank Cass.

Karis, Thomas and Gwendolen M. Carter, eds. (1973), *From Protest to Challenge: A documentary history of African politics in South Africa, 1882-1964*, Vol. 2, Stanford: Hoover Institution.

Karis, Thomas and Gwendolen M. Carter, eds. (1977a), *From Protest to Challenge: A documentary history of African politics in South Africa, 1882-1964*, Vol. 3, Stanford: Hoover Institution.
Karis, Thomas and Gwendolen M. Carter, eds. (1977b), *From Protest to Challenge: A documentary history of African politics in South Africa, 1882-1964*, Vol. 4, Stanford: Hoover Institution.
Kasrils, Ronnie (1993), *"Armed and Dangerous": My undercover struggle against apartheid*, Oxford: Heinemann.
Kies, B. M. (1953), *The Contribution of the Non-European Peoples to World Civilisation*, Cape Town: Teachers' League of South Africa.
Kline, Mary-Jo (1987), *A Guide to Documentary Editing*, Baltimore and London: Johns Hopkins University Press.
Lazerson, Joshua N. (1994), *Against the Tide: Whites in the struggle against apartheid*, Boulder, CO and Oxford: Westview and Bellville: Mayibuye.
Lerumo, A. [Michael Harmel] (1971), *Fifty Fighting Years: The Communist Party of South Africa 1921-1971*, London: Inkululeko.
Lewin, Hugh (1976), *Bandiet: Seven years in a South African prison*, Harmondsworth, Middlesex: Penguin.
Lodge, Tom (1977), "The Pan Africanist Congress: Positive action and the Poqo uprising", in Christopher R. Hill and Peter Warwick, eds., *Southern African Research in Progress: Collected Papers 2*, Centre for Southern African Studies, University of York, 95-113.
Lodge, Tom (1978), "'Izwe-Lethu' (The Land is Ours): Poqo and the politics of despair", in Anne V. Akeroyd and Christopher R. Hill, eds., *Southern African Research in Progress: Collected Papers 3*, Centre for Southern African Studies, University of York, 93-115.
Lodge, Tom (1983), *Black Politics in South Africa since 1945*, London and New York: Longman.
Majeka, Nosipho [Dora Taylor] (1986) [1952], *The Role of the Missionary in Conquest*, Cumberwood: APDUSA.
Mandela, Nelson (1956), "In Our Lifetime", *Liberation*, 19, June, 4-8.
Mbeki, Govan (1964), *South Africa: The peasants' revolt*, Harmondsworth, Middlesex: Penguin.
Mettler, R. [Baruch Hirson] (1957), *It is Time to Awake!*, unpublished manuscript, November, Carter-Karis Microfilm Collection, 2:DA 13:84/9.
Mnguni [Hosea Jaffe] (1952), *Three Hundred Years*, Cape Town.
Musson, Doreen (1989), *Johnny Gomas, Voice of the working class: A political biography*, Cape Town: Buchu.
Nasson, Bill (1990), "The Unity Movement: Its legacy in historical consciousness", *Radical History Review*, 46/7, 189-211.
National Liberation Front (1963a), "The New Line of the Non-European Unity Movement", *Liberation*, 1, 2, April, 10-11 (editor's possession).
National Liberation Front (1963b), "Report on Poqo", *Liberation*, 1, 2, April, 12 (editor's possession).
No Sizwe [Neville Alexander] (1979), *One Azania, One Nation: The National question in South Africa*, London: Zed.
Ntantala, Phyllis (1992), *A Life's Mosaic*, Claremont: David Philip and Bellville: Mayibuye.
Phahle, Roseinnes (1987), "Mass Politics for the NEUM in Johannesburg?"; unpublished paper (editor's possession).
Pogrund, Benjamin (1990), *How can Man die Better ... Sobukwe and Apartheid*, London: Peter Halban.
Potekhin, I. I. [c. 1953], "Extract from 'The Formation of the South African Bantu into a National Community'", mimeo (editor's possession).
Roux, Edward (1964), *Time Longer than Rope: A history of the black man's struggle for freedom in South Africa*, Madison: University of Wisconsin.
Roux, Eddie and Win Roux (1972), *Rebel Pity: The life of Eddie Roux*, Harmondsworth: Penguin.
Roux, Edward (1993), *S. P. Bunting: A political biography*, introduced and edited by Brian Bunting, Cape Town: Mayibuye.
Sachs, Bernard (1949), *Multitude of Dreams: A semi-autobiographical study*, Johannesburg: Kayor.
Sachs, Bernard (1959), *South African Personalities and Places*, Johannesburg: Kayor.
Sachs, Bernard (1961), *The Road to Sharpeville*, Johannesburg: Dial, London: Dennis Dobson, New York: Liberty.
Sachs, E. S. (1952), *The Choice before South Africa*, London: Turnstile.
Sachs, E. S. (1957), *Rebels' Daughters*, London: McGibbon and Kee.
Saunders, Christopher (1988), *The Making of the South African Past: Major historians on race and class*, Cape Town and Johannesburg: David Philip.
Saunders, Christopher C., consultant editor (1994a), *Illustrated History of South Africa: The real story*, Cape Town, London: 1994, 3rd edition.

Saunders, Christopher C., advisory editor (1994b), *An Illustrated Dictionary of South African History*, Sandton: Ibis Books and Editorial Services.
Simons, Jack and Ray Simons (1983), *Class and Colour in South Africa, 1850-1950*, International Defence and Aid Fund for Southern Africa.
Simons, Mary (1976), "Organised Coloured Political Movements", in van der Merwe, H. W. and C. J. Groenewald, eds., *Occupational and Social Change among Coloured People in South Africa*, Cape Town: Juta.
Slovo, Joe (1995), *Joe Slovo: The unfinished autobiography*, Johannesburg: Ravan.
South African Communist Party [1990], *The Red Flag in South Africa: A popular history of the South African Communist Party, 1921-1990*, Johannesburg.
Tabata, I. B. (1950), *The All-African Convention: The awakening of a people*, Johannesburg: People's Press.
Tabata, I. B. (1980) [1959], *Education for Barbarism: Bantu (apartheid) education in South Africa*, Lusaka and London: UMSA.
Turok, Ben (1974), "South Africa: The search for a strategy", Ralph Miliband and John Saville, eds., *The Socialist Register 1973*, London: Merlin, 341-376.
Unity Movement of South Africa (1972), "Terrorism Trial", *Intlaba-Mkhosi*, 1, 1, May.
Vigne, Randolph (1971), "Eddie Daniels", *United Nations Unit on Apartheid Notes and Documents*, 44/71, November.
Walker, Cherryl (1991), *Women and Resistance in South Africa*, 2nd edition, Cape Town and Johannesburg: David Philip and New York: Monthly Review.
Wallerstein, Immanuel (1968), *Africa: The politics of unity*, London: Pall Mall.
Wheare, K. C. (1963), *Federal Government*, 4th edition, London, New York and Toronto: Oxford University.
Witz, Leslie (1987), "A Case of Schizophrenia: The rise and fall of the Independent Labour Party", in Belinda Bozzoli, ed., *Class, Community and Conflict: South African perspectives*, Johannesburg: Ravan, 261-291.
Yawich, Joanne (1977), "Natal 1959: The women's riots", *Africa Perspective*, 5, 1-16.

## Collected papers and archives

Abdurahman Family Papers, Manuscripts and Archives Department, University of Cape Town Libraries.
African Collection (South Africa), Manuscripts and Archives, Yale University Library.
Communist Party of South Africa Collection, Hoover Institution Archives and Hoover Institution Library, Stanford University.
Ruth First Collection, Institute of Commonwealth Studies, University of London.
Jack Simons Papers, Manuscripts and Archives Department, University of Cape Town Libraries.
Southern African Archives, Borthwick Institute of Historical Studies, University of York.
Trotsky Archives, Houghton Library, Harvard University.
Workers' Party of South Africa Papers, Mayibuye Archives, University of the Western Cape.

## Interviews

Kenneth Abrahams, Windhoek, February 1988
Neville Alexander, Cape Town, July 1987
Eddie Daniels, Hout Bay, March 1988
Sadie Forman, Ringmer, June 1990
K. A. Jordaan, Harare, December 1987
Ismail Mohamed, Johannesburg, May 1988
Livingstone Mqotsi, Eltham, September 1996
I. B. Tabata and Jane Gool, Harare, December 1987
Ben Turok, London, June 1990

# INDEX

Abader, Y. 196
Abdurahman, Dr A. 49, 66, 69, 155 n. 7, 156 nn. 14-15, 239
Abdurahman, A. E. 81, 97, 98, 157 n. 24
Abdurahman, I. 194
Abrahams, Dr K 35, 391 n. 16
Abrahamse, Rev. 64, 71, 72
Adoula, C. 387-8
African Democratic Party 16, 36 n. 3
African Freedom Movement 35
African Mineworkers' Strike 1946 20, 21, 206, 223-4
African National Congress 15-16, 18, 22-5, 135; and AAC 17, 18, 75, 86-94; and APO 375-6; and armed struggle 32, 33 (*see also Umkhonto weSizwe*); and CPSA 13-14; and SACP 14, 360-2; banning of 32, 34, 354-5, 360, 364; criticism of 49, 124-30; stay-at-home 20, 22, 220-1, 224-5, 228, 231-2
African National Congress Youth League 16, 17, 20, 25, 223, 224
African People's Organization 17, 18, 38, 75, 99, 103, 156 n. 15; and ANC 375-6; criticism of 49, 105
African Resistance Movement 35-6, 344, 389
African Voters' Association 86
agrarian question 27-32, 296-341
Ahmed, H. H. 46, 55, 72, 154 n. 3
Alexander, N. 35, 391 n. 15
Alexander, R. 14, 21-2, 116-17, 161 nn. 56-7, 206-12
All African Convention 14, 16, 28, 35, 96, 313-14, 356-7; and agrarian question 29-31, 335-7; and ANC 17, 18, 75, 86-94; conferences 57-9, 73, 75; criticism of 149-54; *see also* Society of Young Africa
Amra, I. 65, 66, 68, 69, 71
*Analysis* 140-1, 163 n. 78
Andrews, W. H. 181, 202 n. 7 209
Anti-CAD Movement 16, 20, 40-6, 55-7, 73-5; and boycott 191-2, 194-6; and FRAC 103, 104; and trade unionism 218-19; conferences 14, 21, 46-7, 48-54, 57-9, 63-72; land policy 30-2, 337-8
Arendse, M. 70
Arenstein, R. 33, 351, 390 n. 4
armed struggle 32-6, 344-89; *see also* under specific organisations e.g. ANC
Atlantic Charter 40, 139, 163 n. 76
Averbach, M. N. 29, 31, 297-304, 340 n. 4
Azikiwe, Dr N. 286, 292 n. 20

Bach, L. 158 n. 31
Ballinger, M. 156 n. 10, 172, 173, 179, 202 n. 4
Ballinger, W. G. 51, 156 n. 10, 172-3, 202 n. 4
Baloyi, R. G. 158 n. 29, 179
Bantu Authorities Act, 1945 29
Bantu Education Act, 1953 117, 161 n. 58
Bantu National Congress 124, 126, 162 n. 62
Basner, H. 36 n. 3, 172-3, 201-2 n. 4
Basson, Mr 64, 65, 70
Basutoland Congress Party 387, 392 n. 21
Benjamin, Mrs E. 87
Berman, M. 35
Bevin, E. 80, 157 n. 22
Beyleveld, P. 202 n. 12
Bhengu, S. S. 126, 162 n. 62
Black Sash 138, 151, 163 n. 74

Bokwe, Dr R. T. 158 n. 29, 179
Boshielo, F. 28
boycott, use of 17, 19-20, 68-9, 90, 168-201, 266, 353; *see also* Anti-CAD Movement
Buchanan, Adv. 177
Bunting, B. 130, 133-9, 163n n. 70, 72
Bunting, S. 163 n. 70
Bunting, S. P. 162 n. 67, 340 n. 2
bus boycott 188, 226-7

Cachalia, Y. 25, 157 n. 17
Canca, R. M. 87, 89, 91, 94
Cape African Teachers' Association 114, 151, 373
Cape Federation of Labour Unions 209
Cape Flats Educational Fellowship 150
Carneson, F. 18, 103-6, 160 n. 47, 163 n. 70
Champion, A. W. G. 155 n. 7, 158 n. 29, 179
*The Citizen* 140-1, 163 n. 77
Close, R. 66, 66-7, 70, 71, 72
Coe, A. 340 n. 2
Coloured Affairs Council 16, 18, 20, 38-40, 55-7
Coloured Affairs Department 20; *see also* Anti-CAD Movement
Coloured People's Congress 18, 360; *see also* South African Coloured People's Organisation
Coloured People's National Union 104, 105-6
Communist International 13; policy, People's Front 28
Communist Party of South Africa 13-14, 17, 20, 26, 28, 78, 180; and Coloured Affairs Council 38-40; and TARC 17-18, 84-5, 99-102
Congress Movement 15, 18, 21, 38, 133-5; and armed struggle 32-4, 360-1; *see also* ANC; Multi-Racial Conference,1957
Congress of Democrats 21, 25, 125, 138, 140, 196-7, 360
Congress of the People 25, 121-4
Council of Non-European Trade Unions 21, 22, 233 n. 6
Creswell, Col F. H. P. 155 n. 8, 208, 233 n. 3

Dadoo, Y. M. 16, 73-6, 125, 156-7 n. 17, 269, 340 n. 2
Daniels, E. 35, 114
Davids, A. 160 n. 45
Davis, J. 165 n. 87, 340 n. 6
Defiance Campaign 18, 25, 134, 225, 266
Desmore, A. J. B. 47, 64, 72
du Plessis, B. 340 n. 2
du Plessis, I. D. 194
Dube, J. L. 49, 155 n. 7
Dubois, W. E. B. 287, 293 n. 24
Dudley, R. O. 195, 203 n. 14
Duncan, P. 34, 131, 162-3 n. 69, 392 n. 18

Edross, S. 72
Eiselen Commission *see* Native Education (Eiselen) Commission
Eiselen, W. W. M. 160 n. 52, 200
Ernstzen, E. W. 21, 65, 67, 69-70, 71, 72, 160 n. 45

farm labour 28, 296-7, 301
Fataar, A. 65, 66, 67, 69, 70, 71, 72, 85
federation 283-4, 292 n. 18
Federation of South African Women 116, 161 n. 56
First, R. 28, 86-7, 157-8 n. 26, 163 n. 70, 296-7, 340 n. 2

Food and Canning Workers' Union 21, 22
Forman, L. 26-7, 163 n. 70, 280-4, 291-2 n. 16, 340 n. 2
Fortein, C. I. R. 96-7
Forum Club 14, 15, 18, 22, 23, 26, 98
Fourth International Organisation of South Africa 14, 17, 19, 29, 78-9, 172
Franchise Action Committee 103-6, 160 nn. 44, 48
franchise question 16, 43, 168-72, 192-3; *see also* boycott, use of
Freedom Charter 27, 35, 121-4, 133-4, 139; and ANC 18, 25, 129-30, 225-6, 376; criticism of 25, 135-8, 161-2 n. 60

Gamiet, Z. 66, 67, 72, 112-13, 115, 160 n. 45
Gandhi, M. M. K. 17, 135, 225, 231
Ganyile, A. K. 352, 390 nn. 4-5
Garment Workers' Union 36 n. 4
Godlo, R. H. 158 n. 29
Goldberg, M. 161 n. 56
Goldberg, V. 163 n. 73
Golding, G. J. 18, 97, 103, 104-6, 159 n. 43 193
Gomas, J. 18-19, 130-2, 217-18, 156 n. 14, 159 n. 41; and Anti-CAD Movement 20, 96-7, 192-3
Gool, Dr G. H. 85, 155 n. 4, 156 n. 12; and Anti-CAD Movement 46, 63-4, 72, 159 n. 42; and Unity Movement 59, 87, 91, 92, 94
Gool, H. *see* Ahmed, H. H.
Gool, Miss J. 69, 151, 156 nn. 12, 16
Gool, Mrs Z. 59, 64, 65, 68, 70, 71, 72, 155 n. 7, 156 n. 14
Gordon, M. 156 n. 12, 233 n. 6
Gow, F. H. 49, 155 n. 7
Grammer, F. 64, 67, 68, 70
Group Areas Act 138, 225
Gumede, A. 126
Gumede, J. T. 155 n. 7
Gwala, T. 340 n. 2

Harmel, M. 26, 163 n. 70, 234 n. 12, 262-9, 290 n. 5
Hemming, G. K. 175
Hendrickse, K. 140-1
Hertzog, J. B. M. 39, 56, 75, 84, 96
Hirson, B. 144-7, 163 n. 73, 164 n. 81, 165 n. 87, 234 n. 12, 340 n. 6
Holmes, Mr 72
Hurley, Abp 163 n. 73

imperialism 262-9
Independent Labour Party 16, 36 n. 4
Industrial and Commercial Workers' Union 50-1, 155-6 nn. 9-10, 207, 208-9, 218, 233 nn. 4-5
Industrial Conciliation Act 1924 81, 157 n. 23 207-8, 209; 1956 21, 132, 163 n. 71
Industrial Conciliation ("Native") Bill, 1947 81, 157 n. 23 172, 180, 181
Ismail, A. 59, 64

Jabavu, D. D. T. 59, 65, 73, 86, 158 nn. 28-30
Jabavu, J. T. 49, 155 n. 7, 159 n. 39
Jacobs, Mr 67, 68
Jaffe, H. 31, 65, 67, 70, 155 n. 5, 160 n. 45, 321-5, 341 n. 8
Jason, Rev. E. 65, 66, 68
Jayiya, S. A. 59, 87, 91, 93
Johannesburg Discussion Club 26, 28, 213-17, 233 n. 9, 316-21
Jones, J. D. Rheinallt *see* Rheinallt Jones, J. D.
Jordaan, K. A. 26, 97-103, 113-14, 168-72, 249-62, 160 n. 45, 161 n. 53; and agrarian question 31-2,
325-39; and nationalism 24, 27, 270-4
Jordan, A. C. 151, 165 n. 85
Joseph, H. 161 n. 56

Kadalie, C. 155 n. 9, 207
Kahn, S. 106, 160 n. 49
Kajee, A. I. 49, 59, 155 n. 7
Kalk, W. 340 n. 2
Kies, B. M. 14, 24, 155 n. 5; and Anti-CAD Movement 47, 48-54, 59, 65, 66, 68, 72, 195-6; and Unity Movement 74, 85, 341 n. 8
Kobus, C. M. 87, 91, 94, 195, 203 n. 13
Kotane, M. M. 87, 89, 91, 92, 93, 158 n. 31, 173-7
Koza, D. R. 36 n. 3, 59, 156 n. 12, 201 n. 4

La Guma, J. 156 n. 14
land *see* agrarian question; Natives' Land Act
Langa Educational Fellowship 150
Lavis, Bishop S. W. 70
Lawrence, H. G. 38-40, 55
Leballo, P. 34, 387, 392 nn. 18-19
Leftwich, A. 392 n. 22
legislation *see* under names of specific acts
Legwate, B. M. 221
Lembede, A. M. 173, 202 n. 6, 223, 392 n. 19
Lepolesa, A. 165 n. 87
Letele, Dr A. E. 126
Liberal Party 32, 35, 127, 134, 137, 138, 265
*Liberation* 124-30, 162 n. 61
Louw, E. 39, 154 n. 2, 355, 390 n. 7
Lukele, A. 165 n. 87, 340 n. 6
Luthuli, A. J. 124, 126, 127-8, 162 n. 61, 200, 230, 351

Madeley, W. B. 209
Madzunya, J. 163 n. 73
Mafora, J. B. 126
Mahabane, Rev. Z. R. 87-9, 91, 94, 158 n. 29
Mahomo, N. 391-2 n. 18
Makabeni, G. 89, 93, 158 n. 34, 179, 223, 233 n. 6
Malan, D. F. 39, 99, 154 n. 2
Malangabi, J. 87
Maliba, A. 28
Mampuru, S. 36 n. 3, 201 n. 4
Mandela, N. 27, 33, 159 nn. 36, 39, 40
Mao Zedong (Mao Tse-tung) 138, 163 n. 75 286
Marais, J. 71
Marks, J. B. 87, 88, 158 n. 32, 223, 233 n. 6
Marthinus, E. 59, 65, 66, 67, 71
Matthews, Z. K. 87, 91, 158 nn. 29, 30, 179
Maurice, E. L. 106-15, 160 n. 51
Mazwai, A. K. 87, 93
Mbeki, G. 28, 30, 163 n. 70, 346, 390 n. 3
Mboya, T. 286, 292 n. 21
Mda, A. P. 87, 90, 91-2, 127, 158-9 n. 35, 392 n. 19
Mda, M. 87
Mdatyulwa, J. 87
Meissenheimer, P. 76-9
Mettler, R. *see* Hirson, B.
Mitchell, D. 200
MK *see* Umkhonto weSizwe
Mkabeni, G. 87
Mkhize, F. 161 n. 56
Mntwana, Mrs I. 116, 161 n. 57
Mofutsanyana, E. T. 173, 179, 202 n. 5
Mohamed, I. 165 n. 87
Mokhehle, N. 387, 392 n. 21
Mokone, S. *see* Wessels, V.
Mokonyane, D. 340 n. 6
Molotski, P. 392 n. 18

Mon, A. *see* Averbach, M. N.
Moroka, Dr J. S. 59, 224, 269, 291 n. 9
Mosaka, P. 36 n. 3, 158 n. 29, 172-3, 201 n. 4
Mpama, J. 173, 202 n. 5
Mpanza, S. 223
Msimang, S. 179
Mugabe, R. 159 n. 39
Multi-Racial Conference, 1957 133-41, 163 n. 73
Murison, Dr N. 194, 196

Naicker, Dr G. M. 16, 155 n. 7, 157 n. 17 269
Naicker, M. P. 163 n. 70
Naidoo, H. A. 16
Naidoo, M. D. 163 n. 73
National Committee for Liberation 35, 344, 357-8
National Liberation Front 34, 35, 344
National Party 17, 18, 50, 136-7
nationalism 23-7, 270-89
Native Education (Eiselen) Commission 107-8, 111, 160 n. 52, 161 n. 58
Native Labour Act, 1953 21
Native Representative Act, 1936 172-8, 180, 305
Native Representative Council 16, 20, 24, 81, 174, 176-9, 181, 224
Native Republic thesis 26, 28
Native Trust and Land Act, 1936 28, 80, 117, 305
Natives' Land Act, 1913 27, 301, 304
New Age 132, 163 n. 70
New Era Fellowship 14, 150, 164 n. 84
Ngoyi, L. 161 n. 56
Ngubane, J. K. 127-8, 130, 162 n. 65
Ngwenya, T. 26, 279-80
Nhlapo, Dr 126
Nkrumah, K. 145, 164 n. 82, 278, 286
Non-European Unity Movement 14, 15, 16, 19-20, 25, 314-15; 10-Point Programme 16, 19, 59, 62-3, 74, 143-8, 149, 152; and armed struggle 32-3, 34-5, 344; and FRAC 18, 103, 104; and nationalism 23-4, 25; and TRAC 17-18, 84-6, 97, 99-102; criticism of 19, 21, 23, 34-5, 77-9, 85-6, 144-5; land policy 321-5, 333-5; *see also* AAC; Anti-CAD Movement; WPSA
Ntantala, P. 161 n. 53, 165 n. 85, 202 n. 9
Ntlabati, L. K. 87, 91, 92-3, 94, 158 n. 29

Omar, A. 194, 202-3 n. 13

Padmore, G. 159 n. 41, 286, 293 n. 23
Palmer, J. *see* Mpama, J.
Pan-Africanist Congress 35, 226; and armed struggle 34, 374, 387-8; anti-pass campaign 22, 225, 230-2 (*see also* Sharpeville massacre); banning of 32, 364; formation of 15, 25, 285-9; *see also* Poqo
Pan-African Freedom Movement of East, Central and Southern Africa 390 n. 8
Papert, S. 19, 320-1, 340 n. 6
Parry, W. 66, 72
pass laws 72, 75, 138, 222, 229-31, 308-9
Paton, A. 163 n. 73
Pegging Act, 1943 55, 59, 64, 73, 75, 76, 156 n. 11, 225
Phahle, R. 165 n. 87, 340 n. 6
Phillips, J. 70
Phillips, L. S. 72, 87
Pienaar, Miss R. 69
Pirow, O. 39, 154 n. 2
Pondoland revolt, 1960-1 29, 30, 32, 35, 344-53, 356, 365, 370-1
*Poqo* 25, 34, 344

Potekhin, I. I. 26, 292 n. 17
Progressive Forum 19, 30, 316, 340-1 n. 6
Progressive Labour Group 36 n. 4

Quisling, W. 155 n. 6

Rahim, S. 64, 66, 67, 72
Railoun, E. 71
Ramahanoe, 172
Ramsdale, E. 59, 64, 69, 72
Rand Revolt, 1922 207-8, 212, 233 n. 2
Reddy, S. 340 n. 2
Rehabilitation Scheme, 1945 29-30, 80, 198, 304-16, 320-1, 329
Reitz, D. 340 n. 5
Rheinallt Jones, J. D. 297, 340 n. 1, 340 n. 3
Rivonia raid 33, 35
Roberts, E. C. 46, 59, 65, 69, 70-1, 71-2
Roux, Dr E. R. 30, 130-1, 316, 320-1, 162 n. 67, 340 n. 2, 390 n. 3
rural protests 29-30, 229, 296, 344, 367, 369-72; *see also* Pondoland revolt
rural workers 316-21

Sachs, B. 162 n. 68
Sachs, E. S. 36 n. 4, 130, 162 n. 68, 265, 290 n. 6
Saloojee, Dr 165 n. 87
Sanders, Dr Z. *see* Susser, Z.
Schermbrucker, I. 163 n. 70
segregation, history of 236-62
Sello, R. 87
Selope-Thema, R. V. 87, 88-9, 91, 94, 158 n. 29, 162 n. 62, 179, 223
Seme, P. ka I. 49, 155 n. 7
Separate Representation of Voters' Act, 1950 18, 118
September, D. 35
Sesedi, S. P. 59, 179
Sharpeville massacre 22, 32, 230, 344
Shedrin, J. 340 n. 2
Sigcau, B. 348-9
Sihlali, L. L. 87, 93, 151, 165 n. 86
Simons, H. J. 14, 26, 161 n. 57, 275-9, 291 n. 14
Simons, R. A. *see* Alexander, R.
Sinyogo, T. 59
Sisulu, W. 25, 127, 188-91, 319
Slovo, J. 158 n. 26, 321, 341 n. 7
Smuts, Gen. J. C. 39, 40, 42, 76, 99, 175, 178, 305, 340 n. 5
Snitcher, H. 38-40, 154 n. 1
Sobukwe, R. M. 25, 34, 95-6, 159 n. 37 285-9, 387
Socialist League of Africa 20-1, 22, 35, 222-32, 234 n. 12
Society of Young Africa 19, 20, 149-54, 164 n. 83 197-201
Sondlo, V. 59, 165 n. 87
South Africa Club 26
South African Coloured People's Organisation 18, 125, 135, 196, 203 n. 15; *see also* Coloured People's Congress
South African Communist Party 14, 25-6, 27, 33-4, 358-64, 360-2
South African Congress of Trade Unions 22, 125, 228-9, 360
South African Indian Congress 16, 18, 59, 64, 73-5, 103, 125, 135, 360; criticism of 49, 76, 105
South African Institute of Race Relations 296-7, 340 n. 1
South African Labour Party 50, 155 n. 8
South African Socialist Party 36 n. 4

South African Trades and Labour Council 22, 208, 209-112
South West African People's Organisation 391 n. 16
Spear of the Nation *see* Umkhonto weSizwe
State of Emergency 22, 32, 364-5
strikes 21, 206-8, 220-1; *see also* African Mineworkers' Strike
Suppression of Communism Act, 1950 14, 21, 32, 225
Susser, Z. 316-21
Swart, V. 341 n. 6

Tabata, I. B. 19, 28, 35, 95-6, 155 n. 5, 156 nn. 12, 16, 390 n. 8; and AAC 88, 90-2, 94; and Anti-CAD Movement 67, 69, 70, 72; and boycott 182-8; and Rehabilitation Scheme 29-31, 304-15; and Unity Movement 59, 74, 87, 144, 147-8
Tambo, O. R. 25, 87, 90, 93, 94, 159 nn. 36, 39, 179
Taylor, D. 36 n. 6
teachers as vanguard 14-15, 28, 53-4, 106-15
Teachers' League of South Africa 14, 16, 99, 108, 113-15
Tloome, D. 22, 213-17, 223, 233 n. 8
Tomlinson Commission 142, 143, 163 n. 73, 164 n. 80
*The Torch* 112, 160 n. 50
Trade Union Council 22
trade unions 21-2, 206-12, 213-17, 223-4; and Anti-CAD Movement 69-70; and racialism 210-12, 217-18
Train Apartheid Resistance Campaign 17-18, 21, 81-6, 97-103, 104, 106
Transkei Organised Bodies 30, 81, 174
Transkei Voters' Association 30, 81
Transvaal Agricultural Union 28, 296-7, 305
Traub, N. 165 n. 87
Treason Trial 23, 147
Treason Trial Defence Fund 134
Trotsky, L. 16, 77, 157 n. 20 297-304
Trotskyism 14, 23, 26-7, 28-9, 139; *see also* FIOSA; Forum Club; Workers' International League; WPSA
Tsotsi, W. M. 59, 87-8, 92, 93, 141-8, 164 n. 79
Turok, B. 344-53, 390 n. 1

*Umkhonto weSizwe* 33, 34, 35, 344, 365-6, 374-7
United Party 50, 136-7
Unity Conference 57-63, 73-6, 79-81, 86; *see also* NEUM
Uranovsky, B. 340 n. 2

van Gelderen, H. 67, 70
van Huzer, T. 340 n. 2
van Noie, Mr 67, 70
van Rensburg, J. F. J. 39, 154 n. 2
van Riebeeck Tercentenary 109, 160-1 n. 53, 186-7
van Schoor, W. P. 160 n. 45, 165 n. 86, 290 n. 1; and Anti-CAD Movement 67, 68, 71, 194-5; and nationalism 24, 236-62
Verwoerd, H. F. 142, 151, 161 n. 58, 164 n. 80, 345, 353, 355, 390 n. 7
Viljoen, E. 68, 70, 72
Viljoen, Mrs R. E. 69
Viljoen, R. E. 194
Vutela, S. 154, 165 n. 87

Watts, H. 340 n. 2
Wavell, A. P. 76, 157 n. 19
Welensky, R. 293 n. 25, 360, 391 n. 11

Wessels, Rev. D. M. 70, 71, 195
Wessels, V. 81-3, 157 n. 24
Wilcox, E. 165 n. 87
women 36 n. 1; conferences 115-21; passes 138, 227; use of boycott 20, 197-201
Women's Charter 118-21
Women's International Democratic Federation 115, 117, 161 n. 55
Workers International League 14
Workers' Party of South Africa 14, 16-17, 28, 29, 35
*Workers' Voice* 157 n. 18

Xuma, Dr A. B. 16, 157 n. 17; and boycott 20, 173, 177-8, 179; and Unity 86, 87-8, 92; criticism of 125-7, 130, 223

Yergan, M. 390 n. 3
Young Communist League of South Africa 297-8, 340 n. 2
Yu Chi Chan Club 34, 35, 344, 377-86, 391 nn. 15-16